Gale Encyclopedia of
U.S. History: War

Gale Encyclopedia of U.S. History: War

VOLUME 1

GALE
CENGAGE Learning

Detroit • New York • San Francisco • New Haven, Conn • Waterville, Maine • London

Gale Encyclopedia of U.S. History: War

Project Editors: Anne Marie Hacht and Dwayne D. Hayes

Editorial: Ira Mark Milne

Rights Acquisition and Management: Leitha Etheridge-Sims, Lisa Kincade, Jacqueline Key, and Timothy Sisler

Composition: Evi Abou-El-Seoud

Manufacturing: Wendy Blurton

Imaging: Lezlie Light

Product Design: Jennifer Wahi

For product information and technology assistance, contact us at **Gale Customer Support, 1-800-877-4253.**
For permission to use material from this text or product, submit all requests online at **www.cengage.com/permissions.**
Further permissions questions can be emailed to **permissionrequest@cengage.com**

Cover photographs reproduced by permission of Corbis (picture of the mushroom cloud from "Grable," the first nuclear artillery shell) and public domain (picture of Civil war image of soldiers with cannons).

While every effort has been made to ensure the reliability of the information presented in this publication, Gale, a part of Cengage Learning, does not guarantee the accuracy of the data contained herein. Gale accepts no payment for listing; and inclusion in the publication of any organization, agency, institution, publication, service, or individual does not imply endorsement of the editors or publisher. Errors brought to the attention of the publisher and verified to the satisfaction of the publisher will be corrected in future editions.

Library of Congress Cataloging-in-Publication Data

Gale encyclopedia of U.S. history : war
   p. cm. --
  Includes bibliographical references and index.
   ISBN 978-1-4144-3114-7 (set hardcover) -- ISBN 978-1-4144-3115-4 (v. 1 : hardcover) -- ISBN 978-1-4144-3116-1 (v. 2 : hardcover)
   1. United States--History, Military--Encyclopedias. I. Gale Group. II. Title: Encyclopedia of U.S. history, war. III. Title: War.

E181.G16 2008
355.00973--dc22   2007033628

Gale
27500 Drake Rd.
Farmington Hills, MI, 48331-3535

978-1-4144-3114-7 (set)   1-4144-3114-7 (set)
978-1-4144-3115-4 (vol. 1)   1-4144-3115-5 (vol. 1)
978-1-4144-3116-1 (vol. 2)   1-4144-3116-3 (vol. 2)

This title is also available as an e-book.
ISBN-13: 978-1-4144-3117-8 ISBN-10: 1-4144-3117-1
Contact your Gale sales representative for ordering information.

Printed in the United States of America
1 2 3 4 5 6 7 11 10 09 08

Contents

VOLUME 2

Introduction

How To Use This Book

The history of the Americas is fraught with conflict, from the great empires of the Aztecs and the Incas to the arrival of gun-carrying Europeans and their new way of making war, continuing on to the creation of the United States in the crucible of revolution, and on into its many wars, both foreign and domestic. Over more than five hundred years of recorded history, the scale of warfare in the Americas has grown exponentially, from skirmishes fought with flint axes and matchlock arquebuses all the way to atomic warfare—the United States being, to date, the only country to use nuclear weapons in war—and a military powerful enough to project its strength and influence around the globe.

Although virtually every corner of the Americas, from the Aleutian Islands to the Falklands, has been touched by conflict, the *Encyclopedia of U.S. History: War* focuses on the military history of the United States specifically, as it is that nation that has come to dominate both the theory and the execution of the wars of the last century. As dramatic as the last hundred years have been, this book also spends as much time focusing on the conflicts of the United States in previous centuries, as it grew from a colonial frontier populated by independent-minded sharpshooters and scouts to a power on par with Europe with armies that marched and fought in the European styles of the times.

In-depth coverage is also given to the evolving nature of conflicts and encounters between the growing United States and the native nations of North America. From the early skirmishes all the way through to the watershed events of the nineteenth century, the role and scope of the "Indian Wars" is examined over the course of several chapters.

Organization

Each chapter is arranged in such a way as to assist the student and generalist reader in gaining an in-depth appreciation of one phase of American warfare. Arranged chronologically, the chapters all follow the same structure, beginning with a short overview of the chapter and an examination of the causes that paved the path to war. The *Encyclopedia of U.S. History: War* then uses both biographies and descriptions of key battles to further illuminate the overarching nature of the phase or conflict under consideration. It is in the personal stories of the generals, leaders, soldiers, and innovators, and their role, for good or ill, on the battlefield that the true drama of America at war comes into play. Each chapter then concludes with an examination of the war's aftermath and its impact on the bigger picture of U.S. and world history.

The bigger picture is also examined in the "Homefront" and "International Context" sections. Perhaps more than any other nation, the United States' military policies have been strongly and consistently driven by events on both the domestic and international scenes. From the Great Awakening to Women's Suffrage to the Anti-War Movement of the 1960s and beyond, the Homefront articles detail the impact of non-military events at home on America's wars. Similarly, despite efforts in the past to make it so, our country has never been able to isolate itself from world politics; the United States' wars have been intrinsically linked to global events since the Seven Years War touched off the French and Indian War in colonial America.

What's Inside

The French and Indian War was but one facet of a greater conflict that is the subject of the first chapter, which focuses on conflicts with the Northeastern tribes of Native Americans. This often-overlooked period of the Indian Wars was also, demographically speaking, one of America's bloodiest conflicts.

The American Revolution, that great turning point in history, comprises the next chapter. A time of legendary leaders and battles, the epic sweep of this conflict is balanced by a focus on the simple human drama that resulted in the birth of a new kind of government and a nation quite unlike any seen before.

The focus shifts back to Native American matters with the next chapter, which examines conflicts with the tribes of the West and South as the newly-born United States began to expand westward. A crucial time in early American history, some of the country's first post-Revolutionary heroes were made in these wars, as well as some of the first enduring symbols of Native American resistance and disenfranchisement.

America once again found itself at war with Britain in 1812. A sideshow of the Napoleonic Wars then raging in Europe, the conflict was the United States' first official international war and witnessed the dramatic burning of Washington, D.C. and the equally dramatic American victory at the Battle of New Orleans, which was a tremendous morale boost for the young country even though it had no bearing on the outcome of the war, which had already concluded!

The greatest war-related territorial acquisition in U.S. history came with the subject of the next chapter, the Mexican-American War. Manifest Destiny in action, the war brought the boundaries of the United States to the Pacific Ocean (just in time for the California Gold Rush) and launched the military careers of many future Civil War generals.

The Civil War almost spelled the end of the Union a mere "four score and seven years" after its foundation. The costliest of American wars receives full coverage, from the generals and politicians who shaped the conflict on both sides to the monumental battles that determined the fate of a nation and the freedom of a people.

With the Civil War over, America turned to pacifying the last native tribes. The last phase of the Indian Wars, the conflicts with the Western tribes, is also the best known. The names and battles—Custer, Little Big Horn, Geronimo, Sitting Bull, Wounded Knee—quickly became part of the growing American mythology as the longest, and one of the most tragic, conflicts in the nation's history came to a close.

The Spanish-American War, the subject of the next chapter, marked America's true emergence onto the world stage and the country's first encounter with the complex issue of imperialism. The war was also the first great "media war", drummed up largely by competing newspaper interests. By war's end, Theodore Roosevelt had gained national notoriety and America had gained its first overseas possessions, along with the many problems that go with such acquisitions.

If the Spanish-American War constituted America's first small entry into the global scene, the two World Wars heralded its arrival in a big way. Each gets its own chapter, and each chapter examines the relevant conflict in exhaustive detail, covering not just the American soldiers and battles, but every facet of these massive wars, as well as their complex causes and the vast changes that came in their aftermath.

From the muddy fields of the Somme to the sinking of the *Lusitania* to the Russian Revolution and the Treaty of Versailles, from the rise of fascism in Europe and the Japanese invasion of China to the specter of the Holocaust and the atomic bombings of Hiroshima and Nagasaki, the tremendous scope and sweep of these two global conflicts, the costliest and deadliest in the history of the world, are captured. The immense changes brought about in America by these wars are also examined, including the rise of the first civil rights organizations, the tremendous gains made by women in political and economic arenas, and the sad legacy of Japanese internment in the Second World War.

Having become a superpower in the wake of World War II, America's subsequent wars were fought in the shadow of the Cold War, which gets its own chapter. This section covers the politicians and high-ranking generals who played out a deadly game of move and countermove for fifty years, as well as the times when the Cold War nearly became "hot", most notably during the early 1960s with such dramatic events as the Cuban Missile Crisis, the Bay of Pigs invasion, and the raising of the Berlin Wall.

The two big American wars of the Cold War era, Korea and Vietnam, are covered in two separate chapters. Both conflicts were part of much greater social and political upheavals—the de-colonialization of Asia and the burgeoning Peace Movement, for example—and these are covered in detail, as is the nuclear escalation and Cold War brinkmanship that formed the backdrop to the wars.

In the wake of the Cold War, America's military interests turned increasingly towards the Middle East starting with the Gulf War, which is covered in its own chapter. The War on Terrorism chapter is broken down into two sections: the first covers the invasion of Afghanistan which followed in the wake of the September 11 attacks; the second covers the ongoing conflict in Iraq.

The book wraps up with a five-section look at America's relations with the rest of the world, both past and present, covering covert operations, proxy wars, and U.S. political involvement in various regimes and movements.

Conclusion

The objective of this book is to take the reader on a journey through the history of the United States and the military conflicts that have shaped it and the world. Through studying America's wars and the people who have waged them, the impact history has on our lives today will hopefully become apparent to the reader.

At the very least, it is hoped that the reader will appreciate the great drama and sacrifice contained within the following chapters and will come to recognize the tremendous cost of war for those who wage it.

Chronology

c. 11,000 BCE:
Native Americans use flint-tipped spears to hunt mammoths.

c. 7,000 BCE:
Disappearance of mammoths and other "big game" in the Americas; beginning of food cultivation.

c. 1,500 BCE:
Appearance of Olmec culture in Central America.

c. 350 CE:
Rise of Old Mayan Empire.

c. 700 CE:
Rise of Mississippian culture, last of the mound building cultures of North America.

c. 1000:
Viking settlements briefly established in Newfoundland.

c. 1325:
Tenochtitlan, capital of the Aztec Empire, is constructed.

1438: Inca Empire founded in Peru.

1492: First voyage of Christopher Columbus. Funded by Spain, the Italian-born Columbus discovers "The New World."

1497: Backed by England, explorer John Cabot sails along North American coast.

1507: First reference to the New World as "America."

1513: Spaniard Ponce de Leon conducts slave raids and explores Florida and the Gulf Coast. Another Spaniard, Vasco de Balboa, crosses the Panamanian Isthmus to the Pacific Ocean.

1519: Spanish adventurer Hernán Cortés begins his conquest of Mexico. Aztec Empire falls by 1521.

1533: Spanish adventurer Francisco Pizarro conquers Peru.

1540s: Spaniard Francisco Coronado leads explorations throughout modern-U.S. Southwest.

1565: St. Augustine, oldest European settlement in the future United States, is established.

1579: Englishman Sir Francis Drake explores the California coast during his circumnavigation of the world.

1607: The English colony of Jamestown, Virginia, is founded by Captain John Smith.

1608: City of Quebec founded by Frenchman Samuel Champlain.

1609: Santa Fe, New Mexico, founded by Spanish. Henry Hudson explores Hudson River Valley.

1619: First African slaves arrive at Jamestown.

1620: Puritan settlers land at Plymouth, Massachusetts.

1626: Dutch settle on Manhattan Island, naming their colony New Amsterdam.

1630: Boston founded.

1634: Maryland established as Catholic colony.

1637: Fighting flares up between colonists and the Pequot Indians in New England.

1664: New Amsterdam seized by English, who rename it New York.

1692: Start of the Salem Witch Trials.

1699: French settlement of Louisiana begins.

1713: Queen Anne's War, a colonial conflict between France and England, ends after eleven years of hostilities.

1732: Benjamin Franklin begins publishing *Poor Richard's Almanac.*

1748: Another colonial struggle, King George's War, ends after four years.

1763: The French and Indian War, the North American portion of the Seven Years' War, concludes with French loss of all territorial possessions in Canada and the Mississippi region to the British.

1764: Stamp Act passed by the British Parliament. An effort to raise money after the costly Seven Years' War by taxing colonists on sugar and stamps, the Stamp Act proves wildly unpopular in North America and is repealed two years later.

1770: The Boston Massacre: British soldiers open fire on Bostonian mob protesting against further taxes.

1773: A group of protesting Bostonians throw English tea into the harbor in what is later dubbed the "Boston Tea Party."

1775: The battles of Lexington and Concord mark the beginning of the American Revolution.

1776: The Declaration of Independence signed on July 2 and approved on July 4, signaling the British colonies' formal break from the mother country and laying out an agenda to create a more democratically-based government. December 26: Washington's surprise victory at Trenton.

1777: Winter at Valley Forge, the low point for Washington's army.

1778: Beginning of French-American alliance.

1781: Articles of Confederation adopted. Surrender of the British General Cornwallis marks the effective end of the Revolutionary War.

1783: September 3: Treaty of Paris signed, the formally ending the American Revolution; Britain cedes all territory east of the Mississippi River. Eighty thousand Loyalists emigrate to Canada.

1786: Shays' Rebellion in Massachusetts.

1787: May 14: Constitutional Convention convened to rewrite Articles of Confederation.

1789: New U.S. Constitution ratified and put into effect. George Washington becomes the first president.

1790: U.S. population stands at 3,929,214.

1798: Alien and Sedition Acts, designed to bolster national sovereignty, are passed. Dissolution of French alliance.

1800: Federal government's capital moved to Washington, D.C. from Philadelphia. U.S. population stands at 5,308,483.

1801: American shipping encounters increasing trouble from the Barbary Pirates of North Africa.

1803: The Louisiana Purchase doubles the size of the United States.

1804: Beginning of Lewis and Clark expedition to explore the territory encompassed by the Louisiana Purchase.

1808: Slave trade outlawed by Congress.

1810: U.S. population stands at 7,239,881.

1811: Native Americans defeated in Battle of Tippecanoe in Indiana Territory.

1812: June 18: Beginning of the War of 1812 between the United States and Britain. August 19: The *Constitution* ("Old Ironsides") defeats the British *Guerriere.*

1813: September 10: Battle of Lake Erie. American forces maintain control over this body of water.

1814: August 25: British capture Washington, D.C. and put it to the torch. September 11: British defeated on Lake Champlain. December 24: Treaty of Ghent signed, ending war in stalemate.

1815: January 8: Battle of New Orleans, fought after peace declared, ends in a resounding U.S. victory.

1817: First Seminole War.

1818: U.S.-Canadian border established at 49th parallel.

1819: Florida purchased from Spain.

1820: Missouri Compromise restricts further expansion of slavery west of the Mississippi or north of the Mason-Dixon Line (except in Missouri). U.S. population stands at 9,638,453.

1821: Mexico declares its independence from Spain.

1823: President James Monroe outlines the Monroe Doctrine, creating a U.S. "sphere of influence" in Central and South America.

1825: Erie Canal opened, bringing trade to inland regions.

1828: Construction begins on first U.S. passenger railway.

1830: U.S. population stands at 12,866,020. Indian Removal Act mandates removal of Eastern Native American tribes.

1832: Black Hawk War.

1834: Indian Territory established.

1835: Second Seminole War.

1836: Battle of the Alamo and San Jacinto; Texas breaks away from Mexico, forming an independent republic.

1837: The telegraph is patented.

1838: The entire Cherokee Nation forced by American government to move from Georgia to Indian Territory, a journey known as the Trail of Tears. Thousands die along the way from disease, exposure, and privation.

1840: Opening of Oregon Trail. U.S. population stands at 17,069,453.

1844: First telegraph line established, connecting Baltimore and Washington, D.C.

1845: Republic of Texas admitted as U.S. state.

1846: 49th Parallel border with Canada extended to Oregon. Beginning of Mexican War.

1847: March 29: Capture of Veracruz by General Winfield Scott. U.S. victories in California and the taking of Mexico City follow.

1848: Treaty of Guadalupe-Hidalgo concludes U.S. war with Mexico. Mexico cedes nearly half its territory, extending U.S. border to Pacific coast.

1849: Gold discovered in California; ensuing "gold rush" brings mass movement of settlers out west.

1850: U.S. population stands at 23,191,876.

1851: Fort Laramie Treaties outline Plains Indian tribes' territories and rights. The conditions of the treaties will be systematically ignored or negated over the next forty years as white settlers stream west into Native American lands.

1853: With the Gadsden Purchase, the continental U.S. border attains its modern outline.

1857: Supreme Court issues Dred Scott decision. Tensions between pro- and anti-slavery factions escalate.

1858: Mountain Meadow Massacre in Utah.

1859: Abolitionist John Brown leads a raid on a federal armory at Harper's Ferry, Virginia.

1860: Abraham Lincoln elected president. South Carolina secedes from the United States on December 20. U.S. population stands at 31,443,321.

1861: January-June: Secession of Mississippi, Florida, Alabama, Georgia, Louisiana, Texas, Virginia, Arkansas, North Carolina, Tennessee. April 14: Firing on Fort Sumter; the American Civil War begins. July 21: First Battle of Bull Run.

1862: Ulysses S. Grant first gains notoriety with the taking of Fort Donelson in February. March 9: *Monitor vs. Virginia,* first encounter between ironclad warships. April 6–7: Battle of Shiloh. April 25: New Orleans captured by Admiral David Farragut. August 30: Second Bull Run. September 17: Battle of Antietam. December 13: Battle of Fredericksburg.

1863: January 1: Lincoln issues the Emancipation Proclamation, guaranteeing the freedom of slaves in the Confederate States. July 1–4: The Battles of Gettysburg and Vicksburg mark a turning point in the Civil War in favor of the Union. November 19: Lincoln delivers his Gettysburg Address.

1864: May 6: Battle of the Wilderness. May 11: Battle of Spottsylvania. September 2: Union General Sherman captures Atlanta and burns it; his "March to the Sea" begins in November.

1865: April 3: Richmond evacuated by Confederates. April 9: Surrender of Lee at Appomattox Courthouse, Virginia. April 14: Lincoln is assassinated. The Civil War ends; twelve-year period of Reconstruction begins in the South.

1867: "Seward's Folly" the U.S. purchases Alaska from Russia.

1868: President Andrew Johnson impeached but not convicted.

1869: Completion of Transcontinental Railroad.

1870: U.S. population stands at 38,558,371.

1876: Battle of Little Big Horn results in the death of American General Custer along with all of the men fighting with him that day.

1880: U.S. population stands at 50,189,209.

1881: July 2: President Garfield shot, mortally wounded; dies on September 19.

1886: Statue of Liberty unveiled.

1889: Oklahoma (formerly Indian Territory) opened to settlers.

1890: Wounded Knee Massacre marks an end to open warfare between the U.S. and Native American nations. U.S. population stands at 62,979,766.

1896: Supreme Court rules that "separate but equal" facilities are legal.

1898: February 15: The battleship *Maine* blows up in Havana harbor. April 25: Congress declares war on Spain. May 1: Battle of Manila. July 3: Battle of Santiago. December 10: Peace treaty signed with Spain. U.S. victory in the Spanish-American War grants America control over Cuba, Guam, Puerto Rico, and the Philippines. Beginning of fifteen-year Philippine insurgency. Hawaii annexed.

1900: American forces assist in ending Boxer Rebellion in China. U.S. population stands at 76,212,168.

1901: September 6: President McKinley assassinated; Theodore Roosevelt becomes president.

1902: Cuban Republic established.

1903: United States backs Panamanian secession from Columbia. Panama leases Canal Zone to United States.

1906: San Francisco Earthquake (and subsequent fire) destroys most of the city.

1908: Model T Ford, the first affordable, mass-produced automobile, offered for sale.

1910: U.S. population stands at 92,228,496.

1914: Opening of the Panama Canal under U.S. control.

1917: April 6: United States enters into World War I.

1918: Spanish Flu epidemic spreads worldwide, killing millions.

1919: President Woodrow Wilson promotes his Fourteen Points at Versailles. U.S. Congress fails to ratify the Treaty of Versailles and stays out of the League of Nations when it is established in 1920.

1920: Women granted the right to vote in the United States. U.S. population stands at 106,021,537.

1925: Scopes "Monkey Trial" debates the teaching of Darwinian evolution in schools.

1928: First Mickey Mouse cartoon.

1929: February 14: Mob-related St. Valentine's Day Massacre in Chicago captures nationwide attention. October 29: Crash of the New York Stock Exchange, beginning of the Great Depression.

1930: U.S. population stands at 123,202,624.

1931: Criminal kingpin Al Capone jailed for income tax evasion.

1932: Franklin D. Roosevelt elected president.

1933: Beginning of "New Deal" policy. End of Prohibition after thirteen disastrous years.

1935: Passage of Social Security Act.

1937: Golden Gate Bridge opened. May 6: *Hindenburg* disaster spells the end of lighter-than-air passenger service.

1940: U.S. population stands at 132,164,569.

1941: Mount Rushmore completed. December 7: Japanese surprise attack on Pearl Harbor, Hawaii, catalyzes U.S. entry into World War II.

1942: Japanese-Americans placed in internment camps for duration of the war. June 4–7: Battle of Midway marks turning point in Pacific War in favor of America.

1943: U.S. invasion of North Africa, Sicily, Italy. Italy surrenders and joins the Allies, but is occupied by German troops.

1944: June 6: D-Day landings in Normandy. Allies reach German border by December. German counterattack launched in last week of December, leading to "Battle of the Bulge." U.S. forces land in the Philippines beginning in October.

1945: February: Battle of Iwo Jima. April–June: Battle of Okinawa. April 12: Death of Franklin Roosevelt. May 8: "V-E Day"; end of hostilities in Europe. August 6 and 9: Dropping of atomic bombs on Hiroshima and Nagasaki. August 15: "V-J Day"; end of World War II.

1947: Marshall Plan implemented to assist in rebuilding of Europe.

1948: Berlin Airlift. Harry Truman wins the presidency in a surprise upset.

1949: NATO established.

1950: United States leads U.N. forces in Korean War. Stalemate largely reached by end of year, although the war drags on for two more years. Height of anti-Communist paranoia; McCarthy hearings begin. U.S. population stands at 151,325,798.

1953: Julius and Ethel Rosenberg convicted of spying for the Soviet Union and executed.

1954: Segregation declared illegal in Supreme Court's *Brown v. Board of Education* ruling.

1955: Disneyland opens. Rosa Parks touches off Montgomery Bus Boycott when she refuses to give up her seat on a public bus.

1959: Communist revolution in Cuba; Fidel Castro becomes dictator.

1960: U.S. population stands at 179,323,175.

1961: Soviets put first man into orbit.

1962: Cuban Missile Crisis brings world to the brink of nuclear war.

1963: November 22: Assassination of John F. Kennedy.

1965: Race riots in Los Angeles. Escalation of U.S. involvement in Vietnam. Malcolm X assassinated.

1966: Black Panther party founded. Anti-draft protests on college campuses across the country.

1968: Martin Luther King assassinated. Robert Kennedy assassinated. Tet Offensive begins turning general American opinion against the Vietnam War. Lyndon Johnson announces he will not seek re-election; Richard Nixon elected president.

1969: July 21: Neil Armstrong becomes the first man to walk on the Moon.

1970: Accusations surface of U.S. soldiers massacring Vietnamese women and children at My Lai. Kent State shootings kill four student protesters. U.S. population stands at 203,302,031.

1973: Last U.S. troops withdrawn from Vietnam. Vice President Spiro Agnew resigns amid accusations of corruption.

1974: President Richard Nixon resigns in the wake of the Watergate Scandal.

1977: Elvis Presley found dead.

1979: Iranian Revolution results in American hostages being taken in Tehran. Nuclear accident at Three Mile Island.

1980: Failed rescue attempt for Iranian hostages. May 18: Mount St. Helens erupts in Washington. Ronald Reagan elected president; his administration will drastically increase defense spending and launch the "War on Drugs." Hostages released. U.S. population stands at 226,542,199.

1981: Assassination attempt on President Reagan. AIDS first identified.

1983: Bombing of U.S. embassy in Beirut, Lebanon.

1984: Vietnam Memorial opens in Washington, D.C.

1986: 1986 Space shuttle *Challenger* explodes. Iran-Contra scandal comes to light. U.S. bombs Libya.

1988: Pan Am Flight 103 bombed over Lockerbie, Scotland.

1990: U.S. population stands at 248,709,873.

1991: The Persian Gulf War: A U.S.-led coalition defeats Iraq after that country's invasion of Kuwait.

1992: Riots in Los Angeles in wake of Rodney King verdict.

1993: World Trade Center bombed.

1995: Oklahoma City bombing; largest domestic terrorist act to date.

1999: President Bill Clinton found not guilty by the Senate after an impeachment trial.

2000: George W. Bush elected president after a controversial and divisive election. U.S. population stands at 281,421,906.

2001: September 11: Terrorists carry out the largest attack on American soil to date, hijacking planes and piloting them into the Twin Towers of the World Trade Center in New York City and the Pentagon building in Washington, D.C. America invades Afghanistan a month later.

2003: U.S. and British forces invade Iraq.

2005: Hurricane Katrina devastates New Orleans.

2006: Former Iraqi dictator Saddam Hussein executed.

2007: U.S. Coalition casualties for Iraq invasion and occupation top 4,000.

Glossary

A

AIRBORNE: Troops trained in deployment by air, either by parachute, glider, or similar assault aircraft. Can also refer to any equipment or operations related to or involving air-dropped troops.

ARMORED PERSONNEL CARRIER: Often abbreviated APC, a vehicle designed to transport troops to the battlefield in a protected environment, often alongside tanks and other armored vehicles.

ARMY: From the Latin *armata*, or "act of arming," a term that describes any land-based military force and sometimes including other branches of service as well. In modern military usage, an army is defined as a group of two or more corps. During the World Wars, the massive scale of the conflicts often saw armies being organized in turn to form Army Groups.

B

BARRAGE: A coordinated mass of artillery fire, often fired indirectly.

BATTALION: In modern military usage, a grouping of multiple companies totaling around one thousand soldiers. The smallest unit considered capable of independent, unsupported action.

BAYONET: A dagger-length blade fitted to the end of a rifle or musket. Originally developed to arm slow-firing guns with a secondary use in close combat, turning the firearm into a spear, the use of bayonet tactics was taught in European-style armies from the mid-seventeenth to the mid-twentieth century.

BEACHHEAD: A small footing gained by an army landing on enemy shores or crossing a river. Often the target of determined counterattacks.

BRIGADE: First developed by Swedish king Gustavus Adolphus during the Thirty Years War, the brigade was originally an early version of a combined arms task force consisting of several regiments of infantry, cavalry, and artillery. Modern usage places the brigade roughly on par with the regiment in terms of size.

C

CALIBER: The diameter of the bore, or inside, of a gun's barrel. Can be expressed in millimeters (i.e. 9 mm) or fractions of an inch (i.e. .50 caliber, meaning half an inch bore).

CAMPAIGN: A series of military operations, often designed towards a single objective.

CAVALRY: Soldiers who move and fight primarily from horseback. Does not generally extend to troops who use mounts to move into battle but dismount to fight, who are instead referred to as "mounted infantry."

CIVILIANS: Also called noncombatants, any non-enlisted person. As war became increasingly driven by industry in the late nineteenth and early twentieth centuries, civilians became targets of armies and the weapons of war.

COMMANDER-IN-CHIEF: A general or other leader vested with control of a nation's military forces. The United States Constitution reserves this role for the President, although only two—George Washington and James Madison—have actually led troops in the field while in office.

COMPANY: A military unit consisting of platoons, usually three or four in number, totaling anywhere from 100–200 enlisted men and officers.

CORPS: An organization of two or more divisions, grouped in turn to form armies.

D

D-DAY: A general code term for an unspecified day upon which a planned event is to take place in any given operation; the specific time is referred to as "H-hour." Since June 6, 1944, the term has become synonymous in the popular imagination with the Normandy Invasion.

DEFILADE: A position that protects a unit from direct enemy fire.

DIVISION: A concept that first emerged during the Seven Years War of the mid-eighteenth century, the division organizes ten to twenty thousand soldiers into a single unit, forming the building block of larger armies and corps. Napoleon Bonaparte was the first general to fully adopt the divisional system; by the end of the Napoleonic Wars, all of Europe's armies would be organized by divisions, as are all modern armies.

E

ENFILADE: Also known as "flanking fire," the condition whereby a unit's flank becomes exposed to enemy fire, exposing troops beyond the front rank.

ENLISTED MAN: A term used in modern military organization to refer to the lowest ranking soldiers, often including non-commissioned officers.

F

FILE: A line of troops standing one in front of another.

FLANK: As a noun, flank is a term used to describe the side of a military unit. As a verb, the action of moving against an enemy's side or rear.

FRIENDLY FIRE: Used to describe casualties arising during battle caused by friendly forces either through mistake or accident.

FRAG: A term that became well known during the Vietnam War to describe the murder of a superior officer, usually while out in the field. "Frag" is short for "fragmentation grenade," the supposed weapon of

choice in such situations, since it would leave behind no fingerprints or other ballistic evidence and could easily be chalked up to friendly fire.

FRONT: Also called a battlefront, this is the point along which two opposing forces meet. The term can be applied to anything from local engagements up to entire theaters of war.

G

GRENADE: An explosive devise originally designed to be hurled by hand, which also sends shards of metal flying through the air.

H

HALFTRACK: A vehicle utilizing caterpillar tracks for rear propulsion and standard road wheels for front propulsion. Designed to offer the cross-country capabilities of a tank and the maneuverability of a road vehicle, military halftracks were used extensively in the Second World War as some of the first armored personnel carriers.

I

INFANTRY: The backbone of most armies throughout history, the infantry is characterized by soldiers who fight and move primarily or exclusively on foot and who are armed with relatively light weapons such as spears or rifles.

IRREGULAR: A soldier trained in non-standard military techniques, often making use of loose, open deployments.

M

MEGADEATH: A term coined in 1953 meaning one million deaths. Used to describe potential death yields from various nuclear war scenarios.

N

NO MAN'S LAND: The ground between opposing forces along a front. Can be anywhere from a few yards to a mile or more in width.

NON-COMMISSIONED OFFICER: Commonly abbreviated NCO, an enlisted man given battlefield authority by a commissioned officer. The most well-known "non-com" rank is sergeant.

O

OFFICER: Also called a commissioned officer, these are individuals vested (or "commissioned") with the ability to issue commands on the battlefield. Up until relatively recently, commissions were commonly bought and sold and did not necessarily reflect actual military skill.

P

PLATOON: Originally used to describe a small detachment of men, the platoon evolved into a modern military unit usually consisting of two to four squads totaling thirty to fifty soldiers. Usually led by a low-ranking commissioned officer such as a lieutenant.

R

RANK: A line of soldiers standing shoulder to shoulder. Most regular military units up until the First World War were trained to fight in ranks.

REGIMENT: The first post-feudal military unit, developed as armies became increasingly professional and organized during the sixteenth century. Early regiments often acted as independent military entities, conducting their own recruiting and commissioning their own officers. The modern British Army still has traces of this "regimental system" in its training and deployment of its units. Modern regiments vary widely in size depending on the army and their perceived tactical usefulness and range, anywhere from a few hundred up to three thousand soldiers.

REGULAR: Term used to distinguish trained soldiers who follow commonly accepted forms of military organization and tactical deployment.

S

SQUAD: In modern military organization, the smallest recognized unit on a battlefield, most often consisting of between eight and fourteen soldiers. Called a "section" in British and Commonwealth armies.

STRATEGY: The deployment and movement of large units, from divisions up through entire army groups, to achieve a military goal.

T

TACTICS: Military methods for defeating an enemy in individual battles.

Introduction to Conflicts with Northeastern Tribes (1621–1697)

The permanent British colonization of North America began with a meeting and a peace treaty between the Plymouth colonists and Massasoit, the great sachem (leader) of the powerful Wampanoag Nation. It ended in flames and death, with the Wampanoag and other tribes dead, scattered, or sold into slavery. Generational differences, short-term memory of debts owed, and a basic need for land to support a burgeoning population drove the shift from peace to war.

When Massasoit and William Bradford, Plymouth's long-serving governor, signed their peace treaty in 1621, they did so for complex but sensible reasons. Each wanted the protection the other had to offer. Bradford wanted the security of having a powerful Native American group as an ally and Massasoit wanted the benefit of having the well-armed colonists on his side. Their treaty stood for forty years, with the Plymouth colonists demonstrating their trust in the relationship by aiding Massasoit in a time of desperate need, and Massasoit doing the same by providing the colonists with warning of impending attacks from unfriendly native groups.

But the constant arrival of new settlers coupled with changing leadership as one generation aged and the other took power led to a struggle over land that the Native Americans ultimately lost. In their quest to acquire acreage to support the exploding population, the generation of colonists forgot or chose to ignore any debt owed to Native Americans like Massasoit and his people. As insults, both intended and perceived, against the native people accumulated, Massasoit's sons, first Wamsutta (also known as Alexander) and then Metacom (also known as

Philip), became unwilling to try to work with the colonists any longer and began agitating with other tribes to join them in an uprising. After Wamsutta's death in 1662, Metacom took over leadership, and following an initial period of trying to maintain a treaty with the colonists, he gave up and started recruiting neighboring tribes, including the powerful Narragansett people.

In 1675, before Metacom succeeded in amassing the necessary number of warriors, native outrage against the colonists prematurely triggered one of the most terrible wars in New England's history, which came to be known as King Philip's War. By the time the war ended, Metacom had been killed, his people and those of many other native nations were dead, dispersed, or enslaved, and Native American tribes and culture had essentially vanished from the area. The only large group to remain standing in the northeast was the Iroquois Confederacy, which included the Mohawk and Oneida people. This Confederacy managed to work as allies with the British colonists well into the eighteenth century.

The Native Americans lost to the colonists for many reasons, but the chief imbalance between the two groups consisted of organization and the ability to replenish resources. The English had the upper hand with both, having their motherland of Britain to back them up, and having well-organized and trained troops to engage in battle. The efforts of the Native Americans were sporadic and not synchronized, and they had only the land and themselves for support in any conflict. The colonists took the land, leaving nothing behind but the memories of the relatively few Native American survivors.

Conflicts with Northeastern Tribes (1621–1697)

✪ Causes

Early Conflict in the New World

In the seventeenth century, the New World experienced the growing pangs of conflict between the native peoples and new arrivals, tensions that arose first through the need for more land to support a rapidly exploding population. More food, more housing, and the trade associated with these demands, which resulted in expanded trade and transportation networks, also contributed to the wars that sprang up during this century.

This chapter of American history opened in a surprisingly peaceful way in 1621 with the completion of a treaty between the Plymouth settlers and Massasoit (c. 1580–c. 1661), leader of the Wampanoag, the largest Indian nation in the region. Although these two parties managed to keep their bargain for forty years, other Native American tribes and newly arrived Europeans were not so amenable to peaceful agreement.

The century neared its close with a great war, brought about by a confluence of factors, including ignored treaties. It ended with Native Americans scattered and their native lands fractured. As colonists continued trying to satisfy their voracious need for more and more land, mistreatment of Native Americans escalated, as did their enslavement. The Indian nations also fought among themselves, often over whether or not to ally with the new arrivals. Even the much-vaunted treaty of peace that was upheld for forty years really resulted from a combination of Native American maneuvering to use Puritan firepower for security, and Puritans using Native American connections to expand their presence and ensure their safety.

Acrimony and dissension were no strangers to the colonists either. Originally establishing themselves in the New World to worship freely, the colonists found themselves at odds with those who did not share their beliefs. Colonists fought among one another because of religious differences and land and class conflicts. Plymouth Colony was founded on a base of religious cohesiveness and central authority, but this cohesion collapsed with the appearance of newcomers whose agendas were grounded in acquisitiveness and survival, rather than religion. To many new arrivals, the treaty between Plymouth colonists and Massasoit was almost quaint and not worth consideration. As new generations emerged, this disregard for previous agreements grew, and the New World became increasingly unstable with each arriving newcomer and each deed of mistrust between settlers and the Native Americans. Great conflict was inevitable, and two major conflicts bracket this period of American history: the Pequot War of 1637 and King Philip's War in 1675–1676.

The Pequot War

The first major conflict to break out between Indians and colonists was the Pequot War. Settlers arrived and began clearing huge tracts of land, which was contrary to native traditions of preservation. They brought with them smallpox and other diseases that decimated the native peoples, who had no natural resistance. In addition, many native tribes became dependent on European goods, including weaponry. Heightened tensions, bolstered by resentment over land and health issues and combined with access to guns, finally led to an outbreak of war in 1637.

At that time, the New England European population had peaked at about four thousand people. Within four years, it would almost triple. With the burgeoning growth, the settlers were encroaching westward, into Pequot lands. The Pequots already had reason to dislike the colonists because of their shaky alliance with their traditional enemy, the Narragansetts. The settlers just wanted the Pequots out of the way, but the economic power of the tribe was at least as great as that of the colonists.

The colonists, eager for an excuse to attack, found one when the captains of some English trading vessels turned up dead. Pointing the finger at the Pequots, the enraged colonists demanded that they turn over the murderers, even though the murderers' origins were, in fact, unknown. The Pequots claimed ignorance and even

The Pequot War, fought in 1637, resulted from conflicts between European and Native American powers over control of trade. *Stock Montage/Getty Images*

offered to negotiate with the colonists. However, seeing their chance, the Europeans sent a colonial force led by John Endecott (c. 1588–1665) from Massachusetts to attack the tribe. The army made its attack on Block Island (which lies off of the coast of Rhode Island) the first salvo in the Pequot War.

Striking back, the Pequots laid siege to a colonial fort. After a lull and some sporadic sorties, the settlers hit back hard with an attack in 1637 in what is now Mystic, Connecticut, in which almost every Pequot was killed and their entire village burned to ashes. Behind this raid was an alliance between the English and the Mohegan leader Uncas (c. 1588–c. 1682), who was well on his way to becoming leader of the most powerful tribe in Connecticut after the fall of the Pequots. In addition, the settlers talked the Narragansetts, their reluctant allies, into joining forces with the Mohegans against the Pequots.

With this combined force, the colonists attacked the Pequots on the Mystic River, hacking to pieces or shooting anyone who tried to escape the conflagration. The death count for the Pequots was about four hundred men, women, and children. William Bradford (1590–1657), governor of Plymouth Colony and witness of the peace treaty with Massasoit, described this toll as a "fearful sight," yet as a victory that seemed a "sweet sacrifice."

The Narragansett and Miantonomoh

The colonists' reluctant allies, the Narragansett, saw things differently. They did not fight like Europeans, razing villages and annihilating every living thing in sight. Their emphasis in fighting was on bravery, not body counts. The Narragansett leader, Miantonomoh (c. 1565–1643), had demanded assurances from the colonists that women and children would not be killed in the attack, but the assurances were not granted. When the Narragansett witnessed the brutal and merciless tactics of the colonists, he and his people were horrified. The sachem turned against the colonists, recruiting other tribes to fight with his people against them. Although this pan-Indian alliance was visionary, the sachem failed to execute it successfully because he was too focused on attacking Uncas and the Mohegans for their alliance with the colonists.

This distraction proved to be his demise. During a great battle with the Mohegans, Miantonomoh was captured. Uncas, the Mohegan leader, was eager to demonstrate his trustworthiness to the Puritans. He asked the colony authorities what he should do with the Narragansett sachem. The authorities left the decision to Uncas, and taking quick advantage, his brother dispatched Miantonomoh with a hatchet as they walked the path between

Hartford and Windsor, Connecticut. The few Pequot survivors of the Pequot War either were later killed or scattered across the countryside. The Treaty of Hartford officially declared the end of the Pequot Nation in 1638.

King Philip's War

King Philip's War, begun by Massasoit's son and heir, Philip (c. 1640–1676; also known as Metacom), closed this chapter of discord. Philip initiated the violence after becoming angry with the colonists' treatment of Native Americans and violations of treaties. Philip also carried a powerful hatred for the colonists because his older brother, Alexander (1634–1662; also known as Wamsutta), had died under somewhat strange circumstances while in their custody. Philip responded to these offenses by arranging an uprising known as King Philip's War.

The bloody attacks against the colonists during King Philip's War engendered hatred against the Indians that ended in a vicious campaign of search and destroy. After the war ended with the colonists as victors, surviving Native Americans were killed or sold as slaves, some of whom had surrendered under promises of mercy from the colonial governments. In a very brief period of time, the northeastern landscape, once the domain of vast and powerful tribes, was devoid of Native American life and culture.

✪ Major Figures

Massasoit

Massasoit (c. 1580–1661) was the leader of the Wampanoag. He was best known as the Native American who helped the original colonists forge and keep a peace treaty with the Wampanoag that lasted for forty years. Although history books have portrayed him as the beneficent and high-profile Indian who attended the first Thanksgiving, a closer look at his decisions and maneuvers reveals a shrewd leader who made some smart moves to position his people and himself in the best possible way given the rapidly changing landscape—literally and figuratively—of the world around them. Adding to this more nuanced understanding of the great sachem is the perception by his Native American contemporaries that he accommodated the settlers too much and primarily for his personal advantage.

Before the Settlers Massasoit was born in about 1580 and grew to become leader of what is today known as the Wampanoag Nation, although the tribe may not have achieved its massive status until Massasoit was well into his tenure as leader. He had several names, including Ousamequin (Yellow Feather), but Massasoit is the name that has survived in English-language histories. The central seat of his people was Pokanoket, or Mount Hope (present-day Bristol, Rhode Island). Massasoit was also leader of some other related tribes in southeastern New England.

No one really knows what Massasoit looked like. The only existing descriptions detail the traditional dress of a leader of his people: red face paint and a thick white-bead necklace. The settlers caught their first glimpse of this formidable figure as he stood atop a hill overlooking their colony. His appearance, with the red paint and his accompanying band of sixty warriors, struck the colonists with fear and sent them rushing for weapons. But his arrival really signaled their salvation. They had come to the New World without an inkling of how to plant appropriate crops, hunt the game that lived there, or fish the waters that surrounded them. Only half of them survived the first harsh winter of 1620–1621.

Cultures Meet Although the sight of a "very lusty man" with an "able body" standing on a hillside with sixty warriors at first frightened the winter-weary settlers, they soon realized that Massasoit intended no harm. He gave them food in exchange for what they considered to be mere trinkets and offered protection for them against bands of warriors from other tribes.

Massasoit had made his appearance in March 1621 with two other famous Native Americans, Squanto (c. 1585–1622) and Samoset (c. 1590–1653). Both knew how to speak English, Squanto because he had been kidnapped by a sea captain, sold into slavery in Spain, and freed by some monks who taught him English. Squanto managed to make his way back to his homeland, only to find that his people had been completely wiped out by diseases brought across the ocean on European ships. Squanto joined the Wampanoags. When he and Samoset emerged from the forest for the first time, Squanto greeted the settlers in their own language. Tradition holds that Squanto served as a bridge to friendship between the colonists and Massasoit.

Treaty with the Colonists Massasoit himself knew the costs of disease brought from overseas, having lost a substantial number of his people to foreign illnesses, such as smallpox and measles. He also was no stranger to the Europeans themselves, having encountered Captain John Smith (1580–1631) and others prior to the arrival of the Pilgrims. Whatever his agenda, Massasoit managed to see beyond the dangers of disease and land acquisition associated with Europeans and produce the peace treaty with the Plymouth colonists in which they agreed to live harmoniously and defend one another from outside attacks. The treaty had obvious benefits for both sides: The Native Americans could take advantage of the superior European weaponry, while the settlers had the advantage of friends on their home turf.

Even though Massasoit stuck to this treaty for so long, he did not earn accolades among other Native American tribes. They viewed his pact with the Europeans as a weakening of his own people for material goods, personal fame, and security against his greatest native enemy, the Narragansetts. Massasoit made his decision

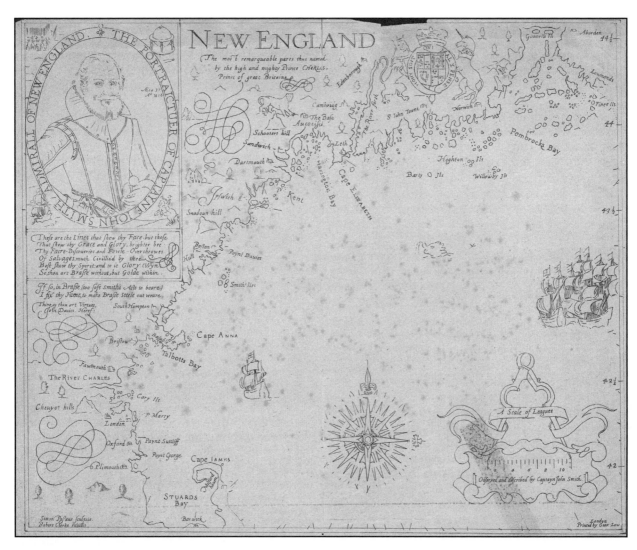

This detail of a 1650 map of New England shows the coast of the thirteen colonies as observed by John Smith. *Mansell/Time Life Pictures/Getty Images*

against a backdrop of death from European-borne disease and a history of previous conflict between Europeans and the native peoples. But Massasoit had a tough decision to make. The future seemed inevitable—Europeans were arriving no matter what he decided to do. Many of his people had died from disease, and other tribes may have wanted to attack his. With a choice between losing to another sachem or treating with the English and their superior weapons, he made the more secure choice.

Diplomacy and Disease Massasoit's willingness to enter into an alliance with the Plymouth colony left open the way for the colonists to use the Wampanoags just as the Wampanoags intended to use the colonists. Two Plymouth leaders, Edward Winslow (1595–1655) father of Josiah Winslow, who would clash with one of Massasoit's sons, and Stephen Hopkins (c. 1582–1644) traveled to the Wampanoag home seat to visit. They were shocked to find the grounds littered with human skel-

etons, the remains of those who had died of disease in such great numbers that not enough survivors remained to bury them all. They also were shocked and displeased to spend two sleepless nights fighting off lice and other vermin in their sleeping quarters before returning to the colony. Yet, they and the leaders back at Plymouth believed that maintaining this friendship with Massasoit was of great importance, as subsequent events showed.

Winslow again went beyond the call of diplomatic duty when he was sent in response to a message from Massasoit in 1623 that he was dying. As Winslow approached the settlement, Massasoit sent word that he was actually dead, explaining to the perplexed diplomat after his arrival that this tactic was a custom intended to make people even happier when the "dead" person turned up alive. But Massasoit was, in fact, near death. His tongue was furred and he could not swallow food. Winslow did more than probably any diplomat before or since by scraping the furring off of the dying sachem's tongue and then administering some fruit preserves to the starving man. Massasoit probably had contracted typhus, which was then called "pestilential fever." It was spread by lice, and Massasoit, after a surprisingly quick recovery, requested that Winslow administer the same scraping treatment to other afflicted members of his tribe. Winslow reluctantly did so, but was apparently well repaid when Massasoit's interpreter, Hobbamock, reported to him that the Massachusetts tribe planned to attack Plymouth.

The Plymouth leaders were at first unsure what to do with the information, but following a violent and vengeful raid by Captain Miles Standish (c. 1584–1656) against some Native Americans, the Massachusetts tribe solved the issue themselves by fleeing into the security of the wilderness. However, their safety was short-lived because they could not farm the land or otherwise accomplish their usual tasks to ensure food for the people. Hiding in the woods, they starved. Standish's brief but decisive attack had, in fact, ended in the deaths of some of the most influential Indian leaders on Cape Cod, which, as it turns out, left the way open for Massasoit to step in and establish his Wampanoag nation as the most powerful in the region.

Massasoit eventually came to have less trust in his English partners. A few years before his death, he entered a kind of retirement away from the spotlight. His older son, Wamsutta, also known as Alexander, briefly took his place as leader. Massasoit died in the winter of 1661. Fourteen years after Massasoit's death, his son Metacom, also known as King Philip, initiated one of the most devastating wars in New England's history in rebellion against the colonists' encroachment on native lands.

William Bradford

Early Life William Bradford (1590–1657) was the second leader of the Pilgrims and its governor. Bradford was born in March 1590, in Austerfield, Yorkshire, England, to a family of yeomen farmers. His mother, Alice Hanson, was the daughter of the village shopkeeper, and William was the third child and only son.

Bradford exhibited preternatural solemnity even at a young age. By the time he was twelve, both of his parents, his sister, and his grandfather had died. Because of an illness of his own, the young Bradford was unable to engage in the usual work and play of children his age and instead turned to books for solace. He discovered the *Geneva Bible*, an annotated version of the Christian religious texts from the previous century, and also fell under the influence of John Foxe's *Foxe's Book of Martyrs* (1563). In his book, Foxe argued that England was a chosen nation and that a godly Englishman might sometimes be called on to die as a martyr in the cause of the true religion.

Religion Just what exactly the true religion was formed the subject of life-or-death debate during Bradford's childhood in northern England. Traditionalists—Catholics and conservative Protestants alike—held that the entrenched rituals and hierarchy of the church were the true roads to understanding God. But others formed a dedication to purifying the church, replacing the formalities and middlemen with a direct relationship between the individual and God. Some of these Puritans came to feel that the traditional church was not salvageable and that a complete separation was in order. These Separatists held that their congregations must consist of those who were "Elect," God's chosen at birth, with their godliness manifest in every aspect of the way they lived their lives. Although no one truly knew whether a person was Elect, members of the congregation closely monitored one another and themselves to ensure that members adhered to the true path. Willful, uncorrected straying ended in excommunication.

Separatists and Puritans were never completely welcome in England, but when James I took the throne following the death of Elizabeth I in 1603, he swore to "harry" these rabble-rousers off the island. In spite of this oath, he made it almost impossible for them to leave, forcing anyone who traveled to other lands to freely practice their chosen form of worship to do so in secret. Bradford, at age seventeen, escaped with members of a congregation he had joined at age twelve, a move he made against the wishes of his uncles, who had become his guardians. Not only had he joined the congregation at that young age in the face of serious personal danger, but he also left for new lands in the face of strong counterarguments from his relatives. Among their points, they insisted that Bradford was due to come into his inheritance at the age of twenty-one. His connection to his church proved stronger, and he sailed with the congregation to Holland.

Travels The congregation ultimately ended up in Leiden (or Leyden), Holland, in 1609, where Bradford became a fustian, or corduroy, maker. He came of age while living there, also coming into his inheritance, which he used to purchase a home and to marry Dorothy May. In the end, he suffered severe financial losses, which he interpreted as corrective messages from God. He continued to interpret events always in the context of God's guiding hand.

By 1620, the congregation in Leiden, which consisted of about five hundred people, was no longer welcome in Holland because of shifting relations in the European map, and Bradford was with the first group that sailed on the *Mayflower* for the New World. After playing a leading role in insisting that the tradesmen involved in the *Mayflower* venture adhere to their original terms and not cheat the colonists, he took his first steps toward becoming a major figure in the new colony. He also was a signer of the Mayflower Compact, the

Massasoit and Governor John Carver signed the earliest recorded treaty in New England. *MPI/Stringer/Hulton Archive/Getty Images*

document that the settlers drew up to ensure representative government and rule of law. This compact was, in fact, the first written constitution in the New World. His life was not, however, a series of positive events and successes. He lost his first wife almost immediately after their arrival in Plymouth Harbor, where she mysteriously drowned as the *Mayflower* stood anchored more than a mile off shore.

Bradford and the Native Americans The colonists barely scraped through the terrible winter of 1620–1621 during which many of their group died. As new arrivals, the people had no idea how to hunt, fish, or grow the food they needed to subsist. The survivors of that first dreadful, demoralizing winter elected Bradford their governor when he was only thirty years old, after the death of their first leader, John Carver (c. 1576–1621). One of Carver's most important acts as governor was negotiation of a peace treaty with Massasoit, shortly before his death. Bradford oversaw the peace that Carver negotiated, and probably dined with his couonterpart Massasoit at what was to be known as the first Thanksgiving.

Another of Bradford's major achievements was his book *Of Plymouth Plantation*, in which he detailed the

events of his life as a colonist and governor. Among other things, this chronicle traces Bradford's own evolution in attitude regarding the Native Americans. When he arrived in the New World, he described the native people as savages, wild beasts, and cannibals. By the end of his chronicle, however, he was using the term "Indian" in almost every case. By that time he had so much experience with untrustworthy Europeans who had tried in various ways to swindle the colony that the Native Americans compared favorably. As an example of his change in perspective, Bradford listened to a case in which several colonists murdered an Indian, and he upheld the court's decision to sentence the perpetrators to death, even though some members of the colony felt the sentence was too harsh.

Leadership Even though Bradford attributed the positive events of his tenure as governor to divine Providence— including meeting Squanto and Samoset, whose help pulled the colony through the first rough years—the successes were also due to his leadership. He proved clever at obtaining information about different tribes by playing informants off one another and maintained a policy of fairness to the native people that earned their friendship in many quarters and kept his own people safe. He also managed to find the best use for people who were not in Plymouth for religious reasons, including adventurers like Miles Standish and John Alden (c. 1599–1687). Bradford maintained Plymouth colony's position and rights in the face of difficulties with other, newer colonies who did not care as much about good relations with the native peoples or even with other colonies. The Plymouth people liked his leadership enough to elect him governor of their colony thirty times. After a life of adventure, loss, gain, and the stressful decision making required of a leader under great pressure, Bradford enjoyed some quiet sunset years, dying peacefully at his home in May 1657.

Wamsutta

Wamsutta (c. 1634–1662), also known by the Christian name he selected, Alexander, was the older son of Massasoit. Wamsutta and his brother, Metacom (also called Philip), were not as strongly interested in keeping the peace as their father. Indeed, by the time they became leaders of the Wampanoag, William Bradford and similar leaders of the previous generation had been replaced by less peace-oriented colonial leaders, as well.

Early Events Although his father survived into his eighties or nineties, Wamsutta lived a comparatively short life, meeting an early, violent death before the age of thirty. He was born around 1634, a prince among the Wampanoag, which came to be the largest tribe living among the colonists. The tribe's principal seat was in Pokanoket (present Bristol, Rhode Island), and Wamsutta and his followers consistently returned to these lands in times of trouble or great success, especially Mount Hope overlooking Hope Bay.

He encountered plenty of trouble in his short, violent life. At first, Wamsutta followed his father's lead, confirming with his father in 1639 an original treaty with the colonists at Plymouth pledging mutual support and assistance. He and his father also worked together in selling off some of the native lands, including Dartmouth in 1652 for thirty yards of material, eight moose skins, and some axes, hoes, shoes, and an iron pot. The next year, the two sold more lands of their people for twenty-five pounds (almost $10,000 today).

Interaction with Colonists Massasoit, world-weary and in need of rest, entered a quasi-retirement with the Quabaugs in 1657, leaving a void that Wamsutta willingly stepped in to fill as the new leader of the Wampanoag. Prior to this, in 1654, Wamsutta had sold Hog Island, which lies in Narragansett Bay, to a Rhode Island man named Richard Smith. He made this sale without the approval of either his father or of the Plymouth leaders, which was required for such transactions. Smith, who had been booted from Plymouth, claimed ignorance about the rules. Even Massasoit eventually came around and approved the sale in 1657, right about the time he entered his retirement phase.

A colored engraving shows Mary Rowlandson's kidnapping and captivity during King Philip's War. *The Granger Collection, New York. Reproduced by permission*

Just following this transaction, Wamsutta rebelled and attracted further attention by refusing to sell land his father had promised to the people of Taunton. The documents for the sale had listed as a witness John Sassamon (c. 1620–1675), a Native American who had become one of the "Praying Indians," converts to the settlers' Christian faith. Sassamon was also an interpreter who had attended Harvard College and served as a scribe for Wamsutta. It may have been at Sassamon's urging or suggestion that Wamsutta and his brother, Metacom, came before a Plymouth court in 1660 to change their names to Alexander and Philip, respectively.

His Confidant Wamsutta had also placed his faith in a merchant from Plymouth named Thomas Willett (1611–1674), who traded with the Dutch colony New Netherland, destined eventually to be New York. Willett had married the daughter of John Brown, who was Massasoit's close confidant among the colonists. Willett eventually became the first mayor of Manhattan because of his frequent trade with the Dutch and his fluency in the language. As he began to spend more time in and eventually move to New York from Plymouth, Wamsutta lost his confidant and saw Willett's replacement, Josiah Winslow (c. 1629–1680), as no replacement for his friendship with Willett.

Josiah Winslow and the New Generations Winslow was a different breed from the Bradfords, Browns, and Willetts who had preceded him. Well educated at Harvard, married to a beautiful wife, Winslow viewed the Native Americans with eyes very different from those of previous colonial leaders like William Bradford. This new generation saw the native peoples as an obstacle to prosperity, whereas William Bradford had wisely seen how the native peoples could help the colonists. The younger generation had forgotten the debt of gratitude they owed the Indians for their very existence in the New World.

At the same time, the new generation of Native Americans also differed from their elders. Wamsutta had already shown himself able to dismiss his father's previous promises, not once but twice selling land that his father had agreed to dispose of otherwise. There also were rumors circulating that Wamsutta was agitating the Narragansetts, trying to get them to join forces with him to fight the English. The English, for their part, were becoming increasingly fearful and summoned Wamsutta before the court to explain his behavior regarding the illegal land sale. Wamsutta did not appear as summoned.

Wamsutta's Death Josiah Winslow saw Wamsutta's failure to appear as an opportunity to deal with this upstart, agitation-fomenting Wampanoag leader, and he set out in July 1662 with ten armed men on horseback. They tracked Wamsutta to his fishing and hunting lodge on Monponsett Pond (present-day Halifax, Massachusetts), arriving in the morning to find the sachem and his wife, Weetamoo, enjoying a breakfast as their weapons rested out of reach. Winslow's group immediately surrounded them and seized the weapons. A tense confrontation both inside and outside the lodge ended with Winslow holding a pistol to Wamsutta's chest, saying, "I have been ordered to bring you to Plymouth, and by the help of God, I will do it."

The interpreter intervened at this point, suggesting that Wamsutta go with Winslow, which the sachem agreed to do as long as he was escorted like the leader he was, not as a prisoner. He and his attendants walked long miles that hot July day. Shortly thereafter, while lodging in Winslow's home, Wamsutta became ill with a fever that some historians today believe may have been appendicitis. If it was, the treatments he received, primarily powerful purgatives, could only have worsened his condition. His attendants were allowed to transport him back to Mount Hope, where he died a few days later. Hundreds and possibly thousands of Native Americans assembled at this gathering place of their homeland to mourn the death of their leader and celebrate the ascendancy to leadership of his younger brother, Philip.

Naturally, many suspicions arose about the circumstances of Wamsutta's death, with blame assigned to the hot July march or suggestions that Wamsutta was starved in custody. His younger brother, Metacom (Philip), was convinced that Winslow had poisoned the sachem, and

his hatred against Winslow was so bitter that when the inevitable war finally broke out, Winslow felt compelled to secure his wife in another settlement and to fortify his home against Philip's wrath.

Metacom

Metacom (1640–1676) was the younger son of Massasoit and the leader of the most severe Indian war in the history of New England. Metacom was also known by his British-bestowed name of Philip. He was a complex figure during his lifetime, and to historians who have studied him since.

Early Life Metacom's older brother, Wamsutta (Alexander), became sachem when Massasoit retired, and from the time of his accession, relations between the Wampanoags and the colonists deteriorated rapidly. The previous generation, led by Massasoit and Plymouth's John Carver, had forged a forty-year peace treaty, but the peace fell in tatters as the new generation stepped in.

Metacom as Leader and Legend Wamsutta's brief rule came to an abrupt end after he died following a short stint in colonial custody. His death led to charges of murder, and Metacom never forgave the colonists for what he believed was their role in his brother's death. Metacom took his brother's place as sachem in a memorial service/celebration at his people's seat of power on Mount Hope. He renewed his alliance with the English, yet rumors that he was planning an uprising soon circulated. Although it was true that several tribes were planning rebellions of some kind in 1667, 1669, and 1671, no one knew with certainty whether the Wampanoags were involved.

Metacom began his rule with an aura of legend that only grew with time. His people said that when he stepped into his brother's shoes as sachem, he stood on top of Mount Hope and hurled a stone two miles to the other side of the peninsula. He was only twenty-four years old and destined to live only a few years more.

Serious conflict over land rights emerged in 1667 when the Plymouth colonists decided to violate an agreement and allow a land purchase in Wampanoag borders. The Native Americans tried to intimidate the colonists by assembling war parties around the disputed territory. In 1671, the worried colonists demanded a meeting with Metacom. They couched the meeting as nonthreatening and diplomatic, yet when Metacom arrived with his well-armed entourage, the colonists held them at gunpoint and bullied them to sign a document admitting Metacom's "naughtiness" in his heart. The sachem ultimately was forced to sign a treaty placing the Wampanoag under colonial rule.

Metacom's response was to really begin planning an uprising, and the ensuing conflict became known as King Philip's War, which lasted from 1675 to 1676. His strategy was to enlist help from other native peoples, including the Nipmuck (or Nipmuc), who were unhappy

Puritans attacking King Philip's Fort.

By the summer of 1676, the New England Puritans were able to capture Metacom's family and overcome the sachem himself in battle. *Picture Collection, The Branch Libraries, The New York Public Library, Astor Lenox, and Tilden Foundations*

with the colonists' attempts to acquire more lands. His efforts to recruit the Narragansetts, erstwhile English allies, and traditional Wampanoag enemies, were unsuccessful. This failure would end in tragedy for Metacom and the Narragansetts and victory for the colonists.

Strangely enough, the British could claim as their allies the Pequots, in spite of the outcome of the Pequot War. Also on the British side were the Mohegans, loyal allies of the Connecticut colonies. Without the Narragansett, who were the most powerful group in the region, Metacom did not have the fighting force he needed to defeat the English, and when the war began, he was unprepared. Tensions reached the snapping point in 1675 with the death of John Sassamon, a Native American and convert to Christianity who had attended Harvard College and spoke fluent English. Sassamon had served as Metacom's assistant and translator before returning to the "Praying Indian" community, where he eventually became a preacher. Metacom despised Sassamon for turning his back on his people and ordered Sassamon's murder, if the scaffold confession of one of three Wampanoags executed for the crime is to be believed. Sassamon had been found dead in a pond, and the three suspects had been convicted by both British and Native American juries, based largely on the testimony of a single witness. Although two of the men

died without confessing, the third did not die instantly when the rope around his neck drew taut, and he attempted to save his life by implicating the other two men. The colonists later hanged him anyway.

King Philip's War Begins The outrage over this execution triggered the war, whether Metacom was ready or not. The colonists had the opening they needed to achieve their real goal of removing the Native Americans completely. On June 23, 1675, an Englishman shot and killed a Wampanoag who was thought to have looted some of the homes in the settlement of Swansea. In response, Metacom's people killed nine members of the Swansea settlement. Attacks on towns in Massachusetts Bay and Plymouth followed, in a wave of violence that trapped both colonists and Native American groups who initially had no intentions of engaging in conflict. King Philip's War spread through the colonies like a plague, coming at one point within twenty miles of Boston, the largest colonial city. In addition to natives attacking colonists, tribes were attacking tribes, as the Mohawks did at the behest of the New York colony's governor.

Metacom was not ready for the war: His planned alliances were not in place, and he did not have enough people to fight the larger colonial forces. Helpless to stop an uprising and touched off by rage instead of calculation, he turned to escape. When the colonial army attempted to lay siege to Metacom and his people near their home on Mount Hope, Metacom slipped away with a group of his warriors and their families. After attacking and burning some villages, Metacom finally managed to join forces with the Narragansetts, who had been goaded into the alliance by the colonists' behavior. During the ensuing winter of 1675–1676, these allied tribes burned several colonial towns, sending a river of refugees streaming into Boston.

Nevertheless, a lack of coordination would be the downfall of the native peoples. Even though the war bears his English name, Metacom was no protogeneral, organizing and directing troops. The course of the war meandered through random surprise attacks and ambushes, with few attempts at organizing them for maximum effect. For the first time, the Native Americans could use firearms in battle, but the colonists simply responded with better-defended garrisons. The colonists also always had their overseas motherland to turn to for supplies and to replenish their arms, whereas the Native Americans had only themselves.

Metacom Is Killed Even as Metacom sought more alliances, some tribes grew weary of their losses and sought terms of surrender or tried to take advantage of colonial offers of mercy, many by the spring of 1676. On a single day in Boston, 180 Native Americans surrendered, having run out of food and weapons. By the time August rolled around, the war had fizzled to its end. That month, Captain Benjamin Church (1639–1718) encountered Metacom in disguise by the Taunton River, but the sachem escaped. Captain Church instead captured Metacom's wife and son and transported them to Boston. Shortly afterward, a Native American informant—bitter against Metacom for killing a relative for suggesting a truce—told Captain Church where to find the sachem.

On August 12, 1676, Captain Church and his troops surprised Metacom at Mount Hope, where Metacom met his end, killed by a single shot from a Native American named Alderman who was fighting with Church's troops. Metacom's body was quartered and the pieces sent for display around the colonies, his head ending up on public display in Boston. Alderman received the sachem's hand and preserved it in a bottle of rum, making a tidy sum from exhibiting it to curious colonists. Metacom's wife and son were sold into slavery in the West Indies.

Metacom's people were not the only ones to pay a heavy price for the war. The hatred engendered against the native peoples resulted in a campaign of search and destroy in which surviving tribal members were killed or sold as slaves. Many of the Native Americans who surrendered under the mercy offered by the colonial leaders ended up sold into slavery, while others barely hung on in isolated settlements. In the short period of King Philip's War, Native American life had essentially vanished from the northeastern landscape.

Benjamin Church

Early Life Benjamin Church (1639–1718) was responsible for the capture of Metacom. Church was born in 1639 into a well-connected Plymouth family. He was the son of Richard and Elizabeth Church and reared to be a carpenter, like his father, an apprenticeship that took him all over Plymouth Colony in his early years. By 1674, he had acquired a patch of land of his own near the southeastern edge of Narragansett Bay, at Sakonnet (present-day Little Compton, Rhode Island), and had taken Alice Southworth for his wife. As he began building his family a home, he became well acquainted with the native Sakonnet people who lived in the area, befriending especially their female sachem (leader), Awashonks. The Native Americans, for their part, greatly respected Church. His fellow Puritans, on the other hand, eyed him suspiciously for his friendship with the native peoples and with the possibly even more suspect Baptists and Quakers who lived nearby.

Church was an ambitious man who became a soldier, rather than entering into the carpentry trade in which he was trained. His homestead lay only five miles away from where Metacom began agitating for a rebellion against the colonists. These rumors reached Church thanks to his friendship with Awashonks, who warned

Benjamin Church (1639–1718) led the colonists in the Great Swamp Fight, a bloody battle in King Philip's War. *The Granger Collection, New York. Reproduced by Permission*

Defeat of the Iroquois by Samuel de Champlain and Algonquin warriors in 1609. © *Corbis*

Church of Metacom's intentions, telling him that Metacom had asked her people to join forces with his Wampanoags. Metacom's warriors were, in fact, threatening Awashonks. When Church arrived to consult with her, he found himself serving as a negotiator between the female sachem and Metacom's intimidating emissaries. He also attempted to seek aid for Weetamoo, the widow of Metacom's brother Wamsutta, who was reluctant to go along with Metacom's agenda and sought safety. Before Church could execute either of his plans to help Awashonks, Weetamoo, and their people, the war began. This tendency to negotiation and aid, however, would become a trademark of his impulse to confer and compromise, rather than to kill and brutalize.

King Philip's War When King Philip's War broke out in June 1675, Church joined up with the Plymouth forces and fought in several skirmishes over the course of the ensuing summer, leading small groups of soldiers. For some time, he did not participate in any major battles, although he managed to glean quite a bit of information about native tactics, including their technique of spreading themselves thin and wide across a large area to make it difficult for the enemy to destroy their core. Church also campaigned vocally in favor of taking the offense and actively pursuing and destroying the enemy, rather than taking a defensive position and focusing on fort building; however, his superior officers failed to listen to him, not for the last time.

One of Church's chief characteristics that emerged during the course of this war was his almost foolhardy recklessness and bravery in battle. Accompanying this Churchill-like disdain for flying bullets was an apparently endless run of good luck. In one battle, a comrade, Andrew Belcher, was gravely injured. The other troops, who had taken frightened cover, were too scared or too sensible to risk their lives to rescue Belcher in a rain of native weapons fire. Church, scorning their fear, braved a volley of bullets from the native fighters to rush into the field and pull his fellow soldier out from under the horse that had pinned him to the ground. Church also retrieved the body of another fallen soldier at the same time and sent the two back on the horses he had brought with him. Not satisfied with these acts of bravery, he then rescued Belcher's horse, completely ignoring a second volley of fire. Not a single bullet hit him. This aura of invincibility followed him to the end of his long life, when ironically, he died as a result of a fall from his horse.

It was during the Great Swamp Fight, a major battle during King Philip's War, that Church made his name as a fighter and as a man with powers of foresight. The battle, which took place on December 19, 1675, in a swamp near the site of a large Narragansett fort near present-day South Kingston, Rhode Island, was devastating both for the colonial troops and the Narragansetts they fought.

Church was captain of a Plymouth company and was wounded twice in the battle. After the fighting ended and the colonists had prevailed, Church lobbied to have the troops remain at the Narragansett fort to recuperate. Yet again, the colonial leaders refused to heed him. They chose instead to burn the fort to the ground, along with hundreds of native elderly, women, and children who died terrible deaths in the flames. As a result of this decision, the number of colonial troops who died on their return march from the battle, lugging more than two hundred of their dead and wounded with them, was much greater than it would have been had they rested at the fort. In the end, the English lost a fifth of the troops who had engaged in the Great Swamp Fight. Between 250 and 600 Narragansetts died that day.

As the war dragged on with hit-and-run attacks from the native troops and bloody responses from the colonists, Church expanded the ranks of Native Americans allied with the troops by offering his captives the choice of fighting by his side or being sold into slavery. Many opted to risk their lives in battle rather than succumb to a brutal death in the heat of a Caribbean sugarcane plantation. With his expanded force, Church managed to capture one of Philip's wives and one of his sons, both of whom were transported to Boston and sold into slavery.

The Capture of Metacom   In August 1676, Captain Church accidentally stumbled across a disguised Metacom lurking near the Taunton River, but the Wampanoag sachem escaped after being recognized by one of Church's native companions. The English captain then learned from a vengeful informant that Metacom had returned to Mount Hope, the seat of the Wampanoag Nation. The informant said he was revealing Metacom's whereabouts because the sachem had killed his relative for suggesting a truce.

On August 12, 1676, Church and his troops surprised Metacom at his home-base camp at Mount Hope, and the native leader died from a single shot delivered by a Pocasset who was accompanying Church's troops. This Pocasset, who went by the name of Alderman, was one of the Native American captives who had chosen to fight with Church rather than be sold into slavery.

Church swore that no bone of Metacom's would find rest in a grave. The body of the Wampanoag sachem ended in pieces that were sent to colonial capitals for decades of public display, his head being placed for public viewing in Boston. The war was over.

After King Philip's War ended, Church went on to lead five expeditions against the French and Indians in Maine and Nova Scotia on behalf of King William III (1650–1702) and then Queen Anne (1665–1714) from 1689 to 1704. The loyalty of the Sakonnets he

had known was so great that many of them joined him in these forays. He achieved the rank of colonel but was not well compensated for his hard work and retired in 1704. He became obese in later age and required two aides to help him get over fallen trees. In spite of his heft, he could apparently still ride a horse. He died of injuries sustained from a fall from his horse on January 17, 1718.

A Different Point of View   One of Church's archrivals was Samuel Mosley (1641–c. 1680), an English captain who believed in the idea that "the only good Indian is a dead Indian." Church had a very different attitude, choosing to try to understand another culture and reach compromises, rather than brutally slaying every Native American in sight. His final act of the war underscored his attitude, which was distinctive for his time. Church's men had captured a Native American elder who called himself "Conscience." The Puritan captain took such a liking to the older man that instead of allowing the captive to be taken to Plymouth and sold into slavery, Church instead quietly released him to one of the man's friends in Swansea.

Plymouth officials had offered clemency to any Native Americans who surrendered to them during the course of the war and its aftermath. However, many of those who did surrender were sold into slavery instead. The colonial leaders felt that this reneging on a promise was justified, reasoning that because some Native Americans were guilty of attacking settlers, all of them were guilty. Benjamin Church strongly demurred, being repulsed by the decision and writing that he had opposed it "to the loss of the good will and respect of some" who had previously been his friends.

As this iconoclasm illustrates, Church was a new kind of man fit for the New World, an amalgam of the civilized and the frontier, someone who knew his way around the wilds and understood Native American culture. He provided the prototype for the American frontiersmen who followed him. Church also satisfied his strong ambition by personally reviewing and approving his son's hair-raising accounts of his exploits, *Entertaining Passages Relating to Philip's War* (1716), which cast the older Church as the first American hero—brave, smart, and lucky beyond belief.

✪ Major Battles

The Battle of Bloody Brook

The battle between settlers and Native Americans over land and ascendancy in Massachusetts Bay began in earnest in August 1675 when the Nipmucks (also given as Nipmuc) attacked the town of Brookfield, Massachusetts, an isolated settlement in the colony. The tiny town, consisting of only twenty houses and lying at

This monument memorializes the 1675 Battle of Bloody Brook between colonists and Nimpuck Native Americans. *Photography Collection, Miriam and Ira D. Wallach Division of Art, Prints and Photographs, The New York Public Library, Astor, Lenox, and Tildon Foundations*

least a day's travel from its nearest neighbor, saw the beginning of its end with an ambush. The Nipmucks laid in wait for a diplomatic delegation from Boston that had ventured into their territory to try to make peace with them. Instead, eight colonists died in the attack, including three townsmen from Brookfield. To the horror of the remaining inhabitants, hundreds of Nipmuck then emerged from the surrounding countryside and laid siege to the town. Eighty townspeople hunkered down in the home of a man who had died during the initial ambush. They fended off the Nipmucks for twenty days. For their part, the Indians tried various tactics to burn out the settlers, including firing flaming arrows into the house and rolling a cartful of burning rags into the side of the home at one point. Luckily for the settlers, a quick squall of rain doused the flames.

The siege ended when fifty troopers arrived and battled off the Nipmucks, but the tribe surfaced only two weeks later in an attack in Lancaster, Massachusetts, that killed eight people. To add to the injury, a hurricane slammed into the east coast at the end of August, an event that the Indians saw as the fury of the gods targeting the settlers.

Bloody Brook Gets Its Name At the beginning of September 1675, Richard Beers (c. 1616–1675) took thirty-six men to evacuate the town of Northfield, Massachusetts, which was under threat of attack. Beers apparently was unaware of the Native American battle tactic of using concealment and walked straight into an ambush in which twenty-one people died.

Following on the heels of this attack only two weeks later, a military company accompanied a group of carts carrying grain straight through Nipmuck territory. The wheat was the fruit of the harvest of Deerfield, a settlement that had been abandoned under threat of Indian attacks. A military garrison at Hadley would benefit from these cartloads of wheat, which warranted saving. On September 19, Captain Thomas Lathrop (c. 1610–1675) conducted his eighty men toward Hadley, which had a mill for grinding the grain. They approached a small brook known as Muddy Brook, where the early autumn grapes bending their vines apparently were so irresistible that many members of the company laid down their weapons to pick them. This foolhardy choice in the midst of an area known to be packed with hostile Native Americans ended in tragedy for the garrison. As Lathrop's soldiers plucked the grapes, a huge force of several hundred Nipmucks emerged from the dense forest and attacked.

The soldiers did not have a chance. Lathrop died instantly. Bullets and arrows seemed to come from all directions, taking out colonial troops before they could even reach for their discarded weapons. All of the cart drivers died, and only a few of the soldiers survived the attack. Within minutes, the rest lay bleeding to death or dead, their blood flowing red into the muddy stream that had halted their progress. From that time, the brook became known as Bloody Brook, where the waters mingled with the blood of the fallen troops.

Samuel Mosley The Native American victors took the moment to celebrate, joyfully beginning to plunder the soldiers and the wagons. Their celebration was short-lived. As it turns out, Captain Samuel Mosley was nearby with his men and heard the gunshots. Unfortunately for the Nipmucks, he also ascribed to the idea that the "only good Indian was a dead Indian," and was the most fierce Indian fighter in Massachusetts Bay. His hatred for Native Americans extended so far that he never believed in the genuineness of the "Praying Indians," those who had converted to Christianity, and he always distrusted Native American scouts. Even though just the year before he had burned to the ground the wigwams of a friendly tribe in New Hampshire and also had strung together a group of Praying Indians with a rope and marched them into Boston, no one had ever moved to stop him. Part of his power lay in the fact that the governor was a relative, and Mosley himself had achieved popularity for his exploits. His cruelty was breathtaking—in one letter, he

Though the British sustained heavy casualties during the Great Swamp Fight, they succeeded in destroying the Narragansett fort. *The Granger Collection, New York. Reproduced by permission*

casually dropped that he had ordered a captive Native American woman to be torn to pieces by dogs.

Mosley hurried to the scene of the bloody ambush, only to be greeted with shouts of "Come on, Mosley. Here are enough Indians for you," from the Nipmucks. His response to these taunts was to battle the Native Americans for six hours, keeping his men together and moving as a single unit, moving back and forth in front of the Nipmuck lines, firing away. Even though the Nipmucks greatly outnumbered Mosley's sixty troops, the English soldiers held off the Indians until Major Robert Treat (1622–1710), commander-in-chief of the Connecticut troops, arrived just at sunset with one hundred English fighting men and enough Mohegan allies to bring a stop to the action. In the end, the settlers buried sixty-seven of their own in a single mass grave at Bloody Brook.

The evening after the battle, the Nipmucks, who had vanished into the forest, taunted Mosley and his men by emerging periodically and waving articles of clothing from their dead comrades. The colonists ultimately abandoned Deerfield completely, which was then destroyed by Metacom and his warriors during the course of King Philip's War.

The Great Swamp Fight

This key battle of what became known as King Philip's War took place on a freezing winter day on December 19, 1675. The colonial forces attacked a fort held by the Narragansett people in the middle of the Great Swamp (near present-day South Kingstown, Rhode Island), near Narragansett Bay. This tribe had initially been the colonists' shaky ally against the Wampanoags, but eventually turned against the English, who had decided on somewhat flimsy evidence to view the Narrangansetts as enemies.

Rampant rumors drove the British to attack the Narragansetts, who compounded the perceived threat by refusing to surrender to the English any Wampanoag refugees taking shelter with the Narragansett people. Slogging through the snow, one thousand British troops under the leadership of colonial Governor Josiah Winslow (c. 1629–1680) made their way to an island in the Great Swamp where the Narragansett fort stood. The first British assault at one in the afternoon was a disastrous failure initially; the colonists sustained tremendous losses. By five that evening, however, they had breached the rear of the fort and ordered it set on fire after fighting within the structure. Women and children screamed as they died in their flaming homes.

Before the fort was set aflame, Captain Benjamin Church, who fought in this battle and was wounded twice, urged Winslow and his other superiors to let the wounded spend the night in the fort. Winslow declined to take Church's advice, a decision that undoubtedly led to more deaths among his men as they made the difficult march back to their garrison, carrying their two hundred dead and wounded with them. By the time the Great Swamp Fight ended, twenty percent of the colonial soldiers lay dead, as did several hundred Narragansett people.

The destruction of the fort by fire not only destroyed any potential shelter for the injured soldiers from the cold of a December night, but it also reduced to ashes the huge store of food and supplies the Narragansetts had accumulated. The English lost six captains and 120 men in the fighting, but they lost many more during the arduous and deadly march back to their garrison in what is now Wickford, Rhode Island. The march incapacitated another four hundred soldiers so seriously that the army had to halt its winter campaign, although Winslow had mustered another large army within a month. These troops, however, were so poorly supplied that after a few weeks of chasing the remaining Narragansetts all over the colonies, the soldiers were forced to eat their horses and the pursuit itself became infamous as the Hungry March.

In spite of the large number of casualties, the English had achieved their primary goal, which was the routing and destabilization of the Narragansett people, one of the most powerful Native American groups in the region.

✪ The Home Front

Salem Witch Trials

One year in the early 1690s, a group of girls gathered around a bowl in a house in Salem, Massachusetts. Among them was the daughter of the house, nine-year-old Elizabeth (Betty) Parris, whose father was a Puritan minister, and her cousin, eleven-year-old Abigail. Most of the other girls worked as servants in the village of Salem. The girls had secretly convened a few times, to try out some of the magic rites the Parris girls had picked up from their West Indian slave, Tituba. One girl cracked an egg into the bowl, and they all leaned forward to see the egg white. Gradually and to their horror, the albuminous white took on the shape of a coffin, a sure sign of death approaching. The girls began having hallucinations and strange physical ailments, some of them babbling incoherently. Doctors were called in and diagnosed witchcraft.

Many people consider their behavior to be the kick-off of the infamous events known as the Salem witch trials. But the atmosphere necessary for a doctor to diagnose witchcraft as a serious cause of illness began forming long before the Parris girls and their friends met for their secret magic ceremonies.

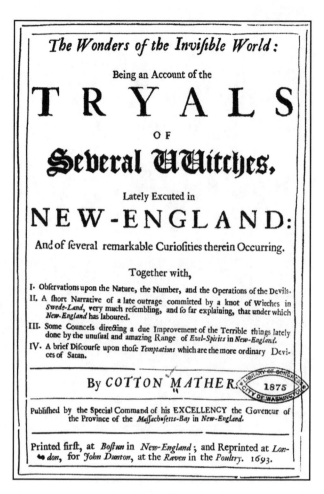

The Wonders of the Invisible World:

Being an Account of the

TRYALS

OF

Several Witches,

Lately Excuted in

NEW-ENGLAND:

And of several remarkable Curiosities therein Occurring.

Together with,

I. Obfervations upon the Nature, the Number, and the Operations of the Devils.

II. A fhort Narrative of a late outrage committed by a knot of Witches in *Swede-Land*, very much refembling, and fo far explaining, that under which *New-England* has laboured.

III. Some Councels directing a due Improvement of the Terrible things lately done by the unufual and amazing Range of *Evil-Spirits* in *New-England*.

IV. A brief Difcourfe upon thofe *Temptations* which are the more ordinary Devices of Satan.

By COTTON MATHER.

Publifhed by the Special Command of his EXCELLENCY the Governcur of the Province of the *Maffachufetts-Bay* in *New-England*.

Printed firft, at *Bofton* in *New-England*; and Reprinted at *London*, for *John Dunton*, at the *Raven* in the *Poultry*. 1693.

Although Puritan minister Cotton Mather's writings on witchcraft fed the anti-witch sentiment in Salem, Massachusetts, he also led the movement to disprove the claims against those convicted and executed in 1692. © *Corbis*

The Cultural Backdrop of the Trials As many cultures have done, the colonists tended to attribute anything they could not readily explain to supernatural phenomena, especially to beneficent or malevolent forces. Their strong religiosity fed their belief in magic, as it has done in many cultures, including the Native Americans and Africans brought into slavery in their homes. Beliefs in evil spirits and in the ability to inhabit animals or use talismans for healing were widespread and considered the norm. Research has shown that these beliefs generally help people feel some measure of control over phenomena that affect them. These beliefs are held especially by spiritual people, such as shamans or ministers, who might even have special powers of healing.

Thus, to the colonists, witchcraft was very real and a very real threat. They believed that witches could control peoples' thoughts and force them to behave in evil ways. An old woman, probably childless and living alone, usually fit the typical profile of the European witch, and these women were thought to fly through the air, engage in orgies with the devil, and cause any number of terrible things to happen, including a child's death, crop failure, or birth defects. In short, witches and their evil intent and activities explained what otherwise was inexplicable.

With witchery all around them, people devised ways to determine whether or not someone was a witch or had been affected by a witch's spell. One way to pinpoint a witch was to bake into a cake of grain something from a victim's body, such as urine. When the victims consumed the cake, they would then utter the name of the sorceress. Among colonists, people suspected of being witches had the opportunity to confess their sins and be welcomed back into the religious fold after repenting. The outcome of the Salem witch trials was an exception to this practice.

Accusations Begin Betty Parris was well aware that her religion forbade her from taking part in witchery, but as a curious young child, she did so anyway. When the doctors diagnosed witchcraft, Betty and her counterparts eventually "confessed" that the perpetrators were Tituba and two other old women from the village.

What followed was a witch hunt in the original sense, as the girls went on a spree of witch identification, even pointing the finger at a former minister. The frenzy spread across the colony as newly identified and confessed witches then turned around and named more witches. By the time the uproar had quieted, 156 people sat in prison, charged as witches.

The Trials The trials themselves were an infamous circus conducted by men who were not trained lawyers, and who judged suspects who had no legal representation. In addition, the judges decided to allow "spectral evidence" as valid, even though it was evidence from only one witness, the victim. The wisdom held that only victims could see the witches in spirit form committing their evil deeds, so by definition, spectral evidence could be given only by single witnesses, regardless of whether or not others were around at the time of the "crime."

In what amounted to the peak of witchcraft hysteria that had been building in Europe and the New World for more than two centuries, a special court was convened in June 1692 to judge the accused. Increase Mather (1639–1723) and his son, Cotton (1663–1728), had contributed to this backdrop of hysteria that allowed the wild imaginings of young girls to bear fruit. Their writings included a collection of proofs of witchcraft that had helped inflame feelings against witches and created an army of experts. In spite of their belief in witchcraft and their claim to expertise, however, the Mathers decried the conduct of the trials, and Increase Mather called for dissolution of the courts trying the case. He also disapproved of allowing spectral evidence as valid in the court.

Not heeding the Mathers, the authorities continued the trials, which ended in one hundred guilty verdicts and twenty executions, most of them women. Of those

sentenced to death, nineteen were hanged, and one accused witch was crushed to death by stones during "questioning." An additional four people died during their imprisonment; some of the prisoners learned about the capital punishment and managed to escape. Many of the accused were offered the chance to confess and repent, but being staunchly pious, they refused to lie in this way to save themselves.

Public Backlash Even before the trials ended, public distaste for the court conduct and outcome had begun to grow. Feeding this sentiment were the gallows statements of those executed, many of whom refused to confess but still forgave their accusers and judges. Within a year, people began publicly doubting the conduct and results of the trial, and interestingly, the Mathers again led the public sentiment, this time in opposition to the proceedings.

The authorities conducted retrials for some of the prisoners, but excluded spectral evidence. The result was that forty-nine of fifty-two accused prisoners were released because of a lack of evidence. By 1697, Massachusetts leaders had realized the terrible error of the trials. The governor ultimately pardoned the condemned, and the legislature eventually designated a special day of atonement for the sin of executing innocent people. Samuel Parris, the father of Elizabeth, lost his salary.

The Causes of the Hysteria In seeking to identify the causes of this hysteria and the willingness of presumably rational people to believe the outrageous claims of a group of young girls, historians have turned primarily to socioeconomic causes. Many of the accusers were girls from rural Salem, some from the same family, who worked in the town as servant girls. Many of the accused were well-to-do older women who lived in Salem Town. Quite a few of the girls who made the initial accusations also had lost a parent to Indian raids, and the colony itself was in a state of transition and upheaval, awaiting the arrival of a new governor. The ailing current governor, Simon Bradstreet (1603–1697), had done nothing to stop the growing hysteria, even as the accusations began reaching to the town's borders. The new governor, Sir William Phips (c. 1651–c. 1695), tried to address the issue by establishing what he perceived to be proper courts to conduct the trials. Yet his courts, in addition to allowing spectral evidence, also revived an old law that made practicing witchcraft a capital offense, resulting in the death penalty.

Thus, many historians conclude that issues of social upheaval and class standing may have operated under the surface of the hysteria, although that does not explain Elizabeth Parris's involvement. Her participation as an accuser, however, is attributable to her probable fear of having violated the sacred tenets of her religion, in which her father was a recognized leader. One of the

MAGNALIA CHRISTI AMERICANA

Cotton Mather, son of Increase Mather, authored *Magnalia Christi Americana* (1702) the story of Christ's works in the New World. His book has tormented and fascinated historians ever since, although at its initial publication, it failed to impress some critics.

Mather himself described his writings as a history and a rhapsody, and historians have argued since about whether or not the book is truly a history or more of an extended hosannah. In the conventional sense, it is not a history—it lacks order or chronology and throughout climbs to heights of religious ecstasy and celebration or descends to condemnation as the occasion requires. The book has been criticized for its mercurial tone, and Mather relied heavily throughout the writing on boilerplate quotes and proverbs typically associated with tract writings and sermons of the time. In fact, some scholars have argued that the book is much less history than one long, extended sermon filled with examples of what Mather perceived to be Christ's work.

In spite of these criticisms, *Magnalia Christi Americana* may be, more than anything else, a serial biographical look at the people of the New World. Two of its seven books focus on biographies—in fact, they are packed with biographies, some extremely sparse, others extensive. In Book II, Mather focused on the lives of the godly New England magistrates, and in Book III, on the lives of ministers in the New World. Even his Book IV, which he intended as a history of Harvard College, devolves primarily into a series of yearbook entries of the school's famous alumni.

His approach to documenting the people and times has, to some historians, come to exemplify a uniquely American form of biography. Even though Mather fell into inaccuracies and lapsed into strange but interesting asides, his intensely personal approach to his historical writing is perceived to be an American invention and to mark a turning point in biographical writing.

He did stick to the conventional, formulaic approach through much of the tome, however, tossing in classical and biblical references aplenty, and also including bizarre but interesting allusions that required some genuine facility with lateral thinking. For example, he quotes Pliny's description of the lantern fish or lucerna fish, "whose *Tongue* doth shine like a *Torch*," as an analogy for a minister whose speech was so spectacularly glowing that his tongue appeared also to have been illuminated from within.

As these allusions indicate, Mather litters his text with references to primarily European sources, yet scholars consider his work to be a uniquely New World production. This paradox is not the only confusion that arises over *Magnalia Christi Americana*. In addition to his extensive list of biographies, Mather tosses in a kitchen sink's worth of other information, including his opinions about the Salem witch trials. Historians have disagreed about the role that Mather played in setting the stage for the hysteria that surfaced during this time and about his and his father's efforts to halt the trials or condemn them.

Before writing *Magnalia Christi Americana*, Cotton Mather expressed disapproval over the conduct of the trials and the treatment of the "witches," yet he also included in his book a spirited defense of the judges who oversaw the proceedings. This latter has left the erroneous impression that he did, in fact, approve of the trials themselves.

Early reviews of his work were not necessarily favorable. One reviewer, William Tudor, who was the first editor of the *North American Review*, compared Mather's liberal use of quotes from the Latin, Greek, and Hebrew to "so many decayed, hideous stumps" that "deform the surface" of the writing. He also dismissed Mather as pedantic and wordy. Some later critics have agreed with this assessment, whereas others have found much that is worthwhile and interesting in Mather's rhapsodic history.

Mather himself had lofty goals for his book. His opening to *Magnalia Christi Americana* is famous: "I write the *Wonders* of the CHRISTIAN RELIGION, flying from the Depravations of *Europe*, to the *American Strand*." His pages begin with a history of the New World as told through his filter, starting with its discovery and covering the founding of Connecticut and New Haven. Perhaps not surprisingly, he dedicated his book to Jesus Christ.

---

trial judges, Samuel Sewall (1652–1730), felt such great regret about his role that he made a public statement in which he took the "blame and shame" of having been associated with the proceedings and asked for God's pardon for "that sin."

✪ International Context

French and English Conflict in North America

The British founded Jamestown, Virginia, in 1607, and only a year later, the French settled the capital of "New France" in Quebec. These two New World settlements lay separated by a vast and tangled wilderness that ensured few encounters between representatives of these archrival European countries.

Different Intentions The two nations initially had very different intentions for the New World. To the French, the Canadian territories were a rich repository of furs and other natural resources to exploit, but not a place to establish permanent settlements. The British, on the other hand, looked further into the future and saw the New World as a vast territory where they could deposit the disgruntled of their people while reaping the bounty of resources the rich lands had to offer. From the beginning the British aimed to promote emigration and establish settlements they intended to be permanent and even installed a king-appointed governor to oversee each colony.

Credit: The Granger Collection, New York

This engraving, by Theodore de Bry, shows Native peoples caring for their sick, who became infected with European disease. *The Granger Collection, New York. Reproduced by permission*

Once the vast resources of North America—including wood, fur, agriculture, and ore—became more evident overseas, the heads of Europe's nations turned toward the New World. Competition for control began in earnest, involving not only France and England, but also Spain and Denmark. England and France were the clear front-runners in the north and east of the continent, having acquired dominion over most of the land east of the Mississippi by the early 1700s. British settlements dotted the landscape from Maine to Georgia, marching north to south along the Atlantic coast. The French, for their part, had control over eastern Canada, the Great Lakes, and the Mississippi River basin.

Native Americans Caught in Between Caught between these occupying countries were the Native Americans, who had, of course, been living in the Americas for thousands of years. Over that time, many different cultures and traditions had arisen, shaped in part by the

natural resources around them. The French, initially lacking interest in land acquisition and focusing primarily on trade, did not seek to remove the Native Americans from their lands and established good relations with them. The British settlers, on the other hand, had a completely different agenda. Only a few decades had passed since the establishment of Jamestown before all-out war broke out between the colonists and the native peoples. These devastating conflicts, including King Philip's War, ended in the decimation of the native peoples and cultures in the northeastern colonies. In the end, the only groups that remained on friendly terms with the colonists were the members of the Iroquois Confederacy, which included the Cayuga, Mohawk, Oneida, Onondaga, Seneca, and Tuscarora nations. The Iroquois and French had been enemies since the French explorer Samuel de Champlain (c. 1567–1635) had shot several Iroquois people during one of the first French expeditions to the New World in the early 1600s. His weapons were the first guns the Iroquois had ever seen.

In a New World reflection of tactics used for centuries in Europe, the British and French allied themselves with tribes who were in turn traditional enemies of one another. The greatest Native American allies of the French colonies were the Algonquian peoples, longtime enemies of the Iroquois. The Iroquois, in their alliance with the British, sought to control trade in the region and keep the French from acquiring any more territory. At the same time, across the Atlantic, England and France continued their centuries-long struggle for European dominance, fighting three wars from the late 1600s to the early 1700s. The effects of these conflicts reverberated across the waters to the New World colonies.

European Wars Carried Across the Atlantic   One of these wars, King William's War (known as the War of the League of Augsburg in Europe), lasted from 1689 to 1697. King James II of England (1633–1701), a staunch Catholic, had fled to France after unsuccessful attempts to convert his largely Protestant nation to his religion. The French King Louis XIV (1638–1715) sided with James II against James's daughter, Mary II (1662–1694), and her husband, William III of Orange (1650–1702), who jointly stepped up to the English throne to become William and Mary of England. The North American version of this war involved conflict between the British and French over who would control the rivers—highways to the colonists—through the Appalachian Mountains. The French leaders triggered the American war with their encouragement of Indian raids that ended in the deaths of hundreds of British settlers. In revenge, the British attacked New France and took Port Royal in Nova Scotia, although they did not take Quebec. When the two sides agreed to a peace settlement, the British returned Nova Scotia to France.

This fragile peace broke with the onset of Queen Anne's War (called the War of Spanish Succession in Europe), which began in 1701. As with many European conflicts, this war began with a vacant throne, this time in Spain. Each major European power wanted to place an ally in the Spanish seat. Again, the clash spread across the Atlantic and began with French-triggered Indian raids on British settlements, which again set off a series of British attacks on Canada. The British were serious this time, going to Canada with the goal of taking over the territory, and took six thousand troops on ships up the coast to the St. Lawrence River, which they expected to travel into the heart of French-Canadian territory. But their plan fell apart when several ships foundered on rocks in heavy fog and more than one thousand people drowned.

The British never made it to Canada on that expedition, but they did win the war in Europe in 1713, leading them to claim supremacy over French-Canadian

territories, including the resource-rich Hudson Bay region. Another peace treaty followed, but its language was so vague that further conflict was inevitable. Eventually, the tensions would erupt again in the French and Indian War from 1754 to 1763.

Subjugation of the Northeastern Tribes

With the end of King Philip's War, Native American lands and cultures lay fractured, never to be made whole again. In the war's aftermath, the colonies engaged in a systematic destruction of corn, the food base for the native peoples, as well as the tracking and capture of Native Americans throughout the summer of 1676.

During the war, the colonists had invited the native peoples to surrender to them, promising mercy for anyone who did so. Yet the Native Americans who accepted this option found themselves sold into slavery instead of receiving mercy. The authorities rationalized that because some of the native peoples had participated in attacks on settlers, all of the native peoples were guilty by association.

Slavery   Slave ships carrying Native Americans began departing from the northeast as early as 1675. The Plymouth colonial leaders had formalized a process by which Native American males over the age of fourteen were automatically deported as slaves to the sugarcane plantations in the Caribbean. There was some dispute about what to do with Metacom's nine-year-old son, who had been captured along with his mother. Execution was considered, but the boy was instead made a slave.

At least one thousand Native Americans were shipped to Caribbean sugarcane plantations during King Philip's War, where most of them died in the brutal, unfamiliar heat. Mount Hope, the seat of the once-sprawling and powerful Wampanoag Nation, lay empty. By 1680, after a methodical and merciless purge, the Native American population had plummeted by more than fifty percent, the result of death in battle, disease, and slavery. In the southern parts of New England, losses reached between 60 and 80 percent.

The Fate of the Remaining People   The Narragansetts, who had remained ostensibly neutral for so much of the war, paid a heavy price for shifting their loyalty to the side of the native peoples. At one point during the war, the colonists tested the loyalty of the Narragansetts by demanding that they turn over any Wampanoag refugees taking shelter with them. The colonial authorities were most interested in getting their hands on Weetamoo, the female sachem of the Pocasset people. When the Narragansetts failed to meet the colonial deadline, the English used this as yet another excuse to remove the Narragansetts as an obstacle to their ability to acquire native lands.

In reality, the colonists were relieved that the tribe had not joined forces against them before that point. If they had allied themselves with Metacom's people at an earlier time, the combined power of the tribes in the opposition would have overwhelmed the colonial forces. Yet, even though the colonists owed the Narragansetts a modicum of patience for not having taken the opportunity to destroy them, they saw their chance and wiped the Narragansetts off the New England map, along with most of the other Native American peoples.

Of the remaining Native American groups, only the Iroquois Confederacy, which included the Mohawk and Seneca nations, survived colonial efforts to eradicate the native peoples. The Iroquois worked as allies with the English settlers well into the mid-eighteenth century.

BIBLIOGRAPHY

Book

Philbrick, Nathaniel. *Mayflower: A Story of Courage, Community, and War.* New York: Viking, 2006.

Periodicals

Schultz, Eric B. "Time Line of Major Dates and Events." *Cobblestone* 21.7 (2000).

Stievermann, Jan. "Writing to 'Conquer All Things': Cotton Mather's *Magnalia Christi Americana* and the Quandary of Copia." *Early American Literature* 39.2 (2004): 263–98.

Introduction to the American Revolution (1775–1783)

The American Revolutionary War (1775–1783) resulted from a conflict between the British government and British subjects living in the thirteen American colonies. Between the years 1764 and 1774, the crown and his majesty's legislature passed a number of tax measures, which the colonists fiercely opposed. Outspoken American leaders took a principled position against taxes because the government that created the laws offered no representation for those being taxed. At the time, only propertied, upper-class men could vote in England and in most elections within America. But even the American voting class could not express on ballots their views on the actions of Parliament.

"No taxation without representation" became the mantra for colonists. The British government responded unapologetically. The king and members of Parliament held that the colonists were *virtually represented* like most British citizens residing throughout the British Isles. That is, fewer than ten percent of men living in the mother country could legally vote. But when Parliament passed laws, Britons contended that it considered the best interests of those without a vote.

Colonists organized opposition to English rule. In Boston, revolutionaries created the Sons of Liberty, an opposition group that began several chapters in cities throughout the colonies. Respected leaders from Philadelphia, like Benjamin Franklin, began to speak for the cause. Patrick Henry and Thomas Jefferson, both from Virginia, became vocal against the British lawmakers.

These men followed ideas proposed by philosophers from the Enlightenment, including John Locke. One Lockean concept that became synonymous with the American cause was that government may not justly take life, liberty, or property without the consent of the governed. The idea made its way into the Declaration of Independence, the Bill of Rights, and several state constitutions.

After the Port of Boston was closed to punish the Boston Tea Party protesters, delegates from twelve of the thirteen colonies met in September 1774 at the First Continental Congress to respond. By the spring of 1775, the British army was an ever-present force in the colonies. In an attempt to seize American weapons near Boston, British soldiers and colonial minutemen fought at the battles of Lexington and Concord. A Second Continental Congress met in May 1775 and established the Continental Army under George Washington. After the battle of Bunker Hill the following month, colonial leaders offered the Olive Branch Petition for peace to King George. It was rejected.

The fledgling Congress commissioned a committee of five men to draft an official statement of its position. The Declaration of Independence signaled the separation from the monarchy and the creation of a new nation dubbed the United States of America.

The world was surprised when this infant nation of militiamen overpowered one of the finest armies in the world. Most of the fighting ended after the British defeat at the Battle of Yorktown in 1781. The Treaty of Paris officially ended the war in 1783. The United States began operating under the Articles of Confederation before the war was over. In 1789, a stronger union was created with the ratification of the Constitution. The Bill of Rights, ratified in 1791, guarantees Americans many of the liberties that Britain had failed to recognize.

American Revolution (1775–1783)

✪ Causes

Sugar Act

The English Empire was a costly endeavor that drained Great Britain's Treasury. Financing exploits in the Americas and across the globe required creative sources of revenue. British politicians had suggested passing part of the tax burden on to colonists, but like the distinguished Sir Robert Walpole (1676–1745) had said with a smile in preparing to depart his position as overseer of the Treasury, "I will leave that for some of my successors, who may have more courage than I have."

George Grenville (1712–1770), England's new chancellor of the exchequer, a humorless statesman with a knack for financial figures, had no problem in requiring Americans to pay taxes. He and Parliament had made the point that much of the 140 million-pound debt the English government faced was borne by the colonies. Grenville prepared a bill for Parliament that placed a tax on sugar products meant to earn revenue for customs.

Part of the justification for the new law was that defending Americans cost the government about 320,000 pounds per year. In the preamble of the Revenue Act, or the "Sugar Act" as it was called in the colonies, Grenville had frankly stated the act's purpose: "That revenue be raised in Your majesty's Dominions in America for defraying the expenses of defending, protecting, and securing the same." In reality, the law taxed more than sugar and it was meant to stop the smuggling of molasses and sugar that had been taxed on paper, but from which revenue was seldom collected. Grenville did not intend to harm the rum industry. In fact, he had lowered the duty on molasses imported from the French or Dutch West Indies from six cents to three cents per gallon. Knowing that most colonial merchants were paying a penny and a half per gallon in bribes, Grenville figured that they could pay three cents in an honest tax. With the actual reduction, he became determined to accurately collect this lower charge. To put teeth in the new act, an elaborate system was designed, involving

papers to be filled out by shippers. Cargo was tightly inspected and violators were tried in admiralty courts without juries, as colonial juries had proven friendly to American smugglers. The new act also taxed other merchandise, however, including coffee, raw silk, and skins.

To Grenville and British lawmakers, the new policy seemed fair and an adjustment to what was meant to have been going on for years. To merchants, it seemed a high-handed and arbitrary act that assumed every colonist engaged in commerce as a thief unprotected by the right to a jury. Additionally, the admiralty court in Halifax, Nova Scotia, the venue for any relevant trials, was a great distance to travel for potential violators. And merchants who were falsely accused by inspectors or other government officials had no recourse. Because so many distillers and merchants had refused to pay the original tax, the now-enforced act came as somewhat of a shock. There was an outcry against the tax, and began the onset of the colonial argument against taxation without representation. But the Sugar Act was largely overshadowed by the Stamp Act and the crisis that followed it a year later.

Stamp Act

The Stamp Act crisis set the stage for the inevitable conflict between American colonists and the British government ten years before the first shots were fired in the American Revolutionary War. The act itself was passed by Parliament to raise revenue for the British Empire. Colonists became outraged and expressed their dissatisfaction in the streets and in the halls of government, challenging the law on both practical and principled grounds. Other parliamentary acts had upset colonists before the Stamp Act. The Navigation Acts, the Proclamation of 1763, and the Sugar Act had all been unpopular. But the Stamp Act dispute encouraged colonists to develop an argument against taxation without representation and let the Americans prove their ability to organize and oppose the mother country.

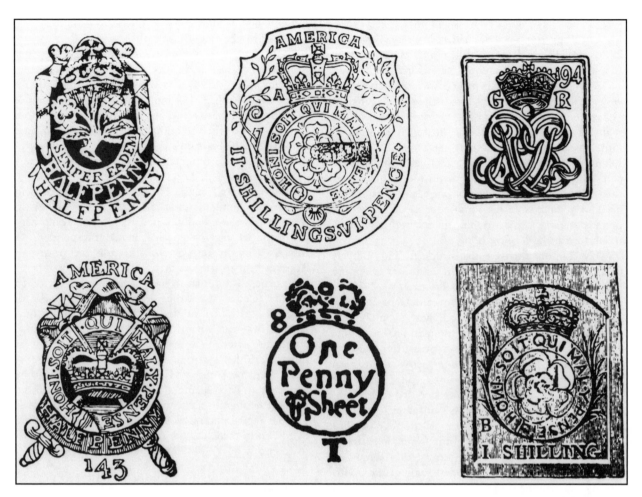

Tax stamps, required for nearly every piece of printed material in New England in the mid-1760s, played a major part in pushing the colonies toward revolution. © *Bettmann/Corbis*

The Sugar Act had not put much of a dent in the financial burden the empire faced, so Grenville engineered the Stamp Act in March 1765. The law mandated that all legal documents—deeds, wills, mortgages, college diplomas—had to be printed on government-stamped paper to be legally binding. Even newspapers and playing cards were subject to this tax. Almost anything formally written or printed would have to appear on special paper shipped from a central stamp office in London and distributed in America by local agents after payments of specified taxes.

Word of the new law arrived in the colonies not through the official channels of government, but far in advance of the actual law taking effect. American newspapers carried the lengthy details of the new act as early as May 1765. Colonists became outraged because they foresaw paying increased fees at every stage of a lawsuit, for advertisements, for bills of sale, and for any other custom papers. Members of Parliament viewed America's loss as England's gain. Colonial leaders, as they did with the Sugar Act before it, opposed the Stamp Act but

with greater effort and organization from several levels of society.

One of the first official responses to the unpopular tax came from Virginian Patrick Henry (1736–1799), who introduced a series of resolutions into the Virginia House of Burgesses that bluntly denied Parliament's right to levy the tax. These Virginia Resolves, as they were called, were printed in newspapers and encouraged other colonial legislatures to pass similar resolutions. The opposition became widespread and obvious. British Commander General Thomas Gage (1719–1787), who later was charged with quelling the Revolution, declared that this opposition was a "signal for a general outcry over the continent."

Outraged colonists in Boston expressed themselves a little more violently in August 1765. An angry mob stoned and pillaged the house of Andrew Oliver (1706–1774), the stamp tax collector who had yet to even officially receive this new post. Members of the mob visited him the following day to suggest that further damage would be inevitable unless he resigned the office that Grenville had yet to even assign him. Oliver was also hung in effigy from a stately elm tree in a very visible spot in Boston. He could not officially resign, but assured the mob that he would not enforce the Stamp Act.

The Boston approach proved successful and more violence followed, especially against the royal Lieutenant Governor Thomas Hutchinson (1711–1780). On the night of August 26, 1765, the Boston mob stormed Hutchinson's house, smashing his front door into splinters, chopping down the fruit trees in his garden, and destroying a manuscript of the history of the colony that Hutchinson had worked on for years. They ruined his library, and stole his furniture and nine hundred pounds sterling. At dawn, the rioters were still at it, trying to tear the roof off of his house.

Hutchinson survived the wreckage and publicly declared he had done everything in his power to oppose the Stamp Act. Governor Francis Bernard (1712–1779) had escaped the attack and contacted General Gage, declaring that he had no force to oppose the mob.

The Boston riots served as inspiration to encourage violent protests in other American cities from Newport to Charleston. Colonists in villages across the eastern seaboard organized themselves into groups called the Sons of Liberty. These associations declared their intentions of refusing to abide by the Parliament's unethical tax. Meanwhile, in response to a call from Massachusetts, nine of the colonies sent twenty-seven delegates to New York for what would be termed the Stamp Act Congress. This gathering reiterated some of the points already made about Parliament's lack of authority to tax these unrepresented colonists.

By November 1, the date that the tax was meant to begin, no single stamp tax collector was prepared to face the kind of damage done against officials in Boston. Americans also announced that not a single ship would set sail for England, nor would one be welcomed in the colonies, until this Stamp Act was repealed. One Virginia merchant planned to send several cargoes of wheat to London, but four hundred members of the Sons of Liberty persuaded him to not do so. The colonists were prepared to use economic boycotting to make their position known.

Once the violence subsided, ideological arguments against the Stamp Act could be refined, and the debate continued. Colonial leaders and statesmen clearly argued that such a tax was illegal, for the British who voted for the tax did not represent the colonists. Grenville and his British supporters argued, quite simply, that though the Americans did not vote for members of Parliament, these members were representing the colonists' best interests much like they represented scores of Englishmen who also lacked a vote under property requirements at the time. This "virtual representation" argument was not well received by the colonists, nor did they really want token representation in Parliament. Such representation would be impractical as Americans would easily be outvoted by the English majorities.

Although most did not favor permanent representation in the British legislature, they did send Benjamin Franklin (1706–1790) as a representative to testify on the colonists' behalf. The mob violence, organization of the Sons of Liberty, and the reality of an American boycott caught the attention of lawmakers in England who welcomed Franklin's presentation. The Pennsylvanian rehearsed to refute all arguments thrown his way before his arrival in London. On February 13, 1766, Franklin appeared in the House of Commons to field nearly two hundred questions from Parliamentarians, most of them unfriendly. When asked what would happen if the act was not repealed, Franklin responded, "A total loss of the respect and affection the people of America bear to this country, and all of the commerce that depends on that respect and affection." When another asked what was the pride of the colonists, Franklin responded, "To indulge in the fashions and manufactures of Great Britain." And what is their pride now, another retorted, to which Franklin replied, "To wear their old clothes again, till they can make new ones." A week later, the House of Commons voted to repeal the Stamp Act. This dilemma had ended, but the debate about Parliament's general right to tax the colonists without representation would continue through a series of additional taxes and the American's principled refusal to accept them.

Boston Massacre

The Boston Massacre resulted from an encounter in early March 1770 between an angry mob of Bostonians and British soldiers who had been assigned to tame the disgruntled city. The killings were followed by a unique trial that pitted one colonial leader, John Adams (1735–1826), against his cousin, Samuel Adams (1722–1803), in a quest for justice. The massacre and its aftermath served as another event that pushed the colonists toward revolution. The trial offered some principled irony as a leading revolutionary insisted on defending the very unpopular British soldiers.

With organized opposition to unpopular taxes, confrontation and violence between British soldiers and Americans had occurred in the other colonies before the Boston Massacre. An eleven-year-old boy had been killed in one skirmish. From March 2 through March 4, hostilities between working men and the English guards had taken place in Boston. By the evening of March 5, 1770, a series of events led to a showdown between the soldiers and colonists that left five colonists dead and more wounded.

Many soldiers stationed in Boston had been removed, but two regiments still remained. One, the Twenty-Ninth, was considered an especially tough lot. After some verbal exchanges between laborers and soldiers around

A chromolithograph by John Bufford shows the events of the Boston Massacre. *National Archives and Records Administration*

the harbor, March 5 proved a deadly day. Private Hugh White was guarding the Boston customhouse when some young apprentice wigmakers began to taunt him. One young lad, Edward Garrick, was particularly insulting. He accused one of White's officers of being a shifty fellow who refused to pay Garrick's master for a wig. White defended his superior and declared him a gentleman, to which Garrick replied there were no gentlemen in the regiment. Having heard enough, the private struck the apprentice harshly across the side of the head with the butt of his rifle. Garrick let out a harsh cry and fled the scene. White and another soldier, whose bayonet was exposed, chased him through the streets and discovered the victim seeking safety in a shop. White struck the cowering boy again.

Word of this abuse spread rapidly. Back at his post at the customhouse, White was surrounded by a half-dozen boys shouting more insults at him. Someone began to ring the bells of a church as if a fire or some other emergency required the attention of the townspeople. The gathering of angry boys turned into a huge mob of outraged Bostonians. Nearly a foot of snow lay on the ground, which had partially melted and refrozen, creating large chunks of ice. Snowballs and ice chunks began to fly toward White, occasionally hitting him in the head.

The sentry stood his ground, but soon had to call for help to protect himself from the unruly protestors. Six men responded, led by a corporal. Captain Thomas Preston also arrived on the scene.

The angry crowd had grown to nearly four hundred men, many members of the Sons of Liberty. The daring horde, some drunk, surged dangerously close to the fixed bayonets and dared the soldiers to fire at them. The protestors predicted that a British soldier could not, and would not, fire onto rioters without a magistrate reading the Riot Act, a procedure required by British law to disperse crowds and restore the king's peace. No magistrate would enforce the Riot Act with the Boston crowds, which had proven strong. Any soldier firing into a crowd without a magistrate's prior warning would face charges of murder.

As Captain Preston approached, the men began to load their muskets. Preston tried to prevent the inevitable encounter, but with the pressure increasing, ice and insults flying, Preston could do little to stop it. Alcohol and darkness complicated matters further. Amid the confusion, Preston could hardly be heard. A club was hurled into the crowd of soldiers, knocking one off his feet. He recovered and fired his weapon. His shot hit no one and brought some distance between soldiers and colonists. Another soldier shot into the crowd and hit a victim in the head. Additional shots were fired, hitting Crispus Attucks in the chest. Attucks, a large, strong man of African descent, had been leading the crowd all evening. When the smoke cleared, Attucks and four others had been killed. Six more colonists were wounded.

For a few hours, Boston had the potential for becoming a complete bloodbath. The Sons of Liberty, who outnumbered the British soldiers by five-to-one, could have quickly armed themselves against both remaining regiments. Only a speech by Lieutenant Governor Thomas Hutchinson, promising to try these men for murder, quieted anxieties. Hutchinson could not find a lawyer in Boston willing to defend the soldiers. Preston maintained that he never gave the order to fire while his men claimed he did.

The massacre was over, but justice hung in the balance. One of Preston's friends begged attorney John Adams to defend the captain. Adams, caught between defending the lives of American victims and feeling that even these soldiers should have a defense, decided to take the case. Two colleagues had promised to assist Adams if he agreed. "Counsel," Adams said, "ought to be the last thing that an accused man should lack in a free country." Adams, who would later rebel against the British government in the Revolution and serve as the United States' second president, was taking an extremely unpopular position. To complicate matters more, his cousin Samuel Adams, a founder of the Sons of Liberty and a popular leader in Boston, aggressively prosecuted the case.

John Adams faced an uphill legal battle, but stubbornly persevered. He assured that Preston and the men would be tried separately and chose jurors from the country, rather than from the irate Boston citizenry. He also found a delicate way to prove that the Sons of Liberty, and his cousin, had partially instigated the matter. He saved the necks of Preston and his soldiers.

Although a public rift occurred between the cousins, the two grew closer privately. Samuel Adams had written scathing articles regarding the trial and its outcome under an alias in the *Boston Gazette*, but began to realize how his Sons of Liberty needed to be tempered. The mob mentality that brought on the Boston Massacre served as a lesson for how colonists should properly oppose the British government. Crispus Attucks and the others died as martyrs. Few Bostonians forgot the incident from which justice was defined as was a more logical approach to the eventual revolution.

Boston Tea Party

The Boston Tea Party, an organized colonial protest against the British government over a tax placed on imported tea, was no party at all. Rather, outraged Boston residents boarded British merchant ships and dumped thousands of pounds of tea into the harbor in the middle of a December night in 1773. This action was a slap in the face to the mother country, which responded with greater restrictions on the Boston townspeople. Like so many other taxes that had been placed on commodities arriving to the American colonies, leaders and townspeople thought this one unfair because the colonists had no vote in the passage of the law.

The earlier Townshend Acts had placed a tax on tea and other items, but most of these taxes were repealed. In 1771, Boston imported 265,000 pounds of tea alone, and the other colonies enjoyed the brew immensely. Americans, however, began to cut down on their consumption and boycotted the product. The British government's concern for one of its companies engaging in the tea trade brought on additional laws that would preserve the company and bring in additional revenue for the Crown. Prime Minister Lord North and King George III had gained support for the Tea Act, a 1773 law that further taxed commodities headed for America and protected a large English company.

The English East India Tea Company, a mammoth corporation that represented England's interests in India, was in financial trouble, partly because of colonial boycotts and partly due to company mismanagement. Roughly nine thousand tons of the product sat in London warehouses ready for the American market. Parliament had invested too much into the company to let it collapse. So the House of Commons passed the Tea Act in May 1773, which allowed the company to appoint its own agents in America to distribute tea directly to retailers. Colonists in Boston did not approve the law and became even more disturbed when the company assigned Governor Thomas Hutchinson's sons as the local authorized distributors. In addition to violating the "no taxation without representation" argument, the law also favored a monopoly.

As the first shipments of tea arrived on three ships in Boston Harbor in late 1773, townspeople urged the ship captains to turn around and not bring the tea into the American markets. In other ports, many took this advice. But in Boston, Governor Hutchinson would not permit the ships to leave before unloading the cargo. A showdown between these two forces began and continued for days. Citizens of the city and neighboring towns were informed by handbills that stated, "Friends! Brethren! Countrymen! That worst of plagues, the detested TEA . . . is now arrived in this harbour. The hour of destruction, or manly opposition to the machinations of tyranny, stares you in the face." The notice invited colonists to a meeting that was to take place in Faneuil Hall. Thousands showed up for the gathering, and a later meeting took place as well. The Sons of Liberty and so many others were prepared to stand up on principle against the importation of the government-

This nineteenth-century engraving depicts the December 1773 Boston Tea Party, in which the Sons of Liberty threw tons of tea into Boston Harbor to protest the Tea Act. *Archive Photos, Inc./Getty Images*

protected tea. One leader posed the question at a later meeting, "Who knows how tea will mingle with salt water?"

The answer to that question came late on the night of December 16, 1773. About fifty men dressed as Indians boarded the three ships and ordered the customs officers ashore. In three hours of furious work, 342 chests of tea worth roughly ten thousand pounds were destroyed. Bostonians had soundly rejected the law that protected the East India monopoly and showed their ability to organize and take drastic action. The king and Parliament did not take the action lightly. They closed the Boston port and passed additional restrictions to punish the colonists known as the Coercive or Intolerable Acts.

Intolerable Acts

The Intolerable Acts (also known as the Coercive Acts) were a series of laws passed by British Parliament after the Boston Tea Party. The so-called party was the colonists' bold protest against what they perceived as an unfair tax on imported tea. Protestors had dressed as Native Americans and boarded three merchant vessels to dump a large shipment of tea into the harbor. When loyal officials reported these acts back to London, King George III (1738–1820) and Prime Minister Frederick Lord North (1732–1792) reacted by punishing these violators and the Boston community at large.

The colonists referred to these laws as the Intolerable Acts because, like the tax that preceded them, Americans could not tolerate them. The English called this legislation the Coercive Acts, which better reveals Parliament's view of Bostonian behavior that led to the Tea Party. The first such law was the Boston Port Act, passed in March 1774. This act was meant to starve the Bostonians into submission. It stopped all shipping into or out of the port until the violators made payment for the destroyed tea, as well as the tax on it. The king also sent additional troops to Massachusetts to enforce the measure. An American onlooker residing in London wrote a friend about the new act. "I was in the Parliament House and heard the bill brought in and read," the witness declared. "I beg you to encourage your people to be strong in opposing this diabolical proceeding. Don't expect any mercy."

To prevent agitators from rising again, the Parliament passed the Massachusetts Government Act, which drastically redefined how the colony would be governed. The original 1691 Massachusetts charter had provided for a representative body of elected colonists, but the law gave the king the power to appoint the colony's representatives. Governor Thomas Hutchinson had pushed for the law, which also empowered him to appoint and remove judges, the attorney general, sheriffs, and other law enforcement officials without the consent of the council. In short, representation—the central right the

Popular anger at the Crown in the wake of the Intolerable Acts is evident in this engraving of rioters chasing Thomas Hutchinson after he demanded Stamp Tax from them. *Hulton Archive/Getty Images*

colonists felt they had lost since the taxes began in 1764—was thrown out the window.

The Administration of Justice Act, passed in May 1774, relocated trials for capital offenses that involved British officials or soldiers. Any officers of the Crown would be tried either in another American colony or in England. Parliament assumed juries in Boston could not offer these defendants a fair trial. The colonists, on the other hand, assumed this meant a pass for any accused British officer. They feared soldiers' treatment toward them could only worsen with no real threat of conviction.

With the new troops arriving to control these agitating colonists, Parliament had to find a way to house them. So came the fourth intolerable measure: the Quartering Act, which gave British General Thomas Gage the authority to house his soldiers in Boston homes. Colonial hosts of these soldiers would be paid rent, but did not have the right to turn the troops away, a right that had been granted in the Quartering Act of 1765.

Another infringement, though not one of the Coercive Acts, came in the Quebec Act. This law created a new government of the former province of French Canada. It altered the map and extended Quebec south to the Ohio River. One supporter acknowledged that it was to tighten the American colonies and keep them closer to the Atlantic where they could be controlled. It established the rights of French-speaking residents to worship as Roman Catholics and made a royal governorship for the area. The act irritated colonists beyond Massachusetts because it denied land claims that colonial governments had on western territory.

Some British leaders denounced the reaction by Parliament. Edmund Burke (1729–1797), a noted member and legal philosopher, urged his fellow lawmakers to "reflect on how you are to govern a people who think they ought to be free and think they are not." William Pitt (1708–1778), a member of the House of Lords and generally respected by the American colonists, felt these were unfair measures because they punished the innocent as well as the guilty. But Prime Minister Lord North strongly disagreed, stating, "We must either control them or submit to them." The Coercive Acts passed through Parliament by great majorities, more than four to one in most cases.

The laws were not initially so intolerable to colonists in the other parts of America, but when word of these policies and the horrible conditions that their Bostonian brothers faced reached Virginia, New York, and other colonies, sympathy for the Boston people soon emerged. Many Americans feared that the Crown would take away similar rights as those denied the violators in Boston. These policies had denied representation, supported military law over civilian law, and gave the governor unchecked powers in judicial appointments. In addition to supporting the residents of Boston, the measures resulted in the gathering of the First Continental Congress. The Intolerable Acts had served as one of the final conflicts before these two sides would erupt in the American Revolutionary War.

✪ Major Figures

Benjamin Franklin

Benjamin Franklin (1706–1790) was a printer, author, philanthropist, inventor, statesman, diplomat, and scientist. Through his written word, political action, and diplomatic skill, Benjamin Franklin played a significant role in supporting the American Revolution. Born on January 17, 1706, in Boston, Massachusetts, Franklin was one of thirteen children of Josiah and Abiah (Folger) Franklin. His father worked as a candlemaker and mechanic, had his own shop, and was a respected citizen in Boston. Franklin's formal education was limited, ending at age ten, after which when he began working for his father.

Because he did not particularly like making soap and candles, Franklin found other, more intellectually stimulating employment. Working for his brother James, a newspaper printer, Franklin became immersed in the printing business at the age of twelve. He had already educated himself by reading all the books he could obtain. Now, Franklin even began writing and publishing critical pieces himself.

When James Franklin was arrested for publishing his own critical works, Franklin took over running the print shop until 1723. He relocated to Philadelphia and worked for another printing business. After a brief tenure in Britain in 1724 where he became a master printer and bought his own printing press, Franklin returned to Philadelphia and founded a newspaper, the *Pennsylvania Gazette*, and the annual *Poor Richard's Almanack*.

Public Positions Franklin continued to expand his business interests to include a bookshop, as well as partnerships with other printers. He also invented the Franklin stove and conducted scientific inquiries into electricity. In addition, Franklin began taking on public positions in the mid-1730s, including serving as the postmaster of Philadelphia and as clerk of the Pennsylvania Assembly. By 1748, Franklin was able to retire from his business interests and focus on public life.

In 1751, Franklin, by this time well known for his electricity experiments as well as his writings, was elected

Benjamin Franklin. *Franklin, Benjamin painting, photograph. National Portrait Gallery/Smithsonian Institution. Reproduced by permission*

to his first public office. He took a seat in the Pennsylvania Assembly as a member of the Quaker party, and soon became the party's leader. Franklin believed that representatives elected by the people, such as himself, had the right to regulate their state's government.

Although he did have some unease on occasion about British apathy toward colonists' concerns, Franklin behaved as a loyal subject of the Crown and encouraged colonial support of Britain's interests and activities in North America. He convinced the Pennsylvania legislative body to use money and people to help defend British interests in the French and Indian War. His primary allegiance, however, was to the colonies, which he represented in disagreements with the mother country. Franklin acted as an agent for the colonies, including Pennsylvania, on various trips to Britain from the late 1750s to the mid-1770s.

Emissary to England After losing his seat in the assembly in 1764, Franklin remained in public office as the postmaster general for North America, a position he had held for a decade. Beginning in 1764, he also represented Pennsylvania on yet another trip to Britain. He was charged with the task of asking that Pennsylvania become a royal colony. Noting the perilous change in government, Franklin declined to complete his mission. Instead, while still in England, he spoke out against the 1765 Stamp Act that the colonists so violently opposed.

Although the Stamp Act was repealed in part because of his words, Franklin remained in Britain for nine more years. He generally remained confident in how Britain treated the American colonies and acted as the voice of the colonists in their mother country. Franklin soon began to doubt British concerns for the colonists and their needs and desires. Parliament distrust in him grew as he continued to argue against the taxation acts being imposed on the colonists. In 1774, his tenure in Britain neared its end when confidential letters from the governor of Massachusetts, which had been obtained by Franklin, were published. Dismissed as postmaster general, Franklin was also threatened with treason charges but was only reprimanded by the British government.

Embracing Independence Franklin's hopes to improve relations between the colonies and Britain were futile as protests continued in the colonies and Britain sent more troops. He returned in March 1775, a mere month before the Revolutionary War began. Franklin believed in the cause and joined the colonists' revolutionary movement, and was selected as Pennsylvania's representative at the Second Continental Congress.

In 1776, he was one of the authors of the Declaration of Independence and also began serving as a representative to France to help gain French support for the revolution. Franklin had already been working to obtain foreign aid for the cause in secret. By 1777, he used his appeal to get war supplies sent to the Americans, and by the end of the year, Franklin gained an alliance with King Louis XVI as well. This action resulted in more supplies as well as some support from the French army and navy for the Revolutionary War effort.

When the Revolutionary War essentially ended with the British defeat at the Battle of Yorktown in 1781, Franklin defined the terms for the peace treaty negotiated in Paris beginning in 1782. He ensured the favorable treaty included American independence and the removal of all British forces from the United States, as well as a defined western boundary and inalienable fishing rights. With the help of John Jay (1745–1829) and John Adams, the treaty was signed in 1783.

Returning to the United States in 1785, Franklin settled again in Philadelphia and continued to be active in civic and political matters. He served a three-year term as president of the Supreme Executive Council of Pennsylvania. In 1787, Franklin attended the Federal Constitutional Convention. Although not supportive of all aspects of the Constitution, Franklin believed it should be ratified and convinced other doubters to do so for the good of the country. Having been ill for some years, Franklin died on April 17, 1790, in Philadelphia.

George Washington

George Washington (1732–1799) was a Revolutionary War hero whose persistence as commander in chief of the combined American and French forces led to victory for the Americans. Washington later served as the first president of the United States and is regarded as the father of the country. Washington was born on February 22, 1732, in Bridges Creek, Virginia, the son of Augustine Washington and his wife, Mary Ball. His father was wealthy and held positions of importance in Virginia, serving as a sheriff, justice of the peace, and a church warden. After his father's death when Washington was eleven, George lived with various relatives throughout Virginia. Primarily raised by his half-brother Lawrence Washington, a rich farmer with some political standing, Washington inhabited the upper echelons of Virginian society. Though erratic in nature, he received what amounted to at least the essential education required of his time.

Early Experience By the time he was seventeen years old, Washington was working in the appointed position of county surveyor. He had already learned much about the frontier by surveying the extensive holdings of Lord Fairfax in 1748, then spending two years in his official capacity throughout northern Virginia. Washington's work as a surveyor gave him valuable familiarity with the frontier and led to the beginnings of his military experiences. In 1752, he was commissioned as a major in the Virginia militia and served during the French and Indian War from 1754 to 1763. Washington played a role in igniting the conflict under the orders of Virginia Governor Robert Dinwiddie (1693–1770).

The governor ordered Washington to caution the French not to march into British territory in the Ohio Valley and then lead about 160 soldiers from Virginia to remove the French from Fort Duquesne. Although the French ultimately bested the Virginians, the clash launched the French and Indian war. Though British troops took charge of the conflict, Washington was promoted to colonel and put in charge of the Virginia soldiers who acted in support of the British regulars. He also served as the personal assistant to the British commander, General Edward Braddock. Among other conflicts, Washington took part in the campaign that resulted in the French loss of Fort Duquesne, Pennsylvania, in 1758.

Political Career After the battle at Fort Duquesne, Washington resigned his commission and went back to his home in Mount Vernon, Virginia, which he had inherited after the death of Lawrence Washington in the early 1750s. While overseeing his farming operations at Mount Vernon, Washington also began his political career. In 1758, he was elected to the House of Burgesses in Virginia, representing Fairfax County. Two years later, he began serving as a judge/justice of the peace for the same county, a position he held until 1774. These experiences led Washington to question British policies toward the colonies and express his opposition

This iconic 1851 image was painted by Emmanuel Leutze and depicts Washington's daring crossing of the Delaware River on Christmas Day, 1776. © *Bettmann/Corbis*

to the Stamp Act of 1765 as well as other British tax policies.

While serving as a representative to the First Continental Congress in 1774, Washington further stated his support of the policy of nonimportation of goods. Washington believed that if the colonies refused to import goods from Great Britain, British policy toward the colonies might change. To that end, the First Continental Congress adopted a plan influenced by the Fairfax Resolves, resolutions partially written by Washington and first adopted by his home county. Through the Continental Association, policies against importing British goods were enforced.

Military Leadership Another aspect of the Fairfax Resolves resulted in the formation of the Continental army. It was proposed that each county create its own militia company that colonists would control, not the governor appointed by Great Britain. Washington helmed the militia company from Fairfax County, and shortly before the Revolutionary War broke out, took on the leadership of the militia from a number of other counties. These militia companies were eventually combined to form the Continental army, which represented the collected colonists during the Revolutionary War after its launch in 1775. The Second Continental Congress named Washington the commander in chief of the Continental

army on June 15, 1775. Washington also functioned as America's de facto chief executive during the same period. He received no salary for his services and was only compensated for his expenses.

During the Revolutionary War, Washington faced challenges as commander in chief from the first. The British troops were more experienced, better armed, and had superior training. Washington sought to maintain discipline among his raw, often tattered soldiers. He also employed effective strategies to keep the enemy moving and smaller confrontations while keeping major engagements with the British to a minimum. Although he made some mistakes as general, such as during the Battle of New York in 1776, he also was capable of unexpected attacks that resulted in wins at Trenton and Princeton, for example. Washington also pulled off unanticipated moves that kept the Americans in the war, such as the winter crossing of the Delaware River.

Washington's position strengthened in 1778 when France became allied with the American cause, and he began serving as the head of the combined forces. However, it was not until the American victory at the Battle of Yorktown in 1781 that Americans seemed to make real progress. Despite low morale among American soldiers, victory was completed when the British completely withdrew by the early winter of 1783. It was Washington's strong character and ability to hold the army together through the sheer force of his personality that ultimately resulted in the American victory.

President of the United States Washington voluntarily stepped down as commander of the Continental army on December 23, 1783, at the end of the war. He then went home to Mount Vernon, where he began focusing on his estate businesses and farming while keeping abreast of land interests in the West and navigating the Potomac River. Washington's political career was not over, however. Noting the failure of the original Articles of Confederation, he was a leader at the 1787 Federal Convention that began the ratification process for the new American Constitution. Within a few years, Washington was unanimously elected to be the first president of the United States and was also selected to serve a second term as well.

During his terms in office, Washington shaped the direction of the new country's government. Between 1789 and 1792, he supported the addition of a Bill of Rights to the Constitution and added several departments to the presidential cabinet. Washington also launched the federal court system and oversaw the implementation of Federalist financial policies. Washing-

ton's second term focused on foreign policy issues, including remaining neutral as a new war broke out between Great Britain and France.

Washington's presidency ended in 1797, and he returned to his home in Mount Vernon, but did not fully retire. War with France appeared to be imminent during the presidency of his successor, John Adams, and Washington was named commander in chief of America's military interests. Diplomacy prevented the war and Washington remained at home, where he died on December 14, 1799.

King George III

King George III (1738–1820) was the British monarch during the American Revolution. His treatment of the American colonies caused the war for independence, and he was held responsible for the loss of the colonies. Born George William Frederick June 4, 1738, in London, England, George III was the son of Frederick Louis, the Prince of Wales, and his wife, Augusta. Frederick was the son of King George II, who was still reigning when Frederick died. George III was twelve years old at the time of Frederick's death. Because of his mother's

By 1776, New Yorkers were illustrating their displeasure with George III by tearing down a statue of the king that stood in that city's Bowling Green. *Pulling Down the Statue of George III in the Bowling Green in 1776, engraved by John C. McRae (engraving), Oertel, Johannes Adam Simon (1823-1909) (after) I(c) The Museum of the City of New York, USA*

Paul Revere's legendary "midnight ride" of 1775 warned American troops about the arrival of the British. *Getty Images*

coddling and overprotectiveness, George III lacked maturity and real-world experience. He was also greatly influenced by his family's German roots, as his great-grandfather, George I, and grandfather, George II, focused much of their interest on their native German states rather than Britain.

Britain's Monarch In 1760, the twenty-two-year-old George assumed the British throne upon the death of his grandfather. As a young king, George III enthusiastically embraced his new duties and played an active role in controlling the actions of Parliament. He enjoyed the political game and expertly played opposing forces against each other to realize his personal goals. George III also used flattery and his friendship as a means of gaining the loyalty of those whom he wanted to use. Although he could be overly trusting of people, he was also inflexible about matters that were important to him.

Within a few years of becoming king, George began directing Parliament to enact measures to better control and increasingly tax the American colonies. The colonists resisted his actions and grew ever more frustrated with Parliament, the king, and his series of prime ministers beginning in the mid-1760s. George III was oblivious to the colonists' intense disgust over the situation, and he continued to tighten his grip. American colonials saw George III as a tyrant against whom they needed to protect themselves. Their attitude further angered the

king and compelled him to take actions he deemed necessary to end their disobedience.

Loss of the Colonies By 1773, George III had his ideal prime minister in office, Lord North, who assisted in getting the Tea Act passed by Parliament. This act gave the East India Company sole control of the market for tea in the colonies, outraging Americans. In response to the act, American colonists tossed hundreds of pounds of tea into Boston Harbor during the Boston Tea Party in December 1773. In response, George III had Parliament pass the so-called "Intolerable Acts" of 1774, which further restricted colonial action but also unified many colonists against the king.

The American colonists soon declared war on Britain and its king. Having declared the colonies in rebellion in 1775, George III welcomed the conflict as a chance to demonstrate to other British colonies the mother country's power. Although British troops did well early on in the war, the frustrated Americans fought tenaciously against their oppressors. Even though they declared their independence from Britain in 1776, George III would not accept losing the colonies.

The Revolutionary War continued through the early 1780s. By this time, George had lost the support of many wealthy British allies who wanted the war to end. George III, however, had no intention of stopping, despite a devastating loss at the Battle of Yorktown in

HENRY WADSWORTH LONGFELLOW'S "PAUL REVERE'S RIDE"

Although Revere was well known for his 1775 ride during his lifetime, it was essentially forgotten after his death. Revere and the ride again took on celebrated status because of Henry Wadsworth Longfellow's well-known 1861 poem, "Paul Revere's Ride." Though the poem contains several historical inaccuracies, it was intended to do much more than celebrate Revere's accomplishment. Longfellow wrote the poem to encourage those in the north to take up arms during the Civil War.

EXCERPT FROM "PAUL REVERE'S RIDE"

Listen my children and you shall hear
Of the midnight ride of Paul Revere,
On the eighteenth of April, in Seventy-five;
Hardly a man is now alive
Who remembers that famous day and year.
He said to his friend, "If the British march
By land or sea from town to-night,
Hang a lantern aloft in the belfry arch
Of the North Church tower as a signal light,—
One if by land, and two if by sea;
And I on the opposite shore will be,
Ready to ride and spread the alarm
Through every Middlesex village and farm,
For the country folk to be up and arm."

SOURCE: *Longfellow, Henry Wadsworth. "Paul Revere's Ride." English Poetry III: from Tennyson to Whitman. Vol. 42 of The Harvard Classics. Charles W. Eliot, ed. New York: Collier and Son, 1904–1914. On Bartleby.com.*

---

deranged. It is now believed he had porphyria, a hereditary condition affecting the metabolism that caused these emotional extremes. George III had several serious, long-lasting episodes of mental illness. The final one began in 1810 and resulted in George III's son, Prince George, acting as regent beginning in 1811. Also both blind and deaf by the end of his life, George III died in London on January 29, 1820. Prince George succeeded him and reigned for the next decade as King George IV.

Paul Revere

Paul Revere (1735–1818) is an American Revolutionary War political leader best known for his night ride in 1775 to inform colonists in Lexington and Concord, Massachusetts, about the approach of British troops. Born January 1, 1735, in Boston, Massachusetts, Revere was the son of Apollos De Rivoire (later changed to Revere), and his wife, Deborah Hitchbourn. His father was a silversmith, and Revere became adept in working both gold and silver while employed at his father's smithy. Upon his father's death when Revere was nineteen years old, Revere took over the business and helped support his family, which included many siblings. During the French and Indian War, Revere also served as second lieutenant in an artillery division. He participated in the Crown Point Expedition of 1756, which failed to achieve its goal of capturing Crown Point, in present-day New York, from the French.

Anti-British Activities In the 1760s and 1770s, Revere's career continued to expand. Because of the large number of silversmiths in Boston, he worked not just in silversmithing but also by creating copperplate engravings, making surgical and dental instruments, and repairing false teeth. By the mid-1760s, especially after the British passed the Stamp Act was enacted, Revere focused much of his energy on anti-British activities. He created a well-known political cartoon-like engraving of the 1770 Boston Massacre that emphasized Boston's blamelessness in the matter. It is also believed that Revere participated in the Boston Tea Party in 1773.

Revere's most significant contributions to the Revolutionary War came by acting as a courier for various political bodies, including the Massachusetts Provincial Congress, Massachusetts Committee of Safety, and the Boston Committee of Correspondence. He was entrusted with the task of telling the New York–based Sons of Liberty that the Tea Party had occurred soon after the event. Revere also made rides to other locales including New York City, Philadelphia, and Durham, New Hampshire, to share information, pass along warnings, and ask for help as needed.

The Legendary Ride On the night of April 18, 1775, Revere became a legendary figure in American history when he took his historic ride to alert American troops

1781. Battles in the American Revolution continued for two more years as George III lost power at home but still insisted he would emerge victorious. Lord North was forced out of office in 1782, and George III signed the Treaty of Paris to end the war in 1783.

Declining Years After losing the American colonies, George III found his political power had decreased. He was compelled to take William Pitt the Younger as his prime minister. As Pitt's influence increased, George III's fell even further until Pitt resigned in 1801. Although George III regained some of his sway at this time, his mental health had not been strong for some time and this problem affected his ability to rule England.

Beginning in about 1788, George III suffered from wild emotional swings and seemed to act mentally

at Lexington and Concord about the British troops marching to the area. Revere was not the only rider that night; Both William Dawes and Samuel Prescott also rode and relayed the same information, and Revere never reached his destination in Concord because the British captured him during his ride. The arriving troops ended up starting the American Revolution with the battles of Lexington and Concord.

In addition to courier activities, Revere supported the revolutionary effort in other ways. He printed currency for the Massachusetts Provincial Congress and, in 1776, founded an important powder mill in Canton, Massachusetts, in which he manufactured gunpowder. In the spring of 1776, Revere's long-standing desire to have a military commission was finally granted.

Military Role Revere became a major in a Massachusetts regiment created to secure Boston, and later was commissioned as a major in a Massachusetts artillery train charged with defending the same city. After being promoted to lieutenant colonel in November 1776, he took command of Castle Island, located in Boston Harbor, a position he held for several years. By 1779, Revere retained his command of the Massachusetts State Train of Artillery after it was reduced to only three companies.

Until the summer of 1779, Revere had not served in the field. He was then given a chance to command troops in what became known as the Penobscot Expedition. Revere's men were to engage the enemy at what is now Castine, Maine, located on Penobscot Bay. The expedition was a total failure, and Revere was charged with disobeying orders as well as other crimes. Relieved of his command a month later, he was eventually court-martialed over the incident, but acquitted.

Later Years Although Revere's military career was undistinguished, his silversmithing became highly regarded in New England when he focused again on the craft in 1780. Revere also owned and operated a hardware store. By the late 1780s, he expanded his business interests by opening a Boston-based foundry and casting bells and cannons, among other items. In 1801, Revere founded a new mill in Canton that produced rolled copper. This venture brought him much wealth and prestige as it produced, for example, the rolled copper used on the dome of the Massachusetts State House. Retiring at the age of 76, Revere died on May 10, 1818, in Boston.

Thomas Jefferson

Thomas Jefferson (1743–1826) played a significant political and philosophical role during the American Revolution, serving as the primary drafter of the Declaration of Independence. Jefferson later served the young United States as secretary of state, vice president, and president. Born April 13, 1743, in Shadwell, Virginia, Jefferson was the eldest son of Peter Jefferson, a farmer, surveyor, and public figure. Through his mother, Jane

Thomas Jefferson's assertion of the right to self-government, proclaimed in the Declaration of Independence, is only one of his many significant contributions to American government. *The National Portrait Gallery/Smithsonian Institution*

Randolph, Jefferson was related to a prominent Virginia family and inherited significant wealth and landholdings, where he built his estate Monticello. Jefferson also received an impressive education for an American of his time. He attended boarding schools, then studied science, history, philosophy, and literature at the College of William and Mary and studied law under George Wythe, the "Father of American Jurisprudence."

Completing his legal education with Wythe, Jefferson began his professional career as a lawyer after being admitted to the bar in 1767. Although he had a thriving legal practice for a number of years, the American Revolution changed his destiny. As the Revolution began in 1774, the courts were suspended and Jefferson could no longer work as a lawyer. Instead, he embraced the revolutionary cause and used his legal know-how to that end.

Toward War Even before the American Revolution broke out, Jefferson served the public in elective office, one of his significant contributions to the movement. Soon after beginning his legal career, Jefferson was elected to the first elected governmental body in the colonies, Virginia's House of Burgesses, in 1768. After the Revolution began, Jefferson served in the First Continental Congress and wrote the precursor to the

Declaration of Independence, *A Summary View of the Rights of British America* (1774), which pushed colonists closer to war with Britain for their freedom. In a significant example of his philosophical contribution to the revolutionary effort, Jefferson claimed in the document that the American colonists had a natural right to self-government.

The Declaration of Independence

Jefferson continued to combine leadership roles in both the political and philosophical arenas as the brewing revolution grew more heated. While serving in the Second Continental Congress in 1775, Jefferson was appointed as the head of the committee charged with writing what became the Declaration of Independence. Nearly entirely composed of Jefferson's words, the legal document officially stated that the American colonies would no longer be part of the British Empire, but its own separate country.

In the Declaration, he built on the ideas first espoused in *A Summary View of the Rights of British America*. Jefferson further claimed that Americans had inalienable rights to equality and freedom, including the right of revolution. For example, while composing the Declaration of Independence, Jefferson contributed the significant phrase "all men are created equal," an idea fundamental to the foundation of the United States. The liberal, freedom-emphasizing philosophies he espoused as the spokesman for the revolutionary cause guided the movement.

Governor of Virginia

Although Jefferson's most significant contribution to the revolution came with the Declaration of Independence, he served in other ways as well. Jefferson was elected to a seat of Virginia's Legislative Assembly, before winning the governor's office. Beginning in June 1779, Jefferson began acting as the governor of Virginia, when the region was significant to the ongoing war.

During his time in office, Jefferson faced some difficulties as the British temporarily won the capital city of Richmond and other territories after a 1781 invasion. Virginia was not prepared for the British assault, and Jefferson himself had little means to defend his state. Jefferson and the government retreated from the British and housed themselves in safer locations. Though Jefferson was absolved of any wrongdoing in a subsequent inquiry conducted by the Assembly, it contributed to questions about his political fitness for years afterward. He also was personally hurt by public criticism of his actions.

Despite quitting as governor by 1782 and vowing to leave public service, Jefferson began serving in the United States Congress in 1783, drafting governmental territorial regulations and helping create foreign policy for the young country. Beginning in 1784, Jefferson spent five years in Europe first as part of a commission charged with negotiating commerce treaties with other countries and later as the American representative in France. When Jefferson returned to the United States in 1789, he continued to negotiate with foreign countries as he became President George Washington's secretary of state. Frustrated by his lack of success in improving America's position and with war breaking out between France and Great Britain, Jefferson resigned in 1793.

National Office

Though Jefferson wanted to end his public life and retire to Monticello, his greatest political offices were yet to come. In 1796, the Democratic Republicans selected Jefferson as their presidential candidate. By losing to John Adams, Jefferson was elected to the vice presidency and served one term before running for president again. Adams lost the 1800 election to Jefferson, who was reelected for a second term in 1804.

During Jefferson's presidency, he doubled the size of the young country through the Louisiana Purchase and enacted numerous governmental reforms during his first term. Jefferson dealt with the potential of war with Great Britain during his second term. During both terms, he had to fight several undeclared wars, including the Barbary Coast Wars of 1801 to 1805, though he personally did not believe in having a significant military.

At the end of his presidency in 1809, Jefferson finally retired to Monticello where he continued to advise members of his Democratic Republican political party, other elected officials, and subsequent presidents, including James Monroe. He also founded and planned the University of Virginia and corresponded with the leading intellectuals of the day. Jefferson died on July 4, 1826, at Monticello.

Benedict Arnold

Benedict Arnold (1741–1801) was an important general for the Continental army during the Revolutionary War before he defected to the British side of the conflict in 1780. Born Benedict Arnold V on January 14, 1741, in Norwich, Connecticut, Arnold was the son of Benedict Arnold IV and his wife, Hannah Waterman King. Although the family was wealthy from land and commerce interests during Arnold's early childhood, his father lost much of the money on failed business schemes and became an alcoholic. Because his father was no longer able to afford it, Arnold's superior education was discontinued and he lacked direction for some time. His life took a turn for the better when two cousins took him on as an apprentice at their apothecary when he was fourteen years old.

Military Career

Arnold's military career began while he completed his apprenticeship. He served in the New York colonial militia as well as during the French and Indian Wars, in which he fought in three battles. He deserted his commission both times, though his desertion during the French and Indian Wars was prompted by his mother's imminent death.

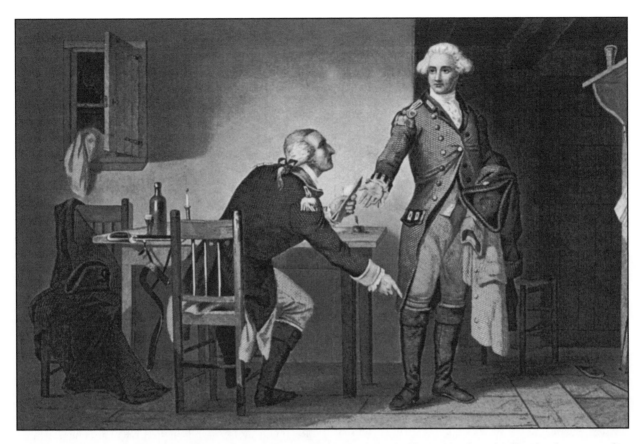

Benedict Arnold's treason was discovered when British Major John André was captured with correspondence detailing the plan to surrender West Point to the British. *Archive Photos/Getty Images*

By the early 1760s, Arnold's father had died, and Arnold had founded his own apothecary in New Haven, Connecticut, with the help of a cousin. A successful business and family man, Arnold made his fortune as a merchant during the 1760s. He accumulated much of his money at sea by trading horses and livestock in Canada and the West Indies on ships he owned. Arnold was also believed to occasionally engage in smuggling. The knowledge he gained from his naval activities would prove useful when the Revolutionary War broke out in the 1770s.

Patriot Army Before the American Revolution began, Arnold served as a captain of citizen soldiers in New Haven in 1774. He later joined the Patriot Army as a colonel in 1775 after the war broke out. Leading men to Boston in 1775, Arnold was involved with battles that led to the capture of both Fort Ticonderoga in New York and a British fort in Canada. In one of his early significant military operations, he led a group of one thousand American soldiers trying to occupy Quebec, Canada.

During the doomed combat in Quebec, Arnold suffered serious injury when he was shot in the leg.

Although Arnold's forces were unable to complete the task and hold Quebec, his spirited, or perhaps obstinate, actions and leadership ensured his promotion to brigadier general in the Continental army. Despite requiring months of recovery time for his leg wound, Arnold was still able to contribute to the war effort by demonstrating his military skill at sea. In 1776, Arnold helmed a fleet of ships that engaged British gunboats at two sites in New York: Lake Champlain and Valcour Island. His ships won both battles. It was his naval triumph at Valcour Island that especially brought him fame during the revolution.

Though Arnold had successes as a military officer for the revolutionaries, his violent temper and personal resentment of higher authorities sometimes created problems for him. He was often in conflict with other officers as well as Congress and faced court-martial on several occasions. In 1777, Arnold considered resigning his commission because other junior officers were promoted ahead of him, though he did eventually receive a promotion to major general. Only the personal intervention of his friend General George Washington ensured that Arnold remained in military service after he threatened to quit on this as well as another occasion.

Despite such issues, Arnold continued to act as a brave leader for the Americans. In 1777, he was in charge of a successful attack on British troops in Danbury, Connecticut. His skills as a military planner also led to the American victory at the key Battle of Saratoga, defeating British General John Burgoyne (1722–1792). However, during the battle, Arnold suffered injuries to the same leg shot in Quebec, and he was unable to command troops in the field again. Instead, in 1778, he became the governor of Philadelphia, a post he used to further his own business and personal interests.

Shifting Loyalties   Arnold's political loyalties started to undergo a transformation during this time. Influenced by his second wife, Margaret "Peggy" Shippen, who came from a secretly loyalist family, Arnold's change of heart also was shaped by the French who joined the American side of the conflict. Though he was court-martialed in 1778 for misusing government property while serving in Philadelphia, Arnold was given a new position of power that same year: fort commander at West Point in New York.

Soon after taking over this post, Arnold made a deal to sell the West Point fort to the British for a significant sum of money, 20,000 pounds sterling. The deal was never completed because Arnold's treason was discovered when the go-between carrying related documents was captured. In 1780, he defected to the British side, which immediately made him a brigadier general. Arnold was put in charge of British forces acting against Americans. British troops under his command raided towns in Connecticut and burned both Richmond, Virginia, and New London, Connecticut.

The British never fully trusted Arnold, and he was not allowed to deal with any military matters of importance or sensitivity. Though the British rewarded him with an audience with King George III in 1781 and a large estate in Canada several years later, his attempts to volunteer again for military service were refused. Arnold focused again on merchant activities in both Canada and England. By the end of his life, however, Arnold's business interests as well as his health were failing miserably. He died in debt in London on June 14, 1801.

Francis Marion

A Revolutionary War military leader from South Carolina, Francis Marion (c. 1732–1795), dubbed the "Swamp Fox," successfully used guerilla military tactics to attack British forces. Born around 1732 in Berkeley County, South Carolina, he was the grandson of Huguenot immigrants. Raised primarily in Georgetown, South Carolina, Marion grew up in an economically modest household. His education was minimal at county schools, and it is believed he was not completely literate. When he was fifteen years old, Marion went to sea, but after being shipwrecked and spending several adrift days at sixteen, he returned to work as a farmer on his family's land.

Early Military Career   Marion first gained military experience, including guerilla techniques, by fighting American Indians in a militia company headed by William Moultrie in 1761. Holding the rank of lieutenant, Marion participated in the Cherokee Expedition. He impressed his superiors by successfully leading a party of thirty men on a mission to remove Native Americans from an important mountain pass. Though twenty-one of his soldiers died, Marion became a highly respected member of his community for these accomplishments. After his service ended, he continued to farm on land he had leased in South Carolina.

By the early 1770s, Marion owned his own plantation located on the Santee River near Eutaw Springs. When the Revolutionary War started in 1775, Marion joined the Second South Carolina Regiment, an infantry unit also headed by Moultrie. Holding the rank of captain, he helped remove the British-appointed governor from his home state and capture British forts in Charleston's harbor. Promoted to major, Marion also played a significant role in the defense of Charleston, South Carolina, by commanding heavy guns at Fort Sullivan in June 1776. Promoted again to lieutenant colonel, Marion was given command of the Second South Carolina Regiment in 1778 and insisted on maintaining a disciplined force despite the lack of significant action. His regiment did fight in Savannah, Georgia, in 1779, but was defeated in its attempted assault.

Marion's Men   When the city of Charleston fell to the British in May 1780, Marion would have been captured had he not been at his home in St. John's Parish because of a broken ankle. The Americans' southern force was then decimated in South Carolina in August 1780 at the Battle of Camden. Because the Americans had few organized troops left in the South and with British forces gaining the upper hand, Marion organized his own small volunteer in South Carolina. It became the primary American military presence in the state for some time.

Marion employed guerrilla warfare techniques to engage the British in 1780 and 1781. Basing his operations in the swamps of South Carolina, Marion commanded small groups of mobile troops in a campaign of harassment against the British. He was able to befoul the British communication system, disrupt supply lines, and take both British scouting and foraging parties hostage. Marion also rescued American soldiers held prisoner and hassled those living in the state who remained loyal to Great Britain. The British hunted Marion, but he was able to use his knowledge of the swamps to evade them. This maneuver led to the nickname "Swamp Fox."

Marion also battled the British with more traditional means, primarily after Marion and his men helped Nathanael

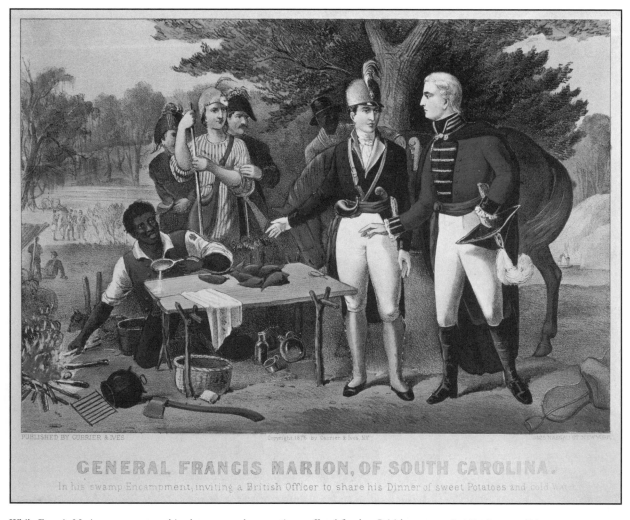

PUBLISHED BY CURRIER & IVES   Copyright 1876 by Currier & Ives. NY   125 NASSAU ST NEW YORK

GENERAL FRANCIS MARION, OF SOUTH CAROLINA.
In his swamp Encampment, inviting a British Officer to share his Dinner of sweet Potatoes and cold Water.

While Francis Marion was encamped in the swamps, he sometimes offered food to British troops. *Scala/Art Resource, NY*

Greene remove the British from North Carolina. Greene's lieutenant, Henry Lee, took troops to Marion, who was by then a brigadier general of the South Carolina militia. Marion also recruited troops and organized a brigade headquartered at Snow's Island. Lee and Marion led troops into battles in 1781, capturing Fort Watson and Fort Motte, among other triumphs. One significant victory came at Eutaw Springs on September 8, 1781, when British troops were forced to retreat to North Carolina. Marion was in charge of the right wing of American soldiers in the successful attack.

In 1781, Marion was also elected to South Carolina's senate and focused most of his attention on politics instead of military matters. Though he had antagonized Loyalists during the war, he acted to ensure they would be treated with mercy. Marion was reelected in 1782 and 1784, but continued to be active in his military brigade on occasion. At war's end, Marion was named the commander of Fort Johnson, a post he held until 1790. He was again elected to the state senate in 1791. Living

on his plantation with wife Mary Videau, Marion died on February 27, 1795.

General William Howe

During the early days of the American Revolutionary War, General William Howe (1729–1814) was the commander of British army troops stationed in America. He was born on August 10, 1729, into a noble family. After receiving some of his education at home, Howe also attended Eton from 1742 to 1746.

Early Military Career When Howe was seventeen years old, he joined the army and soon began distinguishing himself as a soldier. In 1747, he was promoted to lieutenant and was stationed in Flanders during the War of Austrian Succession. Howe's abilities, combined with powerful connections, led to several quick promotions, including captain in 1750, major in 1756, and lieutenant colonel in 1757.

After being chosen to represent Nottingham in the House of Commons in 1758, Howe first went to the

General William Howe, commander in chief of the British forces during the American Revolution, orders the evacuation of his troops after the Siege of Boston. *MPI/Getty Images*

North American continent during the French and Indian War. In 1759, he served under General James Wolfe during the siege of Quebec. Howe himself was the commander of the British attack on and capture of Montreal in 1760. Two years later, Howe was an adjunct general as part of the siege on Havana, Cuba, which was then held by the Spanish. By the end of the war, Howe had distinguished himself as a military officer and was known for his valor and leadership skills.

Command in the Colonies Promoted to major general in 1772, Howe disagreed with British policy in the American colonies and did not want to serve in the American theater of the Revolutionary War. However, when ordered to take a command in May 1775, Howe took on the post as second-in-command to General Thomas Gage because he believed it was his duty to do so. It is believed Howe was also sure that a settlement with the rebel colonists could be negotiated with his help.

After arriving in the colonies, Howe found that negotiations were not possible. Howe demonstrated his courage at the battle of Bunker Hill as well as the attack on Breed's Hill. Although the British won the battles, it was a high cost. In October, his military prowess was

rewarded with two promotions: he was made a full general and named the commander-in-chief of the British forces in the American colonies. Although Howe had some successes as British commander, his failures cost his country important military losses.

Though Howe had to evacuate British troops from Boston in March 1776, he was able to shift his troops first to Halifax then to New York, and later successfully invaded both Manhattan and Long Island. By the end of the year, however, Howe's slow troop movements, inadequate manpower and supplies, and the British inability to break up General George Washington's army resulted in important gains for the colonists. In December 1776, the Americans won unexpected battles at Trenton and Princeton in New Jersey, and Howe again let a chance to capture, if not destroy, Washington slip through his fingers.

By 1777, Howe had devised a new strategy for the British military against the colonial rebels so that he could engage and defeat the army helmed by Washington. Howe's plan involved attacks on both the American capital of Philadelphia and New York state. Although Howe originally planned to move troops over land for the Philadelphia engagement, he changed his mind and decided to move them by sea. Despite failures to position troops until August, the British successfully captured Philadelphia, but this victory did not do as much to further the British cause as Howe had hoped because of defeats in New York.

Howe had accepted General John Burgoyne's word that he had sufficient troops to complete his task. Burgoyne decisively lost the Battle of Saratoga to the Americans in part because no British troops were ready to move in support of him when his men were besieged. Burgoyne was forced to surrender to the Americans in October 1777. The loss at Saratoga deeply damaged the British cause, and Howe sent in his resignation shortly thereafter. It was accepted the following spring, after which Howe returned to Britain.

Post-War Activities At home, Howe was widely criticized, but he defended his actions in America at a Parliamentary inquiry and through the printed word. He asserted that he had acted to best serve Britain's military interests and denied he tried to placate the American colonists. Despite events during the Revolutionary War, Howe continued to have a distinguished military career in Britain, holding significant commands in England during the French Revolution. He also served as governor of Berwick, England, from 1795 to 1808, as well as governor of Plymouth from 1808 until his death on July 12, 1814.

Thomas Paine

Thomas Paine (1737–1809) was an influential writer whose work, especially the pamphlet *Common Sense*, played an inspirational role in starting the American Revolution. Born January 29, 1737, in Thetford, England, Paine was the son of Joseph Pain and his wife, Frances Cocke. (Thomas Paine added the "e" to his surname later in life.) Paine's father made his living farming and fashioning women's corsets and whale-bone corset stays. The family was poor and Paine's education was limited.

When he was thirteen years old, Paine began working. He first joined his father and learned his trade, but soon decided to try other professions. For at least two decades, Paine drifted through a number of jobs, including sailor, manufacturer, tax collector, schoolteacher, grocer, and shop worker. Though Paine's formal education had ended early, he also spent significant time in self-education, often reading about science and politics.

Popular Influence In 1774, the direction of Paine's life changed when he met the important American colonist Benjamin Franklin, who was impressed by Paine's intellect. Franklin convinced Paine that the colonies would be an ideal place for him and even wrote recommendation letters to help him find employment there. When Paine arrived in Philadelphia later that same year,

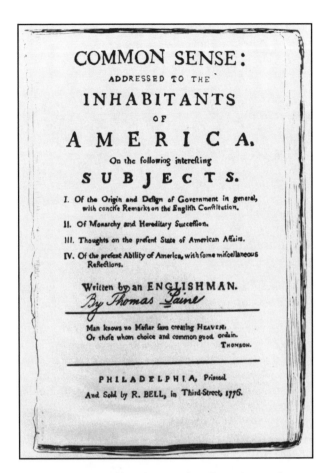

Thomas Paine's pamphlet "Common Sense" urged a complete break with England in early 1776. © *Bettmann/Corbis*

he began working at the *Pennsylvania Magazine* as a writer and editor.

Paine soon played a key role in igniting the Revolution. He used the power of the printed word to influence political events. The colonists were divided on the topic of declaring their independence from Great Britain. Many were open to considering the idea, though some still believed that the colonies and mother country could reconcile differences. One supporter of independence, Benjamin Rush, told Paine that he should pen a publication backing his cause and calling for action. Paine then wrote *Common Sense*, a fifty-page pamphlet published anonymously on January 10, 1776. *Common Sense* was a sensation, with over 500,000 copies eventually purchased. It was also reprinted in several European countries and translated into German.

In the pamphlet, Paine urged his readers to take arms against King George III for a number of reasons. He argued that Great Britain taxed the American colonies to excess, and furthermore, it did not make sense for such a far-off country to oversee political affairs in America. Paine also stated that the British monarchy was an immoral form of government. *Common Sense* achieved

EXCERPT FROM THE FIRST *CRISIS* PAPER

These are times that try men's souls. The summer soldier and the sunshine patriot will, in this crisis, shrink from the service of their country; but he that stands it now, deserves the love and thanks of man and woman. Tyranny, like hell, is not easily conquered.... The heart that feels not now, is dead; the blood of his children will curse his cowardice, who shrinks back at a time when a little might have saved the whole.... [H]e whose heart is firm, and whose conscience approves his conduct, will pursue his principles unto death.

its goal, finally tipping the balance in many colonists' minds toward independence.

Service to the Revolution Paine did not just use the written word to help start the Revolutionary War. He also served as a soldier in the early days of the war when the patriots were losing ground. In 1776, he had a commission in the Continental army. Paine served under General George Washington and was part of the troops' retreat across New Jersey.

In addition, Paine continued to push the revolutionary cause through his writing. From 1776 to 1783, he wrote and published sixteen *Crisis* papers that further encouraged Americans to continue their fight for independence. In the papers, Paine eloquently explained why their patriotism was so important at this critical time.

Though Paine continued to produce influential pamphlets and his writings were popular, he suffered from further financial difficulties in part because he would not take any profits from their publication. During the war, he held posts such as the federal Secretary of the Committee of Foreign Affairs, until he was forced to resign due to his publication of privileged information, and a clerkship for the Pennsylvania General Assembly. But when the Revolutionary War ended in 1783, Paine was impoverished until the grateful states of Pennsylvania and New York provided him with money and a farm, respectively, for his war-related activities.

The French Revolution After living on his farm and focusing on inventing for some time, Paine again used the written word to support a revolutionary movement. After the 1789 French Revolution, he wrote *The Rights of Man* to express his belief in the cause of the rebels who wanted to bring down the French monarchy and King Louis XVI. Paine's book went through several editions in 1791 and 1792 and became a best seller in France as well as Britain and the United States.

In *The Rights of Man*, Paine argued that Europeans were unhappy with their monarchical and hereditary

governments that led to widespread poverty, the inability of people to read and write, high unemployment, and wars that broke out on a regular basis. Paine specifically referenced the situation in Great Britain and called for armed revolt against the king. Charged with treason by the British, Paine made his way to France in 1792.

While in France, Paine faced further difficulties. Though he supported the French rebels, he did not believe King Louis XVI and his wife Marie Antoinette should be executed. When Maximilien de Robespierre became the head of the new French government, he imprisoned Paine in 1794 for espousing such beliefs. Paine's potential execution was deterred by James Monroe, then an American representative in France and later an American president. Paine spent eleven months in jail, during which he began writing his controversial book on religion, *The Age of Reason*, which was published in 1794 and 1796. Like his earlier works, this book sold well in the United States, Ireland, Britain, and France.

Because of the controversy surrounding Paine's book, his public criticism of Washington for not helping him out of prison, and his perceived support of Robespierre's bloody reign of terror, Paine's return to the United States in 1802 was not received well by the American people. He again suffered financial difficulties and spent the last years of his life as an impoverished alcoholic who was often ill. Paine died on June 8, 1809, in New York City.

General Cornwallis

British General Charles Cornwallis (1738–1805) led troops at the decisive Battle of Yorktown in 1781 and surrendered, effectively ending the American Revolutionary War. Born on December 31, 1738, Charles Cornwallis was born into a prominent British noble family. He received his education at Eton College and Clare College, Cambridge, England.

Early Military Career Cornwallis began his military career when he was about eighteen years old. In 1756, he joined the First Foot Guards as an ensign. After a brief stint at a Turin-based military academy in 1757, Cornwallis saw action during the Seven Years War as a part of a regiment assigned to Prince Ferdinand of Brunswick. He took part in battles in Europe, including Kirch-Denkern, Wilhelmstadt, and Lutterberg. By 1761, he was named a lieutenant colonel in the Twelfth Regiment.

While Cornwallis was establishing himself as an experienced, talented military man, he also began a political career. In 1760, he was elected to the House of Commons, representing a family borough in Suffolk. When Cornwallis's father died in 1762, he became the second Earl Cornwallis and took over his father's seat in the House of Lords. While serving in the House of Lords, Cornwallis disagreed with the severe treatment of the American colonies as laid out by King George III and his prime minister, Lord North. Despite this opinion, he

General Cornwallis surrenders to George Washington after the Battle of Yorktown. *Time Life Pictures/Mansell/Time Life Pictures/Getty Images*

did have the king's favor as one of his advisors and a lord of the bedchamber. In 1770, Cornwallis was given the esteemed position of constable of the Tower of London and also joined the privy council.

Service in the Colonies

After being promoted to the rank of major general in 1775, Cornwallis was sent to the colonies in a military capacity in 1776. He had the command of ten regiments of British troops dispatched as reinforcements for Generals Henry Clinton (1738–1795) and William Howe. After arriving in America, Cornwallis saw action in New York in late summer and early fall of 1776. He also had a role in the British occupation of New Jersey. In 1777, Cornwallis participated in the Battle of Brandywine as the commander of a division of troops helmed by Howe.

Cornwallis soon grew frustrated with the British military response to the revolting colonists, primarily because of his new superior. When General Henry Clin-ton became the commander of British military interests in America, he put a conservative strategy into place. Clinton was already critical of Cornwallis for not seizing General George Washington when he had the chance on several occasions. Clinton was also threatened by Cornwallis's position as his designated successor, and he regarded Cornwallis as arrogant. Thus, Clinton and Cornwallis had a tense relationship at best.

Despite this situation, Cornwallis continued to play his role on the battlefield. During the Battle of Monmouth in 1778, Cornwallis commanded some British troops counterattacking men led by Nathanael Greene as Clinton directed the British retreat from Philadelphia. After spending much of 1779 on leave in Britain with his dying wife, Jemima Tulkiens, Cornwallis returned to America and resumed his military position in 1780. He helped plan and take part in the attack on Charleston, which resulted in the city's surrender in May 1780.

Command in the South

By the middle of 1780, tensions with Clinton eased as Cornwallis essentially took charge of British troops located in the South. Although Cornwallis still reported to Clinton, distance and the political support of George Sackville Germaine, the English secretary of state for the colonies, allowed Cornwallis freedom to run his command as he pleased. In addition to turning South Carolina into a supply base desperately needed by the British, Cornwallis led troops to victory at Camden while marching on the Carolinas.

Cornwallis's strategy, however, contributed greatly to Britain's eventual defeat. The bold general believed that the best way to defend the land Britain had regained in the South was to attack Virginia. But Cornwallis had neither enough troops nor the support of enough Loyalists to complete this mission. Cornwallis also kept changing his mind on the approach his strategy would take. By the time he was forced to surrender to General George Washington after being defeated at the Battle of Yorktown in October 1781, Cornwallis had lost about 25 percent of British troops serving in America.

Later Career

In spite of this failure, Cornwallis was generally not blamed for the loss in Britain, and his career continued to thrive. Though he initially refused it several times, he took on the post of the governor general of Bengal in India in 1786, a position of greater responsibility than the one he held in America. Cornwallis was able to build up British rule in India as well as other parts of Asia. As an administrator, he was a reformer who improved Britain's civil administration and took on corruption in Britain's India Company. Also a military leader in the colony, Cornwallis made the best of the troops available from the India Company and essentially won the Third Mysore War in the early 1790s.

After going back to Britain and being given the title of marquess, Cornwallis continued to act in his government's interest as both a diplomat and military expert in several significant hot spots, including Ireland, Flanders, and India. After returning to Bengal in 1805, he died on October 5, shortly after his arrival there.

John Paul Jones

John Paul Jones (1747–1792), arguably the most important American Revolutionary War naval hero, valiantly contributed to significant victories by the Continental navy. He was born simply John Paul in 1747 in Kirkcudbrightshire, Scotland, the son of a gardener who was employed at a local estate. Jones's education was minimal, and at the age of thirteen, he was apprenticed to a ship owner in Whitehaven and went to sea. Jones's employer took him on trading expeditions to Virginia and islands in the Caribbean. Working for other mariners after his master went bankrupt, Jones gained valuable experience as a merchant sailor through the 1760s, including stints with slave traders. By the time of his twenty-first birthday, Jones was a merchant ship captain himself. In the late 1760s and early 1770s, he worked on trading voyages in the West Indies.

Because of a fierce temperament, Jones also faced legal troubles as a young adult. He was once acquitted of murder in Scotland for the death of one of his crewmates a few months after Jones flogged him. In the early 1770s, the crew of another of Jones's ships, the *Betsy of London*, mutinied in Tobago after he decided not to pay them under the expected terms. The mutiny turned into a fight, and Jones murdered the mutineers' leader. He spent the next two years in hiding to avoid being arrested for the crime. By 1774, Jones joined his brother in Virginia and added the Jones surname as a further way to conceal his identity.

Naval Service   About a year after he came to Virginia, Jones joined the Continental navy as a senior first lieutenant. Rejecting a chance to helm his own ship, Jones elected to serve first aboard the *Alfred*, a ship he helped to outfit. He wanted to gain firsthand knowledge of the military skills needed for naval combat. The *Alfred* helped severely damage a powerful British vessel, the *Nassau*.

In the spring of 1776, Jones accepted the captaincy of the *Providence*. Jones soon distinguished himself as a captain and later as the commander of one of the best fleets in the Continental navy. He captured a number of British merchant ships, used his skills as a sailor to get the better of some of Britain's best warships, and destroyed British fishing boats as well. Having developed

John Paul Jones, at the helm of the *Bonhomme Richard*, leads his men during the battle with the *Serapis*.   *The New York Public Library/Art Resource, NY*

a reputation for being an aggressive sailor who acted boldly in battle to engage, not avoid, the enemy, Jones also displayed a sharp sense of seamanship.

International Renown Jones took command of the *Alfred* in the winter of 1776 and continued his distinguished service. His naval career took on a new dimension in 1777, when he became the commander of the *Ranger*. Under congressional orders, he took the ship to France to relay news of the American victory at the Battle of Saratoga in September 1777. After achieving this goal in early 1778, Jones staged raids along the British coast and captured British ships and prisoners over a twenty-eight-day period. These triumphs made his name known internationally.

Remaining in Europe, Jones continued his military service by working for the French against the British while sailing under an American flag. He took command of the *Bonhomme Richard* and headed a small flotilla. Jones continued his military success by capturing a number of British ships as his ships traversed the seas around Britain. Again showing his prowess as a captain in the battle off Flamborough Head, Jones cemented his reputation as a naval hero in September 1779. He won his famous clash with the *Serapis*, a British fighting ship that was quicker and carried more arms than the *Bonhomme Richard*. Jones won his victory through boldness and bravery.

It was during the battle with the *Serapis* that Jones was asked to surrender and uttered his legendary response: "I have not yet begun to fight." Although Jones did refuse to surrender to the British captain, it is unlikely that he spoke that specific phrase because it was not mentioned in accounts of the battle until a half-century later. But, as with many of his other victories, Jones showed he understood that a battle could be won in part by wearing the enemy down and winning psychological advantage. After his triumph, the U.S. Congress honored Jones with a resolution indicating America's gratitude.

Later Years Now famous, Jones continued to be lauded in the United States and France. Helming the *Ariel*, a ship on loan from the French for carrying military goods to America, Jones returned to the United States in early 1781. He campaigned to be promoted to rear admiral in the Continental navy, but was not given the advancement. Lacking other opportunities, Jones went back to Europe as a representative of America, sent to claim the prize monies owed to the United States for his war accomplishments.

Briefly returning to the United States in 1787, Jones was honored with the only gold medal given to a Continental navy officer as voted by Congress. He returned to Europe in 1788 and became a rear admiral in the Russian navy. Serving the Russian Queen Catherine the Great, Jones was stationed on ships in the Black Sea where he fought the Turks and helped capture a Turkish fortress at Ochkov. His stint in Russia ended by the fall of 1789 as court politics and jealous mariners damaged his position.

Jones then moved to Paris, where he spent the last two years of his life in poor health. After his death in 1792, he was buried in an unmarked grave in the French city. In 1905, Jones was re-interred at the American Naval Academy. The academy built a crypt to house Jones's remains in 1913, where his grave remains to this day.

General Lafayette

General Lafayette (1757–1834), also known as the Marquis de Lafayette, was a French military general who helped the Americans win their Revolution and also played a significant role in his native country after the French Revolution. Lafayette was born Marie-Joseph-Paul-Yves-Roch-Gilbert du Motier on September 6, 1757, in Chavagnac, Auvergne, France. His family was wealthy French nobility, and Lafayette was part of their title. After the deaths of his father, mother, and grandfather by the time he was thirteen years old, Lafayette inherited the family fortune. He then received some of his education in Paris, where he studied at the Collège du Plessis.

Lafayette's military career began when he was still a teenager. In 1771, he joined the French army and spent the next five years in active service. Lafayette began his military career as a musketeer. Within three years, he was promoted to second lieutenant, then captain in the Noailles Regiment. He was compelled to retire at the age of eighteen due to reforms of the French military. After marrying Marie Adrienne de Noailles in 1773, Lafayette spent several years in the royal court life of Versailles.

Service in the American Revolution When the American Revolution broke out in the mid-1770s, Lafayette asked King Louis XVI's permission to go to the colonies and assist their cause against the British, France's longstanding nemesis. Louis turned Lafayette down, but the former soldier used his own money to purchase a ship and fill it with supplies. Lafayette then sailed to America to offer his services and military experience to the rebellious colonies.

Arriving in North Carolina in June 1777, the nineteen-year-old Lafayette was given an honorary military commission of major general by the Continental Congress. He had no command, but began serving General George Washington as his assistant. Lafayette encouraged the Americans in their cause, and also saw military action under Washington, participating in battles in Pennsylvania and New Jersey. Lafayette's exemplary performance in these clashes led to his commanding a division of American troops in December 1777 and the summer of 1778.

The Marquis de Lafayette led Americans to victory at Yorktown. *Snark/Art Resource, NY*

Securing French Assistance In 1778, the Americans asked Lafayette to return to France to obtain help for their cause. Because of his earlier disregard of Louis XVI's royal order, Lafayette was arrested when he arrived home in 1779. His punishment was short-lived as Louis XVI decided the political gain from having the Americans as allies was more important. The French king agreed to provide some aid for the Americans, and Lafayette returned to the United States in the spring of 1780.

Upon his arrival, Lafayette took charge of the French auxiliary forces that France loaned to help the Americans fight the British. A year later, Lafayette was put in charge of defending Virginia. Lafayette's actions and military maneuvers helped trap British General Cornwallis, resulting in the decisive American victory at Yorktown in 1781. On October 19, 1781, Cornwallis surrendered and the American Revolutionary War had essentially ended.

Return to France Lafayette was lauded as a hero when he went back to France in 1782. Although he continued to assist American causes in Europe, Lafayette focused primarily on his own country. He was then given the rank of brigadier general in the French army, but spent more of his energies on his political career and served as a member of the Assembly of Notables from 1787 to 1788. When the French Revolution began in 1789, Lafayette was forced to combine his military and political backgrounds.

A believer in the ideals of the Enlightenment, Lafayette played several leadership roles in the beginning of the French Revolution. He successfully suggested the adoption of the "Declaration of the Rights of Man and of the Citizen." After the Bastille prison fell on July 14, 1789, Lafayette was put in charge of the Parisian national guard. His position of power and popularity eroded over time, as he wanted the French rebels to take a more restrained stance and adopt a government modeled on the British Parliament and American Constitution. As radicals ruled the day, Lafayette stepped down as national guard commander in 1791.

French Military Command When France declared war against Austria and Prussia in 1792, Lafayette served as commander of the Army of the Ardennes. He led an invasion of the Austrian Netherlands, but had no backup and was forced to withdraw. Because of his continued political statements against radical action and lack of support among his troops, Lafayette went to Austria, where he was regarded as a prisoner of war. He was released in 1797 when Napoleon Bonaparte came to power in France. Though Bonaparte did not want Lafayette to return to his home country, Lafayette defied this order in 1799. Upon his return, he was recognized as a retired general and given a pension.

After spending more than a decade at his country estate in Lagrange, France, and avoiding political action, Lafayette returned to politics after Napoleon abdicated in 1814. Lafayette then stood for election to the Legislative Chamber, and again influenced French politics. He called for Napoleon's permanent resignation and also served in the Chamber of Deputies as the liberal leader in opposition to the restored monarchy of Louis XVIII and Charles X.

Lafayette's exploits in America had not been forgotten. In 1824, the year he left the chamber, he returned to the United States at the invitation of the American government. There, he was lauded with a tour of the developing country, welcomed by citizens in each state, and given gifts of cash and land by the United States Congress. Fifteen months later, Lafayette returned to France, where his heroism was again acknowledged.

In 1830, Lafayette had his last political day in the sun during the next revolutionary era in France. He again stood as the prominent voice of moderate republicanism and commanded the French national guard, while reluctantly supporting the constitutional kingship of Louis Philippe. After being dismissed in 1831, Lafayette again became a symbol of opposition. Politically, he was essentially irrelevant by the time of his death on May 20, 1834, in Paris.

✪ Major Battles and Events

Lexington and Concord

By the spring of 1775, the dispute between American colonists and the British government had reached a fever pitch. Disagreements over taxes and other acts of Parliament aimed at colonists had raged for ten years. Tensions between those living in and around Boston, Massachusetts, and the mother country were even greater because outspoken Bostonians had protested more actively, which sometimes resulted in violence. They had organized efforts against King George III and his prime minister. Samuel Adams and other leaders had formed the Sons of Liberty, an opposition group that argued "no taxation without representation."

The Boston Tea Party enraged Parliament. The king and Parliament responded by passing a series of laws to punish Boston residents. General Thomas Gage, already the commander of the English forces in the colonies, became the new governor of Massachusetts. The king thought a military commander like Gage could better control these unruly dissenters.

These events drove a bigger wedge between the Americans and the British. Leading up to April 1775, rumors circulated as to when a rebellion would occur. The First Continental Congress had already taken place, and a Second Continental Congress was planned. General Gage had concerns that the Sons of Liberty and others might rebel. He also got word that colonial leaders had stockpiled weapons inland at Lexington and Concord. Concord, about eighteen miles east of Boston, and Lexington a few miles closer, both lay in present-day Massachusetts. Gage and other military leaders constructed a plan to ensure that potential rebels would not have these arms for a possible uprising.

On April 16, 1775, silversmith Paul Revere got word that Gage's troops planned to take the patriot's magazines. He did not know the exact details, but he and other American leaders developed a counterplan to assist the Minutemen of Massachusetts when this mission began. Revere had planned to cross the Charles River and ride into Lexington to warn the militiamen. He also came up with a backup plan in case he could not cross the river. In the Old North Church, which had already become a regular venue for the voices of discontent to organize against the British, lamps would hang to warn that the Redcoats were coming and by what route: "One if by land, two if by sea."

Gage's plan was kept as secret as possible. Lieutenant Colonel Francis Smith was selected to lead a column of twenty-one companies to destroy these American munitions. Smith was to march to Concord, burn and dismantle the stockpile, and return to Boston. Only top commanders were privy to the scheme. British troops had been told to be ready to move at a moment's notice. After the soldiers had turned in for the night of April 18, their sergeants put their hands over the sleeping soldiers' mouths as they awoke them. They slipped out of their barracks and onto the Boston Common. From there, some 600 to 800 soldiers departed at about 10:30 at night. Though the British followed every precaution they could to not disturb townspeople, onlookers noticed their departure from Boston across the water toward Lexington and Concord. Paul Revere had a friend place the two lanterns in the steeple of the Old North Church while he crossed the harbor. Once on land again, he borrowed a friend's horse and headed to warn the Minutemen that the British were coming.

William Dawes, a shoemaker, joined Revere in the effort to warn fellow patriots. They took separate routes from Boston, but met again at Lexington where they informed Captain John Parker's company. The American response to Smith's mission involved communication from several points between the church and the weapons caches at Lexington and Concord. Alarm bells in hamlets along the way and patriot gunshots signaled that the British troops were on the way.

Captain Parker had assembled his militiamen on the Lexington village green, ready for the Redcoat's approach. A detachment from Smith's column came within view of the Minutemen in Lexington. Parker had told his men to stand their ground, but not to fire unless fired upon. He also reportedly said, "If they mean to have a war, let it begin here." Details of events after this are hazy. After shots were fired (who shot first is also disputed), a British officer directed his men to fire toward Parker's militia. Eight Americans were killed and ten were wounded.

The exchange at Lexington took about a half hour. By this time, Smith had rejoined the detachment and wanted to fulfill his mission. At Concord, word of the battle of Lexington soon arrived. Colonel James Barrett was organizing 250 Minutemen from Concord. He knew it would take time for the British to find the hidden ammunition and cannon. So as they filed into Concord, Barrett ordered his men atop a low ridge about 1,000 yards north of the bridge over the Concord River. From here, Barrett's men could see the town.

The British came into Concord and found some of the stored ammunition. Some time after 10:00 A.M., these weapons were placed in the middle of the road and burned. By this time more than four hundred Minutemen had arrived prepared to battle at Concord. Barrett's men, ready to retaliate anyway, saw the smoke from atop the ridge and assumed the British were burning the town. A few minutes later, the militia advanced toward the bridge. The patriots' first shots killed three British soldiers and wounded eight others. After much

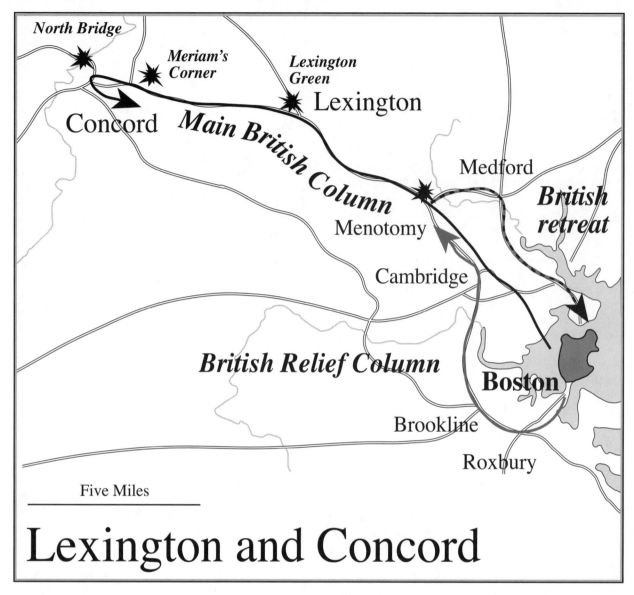

North Bridge

Meriam's Corner

Lexington Green

Lexington

Main British Column

Concord

Medford

British retreat

Menotomy

Cambridge

British Relief Column

Boston

Brookline

Roxbury

Five Miles

Lexington and Concord

Though British forces would attempt to defeat the Revolutionaries by dividing them, American forces were able to win major battles. This map shows the British retreat near Lexington and Concord. *Reproduced by permission of Gale, a part of Cengage Learning*

indecision, Colonel Smith ordered his men to return toward Boston. About one mile toward Lexington, these British soldiers came into view of American marksmen planted out of sight. Their accuracy was devastating, and Redcoats collapsed at the hand of American gunfire.

General Gage sent reinforcements under Commander Hugh Percy. If it were not for Percy, the British would have suffered a complete massacre. Percy arrived at Lexington and provided a safe return for the exhausted Redcoats who had made the journey from Boston to Concord and were now returning.

Before the British soldiers returned to Boston, an estimated 3,500 colonials had responded to the calls to arms from Revere and others. The British suffered a total

of seventy-three casualties and 200 were injured or missing. Colonists lost forty-nine men, thirty-nine suffered wounds, and twenty-six became missing. Percy responded to the fight, "Whoever looks upon them as an irregular mob, will find himself much mistaken." Protecting most of the weapons and running the Redcoats back to Boston gave the colonists high morale. It also signaled to the British that the chances for a peaceful solution to the conflict were basically impossible. The Revolutionary War had begun.

Ticonderoga

Soon after shots were fired to begin the American Revolution, British Fort Ticonderoga became an attractive

British General John Burgoyne with his Indian allies before their successful attack on Fort Ticonderoga in 1777.   *Hulton Archive/Getty Images*

prospect for the American side. The fort, a dilapidated structure that housed only about fifty men, many who were invalids, was probably not seen as the grandest conquest. But controlling such a strategic location could be an advantage in the early stages of the war. It sat in north central New York on the west side of Lake Champlain, north of Albany, where the lake empties into the Hudson River. With Canadians not joining the American rebels, military leaders and onlookers alike predicted that the British would travel southward from Canada to cut off New England from the other colonies. Securing Fort Ticonderoga would decrease the chances for this British strategy. The fort, though short on manpower, held over fifty cannons that could be useful to the colonists.

The taking of Fort Ticonderoga on May 10, 1775, is a unique story from the Revolution. The war effort in 1775 was rather unfocused and uncertain. The Continental army was not a fine-tuned organization. Minutemen and other volunteers received orders from various authorities. The infant Congress, state assemblies, and local committees differed on how to carry out the war. Perhaps more confusing was the question of which offi-

cer was in charge of the attack on the fort. Benedict Arnold and Ethan Allen led the mission. Arnold, known to history as a traitor, was an ambitious young man from a modest background. His first military exploits came in the French and Indian War. As revolutionaries began to dissent against the British, Arnold was an active member of the Sons of Liberty in his native Connecticut. When Arnold arrived in Cambridge, Massachusetts, he offered his plan to take Ticonderoga to the Massachusetts Committee of Safety. With some reluctance, the Committee gave Arnold a provisional commission to gather four hundred men for the mission.

Ethan Allen of Vermont was an equally flamboyant character. He was the eldest of six sons who grew up under the tutelage of their independent-minded father. Ethan Allen thus developed as a freethinker, learning from reading the Bible and Plutarch's *Lives*. When he was about to embark on a formal education at seventeen, his father died, forcing him to take over the family farm. This likely strengthened his self-reliance, but limited his polished language and sophistication. When revolution began, he was a large, strong man, and a self-taught, enterprising philosopher. Allen showed excess in nearly everything he undertook. He became a natural leader of the Green Mountain Boys, rugged soldiers from Vermont who harassed royal officials.

Arnold and Allen met before they each could reach Ticonderoga. Upon their meeting the question immediately arose: Who would be in charge of this mission? Arnold immediately insisted that his commission gave him the authority to lead, but Allen refused to yield. From a practical standpoint, Allen's loyal Green Mountain Boys gave him qualifications to rival Arnold's commission. It was decided that they would jointly share the command. On May 9, 1775, the two officers and about three hundred men waited on the east side of the lake for the right moment to take the fort. After some discussion, about eighty of these men, led by both Arnold and Allen, crossed the lake on a barge and arrived at the fort before dawn. The exact manner in which the fort was taken is of course disputed. Versions told by Arnold, Allen, and their men differ. Apparently, a sleepy sentry lowered his musket at this group, and Allen swatted it away with his sword. The leaders quickly made it to the officers' quarters and announced they were taking the fort. The British commanders were certainly surprised and appeared half-dressed to face the attackers. The result was clear no matter who told the story. The young, disorganized American effort had actually taken Ticonderoga and seized some one hundred guns without a death for either side.

When word of American accomplishments at Ticonderoga reached Congress, a debate about the propriety of the attack began. Surprisingly, delegates were not unanimously elated. At this early point in the war, some still hoped to reconcile with King George III. The battles at Lexington and Concord could be viewed as acts of defense. But this was an aggressive assault on the king's property. Congress decided, over the opposition of the New England delegates, that the successful attackers should abandon the fort. The valuable supplies and weapons should be taken, the Congress said, but only after a careful inventory had been made to guarantee proper payment back to the British when harmonious terms between an independent America and the king resumed. When this decision of Congress reached New York and New England, colonists were shocked at such absurdity. Why would the rebels give up such a strategic point that had been effectively won? With enough prodding, the Congress reversed its decision and colonials maintained the fort until British General John Burgoyne forced them out in the summer of 1777 in his Saratoga campaign.

Bunker Hill

The battle of Bunker Hill took place between the American colonists and regular British troops in Charlestown, Massachusetts, on June 17, 1775. This was the first large-scale battle in the American Revolution. The colo-

nists had yet to officially create the United States and at the time of the battle, there was not yet a unified position for a war against the mother country. The bloody Bunker Hill battle left the British wary of their opponent's strength. The Americans, as well, suffered great setbacks, including the death of one of the most respected revolutionary leaders, Dr. Joseph Warren (1741–1775).

The clash, which actually took place on Breed's Hill, near Bunker Hill, occurred as both British and American military leaders were strategically preparing for war. After the initial shots at Lexington and Concord, the British had sent three major generals—William Howe, Henry Clinton, and John Burgoyne—along with additional reinforcements to tame the colonies. The British commander of the American colonies, Thomas Gage, now had over five thousand troops to quell the colonial uprising. The volunteer American army consisted of about fifteen thousand men under the direction of an overly cautious Artemas Ward (1727–1800). The British generals arrived and began to prod General Gage to act more aggressively toward the uprising. They concocted a scheme to take the American forces on the Dorchester peninsula, which included Bunker Hill, Breed's Hill, and the city of Charlestown, strategically located across the water from the city of Boston. Americans overheard the plan and communicated it to the charismatic and respected Dr. Warren.

American Colonel Israel Putnam (1718–1790) convinced Warren that it was unwise to wait for the British to attack. He convinced Warren to take the high ground on the Dorchester peninsula and to fortify these hills, making the British pay if they attempted to follow through with their plans. Soon, American Colonel William Prescott (1726–1795) was given orders to take three regiments atop the peninsula and protect Bunker Hill. At nine o'clock on the evening of June 16, Putnam, Prescott, and twelve hundred men marched through the largely deserted town of Charlestown with three regiments plus a few hundred men from companies of Connecticut and New Hampshire. Most residents had fled inland for fear that the British might burn the city. Once the commanders arrived, a debate ensued about which hill provided a better position. Both options sat atop this peninsula overlooking Boston. Breed's Hill was lower in elevation, but closer to Boston. The American army had no cannons powerful enough to reach the city or the British ships in the harbor from the higher Bunker Hill. Prescott and Putnam decided to station themselves on Breed's Hill. After hours of diligent work, Prescott's men built an earth bastion 160 feet long and eighty feet high, with enormously thick walls. Two British ships, the *HMS Lively* and the *HMS Somerset*, opened fire on the structure, but neither caused the fort any real damage.

By morning, another four hundred colonists joined the men atop Breed's Hill. That afternoon, General

John Trumbull's painting of the Battle of Bunker Hill commemorates the early loss of Revolutionary leader General Warren.   *Archive Photos, Inc./Getty Images*

Howe and 2,200 British troops headed to displace the Americans from their position. Howe was determined to reassert Britain's power over the colonists, especially after the retreat from the earlier skirmishes at Lexington and Concord. He bombarded the city of Charlestown and launched a frontal assault. The colonials were hardly affected physically by the cannon fire, but became fearful of their aggressive opponent. Many of the officers from two of the Massachusetts regiments announced their exhaustion and withdrew, leaving Prescott with only three hundred of his own men and about two hundred of the Connecticut volunteers. One cannon ball tore the head off a soldier, causing a panic to carry through the garrison. Prescott ordered the corpse to be buried to calm his men.

Then the Redcoats eventually charged the hill. With limited powder and supplies, Putnam issued his famous order, "Don't fire until you see the whites of their eyes." They waited, followed that order, and the enemy began to drop. Sharpshooters killed an estimated ninety-six men, causing the others to retreat. Howe and other British soldiers made additional charges up the hill, facing similar setbacks. Shots were also coming from houses

within Charlestown. At the request of one of the British officers, the Royal Navy began to shoot heated cannon shots into Charlestown homes, burning over three hundred houses. Residents of Boston took to their rooftops to watch the battle.

In the immediate aftermath of this battle, neither side likely viewed it as a victory. Dr. Warren fought to the end, even with a bayonet wound to his arm. Outside the fort he tried to rally his men to take a stand, but was struck in the head by a bullet. He fell and died without a sound. The aftermath to the British army was gruesome as well. Bleeding Redcoats scattered from the hill across the Charles River into Boston. For the British, nineteen officers and 207 men had been killed, 40 percent of its fighting force. The American side lost 140 soldiers and suffered 301 wounded.

Saratoga

The Battle of Saratoga, which took place in the summer of 1777, proved to be a turning point in the American Revolution, especially for the American colonists. The British strategy to advance against the rebellious Americans was simply to divide and conquer by cutting off

Costumes de l'armée Américaine en 1782.

Massachuset. Jersey — Riflemen. Artillerie

A French observer sketched these four types of American Revolutionary soldiers—an infantryman, a musketeer, a rifleman, and an artillery solider—and their weapons in 1782. © *Corbis*

New England from the mid-Atlantic colonies. Saratoga, New York, lay on the Hudson River north of Albany and south of the American-held Fort Ticonderoga. British General John Burgoyne and his fighting force of about five thousand men (some of which were Canadians and Native Americans) were stationed in Canada. He invaded New York by way of Lake Champlain and planned to pursue the enemy down the Hudson. The British master plan included General Barry St. Leger's (1737–1789) maneuvers up the St. Lawrence River through Lake Ontario and then eastward down the Mohawk Valley to Saratoga. A third British group would arrive from New York City on the Hudson. The plan, if successful, could have brought the American rebels to their knees.

From London, Burgoyne was instructed to press on to Albany, a path that would prove treacherous for him.

His Canadian and Native American assistants helped him handle the terrain. By September 12, 1777, a confident American army occupied a position on the west bank of the Hudson, called Bemis Heights. Burgoyne had already reclaimed Fort Ticonderoga and arrived in the area on September 13, but did not encounter Americans until September 18, when a colonial patrol seeking food fired on his men on an abandoned farm. Burgoyne had only a vague idea of the encampment at Bemis Heights, but decided to attack it the following day.

The Saratoga confrontations consisted of two battles, one at Freeman's Farm and one at Bemis Heights. At about ten in the morning on September 19, Burgoyne advanced southward toward the American position with over four thousand of his men, leaving the others behind to guard boats, supplies, and to act as a reserve. The attacking group divided into three columns traveling on the west side of the Hudson. By 1:00 P.M., communicating with gun signals, the three divisions were ready to advance against the Americans.

American General Benedict Arnold felt the best strategy was to meet the enemy in the woods rather than in an open area. Arnold sent a division of riflemen to meet Burgoyne's group coming from the west. The detachment encountered one of the British columns, but was eventually driven back and formed a line along the south end of Freeman's Farm, in a clearing of about fifteen acres. Then Arnold arrived and assumed command. Here, some of the fiercest fighting of the Revolution took place. The real victor in this part of the battle, however, was the German General von Riedesel (1738–1800), a career soldier now fighting for Burgoyne and the British. Americans lost about three hundred in this fight.

The following day, Burgoyne announced that he wanted to attack again, though his senior officers advised against it strongly. On that day he also received a letter from General Henry Clinton, a ranking officer in the king's army, planning to move forward from New York City to assist Burgoyne. Burgoyne decided to wait for him, which proved a fatal decision. It took Clinton two weeks to get his expedition underway, and the second attack did not take place until early October. The British, who enjoyed a degree of success at Freeman's Farm, now suffered from reduced rations, and their horses died of starvation. Burgoyne's men were shivering in the cold fall nights while still wearing their summer uniforms. With over eight hundred sick men—a combination of victims from Freeman's Farm and from cold weather—Burgoyne faced a great setback. American General Benjamin Lincoln (1733–1810) added to Burgoyne's troubles. At a strategic point between Lake Champlain and Lake George, his troops captured 243 Redcoats, freed one hundred American prisoners, and destroyed British supplies. He also disrupted the line between Burgoyne and Canada. Additionally, many of the Native American scouts deserted Burgoyne after facing American rifles.

Meanwhile, the Americans strengthened their position, and General Lincoln, who had been operating on the east side of the Hudson, brought his men across to join Arnold. By early October, the Continental army had a strength of about 11,000 soldiers.

With these setbacks, senior British officers recommended retreat, but Burgoyne would not hear of it. His overconfidence caused him to bet that he would be eating Christmas dinner at his destination in Albany. With this goal, he decided on another attack. On October 7, he took two thousand men and ten cannons to the American left flank. The second skirmish of Saratoga, the Battle of Bemis Heights, was about to take place when the British general sent a reconnaissance team of 1,600 to find a weak point in the American line, to no avail.

Americans soon discovered and mauled this detachment, and twice attacked the main British forts. The British lost 1,200 men while Americans suffered half that. On October 17, Burgoyne formally surrendered his army to General Horatio Gates (1726–1806).

Valley Forge

As the winter of 1777–1778 began, General George Washington decided to move the Continental army into winter quarters at Valley Forge. Soldiers resided at this camp, which was twenty-one miles west of British-occupied Philadelphia. Washington wanted to station his men safely during the cold winter, but also wanted to be able to defend the American interior. Valley Forge was at the junction of the Schuylkill River and Valley Creek. In reality, it was no valley but a two-mile long, thickly wooded high ground above the river.

Valley Forge is most remembered for the horrible condition that soldiers faced there. Upon arrival, one Connecticut doctor recorded he was "sick, discontented, and out of humor," and that none of the basic amenities were available. His descriptive list of inadequacies went on: "poor food, hard lodgings, cold weather, fatigue, nasty clothes, nasty cookery, vomit half the time, and smoked out of my mind."

When the soldiers set up the encampment, Washington's men began to construct huts made mostly from materials they gathered from the local woods. Parties of twelve men erected these makeshift dwellings, and the general offered a prize of twelve dollars for the best and most rapidly built hut in each regiment. These shelters typically measured sixteen feet in length and fourteen feet wide, with walls just over six feet tall. Straw, moss, and mud filled the gaps between logs, but rain often washed this bonding away, leaving openings for the cold winter wind. Washington, trying further to encourage a good design, offered one hundred dollars to the soldiers who could devise the best roof.

The general initially occupied a tent atop an adjacent hill, but once the encampment was established, he and his slave, Billy, moved to a house in the nearby hamlet of Valley Forge. Many officers lived in dwellings similar to those of the rank-and-file soldiers, but not nearly as crowded. To make collecting materials easier, a bridge was built across the Schuylkill River. Desperate soldiers became notorious for stealing anything from locals that was not nailed down. More than a thousand huts filled the camp and depleted the woods.

The lack of supplies and the bitter winter made for widespread illness. The revolutionaries suffered physically, and also mentally. By December 1777, Washington's force had shrunk by over two thousand men, "unfit for duty, because barefoot and otherwise naked," he noted. By February, the total number of soldiers unfit for battle reached nearly four thousand. Many men lost fingers and toes to frostbite. The fires that barely

The National Memorial Arch at Valley Forge at Valley Forge National Historical Park in Pennsylvania commemorates the brutal winter spent there by American Revolutionary troops.   © *Bob Krist/Corbis*

removed the winter chill made the soldiers sick, filling their lungs with smoke. When soldiers had to go on watch, those remaining in the huts lent them clothes for outdoor duty. Smallpox became another issue. Once inoculations were ordered, the remedy itself damaged some receiving it. Lice and bedbugs on the makeshift bunks made for an uncomfortable, itchy rest. Some tried to endure their woes by drinking themselves numb and died frozen outside near a fire. Some very severe cases were sent fifty miles away to the nearest hospital in Bethlehem, Pennsylvania. Many did not survive that journey. One particular bachelors' quarters in the town, designed to sleep 250 men, housed over 750 patients laying practically one on top of the other on straw pallets on the floor.

These conditions brought Washington additional problems, including desertion and resignations. The common penalty for desertion was one hundred lashes. Two chronic deserters were eventually hanged on the parade ground in front of a detachment from every brigade.

The misery at Valley Forge did not result from the lack of wealth in America. During the winter of 1777–1778, Americans feasted on fine food and lived rather comfortably in cities and villages throughout the thir-

teen states, much like during the economic stability before the war started. This became rather obvious to the soldiers when they received letters from their wives and relatives. Realizing this disparity in conditions likely caused additional desertions and resignations. It also showed the inability of Congress, the governing body charged with overseeing and financing the American effort in the war, to provide resources for Washington and his men. This problem marked the beginning of a tense relationship between the government and the military during the war.

Washington received criticism for the decision to go into winter quarters. The Pennsylvania Assembly spoke out against being still rather than driving British General William Howe out of the state. One of his top officers claimed the location must have been chosen based on "advice of a speculator, a traitor, or a council of ignoramuses." Washington was no doubt criticized further when reports of the camp's conditions reached beyond Valley Forge. But the same doctor who recorded the ill conditions assured that the general's conduct was "uncensurable."

The American army finally departed the camp in June 1778. The death toll from starvation and frigid temperatures in the Valley Forge experience was about 2,500.

In the largest sea battle of the American Revolution, the *Bonhomme Richard*, commanded by John Paul Jones, defeated a militarily superior British warship. *© Corbis*

Bonhomme Richard Versus Serapis

The largest sea battle between British and American naval forces during the American Revolution occurred on September 23, 1779, off the coast of Great Britain between the *Bonhomme Richard* and the *Serapis*. American naval officer John Paul Jones had received his orders to lead his first independent command as early as August 1776. By the time of the encounter between his *Bonhomme Richard* and the British *Serapis*, Jones had attained the rank of commodore and had already taken the fight to the enemy across the Atlantic. There he captured seven British ships, raided a Scottish harbor, and defeated a Royal Navy sloop in a fierce fight. In the month before this famous encounter, Jones had circled the British Isles to capture seventeen merchant ships and take more than five hundred prisoners. English newspapers began to ask, "Where is the British navy?"

His long and intense battle against the *Serapis* resulted in an American victory and made Jones legendary. Through bravery, tenacity, improvisation, and will, Jones defeated the *Serapis*, leaving England's newspapers asking the same rhetorical question.

The *Bonhomme Richard* was a converted merchant ship with forty-two twelve-pound guns. It was named in France in honor of Benjamin Franklin's popular and long-running *Poor Richard's Almanack*. Aboard the ship were Jones's officers, crew, and French soldiers acting as marines, totaling about 380 men from various countries. The frigate *Serapis*, captained by Richard Pearson, was a new, double-decked ship with fifty-four guns. Twenty of these were eighteen-pound cannons. Thus, the British ship could discharge three hundred pounds of iron cannonballs, while the *Bonhomme Richard* could manage only 204. Naval historians would assert, too, that heavier cannons were favored to a greater quantity, because they could do more damage. This put the British ship at an even greater advantage. The *Serapis* also had a copper sheathing on its bottom, which made it faster than the *Bonhomme Richard*.

Sailing up the English coast, Jones engaged the enemy ship so closely that a verbal exchange was made between he and Pearson before guns were fired. "What ship is that?" Pearson asked in true English bombast. "Come a little nearer and I will tell you," responded Jones. The *Serapis* fired and the battle was underway. Jones soon rammed his adversary. He then backed off and circled the *Serapis*, coming so close that the muzzles of each ship's guns were almost touching. Knowing the odds were against him, Jones planned to board the ship and take over. The British sailors, however, beat him back.

His first plan did not succeed, but this would be Jones's finest hour. The larger guns of the *Serapis* destroyed those on the *Bonhomme Richard*. But Jones never gave up. He released British prisoners from the galley and forced them to man the pumps to keep his ship afloat. By this point, half of his crew was dead. The chief gunner had abandoned his position to haul down the American flag and surrender. Jones would not have it. To stop him, Jones hurled his own pistol, striking the surrendering sailor in the skull and knocking him unconscious. Jones manned one of his own nine-pound guns in order to take out the sails of the enemy ship.

The American vessel, however, suffered as much if not more than the British ship. It became obvious to Jones that the only way to win was to hold on tight to the *Serapis*. An American who had boarded dropped a grenade on the gun deck of the *Serapis*, hoping to hit enemy sailors below. His grenade landed in the middle of loose powder and cartridges, killing several and igniting the ship. Pearson had had enough. Unable to get his men to take the ship's colors down, he had to do so himself. Night had arrived, and about 150 men of the *Bonhomme Richard*'s crew were killed or wounded in this four-hour battle. The British total of losses and wounded reached 117.

It was early in this clash that Jones, when asked to surrender, reportedly declared, "I have not yet begun to fight." There is no written record of Jones's famous declaration until 1825, and Jones himself never claimed to have said these words. Yet, with his bravery and determination in this battle against Pearson and the British navy, few have questioned if the phrase was worthy. After the surrender, Jones and his crew abandoned the sinking *Bonhomme Richard* and sailed the *Serapis* to neutral Holland.

Yorktown

The last major battle of the American Revolutionary War, the Battle of Yorktown earned the American colonists a victory over the British. Both sides were worn down by 1781. Parliament had partially lost interest in waging this war and the American treasury was depleted. On March 20, British General Charles Cornwallis and his men had arrived from Wilmington, Delaware, in Yorktown, a small town on the banks of the York River in coastal Virginia on Chesapeake Bay. Cornwallis felt that taking the colony of Virginia and advancing on into the Carolinas were the keys to winning the war. He had asked fellow General Henry Clinton, in New York at this time, to assist him in dividing the northeast and mid-Atlantic regions. But miscommunication and differences of strategic opinion—many of the same reasons the British failed at Saratoga—allowed George Washington's army, assisted by the French, to win this battle.

British troop strength at this time numbered about 7,000, because Clinton did send a few men from New York. Washington and American ally French General Lafayette had planned to attack New York City. On August 14, Washington learned that French Admiral François Joseph de Grasse (1722–1788) would arrive from the West Indies to assist the Americans, not in New York, but in the Chesapeake Bay. When the American plans fell into enemy hands, and after receiving news from de Grasse, Washington saw a unique opportunity to pin Cornwallis and about one-quarter of the British forces in America in the Yorktown area. Most of the British force occupied a fortified camp on the south side of the mouth of the York River, with some across the water at Gloucester Point.

By September 1781, the combined French and American forces under Washington's command numbered 14,000. Additionally, patriot forces from Virginia arrived, taking the total toward 20,000 against Cornwallis's troops still under 10,000. The British were hemmed in with two options: starve or surrender.

The American bombardment began on October 9 after the army positioned heavy cannons aimed toward the British. At 3 P.M., the Americans began heavy firing toward Yorktown that lasted six days. Cornwallis was shocked by the American capability. He had erroneously assured his men that their only opposition would be light artillery. On the contrary, one of the initial targets was the general's headquarters in town. The American cannons shattered the three-story Georgian house that he had occupied. By October 14, the American forces had advanced within 200 yards of the British fortifications. British redoubts (forts) nine and ten were especially crucial to Washington's success. He assigned two light infantry units to take them, one American under Colonel Alexander Hamilton and one French commanded by Lafayette. Soon, nearly one hundred heavy guns faced the enemy at point-blank range. The allied effort proved a rather easy task.

Cornwallis became desperate. Clinton's reinforcements from New York, meant to arrive by sea, were delayed by indecision and horrible weather. Cornwallis gambled by trying to take his army out of Yorktown across the river and to the British outpost in Gloucester. He knew he would have to face his enemy to retreat northward, but felt he could overcome the smaller French and Virginian units. In the middle of the night on October 16, British troops boarded sixteen Royal

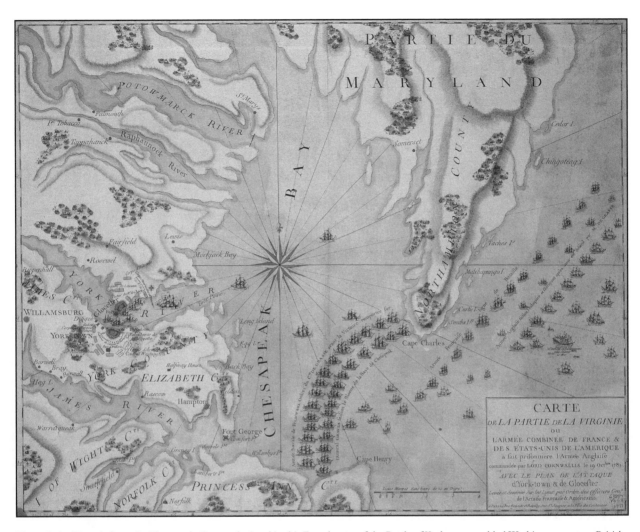

The arrival of French forces in Chesapeake Bay, as depicted in this French map of the Battle of Yorktown, enabled Washington to trap British forces. © *Corbis*

Navy flatboats and ferried across the river successfully. Empty boats made their return to Yorktown for another round, but faced a heavy storm, which put a stop to this retreat plan. Soon after this delay, the general's men informed him that they had only one hundred mortar shells remaining. The numbers of sick and wounded were growing. Cornwallis sought advice. Every one of his officers suggested surrender. As ignoble as it may have seemed, these men were confident that they had done all they could do. Cornwallis accepted the advice and began to dictate a historic letter to Washington offering a formal surrender: "Sir, I propose a cessation of hostilities for twenty four hours, and that two officers may be appointed by each side . . . to settle the terms for the surrender of the posts at York and Gloucester."

The fighting was over. Soon not only the battle, but the entire conflict would end. The surrender ceremony was most formal. At 11 A.M. on October 19, Cornwallis signed the final draft of the surrender document, and over

7,000 British soldiers became prisoners of war. At roughly the same moment, General Clinton finally departed New York expecting to either assist his fellow general, or to arrive to greet a victorious Cornwallis. Like much of the world, Clinton was surprised to find how the Americans had finally defeated the British, several miles and two hundred years from the first British colony founded in America.

Later in the day on October 19, 1781, the failed British troops marched out to the field designated for formal surrender. The British bands played an ironic tune, "The World Turned Upside Down," expressing their surprise and dismay of this turn of events. With French soldiers lined up on one side and Americans on the other, Lafayette noticed how the Brits looked only in the direction of the French forces. The French, a world power and a challenging adversary before, were easier for the defeated British to stomach, while they could not easily look the once-underdog rebels in the eyes.

Lafayette responded by ordering his musicians to play "Yankee Doodle Dandy," at which time the surrendering soldiers began to face the Americans.

Following the same reluctance, British Brigadier General Charles O'Hara (1740–1802)—Cornwallis had failed to show up for surrender—offered his sword to the French general. Count de Rochambeau (1725–1807) then ordered O'Hara to hand it over to General Washington. The American commander then directed O'Hara to hand over his sword to his second in command. The British soldiers then piled their muskets in the open field. Meanwhile, Washington had sent one of his aides to travel to Congress in Philadelphia to report the good news. The Congress received word in two days. London awaited the results for nearly two weeks of agonizing suspense. When British officers finally received word, they reported the surrender to Prime Minister Lord North, who responded, "Oh, God. It's over. It's all over." The peace agreements would be ironed out by parties from both Britain and the United States at the Treaty of Paris in 1783.

✪ The Home Front

Common Sense

In January 1776, Thomas Paine published a slim pamphlet that was to define the American struggle for independence. The cover read: *Common Sense: Addressed to the Inhabitants of America*. In straightforward language, it laid out the political, economic, and military arguments for a definitive break with England. Within three months, almost 120,000 copies of the tract sold throughout the colonies. Americans found a common resolve in its pages, one that would help change the emerging conflict from a rebellion into a revolution.

Thomas Paine Thomas Paine was born in England in 1737. There, he pursued his father's corset business, but failed. He also tried teaching, shopkeeping, tax collection, and marriage, all with little success. In 1774, he was fired from his post as a tax collector for agitating on behalf of his fellow excise officers. Unemployed, he met and befriended Benjamin Franklin in London. With Franklin's letters of recommendation, Paine immigrated to America. He settled in Philadelphia, writing for the *Pennsylvania Magazine*, where his accessible style and plain reasoning quickly found an audience.

Paine arrived at a time when Americans were not committed to the cause of complete independence. They felt outrage over the Intolerable Acts, partially because such measures were seen as violations of the colonists' rights as British subjects. Despite the siege of Boston, many people thought that the Crown would relent under pressure. Many hoped to return to the conditions that had existed in 1763. Paine, a passionate revolutionary, thought such sentiments were simply wishful thinking.

Betsy Ross sewed the first "Stars and Stripes" after General Washington recommended the design to her. *AP Images*

Common Sense Arguments Paine condensed his thoughts on the American situation into *Common Sense*, a 46-page pamphlet, divided into four sections. First came a reflection on the nature of government and on the British Constitution in particular. Paine argued that all government was at best "a necessary evil," designed to bring freedom and security to the people, in the absence of perfect virtue. The most natural government, he proposed, was a legislative body of elected officials. The British Constitution was burdened by the Crown and Peerage, therefore "imperfect, subject to convulsions, and incapable of producing what it seems to promise."

The second part of the tract attacked the monarchy. Paine invoked the Bible to make a case against the institution, pointing out that God had cursed the Hebrew people for requesting a king. He ridiculed the British monarchy, whose right to rule was based on "a French bastard landing with an armed Banditti and establishing himself king of England against the consent of the natives." Even more than the origin of royalty, Paine deplored its propagation. Hereditary succession was "an insult and imposition on posterity," saddling future generations with idiots, children, and tyrants as leaders.

Paine then shifted from theory to the practical concerns of the time. America could no longer dream of reconciliation, he wrote, after hostilities had broken out at Lexington the previous April. He urged his readers to embrace the opportunity of independence. Britain would never defend America's interest as its own. Union with Britain meant enmity with Britain's enemies, dragging Americans into foreign wars and closing off half of Europe to American trade. Any ties of kinship or affection between the two countries had been severed by King George III's conduct.

Paine further declared that as things stood, all attempts at delay amounted to cowardice. "Wherefore, since nothing but blows will do, for God's sake, let us come to a final separation, and not leave the next generation to be cutting throats."

The fourth chapter set about reassuring readers that America could successfully fight England, both economically and militarily, particularly on the sea. Paine spoke of American expertise in shipbuilding, its enormous store of natural resources, and the necessity of building a fleet and defending its own coast.

Finally, Paine laid out the central thesis of his work: that America should openly declare its independence and immediately form a unicameral, republican government. That way allies and enemies would know where they stood: not as masters and rebels but as two sovereign nations at war.

Common Sense was an instant success, winning praises from many of the nation's leaders, including George Washington. John Adams approved the pamphlet's general sentiments, though he scoffed at the proposed political system. He also worried what effect such a popular pamphlet would have among the people.

The immediate effect was to bring a huge number of Americans into the cause of independence. In two years, more than 500,000 copies had been printed, one for every five colonists at the time. The work contributed to a growing clarity and unity of purpose, which lead to the Declaration of Independence later that year.

Aftermath of **Common Sense** In December 1776, Paine enlisted in the army. In the service he composed a series of "Crisis" essays, which were printed to bolster morale over the course of the war. George Washington had the first of these read aloud to his men before the Battle of Trenton:

> These are the times that try men's souls. The summer soldier and the sunshine patriot will, in this crisis, shrink from the service of their country; but he that stands it now, deserves the love and thanks of man and woman. Tyranny, like hell, is not easily conquered.

After the war, Paine moved to Europe, where he continued to pursue his vision of an ideal society. In 1792, he was given a seat in the Convention by the revolutionary government of France, in recognition of his pamphlet *The Rights of Man*. The English accorded him a different honor for his work, trying him in absentia for treason. Paine later fell out of favor in France for opposing the execution of Louis XVI and was imprisoned in the Bastille at the height of the Reign of Terror.

After his release, Paine wrote *The Age of Reason*, which tore down orthodox Christian doctrine in favor of Deism. He also published his "Letter to George Washington," which denounced the president for silently conspiring in his Parisian imprisonment. Neither made him popular in the United States, and when he returned there in 1802, Paine found himself an outcast. He died in 1809, in poverty and obscurity.

Declaration of Independence

The Declaration of Independence, signed by the Second Continental Congress on July 4, 1776, broke off ties between the American colonies and the British Empire. Thomas Jefferson had drafted the one-page, world-shaking proclamation in a little more than two weeks. But in another sense the Declaration was the product of a long string of fateful events.

Toward Independence American radicals like Patrick Henry and Benjamin Franklin had dreamed of self-determination for years. But public opinion, though increasingly anti-British, was not prepared to cast off the Crown altogether. Samuel Adams had counseled patience: "Wait till the fruit is ripe before we gather it."

The outbreak of armed conflict in Massachusetts, however, significantly changed the national mood. Then, early in 1776, Thomas Paine's pamphlet "Common Sense" triggered a tidal wave of pro-independence sentiment among the people. By March, the British had been driven from Boston by the Continental army, and it seemed possible that they could be driven from the continent altogether.

Crafting the Declaration In April, North Carolina's Provincial Congress passed the Halifax Resolves, authorizing their delegates to vote for independence. On May 27, the Virginia delegate Richard Henry Lee (1732–1794) put forward a resolution to the Continental Congress, calling for the severing of all political connection with Great Britain, the formation of foreign alliances, and the creation of a colonial confederation government.

John Adams, an outspoken Bostonian lawyer, seconded the motion when it was brought forward. Congress created a committee to draft a formal statement, consisting of Adams, Franklin, Jefferson, Robert Livingston (1746–1813), and Roger Sherman (1721–1793). Adams asked Jefferson to write the document. A young, quiet member of Congress, Jefferson was initially reluctant, saying that Adams should do it. Adams gave three reasons for his nomination. First, that Jefferson, a Virginian, should take charge of a Virginian initiative. Secondly, that he himself was "obnoxious, suspected, and unpopular," and third, that Jefferson was the far superior writer.

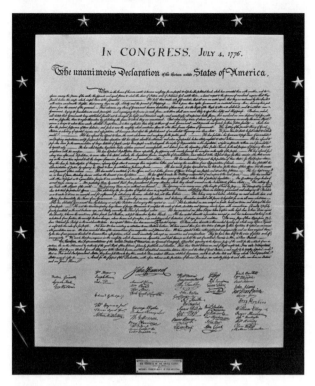

The Declaration of Independence. © *Corbis*

After a few weeks, Jefferson showed his composition to the committee who passed it on to Congress with only minor changes. Adams said he was "delighted" with the work, especially with the passages condemning the slave trade. It contained no original ideas, but summed up the philosophical and practical case for revolution. Echoing the theories of John Locke, Jefferson asserted that all government existed by the consent of the governed, to protect their rights of "life, liberty and the pursuit of happiness." When any government fails in this duty to its people, the people have the right to replace it.

The Declaration then methodically listed the colonies' grievances against King George III, calling him "a Tyrant, . . . unfit to be the ruler of a free people." Some contemporaries expressed discomfort at the charges levied directly at the king, rather than at his Parliament. John Adams considered it too personal, "too much like scolding, for so grave and solemn a document."

In conclusion, the British were reminded that the colonies had sought to resolve their complaints through normal imperial channels, only to have their petitions summarily dismissed. Having no other choice, they proclaimed themselves free states.

July 1–2 Debate began on July 1. John Dickinson of Pennsylvania argued that they should still try to reconcile with Britain, since they were not strong enough to win a war. Adams countered that King George III and his ministers had left no hope of compromise, and that

war had already begun. Pennsylvania and Delaware still held out against independence. The New York delegation had not received the go-ahead from their state legislature.

The next day, key Pennsylvanians opposing independence decided to withdraw from the vote. Caesar Rodney (1728–1784), having ridden eighty miles all night on horseback in the rain, arrived at the last moment to change Delaware's vote. In the end, the Congress voted twelve to nothing in favor of dissolving all ties to England, with New York abstaining for the time being. John Adams wrote to his wife Abigail that July 2 would be "solemnized with Pomp and Parade, with Shows, Games, Sports, Guns, Bells, Bonfires and Illuminations from one End of this Continent to the other from this Time forward forever more."

July 3–4 Even though the colonies—now states—had voted for separation, they still had to publish the official justification of their actions. They devoted the next two days to Jefferson's Declaration of Independence. The document was first read aloud, without interruption. Then the assembled body went through it paragraph by paragraph. Altogether they made over thirty changes, removing a quarter of the original text. The section relating to slavery was struck out entirely; it had accused the Crown of "violating its most sacred rights of life and liberty in the persons of a distant people who never offended him."

Jefferson did not feel that he could objectively participate in the deliberations. He therefore sat silently, "writhing a little," through the severe criticism of his work. Benjamin Franklin took pity on the young author, telling a comic story in an attempt to relieve his suffering.

On July 4, after a long strenuous day plagued by heat and horseflies, the delegates ratified the amended document. According to tradition, John Hancock (1737–1793) joked that his large, distinctive signature ensured that King George could read his name without his spectacles.

The Legacy Everyone present was aware of the personal risks they were undertaking. They understood that the Declaration of Independence contained an implicit declaration of war. The Crown would certainly view all the signatories as traitors and act accordingly. Hancock apparently addressed the members, exhorting them all to be unified, to hang together. "Assuredly we must hang together," Franklin is said to have remarked, "or we will certainly hang separately." Indeed, five of the signers were captured, tortured, and killed by the British. Twelve others had their homes burned to the ground.

The proclamation was then distributed to the public, who received it with public celebrations. In one instance a statue of King George III in Bowling Green, New York, was torn down and melted into bullets. The Declaration's influence reached past the fledgling United States. In France, the Declaration served as a

George Whitefield, a British evangelist who toured the colonies in the time of the Great Awakening, may have cultivated Americans' willingness to challenge the authority of the British. *The Granger Collection, New York. Reproduced by permission*

model for the "Declaration of the Rights of Man" a few years later. It has continued to inspire through the centuries, not only revolutionaries, but those who hold, as self-evident, a belief in the equality of mankind.

The Great Awakening

Thirty years before the Revolution, from about 1739 to 1745, America underwent a revival in religious interest, which came to be known as the Great Awakening. Powerful itinerate preachers and revival meetings sprang up throughout the colonies. Many viewed the phenomenon as an "outpouring of the Holy Spirit."

George Whitefield George Whitefield (1714–1770) had been a member of the "Holy Club" at Oxford University in England, along with Methodist founding brothers John (1703–1791) and Charles Wesley (1707–1788). During an illness in 1735, he felt a moment of inspiration, which he called his "New Birth." He became convinced that true religion was only to be found in a personal experience of God. Whitefield proceeded to stir congregations across England with his emotional sermons. His preaching also attacked the more conventional clergy, berating them for spiritual emptiness. He soon found most of the pulpits of the Anglican Church closed

to him. Undaunted, he organized immensely popular open-air services. In 1739, Whitefield exported his dynamic new church experience to the New World.

Whitefield toured the middle colonies, drawing huge crowds. A magnificent showman as well as a powerful orator, he exhorted his listeners to renew their personal faith and to be united with Christ. He shouted, stomped, acted, sang, and almost always wept. Even his crossed eyes—a result of an early bout with measles—were endowed with spirituality. It was said they allowed him to keep one eye on heaven and another on hell.

Benjamin Franklin, famous for his skepticism, found himself moved by Whitefield's eloquence. Apparently Franklin had attended a revival meeting determined not to give a penny at the collection, but ended up putting all his money in the basket. Whitefield was a very able fundraiser, frequently taking up collections for an orphanage for Georgia's poor, among other things.

Whitefield was also one of the first religious figures to employ new marketing strategies in his evangelism. He distributed printed materials, sent advance publicity, and took out newspaper advertisements to bring people to hear his message. His methods were very effective. Franklin wrote in his autobiography: "It was wonderful to see the change soon made in the manners of our inhabitants. From being thoughtless or indifferent about religion, it seem'd as if all the world were growing religious."

Other Revivalists Christian revivalists were not unknown in the colonies at the time. Presbyterian Gilbert Tennent (1703–1764) had preached throughout the Delaware valley in the 1720s, and he joined Whitefield's ministry with zeal. Perhaps the most famous American of the Awakening era was Jonathan Edwards (1703–1758), a Congregational minister from Connecticut. He did not have the flamboyance of other preachers, generally speaking in a monotone. Nevertheless, when he delivered his sermon, "Sinners in the Hands of an Angry God," he was forced to pause until the crowd calmed down because so many in the audience screamed, sobbed, or fainted.

James Davenport (1716–1757), a Long Island minister, led a wild revival in Connecticut and Rhode Island. His followers built a bonfire to burn their earthly possessions, including theology books and even their clothes. He was brought to court for disturbing the peace, where he was judged "disturbed in the rational faculties of his mind."

New Lights and Old Lights Mainline clergy at first welcomed the renewed interest in religion, but soon found themselves the targets of attacks from itinerant pulpits. Edwards taught that human emotion, not reason, best led the soul to God. This called into question the value of highly educated ordained ministers, who could discuss the finer points of their theology but left the congregation asleep on Sunday. In 1740, Tennent published his sermon "The Danger of an Unconverted Ministry," in which he described most ministers as ungodly hypocrites.

Traditionalists were appalled by new trends in worship: improvised prayers, rejection of liturgy, hymns, and shouting. The revivalists disregarded denominational boundaries, because they insisted that salvation rested with the individual. For the first time, parishioners left their home churches to join another if their old pastor was not charismatic enough.

Local churchmen responded angrily, condemning the revivalists as ignorant rabble-rousers. One Reverend Timothy Cutler described a meeting in these terms: "Came one Tennent, a minister impudent and saucy; and told them all they were damned, damned, damned! This charmed them; and in the dreadfullest winter I ever saw, people wallowed in the snow night and day for the benefit of his beastly braying."

At the time, many colonies still had state-sponsored churches supported by tax money. Some legislatures tried to force the new churches to pay tithes to their old churches, or to fine ministers who preached in someone else's territory. Connecticut went further, refusing to recognize any clergyman without a Yale or Harvard degree.

Soon, almost every denomination in America was split into two camps, dubbed by some the "New Lights" and the "Old Lights." Many, like the Presbyterians, went through official schisms. Other churches were born from the remnants of one camp or another. Unitarianism probably had its roots in the opposition to revivalism, whereas many northern Baptist churches grew from separatists.

The Awakening started to decline around 1743, by which time many people thought that the revivals had gotten out of hand. Even George Whitefield, on his next tour of America in 1745, regretted some of the excesses of his imitators. He later apologized for his part in creating antagonism within the churches, as did Tennent and Davenport.

Historians do not agree on the impact the Awakening had on the Revolution thirty years later. Certainly it weakened Americans' respect for traditional authority. It also fostered a strong belief, especially among the evangelists, in the separation between church and state.

The Federalist Papers

The Federalist Papers were a series of eighty-five essays published in New York newspapers in 1787 and 1788, urging the voters to ratify the United States Constitution. Written by Alexander Hamilton (1755 or 1757–1804), James Madison (1751–1836), and John Jay, the papers tried to push the states toward a stronger federal government.

The Articles of Confederation At the time of the Treaty of Paris, which brought the American Revolution to a formal close, the thirteen states were loosely bound together under the Articles of Confederation. These Articles gave almost total sovereignty to the individual states. Congress itself controlled military and foreign affairs, but could not collect taxes. As a consequence, the country could not repay its debts from the war. This contributed to a general economic downturn and growing discontent.

The Constitutional Convention Many political leaders felt the need for a more powerful central government. In May 1787, a special conference was called in Philadelphia. The conference's stated purpose was merely to revise the Articles of Confederation. James Madison of Virginia, among others, was convinced that stronger measures were called for. He and his delegation proposed an entirely new form of government, with two legislative houses, an executive branch, and a judiciary. Other factions proposed alternate plans, with varying degrees of federal authority and with different ideas for state representation.

After four months of heated debates, the first draft of the U.S. Constitution was passed on to the states for

James Madison, often called the "Father of the Constitution," created the Virginia Plan and contributed to the *Federalist Papers.* *National Archives and Records Administration*

ratification. Nine of the states needed to approve the Constitution before it could become law.

Ratification   Despite all of its compromises, the Constitution faced a vigorous opposition movement called the Anti-Federalists. These included Thomas Jefferson, Patrick Henry, and George Clinton (1739–1812), governor of New York. Anti-Federalists were concerned over the broad authority given to the national government, especially to the executive branch. They claimed that a concentration of power would naturally lead to tyranny, especially in a large and diverse nation. Others rejected the Constitution because it did not contain a bill of rights.

Because the state of New York was strongly divided on the issue, Hamilton, Madison, and Jay decided to publish articles defending the Constitution in local newspapers. They were published anonymously under the pen name *Publius.* Hamilton wrote the majority of the papers.

The Federalist Papers attempted to convince New Yorkers that a strong central government was necessary for the well-being of the United States. Some articles pointed out the political and economic weaknesses of

the Confederacy. Others championed the proposed system of checks and balances between the branches of government. In Federalist No. 10, Madison argued that a federal republic was the most effective safeguard against abuse, precisely because it represented so many different interests.

Hamilton also wrote that a bill of rights was unnecessary. Because the Constitution clearly defined what the government could do, there was no need to reiterate what it could not. Nevertheless, the Federalists promised to amend the Constitution to include the Bill of Rights.

By the time New York voted on ratification, ten states had already endorsed the Constitution. New York's acceptance may have been a simple matter of resignation. Therefore it is difficult to judge the Federalist's success as propaganda. Regardless, the essays are recognized as important works of political science. They were published in book form in 1788 and have been in print ever since. They provide essential insight into the framing of the Constitution.

The Federalist Party   The next year, George Washington was sworn in is as the first president of the United States. He appointed Thomas Jefferson as secretary of state, and Alexander Hamilton as secretary of the Treasury. Hamilton and Jefferson disagreed sharply over the scope of the new federal government. Their respective ideologies split American politics into a fiercely partisan battlefield.

Hamilton was born poor and illegitimate in the West Indies. A self-made man of great energy, he dedicated himself to establishing America as a world economic and military power. To this end, he sponsored legislation favoring banks, industry, and trade. He quickly consolidated and settled foreign debt, creating a strong national currency. Hamilton believed that states should be completely secondary to national rule. He also felt that government policy should not be decided directly by the masses, who tend to be self-interested and ignorant. Rather, the people should choose their leaders from the educated elite. He and his colleagues came to be known as the Federalist Party.

Jefferson, born into the wealthy landowning class, envisioned an ideal egalitarian society based mostly on farming. He believed in direct populist democracy and in greater state sovereignty. Hamilton's strategies, particularly his creation of a national bank, horrified the Anti-Federalists.

Antagonism between the two groups deepened as a result of the emerging revolution in France. The Anti-Federalists (at first) embraced the French insurgents as fellow freedom fighters. The Federalists regarded Paris as the worst example of mob democracy and advocated a closer alliance with Britain.

The split between Federalists and Anti-Federalists (who began to call themselves the Republicans) endured until Jefferson was elected as president. But the struggle

THE BURR-HAMILTON DUEL

Despite the intense rivalry between Hamilton and Jefferson, Hamilton backed Jefferson's bid for the presidency in 1801. He did so because the alternative was Aaron Burr (1756–1836), a fellow lawyer from New York, and a longtime personal enemy.

In 1804, Burr ran for governor of New York. Once again, he met Hamilton's fierce opposition and was defeated. Infuriated, Burr accused Hamilton of slandering him in public. He demanded the satisfaction of a duel.

Hamilton opposed dueling on principle. He wrote that he planned to *delope*, to miss his shot on purpose. When the day came, Hamilton did indeed miss, but Burr did not. Hamilton was severely wounded and died the next day.

The incident effectively finished Burr's political career. Instead, he sought military adventure in the West. He was later turned in by one of his own men, who claimed Burr meant to attack New Orleans and create his own nation in Louisiana. Tried for treason, Burr was acquitted, but he was widely believed to be guilty. In later life he spoke sadly of "my friend Hamilton, whom I shot."

between the advocates of federal authority and the advocates of state rights continued to simmer, until it exploded again in the American Civil War.

✪ International Context

The Age of Enlightenment

Through the seventeenth and eighteenth centuries, new trends of thought emerged in Europe, radically changing the understanding of politics, economics, and religion in the western world. Together, these ideas came to be known as the Enlightenment, which was articulated and spread through the writings of many different thinkers: Voltaire (1694–1778), Jean-Jacques Rousseau (1712–1778), Benjamin Franklin, John Locke (1632–1704), and Adam Smith (1723–1790), to name only a few. Their philosophies deeply influenced the political realities of their time and continue to do so today.

Science The Enlightenment had its roots in the Scientific Revolution, which had begun in the sixteenth century with Nicolaus Copernicus's (1473–1543) vision of a heliocentric solar system. He and his successors, such as Galileo Galilei (1564–1642) and Isaac Newton (1643–1727), successfully challenged old conceptions of the nature of the physical world. They paved the way for an explosion of scientific inquiry, in which human knowledge of physics, chemistry, and biology increased dramatically. Coupled with the expansion of the known world through navigation, these discoveries opened the public imagination to an endless horizon, to limitless possibilities.

In those days, there was often no clear distinction between science (called "natural philosophy") and ideology. Some early scientists, such as Johannes Kepler (1571–1630), Blaise Pascal (1623–1662), and Francis Bacon (1561–1626), viewed themselves primarily as philosophers or theologians. René Descartes (1596–1650), the father of modern geometry, put forward the theory that all philosophy could be reduced to a mathematical progression, beginning with "I think, therefore I am." In other words, all human understanding begins with individual reason.

As time went on, intellectuals increasingly introduced scientific principles—skepticism, imagination, observation, measurement, and experimentation—into other arenas of thought. Just as Copernicus had challenged Aristotle's solar system, the lights of the Enlightenment challenged long-accepted structures of society, government, economics, and religion.

Religion The spirit of the Enlightenment, insofar as it can be distilled, may be described as a questioning of traditional authorities, especially that of the established churches. In particular, the French *philosophes* reflected the strong anticlericalism of France in their writings. Through biting essays and plays, Voltaire (born François-Marie Arouet) condemned Judaism and Christianity as superstitious and ignorant. He particularly questioned how an omnipotent and benevolent God could permit evil in the world. David Hume (1711–1776), a Scottish philosopher, insisted that human reason should be the basis of all opinion and action, and he denied any rational proof of organized faiths. In England, John Locke strongly advocated religious tolerance and the separation of church and state.

The civil and religious authorities of the time were anything but separate, and they did not passively accept criticism. Even Immanuel Kant (1724–1804), a German philosopher sympathetic to Christianity, received a letter from Frederick William II (1744–1797) ordering him to discontinue any commentary on religion. The French police threw Denis Diderot (1713–1784) in solitary confinement for three months following his atheistic *An Essay on Blindness* in 1749.

It should be noted that the Enlightenment encompassed a diverse spectrum of thought. Some writers, like Locke, were devout Christians. Among the rest, very few were outright atheists. Even Voltaire believed in a Designer, though not in a personal God who took notice of human affairs. Others professed a Deity, an impersonal being who created the cosmos and defined morality. This view is loosely described as Deism and was shared in varying degrees by many of the American Founding Fathers.

The Social Contract In 1733, Alexander Pope (1688–1744) wrote, "Know then thyself, presume not God to

Philosopher Jean-Jacques Rousseau's writings emphasized the goodness of humans in a state of nature. *AP Images*

scan; The proper study of mankind is man." Enlightenment thinkers expressed differing theories on the nature of humankind. Thomas Hobbes (1588–1679), an English philosopher, wrote that people were inherently selfish, motivated only by the pursuit of pleasure and the avoidance of pain. The Frenchman Jean-Jacques Rousseau believed that man was naturally good in a primitive state, a "noble savage." Locke argued that the human mind was a *tabula rasa*, a blank slate. He proposed that a person's character was entirely created by that person's experience, not by any inherent qualities of the soul.

From an examination of the individual, philosophers naturally turned to an analysis of the group. Rousseau and Locke both asserted that all human beings were in a "state of nature," free and equal. Therefore no individual had the inherent right to rule over another.

However, if human beings were free to pursue their own good, one's interests would inevitably conflict with the interests of others. Hobbes suggested that, if men lived in perfect liberty, life would be "nasty, brutish, and short." To protect the common good, people entered into a "social contract." Individuals gave up some of their freedom to create a government. In exchange, the government provided justice and order.

The concept of the social contract conflicted directly with the medieval concept of the divine rights of kings.

Nevertheless, some European monarchs partially adopted the notion. Frederick II of Prussia (1712–1786), Catherine II of Russia (1729–1796), and Joseph II of Austria (1741–1790) saw themselves as public servants, pursuing the good of the people by means of their absolute authority. As a result, they have been called "enlightened despots."

It was further asserted that the social contract could be broken. If the government failed in its duties, the people have the right, even the responsibility, to overthrow that government. Thomas Jefferson echoed this concept, along with other Enlightenment themes, in the Declaration of Independence.

Hobbes extended the idea to include the institution of slavery. Since slaves did not consent to their situation or benefit from it, they could use any means, even violence, to escape from it. The Baron of Montesquieu (1689–1755), along with many others, wrote that the institution of slavery was degrading to the masters.

Economics Another staunch opponent to slavery was Adam Smith, a Scot who has been called the father of modern economics. In 1776, Smith wrote *The Wealth of Nations*, in which he argued that trade flourished best when relatively free from government restrictions. Furthermore, because of the nature of competing interests, free trade safeguarded personal freedom. Smith's work was notable for its scientific approach to wealth and labor. Much modern economic theory is based on his concept of the market as a self-regulating system.

Enlightenment thinkers, like Newton, strove to discover the underlying laws of the universe. Their work attempted to formulate the rules that they observed: the laws of human nature, the natural law of morality, the rule of law in politics, and the economic laws of the market.

The Seven Years' War

The Seven Years' War (1756–1763) was the first truly global war. The principal belligerents were Europeans, but the battlefields ranged from Canada to Europe, Africa, the Caribbean, and India. The North American theater of the war came to be known as the French and Indian War.

The American Spark Hostilities began in North America two years before any formal declaration of war. Having obtained land grants in the Ohio River valley from King George II (1683–1760), Virginia traders started to move into the area. This incursion conflicted with the French Canadian land and trade claims. To protect their interests, Canada sent hundreds of men to the valley, building forts and negotiating alliances with local Indian tribes.

The Virginians sent a young officer named George Washington to the newly built Fort Le Boeuf. He delivered a message from the colony demanding that the Canadians leave. When they refused, he returned with a larger force and with royal authorization to use it. During the ensuing skirmishes, Washington's men ambushed a Canadian force, killing ten and taking twenty-one prisoners. Washington's band hastily erected a mud and log fort, dubbed Fort Necessity, to protect themselves from Canadian reprisals. It proved inadequate. For the first and only time in his career, Washington was forced to surrender.

News of this frontier battle reached the courts of Frederick II the Great of Prussia (part of what is now Germany), Empress Marie-Therese of Austria (1717–1780), George II of England, and Louis XV of France (1710–1774). Horace Walpole (1717–1797), an advisor to the English throne, said that Washington had set the world on fire.

War in Europe   Europe had been building up to war for years, but the colonial violence dramatically increased tensions between France and Great Britain. In 1756, to protect Hanover (King George's German territory) from French invasion, England officially allied itself with Prussia. In response, Austria allied with France. This redistribution of power was later called "the diplomatic revolution." The same year, Prussia invaded Saxony, then part of the Austrian Empire (part of Germany today). Frederick of Prussia hoped that he could in this way prevent Austria from teaming up with Russia. The strategy backfired, as Austria, France, Russia, and Sweden declared war against him in 1757.

Great Britain also declared war on France. The first few years proved disastrous for the English. In Europe, they met defeat after defeat. In India, the French-backed Prince Siraj-ud-Dawlah (1729–1757) overran British-held Calcutta. British General Edward Braddock (c. 1695–1755) had been sent to confront the French in America, only to be intercepted and killed. The Marquis de Vaudreuil-Cavagnal (1698–1778), governor of Canada, made effective use of French reinforcements and Indian partners to capture Fort Oswego and Fort William, north of the Hudson River.

British fortunes did not change until the ascendance of William Pitt, later known as Pitt the Elder. An ambitious and able man, he had once said, "I know that I can save this country and that no one else can." He made effective use of the navy, keeping the French fleet occupied in European waters while the British seized control of the shipping routes.

War in the Colonies   Pitt thought globally. He decided to support Prussia mainly with money and take the fight to the frontier. Although France only sent a few divisions to support Canada, thousands of British regulars landed in North America. General Jeffrey Amherst (1717–1797) managed to capture the French fort at Louisbourg, Nova Scotia, in 1758. James Wolfe (1727–1759) managed to capture Quebec in 1759, only to lose it to a French counterattack. The French had to abandon the city a few days later when the Royal Navy appeared on the Saint Lawrence River. They retreated to Montreal, where they were defeated in 1760.

In the meantime, the British secured the West Indies, capturing Guadeloupe, Martinique, Havana, and Manila. These victories, combined with the East India Company's consolidation of British rule in India, established Great Britain as the foremost imperial power in the world.

Peace   Frederick II fought brilliantly and tenaciously, fending off much larger armies. But by 1763, Prussia's manpower and resources were reaching their limit, despite Pitt's enormous financial support. Nevertheless, the French and Austrians knew that Prussia would fight to the bitter end. The European conflict threatened to become a dreary, bloody stalemate.

The British, particularly the newly crowned George III had grown weary of the war. He ousted Pitt the Elder and set peace negotiations in motion. The Treaty of Paris in 1763 put an end to the war.

Aftermath   The Native American tribes had largely broken with the French after 1758. But despite their neutrality, the European powers regarded Indian lands as spoils of war. Anglo American settlers poured into the Ohio River valley. They were more invasive and less

The battle at Fort Duquesne resulted in the death of English General Edward Braddock and the defeat of the British forces.   *Mansell/Time & Life Pictures/Getty Images*

respectful than the French had been. Dissatisfaction with these new conditions sparked armed conflict. Ottawa Chief Pontiac (c. 1720–1769) launched a campaign against the British in 1763, capturing a great many forts. The British responded by sending in reinforcements, who successfully defended Fort Pitt and Fort Detroit until peace settlements were concluded with the various tribes. As part of these treaties, the Crown closed the trans-Appalachian region to white settlers.

The Seven Years' War propelled Great Britain to the zenith of its empire. The victory was a costly one. Pitt had spent money recklessly and had incurred 137 million pounds in national debt. George III, strapped for funds, looked to America to help pay for the war. Parliament passed the Stamp Act in 1765, which levied a small tax on almost all printed materials in the colonies. The colonists reacted by insisting that only their own assemblies had a right to tax them. Resistance was almost universal and often violent. The Stamp Act was repealed, in part because men like Pitt pleaded on the colonists' behalf.

As the tax was meant to pay for the defense of North America, the British regarded the Americans' protests as gross ingratitude. This possibly contributed to the British Empire's stubbornness in regard to the colonists' later complaints. That stubbornness in turn led to Britain's loss of its colonies in the American Revolution.

✪ Aftermath

U.S. Constitution

On the conclusion of the American Revolution, the newly formed United States faced grave financial and political problems. In remedy, the Founding Fathers scrapped the Articles of Confederation, which had served as the nation's framework since 1781. In its place they created the U.S. Constitution, which has been the backbone of American government ever since.

The Articles of Confederation The American people, fresh from their rebellion, distrusted any government with far-reaching authority. They had, after all, rejected the king's right to maintain standing armies abroad, to tax a distant people, and to regulate matters that were none of his business. Accordingly, the Articles of Confederation reflected the spirit of local rule. Instead of forging a strong national leadership, the Articles provided a "firm league of friendship" between the states. Each individual state maintained its "sovereignty, freedom and independence," almost in full.

Congress was to take charge of all foreign affairs, especially the declaration of war or peace. It was also to mediate state border disputes, deal with Native Americans, coin money, and maintain a post office. Despite these broad responsibilities, Congress was given almost no power. The central government had no right to collect taxes, raise an army, or regulate trade. Legislation was difficult to pass and almost impossible to enforce.

The weaknesses of these arrangements became clear rather quickly. Congress had borrowed heavily to support the war and now had no reliable source of revenue to repay its creditors. They had to defray payment of debts, causing a currency crisis. Serious land disputes existed between the states. In addition, British ships poured consumer goods into northern markets. American industries, unprotected by tariffs, could not compete.

In 1786, Massachusetts farmers participated in an armed uprising called Shays's Rebellion, protesting against seizure of land for nonpayment of state taxes. The government had to borrow money from private banks to deal with the crisis.

The Constitutional Convention Alarmed politicians made several attempts to reform the Articles, with little success. In September 1786, a conference was called in Annapolis to discuss the matter. Representatives from only five states attended. The representatives agreed to hold a convention in Philadelphia the following May.

When the convention opened, twelve of the states sent representatives. Rhode Island boycotted the event. George Washington was unanimously called upon to preside over the proceedings. Those gathered agreed to keep the deliberations secret.

The Virginia Plan The advertised purpose of the convention had been to revise the Articles of Confederation. But almost immediately, Edmund Randolph (1753–1813) of Virginia put forward an outline for an entirely new form of government. The Convention agreed to use the proposal as the framework for debate.

The Virginia Plan, as it came to be known, was written almost entirely by James Madison. A small, retiring man, Madison had made a thorough study of historical governments. He was also reputed to know more about the American situation than any other delegate. His framework for the new federal government involved an independent executive and a strong judiciary. It also called for two legislative houses, the House of Representatives and the Senate. Each state would elect members of the House. The larger the population of a state, the more representatives the state would send. The members of the Senate were then to be appointed out of the House of Representatives.

The New Jersey Plan This attempt to base representation on population provoked heated objections from the smaller states. Under the Confederation, each state had one vote in Congress. The Virginia Plan would have drastically diminished the influence of the smaller states relative to the larger states. In response, the New Jersey Plan was advanced. This proposal simply amended the Articles of Confederation, extending the federal government's powers. The states would still

Finalizing the United States Constitution, which took effect in 1789, was the culmination of years of revolutionary activity on the part of Americans seeking an independent government.   *The Library of Congress*

have equal representation regardless of size. The New Jersey Plan was quickly defeated, but the small states remained firm in their opposition to proportional representation.

Roger Sherman of New Haven suggested a middle way, which has since come to be known as "the Great Compromise." The House of Representatives would reflect each state's population size, and each state would have an equal voice in the Senate. This was the course finally accepted by the Convention.

The Convention also faced a fierce contest over the issue of slavery. Southern states wanted to prevent any measure that would threaten the ownership of slaves. On the other hand, they wanted their slaves to count as population, to increase their representation in the legislature. This led them to argue that slaves were both property and people.

Anti-slavery activists like Benjamin Franklin and Governeur Morris (1752–1816) objected strenuously. After bitter debate, the convention agreed to another compromise. Slaves were to count as three-fifths of a person for representation purposes.

The Presidency   The assembly was equally divided over the presidency. Most agreed in the need for an executive to enforce the law. However, some suggested that the task should fall to a council of several people. A single president, one delegate argued, would prove the "fetus of monarchy." Madison argued that a decisive singular executive was needed to check the power of Congress.

They also needed to settle on how the president should be chosen. James Wilson (1742–1798) of Pennsylvania recommended direct popular election. This idea was far too democratic for many delegates. Alexander Hamilton recommended that the president should be elected by the legislature. In the end, the Constitution adopted the compromise electoral college system. Each state was to vote for electors—as many as the number of that state's representatives and senators—and the electors would elect a president. If no candidate received a majority, then the election would be decided by the House of Representatives, with each state receiving one vote.

In the end, the executive branch was given enormous prerogative. Many states rights supporters, notably

The beheading of Louis XVI outraged and worried governments around the world. *Hulton Getty/Liaison Agency. Reproduced by permission*

Thomas Jefferson, worried about such power in the hands of an individual. One delegate wrote that the Convention would probably never have upheld the office of president if they had not believed that George Washington would be the first to fill it. People believed that his virtues would serve as a good example for future generations, as indeed it did.

The Convention closed in September 1787. Not all of the delegates would sign, but Benjamin Franklin summed up the feelings of many present when he said, "I agree to this Constitution with all its faults, if they are such. . . . I doubt too whether any other Convention we can obtain, may be able to make a better Constitution."

French Revolution

The American Revolution had a profound effect on politics in Europe. In the 1780s, the French also threw off their oppressive government. The French revolutionaries were partially inspired by the Founding Fathers' writings and example. However, the French and American Revolutions pursued very different paths, to very different ends.

Pre-revolutionary France Comparison may be unjust, because the two countries had very little in common. America rebelled against a constitutional monarchy; France was ruled by an absolutist monarchy. Socially, the French people were divided into three estates. The first consisted of the clergy, the second of the *aristos* (nobility), and the third included everyone else, from the wealthiest merchant to the poorest farmer. Most clergy were ordained from the nobility, often with little regard to their personal sanctity. The first two estates made up a tiny part of the population, controlled most of the wealth, and paid no taxes. The *philosophes* of the French Enlightenment wrote passionately against the injustice of this medieval system. By the eighteenth century, a great deal of resentment existed in the third estate against the church and the nobles.

The National Assembly When the American Revolution started, Louis XVI's (1754–1793) government offered secret aid to the colonists in the form of money, arms, and uniforms. The French did not share the colonists' belief in democracy. Rather, they wanted revenge for their humiliating loss in the Seven Years War. In

TOUSSAINT-LOUVERTURE

Toussaint was born in slavery around 1743, on the island which is now Haiti. His father was descended from a royal African family, and taught his son his native language, Aja-Fon. Toussaint was freed sometime probably in the 1770s, after which he became a landowner and businessman.

In 1791, conflict broke out between radical and counter-revolutionary colonists in the islands. Toussaint, with many other slave rebels, joined forces with the Spanish in 1793, trying to seize the island from the French. He quickly earned a reputation for bravery and leadership, and was eventually recognized as one of their top military commanders. Around this time he adopted the name Louverture, which means "opening," or "beginning." When the French republic outlawed slavery in 1794, Louverture changed sides, becoming the first black general in the French army in 1801.

Having secured the island, Louverture turned his energies to reconstruction. Though he never declared independence from France, he rebuilt the plantation economy, encouraged trade, and wrote a constitution. When Napoleon tried to reinstate slavery in the colonies, Louverture led his army in the Haitian War of Independence in January 1802. Louverture was captured in battle, and deported to France, where he died in prison. The fight continued without him. The French were driven out, and the state of Haiti was born in December 1803.

1777, with the war starting to turn against the British, France entered into an open alliance with America.

The French monarchy's assistance to an antimonarchal revolution was expensive, to say nothing of ironic. They spent over two billion livres on the American Revolution, and still had debts from the previous war. By 1789, the state was virtually bankrupt. The harvests had been poor and much of the country was starving.

The king's ministers desperately tried to remedy matters. However, the aristocrats were unwilling to surrender any of their privileges, and resisted all attempts at financial reform. With no other option, Louis called for an Estates-General, an assembly in which representatives of the three estates could air their grievances.

It was the first time an Estates-General had been called in more than 170 years. As a result, the structure of the legislative body was not clearly defined. The first and second estates stubbornly strove to establish the rules to their own advantage. They insisted that each estate should have only one vote. Under those conditions, they would win any measure two to one.

Frustrated, the third estate broke away, and declared itself the National Assembly. At this defiance, the king ordered that the assembly hall be locked. Undaunted, the new Assembly met in the tennis courts across the street, where they swore to create a national constitution.

Bastille Day In the meantime, an episode called the "Great Fear" gripped France. Riots swept across the country, fueled by hungry, angry peasants. Rumors spread that the *aristos* planned to squelch the third estate by force. On July 14, 1789, armed Parisians attacked the Bastille prison, killing the warden and guards. The prison was virtually empty, but in previous times the Bastille had held political prisoners, often indefinitely and usually without trial. Its fall had great symbolic importance for the revolutionaries.

In response, the king legitimized the National Assembly, ordering the other estates to participate in it. On August 11, the Assembly produced the *Declaration of the Rights of Man and of the Citizen*, which declared all male Frenchmen equal in the eyes of the law. The Assembly then turned its attention to creating a constitution.

War Over the next two years, many French aristocrats immigrated to England or to Austria. In France they were called *émigrés* and traitors. Abroad, they stirred up anger against the new French government. In June 1791, Louis XVI also tried to escape the country with his family, but they were recognized before they could reach the border. The Assembly forced them to return to Paris and put them under virtual house arrest.

By 1792, Austria and Prussia had massed an army led by *émigrés* who were bent on attacking France and restoring the old regime. To prevent the revolution, France preemptively declared war on Austria. The opening battles went disastrously for the French—Austria overwhelmed them at Verdun. The desperate Legislative Assembly passed a measure to conscript a larger army. Hoping to be rescued by the Austrians, Louis vetoed the bill.

The invasion stirred Parisians to a fever pitch. They blamed French losses on the constitutional monarchy and on the king in particular. On August 9, revolutionaries stormed the palace, killing all the defenders. The next day, the king's power was suspended.

Answering the call of patriotism, thousands of men joined the French army. In September, the Austrian army was pushed back at Valmy. In Paris, the victorious revolutionary government abolished the monarchy entirely and declared the First French Republic. Louis XVI was charged with treason. The convention unanimously convicted him and then sentenced him to the guillotine.

The Reign of Terror The king's death helped push Great Britain and Holland into the war. Monarchal Europe could not tolerate regicide, and they feared that the revolution would spread. In addition, angered by the military conscriptions and food shortages, the western province of the Vendée rose up against the new government. Threatened on all sides, the convention created the Committee of Public Safety. In September 1793, the

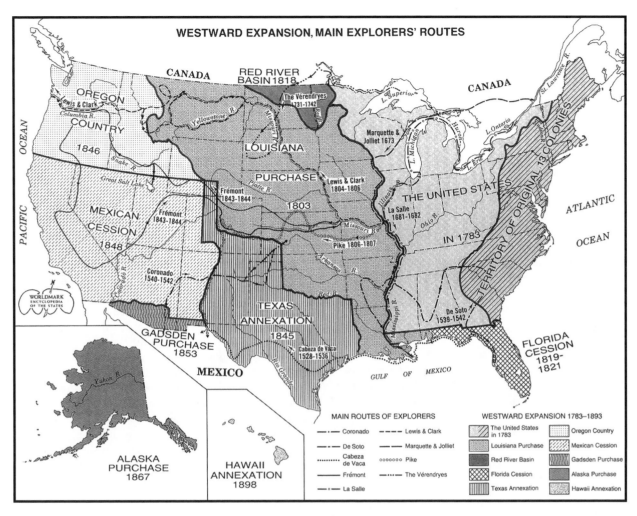

WESTWARD EXPANSION, MAIN EXPLORERS' ROUTES

MAIN ROUTES OF EXPLORERS

- — — Coronado
- — - — De Soto
- ·········· Cabeza de Vaca
- ———— Frémont
- —o—o— La Salle
- – – – – Lewis & Clark
- ———— Marquette & Jolliet
- oooooo Pike
- —··—··— The Vérendryes

WESTWARD EXPANSION 1783–1893

- The United States in 1783
- Louisiana Purchase
- Red River Basin
- Florida Cession
- Texas Annexation
- Oregon Country
- Mexican Cession
- Gadsden Purchase
- Alaska Purchase
- Hawaii Annexation

This map shows the land gained in the Louisiana Purchase. *Reproduced by permission of Gale, a part of Cengage Learning*

Committee was given almost unlimited power to prosecute suspected counterrevolutionaries.

The Committee's rule, known as the Reign of Terror, horrified the world. Led by Maximilien Robespierre (1758–1794), the Committee summarily tried and executed over 17,000 men and women. The victims included the former queen, Marie Antoinette, and members of the old noblesse. But the guillotine claimed commoners as well—political opponents, the indiscreet, the unlucky, even some heroes of the Revolution. The Terror did not end until Robespierre himself was executed in July 1794.

Napoleon After the Terror, a five-member directory governed the country. The war raged on, as France attempted to "liberate" its neighbors from their rulers. After four years, however, morale was low, the economy was bad, and the Constitution was unstable. In 1799, the directory fell in a military coup. General Napoleon Bonaparte (1769–1821) established himself as the new absolute head of state, and by 1804, he crowned himself

emperor. After fifteen years, the French Revolution had shaken off monarchy only to fall into dictatorship.

The Louisiana Purchase

In 1803, Napoleon Bonaparte sold millions of acres west of the Mississippi to the United States. This almost doubled the territory of the young country and set the stage for its expansion to the west.

Spain and France Spain entered the Seven Years War in 1761 on the side of the French and Austrians. The Spanish were not successful; Great Britain quickly captured their islands of Havana and Manila. At the Treaty of Paris in 1763, Great Britain returned control of the islands, but took possession of Spanish Florida. To compensate their ally for this loss, France ceded the Louisiana territory to Spain, including New Orleans.

Since Napoleon had come to power in 1799, he immediately started planning to restore the French Empire. He entered into a secret treaty with Spain, in which Louisiana was returned to the French.

Word of this treaty reached the United States in 1801, where it was rumored that Florida, too, had been given to the French. Thomas Jefferson, then president, viewed this report with alarm. "There is one single spot," he said, "the possessor of which is our natural and habitual enemy.... Every eye in the U.S. is now fixed on this affair of Louisiana." No one doubted Napoleon's ambition, or France's rising military strength. America far preferred Spain as a neighbor.

Secretary of State James Madison asked Robert Livingston (1746–1813) to make inquiries. As U.S. minister to Paris, Livingston was given permission to try to buy Florida, if necessary. He discovered that Louisiana had been transferred, but not Florida.

Crisis Over the Mississippi

In 1802, the Spanish Intendant of Louisiana at New Orleans, Juan Morales, closed the port of New Orleans to American trading vessels. American merchants on the Mississippi could no longer transfer their goods to oceangoing ships at the mouth of the river. The impact of this decision would have been devastating to Western traders; the river was their economic life. Their representatives protested vocally in Congress and even advocated taking New Orleans by force.

James Monroe was dispatched to Paris to negotiate with Napoleon's consulate, even though France had not yet taken control of New Orleans. His instructions were to purchase New Orleans and Florida if possible, for no more than nine million dollars, and to secure rights on the Mississippi River.

Louisiana for Sale

Napoleon had indeed hoped to restore France's former empire in North America. He attempted to restore white rule to Santo Domingo in the Caribbean, where slavery had been abolished in 1794. However, the Santo Domingo black population rallied under the leadership of former slave Toussaint-Louverture (c. 1743–1803) in 1802. By 1803, the French were forced to abandon the island, which the victorious blacks renamed Haiti.

Santo Domingo, with its lush plantations, had been the richest island in the Caribbean before the uprising. Without it, Napoleon had no hope of conquering North America. He saw no further use for Louisiana, and he did not want to spare troops to defend the territory.

Furthermore, the sale could gain the goodwill of the United States. Napoleon was already planning war with Great Britain, and he hoped America would remain neutral. Finally, the French Empire needed money for its armies.

In April 1803, the Marquis de Barbé-Marbois (1745–1837), French minister of finance, was given permission to sell Louisiana to the United States. He entered into negotiations with Monroe and Livingston, then in Paris. They had no instructions to buy all of Louisiana, but nevertheless they bargained hotly for almost a month. In the end, they agreed to pay about fifteen million dollars. They also promised to grant the inhabitants of Louisiana all the privileges of American citizenship.

America Expands

When Jefferson received news of the agreement, he hesitated. As leader of the Anti-Federalist Party, he had fought hard against the expansion of federal power. Under the Constitution, neither he nor Congress had the right to purchase land. Nevertheless, the president approved the purchase, and Congress agreed. By March 1804, Louisiana was formally a territory of the United States.

The exact boundaries of the new territory were not precisely known at the time of purchase. America was to acquire whatever France had acquired from Spain. When pressed for details, French Prime Minister Talleyrand-Périgord (1754–1838) shrugged it off: "I can give you no direction. You have made a noble bargain for yourselves, and I suppose you will make the most of it."

The vagueness of the contract resulted in a long-standing dispute with Spain that concluded only in 1819. In the end, the land purchased would become the states of Arkansas, Iowa, Louisiana, Missouri, Nebraska, North Dakota, Oklahoma, South Dakota, and parts of Kansas, Minnesota, Colorado, Montana, and Wyoming. The price came to roughly three cents an acre.

Jefferson called for a survey of the area, which resulted in the Lewis and Clark Expedition from 1804 to 1806. It opened the United States to major westward growth. However, political strife continually broke out over whether slavery would be legal in the new territories. In this way each new state was forced to choose a side in the upcoming Civil War.

BIBLIOGRAPHY

Books

Fleming, Thomas. *Liberty! The American Revolution.* New York: Viking, 1997.

Johnson, Curt. *Battles of the American Revolution.* New York: Bonanza Books, 1984.

Lewis, James. *The Louisiana Purchase: Jefferson's Noble Bargain?* Chapel Hill, N.C.: The University of North Carolina Press, 2003.

Marrin, Albert. *The War for Independence: The Story of the American Revolution.* New York: Atheneum, 1988.

Minks, Louise, and Benton Minks. *The Revolutionary War.* New York: Facts on File, 1992.

Morgan, Edmund S. *The Birth of the Republic, 1763–1789.* Chicago: University of Chicago Press, 1956.

Porter, Roy. *The Enlightenment (Studies in European History).* Hampshire, UK: Palgrave, 2001.

Smith, Page. *A New Age Now Begins: A People's History of the American Revolution.* New York: McGraw Hill, 1976.

Zobel, Hillard B. *The Boston Massacre.* New York: W. W. Norton, 1970.

Periodical

Norton, Graham Gendall. "Toussaint Louverture." *History Today.* (April 2003)

Web Sites

Franklin, Benjamin. *The Autobiography of Benjamin Franklin.* Reprinted at Archiving Early America. <www.earlyamerica.com/lives/franklin> (accessed March 10, 2007). Originally published in 1793.

Hamilton, Alexander. *The Works of Alexander Hamilton, (Federal Edition)*, Henry Cabot Lodge, ed. Vol. 7. (18thc). Reprinted at The Online Library of Liberty. <oll.libertyfund.org/Home3/HTML.php?recordID=0249.07> (accessed March 27, 2007).

"INDEPENDENCE: The Birth of a New America." *Time* (July 4, 1976). Reprinted at <www.time.com/time/magazine/article/0,9171,712235-1,00.html> (accessed March 10, 2007).

Paine, Thomas. "Common Sense." Reprinted at the Constitution Society <www.constitution.org/tp/comsense.htm> (accessed March 10, 2007). Originally published in 1776.

———. "The American Crisis: 1, December 23, 1776." Reprinted at the Constitution Society <www.constitution.org/tp/amercrisis01.htm> (accessed March 10, 2007). Originally published in 1776.

Smith, Adam. "An Inquiry into the Nature and Causes of the Wealth of Nations by Adam Smith." Project Gutenberg <www.gutenberg.org/etext/3300> (accessed March 27, 2007). Originally published in 1776.

"Thomas Jefferson's Account of the Declaration." Reprinted at USHistory.org. <www.ushistory.org/declaration/account/index.htm> (accessed March 10, 2007).

Voltaire. "The Philosophical Dictionary." H.I. Woolf, ed. New York: Knopf, 1924. Reprinted at Hanover Historical Texts Project <history.hanover.edu/texts/voltaire/volindex.html> (accessed March 27, 2007).

Introduction to Conflicts with Tribes to the West and South (1811–1832)

America's battles with tribal Indians in the Northwest Territory (the area stretching from Ohio to Wisconsin) and in the Deep South (the Mississippi Territory to Florida) resulted from westward migration of white settlers into Native American lands. Some of the treaties that American officials and Indian chiefs may have peacefully agreed to may not have been respected or even known about by countless other Indians on the same lands.

The resulting wars with Native Americans generally took place in two theaters. In the West, white settlers encountered the Shawnee, Delaware, Miami, Sauk, and Fox tribes. In the South, migrants seeking fertile lands for rice and cotton ran into the Five Civilized Tribes, including the Cherokees, Choctaws, Creeks, Chickasaws, and Seminoles.

By the early 1800s, the United States had already battled in and set up forts along the Ohio River valley. General William Henry Harrison, who also served as territorial governor of both the Northwest Territory and later Indiana, faced the issue of keeping peace between the frontier pioneers and Indians for a good part of his career. The dispute reached a pinnacle when Harrison's militia faced off with the dwellers of Prophetstown, a village headed by Tecumseh and his brother Tenskwatawa, at the Battle of Tippecanoe in November 1811. Many tribes had allied with Britain, which had in fact supplied them with arms. After the official declaration of the War of 1812, the British and Indian alliance became stronger, as did the United States' will to defeat both.

Settlers of the American South also faced hostilities there. Enterprising planters relocated to raise cotton and other cash crops for European markets. As these farmers, their laborers, and slaves arrived, some southern Indian tribes did agree to live in peace with them, but the Red Sticks faction of the Creek tribe did not. After these Indians procured gunpowder and munitions from a Spanish governor in Pensacola, Florida, an American militia outfit stationed in southern Alabama attacked them. The Indians retaliated and slaughtered hundreds of soldiers and innocents at the Fort Mims massacre, north of Mobile, Alabama. The United States and Tennessee Militia sent General Andrew Jackson through Alabama to conquer these unfriendly Creek Indians. With mostly successful campaigns, Jackson used a heavy hand to subdue the Creeks. After major defeats, the Red Sticks surrendered and ceded much of their lands. Jackson went on to defeat their British allies at New Orleans, to end the War of 1812. Soon after, he raided Seminole villages in Spanish-controlled Florida, which resulted in the Florida's annexation into the United States.

Successful military campaigns against the Indians gave Jackson and Harrison successful political careers that both climaxed with winning the presidency. The drive for economic success and quasi-legal treaties caused most Americans to view moving into these Indian lands as justified. Millions of acres of land went to the United States from 1790 to 1830. For those Indians who remained, Congress and President Jackson forced their removal with the Indian Removal Act and military force to relocate them, mainly to Oklahoma. Thousands died in that journey, which became known as the Trail of Tears.

Conflicts with Tribes to the West and South (1811–1832)

✪ Causes

European Encroachment on Native American Land

Conflicts between Americans and tribal Indians came after centuries of European encroachment onto Indian lands. Since the Age of Exploration, European powers had penetrated the North American continent from several angles. Primarily, the Spanish, English, and French had made their way, at different points in time, into the American South and modern-day Midwest. The story of European exploration of these lands and diplomacy with Native Americans is a complex one. Over two centuries, the European states competed for control over these regions that involved several imperial wars, various methods of diplomacy with the Indians, and constantly changing political borders after multiple conquests, losses, and treaties. Although it is tempting to generalize, no one characterization of how European and native relations played out is apt.

Spain had sent successful missions to the Americas for gold, God, and glory since the days of Christopher Columbus (1451–1506). Their most successful and long-term conquests came in the American West, extending south into Mexico and in Florida. But they also entered the Southeast. Hernando de Soto (c. 1500–1542) went as far inland as modern-day Atlanta and encountered Cherokee Indians during the mid-1500s. Spain showed interest in southeastern United States, particularly the Mississippi Valley, until the late 1700s.

The French explorers and missionaries entered North America and began to dominate the middle region from the Great Lakes to the Gulf of Mexico. Fishing and furs enticed the French, though the official position of the French government was that its people came to the Americas on a religious mission. Since Jacques Cartier (1491–1557) traveled west up the Saint Lawrence River in 1535, the French began to establish outposts and missions along the Northwest Territory. By the time of the French and Indian War, France had established relationships with Indians for military, matrimonial, religious, commercial, and cultural purposes. They maintained control of much of this region and especially the lands west of the Mississippi River until these were sold to the United States in the Louisiana Purchase in 1803.

British imperial endeavors resulted in acquisition of most of the eastern seaboard. Beginning in the late 1500s, England began to dominate the Atlantic coast, forming colonies in Virginia, Massachusetts, and several points in between. Several Native American tribes had already been pushed westward from their homes in the eastern states prior to the American Revolution. The French and Indian War pitted the British against the French, with most natives siding with the latter. After this conflict, and with rising problems between Indians of the Appalachian Mountain range and American colonists, the British government saw fit to restrict any westward expansion with the Royal Proclamation of 1763. This simply forbade the colonists from interfering with natives to the west. After the American colonists had successfully won their revolution for freedom from England, the Treaty of Paris defined the official boundaries of the new United States in 1783. The United States stretched from the Atlantic seaboard to the Mississippi River, and from the Great Lakes to Spanish Florida. The thirteen colonies had tripled their real estate, and pioneering and enterprising Americans were now ready to head west.

Those who encountered the Indians had various ways in which to handle this relationship. The early Spanish conquistadors had a reputation for being excessively harsh, and explorers and colonists from the other European nations used excessive force from time to time. But they found success with friendly diplomacy as well. The French forged impressive connections with natives from the Saint Lawrence to the Mississippi River, sending trade goods to the Indians. Many Indians referred to the French as their "fathers" and "brothers." Many Native American leaders traveled to European

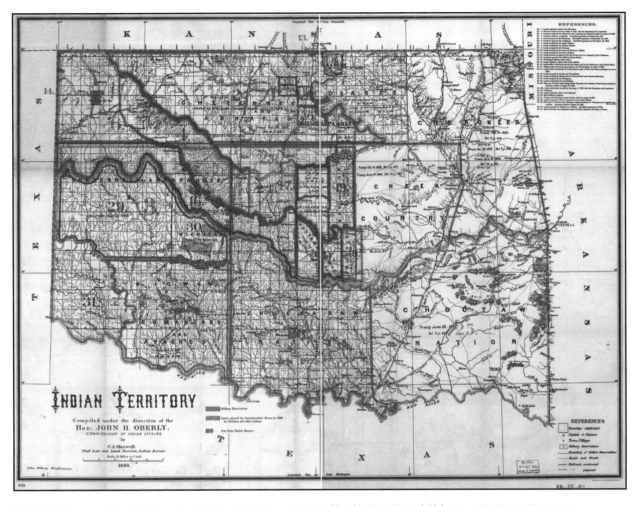

By 1832, after many bloody battles, the Creeks ceded major portions of land in Georgia and Alabama. *The Library of Congress*

nations to be received by heads of state. Cherokee delegations arrived in London in 1730, 1762, and in 1764. A later delegation of Creek and Cherokee Indians visited England in 1790 and 1791. These guests received considerable attention. It was also not uncommon to see Indians in council dress walking streets in the capitals of English, French, and Spanish colonies.

✪ Major Figures

Benjamin Hawkins

Benjamin Hawkins (1754–1816) was an American revolutionary, statesman, and planter, but is most remembered for his role as advocate for the Native Americans in the southern United States. He served much of his career as an agent for the Creek Indians and as a liaison between the Creek Nation and the federal government.

Hawkins was born in 1754 in North Carolina. When the American Revolution began, he was finishing his college degree at Princeton University. He had mastered the French language, which convinced General George

Washington (1732–1799) to call on him to serve as an interpreter with the French allies. He was elected as a delegate to the Confederation Congress more than once and served as one of North Carolina's first two senators under the ratified Constitution. During these times, and well after the United States was established, Hawkins served the United States in its relations with the Cherokee, Choctaw, and Chickasaw tribes, among others.

In 1785, Hawkins was appointed commissioner to negotiate treaties with the Indians. The Treaty of Hopewell resulted largely from his efforts. This agreement defined the Cherokees' borders and recognized their right to expel white squatters. In reality, however, American settlers ignored the agreement and encroached on the Indian lands. Hawkins worked out additional treaties, and eventually President Washington appointed him to negotiate with the Creek Confederacy. His interest in the United States's relationship with tribes and Washington's confidence in Hawkins earned him positions as agent and superintendent of Indian tribes south of the Ohio in 1796.

ALEXANDER MCGILLIVRAY

Alexander McGillivray (c. 1759–1793) served as one of the chief diplomats for the Creek Indians with European and Americans during the late 1700s. He was born around 1759 at Little Tallahassee, Alabama, near present-day Montgomery. The son of Scottish trader Lachlan McGillivray and Sehoy, a Creek woman of the Wind Clan, the young McGillivray was destined to be successful. His father came to America at age sixteen and began trading with Indians in 1735. He married a native woman, "cheerful in countenance, bewitching in looks, and graceful in form," after he gained some property. His father's success allowed for Alexander to receive a quality education. He was schooled in Augusta and Savannah, Georgia, learning to read and write in English at a young age. He also apprenticed in business. But his mother's heritage encouraged McGillivray to live the lifestyle of a Creek Indian. With these two attributes, and his intelligence and savvy for politics, McGillivray became active in diplomacy with various political entities over the course of his rather short, but unique life.

He sided with the British during the American Revolution, returning to Little Tallahassee in 1777 to organize the Creeks on the side of the British to fight in southern battles. Though the Creeks were not totally united with England, McGillivray impressed many chiefs and warriors as an interpreter of the outside world. Once the war ended and Britain ceded southern lands to the United States, he took the position that, although the Creeks sided with the Britons, they never gave their lands to them, and thus these lands could not be given by the British to the now-independent Americans. He was involved with negotiating with Spain for the Treaty of Pensacola, which guaranteed Florida Creeks their territorial rights. He also met with officials from the United States and Georgia to convince both that if the encroaching Americans did not respect Creek boundaries, they would be met with force. In 1785 and 1787, Creek warriors kept McGillivray's promise, attacking and expelling American invaders.

As local chiefs began ceding lands for payments, McGillivray claimed they did not have the political authority to do so. No Creek chief or tribe alone could enter treaties or sell these lands, McGillivray posed, without the consent of the entire Creek Nation and a national council. With his influence over the Wind Clan McGillivray sent warriors into these passive tribes to harass them and destroy their property. With his authority under the Treaty of Pensacola, he prevented trade goods and weapons from reaching the warriors. All this in hopes of creating a strong national government to preserve and protect the Indians from westward-bound Americans.

His final shining moment was representing the Georgia Creeks in the Treaty of New York with the United States. This move sidestepped the reluctant Georgia government and brought the United States recognition. This treaty also gave him control over commerce with these tribes, thus empowering him to subordinate Creek towns for his purposes. McGillivray died on February 17, 1793. Native Americans, especially Creeks, followed his ideals and kept them alive into the resistance to Indian removal in the 1820s and 1830s.

His jurisdiction covered thousands of square miles, while his relationship with the natives earned their respect. He abandoned a potential career and instead immersed himself in Indian life, becoming a diplomat as well as a teacher and an advocate. His kind attitude earned him the title "Beloved Man of Four Nations." He began a plantation and taught Creek Indians the art of modern farming. His farm became an academy of agriculture for his Indian followers. Hawkins became so respected that his brand, the mark found on his livestock, prevented any losses. Area peoples returned any farm animals that wandered off his lands. For twenty years, Hawkins's influence allowed for peace between these southern Indians and the United States. He fell in love with a Creek woman, who he took as a common-law wife.

As the War of 1812 approached and as greater numbers of whites encroached on Creek lands in the South, this peaceful relationship between the two nations was soon in jeopardy. Some tribes sided with the British, for they posed less of a threat to their lands. Additionally, Shawnee leader Tecumseh (c. 1768–1813) preached a defense of the Indian homeland and a resistance to the white Americans. Those Creeks nearer to Hawkins joined him and allied themselves with the United States. He raised a regiment of Indian warriors and placed William McIntosh (c. 1778–1825), a chief of mixed heritage, as commander of the regiment.

After General Andrew Jackson (1767–1845) marched under federal orders on an anti-Creek campaign through Alabama and defeated the hostile Red Sticks tribe, the general forced the suppressed natives into a treaty with unfavorable conditions. They were forced to cede large portions of their lands. Even Creeks who had been friendly to the Americans and had all along sided with Hawkins, were compelled to give in to Jackson's demands. Hawkins was at the great council at Fort Jackson, but could do little to advocate for the Creeks he so admired. Between Jackson's forceful approach and the white settlers' push to overcome them, the Creeks' spirit was broken.

During his time with the Indians, Hawkins recorded authentic accounts of Creek customs that were later published by the Georgia Historical Society. Hawkins finally married his common-law wife on his deathbed and thereafter died on June 6, 1816.

William Henry Harrison

William Henry Harrison (1773–1841), perhaps best known for his short service as president of the United

States, first reached national fame as a military general against the Indian tribes of the West (in modern-day Indiana and the surrounding area) and through his service in the War of 1812. Harrison was a native Virginian and son of Benjamin Harrison, a signer of the Declaration of Independence. His grandson, also named Benjamin Harrison, was elected president of the United States in 1888.

Settling the West William Henry Harrison joined the U.S. Army and was stationed at Fort Washington in 1791, in what is today Cincinnati, Ohio. This exposed him to the conflict that he would deal with for much of his military and political career—the conflict between white American settlers and Native Americans, including the Shawnee, Miami, and Delaware tribes. By 1793, the young Harrison sold his Virginia property and relocated to Ohio, beginning his influence as a founder of the Northwestern Territory, first as a soldier and later as a commander and governor.

The infant United States had decidedly defeated the British army and was now faced with encounters between its citizens and Indian tribes. Revolutionary War General Arthur St. Clair (c. 1734–1818) had already lost about one thousand men in a devastating defeat in November 1791 at the Battle of Wabash at the hands of Shawnee and Miami Indians. Harrison now held the rank of lieutenant and served as General Anthony Wayne's (1745–1796) aide-de-camp. Wayne took Harrison, his other officers, and soldiers to avenge the American defeat and St. Clair's loss. On this journey, he burned Indian villages and destroyed their crops along the way. Wayne and Harrison met Indians at the Battle of Fallen Timbers, an area north of the American Fort Greenville and just five miles south of Fort Miami, where the trees had been cleared by a strong tornado. Wayne's army and Harrison came under the attack of the Ottawa tribe. A young Shawnee Indian, Tecumseh, was also in the battle. Wayne's troops defeated the natives, which eventually led to the Treaty of Greenville, quieting the conflict north of the Ohio River. This outfit eventually established Fort Wayne on the Wabash River, which became the center of American military power in this region.

Harrison became a captain in 1797, but soon resigned his military position to serve in a civil capacity as territorial secretary in June 1798. He served as a chief delegate from the Northwest Territory to the U.S. Congress at the turn of the century. When his term expired, he became the governor of Indiana Territory and settled in the capital of Vincennes. He built a large Georgian home on his new estate called Grouseland. The property served as both a governor's mansion and a site for several diplomatic encounters with area Indian tribes. As governor, Harrison was absolute ruler. He served as commander-in-chief of the territorial militia and superintendent of Indian affairs. This combined author-

ity caused several Native Americans to bring their grievances to him at Vincennes.

Over the next decade, the territory transformed as Harrison and the United States acquired quasi-legal rights to much of these Indian lands and as more white Americans moved into the region. In September 1801, Harrison worked out a treaty that resolved conflicts between the Shawnees, the settlers in the Vincennes area, and the Piankeshaws, who were few in number by this time. The Treaty of Fort Wayne, which ceded additional lands to Americans, was formalized in 1803. In August 1804, a treaty with the Delaware tribe and Piankeshaws cleared lands between Vincennes, Indiana, and Louisville, Kentucky. Other agreements followed.

Though these peace offerings were declared formal at councils hosting American officials and Indian leaders, the diplomatic policies that forged relationships between the settlers and the Indians did not make for a completely harmonious relationship. Harrison followed the primary objective of securing Indian-occupied lands in and around Indiana in return for money, liquor, and other goods, and often with a promise of more distant western lands. The United States, through Harrison and others, began negotiating with civil chiefs who often agreed to the conditions of these treaties. The assumption that these chiefs were heads of state like European leaders with binding authority over countless others in their nation was a mistake. In reality, various tribes in the West did not always have a hierarchical relationship under a chief who could speak for all Indians in the area. Harrison and other officers took these treaties at face value, although many Native Americans not privy to the agreements did not.

Handling Hostilities As more and more white settlers entered the area and encountered tribesmen who ignored these treaties, it became increasingly difficult for these two societies to live side by side. By 1805, five thousand white inhabitants occupied Indiana, which put it on the road to statehood and caused other problems. Alcohol became a real problem. It was a commodity that accompanied treaty agreements. However, it became a social problem within the tribes of the Northwest Territory and a symbol of the white man's poison, a reminder of how American settlers were destroying the Indian nation. When Indians and white civilians had deadly encounters, the treaties stated that aggressive attackers, whites or natives, should be brought to justice, and properly punished if guilty. But this agreement resulted in anything but a two-way street. Much to Harrison's dismay, American courts quickly convicted accused Indian murderers, while accused whites rarely met justice. Fellow whites refused to testify, and white juries refused to convict their own. To combat the inequity, Harrison offered rewards for the arrests of white murderers who were never punished when arrested. He reported to President Thomas Jefferson (1743–1826)

William Henry Harrison's victory at the Battle of Tippecanoe would propel him all the way to the White House. *The Library of Congress*

after the Delawares complained of six non-prosecuted murders, "All these injuries the Indians have hitherto borne with astonishing patience." He warned his commander-in-chief, "though they discover no disposition to make war on the United States at present ... [they] would eagerly seize any favorable opportunity for that purpose." He warned the president that if America came into any war with a foreign European power, that nine-tenths of the Indians in the region would side with an enemy of the United States.

By 1806, Harrison learned that a Shawnee Indian, Tecumseh, and his brother, who claimed to be a prophet, were preaching against him and the white settlers. Trouble was on the rise. Tecumseh's goals went beyond seeking immediate revenge. He wanted to create an Indian confederacy among several tribes of the West, and include those from the South. By 1808, these Shawnee had established a village on the Tippecanoe River in present-day Indiana. Tecumseh's brother, who went by the name Prophet (c. 1775–c. 1837), visited Harrison at Vincennes for two weeks, explaining his complaints.

With the settlers of the Indiana Territory strongly behind a policy of forcing the Indians out, and after Tecumseh refused to accept a delivery of salt by Harrison's men, the governor and commander felt he had no choice. The safety for the people he represented could,

he thought, only come by crushing Indian resisters. On June 24, 1811, Harrison wrote Tecumseh, accusing him of conspiring with other tribes up and down the Mississippi River and of planning to murder Harrison. Except for seizing five barrels of salt, the Shawnee had committed no overt act of war. Additional murders in the area brought support for American action against Tecumseh. But Tecumseh, instead, arrived at Vincennes with three hundred warriors for a discussion with the governor. The meeting became hostile, and the Shawnee warrior departed in a rage. This prompted Harrison to lead an expedition of one thousand forces of regulars, militiamen, and a mounted force from Kentucky north toward Tecumseh's village of Prophetstown on the Tippecanoe River. On the way, Harrison's force constructed a fort at Terre Haute as an advance point and named it in his honor as Fort Harrison. The Battle of Tippecanoe was a bloody one that left both sides damaged. Tecumseh was absent. He had traveled south to create alliances with other tribes.

Soon after Tippecanoe, the U.S. Congress voted to declare war with Britain in the War of 1812. Harrison served as a major general in this conflict, starting from Cincinnati and heading north to meet British and Indian enemies. Tecumseh harassed Harrison and his men at Fort Meigs, Ohio, in April 1813. The fort withstood pressures from both British cannon and Shawnee warriors. Tecumseh challenged Harrison to come out and fight, but Harrison wisely declined. Their final confrontation occurred in the Battle of the Thames. Tecumseh had persuaded the English General Henry Procter to fight the Americans, what Tecumseh thought would be the final chance to save his homeland. On October 5, 1813, Harrison and his army defeated their opponents. Tecumseh was killed.

Political Life Harrison's wartime successes made him a military hero and catapulted him into a successful political life. From 1816 to 1836, Harrison served at different points in the U.S. House of Representatives, the Senate, as ambassador to Columbia, and in some state and local offices. He made an impressive run for president in 1836, but fell short of victory. In 1840, he was elected on the Whig ticket with Vice President Virginian John Tyler (1790–1862) with the campaign slogan, "Tippecanoe and Tyler too." He became ill after his inaugural address in the cold and died one month into his term, leaving no legacy as president.

Tecumseh

Tecumseh (c. 1768–1813) was a Shawnee warrior who led an effort to unite North America tribal Indians against the growing United States. He was born in the Ohio River valley around 1768 to a Shawnee father, Puckeshinewa, and a Creek Indian mother. As white settlers began moving westward, they violently encountered the Shawnee and surely influenced Tecumseh in

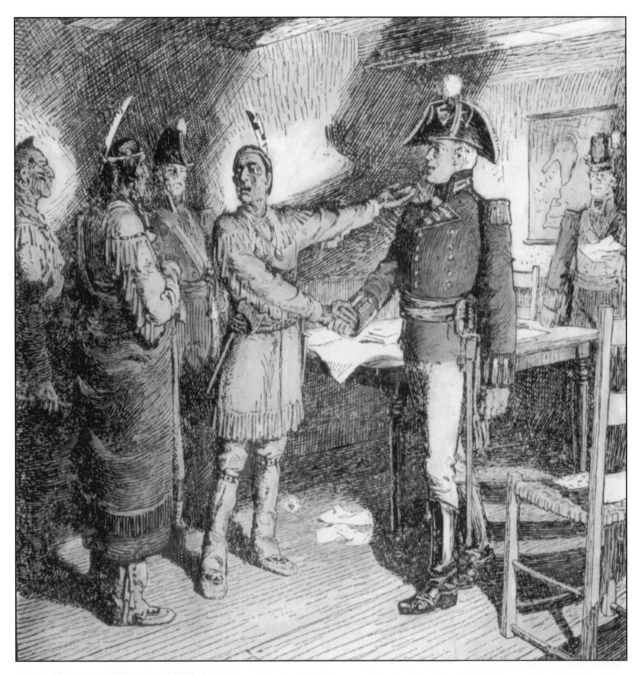

The Shawnee leader Tecumseh accepted an officer's rank in the British Army and fought alongside the British in the War of 1812. *The Granger Collection, New York. Reproduced by permission*

his lifelong pursuit of protecting the Indian lands against them. American colonists killed his father in the Battle of Point Pleasant along the Ohio River in 1774. In 1779, Tecumseh's village was attacked, forcing scores of Shawnee from their home villages.

Tecumseh was a warrior from an early age. He excelled at war games that young Indians played. He was skilled with the bow and the musket, and he would go on hunts and fight mock battles with his boyhood friends, which prepared him for real battles later in life. He also had a humanitarian side. The generous Indian provided food and meat for tribal members who had none. And, though he was foremost a warrior, he opposed torture of captives, a common practice with both Indians and whites on the frontier.

As more and more whites and American soldiers began to occupy the Ohio country, Tecumseh and the Shawnee people were forced westward. After defeats like

TECUMSEH'S SPEECH AT VINCENNES

Tecumseh denounced the Treaty of Greenville (Ohio), in which Indian chiefs sold millions of acres of natives' lands for $10,000. He and other Indians did not know of the agreement. These chiefs, Tecumseh claimed, did not speak for all Indians on this land. In a speech addressed to Indiana Territorial Governor William Henry Harrison at Vincennes, Tecumseh outlined his reasons for not agreeing to the treaty:

> Houses are built for you to hold your councils in; Indians hold theirs in the open air. I am a Shawnee. My forefathers were warriors. Their son is a warrior. From them I take my only existence. From my tribe I take nothing. I have made myself what I am. And I would that I could make the red people as great as the conceptions of my own mind, when I think of the Great Spirit that rules over us all . . . I would not then come to Governor Harrison to ask him to tear up the treaty. But I would say to him, "Brother, you have the liberty to return to your own country."
>
> You wish to prevent the Indians from doing as we wish them, to unite and let them consider their lands as the common property of the whole. You take the tribes aside and advise them not to come into this measure. . . . You want by your distinctions of Indian tribes, in allotting to each a particular, to make them war with each other. You never see an Indian endeavor to make the white people do this. You are continually driving the red people, when at last you will drive them onto the great lake, where they can neither stand nor work.
>
> Since my residence at Tippecanoe, we have endeavored to level all distinctions, to destroy village chiefs, by whom all mischiefs are done. It is they who sell the land to the Americans. Brother, this land that was sold, and the goods that was given for it, was only done by a few. . . . In the future we are prepared to punish those who propose to sell land to the Americans. If you continue to purchase them, it will make war among the different tribes, and, at last I do not know what will be the consequences among the white people. Brother, I wish you would take pity on the red people and do as I have requested. If you will not give up the land and do cross the boundary of our present settlements, it will be very hard, and produce great trouble between us.
>
> The way, the only way to stop this evil is for the red men to unite in claiming a common and equal right in the land, as it was at first, and should now be now—for it was never divided, but belongs to all. No tribe has the right to sell, even to each other, much less to strangers. . . . Sell a country! Why not sell the air, the great sea, as well as the earth? Did not the Great Spirit make them all for the use of his children?

SOURCE: *Eyewitnesses and Others: Readings in American History.* Austin: Holt Rinehart and Winston.

---

the one at the Battle of Fallen Timbers, Tecumseh, his brother—known as Prophet—and scores of Ohio Indians moved into the Indiana Territory. As the American military proved its might against the Indians, tribes across the region began to cede lands to American agents at councils like the one that took place at the Treaty of Greenville. Dozens more followed. Tecumseh refused to participate at such negotiations and did not agree to any promised relations with the Americans. The United States, however, had secured these lands in what they saw as legal means, giving up federal funds and goods in return. Tecumseh and many others did not support, and in many cases did not even know about, these treaties. Indian tribes were not arranged in a singular hierarchy that representatives of the entire United States or European states could engage in diplomacy. Thus, Tecumseh did not feel bound by these agreements. He watched as his way of life was overrun by the Anglo-American culture. White men's alcohol, a common tool in persuading Indians, became recognized as a poison by Tecumseh.

By the early 1800s, Tecumseh had relocated near the Tippecanoe River to a village known as Prophetstown near present-day Lafayette, Indiana. The village's namesake, Prophet, had proven a spiritual and religious leader among the Shawnees, but Tecumseh was certainly the political leader. Tecumseh became the chief nemesis of Indiana Governor William Henry Harrison. As whites and tribesmen clashed in the area, resulting in disputes that often led to murders, Tecumseh began relations on two fronts. He wanted mainly to unite native tribes living in the southern United States with those of the North and West. He traveled frequently hoping to create alliances and perhaps a formal Indian Confederacy. He also began normalizing relations with the British, with whom the United States was at odds. The natives could be a promising ally or a dreadful enemy if the disputes between the two countries resulted in war. The Shawnee warrior began to side with the British and the British accepted him. As this relationship developed, encounters between Tecumseh, his brother, and Governor Harrison caused the peace between area Indians and whites to deteriorate. On more than one occasion, the Shawnee leaders, including Tecumseh, traveled to Vincennes to address Harrison and present their grievances.

Petitioning the governor, sometimes threateningly, only drove the wedge further between these two sides and brought Tecumseh closer to the British. Royal

Canadian warehouses began to supply his people with food, supplies, and arms. The climax of tension between Harrison and the Indians came at the Battle of Tippecanoe. Tecumseh was actually away from Prophetstown trying to organize southern tribes when Harrison and his army approached. The winner of the battle is a matter of debate, but it likely harmed Tecumseh's people and disturbed his following while it rallied American settlers in the region to defeat the Indians. It was also one of the final steps toward the War of 1812. Tecumseh returned to Indiana to find his tribe damaged and war imminent.

He was given an officer's rank in the British army. He went on to fight with great courage at Brownstown, Fort Meigs, and Fort Stephenson. But Tecumseh did not survive the Battle of the Thames in October 1813, where Harrison's forces defeated the British and their Indian allies.

Andrew Jackson

Andrew Jackson (1767–1845) was a lawyer, general, and president of the United States. He spent much of his career controlling Native Americans, both on the battlefield and as president. Jackson was born in South Carolina and moved to Nashville, Tennessee, to open a law office at age twenty-one. Before entering politics, Jackson was a successful field commander in campaigns against the Creek Indians throughout Alabama and against the Seminoles in Florida. He is noted for defeating the British at the Battle of New Orleans in the concluding days of the War of 1812. But Jackson spent more time conquering the Indian tribes of the growing American South as general and chief executive than he spent defeating the British.

The Creek War   The Creek Indians, one of the "Five Civilized Tribes" of the American South, became a challenge to the United States as the country waged war with Britain in the War of 1812. The Creeks generally had positive relations with the British, so between animosities caused by white Americans encroaching on their lands, and their siding with the British, they became a key adversary of the United States. A particular faction of the Creeks, the Red Sticks, were particularly aggressive toward white settlers. In August 1813, the Red Sticks killed hundreds of Americans in the Fort Mims massacre near Mobile, Alabama, after which the military increased efforts to crush this tribe.

Both President James Madison (1751–1836) and Tennessee Governor William Blount (1749–1800) decided that actions against the Creeks were necessary. The Tennessee state legislature authorized Governor Blount to summon five thousand volunteers for this mission. Major General Andrew Jackson organized the soldiers and departed on October 7, 1813, to avenge the attack and to settle the question as to who would occupy and rule this territory. Jackson marched his men southward through Alabama, slicing the Creek Nation in half on his way to Mobile.

Andrew Jackson's enormous political popularity was based in part on his military victories, such as his defeat of the British at the Battle of New Orleans.   *The Library of Congress*

General John Coffee (1772–1833) and other soldiers-turned-statesmen accompanied Jackson, including David Crockett (1786–1836) and Sam Houston (1793–1863). Their first encounter took place on November 3, when Jackson's men encircled nearly two hundred Red Stick warriors at Tallushatchee in northern Alabama. Jackson ordered Coffee and his men to destroy the village. Coffee lost only five men and suffered only forty-one wounded. The Americans slew 186 Indian warriors and brought the captured women and children back to camp as prisoners. The army's success convinced many Red Stick villages to switch their allegiance to Jackson. William "Red Eagle" Weatherford (c. 1781–1824), a Red Stick chief of mixed ancestry, learned of the local village turning on him and brought a thousand of his tribe to burn it to the ground. Jackson prepared well and met the enemy attackers at Talladega. He and Coffee handily defeated the Indians in this battle, killing over three hundred.

Jackson headed for the important Creek stronghold of Horseshoe Bend, a 100-acre peninsula formed by the Tallapoosa River. A mid-January 1814 battle proved challenging for Jackson when the Red Sticks struck his camp at dawn, but Old Hickory, as the hardened Jackson was known, was ready for them. The Indians attacked, firing guns and arrows. By the time the battle ended, twenty Americans lay dead and seventy-five were wounded. On the Creek side, about two hundred died.

Additional successes followed, but sickness and disgruntled troops caused Jackson some problems. Governor Blount and the U.S. War Department sent reinforcements, giving Jackson several thousand men. On March 14, 1814, Jackson was ready for a full assault on the Creeks that he hoped would end the conflict. He left one of his commanders and 450 men behind to guard Fort Strother, the advance point Jackson had set up in central Alabama. With the additional troops and quite a few friendly Creeks, he headed for Horseshoe Bend. At 10 A.M. on March 27, he arrived to find a heavily fortified breastwork. Within a half hour he began artillery fire at the fort to break down the walls. Soldiers began to fire muskets and rifles into the fort. One regiment eventually charged. The Indians began to retreat, but the killing became savage. "The carnage was dreadful," Jackson wrote. The next day the general ordered a body count, which totaled some 557 dead on the battlefield and several hundred more in the river.

Much to Jackson's surprise, Chief Red Eagle was not present at Horseshoe Bend. Jackson and his men rested for a short period and then moved on to set up in an old French fortress that became known as Fort Jackson. Area chiefs got word of the slaughter at Horseshoe Bend and came to Jackson with peace offerings. Red Eagle himself, with bravery and audacity, walked into the fort to surrender. "I am in your power. Do with me what you please," Red Eagle told Jackson. He continued, "If I had an army, I would yet fight and contend to the last. But I have none. My people are all gone." Horseshoe Bend proved decisive in quelling the Red Sticks. Jackson was so impressed by the enemy general, that he only gave Red Eagle a strong warning, but promised to protect him if he promised never to rise against the white Americans again.

Seminole Wars Jackson had handled the Indian dispute in Alabama as a theater of American operations during the War of 1812. He went on to New Orleans to defeat the British there. But within a few years, he returned to deal with the Indians in Spanish Florida, which eventually led to additional white settlement and statehood. U.S. troops attacked Fort Gadsden in the panhandle of Florida to recapture runaway slaves the Seminoles harbored there. After a series of raids by American Major David Twiggs (1790–1862) and the Indians' counterraids, Andrew Jackson was sent into the area with 3,500 men to repeat what he had done in Alabama.

At this time, Florida was still controlled by Spain. But Jackson and American policymakers in Washington asserted the right to enter the territory, justifying their actions with the effort to commandeer runaway slaves and to control Seminoles who had allegedly been harassing settlers across the border in Georgia. The Spanish were not terribly offended by the act. Most of the encounters were between Jackson's force and Seminole victims. He slashed through Florida burning villages, crops, and seizing livestock. In April 1818, the general captured the Spanish garrison at Saint Marks, and another Red Sticks village. He then moved on to take Nero, a settlement on the Suwannee River named for a runaway mulatto leader by the same name who had set himself up as chief to several fugitive slaves.

More of Jackson's exploits led to international disputes with the Spanish and English. Differences of opinion in Washington made for a contentious and suspenseful period. As Jackson conquered the natives, others wondered if another American-European conflict would take place. But with Jackson's tenacity and proven American might, this campaign ended with the Seminoles defeated, at least temporarily, and with Florida becoming a state.

Jackson left military life and entered politics. After a few years serving as governor of the Florida Territory and in Congress, Jackson won the election as U.S. president in 1828. His policy toward the Indians as Commander in Chief paralleled those as field commander. The Creeks and Seminoles had been put down early in Jackson's career but had not completely succumbed to American rule. With the president's support, the Congress narrowly passed the Indian Removal Act in 1830, which relocated scores of Creek Indians to the area west of the Mississippi River.

John Coffee

John Coffee (1772–1836) served as an officer in the Tennessee Militia during General Andrew Jackson's campaign against the Creek Indians during the War of 1812. After an Indian attack on a southern Alabama fort, Jackson, Coffee, and thousands of American troops marched from Tennessee through Alabama, vanquishing the Creeks. Their primary adversary was the Red Sticks tribe, led by Red Eagle and Chief Menawa (c. 1765–c. 1836). Coffee achieved the rank of general and later fought Indians in southern Georgia and northern Florida.

Coffee was born in Prince Edward County, Virginia, in 1772, and was formally educated as a young man. He was also skilled in agriculture, which he learned from his father. After his father's death, Coffee sold the family property and purchased a valuable tract of land on the Cumberland River in Tennessee, near Nashville in 1804. There, he entered into various businesses, including running a dry goods store, a riverboat operation, and a racetrack. He became a close friend and business associate of Andrew Jackson. In fact, Coffee married Jackson's wife's niece. His mentor, business partner, and uncle by marriage, Jackson tore up several of Coffee's notes of debt as a wedding gift.

Coffee became an experienced surveyor and land speculator. He engaged in the development of the Mississippi Territory and northern Alabama. After the Indian treaties of 1805 and 1806, Coffee was called on to design the town of Twickenham, which later became Huntsville, Alabama.

As more white settlers moved into these southern lands, some Indian tribes reacted violently. Meanwhile, Anglo-American conflicts brought Britain and the United States into war. Coffee served in this two-front war from 1813 to 1815. After the Red Sticks slaughtered a few hundred white settlers at Fort Mims in Alabama, General Andrew Jackson was called on to put down the Indians, who were allying with the British. He relied on Coffe, his trusted friend, to accompany him and lead several missions ahead of Jackson's main column. They departed Fayetteville, Tennessee, in late 1813, and began attacks on unfriendly Creek Indians, especially those led by Red Eagle.

In one of his early missions, Coffee took nine hundred men from Fort Strother eastward into central Alabama to one of the Creek villages known as Tallushatchee. Early on November 3, 1813, Coffee surrounded and destroyed the Indian village. After the battle, his men counted 186 dead Indians, this from a village of about 284 inhabitants including women and children. "I lost five men, and forty-one wounded," General Coffee reported, "none mortally, the greater part slightly, a number with arrows ... this appears to form a very principal part of the enemy's arm for warfare, every man having a bow with a bundle of arrows, which is used after the first fire with the gun until a leisure time for loading offers." At a later encounter at Enotachopco Creek, further south on the Coosa River, Coffee repulsed the Indians after they tried to attack the encampment. He was successful, but suffered a wound himself.

Perhaps the most successful battle that Coffee contributed to was the attack on the Red Sticks stronghold of Horseshoe Bend on the Tallapoosa. In the early morning hours of March 27, 1814, Jackson sent Coffee and his cavalry ahead of his main column to the impressive Indian fort. Coffee arrived with his regulars and several Cherokee allies to guard against the Red Sticks' escape. Jackson also ordered Coffee to create a diversion so the enemy would not realize the principal attack. Coffee was simply to contain the fort and distract the warriors while Jackson smashed through the fort and destroyed them. After getting into position, Coffee ordered his men to commandeer the Indian canoes, ferrying these across the river to prevent escape by that means. Then his men set fire to huts outside the fort. This diverted them and signaled to Jackson that the moment for attack had come. His forces began the raid and won handily. Jackson relied on Coffee to report the details of the aftermath. "The slaughter was greater than all we had done before," he wrote, "We killed not less

Creek Chief Menawa. *MPI/Getty Images*

than eight hundred and fifty or nine hundred of them, and took about five hundred squaws and children prisoners."

Coffee marched on with Jackson to New Orleans and participated in the final battles of the War of 1812 against the British. He also campaigned against the Indians in southern Georgia and into Florida during the Seminole Wars. By the time his commander and friend had reached the White House, Coffee served as an Indian commissioner and was instrumental in the United States' relations with many Creek Indians, including the Chickasaw and Choctaw tribes. He died in Alabama in 1833.

Menawa

Chief Menawa (c. 1765–?) was a leader of the Creek Indians who occupied the southern United States. Menawa was a member of the Red Sticks tribe, a faction that split from other tribes within the Creeks to aggressively oppose American settlement onto the natives' lands. Menawa resisted the white domination of his area until he and the Red Sticks were forcibly put down and controlled by the federal government during the War of 1812 and into the 1830s.

Menawa was born around 1765 at the village of Oakfuskee on the Tallapoosa River in central Alabama. He was of mixed ancestry. His mother was also a Creek Indian, and his father was of Scots descent, a heritage not uncommon during Menawa's generation. He was originally known as "Crazy Trouble Hunter," and developed a reputation for living recklessly on the edge. Tales of his escapades, which included his marauding into southern Tennessee, earned him a place in local folklore among tribes in the northern Alabama area. He was hated and feared, yet respected by white settlers in the Cumberland River valley.

He settled to a degree and began to somewhat follow the white man's economically lucrative customs—raising cattle, farming, and trading with Indians. At one point he loaded a train with over fifty horses to sell far south of his home in Florida.

But as the conflict between the overcrowding white American settlers and the natives intensified into the early 1800s, Menawa sided with his Red Sticks tribe not only in custom, but also in war. By this point, he had become second chieftain in his tribe and assumed the name Menawa, meaning "The Great Warrior." General Andrew Jackson had led an aggressive campaign against the Creek Indians during the War of 1812. His troops and Menawa's tribe clashed at the Battle of Horseshoe Bend on March 27, 1814. The battle was a one-sided affair that proved a turning point in the United States' fight both against the British and the southern Indians. Over nine hundred Red Sticks were slaughtered at the Red Sticks fort at the bend of the Tallapoosa River. Menawa fought hard to defend the fortress and to stave off the American soldiers. He was wounded seven times. He lay on the ground until it was safe for him to crawl into a canoe. He then floated down the river to safety. Some Creek women who had also escaped the carnage pulled the wounded Menawa from the canoe and nursed him back to health. After months of healing, he returned to his Oakfuskee village only to find his home and settlement destroyed.

This sight only stirred Menawa to fight to defend his peoples' lands against the powerful American forces. When his adversary, William McIntosh, another Creek of Scots ancestry, signed a treaty to give additional lands to the United States, Menawa became furious. He led other Creek chiefs to hunt down and assassinate McIntosh.

The Great Warrior watched as the tide turned against his tribe and the entire Creek Nation, preventing his goals of protecting his lands and preserving the culture. He was involved in some negotiations in Washington, D.C., and even compromised to a degree to keep their southern lands. He lived long enough to be a victim of the forced removal of Indians under President Jackson's administration. On the eve of his departure from his Alabama home, he stayed up all night enjoying his home for the final time. The next day he reportedly said, "Last evening I saw the sun set for the last time and its light shine on the treetops and the land and the water, that I am never to look upon again." Menawa died during the relocation to western lands.

Black Hawk

Black Hawk (1767–1838) was a Sauk Indian who resisted white settlement in his homeland that is present-day Illinois. He is most known for leading a fight against the United States in 1832, a short-lived but bloody conflict that became known as the Black Hawk War. He certainly opposed white settlement into Midwest Indian lands throughout his life. As a young warrior, he was influenced by the ideas of Tecumseh and fought American soldiers trying to control natives.

Black Hawk was born in 1767 at the confluence of the Rock River and the Mississippi River near present-day Rock Island, Illinois. He earned the reputation as a brave warrior by the time he was a teenager. At fifteen he was given the status of brave, having wounded the enemy in battle. At nineteen, he assumed the sacred

George Catlin painted this portrait of Black Hawk in 1832, the year Black Hawk fought his ill-fated rebellion, culminating in the Indian Creek Massacre. *The Library of Congress*

duties of tribal medicine man, a role he inherited from his father.

By 1804, countless white settlers had moved westward into Indiana and Illinois, and the United States had purchased the vast Louisiana Territory. America's westward expansion became the bane of Black Hawk's existence. Indiana Governor William Henry Harrison had already compelled several bands of Indians to agree to peace terms, which typically included ceding lands for money and alcohol. Black Hawk began to agree with the Shawnee leader, Tecumseh, and others who refused to give in to the whites' demands. As the War of 1812 began, these Indian leaders joined with Britain to defeat their common enemy.

Harrison, the growing white population, and the U.S. military proved too strong for the Sauk and other resisting tribes. Defeats in the War of 1812 and the treaties that followed ended any real threats from Tecumseh and Black Hawk. Tecumseh was killed and Black Hawk's desires to maintain his lands became more and more difficult to attain. During the interim between Indian defeats during the War of 1812 and his Black Hawk Wars, the Sauk leader came to a degree of acceptance of the white man. One of Black Hawk's Indian rivals, Chief Keokuk (c. 1767–1848), convinced many Sauk people to negotiate with the United States. As the federal government treated with Keokuk, greater dissention came to the Sauk Nation. Keokuk ceded the Rock River country to the United States in exchange for an annuity and promises of lands west of the Mississippi River.

After a winter hunt in 1829, Black Hawk returned to his village only to find that white settlers had taken up residence in his Indian lodges. The two groups temporarily coexisted. But after his return on a hunt two years later, Black Hawk and his followers were not welcomed. The Illinois governor called out the state militia against the warrior and ran him off, forcing his tribe to cross the Mississippi River. Black Hawk said of the white occupants of his settlement, "They are now running their plows through our graveyard, turning up the bones and ashes of our sacred dead, whose spirits are calling on us from the land of dreams for vengeance."

Revenge is exactly what Black Hawk wanted. The very ideals he supported at the turn of the century remained deep in his heart in the 1830s. In 1832, he tried to rally support from other Indian tribes who had been abused or displaced. He consulted with the Winnebago, Kickapoo, and Potawatomi tribes in an attempt to fight for the return of their lands and to preserve their way of life. He had little success. These tribes had already been subdued and knew the odds were greatly against them. Black Hawk could only muster a force of about two thousand—a large force during his early days as a warrior, but rather small as these western lands filled with militiamen pressing to remove the Indians.

Black Hawk's force began to attack white settlements and family farms. In the battle known as Stillman's Run, Black Hawk defeated a militia unit that had earlier fired on and killed some of his men. In May 1832, his army attacked a farm at Indian Creek, killing fifteen, including women and children. These victories for Black Hawk resulted in widespread support for the cause against him from the frontier, the Illinois governor, and the U.S. military. General Henry Atkinson (1782–1842) had already begun to put Black Hawk down with his force of about two thousand militiamen. The Indian Creek massacre convinced President Andrew Jackson to send General Winfield Scott (1786–1866) from Chicago with eight hundred soldiers to assist the endeavor. With this reaction from the Americans, it became apparent to the vengeful warrior that he had no hope in defeating his enemy. By August, he surrendered.

After his surrender and capture, additional treaties confirmed the concession of lands to the United States. Black Hawk was taken to Washington, where he met President Jackson. The president scolded the warrior for the unnecessary and mindless slaughter in what Jackson saw as a futile effort to regain lands that had already been ceded. Black Hawk was imprisoned at Fortress Monroe in Virginia under the condition that he would be released once he persuaded his Sauk followers to lay down the hatchet. He eventually declared, "It is best to obey our Great Father [President Jackson] and say nothing contrary to his wishes." This marked the end of Black Hawk's resistance to the authority of the United States. After his release, he toured the eastern United States and was exposed to the more developed civilization that would eventually envelop his Sauk lands. Only after his unconditional surrender and his promise to live under the rule of his rival Keokuk did Black Hawk return to the Midwest a free man. He died in 1838.

✪ Major Battles

The Battle of Tippecanoe

The Battle of Tippecanoe took place on November 7, 1811. William Henry Harrison led the American forces against the Tecumseh-influenced Shawnee tribe in this indecisive, but notable encounter. By this time, the United States had begun settling land in the Northwest Territory, which heightened the tensions that existed between the Native Americans and whites. The Battle of Tippecanoe was an inevitable skirmish between these two sides that shed light on the two forces and led to the War of 1812.

Tecumseh Refuses to Yield   Harrison, a general and governor of the Indiana Territory, had already worked out the Treaty of Fort Wayne, where he summoned area chiefs to the Indiana town and exchanged $7,000, a complete store of liquor, and an annuity for three

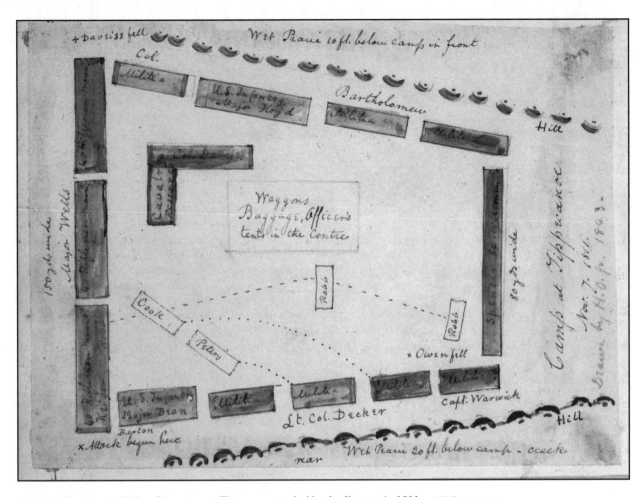

This map illustrates the U.S. military camp at Tippecanoe attacked by the Shawnee in 1811.   *MPI/Getty Images*

million acres of Indian lands. Tecumseh, not present for the deal, became enraged at how his contemporaries and those from neighboring tribes bowed to the American officers. He began a campaign to denounce the white man's liquor and culture in general. The Shawnee chief also took four hundred of his warriors in canoes to Governor Harrison's home at Vincennes. Around a council fire, Tecumseh made his case to the governor about how his people did not agree to the terms of Fort Wayne, among other grievances. The general replied that the agreement was between President James Madison and the vast majority of Indians throughout the region, who had consented to the treaty and had partially collected on the annuity. With emotions taking over, Tecumseh became hostile with Harrison and called him a liar. After an interpreter translated for Harrison, the general rejected the claim and drew his sword. The Shawnee leaders around the fire rose ready to fight. After a tense moment of the two leaders staring each other down, the council fire was put out and both sides went their separate ways.

The following day, Tecumseh sent Harrison a partial apology, but maintained that each side may have to fight it out. One rumor circulated that the chief put a reward of two thousand beaver skins on Harrison's head. Receiving only a half-hearted apology, and insisting that the land was now federal property, Harrison took steps to assert the United States's authority over the warriors who refused to yield.

Harrison Marches to Tippecanoe   There can be little doubt that Harrison, with strong support from Indiana's citizenry, took the offensive against the Shawnee people. Orders from President Madison and the War Department show no aggressive federal policy against Tecumseh's people. "I have been particularly instructed by the President," Secretary of War William Eustis (1753–1825) wrote Harrison, "that peace may, if possible, be preserved with the Indians." Communiqués from Washington, D.C., and the governor's role as commander-in-chief of the Indiana Territory, did, however, place a degree of discretion in Harrison's hands. He gathered one thousand men, regulars, and militiamen, and departed Vincennes on

September 26, 1811. Tecumseh had left his village, also known as Prophetstown, to rally other Indian tribes to unite against the Americans encroachment on their lands. Harrison marched toward the Shawnee settlement, near present-day Lafayette, Indiana, at the confluence of the Tippecanoe and Wabash rivers. While building Fort Harrison at Terre Haute, one of Harrison's soldiers was shot by an unknown gunman. This gave Harrison more justification to sustain an attack on the Shawnee. His soldiers' march resumed. Harrison, trying to bait the Indians, camped within a mile of Prophetstown. After Harrison refused Indian appeals for a conference, Tecumseh's brother, Tenskwatawa, a self-proclaimed mystic known simply as Prophet, drove into Harrison's camp before dawn.

The U.S. forces awoke to the attack and began to defend themselves. Prophet, left in charge while his brother tried to forge Indian alliances, promised his warriors that his medicine would strengthen the Shawnee and render Harrison's men helpless. Before the battle was over, over sixty Americans had been killed, and scores more wounded. The Indians lost only about thirty men, but were driven off. Harrison responded by razing the Indian village.

Considering the capabilities of these two forces and the result of the encounter, this battle was somewhere between a draw and a loss for Harrison. But the battle served as a propaganda victory for Harrison and the United States. News of Tippecanoe rallied white settlers further against the natives and brought attention to conquering them. It also gave more support to Americans willing to fight the British in what would become the War of 1812. The British, it was already suspected, were in an alliance with many Indian tribes. British firearms were found on the battleground in the aftermath, making the future enemy look partly responsible for the damage done to Harrison's army. Tecumseh soon allied himself officially with the British in the war and was later killed at the Battle of Thames. His brother, having failed his followers with false promises, fell into obscurity. Harrison earned quite a reputation from this battle in what became recorded as an effort to protect Americans from both hostile natives and the encroaching British enemy. He later departed his military career for a life in politics, and rode the legacy of the battle all the way to the White House. In 1840, "Tippecanoe and Tyler too" was the slogan for the successful presidential campaign of Harrison and his vice presidential running mate, John Tyler.

The Battle of Burnt Corn

The Battle of Burnt Corn occurred on July 27, 1813, in northwestern Florida, about eighty miles north of Pensacola. The Creek Indians generally fell into two camps, divided on how to relate to the white Americans who were moving into their territory. The Lower Creeks generally decided against any kind of war against the settlers, but twenty-nine of the thirty-four Upper Creek towns declared for war. The two factions became known respectively as the White Sticks and the Red Sticks. The latter painted their war clubs red, indicating that they wanted to spill Americans' blood. The Burnt Corn encounter pitted a disorganized frontier militia against members of the Red Sticks tribe lead by Peter McQueen (c. 1780–1820), a Creek chief of a Scottish father and Creek mother.

Americans had begun to settle the Mississippi Territory, and especially southern Alabama, near Mobile. The Spanish still controlled Florida. As the conflict between the warring Creek faction and the settlers began, the United States was on its way to declaring war against Britain. With a common enemy in the United States, the British and the Red Sticks ultimately joined forces. The Battle of Burnt Corn began the Creek War.

McQueen led a large group of his Red Stick warriors to Pensacola with four hundred dollars to procure ammunition and weaponry from Spanish Governor Manique to fight the Americans. On their trip, the Red Sticks ran off any of their own who did not take up a position of war against the United States. They also burned down the home of one American settler and kidnapped his wife, leaving her at Pensacola.

Colonel Joseph Carson, who commanded Fort Stoddert, north of Mobile, learned of McQueen's intentions and sent spies to see if the Spanish Governor complied. Manique provided the Red Sticks with three hundred pounds of powder and an appropriate amount of lead. On their return from Pensacola, McQueen's warriors held a war dance, signaling their formal declaration of war. Carson's spies returned to Fort Stoddert to report some of these details. Local settlers became alarmed and began fleeing from their homes to take refuge into area stockades. Colonel James Caller ordered out the militia to intercept the enemy Creeks on their return from Pensacola. Caller left to meet the Red Sticks on July 25, and picked up additional forces along the way. Dixon Bailey, a Creek who sided with the Americans, joined him. The total force numbered about 180, including whites and Indians.

Spending the night at a site not far from the Red Sticks' camp at Burnt Corn Creek, Caller and his officers were informed of the Indians' encampment. Caller's force caught the Indians totally off guard, as they were eating and relaxing. The ill-prepared militia dismounted their horses and took aim at the Indians. The Creeks temporarily stood their ground and fired back before they were forced into wild confusion, scrambling for safety. The battle has been characterized as a series of charges and retreats by both sides. After the majority of his force fled the battle, Caller made a second attempt with fewer than eighty men. The Americans proved to be

The Creek attack on Fort Mims resulted in the deaths of over 300 people. *Hulton Archive/Getty Images*

better marksmen, but the hectic nature of this battle left many wondering who really won.

The Battle of Burnt Corn was the first official engagement in the long and bloody Creek War. The Americans lost only two men and suffered fifteen wounded. About ten Creeks were killed, and approximately a dozen were wounded. The attacking force did commandeer most of the Indian packhorses and two hundred pounds of the gunpowder obtained at Pensacola, but politically, it probably did more harm to the American side. Few respected the disorganized manner in which the militia approached the battle and the fact that most who participated in the skirmish fled the scene and later dropped out of the service. Caller and other officers had lost their horses and therefore lost their way in the forest. When Caller resurfaced, he wore nothing more than his shirt and his underwear. In retrospect, many felt the tactic to meet the Indians was in haste. White residents in the area contemplated whether a diplomatic course had been taken with the war-declaring Creeks and if hostilities could have been avoided. And to avenge the battle, the Red Sticks fiercely attacked the Americans at Fort Mims, killing hundreds of soldiers, women, children, and slaves.

The Fort Mims Massacre

The massacre at Fort Mims took place on August 30, 1813, about thirty-five miles north of Mobile on the Alabama River in southwest Alabama. The Red Sticks made the attack, which resulted in the death of hundreds of soldiers and other innocent victims. The fort was merely an extension of Sam Sims's home. It housed more than five hundred people, including soldiers, blacks, refugees, women, and children. Some of those living in the fort came from the White Sticks tribe that had befriended the American settlers. Many Creek Indians, both friends and foes of the Americans, had intermarried and borne children with white settlers. The son of a Scottish trader and a native Creek, Chief William Weatherford, also known as Red Eagle, led the attack. He and his Red Stick followers sided with the British in the War of 1812. Tecumseh, Red Eagle's Shawnee counterpart, met with Red Eagle to encourage a great native confederacy. Both opposed the aggressive white settlement into Indian lands and sought to resist American expansion.

Red Eagle led the Red Sticks to the Fort Mims stockade. When the alarm came that Indians were approaching,

William McIntosh was a Creek chief whose forces fought with Andrew Jackson against the Red Stick Creeks in 1813 and 1814. *MPI/Getty Images*

roughly 573 whites quickly gathered for safety. Major Daniel Beasley commanded the militia of about 150. Beasley had disregarded warnings that the Indians were approaching. At noon on August 30, Red Eagle and about one thousand of his followers raced stealthily toward the fort. The gates were open. By the time those on watch sounded the alarm, many of the Red Sticks had made their way into the stockade. Once inside, they howled their war cries and began to slaughter those inside.

The massacre resulted in the deaths of over three hundred victims, who were quickly butchered. According to historian Albert J. Pickett, "The children were seized by the legs, and killed by batting their heads against the stockade. The women were scalped, and those who were pregnant were opened, while they were alive, and the embryo infants let out of the womb." The few American whites who made their way into the fort cabins were set afire. Red Eagle allegedly tried to stop these savage acts, but could not control his warriors, and eventually faced threats himself.

About thirty-six people were lucky enough to escape the carnage. Several of the fort's black tenants were taken as slaves for the Red Sticks. One young girl was placed in a canoe and floated downriver to safety. She reported the massacre, and the horrific details traveled throughout the area and to military leaders in Washington. The news shocked government leaders. A committee of public safety called on General Andrew Jackson to retaliate against the violent Creek faction. He soon began a march from his home state of Tennessee through Alabama to conquer the warring Creek Indians. After a series of battles throughout Alabama, Jackson eventually subdued the Creeks, with support from both Tennessee volunteers and federal troops. Red Eagle surrendered in April 1814, when he bravely walked into Jackson's fort. The mastermind of the Fort Mims massacre had come under the control of the United States.

The Battle of Horseshoe Bend

The Battle of Horseshoe Bend pitted American volunteers against the Red Sticks at a major bend in the Tallapoosa River in west-central Alabama. The battle took place on March 27, 1814. At the time, the United States was at war with Great Britain in the War of 1812. The Red Sticks tribe, led by William "Red Eagle" Weatherford, opposed the Americans and sided with the British. They had already massacred hundreds of people, including innocent women and children, at Fort Mims in southern Alabama. This prompted a response from both the U.S. War Department and from the Tennessee Militia. General Andrew Jackson was called to lead troops southward to conquer the Indians.

Avenging Fort Mims Jackson had traveled with his army from Tennessee since October 1813. He set up Fort Strother on the Coosa River on his way southward, a position from which several of his raids would take place. Jackson suffered some setbacks in the expedition. Many men wanted to return after their terms expired. But by early 1814, reinforcements of both regular militiamen and additional volunteers arrived, swelling Jackson's army to five thousand men. By January 21, Jackson camped at Emuckfaw Creek, three miles from the Red Stick fortification at Horseshoe Bend. Jackson, as he often did, sent spies out ahead of time to determine the Indians' intentions. His investigators returned to camp and reported that their whooping and dancing indicated that they knew of the white army's presence, and their attack was on the way. At dawn, the Red Sticks struck the Americans at Emuckfaw Creek. Ready for them, Jackson's fighters drove them back after about an hour of battle. After the Indian retreat, the general sent one of his officers, John Coffee, with four hundred men to attack their base at Horseshoe Bend.

The Red Stick fortification, however, was too strong for the detachment to do any real damage to it. Coffee returned to camp to report that a different strategy was necessary. In the meantime, the Red Sticks struck again, peppering the Americans with musket shot. Jackson's

Andrew Jackson accepting the surrender of Chief William Weatherford at the Battle of Horseshoe Bend in 1814.   *MPI/Getty Images*

men defended themselves once again, but the damage during these encounters encouraged Jackson to temporarily retreat back to Fort Strother. On his way, the Red Sticks followed and delivered more relentless attacks. Another skirmish occurred at Enotachopco Creek. The retreating volunteers did well to defend themselves—twenty Americans were killed compared to about two hundred Indians—but still backpedaled away from Horseshoe Bend. After the battle, Jackson received word that two thousand soldiers from East Tennessee would join him. On February 6, the Thirty-Ninth Regiment arrived at Fort Strother, giving Jackson enough men to take Red Eagle's strong fort.

The Seige   On March 14, Jackson began his move. Jackson left officers and 450 men behind to guard Fort Strother. He took a force of four thousand, including Cherokees and friendly Creek Indians, to attack the eight hundred or so Red Sticks at their headquarters at Horseshoe Bend. The bend was a 100-acre wooded peninsula almost completely surrounded by water, with a stout breastwork protecting it across its 350-yard neck. Earlier reports estimated that a thousand hostile Red Sticks occupied the fort, plus about three hundred

women and children. At 10 A.M. on March 27, Jackson began artillery fire on the structure. Cannonballs simply bounced off. He reported later to his superiors that the strength of the breastwork was "astonishing." For two hours, Jackson kept firing cannons harmlessly at the fortified walls, as Red Sticks fired muskets at the soldiers while they reloaded.

General Jackson sent John Coffee and a detachment to cut off the Red Sticks' options for retreat. With allied Cherokee scouts, Coffee stole the enemy canoes. He brought these back to the front line, and Jackson's foot soldiers used the canoes to ferry over to the fort. He also ordered his men to set fire to adjacent huts clustered at the turn of the bend. When he saw the smoke, and the diversion he needed, Jackson ordered his light infantry to charge the garrison. Running into flying bullets and arrows, Americans pushed the muzzles of their rifles through the portholes of the fort and began firing at very close range. Others began to leap the wall. The carnage had begun. Some Indians escaped, but most did not. By the time the battle ended, the Red Sticks' losses far outweighed those of Jackson's men. The general ordered a body count the following day. Some 557

Indians were found dead on the ground and about three hundred bodies were discovered in the river. Additional Red Sticks were discovered in the woods. About nine hundred enemy Indians were killed in the battle. Jackson's forces lost about forty-seven uniformed dead, and 159 were wounded. Of his Creek allies, twenty-three were killed and forty-seven were wounded.

Much to Jackson's dismay, Chief Red Eagle was not at the fort and therefore still remained to lead fighting forces against Americans. But this victory proved a turning point in the War of 1812. The Indian's threat as a British ally began to decline. The victory at Horseshoe Bend also furthered American interest in settling the South. Local white settlers became more confident that the so-called Indian menace would eventually subside, and these lands would be ceded to them. It also marked Jackson's rise in military stardom. He received a promotion to major general in the regular army.

✪ The Home Front

The Rise of Plantations in the South

The conflicts between Indians and white settlers in the American South were inevitable in the face of political and economic changes that occurred from the late 1700s through the period leading to the U.S. Civil War. The swath of land from the Mississippi River to Georgia had changed hands many times over the prior century. The Chickasaw, Choctaw, Cherokee, and Creek Indian tribes, among others, occupied this land before European contact. At different points, British, French, and Spanish claimed these lands. In 1763, France ceded the land to Great Britain after its victory in the French and Indian War. American colonists, however, were prevented from entering the area with the Royal Proclamation of 1763. Certainly some aggressive frontiersmen violated this parliamentary act, which was haphazardly enforced. But for the most part, Creek and other tribal Indians dominated the region west of the base of the Appalachians Mountains. After the American Revolutionary War, the victorious American colonists acquired the Mississippi Territory with the Treaty of Paris in 1783.

This unsettled area became attractive to land speculators and enterprising planters. Over the next twenty years, it would begin to populate as the United States issued land grants to Revolutionary War veterans, but more so as the demand for cotton began to rise. The

The expulsion of Native Americans from the Southeast made way for the establishment of stately homes for a new planter class, such as this one in Thomasville, Georgia. © *Kevin Fleming/Corbis*

plantation system had its roots in the colonies to the east and north, where tobacco and other lucrative crops were grown. At the turn of the nineteenth century, Eli Whitney's invention of the cotton gin caused tobacco to take a backseat to America's new primary cash crop. The textile industry in England was the destination for much southern cotton. Plantations emerged as American settlers entered the Deep South from Tennessee and Georgia, and from the Gulf of Mexico up the Mississippi River valley. With the fertile soil and navigable southern rivers, the wilderness frontier was eventually replaced by organized farms and plantation culture.

Slaves came with these planters. One provision in the U.S. Constitution prevented the international slave trade after 1808. Slave traders brought over 400,000 slaves into the interior of the United States prior to that year. Afterward, illegal international trading, domestic trading, and births of slaves on southern plantations increased the slave population. White inhabitants, too, began to fill the southern landscape. Federal roads allowed for migration into the region. By 1820, Tennessee, Louisiana, Mississippi, and Alabama had populated and entered the Union as states. The 1820 census reported that these states ranged in population; Mississippi had over 75,000 inhabitants and Tennessee had more than 422,000.

This growth of white population threatened Native Americans, while the economic bounty from the plantation system caused Southerners to press even harder for rights to operate these lands. Violent encounters between pioneers of the South and southern Indian tribes were not uncommon. As greater numbers of settlers encroached on these Indian lands, tensions between Americans and the natives grew. Having had some amicable relations with the European powers in the decades and generations prior, the southern natives began to ally with the British and Spanish, viewing these nations as less aggressive in desire for their lands. Skirmishes between white American settlers and Indians in southern Alabama and northern Florida brought the conflict to a head. The militia attacked Indians at the Battle of Burnt Corn near Pensacola, and the Red Sticks tribe of the Creek Indians retaliated by slaughtering American soldiers, women, and children at Fort Mims, north of Mobile. This essentially solidified the Red Sticks' anti-American position and alliance with the British in the ensuing War of 1812.

What followed was General Andrew Jackson's march through Alabama to put down the Creeks and defeat the British at New Orleans. This removed many of the Indians to lands further west and opened the door for more plantation settlement of the region. Conflicts between Southerners and Indians, however, did not cease with these defeats. Many Cherokee, Creeks, and others refused to bow to the planters and the whites populating the region. As late as 1830, the Congress addressed the issue. What resulted was a sectional debate that paralleled the debate around slavery. The southern bloc, having witnessed atrocities between whites and Indians and insistent on protecting their plantation livelihood, argued for swift removal of the Indians. Northerners, influenced by the same religious and moral ideals that sparked the abolition movement, felt that Southerners should respect the natives, who occupied the land first. With the support of then-President Andrew Jackson, the Southerners won, and the federal government began forcing the Indians away from the plantations in what became known as the Trail of Tears. The plantation economy that dominated the region throughout the Civil War had superceded and pushed out the Indian culture from the Deep South.

✪ International Context

Spanish Presence in the Americas

As Europeans discovered and explored the Western Hemisphere in the sixteenth century, Spain dominated. Under the Spanish flag, Christopher Columbus, Ponce de León (c. 1460–1521), Hernán Cortés (c. 1485–1547), and Hernando de Soto voyaged into the Americas, claiming lands in the name of Spain, God, and gold. Columbus arrived first in 1492, planning to reach the East Indies and believing that he had. In reality, he landed on a Caribbean island and erroneously named the natives "Indians," assuming he had landed on or near the country of India. Columbus made three more voyages from Spain to the New World, reaching the mainland of South America. The conquistadors that followed Columbus discovered additional parts of the Americas. Landing on Easter Sunday in 1513, de Leon dubbed the newfound territory La Florida for the beautiful and unique flora that he discovered on the peninsula. A dozen additional voyages from Spain to the New World resulted in Spanish dominance of much of North and South America. Cortez began his conquest of Mexico in 1519 and established Spain as a ruler of much of Mexico and the American Southwest. Hernando de Soto explored the west coast of Florida and the coast along the Gulf of Mexico from the late 1530s to the early 1540s. He also made his way to the interior with impressive expeditions, encountering natives several miles inland. His discoveries and exploits carried him from southern Georgia westward into Texas and Oklahoma.

One hundred years after Columbus's initial voyage, Spain claimed thousands of square miles of American land. The conquistadors who conquered these lands, and the hidalgo, or noblemen, who ruled locally, often did so brutally. Though the Spanish Crown had strictly instructed to use diplomacy before force, explorers and their armies did not follow those directives. Columbus and the others earned a reputation for brutality with the natives, and often with their own subordinates. Their

Americans, such as the ones shown here at a trader's camp on the Santa Fe Trail, put pressure on the Spanish and Mexican governments by moving into Texas and New Mexico by the tens of thousands. *MPI/Getty Images*

ships carried women, slaves, friars, and priests, but these missions were decidedly military in nature. Soldiers also departed these ships with lances, crossbows, and later, muskets. Large vicious dogs of war sometimes accompanied the columns of Spanish warriors to fight off any unfriendly Indians. Native villages were plundered, women raped, and people taken into slavery. One tactic was to lure the tribal chief into the Spanish council and hold him hostage until their demands were met. Such an approach caused these explorers to be embroiled in battles with the natives. Columbus faced an immediate revolt in his camp known as Villa de la Navidad (town of the Nativity). De Soto's clash with Choctaws in the battle at Mabila was likely the deadliest encounter of the period.

Spain's exploration of the southwestern United States continued as Francisco Vásquez de Coronado (c. 1510–1554) searched the region for cities of gold. All told, Spain claimed most of the southern and western United States, Mexico, and many lands south of the equator before England or France could realistically compete with the Spanish. However, during the seventeenth century, these other European powers did compete with Spain. The French entered the continent through the Saint Lawrence River in the northeast to the Great Lakes and eventually down the Mississippi River. The English began to settle the Atlantic coast. Over the next century, a series of imperial wars between

these nations and peace treaties resulted in a frequently changing map of North America. In 1800, Spain still controlled Florida and the landmass from California to Texas, and extending south into Mexico. France held the Louisiana Territory that stretched from the Gulf of Mexico to modern-day Washington State and Oregon. During the American Revolution, the English lost the area from the Mississippi River to the Atlantic Ocean, and south of the Great Lakes, to the American colonists.

The French sold the Louisiana Territory to the United States in 1803, which brought border disputes between the United States and Spain. The American government contended that the purchase included lands southwest to the Rio Grande and into parts of Florida. Spain disagreed, holding fast to Texas and Florida. This caused great tension between the two nations, but Spain faced a greater dilemma in the Peninsular War. France attacked Spain, causing King Ferdinand VII (1784–1833) to abdicate and hand the Spanish throne over to Joseph Bonaparte (1768–1844), Napoleon's brother. The Spanish people, however, refused to accept him. The fallen state was not strong enough to defeat the experienced and well-financed French. The British, however, came to Spain's rescue to once again fight their long-time French enemy. These battles on the Iberian Peninsula weakened Spain in world politics and caused the United States to cease relations with the country until a more stable government was in place. With the

English assistance, that time finally came. By 1819, the Adams-Onís Treaty, named for Secretary of State John Quincy Adams (1767–1848) and Spanish Foreign Minister Luis de Onís (1769–1830), gave Florida to the United States and defined the borders of Louisiana Territory along the Sabine, Red, and Arkansas rivers to Spain's liking.

Meanwhile, revolutionaries in Mexico had already shown interest in ousting their mother country. By 1821, they succeeded and eventually set up a republic. An influx of Americans into Mexican-controlled Texas followed. Mexico initially accepted these contractors and planters, but later deemed them unwanted. The Mexican government did not want Protestantism or slavery to enter its lands. But the Americans kept coming. By 1835, about 28,000 Americans lived in Texas, far more than the Mexican population there. Tensions increased that led to Texas's fight for independence, which it earned in 1836. It operated as an independent republic until the United States annexed the state in 1845.

Spain had certainly dominated vast amounts of lands in North America since its early conquests. The Spanish invaders dominated the Indians of Florida, the southeastern woodlands, and the lands from Louisiana to California and south into Mexico. The Spanish culture can be seen throughout this region today. But by the early to mid-1800s, Spain had lost much of the control it once had on the New World.

✪ Aftermath

Indian Removal Act

The Indian Removal Act passed the U.S. Congress on May 28, 1830. The primary idea behind the law had been discussed since Thomas Jefferson's administration offered a similar bill in 1803: to remove Native Americans from their original lands east of the Mississippi River and relocate them in the U.S. territories to the west. The plan was reintroduced in 1825 after a series of problems that resulted from encounters between the tribal Indians of the southern states and the federal government. President Andrew Jackson, who had conducted military campaigns against the Creek Indians and other tribes, supported the law. He first called for it in his initial message to Congress. He felt the Native Americans constituted a distinct threat to American interests, and he honestly felt that removing them from within the white settlements in the South was in the Indians' best interest, believing that they could not live surrounded by a sovereign white nation.

The legislation recommended the area west of the Mississippi River to be divided into enough districts to accept as many tribes that would be relocated to this area. The bill also offered an exchange of Indian lands from the South for those in the Midwest. In both the House of Representatives and in the Senate, this proposal sparked a heated debate. Senator Theodore Frelinghuysen of New Jersey, a deeply religious man, claimed the Indians had the right to refuse the taking of their lands. "We have crowded the tribes upon a few miserable acres of our Southern frontier ... and still, like the horse-leech, our insatiate cupidity cries, give! Give! Give!" Members from the southern states, who felt more threatened by the Native Americans, spoke in favor of the bill. The Senate voted for the law by a vote of twenty-eight to sixteen on April 26.

In the House, the debate was even more contentious. Religious leaders and organizations back home in the congressmens' districts had expressed their opposition to the bill, and several House members worried about how voting for the measure would affect their next election. Some of these lawmakers leveled accusations at President Jackson for defying the Constitution. Others claimed that Jackson exercised a paternalistic approach toward the natives, believing, as Georgia Congressman Wilson Lumpkin said, "No man entertains kinder feelings toward the Indians than Andrew Jackson." The bill barely passed the House by a vote of 102 to 97.

Jackson and his administration negotiated the treaties that removed the so-called Five Civilized Tribes. Many of the relocated Indians were moved to what was commonly called Indian Territory, in present-day Oklahoma. The relocation journey, harsh and unexpected, became known as the Trail of Tears. Thirteen tribes made the one-way trip. Some resisted. Federal troops had to remove some Cherokees. As late as 1838, General Winfield Scott was assigned this duty. He and seven thousand U.S. troops rounded up the remaining Cherokees and forced them to the new Indian Territory. The Seminoles of Florida fought the United States in the Second Seminole War (1835–1842) before the act was completely carried out.

BIBLIOGRAPHY

Books

Adams, Henry. *History of the United States of America During the Administrations of James Madison.* New York: Library of America, 1986.

Calloway, Colin G. *New Worlds for All: Indians, Europeans, and the Remaking of Early America.* Baltimore: Johns Hopkins University Press, 1997.

Dillon, Richard H. *North American Indian Wars.* New York: Facts on File, 1983.

Green, Michael D. "Alexander McGillivray." *American Indian Leaders: Studies in Diversity.* Lincoln, NE: University of Nebraska Press, 1980.

Griffith, Benjamin W., Jr. *McIntosh and Weatherford, Creek Indian Leaders.* Tuscaloosa: University of Alabama Press, 1988.

Halbert, H. S., and T. H. Ball. *The Creek War of 1813 and 1814.* Tuscaloosa: University of Alabama Press, 1969.

Hoxie, Frederick E. *Encyclopedia of North American Indians.* Boston: Houghton Mifflin, 1996.

Keenan, Jerry. *Encyclopedia of American Indian Wars.* Santa Barbara: ABC-CLIO, 1997.

Nies, Judith. *Native American History.* New York: Ballantine Books, 1996.

Painter, Sue Ann. *William Henry Harrison: Father of the West.* Cincinnati: Jarndyce and Jarndyce, 2004.

Pickett, Albert J. *History of Alabama, and Incidentally of Georgia and Mississippi, from the Earliest Period.* Charleston, SC: Walker and James, 1851.

Remini, Robert V. *The Life of Andrew Jackson.* New York: Harper and Row, 1988.

———. *Andrew Jackson and His Indian Wars.* New York: Viking, 2001.

Web Sites

Calvert, J. B. "William Henry Harrison and the West." University of Denver, 2001. <www.du.edu/ ~jcalvert/hist/harrison.htm>

Fowler, Mariam R. "Menawa: A Chief of the Upper Creeks." Shelby County Museum, Columbiana, AL. <www.rootsweb.com/~alshelby/ Menawa.html>

Introduction to the War of 1812 (1812–1815)

The War of 1812 may be the most paradoxical war the United States ever fought. It was a war neither the United States nor Great Britain really wanted. A major cause for war—the British Orders-In Council—was vacated two days before Congress voted to declare war. The war's most decisive battle—at New Orleans—was fought after the peace treaty, the Treaty of Ghent, had been signed. In that treaty, both sides agreed to return to the status quo that existed prior to the war.

The war had its origins in the long series of European wars ignited by the French Revolution. By 1812, the French revolutionary republic had been replaced by a French empire, but the fighting continued, growing into a world war. Economic warfare accompanied military action, disrupting American trade. American sailors were forced into the British Royal Navy. The United States suspected Britain of inciting Indian nations within the United States. War sputtered to a start over these issues, fed by an American desire to grab Canada from Britain.

Britain's initial reaction was to ignore the war and hope it went away. The Orders-in-Council, to which the United States objected, had been vacated. Britain hoped that when this news reached the United States, peace would result. Instead, the United States invaded Canada.

The American invasion was bungled. Britain repulsed American advances and then chased the United States out of what later became Michigan. American land defeats were balanced by a small string of American naval victories in 1812, which stung British pride and encouraged America to continue the war.

In 1813, a series of British victories led the United States to return to diplomacy and seriously negotiate peace terms. By this time, British attitudes had hardened, and Britain sought terms that would make it impossible for the United States to threaten Britain again. These involved territorial concessions the United States was unwilling to make.

The war continued into 1814. The United States regained its previously lost territories and again threatened Canada. Britain countered with a series of raids along the American eastern coastline. Both nations could make the other miserable. Neither could achieve a decisive, war-ending result at a price it was willing to pay. The Napoleonic Wars in Europe ended in the summer of 1814, rendering issues over free trade and sailors' rights moot. The military capabilities of Indian nations within the United States had been decisively destroyed. British support had become a non-issue.

The United States and Britain were war-weary. A peace treaty was negotiated in Ghent, Belgium, which settled all territorial claims on the basis of the status quo prior to 1812. Trade issues and impressment were simply ignored, in the hope that peace would continue.

The War of 1812 sealed the national identities of both Canada and the United States. Both sides won sufficient victories to make them happy and provide fodder for historical legend. Over the following century, Britain and the United States ceased to be adversaries, becoming instead firm allies.

The War of 1812 (1812–1815)

✪ Causes

Impressment

A major cause of the War of 1812 was British impressment of American sailors. Impressment—a form of naval conscription—generated more controversy and greater outrage than any other aspect of naval life in the eighteenth and nineteenth centuries.

During peacetime, the Royal Navy, along with most national navies, relied on volunteers to man its ships. In 1792, the last year of European peace before the wars stemming from the French Revolutionary Wars, only 20,000 sailors were required. When Great Britain joined the wars against France in 1793, the number of sailors needed jumped dramatically. By the end of 1794, the Royal Navy needed 73,000 sailors, and in 1813, after twenty years of warfare, the Royal Navy had swelled to 109,000 seamen. To meet this manpower need, the Royal Navy used impressment—involuntary recruitment into the Royal Navy.

There were strict rules over who was subject to impressment and who was not. The object was to find men capable of sailing a ship. Seamanship was a skilled trade, and while a warship could use some unskilled landsmen, the real need was for those that knew which lines to pull (handle), knew how to work with sails (reefing), and knew how to stand a watch at a tiller or wheel (steer).

Only mariners subject to the British crown could be pressed into service. Foreigners—including Americans—were exempt. Some maritime activities—fishermen or watermen (those who handled small boats in harbors and rivers)—were also exempt, as were the officers and petty officers of merchant vessels. Any other British sailor could be seized and forced to serve on a Royal Navy ship for the duration of the time the ship remained in commission.

While impressment sounds harsh, it differed little from military conscription used by the United States during the Civil War and in the twentieth century. It worked well for most of the eighteenth century, when few naval wars lasted more than four years. Conditions aboard a British warship, while difficult by modern standards, were actually easier than those on the average merchant vessel of the same period.

Impressment was ill adapted to a long war, however. By 1808, Britain had been at war with France for more than a decade. The pool of available sailors was drained, and the war seemed to have no end. Service in the Royal Navy appeared to be a life sentence, discouraging volunteers.

Royal Navy captains became increasingly desperate to find men. Sometimes they illegally pressed landsmen. Other captains gave in to the temptation to impress American sailors. Often, those Americans had been born in Britain and immigrated to the United States. In the eyes of the Royal Navy, such sailors were still British and subject to impressment.

Some British officers made honest mistakes. It was difficult to differentiate between the accents of someone born in New England—part of the United States—from someone born in Nova Scotia—part of Canada. On other occasions, Royal Navy officers simply did not care. They needed men. In their view, the United States was being protected from Napoleon's ambition by the British fleet. The tariff of a few sailors was a small price for that protection and the money the United States made as a neutral carrier.

Quite reasonably, the United States did not see things the same way. American citizens had no obligation to serve in the Royal Navy, even if those American citizens had been born British. In 1812, all Americans over the age of thirty-one had been born British citizens. Failure to protect the rights of its citizens could lead to a loss of American sovereignty, something about which the young republic was highly sensitive.

Neither side would yield. The British were willing to return native-born Americans, but needed men too badly to concede immunity to Britons claiming to be American, even those that had legitimately moved to the

This engraving shows American seamen being impressed into the chronically short-handed British Navy.   © *Bettmann/Corbis*

United States. Taken with incidents where overzealous Royal Navy captains pursued deserters onto American soil, or on one occasion onto an American Navy warship, and there was a complaint worth fighting over.

As with much associated with the War of 1812, the impressment issue was not resolved by the war or the peace treaty. Britain was at peace with every nation except the United States by 1815. It would not again need conscription until World War I began in 1914. Yet it never forswore either impressment—or the right to conscript British sailors who became American citizens.

Trade Restrictions

A major cause of the War of 1812 was trade restrictions. While the plight of impressed sailors struck an emotional chord, it affected few. British alliances with the Native Americans only affected those on the frontier, another minority. Few in the United States would profit from adding Canada to the country. However, trade affected the lives of all Americans. When trade flowed freely, the whole of the United States prospered. When trade was restricted, the entire country suffered.

By 1812, Europe had been at war for almost two decades. The two main antagonists, Great Britain and

France, could not defeat the other through force of arms. The war had stalemated in the late 1790s. The French military was too weak to defeat the British Royal Navy at sea and reach England. The British Army was too small to overcome the French Grande Armée. Each side turned increasingly towards trade restrictions, hoping to weaken its foe by ruining the enemy's economy.

In the early nineteenth century, there were conflicting views about what type of trade was allowed. Everyone agreed that a nation at war had the right to stop and capture ships that belonged to nations with which it was fighting. Beyond that was confusion about the rights of ships of neutral nations.

The United States held to a theory originated by the Dutch, that free ships meant free goods. In other words, a neutral ship could carry any cargo to any port. Nations with small navies and large merchant fleets liked this doctrine because it allowed them to carry goods into blockaded ports.

The major European nations rejected this doctrine, as would the United States once it developed a powerful navy. They held that belligerent nations had the right to blockade enemy ports and to seize neutral ships carrying military cargoes to enemy countries.

AN IMPRESSED SEAMAN'S STORY

James R. Durand was born in Connecticut in 1786. He took to a life at sea, serving on numerous merchant vessels and three American warships. He was serving as mate aboard a British merchant ship when caught by a press gang in Plymouth harbor, in England.

As an American and a ship's officer, he should have been doubly exempt from impressment, but neither status protected him. The frigate *Narcissus* badly needed men, and his claim of being an American was ignored since he was on a British ship. In his memoirs, Durand gives a vivid account of being impressed:

About 11 o'clock at night, there came along side a boat belonging to the *Narcissus* frigate. They boarded our brig and came below where I was asleep. With much abuse, they hauled me out of my bed, not suffering me to put on or take anything except my trowsers.

In this miserable condition I was taken on board their ship but did not think to be detained there for seven years.

Trade Legislation The British carried this one step further with the Rule of 1756—which was first used in a war started that year. It stated that trade closed to a nation in time of peace could not be opened during wartime. If France did not let the United States carry sugar from Guadeloupe to Bordeaux during peacetime, the British could seize American ships doing that when Britain and France were at war.

While the United States officially held to its free ships–free goods position, it recognized these accepted European rules of blockade, including the Rule of 1756. The United States was unwilling to fight for unlimited access to belligerent ports. Then the French and British changed the rules.

In November 1806, French Emperor Napoleon Bonaparte (1769–1821) issued the Berlin Decree. It stated that no ship could sail directly to French-controlled portions of Europe directly from England or an English colony. If it did, it would be seized in port. This, and the subsequent Milan Decree, further restricted neutral trade with Britain and formed the heart of what Napoleon called the Continental System.

The British retaliated. It issued the First Order-in-Council in January 1807, which forbade neutral ships from trading between enemy ports—even if the cargo carried were allowed during peacetime. At the time, the United States was the only neutral country with a significant merchant fleet.

Then, in November 1807, the Second Order-in-Council required neutral shipping cargoes to the European continent to stop in Britain first. Ship owners were thus forced to abide by either the Second Order-in-Council or the Berlin Decree; it was impossible to comply with one without violating the other.

The United States countered these actions with the Embargo Act in 1807. It closed United States ports to international commerce. It threw the United States into a deep recession, because much of the economy was based on foreign trade. It failed to coerce either Britain or France to change its policies. The Embargo Act served the purposes of the Orders-in-Council and the Continental System better than Britain or France could. Realizing this, the Embargo Act was repealed in 1808.

In 1809, Britain again modified its trade policies. It issued a Third Order-in-Council, imposing a strict blockade on French-controlled Europe. This actually had an adverse affect on the British economy, because it blocked British shippers from trading with European nations that were allied with France but were not fighting Britain.

The United States retaliated with the Non-Intercourse Act of 1809. It banned trade with Britain and France while they blocked United States shipping. It was as ineffective at modifying British and French policy as the Embargo Act.

It had less effect on the United States economy than the Embargo Act, however, because it was easy to evade. Merchants simply claimed to be sailing for a destination not barred by the Act. They then went to a British (or French) port due to some purported emergency that forced them to anchor. While there, they sold their cargo, claiming their host would not allow them to leave with it.

Because it was ineffective, the U.S. Congress modified the law in 1811 by passing the Non-Importation Act. It forbade imports from countries that blockaded United States ships. It, too, failed to modify British trade policy.

War Erupts Congress resorted to the only action that could affect British behavior: threatening war. By early 1812, Britain's resources were stretched to the limit by the war with France. It wanted to avoid a North American distraction. The Orders-in-Council were as unpopular in Britain as the Embargo and Non-Intercourse Acts had been in the United States. The reason was the same—it hurt the country initiating the rule more than its intended victim.

In 1812, Britain offered a compromise. It offered to issue American ships licenses to trade with Europe. The United States rejected that offer, feeling it was too difficult to control. At that point, the British government gave in. Rather than go to war, on June 16, 1812, it anounced that it would repeal the Orders-in-Council if the United States repealed the Non-Importation Act. Since the Non-

This 1811 cartoon celebrates the embargo on foreign trade passed in response to French and British trade restrictions. *The Granger Collection, New York. Reproduced by Permission*

Importation Act was aimed at removing the Orders-in-Council, the offer should have been acceptable.

American patience had run out. On June 18, 1812,—after the British lifted the Orders-in-Council, but weeks before Congress would hear about it—President James Madison (1751–1836) signed into law a declaration of war against Britain. War, once started, was not easy to stop.

British Alliance with Native Americans

One reason cited by the U.S. Congress for going to war with Britain in 1812 was that the British government was "exciting the Indians to hostilities against the United States." In reality, prior to the war, the British government had been trying to restrain its Native American allies from attacking the United States. However, it was hard to convince an American settler in the western territories of that. The period immediately prior to the War of 1812 was marked by Native Americans on the frontier resisting westward expansion of American set-

tlers by force of arms. Many of the arms they used were supplied by British traders.

The British cultivated ties with the Native American nations on the western frontier for economic and strategic reasons. The Native Americans were valued as trading partners. A large part of Canada's economy was then based on furs. Native Americans on both sides of the border trapped animals and sold pelts to British agents.

The Native Americans bought needed or desired goods from the British that they could not manufacture. The Native Americans of the Old Northwest (in present-day Ohio), lacking the capability to smelt metals, had grown dependent on trade for iron cookware, steel knives, hatchets, animal traps, and the firearms that they needed. Britain made a good profit from both the furs exported to Europe and the goods they sold to their Native American allies.

The British also viewed the Native Americans as a bulwark that would help shield Canada from the United States. Many of these tribes had fought alongside Great

DEFENSE

FORT DEARBORN STOOD ALMOST ON THIS SPOT.
AFTER AN HEROIC DEFENSE IN EIGHTEEN
HUNDRED AND TWELVE, THE GARRISON TOGETHER
WITH WOMEN AND CHILDREN WAS FORCED TO EVACUATE
THE FORT LED FORTH BY CAPTAIN WELLS, THEY
WERE BRUTALLY MASSACRED BY THE INDIANS
THEY WILL BE CHERISHED AS MARTYRS IN
OUR EARLY HISTORY

ERECTED BY THE TRUSTEES OF THE
B. F. FERGUSON MONUMENT FUND
1928

This monument at the site of Fort Dearborn commemorates those who were massacred by Pottawatomie Indians allied with the British during the War of 1812. © *Lowell Georgia/Corbis*

Britain in the American Revolution. They had provided Britain with a militarily useful auxiliary force.

Britain was not seeking a war with the United States in the first decade of the nineteenth century. British military resources were committed to the war against France that Britain was then fighting. Britain did not want the expanded military commitment a war with the United States would entail. That included getting dragged into a war by their Native American allies.

Britain did not—and could not—control its allies. Tribes often had their own agendas, especially the militant tribes that were determined to stop settler encroachment on their lands. Frequently, lawless Americans would rob or otherwise injure Indian tribes allied with Britain. The tribe would retaliate—drawing a response from the United States, which then triggered a cycle of increasing violence.

Often, British citizens would be involved in these retaliatory actions. Many traders and agents acting for the British had married Native Americans. Family ties often caused them to go further in their support for the tribe than British policy permitted. U.S. citizens that suffered from Indian raids interpreted this unofficial support as representing British government policy.

Once war was declared, Britain used its Native American allies widely and sought out new allies as well. Native American forces assisted the British in capturing the frontier forts of the United States. For example, Fort Mackinaw, which guarded the straits connecting Lake Huron and Lake Michigan, was captured by forces that were almost exclusively Native American.

Britain sought the assistance of Native Americans in the southwestern United States as the war progressed but met with mixed success. Of the five major tribes in the gulf states, the Choctaw and Chickasaw actively supported the United States. The Choctaw sent a group to help defend New Orleans in 1814. The Cherokee remained friendly with the United States, but offered limited military assistance.

The Creeks split. One faction favored the United States, while another fought an independent war against the United States. The Creek War ended decisively in favor of the United States before the British began serious recruiting of Indian allies in 1814. Many surviving Red Stick Creeks, from southern Alabama, and Seminoles, a closely related tribe from northern Florida, allied with the British.

✪ Major Figures

James Madison

James Madison (1750-1836) was the fourth president of the United States. To Federalists, the War of 1812 was "Mr. Madison's War." However, it would be more accurate to describe Madison as the man who happened to be president when the war was fought than as the man who shaped the War of 1812.

Early Career Madison's presidency was an undistinguished capstone to what had hitherto been an illustrious career. Madison was born on March 16, 1751, in Port Conway, Virginia. He was a contemporary of, and neighbor to, Thomas Jefferson and James Monroe. Educated at the College of New Jersey at Princeton, he considered entering the ministry, but chose instead to return to Virginia, where he became involved in politics. He served in both the Continental Congress and in the Virginia Assembly during the American Revolution and was an active supporter of the Revolution.

A Founding Father The apogee of his career came during the Constitutional Convention of 1787 and its immediate aftermath. He took a leading role in the framing of the Constitution and is often refered to as its "father." He was one of the main advocates of a strong central government and helped develop the system of checks and balances written into the Constitution.

After the Constitution was drafted, he was one of the leading figures in the successful struggle to ratify the document. Along with John Jay (1745–1829) and Alexander Hamilton (1755 or 1757–1804), he wrote the *Federalist Papers*, a series of eighty-five essays that still form a cornerstone of constitutional law. Additionally, Madison drafted the Bill of Rights—the first ten amendments to the Constitution. It is a testament to Madison's ability as a lawmaker that the Constitution has endured in one of the oldest continuous governments in the world.

Following the Constitution's ratification, Madison served in Congress until 1798. Along with Thomas Jefferson, he helped found the Republican-Democratic Party (today's Democratic Party, but often called the Republicans during the War of 1812). A Francophile (and Anglophobe), Madison opposed the Jay Treaty, ratified in 1795, which provided closure to the American Revolution. Madison feared it would bring the United States too close to its mother country.

Madison returned to national politics in 1800, when he became President Thomas Jefferson's (1743–1826) secretary of state. Madison was instrumental in securing the Louisiana Purchase in 1803 and in suppressing the Barbary Pirates from 1803 through 1805. However, Madison also supported the pro-French, anti-British foreign policy of the Jefferson Administration that led to the Embargo Act of 1807.

THE FORGOTTEN CLAUSE

The British remembered their Native American allies in the Treaty of Ghent, which ended the War of 1812. Article 9 of the Treaty of Ghent stated, in part:

> The United States of America engage to put an end immediately after the Ratification of the present Treaty to hostilities with all the Tribes or Nations of Indians with whom they may be at war at the time of such Ratification, and forthwith to restore to such Tribes or Nations respectively all the possessions, rights, and privileges which they may have enjoyed or been entitled to in one thousand eight hundred and eleven previous to such hostilities.

For many tribes, this clause proved hollow. They often did not have the possessions, rights, and privileges they enjoyed previous to the war restored. Britain did nothing to help them. The United States posed less of a military threat to Canada, and the fur trade was diminishing in value. As the military and economic value of the native peoples faded in importance to Britain, the value of the United States's goodwill increased. As typical in diplomacy, interests proved more important than friendship.

Presidency James Madison took the then-conventional route to the White House, being elected to the presidency in 1808 after serving as secretary of state. He inherited the presidency at a time of turmoil. The country was in a depression due to the effects of the Embargo Act. The act had been repealed prior to Madison's taking the oath of office, but Madison continued the Anglophobic policies of the Jefferson Administration. This hastened the slide to war.

When the British issued the retaliatory Third Orders-in-Council in 1809, which restricted the United States's ability to freely trade with Europe, Madison supported passage of the Non-Intercourse Act that same year, followed by a less restrictive non-importation act in 1811. Neither act damaged Britain financially, although both hurt American commerce. Madison also allowed the charter for the national bank to lapse in 1811. Both weakened the American economy in the years immediately preceding the war, undermining the government's ability to prepare for war.

Additionally, he failed to delay momentum toward war until the United States was prepared militarily for a conflict. He instead allowed the ambitions of congressional "War Hawks" to dictate the pace of events.

Madison's leadership during the war was as uninspired as his performance prior to the war. He pinned success on Canada succumbing to American military might before Britain could move reinforcements to that province. Considering the performance of Continental

DOLLEY MADISON

Dorothy (Dolley) Payne Todd Madison (1768–1849) married then-Representative James Madison in September 1794. Dolley would be the love of Madison's life. She was also a political partner that would not be repeated on a national scale for another hundred years, when Franklin and Eleanor Roosevelt took America's political stage.

Dolley Payne, born into a Quaker family in 1768, married John Todd of Philadelphia in 1790. He died of yellow fever less than three years later, leaving Dolley a widow with a small son. Dolley met James Madison in 1794, and they married that year.

After their marriage, both blossomed. Dolley became a fashionable society hostess. James Madison, a reticent, private man before marriage, became more outgoing. When James Madison became secretary of state for Thomas Jefferson, a widower, Dolley made the Madison home the capital's social center. It was a role she continued after becoming First Lady. Dolley was also one of James Madison's closest and shrewdest political advisors. Her gracious tact was one of Madison's diplomatic assets during his presidency.

During the War of 1812, Dolley performed two important services for her country. She nursed James Madison back to health after a serious illness in 1813. She also oversaw the evacuation of the White House in 1814, taking a portrait of George Washington attributed to Gilbert Stuart. It would otherwise have been burnt along with the White House after the British occupation.

Dolley Madison died in 1849, thirteen years after her husband.

militias during the Revolution, and the dependence upon similar militias for any invasion of Canada, it represented a triumph of hope over experience.

Madison also failed to field good commanders, particularly in the army. He was slow to replace bunglers like James Wilkinson (1757–1825) or William Winder (1775–1824). The lackluster performance of the U.S. Army in 1812 was a major reason for Madison's narrow presidential victory in the 1812 election.

After the War of 1812 ended, Madison led a set of internal improvements that restored his popularity, including provisions for a national bank and interstate travel. Retiring from public life in 1817, he focused his attention on scientific agriculture at his estate at Montpelier, Virginia. With Jefferson, he helped found the University of Virginia. He died in 1836, then the last of the great founders of the United States.

Alexander Cochrane

Alexander Cochrane (1758–1832) was in command of British naval efforts in the War of 1812. Born in 1758,

he was the son of Thomas Cochrane, the eighth Earl of Dundonald. Alexander Cochrane entered the Royal Navy as a teenager, in the early 1770s.

Early Career In 1778 he was promoted to lieutenant and appointed to the *Sandwich*, Admiral George Rodney's (1718–1792) flagship during Rodney's West Indies campaign during the American Revolutionary War. Cochrane distinguished himself, and in 1789 was promoted to commander and given command of a sloop-of-war. Just before hostilities ceased, Cochrane was promoted to captain—"made post" in the parlance of the Royal Navy. Once a man became a post captain, future promotion was based on seniority.

Unemployed by the Royal Navy during most of the peace between the American and French revolutions, Cochrane received command of a frigate in 1790. Thereafter, and until the Peace of Amiens in 1801, Cochrane was continuously at sea, first as a frigate captain, and later commanding a ship-of-the-line. After the Napoleonic Wars resumed in 1803, he was given command of another ship-of-the-line and then promoted to rear-admiral in 1804. From there, he commanded increasingly larger numbers of ships, primarily in the Caribbean.

Cochrane conquered Guadeloupe in 1810, taking it from the French. It was the last French possession in the Caribbean. Cochrane had been continuously in the Caribbean since 1805, spending the time capturing islands held by France and its allies.

Command in North America Vice Admiral Alexander Cochrane took command of the North American Station (the headquarters of the Royal Navy ships stationed in North American waters)—and through that, command of British naval efforts in the War of 1812—in late 1813. Cochrane replaced Admiral John Borlase Warren (1753–1822) because the British government had finally decided to more aggressively seek a military solution to the war.

The British government, focused on the war against Napoleon, had initially tried to ignore the American declaration of war, hoping the problem would go away. When it did not, Britain then attempted to negotiate a peace based on the status quo before the war. That failed, despite American military losses in Canada, primarily because of American success at sea. Napoleon's empire began collapsing following a failed invasion of Russia in 1812. By 1813, this released Royal Navy resources for use against the United States. Britain determined to compel a settlement through force of arms.

The Admiralty chose Cochrane for three reasons: He was competent, he was aggressive, and no other admiral then serving had as much experience conducting joint and amphibious operations. At the time of his promotion, Cochrane had been serving as governor of Guadeloupe.

First Lady Dolley Madison is credited with saving the Gilbert Stuart portrait of George Washington from the White House as British forces neared Washington, D.C., in 1814. *MPI/Getty Images*

Cochrane exceeded Admiralty expectations. He instituted a successful blockade of the American coast. While unable to stop American privateers from sailing, Cochrane successfully bottled up American merchant shipping and the U.S. Navy. Between July 1813 and the end of the war, only two squadrons of American warships evaded the British blockade.

In 1814, Cochrane initiated a series of successful raids on the American coast. From Stonington, Connecticut, to the Louisiana coast, British fleets would suddenly appear, land British soldiers, destroy structures, and burn or carry off materials that could aid the United States' war effort. The British would usually be back aboard ship and sailing to a new destination before American forces could react.

Later Career   After the War of 1812 ended, Cochrane returned to England. He was promoted to admiral in 1819 and appointed commander-in-chief of the naval base at Plymouth, England, in 1821. He died in 1832.

Robert Ross

Robert Ross (1766–1814) was a commander of one of Wellington's brigades in North America. Ross was born in 1766 in Rosstrevor, Ireland, and was a member of the Scots-Irish aristocracy. After graduating in 1784 from Trinity College, Dublin, he joined the British Army as an ensign in 1789. After progressing through the officer ranks, he purchased a major's commission in the Twentieth Foot in 1799.

Service in the Napoleonic Wars   Ross remained with the Twentieth Foot regiment until 1813, becoming its commanding colonel in 1809. During that time he saw action in Holland, Italy, Portugal, and Spain. In 1813, he was promoted to command of the Fusilier Brigade in Wellington's Army, which included the Twentieth. He led the brigade ably at the battles of Vittoria, Pampeluna, Sauroren, Nivelle, and Orthes. He received a gold medal for Vittoria. Wellington (Arthur Wellesley, 1st Duke of Wellington) (1769–1852), who led British forces against Napoleon, cited Ross's brigade for its bravery at Sauroren. At the Battle of Orthes on February 27, 1814, Ross was badly wounded—again leading from the front—which took him out of the rest of the campaign. His ability and availability led to his appointment as a brigade commander in North America.

Command in North America   Ross was given command of one of four brigades of Wellington's veterans sent to North America in June 1814. Three brigades were sent to Canada. Ross's brigade, which consisted of three regiments from Europe and one added at Bermuda, was sent to raid the American coast.

Ross proved to be an imaginative, aggressive, and competent commander. Working closely with his naval counterparts—Vice Admiral Alexander Cochrane, who commanded the North American Station, and Rear Admiral George Cockburn (1772–1853), commanding inshore forces—Ross led a series of successful raids in Chesapeake Bay.

The high point of the Chesapeake campaign occurred in the week between August 19, 1814 when British forces landed at Benedict, Maryland, and August 24, when they took Washington, D.C. Ross bypassed two strongly held positions on the Eastern Branch of the Potomac at bridges on the direct route to Washington, looping north to Bladensburg, Maryland. He outmaneuvered and routed an American militia force fortified there, allowing uncontested possession of the American capital.

Ross dined at the White House on August 24, writing "so confident was Madison of the defeat of our troops that he had prepared a supper for the expected conquerors." Ross was probably mistaken as to the nature of the meal he found at the president's abandoned residence. There is no evidence that Madison planned a victory dinner. Madison's valet Paul Jennings wrote in his memoirs that a state dinner had been prepared for that night. Ross mistakenly assumed it was a victory meal.

After the capture of Washington, D.C., Ross attempted to duplicate the feat at Baltimore. He landed forces at North Point, Maryland, and planned to march them twelve miles to Baltimore. At a narrow spot on the peninsula, Ross's forces encountered six thousand militia

This engraving shows the death of famed British General Ross at the Battle of Baltimore in 1814.   *Hulton Archive/Getty Images*

in prepared positions. As was common with British generals schooled in Wellington's army, Ross led his troops from the front. Ross had had a horse shot out from under him during the march on Washington. His luck ran out at the Battle of North Point in September 1814. The British routed the Americans, but Ross had been shot and mortally wounded while scouting the American positions.

Jean Lafitte

Jean Lafitte (c. 1780–c. 1826) was portrayed as a sea-going Robin Hood, a patriot pirate who helped the United States win its most decisive battle in that war. Lafitte's contribution to the Battle of New Orleans, while real, was much smaller than his legend recounts.

Early Career   Jean Lafitte and his brother Pierre were born in France but had moved to San Domingue (colonial Haiti). Chased out of San Domingue by slave revolts, and out of the French Caribbean by British conquests, the brothers appeared in New Orleans around 1803. They started as traders, but began fattening their profit margins through smuggling. From there it was an easy slide to smuggling slaves and stolen goods.

Gentleman Pirate   Around 1811, Jean Lafitte decided to eliminate his middlemen. He acquired first one, then more armed ships, and acquired goods through force of arms. He was technically a privateer authorized by a port on the Colombian coast that had declared itself independent of Spain. This port, the Republic of Cartagena, issued licenses to ship owners, allowing them to seize Spanish merchant ships.

Lafitte set up a base in Lake Barataria, Louisiana, and was selling seized goods on the U.S. gulf coast, where he could get better prices than in Cartagena. Few nations recognized the Republic of Cartagena—which made him a pirate in the eyes of the owners of the seized goods. He made money initially, but by 1813, legal complications threatened his freedom and his finances.

Service to the United States   Lafitte tried unsuccessfully to get licensed as an American privateer when the War of 1812 broke out. By then, he was viewed as a

Famed privateer Jean Lafitte, who aided the U.S. military at the Battle of New Orleans, was later pardoned for his piracy by President Andrew Jackson.   © *Bettmann/Corbis*

pirate by United States and Louisiana authorities. He thus remained a Cartagenian privateer. The British attempted to recruit him to their side in August 1814, offering him a captain's commission in the Colonial Marines. Lafitte turned the offer down. Instead, he reported the British offer to the Louisiana governor, motivated by his dislike for the British and expectation that the Americans would control Louisiana after the war.

Lafitte's action on behalf of the United States did not save his ships or his Baratarian base. In September 1814, the U.S. Navy took time out from the war to attack Lafitte's base. It captured his ships and stolen goods and destroyed the base.

Lafitte and the few Baratarians that escaped the attack hid out in the bayou country for the next two months. In December, Lafitte again offered his services to the United States against the British. He and three dozen surviving Baratarian pirates agreed to serve in the U.S. Army in exchange for a pardon. The men provided crews for two of the fourteen artillery pieces the Americans used during the Battle of New Orleans. Jean Lafitte served as a staff officer.

Contrary to legend, Lafitte supplied the American army with neither gunpowder nor artillery. His stocks

had all been seized by the U.S. Navy in September, when Barataria was raided.

General Andrew Jackson (1767–1845), the hero-leader of the Battle of New Orleans, recommended Jean Lafitte, his brother Pierre, and the thirty-six Baratarian artillerymen for pardons, which were granted. Jean Lafitte began 1815 freed of legal complications, but in the years following the war, slid back to his old ways.

Later Career   Dozens of new nations were born around the Caribbean basin between 1815 and 1825. Lafitte accepted privateering commissions from several such young nations and was again viewed as a pirate. He set up a colony at Galveston, Texas, while a privateer for a "Mexican" republic revolting against Spain. That republic disappeared before his colony did, and the United States and Spain chased him out of Galveston in 1820.

Lafitte then went on to become a privateer for Venezuela. Fort the first time in his career, he was a legitimate privateer, operating out of the country from which he held his commission. He disappeared in the 1820s, probably killed in a storm or aggressions at sea.

✪ Major Battles

Invasion of Canada

One of the United States's objective in the War of 1812 was to add Canada to the nation. At that time, Canada was considered to consist of what are today the provinces of Ontario and Quebec—Upper and Lower Canada, respectively. Newfoundland was then a separate colony.

The United States failed to achieve this objective for three reasons: poor American leadership early in the war; American reliance on militia troops, which were rarely steady enough for prolonged offensives; and the awakening of Canadian nationalism. The War of 1812 made Canadians work together to defend their territory—and got them thinking as Canadians rather than colonists.

At the war's outset, the United States launched invasions of Canada from the Michigan Territory and across the Niagara River. Both attempts ended disastrously.

The Michigan invasion was commanded by General William Hull (1753–1825), known as "Granny" Hull by his men because of his timidity. Hull's force was mostly militia, many of whom refused to leave the United States to fight in Canada. Even without these men, Hull outnumbered the British forces and their Native American allies in the area.

It did not matter. Hull's fear of the Native American forces led by Tecumseh (c. 1768–1813) paralyzed American forces. In August 1812, Hull was ignominiously bluffed into surrendering at Detroit by the British commander, Isaac Brock (1769–1812). At the end of 1812, Britain controlled both the Michigan Territory and parts of western Ohio.

American General William Hull surrendering to British General Sir Isaac Brock at Fort Detroit, after a disastrous invasion of Canada, in 1812. *Hulton Archive/Getty Images*

At the other end of Lake Erie, U.S. forces crossed the Niagara River into Canada on October 13, 1812. Colonel Winfield Scott (1786–1866) fought his way onto Queenston Heights with a mixed force of U.S. Army regulars and New York militia. His forces were driven out by a mixed army of British regulars, Canadian militia, and Native American auxiliaries led by General Brock. Brock was killed in the battle, depriving Britain of a talented leader.

Scott was driven from Queenston Heights by lack of reinforcements. Militia units in the American army refused to leave the United States. While possibly motivated by constitutional concerns, these green troops were more likely unnerved by the fighting they had witnessed during Scott's assault.

In 1813, the United States launched a successful amphibious assault at York (present-day Toronto). They captured the fort, but suffered heavy casualties after the battle, when the fort's magazine exploded. The Americans then successfully captured much of Canada around the western side of Lake Ontario.

Instead of reinforcing success, the United States began drawing troops from that front to provide reinforcements for a proposed invasion of Lower Canada, across the St. Lawrence River. Led by General James Wilkinson, one of the most notoriously ineffective and

self-serving American generals ever, the St. Lawrence attack was delayed until 1814. Drawing forces from the Niagara front so weakened the American army that they had to withdraw from Canada.

On December 10, when the United States evacuated Fort George on the Canadian side of the Niagara River, they had burned the fort—and the adjacent town of Newark (now Niagara). Their evacuation balance so tipped in favor of the British that in November, Brock's successor Lieutenant General Sir George Prevost (1767–1816) launched a counteroffensive. It culminated in the capture of Fort Niagara in December. Prevost then raided the American side of the Niagara River, including several towns on the border, as a reprisal after the burning of Newark.

The United States fared well in the west during 1813. The Battle of Lake Erie in September 1813 gave the United States control of that lake. Led by General William Henry Harrison (1773–1841), the U.S. forces, reinforced by a large contingent of Kentucky militia, retook the occupied portions of Ohio and Detroit in the Michigan Territory. The Kentucky militia, under Harrison's firm leadership, was willing to invade Canada.

Crossing the Detroit River, American forces trapped a smaller force of British and their Native American allies at the River Thames. In the ensuing battle, the Native American leader Tecumseh was killed, and Native American military power was shattered. British forces slipped away, but 1813 ended with the United States in firm control of western Ontario.

The war's final year, 1814, proved a year of stalemate. The western frontier became a strategic sideshow once the United States retook its territory. Western Upper Canada's fate depended on military events to the east.

Three fronts developed in the east: the Niagara River, the St. Lawrence near Lake Ontario, and the Richelieu River and Lake Champlain. The end of the war in Europe allowed the British to send three brigades of troops to Canada starting in June—13,000 veterans of campaigns against Napoleon.

This was balanced by the increased professionalism of the U.S. Army. Ineffective officers had been replaced by active leaders, except for Wilkinson, whose main talent was professional survival. After two years of war, the Army had developed a core of first-rate regular soldiers.

A number of bloody actions were fought on the Niagara front in 1814. The United States again invaded Canada with an army commanded by Major General Jacob Brown (1775–1828). With him was Winfield Scott, now a brigadier general. The American army, spearheaded by Scott's brigade, swept the British from the field at the Battle of Chippawa. It was the first time in the war that an American force defeated a British force of equal size on an open field. The two armies fought a few weeks later to a bloody draw at Lundy's Lane.

Lundy's Lane blunted the American offensive, and they fell back to Fort Erie, on the Niagara River, opposite Buffalo, New York. The British besieged, and then on August 15, assaulted Fort Erie. They were repulsed in a battle that saw heavy casualties on both sides.

On the St. Lawrence River, Wilkinson took four thousand men to threaten Montreal. Near the Richelieu, in late March, he encountered a British force of five hundred men, which stopped him. Wilkinson turned around and fell back to his starting point.

In the summer, Prevost sent ten thousand of the veterans from Europe down the Richelieu River. He planned to invade northern New York using Lake Champlain as his supply line. Prevost's army besieged a smaller American one at Plattsburg, New York, but was forced to withdraw after the British lost control of Lake Champlain in the naval Battle of Lake Champlain.

Before the 1815 campaign season could begin, peace was signed. Both sides agreed to return to pre-war boundaries.

The Lakes Campaigns

Canada was the major theater of land operations during the War of 1812. In an era before the steam locomotive, supplies followed waterways—along rivers or across lakes and seas. The northern lakes along the Canadian-American border—Michigan, St. Claire, Erie, Ontario, and Champlain—were highways, not barriers. Whoever controlled those lakes controlled the flow of goods needed to supply an army.

They were seasonal roads. These freshwater bodies froze in the winter, becoming impassable. Communications between the lakes was difficult for anything other than small boats. A warship could not sail from Lake Ontario to Lake Champlain or Lake Erie. Separate naval forces had to be built on each lake that were incapable of supporting the other lakes. The lakes upstream of Erie were strategically insignificant in 1812.

The Canadian side of the lakes was more heavily settled than the American side. The St. Lawrence River served Canada as a highway to the sea. On the American side, goods had to be brought up the Mohawk River and then portaged to Lake Oneida and the Oswego River to reach the lakes.

The war started with the British holding the advantage on Lake Erie and Lake Ontario. They had small groups of warships on both lakes. The United States had one warship on Lake Ontario. In 1812, the Americans armed six schooners on Lake Ontario, giving them rough parity with the British. Both nations moved regular naval officers and resources to Lake Ontario and began building warships. By the spring of 1813, both sides on Lake Ontario had two brigs mounting twenty-four guns each to augment the forces they had started with.

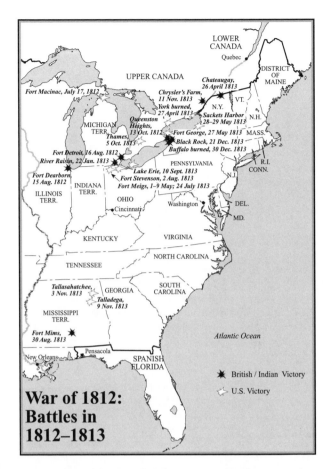

War of 1812: Battles in 1812–1813

Land conflicts of the War of 1812 concentrated in three areas: the northern border of the United States, the Chesapeake Bay area, and New Orleans. *Reproduced by permission of Gale, a part of Cengage Learning*

The results on Lake Ontario were indecisive. Both sides had cautious commanders, Captain James Yeo (1782–1818) for the British, and Commodore Isaac Chauncey (1779–1840) for the United States. The guns mounted by the respective navies gave the Americans an advantage in calm seas and the British an edge in rough weather. Neither commander was willing to cede the advantage to his opponent, so both sides advanced and fell back as weather conditions changed.

Both sides commenced a building war in 1814, first building sloops-of-war, then frigates, and finally ships-of-the-line. None of the largest ships were finished by war's end, and the hulls remained on the builders' stocks for years afterwards. Both commanders remained unwilling to fight unless they had the advantage. The two sides alternated retreating from the lake as the other side added ships.

On Lake Erie and Lake Champlain, results were more decisive. The British dominated Lake Erie in 1812, seizing the one American warship on that lake when they captured Detroit. In 1813, both sides reinforced Lake Erie. The

THE BATTLE OF LAKE CHAMPLAIN

In 1814, both sides began building ships on Lake Champlain at a frantic pace. The Americans ripped the engines out of a steamboat on the lake, converting it into a sailing warship. They built a large sloop-of-war, a brig, and numerous gunboats. They stripped the crews out of American frigates blockaded on the Atlantic coast to provide crews for the lake fleet.

The British matched the Americans by dismantling a thirty-six-gun frigate, moving the pieces to Lake Champlain, and rebuilding it. They also built a seventeen-gun and two eleven-gun brigs, as well as twelve gunboats. In this case, the United States had a disadvantage in men and weight of broadside. The two sides met on September 11, 1814.

Macdonough countered that British advantage by choosing a site for the battle that neutralized the British edge. He anchored his fleet in a tight line, allowing the entire crew of the ship to work the guns. The British had to fight their way to the American line. Eventually, the British battered the exposed sides of the American warships, silencing them.

That should have given the British victory, but Macdonough anchored his ships so that they could pivot 180 degrees. They now did, exposing a fresh set of guns to the enemy. The British attempted to do the same, but had not made the same preparations. Their attempt failed. The British frigate surrendered to the Americans, shifting the balance on the lake to the United States.

United States sent Lieutenant Oliver Perry (1785–1819), along with sailors from the Atlantic coast and shipwrights. The Americans began construction of two big twenty-gun brigs-of-war.

The British sent Commander Robert Barclay (1786–1837), who augmented the existing British force on that lake by building a twenty-gun warship. Both sides finished their ships at roughly the same time. The British outnumbered the American forces in warships and roughly equaled them in men. The Americans had a decisive advantage in guns, however. American warships had a broadside weight of metal that was almost double that of the British.

The two sides met at Put-in-Bay, on Lake Erie's western shore, on September 10, 1813. Despite being outgunned, the British initially held their own. They battered Perry's flagship silent. The second American brig had been slow to join the fight. Perry shifted his flag to that ship. Once it joined the action, the outcome shifted decisively to the United States.

The Battle of Lake Erie became the best-known naval action of the war, in part because of Perry's memorable report of the action. It started, "We have met the enemy, and they are ours—two ships, two brigs, one schooner and one sloop." The results were equal to the drama of the statement. Lake Erie remained in American control for the rest of the war.

On Lake Champlain, an equally decisive result occurred near Plattsburgh, New York. Lake Champlain was a traditional invasion route between the United States and Canada, starting in the Seven Years War. During the American Revolution, the colonies had sent an expedition under Benedict Arnold to capture Canada, and the British used it to invade northern New York, during the Saratoga campaign during the American Revolution.

The United States wrested control of Lake Champlain from the British at the war's outset. With the British shift to a more aggressive policy in 1813, the lake became the scene of an arms race. The British moved veteran regiments from the Peninsular Campaign to Canada to spearhead the invasion.

At the Battle of Lake Champlain (also known as the Battle of Plattsburgh), the U.S. Navy, under the command of Captain Thomas Macdonough (1783–1825), defeated a larger Royal Navy force commanded by Captain George Downie, who died in that battle. Without control of the lake, the British could not supply their invasion of New York, and the attempt to achieve another triumph in New York—as they had during the American Revolution—was thwarted. The war ended with the United States firmly in control of Lake Champlain.

Chesapeake Bay

The British campaign in the Chesapeake in 1814 followed a shift from a purely defensive strategy. The shift was made possible because the war in Europe had ended, freeing resources for the fight in North America. After fighting virtually continuously since it entered war with France in 1793, Britain was war-weary. It wanted to end the War of 1812 and felt the quickest way to do that was to force the United States to seek peace.

The British sent a brigade—four regiments—to raid the eastern seaboard of the United States. These infantry regiments, veterans of the Peninsular Campaign in Spain and France, totaled 3,400 men. The force also had light artillery and a detachment of Congreve rockets. These troops were commanded by Brigadier General Robert Ross, who had commanded a British fusilier brigade in Spain and France.

Vice Admiral Alexander Cochrane, commanding the Royal Navy on the North American Station, assigned a squadron of warships commanded by Rear Admiral George Cockburn to transport and assist the army. In addition to transport and gunnery support that the ships could offer, each warship had a contingent of marines. Seagoing soldiers, the marines upheld authority aboard ship and were used for shore expeditions carried out by

Rather than occupy Washington, D.C., upon their successful invasion of the city in 1814, British forces burned buildings including the Capitol. © *Bettmann/Corbis*

the Navy. When this force was filled out by sailors, it added one thousand men to the force available to Ross.

Ross, Alexander, and Cockburn settled on Chesapeake Bay as the theater for their raids. The Chesapeake sheltered what were then two of the United States's largest seaports, Philadelphia and Baltimore, as well as the capital, Washington, D.C. The Chesapeake provided a highway to European markets for Pennsylvania, Maryland, and Virginia. Valuable tobacco plantations lined the southern Chesapeake. It also gave access to the Atlantic states most strongly favoring the War of 1812.

The Chesapeake Campaign on Water Cockburn spent most of 1813 exploring the Chesapeake with his ships and early 1814 conducting lightning raids on vulnerable towns and plantations. By the time Ross arrived in August 1814, Cockburn's squadron knew the Chesapeake better than many American pilots.

A small flotilla of gunboat barges commanded by Joshua Barney (1759–1818) guarded the bay for the United States. Barney captained a frigate in the American Revolutionary Navy. Barney was pugnacious and capable, but his flotilla of a few dozen boats—mainly small row-barges with single large guns in the bows—were outclassed by the Royal Navy. One seventy-four-gun British ship-of-the-line could fire more ammunition at once than Barney's entire flotilla.

On land, state militias defended the Chesapeake. The federal government called for 93,000 men, but only 15,000 mustered. These troops were scattered among three states and the District of Columbia. On paper, United States forces outnumbered British troops three to one, but the Americans were so widely scattered that the British could gain localized superiority.

From April until August 1814, Barney fought a stubborn rear-guard action against the British. By the time British troops arrived off the Chesapeake in August 1814, Barney's force had been swept from the Bay. Barney formed the surviving sailors into a naval brigade to fight on land.

THE ROCKET'S RED GLARE

The Congreve rocket, invented by William Congreve in 1804, was a gunpowder-filled steel tube, much like skyrockets used in fireworks displays. The rockets had no fins, using a long stick tied to the tube for stability. The British Army deployed Congreve batteries throughout the latter half of the Napoleonic Wars and the War of 1812.

The rockets were noisy, spectacular, and inaccurate. A Congreve rocket gave a piercing shriek in flight and was trailed by a long red flame (the rocket's red glare mentioned in "The Star-Spangled Banner"). Upon impact, they exploded violently. The actual warhead was small, so each rocket did limited damage.

They were more a psychological weapon than a killing tool. An initial exposure to Congreve rockets often caused even veteran troops to panic. Experienced soldiers learned to ignore them. Congreve rockets succeeded in the Chesapeake because American militias—never particularly steady—had no previous experience with them.

The Chesapeake Campaign on Land The British landed their troops at Benedict, Maryland, on the Patuxent River. It was a short march to Washington, D.C. With 4,500 men, and three days' rations, the British Army, led by Ross and Cockburn, moved out to the capital.

The landing drew thousands of militiamen to the defense of the capital. Including the 500 marines and sailors of Barney's force, Brigadier General William Winder, commander of the Washington District, had 6,000 men with which to defend the capital: 2,000 militia from the District, 2,000 from Baltimore, and the rest from the Maryland countryside.

Winder was a political appointee who lacked energy and skill; he lost control of the situation. The British ignored crossings on the direct route, marching around Washington to attack it from the north. James Monroe (1799–1870), then secretary of state, repositioned the defenses at Bladensburg, Maryland. Monroe had no authority to do this, but Winder allowed it.

Monroe scattered the defenders into positions where they could not support each other. When the British attacked on August 24, the American line initially held. The British took the first line of American defenses. A barrage of Congreve rockets caused the militia to flee a second line.

Barney's men held the third line and were stopping the British when Winder ordered the withdrawal of part of the third line's militia. Instead of withdrawing, the militia routed, leaving the flank—and the road to Washington—open. Barney's men retreated in good order, but the rest of the army scattered.

The U.S. government fled the capital in a panic. The Washington Navy Yard was burned to deny the Royal Navy the ships and stores held there. The British occupied the evacuated city that evening.

The British were in a quandary. The landing was a raid. Occupation was not the goal. There was no American government with which to negotiate. Ross ordered the public buildings of Washington burned before evacuating the city as retaliation for the American destruction of the Canadian provincial capital at York (now Toronto). It was an unusual, but legal, order. It denied the enemy resources with which to fight. Cockburn and Ross then marched the British forces back to Benedict where they re-embarked on August 30.

Meanwhile, the British sent a flotilla up the Potomac, where it took the Washington suburb of Alexandria, Virginia. There they confiscated or destroyed 16,000 barrels of flour, 1,000 hogsheads (large barrels) of tobacco, 150 bales of cotton, and $5,000 worth of wine.

The British closed their Chesapeake campaign with an unsuccessful raid on Baltimore. On this occasion, the Americans were led by more resolute commanders and were able to turn back the British invasion.

The Battle of Baltimore

The capstone of the British campaign on the Chesapeake was supposed to be the capture of Baltimore, Maryland. Baltimore was probably the most anti-British city in the United States and was viewed as the heart of the war's support. It was also a wealthy port and home to many of the privateers preying on British mercantile traffic. Admiral Alexander Cochrane believed Baltimore's capture would force the Americans to end the war.

Baltimore, unlike Washington, D.C., possessed both significant defensive works and competent leadership. Instead of the inept General William Winder, forces in Baltimore were under the overall command of the energetic Samuel Smith (1752–1839), and the city was protected from seaborne approaches by Fort McHenry, a masonry fortification completed during the Quasi-War with France in 1799.

The overland approaches were vulnerable, but Smith had virtually all of Baltimore's male population turn out to create a massive earthwork anchored on Hampstead Hill. Known as Rodgers Redoubt, it shielded Baltimore from any overland march from a landing coming from the Chesapeake. It was occupied by ten thousand armed men, including the naval brigade, twelve hundred marines, and sailors commanded by Commodore John Rodgers (1772–1838).

The British tried the overland approach. They landed at North Point, on the tip of a peninsula formed by the Patapsco and Back Rivers. They then marched toward Baltimore, eight miles away. After traveling three miles, they encountered 3,100 American militiamen in prepared positions at a narrow spot in the peninsula. In

Francis Scott Key wrote "The Star-Spangled Banner" after watching the bombardment of Fort McHenry, depicted in this etching. © *Bettmann/Corbis*

the resulting Battle of North Point, they swept the militia aside, but only after the British commanding general, Robert Ross, was shot and killed.

Colonel Arthur Brooke (1772–1843) assumed command of the British forces. After reforming their troops, the British pressed on to Baltimore. When they reached the American defensive works, Brooke decided against a frontal assault. The position was too strong to storm. Instead, he tried to lure the Americans out of their fortifications, but Smith did not accept the bait.

Brooke decided to let the Royal Navy soften up the redoubt. Since it was an earthwork, it would be vulnerable to fire from British bomb vessels. Bomb vessels carried two mortars, each of which fired either a 200-pound, 13-inch shell or a 10-inch shell that weighed 70 pounds. Both were filled with explosive. The mortars could devastate anything they could reach. To reach Rodgers Redoubt, the Royal Navy had to silence Fort McHenry. Unless that was done, the fort's guns would sink the bomb vessels before they could sail close enough to the redoubt to strike it.

On the evening of September 13, 1814, Alexander Cochrane sailed the British fleet up the Patapsco River to attack Fort McHenry. He had four bomb vessels, and one that fired Congreve rockets. Congreve rockets were fueled with black powder, much like skyrockets used for

fireworks. They were inaccurate, but noisy, and could panic troops that had not faced them before.

The British bombarded the fort throughout the night. They fired over 1,500 mortar shells, a quarter of which landed within the fort but failed to do serious damage. The rest, along with the rockets, burst spectacularly, but harmlessly, in the air. By dawn, American casualties numbered twenty-four wounded and four dead.

The fleet withdrew, unable to force passage into the harbor's Northwest Branch, where they could bombard the redoubt. Shortly after dawn, once it became apparent that the fleet had failed, Brooke marched the British troops back to North Point, and re-embarked on the transports. General Smith allowed them to depart unmolested. He did not wish to give the British an opportunity to snatch victory from the jaws of defeat.

The assault on Baltimore proved counterproductive. Instead of disheartening the United States, the victory renewed American spirits. It punctured the reputation for invulnerability the British had developed during the Chesapeake campaign and cost them the life of one of their most talented generals.

The War at Sea

The War of 1812 is best known for a set of spectacular, but strategically unimportant, naval battles fought

THE STAR-SPANGLED BANNER

The most lasting result of the Battle of Baltimore was the national anthem of the United States: "The Star-Spangled Banner." Its author, Francis Scott Key (1780–1843), was a Georgetown lawyer. After a prominent area physician, Dr. William Beanes (1749–1829), had been seized by the British and confined on a warship, Key boarded the British flagship to negotiate the doctor's release. He succeeded, but the British were going to attack Baltimore that night. Key and Beanes were kept behind the British line until the attack ended.

Key watched the bombardment and assault from deck. While not a soldier, Key was patriotic. When the sun rose the next morning, Key was overjoyed to see the American flag still flying over Fort McHenry. He composed a poem to express his intense relief and pride: "The Star-Spangled Banner."

Key and his wife had the poem printed as a broadsheet with the title "The Defense of Fort McHenry." The poem became instantly popular. As was common in that period, the poem was sung using a then-popular drinking song, "To Anacreon in Heaven."

Its popularity grew, despite the vocal challenge it presents to the singer. Its original title was forgotten. Within a few years "The Star-Spangled Banner" became an unofficial national anthem for the United States. It was officially designated the national anthem by Congress in 1931.

weaker ships and second-best captains there. It needed the best to fight France.

The U.S. Navy was also ready for war at sea. It sent out all of its frigates in one squadron, looking to snap up any unsuspecting Royal Navy ships. As a result, the Royal Navy was forced to concentrate its warships, allowing American merchant vessels and privateers—private warships sailing under government license—unmolested access to the Atlantic Ocean.

As the American squadron ran low on supplies, ships from the squadron returned to port individually. En route, two of them came across single British frigates, also sailing to or from the British squadron. In each case a single-ship duel resulted, where the American and British frigate squared off. The American ships mounted much heavier broadsides than their British opponents.

In both cases, victory went to the heavier battery—a pattern that continued virtually unbroken to the end of the war. When the British ship had the advantage of broadside (the total ammunition that could be fired at once), it won. When the United States ship had it, it won.

The results of these spectacular victories—as well as a few others in 1812, actually weakened the U.S. Navy strategically. They encouraged the United States to send out individual warships rather than a squadron. This allowed the Royal Navy to break up its squadrons and send its cruisers out in pairs—which could beat an individual American frigate. After 1812, the United States won only one frigate action on the high seas. On that occasion, the British commanders disregarded orders and attacked a superior force.

The British also shifted stronger ships and better leaders to the North American Station, starting in 1813. In 1814, the end of the Napoleonic Wars allowed Britain to transfer a crushing superiority in warships to American waters. They began a close blockade of the United States's coastline, stopping privateers and capturing any American merchant craft that sailed without a license from Britain. (Britain licensed merchant ships from the United States to carry food from the United States to Wellington's army in Spain.)

By the middle of 1813, the United States realized the futility of trying to match Britain at sea. The three largest American frigates remained in commission to provide a strategic distraction for the British, to force them to use resources guarding against these ships.

Five smaller frigates were laid up, and their crews transferred to the inland lakes, to provide men for the warships being built there. Only two of the small frigates remained in commission. One took the diplomats to Europe to negotiate the Treaty of Ghent. A second was sent to the Pacific to attack the British whaling fleet there. Privateers kept sailing, but the risk of capture soared.

between the Royal Navy and the new U.S. Navy. They are chiefly remembered because they are the stuff of legend. Most of the battles were single-ship duels in which two comparable ships squared off. Adding to the story was a David-versus-Goliath quality to the battles: the Royal Navy had been fighting virtually undefeated for nearly twenty-five years, while the U.S. Navy was in its infancy.

Throughout the War of 1812, the U.S. Navy was tremendously outnumbered by the Royal Navy. It had only a dozen frigates—large cruising warships—and perhaps as many sloops-of-war—used primarily for anti-commerce warfare or as convoy escorts—throughout the war. There were never more than half the fleet ready to go to sea. In 1812, the Royal Navy had 124 frigates and 235 sloops-of-war at sea. Britain also had 102 ships-of-the-line commissioned. A ship-of-the-line mounted from 64 to 120 cannon. It could blow a frigate out of the water with a few blasts.

The U.S. Navy had a few advantages as the war opened. Britain was in a war with France. Most of its navy was tied down blockading Europe or protecting its sea-lanes. The North American Station was a backwater before the War of 1812 started. The Royal Navy sent its

Most of the naval battles in the War of 1812 were single-ship duels, like this engagement between the USS *Constitution* and the HMS *Guerriere*. © *Francis G. Mayer/Corbis*

After the war's end, the captains—on both sides—that fought in the frigate duels became celebrities, and the ships that fought in them were cherished symbols of naval prowess. The United States kept two of the frigates that fought in the War of 1812 for over fifty years after the war. Both the United States and Great Britain made replicas of one of the frigates they captured from the other and kept them as trophies even after the sailing warship became obsolete.

The Battle of New Orleans

Denied at Baltimore, the British sought another way to put pressure on the United States. New Orleans, near the mouth of the Mississippi was an obvious target. It was the outlet, in 1814, for all goods produced by the United States west of the Appalachian Mountains. Whoever held New Orleans held the American economy.

By the fall of 1814, Britain had won its long war against Napoleon. This freed up veteran troops for use in North America in Britain's last active war. Nine regiments were sent from Europe. These veterans had formed the core of the army Wellington had led to victory against the French in Spain and France. Edward Pakenham (1778–1815), Wellington's adjutant general in Spain, took command.

The British included the troops raiding the Chesapeake to these reinforcements and added two regiments from Jamaica to serve as an occupation force once New Orleans had been taken. Pakenham sailed to the Gulf of Mexico with orders to press operations until he received official word of a peace settlement and to disregard any rumors of peace.

British preparations were noticed. General Andrew Jackson commanded American forces in the southern United States. As 1814 progressed, he set about securing the Gulf Coast. He reinforced Fort Bowyer at Mobile Bay just in time to repulse a British attack there in September 1814. Next, Jackson moved into neutral west Florida, then Spanish. He captured Pensacola, chasing out a small British garrison that was not officially there. These actions denied the British the two good gulf coast bases from which to launch an assault on New Orleans.

In August, the British enticed Jean Laffite and the band of pirates he led at Lake Barataria, offering Lafitte a captain's commission if he joined the British. Lafitte spurned the offer, reporting it to Louisiana's governor, William Charles Coles Claiborne (1775–1817). By late November, Jackson was hurrying to New Orleans with every American unit he could gather.

This painting depicts the Battle of New Orleans as General Andrew Jackson and his troops overcome the British in 1815. *AP Images*

On November 22, 1814, the British fleet assembled in Jamaica to sail for Louisiana. By the time the British landed in Louisiana, Jackson had gathered 4,500 men in New Orleans, a mixture of regular units of the U.S. Army; militia units from Kentucky, Tennessee, Mississippi, and Louisiana; and local volunteers. The latter included the Baratarian pirates who volunteered to serve as gunners and a company of Choctaw Indians.

The British had a considerably larger force—7,500 soldiers, all regulars, from ten Army regiments, as well a contingent of Royal Marines and sailors landed by the navy. Well over half of these were veterans of Wellington's peninsular campaign.

The problem was getting this army to New Orleans. The port was nearly one hundred miles from the mouth of the Mississippi River. Fort St. Phillip covered the river approaches halfway to New Orleans. Instead of going up the Mississippi, the British considered taking New Orleans from the north, landing their army on the southern shore of Lake Ponchartrain.

The British fleet swept away a small flotilla of American gunboats guarding Lake Bourne. Once in Lake Bourne, the British discovered Ponchartrain was too

shallow to use. Instead, they landed their army on Lake Bourne at Fisherman's Village, south and east of New Orleans. On December 22, they captured the Villere Plantation and discovered a canal that ran to the Mississippi that could be used as a supply line.

Jackson's army was scattered around New Orleans to give warning of any British approach. Once reports of the capture of the Villere Plantation arrived, and the British army began arriving south of New Orleans through the Villere Canal, Jackson massed his forces on the south side of the city. Because of the swamps, the British could only attack via a plain a few thousand yards across. Jackson planned to hold a line behind a canal where the plain narrowed to only one thousand yards.

Jackson attacked the arriving British in the evening of December 22. He used a complicated three-pronged attack, which proved too ambitious. The British pushed the Americans back, almost capturing Jackson. While Jackson's plan failed, it caused the British to spend time preparing defenses for their base.

Jackson cut a levy between the two armies, flooding the plain with thirty inches of water. This gave him time to build up the earthworks behind the Rodriguez Canal.

As a young man in the early 1800s, Abraham Lincoln navigated the same kind of flatboats that ensured the waterway flow of goods during the War of 1812. *George Eastman House/Getty Images*

A four-foot-high earth rampart was raised and faced with timber to keep it from collapsing. Cotton bales were used to build artillery emplacements.

By December 28, the plain had drained. The British launched a hasty assault on this Jackson line. The American ran from similar positions at Bladensburg and North Point on the Chesapeake. The British thought one quick charge could rout the defenders. They came close to success, but they lacked artillery support and the American line held. The British brought up artillery and attempted to bombard the Americans out of the Jackson line on January 1, 1815, but their ammunition ran out before the Americans did.

Things remained quiet for the next week. The British brought up ammunition and troops. The Americans strengthened their defensive works. Finally, on January 8, the British launched a prepared assault on the American positions.

It proved a disaster for the British. The British landed troops on the west bank of the Mississippi to clear away American batteries that were firing across the river at the British. That attack eventually swept the Americans from the field, too late to affect the outcome on the east bank.

British artillery proved ineffectual against the reinforced mud embankment. American artillery firing at massed troops in an open field cut the British down in rows. The British reached the Jackson line, but troops carrying the ladders needed to climb the embankment had gotten lost. American riflemen picked off British officers. Pakenham was killed, along with other senior officers. The assault faltered, and the British retreated, having suffered 192 dead, 1,265 wounded, and 484 missing of 7,000 attackers. American casualties were less than fifty men.

The British army withdrew from Louisiana. Before they could reorganize for another attempt, word of the peace treaty arrived. The battle's biggest impact occurred four months later, during the Waterloo campaign in Europe. Wellington faced Napoleon without the veteran troops sent to North America. Wellington won, but it was close, and had Napoleon not made mistakes, Wellington might have lost. Jackson emerged as a national hero, eventually becoming president.

The Battle of New Orleans was fought two weeks after the peace treaty had been signed on December 24, 1814, but a month before it was ratified and the war ended. As with much of the War of 1812, it was a battle whose results were overtaken by outside events.

✪ Homefront

Riverboat Travel on the Mississippi

During the War of 1812, bulk goods moved by water—along rivers and across lakes, or by sea, from seaport to seaport. Railroads did not yet exist. Animal-drawn wagons were useful for short distances, but the draft team would eat a wagon's weight of fodder in less than a week. To move low-value, high-bulk goods such as grain long distances over land, merchants had to convert it to a more concentrated form of wealth. They fed the corn to livestock (which moved themselves) that they could sell as meat, or they distilled it into whiskey (which was valuable and compact).

The United States has an excellent inland-waterway system. The Great Lakes basin allowed goods to flow throughout the upper Midwest. Its major limitation in 1812 was that it then had no outlet to the ocean. The Mississippi basin provided a highway to the sea for the southern and central United States. The Mississippi and its eastern tributaries, the Ohio, Tennessee, and Wabash rivers, gave the inland states a market for their goods.

Tennessee, Kentucky, Ohio, and Indiana, as well as the western parts of Pennsylvania and Virginia, could ship corn, timber, and hogs by boat to New Orleans, where they could be loaded onto seagoing ships for shipment to markets. It was easier to send a load of corn from Wheeling to Richmond through New Orleans than directly overland.

During the War of 1812, the boats on the Mississippi were primarily muscle-powered. Sail power was undependable. Going upwind required a ship to beat into the wind. It was slow—they could only go three to four knots—and they could sail no closer to the wind than 45 degrees. If they were sailing upstream, against the current, the river's current often pushed them downstream faster than they could sail upstream. Once they got north of New Orleans, the Mississippi was too narrow to navigate upstream easily.

Thus, most river travel was one-way—downstream. Men would build flatboats, timber rafts that were as much as sixty feet long and twelve to twenty feet across. A crude deckhouse housed the crew—typically four to eight men—who would steer the boat with oars as it drifted down the Mississippi. Flatboats could move tons of goods inexpensively down the river because they did not need to pay for fuel.

The boat itself would be taken apart when it reached New Orleans and sold for lumber. The crew would then walk back home, following the Natchez Trace, an early road that ran from Tennessee to New Orleans. Often, they returned with a small amount of manufactured goods, such as nails or tools. These were items that were portable, necessary, yet not available in the frontier counties.

The *New Orleans*, the Mississippi's first steamboat, appeared in 1811. It was experimental, used primarily as a tugboat, to help sailing ships get to New Orleans. Steamboat technology was emerging but had been interrupted by the war. After the American victory, steamboat traffic on the Mississippi blossomed, with hundreds of river steamboats.

The Hartford Convention

The Hartford Convention was the product of New England's frustrations with the War of 1812. Many, including people living in New England, considered the gathering as treasonous, although most of those most ardently opposed to the war—and those most actively seeking secession from the United States—refused to participate. They viewed the convention's goals as too moderate.

The War of 1812 was never popular in New England. Much of that region's economy depended on maritime trade, or trade with Britain and Canada. War put an end to much of that. Some in New England initially profited from privateering. They sent out privately owned warships, called privateers, that held government commissions to capture British merchantmen. The Royal Navy ended that source of easy money by the end of 1813, protecting their sea lanes with warships freed by the end of the Napoleonic War in Europe.

Reverses in Canada threatened the New England states, making them vulnerable to invasion. By late 1814, several New England states were so war-weary that they were willing to negotiate a separate peace with England. Massachusetts and then Connecticut issued calls for constitutional conventions. In Massachusetts, delegates to this convention were elected by a minority

Frustrated with the impact of the War of 1812, delegates convened the Hartford Convention in 1814. © *Corbis*

of the state's legislators. In Connecticut, the governor, John Cotton Smith (1765–1845), convened the legislature and invited states to send delegates.

The convention called for by Governor Smith met in Hartford, Connecticut, in December 1814. Only Massachusetts, Connecticut, and Rhode Island sent state delegations, although delegates from a single county in Vermont and two counties in New Hampshire also attended. A total of twenty-six delegates attended.

The convention was handicapped from the outset because the delegates were primarily Federalists—the minority party in the United States. Even Federalist John Adams described the Hartford delegates as "intelligent and honest men who had lost touch with reality."

Regardless, the convention indicted President Madison for perceived abuses of federal power in starting and running the War of 1812. It also passed a resolution recommending seven amendments to the U.S. Constitution:

1. Congress would repeal the "three-fifths compromise," which allowed states to count slaves toward representation in Congress and the Electoral College

2. Admission of new states could only occur after a two-thirds vote of both houses of Congress.

3. Embargoes could not be imposed for more than sixty days.

4. A two-thirds vote of both Houses of Congress would be required for declarations of war.

5. A two-thirds vote of both Houses of Congress be required to declare commercial embargoes.

6. Naturalized citizens could not hold any elective or appointive federal office.

7. A president could only serve one term, and no two successive presidents could come from the same state.

All twenty-six delegates signed the resolution and sent it to Washington, D.C., under the care of Harrison Gray Otis (1765–1848), a Massachusetts Federalist who first conceived the idea of holding such a convention.

As with much else associated with the War of 1812, the resolution was overtaken by events. On January 8, 1815, three days after the resolution was signed, the United States won a decisive victory over the British at New Orleans. Word of the victory reached Washington at the same time that Otis arrived there on February 5, 1815. Less than a week later, the Treaty of Ghent arrived in the United States. It was quickly ratified. The Hartford resolutions were withheld, and they were never introduced to Congress.

✪ International Context

The Rise and Fall of Napoleon

The War of 1812 was fought against the backdrop of the Napoleonic Wars. Both impressment of American sailors and free trade issues were the direct result of the war that Great Britain was waging against France. A major cause of that war was French Emperor Napoleon Bonaparte. Without Napoleon, the War of 1812 might never have been fought.

Early Years Napoleon Buonaparte (he changed the spelling to Bonaparte in 1796) was born to a family of minor nobility in Corsica in 1769. This was the same year Corsica was annexed by France. The annexation made Bonaparte French, but he came from a province outside traditional French society of the day.

Educated at military schools in France, in 1784, Bonaparte attended the École Militaire of Paris, the royal military school. Graduating with honors, he entered the Royal French Army in 1785. Although a member of the Corsican aristocracy, he lacked influence in France. He became an artillery officer, the traditional branch of service for bright officers without political connections.

The French Revolution in 1789 transformed Bonaparte's life. An outsider, he was unsympathetic to the French aristocracy. He was willing to serve in the Revolutionary Army when few other trained officers would. The French Revolution triggered a nationalistic rising in Corsica. It split into pro-independence and pro-French factions. Bonaparte's family, siding with the pro-French faction, fled Corsica when the nationalists won. This tied Napoleon to France.

Napoleon rose to prominence during the siege of Toulon. He commanded the artillery key to the Revolutionary Army's victory there. Afterwards, despite occasional bumps, he rose meteorically, successfully leading French armies in Italy on two occasions.

Political Power Napoleon led a coup that overthrew the existing revolutionary government in 1799. Napoleon was named first consul, heading up the new government, and given dictatorial powers.

Despite rising as a result of the French Revolution, Napoleon ruled like a monarch. In 1802, he was named consul for life, with the right to name his successor—giving himself the power of a king, if not the title. In 1804, he crowned himself Emperor of France. In 1810, he annulled his first marriage and married a daughter of the Austrian Emperor, with an eye towards establishing a Bonaparte dynasty in France, with himself as Napoleon I.

Napoleon's military skills earned him the power to name himself emperor in 1804. *Public Domain*

He got away with such naked ambition because was a talented administrator and a brilliant battlefield commander. When he first took over France, he ended the internal fighting between Royalist and Revolutionary factions that had been ongoing since the execution of King Louis XVI in 1793. He also established a rational civil service and laws within greater France. He was also a superb general, defeating the armies of each nation in Europe in turn.

The Napoleonic Empire Bonaparte's greatest fault as a leader was consistently placing personal interests ahead of everything else, including the best interests of France. He ran France like a personal possession, not a nation. He reconstituted a heredity aristocracy with himself as the head, and his immediate family as leading nobles.

He awarded kingdoms to his brothers and brothers-in-law. In 1808, Napoleon alienated what had previously been France's strongest ally, Spain. Napoleon deposed Spain's king, replacing him with a brother, Jerome Bonaparte. Spain rebelled and allied with Britain.

Napoleon also conducted diplomacy as vendetta. Unable to conquer Great Britain (his armies could not reach the island nation), Napoleon negotiated peace with Britain in 1801. It ended a war between Britain and France that began in 1793. Obsessed with humbling Britain, Napoleon used the peace to prepare for a new war with Britain. Realizing that they were the object of French invasion plans, Britain renewed the conflict in 1803.

The next ten years was a duel between the two nations, with neither able to conquer the other. Britain destroyed French and Spanish fleets at the Battle of Trafalgar in 1805. This made it impossible for France to invade Britain. Napoleon turned on Britain's continental allies, beating the Austrians and Russians in an 1805 campaign that ended with a decisive French victory at Austerlitz. He conquered Prussia the following year.

Napoleon controlled most of Europe by 1806, but not Britain. Yet Britain could not beat France. Both sides began conducting economic warfare. The French imposed the Continental System restricting trade with Britain. The British government issued Orders-in-Council choking trade with the French-controlled parts of the continent. Neutrals and allies—on both sides—ignored these trade restrictions at every opportunity.

Napoleon began a set of destructive wars to enforce the Continental System. French armies unsuccessfully invaded Portugal to keep Portugal in the Continental System. Failure in Portugal led to Napoleon deposing Spain's king in 1808. The Spanish war that resulted from replacing Spain's king encouraged Austria to mobilize against France. Napoleon crushed Austria in a campaign waged in 1809.

Downfall In 1812, determined to force obedience to the Continental System, Napoleon invaded Russia. Napoleon's main army chased the Russians to Moscow, but failed to destroy Russia's army. When the Russian winter began, Napoleon had to withdraw his exhausted army. By the time Napoleon reached the Russian border, his army was gone.

In 1813, every major power in Europe attacked France. Napoleon fought a brilliant defensive campaign before losing the Battle of Nations at Leipzig. In 1814, France's enemies were at its frontiers. In April 1814, Napoleon abdicated, and accepted exile in Elba, off the Italian coast.

The end of this war removed many reasons for fighting the War of 1812. By December 1814, Britain and the United negotiated a peace, which was ratified by the United States Congress in February 1815.

A month after the peace between Britain and the United States took effect, on March 20, 1815, Napoleon escaped from Elba and returned to Paris in an attempt to regain his throne. A brief campaign ensued. Napoleon was defeated at Waterloo in June 1815. Napoleon again abdicated, accepting exile to St. Helena, an island in the South Atlantic. He remained in St. Helena until his death in 1821.

✪ Aftermath

Monroe Doctrine

In the War of 1812, the United States held its own—without any major allies—against one of the world's foremost powers. The United States had not beaten Britain, true, but Britain could not beat the United States, either. One of the results of this realization by the United States was increased confidence in its position on the world stage and an increased willingness to assert its interests. The Monroe Doctrine was one fruit of that new confidence.

The decade following the war's end—1815 through 1825—would become known as the "Era of Good Feeling." Restoration of trade relations with Europe following the war's end revived the American economy. President James Madison, continuing the precedent set by George Washington, declined to run for a third term in 1816. Madison was succeeded by his Secretary of State, James Monroe (1799–1870).

The United States had gained respect on the world's stage—and had increased self-confidence. The United States proved able to hold its own against Britain, without European allies. The peace treaty—a return to the status quo prior to the war—demonstrated a measure of respect for American military prowess by Britain, now Europe's leading nation.

With the end of the Napoleonic Wars, the causes of the partisan differences that bitterly divided the United States in the nineteenth century's opening years faded. One measure of how cordial domestic politics had become was that Monroe appointed John Quincy Adams (1767–1848) as secretary of state, a position that then led to the presidency. Adams, son of President John Adams (1735–1826), helped negotiate the Treaty of Ghent, which ended the War of 1812. He was also a former Federalist, the party in opposition to Monroe's Republican-Democrat Party.

While things ran smoothly within the United States, the decade following the War of 1812 was a troubled one in the rest of North and South America. Russia was moving south from Alaska, threatening to exclude other countries from the Pacific Northwest. Spanish and Portuguese colonies in the New World declared independence, intent on following the path taken by the United States in the previous century.

In 1823, rumors circulated that the Holy Alliance—a combination of reactionary European monarchies that included Spain and France—had concluded an agreement to reconquer these breakaway colonies.

Both the Republican-Democrats and Whigs (which had replaced the Federalist Party) found common ground in a desire to prevent this. It could interfere with American territorial ambitions as well as American economic growth—the ex-colonies were trading partners.

President James Monroe, center, announced the foreign policy that became known as the Monroe Doctrine in 1823.   *The Library of Congress*

The rumors also troubled Great Britain, the only nation with significant colonies left in the Americas. In 1823, the British foreign minister invited the United States to issue a joint declaration that supported Latin American independence—and that pledged to abandon further territorial ambitions in the New World. Britain's offer of diplomatic partnership with its former colony was evidence of the increased influence of the United States.

The offer was flattering but constraining. The United States would have to abandon the territorial ambitions it held toward pieces of the former Spanish empire. Adams also realized that Britain would block Spanish recolonization efforts even if the United States failed to support the declaration.

Adams recommended that the United States go it alone and establish a policy that declared that "the American continents, by the free and independent condition which they have assumed and maintained, are henceforth not to be considered as subjects for future colonization by any European powers."

Monroe used this language almost verbatim in his annual address to Congress in December 1823. This policy, that European nations could establish no new colonies in North or South America, became known as

the Monroe Doctrine. It put Russia and Britain on notice that expansion of their colonies would not be tolerated by the United States either.

When announced, the Monroe Doctrine was enthusiastically accepted in the United States and widely ignored by European nations. It had no practical effect during the balance of the Monroe administration. No European nation intended to create new colonies during that time. It was ignored when the British took over the Falkland Islands in 1833.

In the 1840s, President James Polk (1795–1849) reasserted the Monroe Doctrine, threatening military action if either Spain or England established a protectorate in Mexico's Yucatan Peninsula. From then on, the Monroe Doctrine would be increasingly cited as justification for expansion of or intervention by the United States in the Western Hemisphere.

BIBLIOGRAPHY

Books

Borneman, Walter R. *1812: The War That Forged A Nation.* New York: Harper Collins, 2004.

Caffrey, Kate. *The Twilight's Last Gleaming: Britain vs. America 1812–1815.* Briarcliff Manor, NY: Stein and Day, 1977.

Canney, Donald L. *Sailing Warships of the U.S. Navy.* Annapolis, MD: Naval Institute Press, 2001.

Chandler, David G. *The Campaigns of Napoleon.* New York: Macmillan, 1966.

Chapelle, Howard I. *The History of the American Sailing Navy.* New York: W. W. Norton, 1949.

Clowes, Wm. Laird. *The Royal Navy: A History From the Earliest Times to the Present, Vol. 6.* London: Sampson Low, Marston and Company, 1901.

Davis, William C. *The Pirates Laffite: the Treacherous World of the Corsairs of the Gulf.* Orlando, FL: Harcourt, 2005.

Dudley, William S., ed. *The Naval War of 1812, A Documentary History, Vols. 1–3.* Washington, D.C.: Naval Historical Center, Department of the Navy, 1985.

Durand, James R. *The Life and Adventures of James R. Durand.* Sandwich, MA: Chapman Billies, 1995.

Dwight, Theodore. *History of the Hartford Convention: with a review of the policy of the United States Government, which led to the War of 1812.* Freeport, NY: Books for Libraries Press, 1970.

Gardiner, Robert. *The Naval War of 1812.* London: Chatham Publishers, 1998.

Harvey, Robert. *Cochrane: The Life and Exploits of a Fighting Captain.* New York: Carroll & Graf, 2000.

Hickey, Donald R. *Don't Give Up The Ship!: Myths of the War of 1812.* Champaign, IL: University of Illinois Press, 2006.

James, William. *The Naval History of Great Britain: From the Declaration of War by France in 1793 to the Accession of George IV, Vol. 6.* London: Richard Bentley, 1859.

Mahon, John K. *The War of 1812.* Gainesville, FL: University of Florida Press, 1972.

Markham, Felix M. *Napoleon.* New York: New American Library, 1964.

Muir, Rory. *Britain and the Defeat of Napoleon 1807–1815.* New Haven, CT: Yale University Press, 1996.

Pickles, Tim. *New Orleans 1815.* Oxford: Osprey Publishing, 1993.

Pope, Dudley. *Life in Nelson's Navy.* London: Chatham Publishing, 1997.

Ralfe, James. *The Naval Biography of Great Britain: Consisting of Historical Memoirs of Those Officers of the British Navy Who Distinguished Themselves During the Reign of His Majesty George III, Vol. 2.* Boston: Gregg Press, 1972.

Ramsay, Jack C., Jr. *Jean Laffite: Prince of Pirates.* Austin, TX: Eakin Press, 1996.

Reilly, Robin. *The British at the Gates: The New Orleans campaign in the War of 1812..* New York: Putnam, 1974.

Rodger, N. A. M. *The Wooden World: An Anatomy of the Georgian Navy.* Annapolis, MD: Naval Institute Press, 1986.

Stephen, Sir Leslie, and Sir Sidney Lee, eds. *The Dictionary of National Biography.* Oxford, Oxford University Press, 1917.

U.S. Department of the Navy. *Official Records of the Union and Confederate Navies in the War of the Rebellion.* Washington, D.C.: GPO, 1922.

Ware, Chris. *The Bomb Vessel: Shore Bombardment Ships of the Age of Sail.* Annapolis, MD: Naval Institute Press, 1994.

Web Sites

Treaty of Ghent. <www.loc.gov/rr/program/bib/ourdocs/Ghent.html> (accessed April 5, 2007).

State of the Union Addresses of James Monroe. Monroe, James. <www.gutenberg.org/dirs/etext04/sumon11.txt> (accessed April 8, 2007).

Introduction to the Mexican-American War (1846–1848)

Though often overlooked by historians, the Mexican-American War of 1846–1848 presaged dramatic change in America. The conflict emerged out of America's expansionist past and sped the nation on its way to the Civil War.

In the early nineteenth century, thousands of Protestant Anglo-Saxon Americans had poured into the Mexican territory of Texas. These settlers, led by Stephen Austin and Sam Houston declared their independence in 1835. Mexican President Antonio de Santa Anna personally led a punitive expedition to quash the rebellion. Initially, his army fared well, overcoming fierce resistance at the Alamo in San Antonio. But the Mexican victory provoked furious—and sustained—hatred from the American Texans. A month later, Santa Anna was defeated and captured at the Battle of San Jacinto. Santa Anna was released only after he had signed a treaty acknowledging Texas as a sovereign state.

Santa Anna returned home in disgrace. Infuriated, the Mexican government repudiated the treaty and refused to recognize the Republic of Texas. For the next decade, Mexican and Texan troops fought a sporadic border war, with raids, incursions, and atrocities on both sides.

In March of 1845, Texans agreed to annexation by the United States. Mexico immediately broke off diplomatic relations with Washington.

Expecting a Mexican invasion of Texas, U.S. President James K. Polk preemptively sent General Zachary Taylor to the Rio Grande River with four thousand men. Across the river, General Pedro de Ampudia's forces saw Taylor's army as an invasion into their territory. The Mexican government declared war on April 23, 1846.

Congress responded in kind on May 13. Fighting had already begun.

Taylor moved west into the heart of Mexico, winning several bloody victories. On February 24, 1847, at Buena Vista, his army drove back a vastly larger Mexican force commanded by Santa Anna himself.

In the meantime, Colonel Stephen Kearny captured Santa Fe, New Mexico, without resistance. His army then continued to California, where the Pacific Squadron, under Commodore John Sloat, had taken San Francisco and other key ports on the Pacific Coast.

Colonel Alexander Doniphan had traveled with Kearny to Santa Fe and then turned south into Mexico. His forces defeated the Mexicans at El Brazito on Christmas Day, 1846. Two days later they occupied El Paso, and then they marched south towards Monterrey.

General Winfield Scott, with the Navy's Home Squadron, fought from Vera Cruz in March 1847 to Mexico City in September. American troops occupied the city until the peace was concluded. Santa Anna fled the country.

After two years of intense fighting, both armies had suffered enormous losses. The Americans, though almost always outnumbered, had won every battle, largely due to their superior weaponry. By the end of 1847, they controlled New Mexico, California, and a substantial part of Mexico.

On February 2, 1848, the Treaty of Guadalupe Hidalgo officially ended the war. The United States bought New Mexico and California for $15 million, and Mexico recognized the U.S. border at the Rio Grande. The American state of Texas was established—half slave and half free—sixteen years before the country plunged into an even bloodier war.

The Mexican-American War (1846–1848)

✪ Causes

Manifest Destiny

Since the settlement of Plymouth Colony in 1620, white Americans felt their presence in the New World was their deliverance, reward, and providence. In the nineteenth century, some Americans pushed for the annexation of Texas, New Mexico, California, and Oregon. They claimed that the United States had the God-given right and responsibility to fill the continent, no matter who stood in their way. They called it America's "manifest destiny."

From Sea to Shining Sea From a very early date, the vision of American expansion has motivated U.S. policy. Thomas Jefferson (1743–1826) purchased the Louisiana Territory in 1803, saying in his second inaugural address, "Who can limit the extent to which the federative principle may operate effectively? ... is it not better that the opposite bank of the Mississippi should be settled by our own brethren and children, than by strangers of another family?" In 1819, the Adam-Onis Treaty acquired Florida and parts of Alabama and Mississippi.

Still, the phrase "manifest destiny" was not widely used until 1845, when John O'Sullivan (1813–1895), editor of the *New York Post*, used it to support the annexation of Texas. "It is our manifest destiny," he wrote, "to overspread the whole of the continent which Providence has given us for the development of the great experiment entrusted to us."

By "experiment," O'Sullivan meant federal government and self-rule, also "schools and colleges, courts and representative halls, mills and meeting-houses." He believed that the political and social systems of the United States offered the best formula for human happiness. He thought that other peoples should be persuaded to adopt American ways.

This attitude grew partially out of the United States' religious missionary tradition—Christians believed that they possessed the true faith, and they felt called to spread it. Others, like John Quincy Adams (1767–1848), took a more practical approach. Adams said that the United States had a duty to develop the wilderness, since the Indians had failed to do so.

Above all, the mystique of manifest destiny was fueled by the frontier experience. It was the dream of every family who bundled into covered wagons. It drove every grizzled prospector who dug for gold in California. Manifest destiny was the collective expression of a million individual ambitions.

Oregon Country When James K. Polk (1795–1849) made his bid for the presidency in 1844, he ran on an expansionist platform. He particularly championed the American claim to Oregon Country, which had been jointly owned by Britain and the United States since 1818. Polk demanded that the United States should have sole possession of the northwest, up to latitude line fifty-four degrees, forty minutes north, almost to the southern boundary of Alaska. Democrats rallied behind Polk's slogan: "Fifty-four forty or fight."

Great Britain, on the other hand, reacted with scorn, and some fierce saber-rattling ensued. As negotiations with Mexico also broke down, many observers feared that the United States would have to fight two wars at once. However, a compromise was reached with the British government in April 1846. The United States would take Oregon up to the forty-ninth parallel, and Britain would retain Vancouver Island.

The Southwest Meanwhile, the United States annexed Texas in 1845. The Mexican government, which had never recognized Texan sovereignty, immediately broke off diplomatic relations.

In response, Polk sent John Slidell (1793–1871) to Mexico City as minister plenipotentiary of the United States. Polk did not particularly want war, and he thought that Mexico would be willing to bargain. Slidell was given the authority to buy parts of Texas, New Mexico, and California. The United States would pay with a combination of cash and the assumption of Mexican debt.

Mexican President José Herrera (1792–1854), had indicated that he would talk with an American representative, but hardliners in the Mexican government would not accept losing any Mexican territory. They felt that Herrera was a traitor for even considering it. Neither Herrera nor his successor, Mariano Paredes (1797–1849), would receive Slidell during his visit. Thus, unable to make his case for U.S. purchase of the land diplomatically, Polk set about taking them by force.

Destiny and War Not all Americans embraced the theory of manifest destiny, and many saw the Mexican-American War as a bald-faced, thuggish land grab. Ulysses S. Grant (1822–1885), a young officer at the time, labeled the war "one of the most unjust ever waged by a stronger nation against a weaker nation."

Congressman Abraham Lincoln (1809–1865) also opposed the war, a stance that probably cost him his reelection. Lincoln would later say that he "did not believe in enlarging our field, but in keeping our fences where they are."

The rhetoric of manifest destiny died down during the Civil War, but its influence has persevered in the American psyche. It would reemerge with vigor as American Imperialism in the Spanish-American War. Its echo can be heard in American politics even today.

✪ Major Figures

Stephen F. Austin

Stephen F. Austin (1793–1836) organized the Anglo colony in Texas and then was a leader in the Texas Revolution, which allowed the territory to become free from Mexico. He is often called "the Father of Texas." Born Stephen Fuller Austin on November 3, 1793, in Austinville, Virginia, he was the son of Moses Austin, the operator of a nearby lead mine, and his wife, Maria Brown. When Austin was five years old, his father moved the family to the frontier territory of Missouri, then under Mexican control. Moses Austin again successfully worked in the mining of lead as well as land speculation.

Early Years Because of the family's wealth, Austin primarily received his education out of state after 1804. He attended Bacon Academy and Colchester Academy, both in Connecticut, and Transylvania University in Kentucky. When his father asked him to return home after only a year or two of college, in 1810, Austin went back to Missouri. He went to work in his father's businesses and soon showed his management abilities. In 1814, Austin was elected to the state legislature, where he served until 1820. He also served in the state militia

ALL OF MEXICO MOVEMENT

From the outset of the Mexican-American War, Polk intended to claim New Mexico and California as spoils of war. However, many Americans demanded much more. The colorful journalist Jane McManus Storm Cazneau (1807–1878) wrote in favor of "keeping the whole of Mexico." Why should (white Americans) give away territory, she argued, "when they had paid for it in blood and treasure?"

She was not alone in this opinion. Many Southerners wanted to establish a slave-owning empire in Central America. Some Northerners believed that emancipation was inevitable, but that freed blacks would never fit into white society. They suggested that former slaves could migrate to Mexico, where society would accept them.

Newspapers like the *New York Sun* supported the annexation of Mexico. But despite their efforts, most white Americans did not want people of "mixed and confused blood" as United States citizens. They also deeply distrusted the Mexicans' Catholicism.

There were more practical considerations. Union with Mexico meant the assumption of the Mexican national debt—over $10 million.

Interestingly enough, a sizable number of Mexican radicals also advocated annexation by the United States. They hoped that the American government would rid their land of military tyrants and corrupt Catholic priests.

The issue became moot, however, with the ratification of the Treaty of Guadalupe Hidalgo. Nicholas Trist (1800–1874), had failed at one attempt to negotiate an armistice with Mexican General Santa Anna (1794–1876), but remained in Mexico and brokered the agreement even after Polk had recalled him to Washington. The treaty maintained the sovereignty of the Mexican nation, but ceded a third of its land to the United States.

as an officer, worked for a bank in St. Louis, and was briefly a storekeeper.

Austin had total control over the family's mining operations by 1817, when his father decided to focus on other businesses. As the mines failed, the family's debt increased greatly. The family enterprises went bankrupt during the Panic of 1819. Austin then went to Arkansas to try to erase family debts by buying land on credit with the intent of developing a town. This scheme failed, but Austin became an appointed district judge in early 1820. This position did not offer a large enough salary to pay off the money the Austin family owed, which had landed Moses Austin in jail and resulted in the sale of the family mines at auction. By the end of the summer of 1820, Austin was living in New Orleans, Louisiana, and

"Go West, young man!" exhorted *New York Tribune* editor Horace Greely. © *Bettmann/Corbis*

working at a newspaper to help pay the family's debts. He also studied law.

Austin's Colony Moses Austin died in the spring of 1821, but he had already started a new scheme that he hoped would allow his family to repay its debts and restore its wealth. He believed that immigration to Texas and starting a colony there would be profitable. Upon his father's death, Austin inherited the government permit to found a colony with three hundred families in Texas that Moses Austin had obtained from the Spanish, who controlled the area. With the help of his younger brother Brown, he publicized the venture throughout the United States and moved to Texas himself.

In 1822 and 1823, Austin went to Mexico City to make sure that Mexico, which had won its independence from Spain in 1822, recognized the permit. Mexican authorities did so after he pledged his allegiance to their country. Austin later applied for Mexican citizenship. The Mexican government also gave Austin the title of "empresario," which meant that he was the official authority of the colony. As empresario, Austin was given large amounts of the best land as well as the ability to collect a fee for land bought, usually on credit, by other settlers.

Austin maximized the permit and brought three hundred families to Texas in 1823 and 1824. Over the next decade, he was able to acquire more permits and found legal loopholes to bring 750 more white families to the colony. To attract settlers, he allowed slavery, though he personally opposed the practice. The number of whites soon surpassed the Spanish Mexicans living in Texas.

Austin spent the rest of his life working to make the Texas colony viable. He served as the leader of the colonists in Texas, taking charge of coordinating the defenses against the Native Americans in the area as well as acting as a liaison to authorities in Mexico. He also created a land system and served as the translator of Mexican laws for the colony. In addition, Austin was able to survey and map what would become the state of Texas.

Texas Independence Within a decade of the founding of the Texas colony, the white settlers decided they wanted Texas to be an independent state. (It had been named part of a state in Mexico in April 1824.) Continuing to serve the colonists, Austin acted as the president of the first of many conventions to discuss independence and draft a proposal to present to the Mexican government. He also went to Mexico City in 1833 to argue the matter, but he was arrested in early 1834 because such conventions were illegal under Mexican law. Austin was charged with sedition and imprisoned for nearly two years. Released without being tried, he went back to Texas in 1835, and by September, became active in the

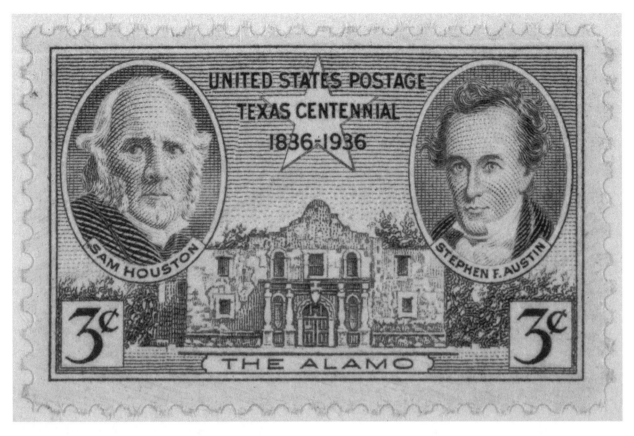

This 1936 U.S. postage stamp commemorating the 100th anniversary of the Republic of Texas demonstrates the lasting stature of Texas heroes Sam Houston and Stephen F. Austin. *The Granger Collection, New York. Reproduced by Permission*

independence movement. While he was in jail, the Anglo population in Texas had continued to grow.

When the Texas Revolution broke out, soon after his release from jail, Austin supported the military operation to seek independence. He took charge of the armed forces organized by the Texas settlers. Austin's time at the top of the military order was short-lived because of his poor health. Taking on a diplomatic role by the end of 1835, Austin was in the United States as a commissioner from Texas to ask for American aid in the white settlers's cause. When Texas declared its independence from Mexico, Austin also asked the American government to recognize Texas's new status.

In 1836, after Texas won its independence and declared itself a republic, Austin was compelled to run for the new country's presidency. His opponent was Sam Houston (1793–1863), who was a military hero of the Texas Revolution. Houston won the election and offered Austin an office in his administration. Austin served in the post for only a short time. Austin died on December 27, 1836, in Columbia, Texas, of pneumonia.

Sam Houston

Samuel Houston (1793–1863) was a soldier, governor of Tennessee and Texas, president of the Republic of Texas, U.S. congressman from two states and senator from one, and was instrumental in Texas's independence from Mexico and annexation by the United States. Houston was the fifth child and fifth son of Samuel Houston and Elizabeth Paxton. He was born on March 2, 1793, at his family's plantation in Rockbridge County, Virginia. Houston was thirteen years old when his father died. In 1807, he moved with his mother, five brothers, and three sisters to a farm near Maryville, in eastern Tennessee, where they farmed and operated a store.

Early Years Houston received about six months of basic education while in Virginia. He attended an academy near Maryville for about a year and developed a love for classical literature there.

In 1809, when he could not tolerate his older brothers's demands that he work both on the farm and at the store, Houston ran away from home. He lived for three years with the Cherokees across the Tennessee River and made occasional visits to Maryville. Chief Oolooteka adopted him and gave him the Indian name "the Raven." This experience gave him great insight into Indian cultures and traditions, which he would draw on repeatedly in later years.

He left the Cherokees in 1812 and established a private school so that he could repay debts. With the outbreak of the War of 1812, he enlisted in the U.S. Army as a private. He was severely wounded at the Battle of Horseshoe Bend in March 1814, and was commended by General Andrew Jackson (1767–1845) for his courage and promoted to second lieutenant. Houston was assigned to Jackson's command at Nashville and named an Indian subagent, and he assisted in the removal of Chief Oolooteka to the Indian Territory. He resigned from the regular army in 1818 to study law, was admitted to the bar, and opened a practice in Lebanon, Tennessee. He also received Jackson's assistance with an appointment as a colonel in the state militia, and in 1821, was named major general of the Tennessee militia.

The Tennessean As a Jacksonian Democrat, Houston was elected to Congress in 1823, was reelected in 1825, and became governor of Tennessee in 1827. He married nineteen-year-old Eliza Allen in January 1829 and announced his candidacy for another term as governor. His marriage lasted eleven weeks. Allen left him and returned to her parents. For the rest of their lives, neither party spoke of the reason for the breakup. On April 16, in the wake of the scandal, Houston resigned his office and moved to Oolooteka's Cherokee clan in present-day Oklahoma.

The Cherokee He lived among the Indians again for three years. He was granted Cherokee citizenship, established a trading post near Fort Gibson, Oklahoma, married Cherokee Diana Rogers Gentry under tribal law, and acted as an emissary between tribes. He maintained contact with the non-Indian world outside the trading post with trips east as well as correspondence with various government officials, including his mentor, who was then President Jackson.

The Texan In 1832, Jackson tasked Houston with presenting peace medals to western Indian tribes. Once he completed this mission, Houston turned his thoughts to Texas. He left Diana and the trading post, and on December 2, 1832, crossed the Red River into Mexican Texas (in the Mexican state of Coahuila y Tejas) and started a law practice in the present day–east Texas town of Nacogdoches.

Within a few months, Houston was elected as a delegate to the Convention of 1833, which advocated making Texas a separate province of Mexico. Relations between Texians (residents of Mexican Texas) and federal authorities in Mexico City deteriorated, and in November 1835, he was appointed major general of the Texas Army. When volunteers refused to obey his orders, the Texas provisional government gave him the task of negotiating peace with the Indians and given a furlough until March 1, 1836. Returning to the Texas provisional government headquarters on March 1, he

arrived in time for the adoption of the Texas Declaration of Independence on March 2, 1836. At last, Texas was fighting for independence from Mexico. He was again named commander of the army. Four days later, General Antonio López de Santa Anna had approximately 2,500 Mexican soldiers assembled to attack the Alamo. All of the defenders (about 180) were killed. A few weeks later, at Goliad, more than 340 Texas volunteers were killed after their capture. Houston was left with about 400 volunteers at Gonzales facing more than 4,000 Mexican troops on Texas soil.

Houston began a march across eastern Texas, trying to drill the recruits along the way. Additional volunteers joined the Texas Army as the withdrawal continued. Heavy rains and swollen streams slowed both armies. When Houston learned Santa Anna intended to cross the San Jacinto River at Lynch's Ferry, he knew that was the place to meet the Mexican Army. On April 21, 1836, Houston led about 900 men against an estimated 1,200 Mexican soldiers. In a mid-afternoon silent march, the Texans caught the Mexicans by complete surprise, approaching within 550 yards of Santa Anna's fortifications before any alarm sounded. The battle lasted eighteen minutes. Nine Texans were killed, and thirty were injured. Houston's official report listed 630 Mexican soldiers killed, 208 wounded, and hundreds taken prisoner. Santa Anna was captured the next day. With the Treaty of Velasco signed May 14, Santa Anna agreed to remove all Mexican forces south of the Rio Grande.

After this military victory, Houston was elected president of the Republic of Texas through 1838, and again for 1841–1844. During his terms, he sought annexation of Texas by the United States, peace with various Indian tribes, and low government spending. In 1837, he formally divorced Eliza Allen. He married twenty-one-year-old Margaret Moffette Lea of Marion, Alabama, on May 9, 1840. Houston became a father at age fifty-five when Sam Houston Jr. was born in 1843. He went on to father three more boys and four girls.

In 1845, after Texas was admitted to the United States, Houston served two terms as a U.S. senator. In 1859, he ran for governor and won, becoming the only person to have been elected governor of two states. He opposed secession, and when he refused to take an oath of allegiance to the Confederacy in 1861, he was thrown out of office. In 1862 he moved the family to Huntsville, Texas. The next year, he contracted pneumonia. Sick and ailing for several weeks, he died July 26, 1863. His last words were reported to be, "Texas! Texas! Margaret!"

William Barret Travis

Early Years William Barret Travis (1809–1836) was the Texas commander at the Alamo. Travis was born in early August of 1809 near Saluda, South Carolina. He was the first of eleven children born to Mark and Jemima

After his capture at San Jacinto, Santa Anna was held first by Sam Houston, then by Andrew Jackson in Washington, D.C., before he returned to Mexico. *The Library of Congress*

(Stallworth) Travis. He grew up on the family farm and received his first education at home. The family moved to Alabama in 1817, and Travis received formal schooling near Sparta. He also attended school in Claiborne, taught other students there, and apprenticed as an attorney under James Dellet. Once he was admitted to the bar, he practiced for a time with Dellet before opening his own office. Travis married a former student, Rosanna Cato, on October 26, 1828. Their first child, Charles Edward Travis, was born about ten months later.

For a while, it looked like Travis would establish himself in business. He started a newspaper, the *Claiborne Herald*, practiced law, became a Mason, and joined the Alabama militia as an adjutant. Despite these outward signs of stability, he was falling deeper and deeper in debt. The paper was not getting the advertising he needed, and his legal practice was floundering. Court records show judgments rendered against him. In 1831, he decided to make a clean break and left for Texas, leaving his pregnant wife and son. He promised to send for the family when he was successful in his new location. Shortly after arriving in Texas, he established a legal practice in Anahuac, a small port on the northeast side of Galveston Bay.

Service to Texas There were few lawyers in this part of the Mexican province, and his practice flourished. In 1832, he had his first brush with the Mexican military. On a pretense, the military commander had Travis and his law partner arrested. When word of the arrest spread, settlers descended on Anahuac to gain the release of the two. Mexican troops were outnumbered, the lawyers were released, and Travis had newfound fame and notoriety.

Travis moved to San Felipe de Austin shortly after being released. San Felipe was headquarters of Stephen F. Austin's colony and the de facto capital of Anglo settlement. He became more involved with politics and the militia, although his main credentials were his law education and passion for Texas independence. Meanwhile, Rosanna Travis allowed Charles Edward Travis to move to Texas to be close to his father. Travis never sent for Mrs. Travis and his daughter, Susan Isabella, to join him in Texas. Mrs. Travis filed for divorce, citing desertion as the reason in her 1834 pleadings. The divorce became final in the fall of 1835. It is not known if Travis knew this, since he was traveling extensively across the settled parts of Texas as the revolution grew ever closer. He pursued many women, promising one he would marry her.

In June 1835, Travis launched a water-borne attack on Anahuac, capturing Mexican soldiers at the port. Reacting to this affront and other disturbances, General Martin Perfecto de Cos (1800–1854), the Mexican military commander for that part of the country, moved troops from Matamoros, on the southern tip of the Rio Grande river, almost 250 miles northwest, to San Antonio, then the largest town in Texas. General Cos was also the brother-in-law of Antonio López de Santa Anna, commander-in-chief of all the country's armed forces. Travis learned General Cos wanted the Anahuac participants delivered to him for a military trial.

When Travis finally came close to San Antonio in late October 1835, it was with hundreds of Texas militia who laid siege to the town. He distinguished himself on November 8, when three hundred mules and horses were captured. He then left the siege and returned to San Felipe, where he served as the chief recruiting officer for the Texas army. General Cos surrendered in December, agreeing to march south of the Rio Grande and not return. Once back in Mexico, he met with Santa Anna. The commander-in-chief told Santa Anna that the agreement to not move north was null and void. Santa Anna ordered a force of several thousand soldiers to march on San Antonio.

In January 1836, Travis was ordered to gather volunteers and go to the Alamo, the former mission, because Santa Anna's arrival there was anticipated. He arrived on February 3 and met commander James Clinton Neill (c. 1790–1848) and James Bowie (1796–1836). On February 8, David Crockett (1786–1836)

TRAVIS'S LETTER FROM THE ALAMO

William Barret Travis was an imperfect man, but one talent he did not lack was the ability to write stirring prose. The day after Santa Anna's forces began their siege at the Alamo, Travis penned one of the most famous heroic appeals for aid ever written. While it did not save him and the other Texas defenders, it rallied support for the Texas cause and the battles yet to come:

> Commandacy of the Alamo—Bexar, Feby 24th, 1836
>
> To the People of Texas and All Americans in the World—
>
> Fellow Citizens & Compatriots—
>
> I am besieged, by a thousand or more of the Mexicans under Santa Anna—I have sustained a considerable Bombardment & cannonade for 24 hours & have not lost a man—The enemy has demanded surrender at discretion, otherwise, the garrison are to be put to the sword, if the fort is taken—I have answered the demand with a cannon shot, & our flag still waves proudly from the walls—***I shall never surrender or retreat.*** Then, I call on you in the name of Liberty, of patriotism, & everything dear to the American character, to come to our aid with all dispatch—The enemy is receiving reinforcements daily & will no doubt increase to three or four thousand in four or five days. If this call is neglected, I am determined to sustain myself as long as possible & die like a soldier who never forgets what is due to his own honor and that of his country—

SOURCE: *The History of the Alamo & the Texas Revolution.* Texas A&M University www.tamu.edu/ccbn/dewitt/adp/history/bios/travis/travtext.html (accessed April 30, 2007).

arrived with a group of volunteers. On February 14, Neill announced he had to take a leave of absence to care for his ill family. After his departure, Travis was voted commander of the members of the Texas regular army, while Bowie commanded the volunteers.

The question of command structure among the different pro-Texas forces took on little to no significance with the arrival of Santa Anna's advance forces and the start of the battle on February 23. Defenders fell back from the town and moved to the limited protection of the Alamo. The siege had begun. On February 24, Bowie became seriously ill, and Travis assumed command of all forces.

Travis continued Neill's attempt to fortify the Alamo by bringing in provisions, building gun emplacements, and appealing to the Texas provisional government for reinforcements. After the siege began, the largest contingent reaching the mission, on March 1,

was thirty-two volunteers from Gonzales. Travis's had a total of 190 defenders against Santa Anna's forces, which eventually totaled almost 2,500 soldiers. As the thirteen-day siege dragged on, Santa Anna moved his cannons closer to the Alamo, crumbling the fortified walls with each shot. On March 3, Travis received word around noon that there would be no reinforcements from Goliad, where James Fannin (1804–1836) commanded almost five hundred Texas soldiers. That same day he wrote a friend, "I am determined to perish in the defense of this place, and my bones shall reproach my country for her neglect."

At approximately 5:30 A.M. on March 6, 1836, Santa Anna ordered his troops to advance towards the Alamo. The mission defenders ran to their positions, alerted either by shouting Mexican troops or buglers sounding the advance. Travis raced to the northern wall, near the steps of the present-day San Antonio downtown post office, about one block northwest of the front chapel door. As he looked over the side, he saw Mexican soldiers already at the wall, putting up scaling ladders. Travis's slave, Joe, stood beside him. One of the few survivors that day, Joe later recounted that Travis emptied his shotgun into the crowd below. Shortly after this volley, he saw Travis stumble backwards from the force of a round of ammunition that found its mark. There was a gaping hole in his forehead. The twenty-six-year-old commander still clutched his sword as he fell down an incline, raised up for a moment, and then died. He was one of the morning's first casualties. After the battle, his body was burned along with that of the other defenders who had been killed. The site of the funeral pyre is not known.

David Crockett

Early Years   David (Davy) Crockett (1786–1836) was a hero at the siege of the Alamo as well as of the American frontier. His backwoods exploits were popularized in print and on stage in his own lifetime, in a 1950s children's television series, and in folklore. Crockett was born on August 17, 1786, in Tennessee, which was on the frontier of the United States. He was born in a cabin located on the Holston River in Greene County. Crockett was the son of John and Rebecca (Hawkins) Crockett. His family, squatters, regularly moved around Tennessee, where his father, an Irish immigrant worked variously as a farmer, mill operator, tavern keeper, and store manager.

When Crockett was still a child, the family put down roots in northwest Tennessee. He had little schooling. When he was twelve, his father sent him to Virginia to work as a cattle driver to help the family's always precarious financial situation. Returning to Tennessee that winter, he went to school for four days before getting into a fight. Crockett then stopped going, but did not

David (Davy) Crockett. *The Library of Congress*

tell his father he was not attending school and ran away from home to avoid being punished.

Crockett spent most of the next three years in Virginia, North Carolina, and Maryland working as a teamster and hatter apprentice as well as traveling. After going back to Tennessee, he determined that he needed some education to find a worthy spouse and spent six months in the employ of a teacher in exchange for a basic education. In 1806, Crockett married his first wife, Polly Findley, and he began farming. Crockett liked hunting better than farming, and in 1811 he began moving west. The family settled in Franklin County, Tennessee, in 1813.

Early Career From 1813 to 1815, Crockett served two stints in the Tennessee militia during the Creek War, which was part of the greater War of 1812. The battles were fought between Creek Indians and settlers after some frontiersmen ambushed a number of Creek warriors in Alabama. The Creek responded by killing five hundred settlers hiding in the undefended Fort Mims. During the conflict, Crockett served primarily as a mounted scout and hunter, and saw only limited, if any, action.

After nearly dying of malaria, Crockett began a career in politics in Tennessee. His first post came in 1817 when he was an appointed, popular justice of the peace. By 1818, he added three more titles: county court referee, Lawrenceburg county commissioner, and colonel of the state militia. Resigning as commissioner in 1821, Crockett decided to make a run for the Tennessee legislature.

One reason for Crockett's political success was his storytelling abilities. Though still only partially literate, he used his formidable storytelling abilities in his successful campaigns. His political campaign speeches were often filled with stories that appealed to his audience of frontiersmen. Elected to the state legislature in 1821, he worked to defend the interests of settlers in the west by reducing taxes, providing for debtor relief, and offering solutions to land claim disputes. He served in the Tennessee legislature again from 1823 to 1825, this time representing his new home of Gibson County, Tennessee.

National Politics After a failed 1824 campaign for U.S. Congress, Crockett ran again in 1826 as a Democrat and was elected to the House of Representatives. He held the seat until 1831. A split with fellow Tennessean Andrew Jackson, then president of the United States, contributed to Crockett's losing the 1830 election. He then joined the Whig party and was again elected to Congress by a close margin in 1832. During his congressional terms, he worked to get frontier settlers land for free through his support of the Tennessee Vacant Land Bill and worked on relief for those in debt.

After continued criticism of Jackson, Crockett lost in the 1834 election. By this time, he had become something of a national celebrity. The popular play *The Lion of the West* popularized his legend while he was a still congressman. He toured the East Coast on speaking engagements, and a number of best-selling books were published based on his life.

Texas Hero When Crockett lost the 1834 Congressional election, he decided to move to Texas. He traveled with his second wife and neighbors in search of land opportunities. At the time, Texas was in transition as a part of Mexico that was primarily inhabited by white American settlers. The settlers soon began fighting Mexico for the freedom to make Texas an independent nation. Joining the Texas Volunteers in January 1836, Crockett participated in the fight for Texas independence as an officer.

By February 1836, Crockett and other volunteers were in San Antonio, defending the Alamo. The former mission was serving as a fort for the Texans. Mexican troops descended on the fort, and the white colonists were martyred in the battle. Among the casualties of the Mexican siege and capture was the Alamo troop commander, Crockett, who was executed by Mexican troops on March 6, 1836. Journalists of the day embellished his life and death at the Alamo. Crockett's fame resurged in the mid-twentieth century, when television series and movies loosely based on his life were popular.

James Bowie

Early Years James (Jim) Bowie (1796–1836) was an important military leader for the Texas Rangers who lost his life during the siege of the Alamo. Born in Kentucky, he was the son of Rezin Bowie and his wife, Alvina Jones. Not much is known about Bowie's childhood other than the fact that the Bowie family, including Bowie's four brothers, moved first to Spanish-owned Missouri in 1800 and then to Catahoula Parish, Louisiana, in 1802.

By adulthood, Bowie and his brother Rezin (1793–1841) ran a sawmill and invested in a successful sugarcane plantation. They were the first in Louisiana to employ steam power in the grinding of sugarcane. Bowie was later believed to be in the slave smuggling business with one or more of his brothers, and he also was a land speculator in Natchez, Mississippi, in the late 1820s.

Moved to Texas By 1828, Bowie was living in Texas. Settling in San Antonio, he spent time looking throughout the nearby region for a lost mine. After becoming a

The large, distinctive Bowie Knife, with its blade guard reportedly inspired by an injury suffered by Colonel Jim Bowie, became a popular weapon and tool in the nineteenth century. © *Bettmann/ Corbis*

Mexican citizen in October 1830, he obtained large amounts of land by convincing Mexicans to ask for land grants, then buying the land tracts from them at a cheap rate.

Though Bowie married Ursula Martin de Veramendi, the daughter of the governor of the Mexican state Coahuila y Tejas, in the spring of 1831, his allegiance was with the other white American settlers who had been colonizing Texas in greater numbers in the early to mid-1830s. These Americans challenged the Mexican government, which had allowed them to move to Texas, and sought more freedom and independence. Bowie's wife, two children, and many members of her family had died of cholera in 1833, so he focused much of his time and energy serving in the Texas Rangers as a colonel in support of the settlers' efforts.

Colonel Bowie Bowie participated in several battles between the white Texans and the Mexican government. In August 1832, he was part of the conflict at Nacogdoches, Texas, in which Colonel José de las Piedras surrendered. Bowie escorted the prisoners back to San Antonio and then spent most of the next two years in private life, but he also fought in Mexico in support of Monclova as capital of the Mexican Texas state of Coahuila y Tejas in 1833.

Texas settlers continued to call for freedom from Mexico. In May 1835, Bowie was selected to be a member of the first committee of safety, which was organized at Mina. The Texas Revolution broke out soon afterward, and Bowie was named a colonel in the settlers's military. He was in command of a small number of troops and helped with war strategy. Bowie helped rid Texas of the Mexican military by mid-December 1835.

Early in 1836, the Mexican Army, headed by General Santa Anna, returned to Texas. Bowie and the other volunteer soldiers under his command were forced to retreat to the Alamo. The former mission gave refuge to the soldiers as they made their failed stand against the Mexicans. Ignoring orders to leave, Bowie and his men stayed and fortified the Alamo. Bowie's command was stymied when he either fell ill with respiratory disease or suffered broken bones while fortifying the Alamo. Thus, he was in bed on March 6, 1836, as the Mexican army besieged the Alamo. Bowie died there, though he managed to inflict casualties on the enemy before he died.

Antonio López de Santa Anna

General Antonio López de Santa Anna (1794–1876) led the Mexican Army to a victory at the Alamo, but he suffered a number of defeats and eventually lost the Mexican-American War. Santa Anna also served as the president of Mexico six times and was generally perceived to be more concerned with gaining glory and advantage for himself than with improving the emerging Mexican nation. Santa Anna was born in 1794 in Jalapa,

Veracruz, Mexico, to Antonio Lafey de Santa Anna and his wife, Manuela Perez de Lebron. His father worked as a mortgage broker and public official, and the family was wealthy. Though Santa Anna longed for a military career from childhood, his family pushed him into an unsuccessful apprenticeship with a merchant.

Early Career When Santa Anna was sixteen years old, he was finally allowed to join the Veracruz Infantry regiment as a foot soldier. Part of the colonial Spanish Army, he later served in the cavalry as well. When Mexicans began rebelling against Spain as they looked for their independence, he fought in support of Spain. Santa Anna proved formidable in battles, including conflicts in Texas against independence leader Miguel Hidalgo (1753–1811). Santa Anna reached the rank of captain by the early 1820s and had a favorable record of service, despite a gambling scandal and accusations that he had stolen money. In 1821, when the rebellion seemed near victory, Santa Anna defected to the pro-independence, yet conservative, side and joined the army of future–Emperor of Mexico General Agustín de Iturbide (1783–1824). Santa Anna was soon named a brigadier general of his forces.

When Mexico gained its independence in August 1821, Santa Anna soon displayed his political inconsistency by revolting against Iturbide's self-declared imperial empire in 1823. After taking the port of Veracruz that year, Santa Anna declared himself in support of a republic for Mexico, even though he did not fully understand what that meant. He then retired to his hacienda, Magna de Clavo, until the late 1820s when political events again drew his interest. He put together an army in support of liberal Vicente Guerrero (1782–1831) to oust the elected conservative president Manuel Gómez Pedraza (1789–1851).

Political Prominence In 1827, Santa Anna gained widespread fame in Mexico when he handled the surrender of Cuba-based Spanish forces that made a feeble attempt to invade Mexico at Tampico. He was regarded as a hero for his actions and became important in Mexican politics. In 1833, Santa Anna became Mexico's president after its Congress elected him to the post. Claiming personal illness, but actually disinterested in governing, Santa Anna remained at home and allowed his vice president, Valentín Gómez Farías (1781–1858) to serve as provisional president. When Gómez Farías's actions and reforms proved unpopular, Santa Anna overthrew him in 1834 and labeled himself "liberator of Mexico."

Santa Anna then became Mexico's dictator for a time, though there was political instability in the country. Amid the revolts and Santa Anna's own resignation and resumption of control, he led Mexican troops into Texas in 1836. White Americans had been forming a colony in Texas with Mexican approval but now wanted their independence. Santa Anna achieved some successes

THE BOWIE KNIFE

James Bowie's name is often associated with the invention of the so-called bowie knife, though claims that his brother Rezin invented it are supported by letters from as early as 1827. Some sources claim that James Bowie did devise the knife, and that he was inspired by a fight with an Indian in which he was carrying a butcher's knife. He hurt himself when his hand slipped from the knife's hilt to its blade. Bowie then is said to have carved a wooden model for a new kind of knife with a guard, a single edge, and an uncurved blade that was fifteen inches long. He showed it to a blacksmith named John Sowell, who made the first one. Sowell named the knife the bowie knife. The weapon became well known after James Bowie used it to kill another man in a fight known as the "Sandbar Fight" in Mississippi in 1827. By 1840, the bowie knife, which was also called the Arkansas toothpick, was being manufactured in England. The bowie knife proved to be a popular weapon in Texas and beyond for mountaineers, Texas Rangers, hunters, and those living on the frontier.

in his military maneuvers, including a victorious siege at the Alamo, but he ultimately suffered a humiliating loss to Sam Houston at the Battle of San Jacinto on April 21, 1836.

Captured as a prisoner of war, Santa Anna was forced to sign the Treaty of Velasco, which granted Texas its independence and withdrawal of Mexican troops. Santa Anna was later held prisoner in Washington, D.C., for a brief time. In February 1837, Santa Anna returned to Mexico to find that he had been deposed in favor of a former president, Anastasio Bustamante (1780–1853). Santa Anna was further disgraced when Bustamente declared the Treaty of Velasco invalid, but he would soon emerge again to help his country.

After spending a year and a half on Magna de Clavo, Santa Anna led Mexican troops to a victory over a French squadron bombing a city in Veracruz. The French had attacked Mexico because of unpaid debts owed to their country, in the so-called "pastry war." Santa Anna lost his leg in the conflict, which demonstrated his courage and only heightened his already growing political attractiveness. By 1839, Bustamente was compelled to name Santa Anna interim president of Mexico, and the general eventually gained the post outright again in 1841. Santa Anna retained the presidency until 1842, then again from March 1843 to July 1844, when he was overthrown once more and imprisoned.

Service in the Mexican-American War Rather than being charged with treason by the new government, Santa Anna instead was forced to go into exile in Cuba in 1845. He was able to convince the United States that if he was allowed to return to Mexico and regain his post, he would settle the disputed border of Texas and negotiate peace. While the Americans had the Mexican coast blockaded, Santa Anna was allowed to slip through. When he arrived in Mexico he reneged on his word and helped Mexico prepare for war with the United States.

Santa Anna once more became president of Mexico in December 1846, and then took charge of gathering and training twenty thousand Mexican soldiers early in 1847. He soon began attacking U.S. troops with his army, battles which were part of the Mexican-American War. However, his leadership proved to be inadequate, if not inept, and the Mexican army lost key battles to the Americans.

One stinging defeat came in the Battle of Buena Vista, in which the outnumbered Americans displayed their superior artillery skills. They compelled Santa Anna to retreat at night after losing many men in one day of conflict. Santa Anna also suffered heavy casualties at the Battle of Vera Cruz and the Battle of Cerro Gordo. As Mexico lost territory to the Americans, Santa Anna resigned his presidency and later abandoned his troops and his military post. He was forced into exile in Jamaica, then a British territory, before spending two years in Central America as a farmer.

Returned to Mexico After conservatives, led by Lucas Alamán, (1792–1853) regained control in 1853, Santa Anna was asked to return as interim president. Santa Anna took the post in April of that year and retained the office even after Almán's death. In April 1854, Santa Anna agreed to sell Arizona to the United States under terms of the Gadsden Treaty.

Because of continued corruption, liberal forces organized a revolt against Santa Anna in August 1855. He fled Mexico, and spent ten years in exile in Cuba, the United States, Columbia, and St. Thomas. He tried to return again in the mid-1860s, but had no support. His banishment lasted until 1873, when he was permitted to return to Mexico because he was not a political or military threat. Already suffering from ill health, Santa Anna died on June 21, 1876, in Mexico City.

James Polk

James Knox Polk (1795–1849) was the eleventh president of the United States, overseeing the country during the Mexican-American War. He was the first president to lead the United States during a foreign war. Born November 2, 1795, in Pineville, North Carolina, he was the son of Samuel Polk, a wealthy farmer, and his wife, Sarah Jane. When Polk was ten, his father moved the family to Tennessee, where he farmed thousands of acres with slave labor. Polk spent the rest of his formative years there.

Early Political Career After receiving the bulk of his education at home, Polk attended the University of

The eleventh president of the United States, James K. Polk, played an active role in the Mexican-American War. *Courtesy of the National Archives/Newsmakers/Getty Images*

North Carolina, where he focused on the classics and mathematics. Upon graduating in 1818, he began studying law with Felix Grundy, a congressman. In 1820, Polk was admitted to the bar and spent two years in legal practice. He then ran for a legislative office in Tennessee in 1822. Winning the seat in the Tennessee legislature, Polk opposed land speculators as well as Tennessee's banks.

After fellow Tennessean and family friend Andrew Jackson won the presidency in 1824, Polk, who supported Jackson's campaign, won a seat in the U.S. House of Representatives. Serving seven consecutive terms, Polk supported states' rights and soon became a Democratic Party leader. By 1833, Polk was serving as the chairman of the House Ways and Means Committee and was a backer of the banking policies espoused by President Jackson.

Polk's political career continued to rise when he was elected speaker of the House of Representatives in 1835. While holding the post, Polk expanded the speaker's powers. Because of his actions, his office of the speaker took charge of overseeing organizational matters as they passed through Congress. Polk left the House in 1839 to take on political challenges in his home state.

Polk became governor of Tennessee in 1839. He held the post through 1841. Though he ran for reelection in 1840, he was defeated. He ran again in 1843 but again lost. During these years, Polk made his living as a farmer.

The U.S. Presidency Though Polk was twice unable to win the governorship of Tennessee, he was nominated by the Democrats to run for U.S. president in 1844. Polk was not the front-runner for the Democrats—divisive Martin Van Buren (1782–1862) was—but a compromise candidate who was able to bring disparate Democrats together during his political campaign. Though the relatively unknown Polk was not expected to win the election against Henry Clay (1777–1852), a more prominent Whig, he was able to capture an upset victory by a slim popular plurality. This victory marked the first time a so-called "dark horse" candidate won the presidential election.

Once in office, Polk proved successful—he had useful administrative organizational abilities and assembled a strong cabinet. In his inaugural address, he defined four goals he wanted to achieve as president—and he was able to achieve them all by the time he left office in 1849. Polk was able to lower the tariff with the passage of the Walker Tariff, and set up an independent federal treasury. Polk also added California to the Union with the Treaty of Guadalupe Hidalgo, which ended the Mexican-American War, and resolved the Oregon border dispute with Great Britain by getting the British to agree to define the border between Oregon and Canada at the forty-ninth parallel. In addition to these issues, Polk had to deal with political and philosophical differences between slave and free states, an issue brought to the forefront by the acquisition of new territories and the inability of either side to compromise.

The Mexican-American War Polk inherited a difficult political situation that soon led to war. On the very last day of the presidency of his predecessor, John Tyler (1790–1862), Texas was annexed to the United States. Though Mexico immediately ended diplomatic relations with the United States because of this action—Mexico believed the United States did not have the authority to annex lands located west of the Sabine River—Polk tried to negotiate with the Mexican government. He sent envoys to negotiate with the Mexican government on several matters, including settling boundary disputes. These negotiations failed, and the Mexican government also ejected an American emissary to Mexico, John Slidell, from the country.

In the spring of 1846, Polk determined that the United States had no choice but to go to war with Mexico. On May 11, 1846, the House of Representatives formally passed the war resolution, though battles had already been fought by troops under the command of General Zachary Taylor (1784–1850). During the war, Polk played an active role in overseeing the actions of army, in part for his own political well-being. He regarded both General Taylor and General Winfield Scott (1786–1866), two heroes of the war who were

instrumental in the American victory, as political rivals. Polk also directed the details of organizing the troops, helped appoint officers, and directed the United States's war strategy.

Polk pursued secret diplomacy with Mexico during the war. He still hoped to acquire both California and New Mexico via this method, but failed. It was not Polk's only disappointment. He had agreed to pay Mexico's former dictator, Antonio López de Santa Anna, to return home in exchange for an agreement to end the war and begin peace negotiations. Santa Anna backed out of the deal after he returned to Mexico. As soon as Santa Anna was back in Mexico, he became the commander of the Mexican army and joined the conflict.

The U.S. Army won the Mexican-American War with military superiority and a decisive strategy that included the capture of Mexico City. The peace treaty negotiated after the war's end in 1848, the Treaty of Guadalupe Hidalgo, saw the United States retaining Texas and gaining both California and New Mexico in exchange for $15 million. Because of this treaty, Polk was able to add more than one million square miles to the United States.

No Second Term Early in his presidency, Polk announced he would not run for a second term. He did this because he hoped it would reduce tensions within the Democratic Party and free him from party politics so that he could represent all Americans. In 1848, he gave his support to Lewis Cass (1782–1866), who became the party's presidential nominee. General Taylor, the Whig candidate, was able to win when Martin Van Buren left the Democrats, offered himself as a third-party candidate, and split the Democratic vote.

When Polk left office early in 1849, he was already suffering from poor health. He died only twelve weeks later, on June 15, 1849, in Nashville, Tennessee. Years after his death, Polk was considered one of the best presidents the United States ever had.

Zachary Taylor

Zachary Taylor (1784–1850) was a hero of the Mexican-American War and the twelfth president of the United States. He was nicknamed "Old Rough and Ready" and was known for his tactical and exceptional leadership skills. Taylor was born November 24, 1784, on the Montebello estate about twenty miles from Charlottesville, Virginia, the son of Richard Taylor, an officer who had served during the Revolutionary War, and his wife, Sarah Dabney Strother.

When Taylor was less than a year old, the family moved to Louisville, Kentucky, where his father had been given land as a reward for his war service. Although his father built a plantation on his land, he also took a job as a customs collector. Taylor received his education from private tutors at home, but it was limited and not

GEN! TAYLOR, AT THE BATTLE OF BUENA VISTA.

Who, from a hill in the vicinity, saw, with exultation, his Spartan Band successfully repel the last charge of the terror-stricken Mexicans!

General Zachary Taylor directed his troops to victory at the Battle of Buena Vista. *Library of Congress*

of high quality. He also worked on the plantation and learned about agriculture.

Early Career Though Taylor's father wanted him to remain on the plantation, Taylor was permitted to act on his interest in the military and enter the U.S. Army after an elder brother died. When he twenty-four years old, he was given a commission as a lieutenant in the Seventh Infantry and sent to New Orleans under the command of General James Wilkinson (1757–1825). After a brief leave when he contracted yellow fever, Taylor was promoted to captain and sent to the Indiana Territory in 1810.

Taylor was put in charge of Fort Harrison during the War of 1812, and was breveted major for the duration of the conflict. While Taylor was in command, the fifty soldiers in the fort survived an assault by four hundred Native Americans led by Shawnee Chief Tecumseh (1768–1813). The victory made him famous. When the war ended, he was demoted to captain. Taylor was insulted by the demotion, resigned, and went home intending to work again in agriculture.

The Indian Wars Taylor's retirement was short-lived, because President James Madison (1751–1836) reinstated his promotion to major in 1816. Over the next twenty years, Taylor served in the Wisconsin Territory as the commander of the Third Infantry and as the head of garrisons in Louisiana and Minnesota. After being promoted to colonel in 1832, Taylor was in charge of four hundred soldiers during the Black Hawk War. He was the recipient of Black Hawk's (1767–1838) surrender.

After Taylor served as the commanding officer of Fort Snelling, in Minnesota, for several years, he was put in charge of the U.S. Army during the Florida-based Seminole Wars in 1837. He was breveted brigadier general after defeating the Seminole Indians in a major victory at Lake Okeechobee. By 1840, Taylor was serving as commander of the Department of the Southwest and was based in Louisiana's Fort Jessup. He then made Baton Rouge his home, though he also bought a plantation in Natchez, Mississippi, in 1841 and became a slave owner.

Service in the Mexican-American War By the spring of 1845, Taylor was positioned in the Republic of Texas as the territory was being annexed by the United States. He was under orders to fend off any attempt by Mexico to interfere or reclaim the territory. Taylor led the four thousand men under his command to Corpus Christi, Texas, during the summer of 1845, and a few months later moved his troops to the Rio Grande's mouth. The Americans wanted the river to be the southern boundary of Texas.

Taylor prepared for war by building Fort Brown (sometimes called Fort Texas, in present-day Brownsville, Texas) in March 1846. After the Mexican army struck the Americans, Taylor fought back even before war was declared by the United States. At the Battle of Palo Alto in May 1846, Taylor's troops won a victory over a much larger Mexican force. Two reasons for the win were the precision of the artillery's and Taylor's own courage and inspiring leadership. A day later, Taylor won another victory at the Battle of Resaca de la Palma. With these victories, Taylor's troops were able to occupy Matamoros, the Mexican town across the Rio Grande from Fort Brown.

After the two battles, Taylor received other honors. He was named commander of the Army of the Rio Grande by President James K. Polk. Taylor was also breveted general and given gold medals by Congress. In September 1846, Taylor led six thousand soldiers to Monterrey, Mexico, and was able to capture the city after a four-day battle. But only Taylor's increasing popularity prevented his being removed as commander by President Polk, who was unhappy with Taylor's merciful attitude toward the Mexicans.

Taylor briefly remained at Monterrey with three thousand troops while General Winfield Scott led the rest of the U.S. Army in the area on an invasion at Veracruz, Mexico. Though Taylor was supposed to stay on the defensive in Monterrey, he soon took his men and marched south to engage the bigger Mexican army—15,000 to 20,000 strong—led by Antonio López de Santa Anna. The Battle of Buena Vista took place on February 22 and 23, and again, the stronger artillery compelled a U.S. victory and a Mexican retreat.

Elected U.S. President After returning from Mexico in November 1847, Taylor was ready to run for the U.S. presidency. Though his supporters considered his political skills abysmal, and he had never voted in a presidential election, Taylor won the nomination of the Whig party in 1848. He unexpectedly defeated Democrat Lewis Cass and took office in 1849.

As president, Taylor's lack of political skill made his short-lived presidency essentially unsuccessful, especially in the areas of foreign policy and congressional relations. Taylor dealt with the growing issue of slavery, however. Though he did own slaves, he wanted California and New Mexico admitted as free states and strongly opposed Texas's claims on lands east of the Rio Grande as well as any talk of secession by southern states. He was

also the last Whig president, in part because he created division within the party.

Taylor developed cholera or gastroenteritis and fever on July 4, 1850, probably as a result of drinking large amounts of water on a hot day. He died shortly thereafter, on July 10, 1850, in Washington, D.C., and was buried in Louisville, Kentucky.

General Winfield Scott

General Winfield Scott (1786–1866) was a hero of the Mexican-American War and eventual general in chief of the U.S. Army. He led U.S. troops to significant victories in Mexico during the conflict. Scott was born on June 13, 1786, near Petersburg, Virginia, the son of William Scott and his wife Ann Mason. The family had inherited significant wealth. William Scott was also a Revolutionary War veteran who worked as a farmer, but died when Scott was six years old. Scott's mother died when he was seventeen, but she had raised him with a strong sense of manners and a love of books.

Scott chose to go to college after his mother's death, attending William and Mary College for a year. Deciding to pursue a legal career, he studied law with well-known attorney David Robinson and was admitted to the bar of Virginia in 1806. Scott practiced law until his military career began.

Early Military Career Scott's military experiences began in 1807 when he heeded President Thomas Jefferson's call for volunteers for a militia to keep British ships away from the American shore. Scott volunteered as a lance corporal and was in charge of a patrol that watched over a small amount of coastline. He soon asked Jefferson for a permanent commission in the military.

In 1808, Scott was appointed a captain in the U.S. Army and stationed in New Orleans. Within a short amount of time, he faced difficulties. He served under a commanding general, James Wilkinson, for whom he had little respect. Scott was court-martialed after he called Wilkinson a traitor to the United States. He was convicted and spent the year 1810 suspended from the Army. He resumed his legal career during this time.

After being reinstated to the Army, Scott was promoted to lieutenant colonel by the time the War of 1812 began. He was in charge of recruiting what came to be the Second Artillery. On the battlefield in Canada, he showed himself to be a superior soldier, both courageous and able to make solid judgments despite being captured at the battle at Queenstown. Scott later led troops to victory at Niagara, Stoney Creek, and Fort George. Scott's valor led him to be promoted first to brevet brigadier general and then brevet major general. He also received congressional thanks and a gold medal.

Though Scott was asked to become President James Madison's secretary of war, the general turned down the offer. Instead, Scott left the army from 1815 until 1821. He returned as the commander of the Army's Eastern

General Winfield Scott led his army into Mexico City on September 17, 1847. *The Library of Congress*

Division until 1825, when he was temporarily relieved of his duties after being court-martialed for refusing orders. In addition to training officers under his command, Scott also wrote military manuals on infantry and tactics, both of which became accepted standards. He twice went to Europe to learn about other countries's military tactics as well.

Leading American General Beginning in the late 1820s, Scott participated in several significant military operations. He took part in the Black Hawk War in 1828 and then was stationed in South Carolina during the nullification controversy of 1832. Scott here showed his burgeoning negotiating skills, which prevented civil war—one of several times his expertise proved effective in preventing battles. Scott was on his way to becoming the leading military mind in the United States.

By 1835, Scott was in Florida to combat the Seminole and Creek Indians under President Andrew Jackson's orders. Because of the lack of material support, Scott's effectiveness was limited, however. Though Jackson relieved him of his command and ordered him to go in front of a board of inquiry, Scott was not only absolved of any wrongdoing, but also praised for his handling of the situation. Scott continued to show his military and negotiating skills in various military operations during the late 1830s, including bringing peace to the Niagara region after the failed Canadian revolt

of 1837, overseeing the removal of Cherokee Indians to the Indian Territory in 1838, and helping negotiate peace in the 1839 Lumberjack War.

Such successes led to Scott being named the Army's general in chief in 1841. He would remain in the post until 1861. Scott was personally responsible for making the U.S. Army more efficient and effective. He also enforced high standards of discipline and dress on troops, including a personal crusade against the consumption of alcoholic beverages.

Service in the Mexican-American War Though General Zachary Taylor had been in charge of U.S. troops through the early part of the Mexican-American War, Scott was brought in by President James K. Polk in 1847 to seal the victory Taylor had been unable to achieve. (Polk had not appointed Scott the head of U.S. forces in the region for political reasons. Scott had already been considered as the Whig nominee for president in 1838, 1840, and 1844, and Polk did not want to heighten Scott's visibility.)

Scott proved effective in the conflict. Beginning in March 1847 with his landing at Veracruz, Mexico, Scott reeled off a succession of victories. He won battles at Cerro Gordo, Molino del Rey, and Chapultepec before securing Mexico City six months after his initial landing in Mexico. While the peace treaty was being negotiated, Scott commanded the U.S. troops occupying and keeping

Though the defeat at the Alamo was initially devastating, a desire to remember it rallied the American Texans at San Jacinto. *Getty Images*

order in Mexico City. Some Mexican citizens even asked Scott to become their country's dictator, but Scott soon returned home and left General William O. Butler (1791–1880) in charge of the troops.

Failed Political Ambitions After coming back to the United States, Scott continued to serve as general in chief of the Army while General Taylor was elected to the White House in 1848. Scott's own political ambitions took hold when he received the Whig nomination for president in 1852. Though he desperately wanted to be president, Scott lost by a wide margin, in part because of the arrogance displayed in his campaign.

While his political career had essentially ended, Scott continued to distinguish himself as a military officer. In 1855, he was promoted to lieutenant general, a rank last held by George Washington (1732–1799). Remaining with the Union Army during the Civil War, Scott proposed the policy of dividing the South to contain it. President Abraham Lincoln adopted the measure, which proved successful. It was one of Scott's last acts as general in chief. He chose to retire on November 1, 1861, at the age of seventy-five. Scott died less than five years later, on May 29, 1866, at West Point, New York. He is buried at Arlington National Cemetery.

✪ Major Battles and Events

The Alamo

The two-week siege at the Alamo saw the Anglo and Mexican Texans fortified therein to stand up to their Mexican colonial overlords. The Texans wanted their independence but suffered a devastating defeat at the Alamo at the hands of the Mexican army on March 6, 1836. Texans had begun organizing militarily after the Mexican president, General Antonio López de Santa Anna, sent Mexican troops in 1835, under the command of General Martín Perfecto de Cos, to the forts located along the Rio Grande River, the border of the Texas colony with Mexico. Cos was attempting to administer new Mexican federal laws in the colony, but failed.

Setting the Stage White settlers began firing on the Mexican troops under General Cos, and the troops fired back. The Texans soon organized their own small militia, which took over two small towns in Texas, Goliad and Gonzales. By the end of October 1835, the Texans's militia had arrived in the fortified city of San Antonio, where General Cos had made his headquarters with four hundred Mexican troops.

The Texans's militia, which now included about three hundred new members, then spent six weeks exchanging fire with the Mexican army in San Antonio. In early December, the Texans grew bold and besieged the fort. By December 10, Cos had lost 150 of his 400 men, and he surrendered San Antonio, to the Texans. Though the victors let the Mexican army, including Cos, go back home without their weapons and with a promise not to return, they knew there would be reprisals. The Texans fortified the Alamo and waited for an attack.

Furious, General Santa Anna decided that the Texas colony must be put in its place. He led six thousand Mexican troops himself to the area in early 1836. The Texans in the militia in San Antonio did not expect an attack from Mexico until spring. Because some of the volunteers in San Antonio had grown restless during the winter and sought battles in other cities, only about one hundred militiamen remained there, though others joined those waiting in San Antonio. By the time Santa Anna arrived in February 1836, there were about 150 militia members in San Antonio, including David Crockett and Jim Bowie. Bowie and another new arrival, Colonel William Barrett Travis, were the joint commanders of the militia's volunteers.

The Siege Begins

On February 23, 1836, a sentry for the Texans saw 1,500 members of the Mexican cavalry nearing San Antonio. With that warning, Travis ordered that all in San Antonio should move into the Alamo. (The Alamo was once the San Antonio de Valero mission, which had later served as a fort, but had been deserted until shortly before the battle.) Surrounded by high walls, the Alamo consisted of several buildings that surrounded a three-acre plaza. To protect themselves, the Texans mounted the fourteen cannons in their possession along the walls. They also set up rifles.

Santa Anna's army did not directly attack the Alamo right away but instead controlled San Antonio and surrounded the Alamo. That same day, February 23, Santa Anna sent a messenger to the Texans demanding their surrender. He and his troops were appalled when the Texans released a cannon shot that nearly hit the messenger.

The Siege Reaches a Stalemate

For the next two weeks, the Mexican army laid siege to the Alamo. From the Alamo, the Texans were able to use their superior Kentucky rifles and other weapons to injure and kill a many Mexican soldiers. The Mexican troops used muskets and cannon fire on the Alamo—to much less effect because the Texans' weapons had much longer range. Reinforcements for the Mexican army continued to arrive during the siege.

While the siege was essentially a stalemate, with no injuries inside the Alamo, the Texans were hoping to hold on until reinforcements arrived. On February 24, Colonel Travis sent a message to Sam Houston, who was organizing a Texas army. Travis told him about conditions inside the Alamo and asked for more troops.

By March 1, thirty-two additional volunteers were able to sneak inside the Alamo. Travis realized that the situation was still dire and that no more reinforcements were arriving. The fewer than two hundred defenders inside the Alamo were no long-term match for the thousands of well-trained Mexican soldiers. Travis informed the defenders on March 3 that they would have to fight to their deaths, but if they wanted to leave now, there would be no loss of honor. At most, only one man left, though even one man leaving is the subject of historical debate.

Final Showdown

On March 6 at 5 A.M., Santa Anna ordered a degüello attack (no prisoners to be taken) on the Alamo. The battle began with Mexican cannon fire creating two enormous holes in the walls of the Alamo. Through these holes, about three thousand Mexican soldiers entered the fortified mission. The Texans defended themselves with a hail of bullets and cannon fire, but they could not hold their positions for long. The battle soon turned to hand-to-hand combat using knives and bayonets. The entire confrontation lasted less than ninety minutes.

Before the end of the March 6 battle, Travis, Crockett, and a bed-ridden Bowie were already dead. Only five of the Texas defenders survived the attack. Though the remaining defenders surrendered to the Mexicans, they and nearly everyone who had sought refuge in the Alamo were killed by the Mexican army. Only Susanna Dickinson (c. 1814–1883), the wife of a Texas soldier, her baby, a few female Mexican nurses, and two slave boys were allowed to live and leave the Alamo. Approximately six hundred Mexican soldiers died in the final siege.

With the Alamo under control, Santa Anna pursued the fleeing Texas army east. The Texans lost again to the Mexican army at Goliad. "Remember the Alamo!" became the inspiring rallying cry as Texas fought for its declared independence from Mexico and began the Texas Revolution.

San Jacinto

The Battle of San Jacinto was fought on April 21, 1836. It was the definitive engagement in the Texas revolution against Mexico. Fought on a slightly crested peninsular plain near present-day Houston, the battle and resulting events created a viable Republic of Texas and set the stage for the annexation of Texas by the United States in 1845. It also helped produce the Mexican-American War of 1846 and led to the eventual transfer of more than one million square miles of territory from Mexico to the United States.

After his victory at the Alamo on March 6, Mexican commander Santa Anna split his army into thirds. He planned to sweep down from the north, secure the coast

The San Jacinto Monument commemorates the overwhelming American Texan victory at the site on April 21, 1836. *Matthew Stockman/Getty Images*

with a detachment moving northeast from Matamoros, and command forces east across the middle of the Texas from San Antonio, destroying any rebel resistance along the way. His combined army of almost 3,500 troops would either eliminate any military threat in Texas or push all opposition across the Sabine River and into the United States. Mexico would again control its northern-most province.

Goliad Texas commander-in-chief Sam Houston needed time to gather strength, train volunteers, and concentrate his forces as he fell back across Texas before the advancing Mexican army. He ordered Goliad commander James Fannin and more than four hundred defenders to leave their garrison and join him on the march east. Fannin delayed and was captured with most of his men. On March 27, Santa Anna ordered the execution of the 342 prisoners. This order was in keeping with a law the Mexican legislature had approved in December 1835 that provided for the execution—as pirates—of all foreigners taking up arms against

Mexico. The Mexican commander at Goliad saved as many Texans as he could and spared anyone with beneficial skills and prisoners captured without weapons. The message to Texas volunteers was clear. After the Alamo and Goliad, any future Mexican victory meant almost certain death.

Coming Together In mid-April, Santa Anna learned the Texas government was in Harrisburg (now Houston). He thought he could move swiftly and capture the civilian rebels and then deal with General Houston. Favoring speed over numbers, he marched with roughly 650 soldiers, about 50 cavalry, and one piece of artillery, leaving his remaining force of 2,800 soldiers and numerous artillery pieces forty miles southwest of Harrisburg at Fort Bend (present-day Richmond) on the Brazos River. When he got to Harrisburg, he found the government was now at New Washington, 20 miles east. He arrived there on April 18, just in time to see the Texas government sailing away across the bay, heading for Galveston Island. On the same day, Texas scout Erastus "Deaf" Smith (1787–1837) captured a Mexican courier, and General Houston (with 1,200 troops) arrived in Harrisburg. Documents in the courier's saddlebags gave Houston Santa Anna's troop strength, overall strength and location of other Mexican forces, and Santa Anna's planned movements. He also knew Santa Anna would soon get about six hundred reinforcements led by his brother-in-law, General Martin Perfecto de Cos. Even counting these additional troops, after the Alamo, Goliad, and the overwhelming desire of his volunteers to avenge these defeats, Houston was ready for a fight against 1,300–1,400 Mexican soldiers. Santa Anna had to cross the San Jacinto River at the Lynchburg ferry in order to move east. Houston raced for the ferry crossing.

On April 19, Houston left almost 250 sick or wounded soldiers in Harrisburg and marched his remaining army northeast on the Lynchburg road, crossing Vince's Bridge along the route. On the morning of April 20, about nine hundred Texans moved onto the plain at San Jacinto, about fifteen miles from Harrisburg. They established their camp on high ground in a grove of oak trees near the confluence of Buffalo Bayou and the San Jacinto River. Santa Anna learned of the Texas troop movements, burned New Washington, and after marching northwest about eight miles, established camp in front of the Texans—about 1,200 yards away. Because of high grass and a small rise in the San Jacinto plain between the two forces, neither army could see the other's encampment. The Texas forces had water to their back (Buffalo Bayou), water to their left (the San Jacinto River), hundreds of Mexican troops in front of them, and General Cos and his troops coming on their right. The Mexicans had the river to their right, swamps and a lake to their back, and the Texans in front. They also had a long plain heading off toward the coast on their left back to New Washington, and the bridge to Harrisburg to the southwest.

There was a short cavalry skirmish on the afternoon of April 20. The main effect of this parry was the demotion of Sidney Sherman back to command of the Second Texas Infantry (240 men) and the elevation of private Mirabeau B. Lamar (1798–1859) to commander of the cavalry (50 men) the next day. Sherman wanted to fight the Mexicans so much that his cavalry movements threatened to start a full battle.

April 21, 3:30 P.M. On April 21, Texans heard reveille at 4 A.M. The sleep of the previous night was their first good rest in days. On the Mexican side, there was little to no sleep. During the night, Santa Anna had his soldiers throwing together hastily built breastworks (aboveground trenches) of boxes, luggage, saddles, and other items. At about 9 A.M., General Cos arrived via Vince's Bridge, not with 600 battle-hardened soldiers as Santa Anna had ordered, but with about 540 new recruits. Santa Anna now had approximately 1,300 troops. Cos's men had marched all night and through the morning to reach the camp. They were dispersed on the extreme right side of the Mexican lines. To their right was the San Jacinto River; behind them were a series of marshes, a small lake, and more river. They were beyond what little protection was afforded by the breastworks to their left (which were supported by about 240 men), the single piece of Mexican artillery in the middle of the defenses, more breastworks and about 340 soldiers, and finally about 50 cavalry completing the left flank. The entire line stretched more than 1,000 yards in an arc that bulged slightly towards the Texas camp.

Aware of growing unease in the Texas ranks, Houston called a council of war around noon that lasted until 2 P.M. He also ordered Deaf Smith to destroy Vince's Bridge. There would be no more reinforcements from the Harrisburg road, and the Texans's only way out of San Jacinto would be through the Mexican defenses. At approximately 3:30 P.M., Houston ordered the officers to parade their commands and advance across the open plain. On the left flank was Sidney Sherman (1805–1873) and 260 members of the Second Texas Infantry. To his right was the First Texas Infantry with 220 men commanded by Edward Burleson (1798–1851). Volunteers brought their own equipment, usually a musket or rifle. On this day, many also had two or three loaded pistols and a bowie knife or sword. Next to Burleson were thirty-one soldiers, commanded by George Hockley (1802–1854), manning the artillery, two "six-pounders" (cannons that fired six-pound balls) known as the "Twin Sisters." To the right of the artillery marched Henry Millard (c. 1796–1844) (240 men) and the Texas Regular Army. Unlike the volunteers, these soldiers were supplied with 1818 Harpers Ferry flintlock muskets and bayonets. Some also had more recently issued U.S. hardware. Millard had been the

chief Army recruiter in Nacogdoches. His group had a large concentration of volunteers with recent U.S. military experience. There were several U.S. Army deserters and recently released soldiers who joined the Texas cause after leaving their posts with the regular army in nearby Louisiana. Next to Millard was Mirabeau B. Lamar at the lead of about sixty cavalry. The combined forces stretched more than one thousand yards from left to right in two lines.

Remember the Alamo! Remember Goliad! At approximately 4:30 P.M., the Texans were within five hundred yards of the Mexican line when they crested the slope and emerged from the tall grass. In a document written after the battle, Santa Anna stated he ordered sentries posted; on that afternoon, there were no sentries. He planned to attack April 22 and did not think the Texans would attack fortified positions across an open plain. Most of the soldiers were resting or asleep. As Santa Anna wrote in his official report, "I yielded to repose." Bareback cavalry horses were feeding on grass or being led to and from water. A bugler saw the Texans approaching and sounded the alarm. The Twin Sisters were wheeled within two hundred yards of the Mexican defenses and opened fire. Cannon fire flew through the front lines. Mexican troops got off one organized volley, but their aim was high and few attackers fell. Texans waited until they were within pistol range and then opened up with muskets and rifles. The results were devastating. After this exchange, the lines fell apart as individual clusters of Texans raced to breach the defenses.

Sherman's infantry hit first. With shouts of "Remember the Alamo!" and "Remember Goliad!" ringing out, the Texans smashed into Cos's men, throwing the recruits into disarray. Those who were not killed in the initial sweep ran into the wetlands to their rear or fled to the left through the rest of the Mexican army, followed closely by attacking Texans. This caused more confusion as seasoned veterans tried to form up and fight. For Santa Anna's army, it was already too late. The Twin Sisters were wheeled within seventy yards of the Mexican lines, fired again, and then fell silent. After these shots, any Texas artillery would hit Texans, because Texas First fighters were already over the breastworks on the left and Millard's Texas Regulars seized the Mexican's only cannon and more breastworks to the right. Lamar's cavalry engaged the far right of the Mexican defenses, against a largely insignificant mounted response. Once at and over the lines, Texans continued inflicting injuries with pistols, swords, knives, captured Mexican weapons, and the butts of their long guns.

Active fighting lasted eighteen minutes. Afterward, Texans continued killing Mexican troops until nightfall. Most of these deaths occurred in the swamps and lake behind the Mexican encampment. Individual soldiers were killed where they stood or were shot in the water.

Aftermath and Prelude Texas losses were nine killed and thirty injured, including Houston, who was shot in the ankle. Reports of Mexican losses are inexact, with generally accepted figures of more than six hundred killed and almost seven hundred taken prisoner. Santa Anna was captured the next day and brought before Houston. Rather than kill the self-described "Napoleon of the West," Houston used Santa Anna to order his remaining forces to fall back to San Antonio and await further instructions. On May 14, with the public Treaty of Velasco and a secret side agreement signed the same day, Santa Anna agreed to move all Mexican troops south of the Rio Grande, to establish the Texas border with Mexico at the Rio Grande, and to not invade Texas again. The Mexican government refused to abide by the treaty, the Texans seized Santa Anna as a prisoner of war, and Mexico would not recognize the Rio Grande as its northern border until it signed the Treaty of Hidalgo in 1848.

Battle of Palo Alto

Though skirmishes between Mexican and U.S. troops occurred before war was officially declared, the Battle of Palo Alto was the first battle afterward. It was fought before the declaration of war was signed by President James K. Polk and is generally considered the first major battle of the war. President Polk had put General Zachary Taylor in charge of bringing about four thousand members of the U.S. Army to the Rio Grande River across from the Mexican town Matamoros. This encampment irritated the Mexicans, who stationed their own troops in Matamoros.

From Fort Brown (also known as Fort Texas), across the Rio Grande from Matamoros, Taylor marched about 2,300 of his soldiers on May 1, 1846 to the U.S. supply depot at Port Isabel, about thirty miles away. At the time, Taylor and his men were in dire need of supplies, and they took advantage of the chance to breach Mexican lines in order to reach their supply depot. After Taylor arrived at Port Isabel on May 2, he had his troops take everything they could transport, including all the cannons that the arsenal could do without.

Arista's Offensive Mexican General Mariano Arista learned of Taylor's supply trip and wanted to engage the American general and his troops in a battle as they made their way back to Fort Brown from Point Isabel. To that end, before the Americans returned, Arista

General Zachary Taylor defeated Mexican forces at Palo Alto.   *Hulton Archive/Getty Images*

positioned his six thousand men on Palo Alto, the flat, broad plain between the two locations. Taylor and his army reached Palo Alto early on May 8, 1846. After the two armies saw each other and formed battle lines in the early afternoon, fighting began.

The combat started with and consisted primarily of cannons and other artillery fire. The Americans gained the upper hand within an hour. Mexican cannons fired low to the ground, and many of their cannonballs landed far in front of the American soldiers. Because U.S. forces could easily dodge the poor-quality Mexican cannons, gunpowder, shot, and musketry, they were able to hold them off.

Superior American Firepower American artillery inflicted heavy damage on the Mexican army. Using siege guns, howitzers, cannons, and the highly maneuverable "flying artillery" (a light, mounted mobile cannon consisting of a howitzer mounted on caissons, used for the first time in battle), American soldiers bombarded the Mexican army with great success.

During the afternoon, other strategies were tried by the Mexicans and by the Americans. Less successful than bombardment was each side's attempt at a cavalry charge, though the Mexican horses were of better quality than their armaments. The Mexicans also tried an infantry charge, but this, too, was repelled by American artillery. By the end of the afternoon, the Mexican army could not gain ground on the Americans.

Fire Ends the Day's Battle Near twilight, the high grass of Palo Alto, which had been trampled all day by both sides, caught fire. The fire emitted a large amount of smoke. Though the smoke temporarily stopped fighting, the Americans used it as an advantageous cover to ambush Mexican soldiers. A truce was later called for the day, and both armies camped for the night. The next morning, the Americans returned to the battlefield. They found that the Mexican army had retreated and was nowhere to be seen. Only 10 Americans were killed and 40 injured during the Battle of Palo Alto, while there were 257 to 400 Mexican casualties.

The Americans found the Mexicans at Resaca de la Palma, five miles from Palo Alto, and again engaged in battle on May 9. The U.S. Army's infantry and cavalry routed their Mexican counterparts, and the Mexican army continued to retreat as U.S. forces, led by Taylor, occupied much of the northeastern part of Mexico.

Battle of Buena Vista

One of the most significant battles of the Mexican-American War, the Battle of Buena Vista, was also the first involving General Antonio López de Santa Anna in a decade. Shortly before the battle, Santa Anna had taken over the Mexican presidency and raised an army of 25,000. Based in San Luis Potoí, Santa Anna ordered about twenty thousand Mexican troops to march for three hundred miles to Buena Vista in February 1847.

After learning of the American war plan from an intercepted letter, Santa Anna made the journey in order to engage U.S. forces commanded by General Zachary Taylor.

For much of the Mexican-American War, American troops were headed by General Zachary Taylor. Primarily for political reasons, President James K. Polk decided to split the command of the U.S. forces in Mexico between General Taylor and General Winfield Scott. Polk gave Scott orders to launch an invasion of Mexico City from the port city of Veracruz. The American troops previously serving under Taylor were split in half, with Scott taking about five thousand to six thousand men. Nearly all of the regular soldiers, as well as a number of volunteers, were transferred to Scott as he prepared to invade central Mexico.

Santa Anna's Plan Santa Anna learned of the plan for Scott's invasion and decided to attack Taylor first, in part because he seemed more vulnerable because of the troop division. By February 1847, Taylor was moving his remaining men—primarily volunteers—westward into the Sierra Madre mountains of Mexico. Taylor was putting his troops into a defensive position. Santa Anna marched twenty thousand of his troops northward with the intent of intercepting Taylor and pushing the Americans back to the Rio Grande. Over the course of the journey, five thousand Mexican soldiers deserted or died of disease before reaching the battle site.

On February 22, 1847, Taylor's men passed through a narrow mountain pass that had mountains on one side and treacherous gullies on the other. (A nearby ranch was called San Juan de Buena Vista and lent its name to the battle.) Though the pass area was difficult to either defend or attack, the U.S. forces knew of Santa Anna's nearby army and took up a defensive position. Santa Anna's troops were stationed beyond the pass, lying in wait for the Americans, who were far fewer in number than their Mexican counterparts.

Santa Anna sent a message to Taylor on February 23 that formally asked for the surrender of Taylor and the Americans. Taylor's response to the message was harshly negative. The first clashes of the Battle of Buena Vista happened later that afternoon, but these were only minor engagements between the Mexican light infantry and American volunteer soldiers who were riflemen and unmounted cavalry. During the rainy night that followed, both sides readied themselves for the primary clash the next day.

The Battle Begins The next morning, the Battle of Buena Vista began in earnest, primarily consisting of gunfire supported by aggressive artillery action. The Americans relied on cavalrymen and riflemen on nearby heights. Santa Anna repositioned his soldiers in order to add to the light infantry soldiers stationed on the mountainside. Artillery was placed in attack position near the

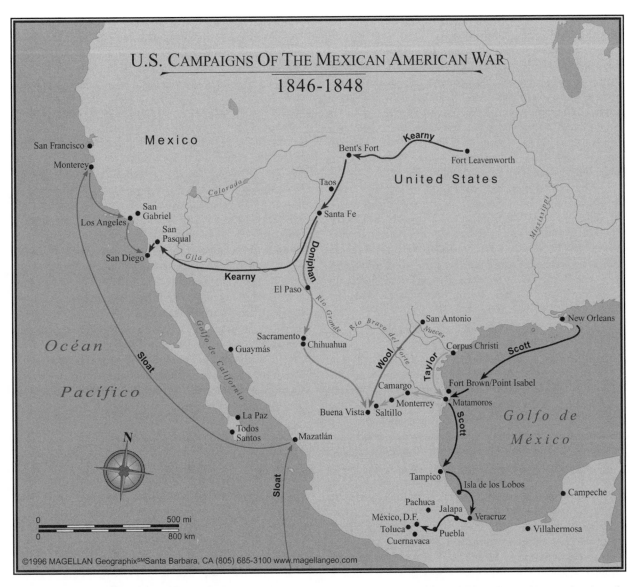

U.S. CAMPAIGNS OF THE MEXICAN AMERICAN WAR
1846–1848

General Winfield Scott's capture of Mexico City in 1847 brought an end to a conflict that had spread across the southwestern portion of North America. © *MAPS.com/Corbis*

pass, ready to strike the Americans. Assault columns and artillery were prepared to hit the American left flank.

The first shots came from the Mexican army as a column traveled up Saltillo Road, which cut through the area. Their efforts were stymied by a battery of Americans. Two divisions of the Mexican army on the right flank had more success early on against the second Indiana Regiment and several pieces of artillery. The regiment's commander became confused during their exchange and ordered a retreat, which forced the artillery commander, Captain John Paul Jones O'Brien, and the troops on the mountain, to back off as well. Though the American left flank could have fallen apart, reinforcements in the form of volunteers from Illinois and Kentucky halted the Mexican advance.

American Momentum U.S. forces slowly found the battle going their way. Troops at the center of combat under General John E. Wool (1784–1869) were forced to withdraw, but did so with a fight. General Taylor rallied all his troops and inserted some fresh soldiers into the battle, including the First Mississippi Regiment. These men, plus the reorganized Second and Third Indiana Regiment, formed the new left flank. Using a "V" formation, the Americans were able to rout the Mexicans, who tried to repel the enemy with a lance attack.

The final assault, led by Santa Anna, to the center of the American troops met with some success. A few U.S. units of infantry and artillery troops from Illinois and Kentucky mistakenly advanced at the same time as the Mexican forward thrust. The Americans found themselves surrounded by the larger Mexican army but were saved by the arrival of more U.S. troops.

The battle continued through the afternoon, but at nightfall both sides agreed to a break and the Mexican Army began retreating. On February 25, the Americans unexpectedly found that the Mexican Army had completely retreated. They could see that Santa Anna's men were on their way back to San Luis Potoí, primarily because of heavy troop loss. About 3,400 Mexican troops were dead, injured, or missing. More Mexicans lost their lives as they marched away.

The Americans lost 267 men, while 465 were wounded and 23 were missing as a result of the battle. Despite the heavy loss of life, the U.S. forces considered the Battle of Buena Vista to be a victory—and an important one—because a prime piece of Mexican territory had been secured. Santa Anna also believed that his army won the Battle of Buena Vista, though many Mexicans disagreed with his assessment, and morale was low among his men.

Battle of Veracruz

During the Mexican-American War, the Battle of Veracruz was a crucial American victory that allowed the United States to control important territory in Mexico and helped lead to the beginning of the end of the conflict. At the beginning of the war, the U.S. Navy blockaded the gulf city of Veracruz as well as the rest of Mexico's port cities. By late 1846, President James K. Polk believed that occupying Veracruz and then marching to Mexico City could bring about the war's end.

Under Polk's orders, General Scott had spent the first months of 1847 preparing for the invasion of Mexico. He had about 14,fourteen thousand troops at his disposal, including five thousand to six thuosand men who were transferred from the command of General Zachary Taylor. The rest of Scott's force was comprised of new soldiers recruited in the United States.

Landing at Collado Beach On March 9, the U.S. troops headed by Scott landed on Collado Beach. The forces had first sailed from the American-controlled Tampico to Lobos Island on February 21, and had then arrived at the American naval base at Antón Lizardo on March 3. They used surfboats, which had been constructed for this landing, to transport ten thousand soldiers to Collado Beach, which was about three miles southeast of Veracruz. Naval ships soon moved off the coast as well in order to support the Army's effort. When the American men arrived on the beach, they were attacked by Mexican lancers who rode along nearby sand dunes. The lancers were soon repelled by gunfire from American ships. The ten thousand American soldiers were able to land without incident or loss of life.

As the Americans continued to organize their operation and bring more supplies ashore on March 10, the three thousand Mexican soldiers stationed at Veracruz remained inside the city under the orders of General Juan Morales. Morales was the Mexican military officer in charge of defending Veracruz. His forces watched as the Americans prepared for a siege. Scott had three divisions of soldiers form a half-moon around Veracruz.

Bombing of Veracruz Because Veracruz, a vital port for Mexico, was highly fortified with high walls and protected by heavy guns, General Scott decided that bombing would be a more effective strategy than an infantry attack on the city, which some had suggested. Scott believed that a bombing siege would result in fewer casualties. As a courtesy, Scott informed General Morales on the day before the bombing began that the city's citizens who were not involved in the fighting could leave. Scott did not receive a reply.

On March 22, Scott ordered the beginning of the bombing of Veracruz. The U.S. military used heavy cannons to shell the city. Other forms of artillery and mortars had been stationed around the city and were also used in the attack. U.S. naval ships contributed to the assault with six heavy cannons located off shore. American naval forces also brought some heavy guns ashore that were operated by naval personnel. Mexican troops responded with their own armaments, but because of their relatively poor quality, the response was ineffective.

U.S. Forces Take the City The American bombings were extremely effective, however, destroying both public buildings and private homes. U.S. forces also had cut off supplies, including water, to Veracruz, further harming those inside the city. Both Mexican soldiers and civilians were killed in the American assault. Over the course of the attack, 180 Mexicans lost their lives. The United States only suffered one hundred casualties, nineteen dead, and eighty-one wounded.

On March 28, after six days of bombing, General Juan Landero surrendered Veracruz to the United States. (Landero had replaced General Morales after his resignation a few days earlier.) Mexican soldiers then marched out of the city and laid down their arms. Mexican authorities in Mexico City were stunned by the loss of Veracruz.

As part of the surrender agreement, American forces specifically stated that the Mexican citizens who remained in Veracruz would be allowed to practice their Roman Catholic faith. Mexicans believed that the Americans were anti-Catholic and would chastise them for their religious beliefs, perhaps even desecrate their churches and physically harm their religious leaders. This provision was expected to improve relations between the American invaders and Mexicans in the land they were conquering. The United States remained in control of Veracruz until the end of the Mexican-American War and used it as a supply port in support of its war effort.

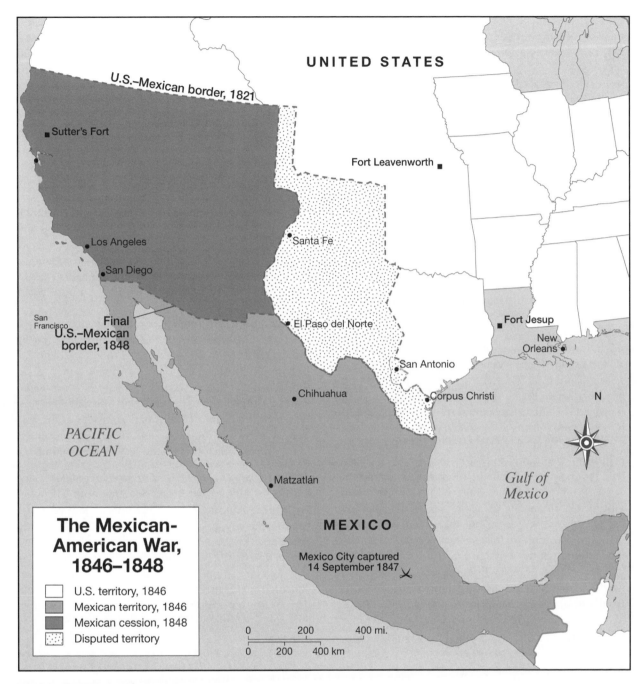

The Mexican-American War, 1846–1848

- ☐ U.S. territory, 1846
- ▨ Mexican territory, 1846
- ▨ Mexican cession, 1848
- ⠿ Disputed territory

UNITED STATES

U.S.-Mexican border, 1821

Sutter's Fort

Fort Leavenworth

Los Angeles

San Diego

Santa Fe

San Francisco

Final U.S.-Mexican border, 1848

El Paso del Norte

Fort Jesup

New Orleans

San Antonio

Chihuahua

Corpus Christi

N

PACIFIC OCEAN

Matzatlán

Gulf of Mexico

MEXICO

Mexico City captured 14 September 1847

0   200   400 mi.

0   200   400 km

As this map reveals, one of the most significant results of the Mexican-American war was a dramatic increase in U.S. territory. *Map by XNR Productions. Reproduced by permission of Gale, a part of Cengage Learning*

March into Mexico City

General Winfield Scott's ultimate conquest of Mexico City sealed the American victory in the Mexican-American War. On April 8, 1847, after he won the Battle of Veracruz, he began marching his men towards Mexico City. It was 225 miles from Veracruz to Mexico City, and Scott's men primarily used the paved National Highway, which ran directly into the city. Scott first wanted to reach Jalapa, about seventy-five miles inland, and then prepare for the assault on Mexico City. On their way, the Americans were forced to engage the Mexican Army in a number of minor battles.

Battle of Cerro Gordo The Mexican forces, led by General Santa Anna, tried to stop the Americans at a narrow mountain pass near Cerro Gordo, which was twelve miles to the west of Veracruz. In an attempt to surprise the U.S. forces, who were weighed down by their heavy guns, the Mexicans fortified one large, steep hill, El Telégrafo, in preparation for an attack on what they hoped would be slow U.S. troops. The Americans were able to evade the Mexicans on April 17 and successfully convey their equipment and men.

On April 18, the Battle of Cerro Gordo broke out when the Americans attacked the Mexicans on three sides. Santa Anna retreated after sustaining heavy losses, about one thousand casualties and three thousand captured as prisoners of war. The Americans lost only 63 men, and 353 were wounded. The U.S. forces also gained forty-three cannons as well as other armaments and supplies from the Mexicans. The Americans released the Mexican soldiers after taking their guns and extracting promises that they would cease fighting in the conflict.

Time of Rest As the Mexican Army retreated to Mexico City, American forces led by General Scott continued their march to the city. On April 19, Scott was able to reach his short-term goal of Jalapa. The U.S. forces were able to occupy Jalapa without engaging in battle. Within a month, the Americans also controlled two additional nearby towns, Perote and Puebla. American troops remained in these communities for several months because more soldiers were needed to replace the volunteers whose commitment terms had ended. By the beginning of August, Scott's army had increased to fourteen thousand men due to the thousands of new arrivals.

This time period was not easy for the Americans. Disease left thousands of soldiers weak and unable to engage in combat. The supply line came through Veracruz, but Mexican guerrilla soldiers sometimes successfully interrupted the arrival of supplies. Scott was able to garner some food supplies from the local area, which was heavily agricultural. All of these problems ended when Scott's troops finally began moving again towards Mexico City on August 7. They traveled between twelve and fifteen miles per day, marching by divisions having a one-day interval between one another.

Nearing Mexico City Mexico City was well protected by its location (in a volcanic crater encircled by lakes, marshes, and villages), by its fortifications, and by thirty thousand Mexican troops. When Scott reached the nearby Valley of Mexico and stopped at San Agustin on August 11, he believed the best way to attack the city was from the south. Scott noted that the eastern gate to the city was blocked by the Mexican army, and an attack from the north would require a longer march and increased vulnerability to Mexican attacks on his rear lines. An attack from the south based in San Agustin allowed the Americans several paths into the city that Santa Anna would have to defend.

Using reconnaissance gathered by engineer (and future Confederate leader) Robert E. Lee and others, the Americans began turning an old mule trail Lee found into a wide road that could support artillery movement. This new road would give the U.S. forces access on the edge of the Pedregal, a large field of rough lava rock. There was much uncertainty if this means of attack would work, but the Americans created the road and crossed the Pedregal with ease.

After traversing the Pedregal, U.S. forces successfully attacked Mexican troops at Contreras on August 19 and Churubusco on August 20. During these two battles, the Mexican Army saw its casualties reach 4,000, while the United States saw only 150 men dead and 800 wounded. On August 21, Scott contacted Santa Anna and suggested the beginning of peace negotiations. Though Santa Anna agreed to a truce and to start negotiations, his excessive demands led to the end of peace talks on September 7.

Scott's attacks on the Mexican Army continued the next day. On September 8, 3,400 U.S. forces, led by General William Worth, successfully took El Molino del Rey and Casa Mata, both only a few miles from Mexico City. The first of these battles was the most costly battle for the United States during the Mexican-American War. About a quarter of all American troops in the area were casualties in the battle, and there was no cannon factory there, which the Americans expected to find.

Taking Chapultepec Hill On September 12, American troops led by Scott began bombing both Chapultepec Hill, an important symbolic landmark located at the edge of the city, and Mexico City itself. The bombing continued for about a day and inflicted death and destruction on the population. September 13 saw American infantry troops, led by General Worth, General Gideon Pillow, and General John A. Quitman, begin their attack on Chapultepec Hill, which was defended by only eight hundred Mexican troops, including fifty teenaged cadets.

The Americans suffered casualties as they charged the hill and attempted to climb it using tall ladders. They were shot at by the Mexicans and had their ladders pushed down. The limited amount of Mexican ammunition soon led to hand-to-hand combat with the Americans in a harsh battle. The U.S. forces triumphed, and nearly all the Mexican soldiers were killed. The remaining Mexican troops surrendered to the Americans about two hours after the battle began.

Mexico City After securing Chapultepec Hill on September 13, the U.S. forces began attacking Mexico City. Two divisions attacked fortified city gates, including San Cosme. Mexican forces again suffered greater losses than the Americans in the fight, with three thousand casualties,

The original caption of this image, depicting the formal joining of Texas with the United States, read "The Republic of Texas is no more." © *Bettmann/Corbis*

including eight hundred who were taken prisoner. The United States counted only 850 dead and wounded. On the night of September 13, Santa Anna took his remaining troops and retreated from Mexico City to Guadalupe Hidalgo. He left at the request of city officials who hoped his retreat would save the city and prevent further loss of life.

General Scott accepted the city's surrender on September 14, and his troops officially marched into the city triumphantly. They then began the American occupation of what was now a chaotic Mexico City. On September 16, 1847, Santa Anna resigned as president of Mexico, though he remained head of the army for some time and used what remained of the Mexican forces to harass the Americans and affect their supply lines. U.S. troops remained in Mexico until June 1848, when negotiations for the peace treaty were completed.

✪ The Home Front

The Annexation of Texas

In 1836, American settlers in Texas declared their independence from Mexico, and in 1845, the United States annexed Texas, triggering the Mexican War.

Mexican Territory Since Mexican independence from Spain in 1821, the territory of Texas had seen a wave of immigration from the United States. Hundreds of Americans packed their belongings, hung a sign on the door reading "Gone to Texas" (or simply "GTT"), and moved out. Soon Anglo-Americans settlers formed the majority of the Mexican Texas's population.

This led to some friction with the Mexican authorities. Many of the newcomers defied national laws—squatting on land, smuggling, trading in slaves, and refusing to convert to Catholicism. Sporadic government crackdowns and rebellious outbreaks continued through the early 1830s.

However, the real breach did not come until 1834, when Mexican President Antonio López de Santa Anna got the legislature to approve the Siete Leyes (or Seven Laws), which amended the 1824 constitution. The laws abolished the Mexican states, consolidating power in the centralist government. They also lengthened the presidential term of office and severely limited suffrage.

Angry protest against the new regime rose up all across Mexico. Santa Anna brutally suppressed a popular uprising in the state of Zacatecas, killing thousands. In Texas, a disorganized but determined resistance movement began. Texians, ethnically Mexican Texans (Tejanos) and white settlers in the area, joined to form a rag-tag rebel army under Stephen F. Austin.

In October 1835, a Mexican cavalry unit tried to reclaim a cannon from a fort at Gonzales, Texas. The Texians refused. Instead, they raised a flag that read: "Come and take it." Hostilities soon began.

In 1836, Santa Anna fitted out an army of 6,000 men and headed north. He was convinced, not unjustly, that the United States had incited these difficulties in Texas. Should the Yankees get in his way, he said, he would storm Washington, D.C., and raise the Mexican tricolor flag over the capitol.

Independence At first, the Texian rebels could not agree on their war aims. Some parties simply wanted a return to the 1824 Mexican Constitution. However, on March 2, 1836, a convention at Washington-on-the-Brazos declared Texan independence. On the same day, Tennessee volunteers slipped through Mexican lines to reinforce the besieged fort at San Antonio, the Alamo.

Days before the siege of the Alamo started, Lieutenant Colonel William Travis wrote to the provisional Texas council. In the letter, Travis swore that he "would never surrender or retreat ... victory or death." On March 6, Santa Anna's army stormed the Alamo. Ordered to take no prisoners, the Mexicans killed all the defenders, including the legendary David (Davy) Crockett.

A few days later, almost four hundred Texians surrendered to Mexican troops near Goliad, Texas. The rebels expected to be treated as prisoners of war. Instead, they were declared under Mexican law to be foreign pirates. They were all summarily executed.

On April 21, Sam Houston and his army fell on Santa Anna's main force at San Jacinto. Caught by surprise, the Mexicans put up a feeble resistance. The Texians continued the slaughter much longer than was necessary, crying, "Remember the Alamo!" Santa Anna signed the "treaty" of Velasco, which recognized Texan sovereignty. The government in Mexico City, however, neither recognized Santa Anna's authority to make such an agreement nor the treaty itself.

Meanwhile, the Republic of Texas elected Sam Houston as its first president. Despite recognition from most world powers, the new nation faced a precarious future. The war had left the government in debt, and the Texas economy was shaky. Internally, Indians and Tejanos rebelled against Texian rule.

Moreover, the Mexican government never acknowledged Texan independence and frequently sanctioned border raids. In 1841, the irrepressible Santa Anna returned to power and promptly swore to retake Texas.

Annexation The American presidential election of 1844 was practically a single-issue contest. James Polk entered the race as a virtual unknown. He won primarily because he supported the annexation of Texas. Never-

theless, he faced determined opposition, especially from the abolitionist movement. Slave-owning Texas would tip the balance of power in Washington in favor of the South.

In his last few days in office, John Tyler signed a joint congressional resolution that offered American statehood to the Republic of Texas and stipulated that slavery should be illegal above the Missouri Compromise line. To no one's surprise, Mexico immediately broke off diplomatic relations with the United States.

Tyler's emissary, Andrew Jackson Donelson (1799–1871), went to Houston with the treaty. Surprisingly, he found that Texan leaders were at best ambivalent towards statehood. Sam Houston and his successor, Anson Jones (1798–1858), would have preferred to retain Texas sovereignty, which they had fought hard to achieve.

Accordingly, Jones sent a message to Mexican President José Herrera (Santa Anna had been ousted again, in 1844). Jones asked Mexico to recognize the Republic of Texas. In return, Texas would promise not to be annexed by any other nation. Herrera agreed to this proposition.

Jones then turned the issue over to the Texan people. Would they prefer independence and recognition, or United States statehood? In June of 1845, the Texas Congress voted unanimously for annexation.

Anticipating trouble (or perhaps to instigate it), Polk sent General Zachary Taylor to Corpus Christi, Texas, and then south to the banks of the Rio Grande River. Americans claimed the Rio Grande as the border of Texas. Mexicans designated the border at the Nueces River, to the north. From their point of view, Taylor's advance represented an invasion of their country and a clear act of war.

The American army waited at the Rio Grande for months, glaring at the Mexican troops across the water. Meanwhile, Taylor exchanged scarcely veiled threats with the Mexican commander, General Pedro de Ampudia.

Ampudia had a reputation for incompetence and cruelty (apparently, he had once fried a man's head in oil for public display).General Mariano Arista took over Ampudia's command in April of 1846, days after Herrera declared a "defensive war" against the United States. Arista sent an advance force across the Rio Grande north of the American position. Captain Seth Thornton was to intercept them, but his party of sixty-three dragoons was ambushed. Eleven Americans were killed, and the rest were captured.

A cry went up in the American press. Polk declared that, "Mexico has ... shed American blood on American soil." On May 12, Congress declared war.

The Missouri Compromise

In 1819, the Missouri Territory applied for United States statehood, prompting an explosive debate over

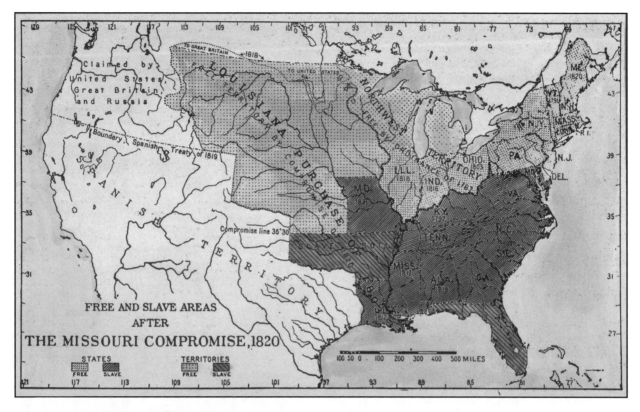

The Missouri Compromise limited slavery to lands south of Missouri. As this map makes clear, the Mexican territories blocked the expansion of the South. *The Granger Collection, New York. Reproduced by permission*

slavery and states rights. The furor was quieted for a time by the adoption of the Missouri Compromise in 1820.

Controversy Slave-owning French colonists had originally settled Missouri in the eighteenth century. By the time Missouri applied for admission into the United States, slaves made up 16 percent of the territory's population. At the same time, eleven existing American states prohibited slavery, and eleven states allowed it. The admission of Missouri would upset the balance of power in the U.S. Senate and give an advantage to the pro-slavery block.

Still, the statehood measure might have passed easily if Congressman James Tallmadge (1778–1853) had not proposed an amendment. Under his plan, Missouri would be admitted, but no new slaves would enter the state. Missourians would retain possession of their existing slaves, but slave children would be freed at the age of twenty-five. In this way, Tallmadge hoped to gradually abolish slavery in Missouri.

The southern states reacted with outrage. Tallmadge's amendment amounted to a moral condemnation of slavery, the first to be presented by the U.S. government since the Constitutional Convention.

On February 6, 1819, the House voted to prohibit the future importation of slaves into Missouri. It also

approved Tallmadge's gradual emancipation scheme. Both measures failed in the Senate.

Compromise The case was further complicated by the fact that Maine, formerly part of Massachusetts, had also applied for statehood. Henry Clay (1777–1852) of Kentucky suggested that if Maine entered the Union as a free state, Missouri should be admitted as a slave state.

For white Americans of the early nineteenth century, slavery posed an extremely complex question, and they developed equally complex answers. Clay owned slaves, yet he was a dedicated member of an abolitionist group. At the same time, Clay highly valued the union of the states. Perhaps because of his own diverse views, he tried to promote solutions that everyone could accept. He would later be known as "the Great Compromiser."

The actual author of the Missouri Compromise, however, was Illinois Senator Jesse Thomas (1777–1853). Thomas did not own slaves, but did not disapprove of those who did. He proposed that Missouri should enter the country as a permanent slave state, and that Maine should come in as a free state. After that, a line would be drawn at Missouri's southern border—latitude 36 degrees, 30 minutes north. North of that line, slavery would be prohibited in all other American territories.

Debate The Missouri issue sparked venomous debate in Washington. The press reported an exchange of angry tirades daily, tirades whose fury caught the country off guard. From retirement at Monticello, Thomas Jefferson wrote that the argument, "like a fire-bell in the night, awakened and filled me with terror."

The issue of slavery had long festered beneath the surface of American politics, however. But now, for the first time, abolitionists brought their agenda into the open. Senator Rufus King (1755–1827) delivered an emotional speech that condemned the institution of slavery everywhere, not just in the new territories. King and his supporters opposed the Thomas compromise. They argued that a showdown over the slavery issue could not be avoided indefinitely.

Southern congressmen responded with equal fervor. In the past, southern politicians had admitted the inherent evil of slavery but denied that there was a practical solution to the problem. Now slavery's defenders lauded the institution as a positive good. South Carolina Senator William Smith (1762–1840) made a biblical case for slavery, saying, "The Scriptures teach us that slavery was universally practiced among the holy fathers." North Carolina Senator Nathaniel Macon (1757–1837) argued that the practice was perfectly morally acceptable.

Prophetically, Georgia Representative Thomas Cobb (1784–1830) warned that "we have kindled a fire which all the waters of the ocean cannot put out, which seas of blood can only extinguish."

Resolution On March 1, 1820, largely because of Clay's efforts, Congress adopted the Missouri Compromise. For a moment, the storm receded.

The accord nearly disintegrated shortly afterward, however, when Missouri submitted its new state constitution. The draft forbade free blacks from traveling into Missouri territory, even though Massachusetts recognized African Americans as citizens.

Clay managed in 1821 to push through the Second Missouri Compromise. This law declared that Missouri could not pass any laws that violated the rights of American citizens. Nevertheless, Missouri defied Congress and passed laws prohibiting black immigration.

The Missouri Compromise maintained the balance of power in the United States for the next few decades. Whenever a slave state was admitted to the country, Congress had to also admit a free state. For example, when Arkansas was admitted as a slave state in 1836, Michigan, a free state, followed in 1837.

The Mexican-American War Many Americans saw the annexation of Texas as an opportunity for the pro-slavery faction to seize power. Indeed, both Texas and Florida were both made states in 1845, giving the South a two-state advantage.

Abolition and sectarianism motivated much of the opposition to the war. As poet James Russell Lowell (1819–1891) wrote:

The annexation of Texas was strongly opposed by abolitionists like Henry Clay. © *David J. & Janice L. Frent Collection/Corbis*

They jest want this Californy
So's to lug new slave-states in
To abuse ye, an' to scorn ye
And to plunder ye like sin.

In August 1846, President James K. Polk asked Congress to appropriate $2 million for a peace settlement with the Mexican government. Everyone understood that he wanted the money to purchase territory. Representative David Wilmot (1814–1868) of Pennsylvania proposed an amendment that stated that slavery would be banned in any lands taken from Mexico. The measure—known as the Wilmot Proviso—narrowly passed the House but was filibustered and killed in the Senate.

From that point on, sectarian squabbles became more frequent and more intense. Southern legislators, including South Carolina Senator John C. Calhoun, (1782–1850) denied the right of the federal government to outlaw slavery anywhere in the country.

Disintegration In 1850, Henry Clay once again tried to calm the waters. Congress passed a series of his compromises: California was admitted as a free state, and New Mexico and Utah were given the right to choose for themselves. In addition, the Fugitive Slave Act went into effect. By this time, however, the national differences could no longer be smoothed over.

In 1857, in the *Dred Scott v. Sandford* case, the U.S. Supreme Court ruled that the Missouri Compromise deprived slave owners of their property without due process and was thus unconstitutional.

✪ International Context

The Irish Potato Famine

In 1845, the potato crop in Ireland suffered a devastating blight. The resulting famine prompted one of the larges exoduses in world history. Millions of Irish men and women left their home country, and a majority of them relocated to the United States.

The Blight Ireland had never been a particularly wealthy country. In 1729, Jonathan Swift (1667–1745) satirically proposed that a cannibalism of starving Irish babies could kill two birds with one stone: feeding the hungry and reducing their number. By the early nineteenth century, the island's people eked out only a meager existence. Historian Alexis de Tocqueville (1805–1859) made a tour of Ireland in 1835. "You cannot imagine," he wrote, "what a complexity of miseries five centuries of oppression, civil disorder, and religious hostility have piled on this poor people."

Nevertheless, the Irish clung to their country, maintaining their identity by means of their language, their tight communities, and their deep Catholic devotion.

Very little industry developed. For the most part, the people lived off the land.

In June 1845, the land failed them. A fungus attacked the potato fields, wiping out the remainder of that year's harvest. The next year's crop would fail entirely. The potato had been the staple crop of Ireland since about 1580, when Sir Walter Raleigh (1552–1618) first brought it from the New World. Potato plants grew well in cool and boggy terrain, and their roots provided far more calories than grain. It was largely due to potato cultivation that the population had almost tripled since 1700. By 1845, about 8.5 million people lived in Ireland, making it one of Europe's most densely populated regions. Over the next decade, more than a million would die of starvation or disease, and two million would leave.

The British The prime minister of England, Sir Robert Peel (1788–1850), eventually bought 100,000 pounds of corn from The United States. This stock was held in reserve and sold at cost to relief societies. His quick action somewhat reduced the severity of the disaster. Nevertheless, the availability of cheap corn created some longer-term problems. Thousands of Irishmen left their farms and poured into urban slums and poorhouses, relying on soup kitchens for their survival.

Not everyone approved of the government's actions. Though the island was technically part of the United Kingdom, many English blamed the famine on the Irish, and called Peel's relief efforts a waste of British time. The *Times of London* wrote, in 1847: "The Celt is less energetic, less independent, less industrious than the Saxon.... [England] can, therefore, afford to look with contemptuous pity on the Celtic cottier suckled in poverty which he is too callous to feel, and too supine to mend."

Accordingly, after Peel fell from power, Britain withdrew any material aid to the stricken island. The chancellor of the exchequer, Sir Charles Wood (1800–1885), justified the action, saying that it would "force [the Irish] into self-government ... our song ... must be—'It is your concern, not ours.'" Furthermore, the legislature amended the Irish Poor Law to penalize small Irish landowners. Thousands of farmers were forced to abandon their land or starve. Entire villages were evicted.

Britain's stubbornness was to stir Irish hatred, and to haunt English consciences, for years. John Mitchel (1879–1918), an Irish patriot, said later that "the Almighty indeed sent the potato blight, but the English created the Famine."

The Ships The potato crop would fail again in 1846, 1848, 1849, and the early 1850s. In addition, Asiatic cholera spread quickly throughout the starving and weakened population. Mass graves were dug across the country, but many of the dead were just left by the side

BOY AND GIRL AT CAHERA.

In the late 1840s, the Irish Potato Famine starved hundreds of thousands of Irish pesants and forced even more to emigrate. This engraving from the time shows Irish children searching for potatoes. *Hulton Archive/Illustrated London News/Getty Images*

of the road. In desperation, one man wrote to his relatives in the United States: "For the honour of our lord Jesus Christ and his Blessed mother, hurry and take us out of this."

Thousands of Irish poured into the port of Liverpool, trying to flee the country. If they could scrape together four pounds, they could procure a transatlantic fare. The ships to the United States were so overcrowded that the emigrants, packed in like cargo, hardly had space to breathe. Sickness, starvation, and misery accompanied the Irish across the ocean.

The Settlers The Irish were not new to American shores. Since the eighteenth century, large numbers of Scotch-Irish Protestants had settled in Canada and the southern part of the United States. In 1817, many young Irish men had sought work digging the Erie Canal. Their poverty made them hard workers and cheap labor. As such, they were both sought after and despised by Anglo-Saxon Americans.

Nativist groups wrote increasingly against the Irish settlers, who were seen as drunken, rowdy, and illiterate. Inventor Samuel Morse (1791–1872) repeatedly warned the public against Catholicism. He and many others believed that the Irish shantytowns harbored a papist conspiracy, which menaced free society. As Irish immigration increased, anti-Catholic violence escalated. A Charleston convent was burned to the ground in 1834. In 1844, a Philadelphia Nativist riot left about a dozen dead.

Negative reaction only increased when thousands of starving, diseased, poverty-stricken Irish men and women descended upon American ports in 1845. Massachusetts Governor Henry J. Gardner (1819–1892) compared the newcomers to a "horde of foreign barbarians." Boston and New York passed laws making it more difficult for immigrants to disembark.

The American Party, formed in 1854, tried to block the entry of foreigners and Catholics into the United States. They also worked to convert immigrants to Protestantism, especially in schools.

Nevertheless, the new arrivals settled in and eventually grew strong. Working at a variety of menial jobs, the Irish often sent money back to the "old country" to buy their families passage to the United States. The immigrants regrouped around the Catholic Church, which created a network of social services. After a century and a half, the Irish had been completely accepted by American society, to which they had contributed many outstanding members.

One Irish immigrant, Herman Melville (1819–1891) wrote this in praise of his new home: "On this Western Hemisphere all tribes and people are forming into one federated whole; and there is a future which shall see the estranged children of Adam restored as to the old hearth-stone in Eden."

The Revolutions of 1848

In the fateful year of 1848, a spate of revolutions broke out Europe, beginning in Sicily, exploding in France, and then spreading across the continent. Popular uprisings broke out in Italy, Prussia, Austria, and Poland. The causes were varied and complex. Working people, suffering from food shortages and displaced by new technologies, demanded economic reform. The bourgeoisie (middle class) hounded their aristocratic rulers for political liberalization. In the meantime, nationalists attacked the crumbling empires of central Europe, seeking autonomy and self-determination.

Conservative forces managed to reverse or crush all of the revolts. Even defeated, however, the bloody struggle inspired a new generation of radical European thought. Socialism, communism, and anarchism came to maturity behind the barricades. Nationalist feelings were brought to a flood tide, and they set the stage for the unification of Germany and Italy twenty-two years later. The revolutions of 1848—sometimes called "the springtime of nations"—represented a turning point in European history.

France The French democratic revolution had proved less stable than its American equivalent. Since 1787, France had been ruled by a constitutional monarchy, a republic, a committee, an emperor, and had returned to a monarchy in 1814. In 1830, the ultraconservative Charles X (1757–1836) was overthrown in the July Revolution. Louis-Philippe (1773–1850), the so-called "bourgeois monarch," ascended to the throne in his place.

King Louis-Philippe was popular with the lower classes—he dressed in modest clothes and frequently strolled around Paris talking with workers. Nevertheless, as time went on, his rule became more authoritarian. Critics began to accuse the court of rampant corruption. In order to secure his power over Parliament, the king resorted to censorship.

Opposition to the monarchy was twofold. Moderate reformists pushed for political reform only. More radical leaders, like socialist Louis Blanc (1811–1882), advocated drastic social and economic change.

In February 1848, the monarchy tried to prevent an opposition banquet in Paris. The workers began to riot in the streets of Paris, and some members of the National Guard joined them. Violence escalated, until Louis-Philippe dismissed François Guizot (1787–1874), his highly unpopular (to liberals) education minister. The king himself stepped down on February 24. The moderates formed a provisional government, and shortly afterward declared the Second French Republic.

Parisians had always held more extreme political views than the rest of France, and Paris had a proud tradition of violent insurrection. Bearing these factors in mind, the new moderate government made some concessions to radical demands. They created the National Workshops, which offered relief to the unemployed. They also established the Luxembourg Commission to discuss issues relating to workers.

However, the radicals hoped for much more sweeping changes, such as workers' associations, state-provided medical insurance, and old-age pensions. To these ends, they staged massive demonstrations in the capital, hoping to stir support. The tactic backfired. Alarmed by Parisian extremism, the French countryside voted overwhelmingly for a moderate liberal government.

Armed with a popular mandate, the Republic disbanded the National Workshops. On June 23, furious Parisians erected barricades throughout the city. The army put down the revolution after three bloody "June Days."

The June revolution led to a sweeping conservative victory in the next elections. However, the Second Republic did not last long. A few years later, Louis Napoleon Bonaparte (1808–1873) seized power and proclaimed himself Napoleon III, Emperor of the French.

COMMUNIST MANIFESTO

A spectre is haunting Europe—the spectre of communism. All the powers of old Europe have entered into a holy alliance to exorcise this spectre: Pope and Tsar, Metternich and Guizot, French Radicals and German police-spies.

Great Britain did not experience any violent revolt in 1848. However, that year the island witnessed the birth of an even more significant revolution. In January 1848, German immigrants Karl Marx (1818–1883) and Friedrich Engels (1820–1895) published the *Communist Manifesto* in London.

Marx wrote the pamphlet as a the mission statement of his secret society, the "Communist League." In the tract, he described the European unrest as a class struggle between the workers and the bourgeois. He prophesied that capitalism would only cause increasing suffering for the people, and that the people would inevitably overthrow their oppressors. The new revolution that he proclaimed would haunt Europe—and the world—for well over a century.

Italy In the mid-nineteenth century, the Italian peninsula was a patchwork of small city-states ruled by feudal princes. The northern part of the country, Venice and Milan, fell under the rule of the Hapsburg Austrian Empire.

Revolution gripped Italy in 1848, beginning with a January revolt in Palermo, Sicily. Ferdinand II (1810–1859), King of the Two Sicilies, acceded to pressure to create a constitution in Naples. This sparked liberal rebellions throughout the kingdoms of Italy. By March, radicals in Rome, Sardinia, Tuscany, and Piedmont had demanded democratic constitutions and individual freedoms. Venice and Milan threw off Austrian rule, and the king of Sardinia, devoted to the cause of Italian unity, declared war with Austria.

Pope Pius IX (1792–1878) could not bring himself to condone war with Catholic Austria. He was forced to disguise himself as a common priest and flee to the south. In his absence, radicals declared the new Roman Republic.

By May, Ferdinand II had revoked his reforms and regained absolute control of the Sicilies. Austria counterattacked and eventually squelched the nationalist movement. France sent in troops to restore the Pope in 1850.

Germany In March 1848, inspired by the Paris Revolution, riots also broke out in Berlin, the seat of King Frederick William IV of Prussia. As in France and Italy, the king initially bowed before the sudden storm and permitted the creation of a constitution and legislature. However, when the nationalist Frankfurt Assembly offered him the crown of a united Germany, Frederick

Henry David Thoreau advanced the ideas that a country's citizens should be "men first, and subjects afterwards." *The Library of Congress*

William flatly refused. He recalled troops to Berlin, dissolved the liberal government, and set up an ultraconservative ministry in its place.

Austria At the same time, students and workers also staged an uprising in Vienna. Emperor Ferdinand I (1793–1875) complied with many of their demands, including the dismissal of the brilliant arch-reactionary Klemens Metternich (1773–1859). Metternich, as Europe's preeminent diplomat, had encouraged the traditional powers to band together against the forces of change. He had further advocated that revolutions should be put down by force. "Order alone can produce freedom," he proclaimed grimly.

Radicals throughout Europe rejoiced at Metternich's removal. Vienna insurgents were not satisfied, however, and Ferdinand was forced to flee. In October, the Austrian army entered the city, killing thousands and ending the rebellion.

At the same time, an independence movement flared in Bohemia (part of today's Czech Republic), but it was also quelled by Austrian troops. In Hungary, a republic was declared, but civil war broke out shortly afterward between the various ethnic groups. That conflict continued until czarist Russia helped Austrian forces to reclaim the country.

✪ Aftermath

Abolitionism

Before the Civil War, American antislavery sentiment took a number of forms. Some people merely wanted to make slavery more humane; others wished to limit its spread into new territories. Abolitionism was a radical movement calling for the total elimination of slavery. Many of those who opposed the Mexican-American War did so for antislavery or abolitionist reasons.

Origins of Abolitionism Many of the founding fathers condemned the practice of slavery, even those, like Thomas Jefferson, who owned slaves themselves. Enlightenment philosophy generally described slavery as an affront to natural law and human liberty.

Most antislavery activism, however, came from the religious establishment, especially from the Quakers (also known as the Society of Friends). Quakers were primarily responsible for the Pennsylvania Abolitionist Society (PAS), founded in 1775, and the New York Manumission Society, founded in 1785. In the northern states, Methodist, Baptist, and Presbyterian ministers also eventually declared slavery to be incompatible with Christianity.

In the beginning, northern abolitionists mainly tried to abolish the African slave trade. They believed that if blacks were no longer brought into the country, slavery would die a natural death. Congress banned the importation of slaves in 1808, but antislavery advocates could not agree on how abolition should be brought about.

Most advocated a gradual emancipation scheme, in which slaves would be freed at a certain age. Others advocated "colonization"—sending freed slaves back to Africa or to the Caribbean. Yet others, such as William Lloyd Garrison (1805–1879), wrote numerous tracts insisting on an immediate and complete end to slavery. *The Liberator*, Garrison's newspaper, circulated widely in the North and gained a number of converts to his cause.

The Turner Rebellion In 1831, Nat Turner (1800–1831), believing himself chosen by Christ, led a slave rebellion in Southampton County, Virginia. He and six fellow-conspirators set out early in the morning of August 22, murdering his owner and his family and taking the house's weapons. Gathering support as they went along, the insurgents killed every white family they came across, including women and children in their beds. The uprising was quelled by white militia troops the same day. Turner was captured and tried, and was executed a few months later.

The incident shook Virginia whites; they made sweeping reprisals. Legislation clamped down on slaves's religious observances. Many southerners grew increasingly suspicious and hostile towards northern activists. Abolitionists, they claimed, incited violence.

Revival In the early nineteenth century, abolitionism represented a fringe political group. However, the movement

Sojourner Truth, an escaped slave, reminded white women of their obligations to black women with her speech at the Women's Convention in Akron, Ohio, 1851. *Getty Images*

witnessed a revival in the 1830s. Reorganized abolitionists distributed tracts and newspapers to spread their message. They also used the techniques of the Great Awakening, the eighteenth-century religious revivalist movement. Young men and women were appointed as missionaries. They spoke at meetings around the country, founding small antislavery societies as they went. Some of the most famous of these were Theodore Dwight Weld (1803–1895), James G. Birney (1792–1857), and the sisters Angelina Grimké (1805–1879) and Sarah Moore Grimké (1792–1873).

Possibly the most influential voices were those of black Americans. In 1841, former slave Frederick Douglass (1818–1895) spoke at the Massachusetts Antislavery Society, describing his life enslaved. Though he began by stuttering, his impassioned speech was roundly cheered at the conclusion. Douglass became a world-famous orator, touring England and Ireland with his message of universal freedom.

Sojourner Truth (c.1797–1883) spoke with more humor and gentleness that did Douglass, but her message was the same: God loves his children, and his children should love each other. She preached women's rights and an end to slavery throughout the North.

Their efforts met with strong opposition. Starting in 1836, Congress imposed a gag rule, forbidding all congressional debates about slavery. Church authorities often condemned abolitionist meetings as divisive and improper. In the south, riots broke out at antislavery rallies. Many blacks and some white abolitionists were killed.

These incidents helped garner sympathy for the antislavery movement, which claimed that their freedom of expression was under attack. In addition, from 1839 to 1841, legal furor over the slave ships *Amistad* and *Creole* brought attention to the international plight of African slaves.

Free Soil Many politicians did not believe that it would be possible, or even desirable, for the federal government to outlaw slavery in the southern states. They saw the religiously motivated emancipation movement as hysterical and impractical. Instead, they concentrated their efforts on preventing the spread of slavery into the western territories. The Free Soil Movement, as it was called, gained widespread support. A growing American middle class viewed slavery as a threat to white labor in the territories. Politically, northern states opposed the creation of pro-slavery states, which would increase the South's representation in Congress.

Benjamin Lundy (1789–1839), a prominent Quaker abolitionist writer and publisher, believed that the southern states had orchestrated the entire movement for Texas independence. In 1836, Lundy published *War in Texas*, in which he argued that the American-backed Texas Revolution was nothing but a plot to extend the slave-trading empire.

James K. Polk and other Democrats blasted the opposition as traitors, who were giving "aid and comfort to the enemy." His critics reacted with scorn, arguing that they had a patriotic duty to oppose injustice. Stephen S. Foster (1809–1881) went so far as to say, "Every true friend of the country . . . will be found fighting in defense of freedom—under the banners of Mexico." Henry David Thoreau (1817–1862) refused to pay taxesto support the war in protest. His essay "Civil Disobedience" would inspire antiwar movements to this day.

The anti-annexation forces failed, however, with Polk's election as president in 1844. Despite the efforts of John Quincy Adams, Horace Greeley, and Daniel Webster, they also failed to stop the Mexican-American War. Abolitionist John Greenleaf Whittier (1807–1892) bitterly described the conflict in these terms: "Christian America, thanking God that she is not like other nations . . . goes out, Bible in hand, to enslave the world." Disillusioned, some abolitionists began advocating a total break with the southern states. "My motto is, 'No union with the slaveholder,'" Frederick Douglass said, "because, I believe there can be no union between light and darkness."

Indeed, union within the United States was impossible, and the abolitionist movement grew in fervor and influence over the next twenty years—as did its opposition.

This engraving shows gold mining prospectors in the Bedwell River during the California gold rush.   *Time Life Pictures/Mansell/Getty Images*

The Gold Rush

Immediately after the Mexican-American War, gold was discovered in the hills of California, prompting the Gold Rush of 1849. A mass immigration began; prospectors and miners filled the territory, and the "Golden State" of California was born.

Discovery   In March 1848, Congressman Daniel Webster (1782–1852) staunchly opposed the annexation of Texas, the Mexican-American War, and the acquisition of new territories. An abolitionist and a powerful orator, he stormed at the Senate:

> I have never heard of any thing . . . , more ridiculous in itself, more absurd, and more affrontive . . . , than the cry that we are getting indemnity by the acquisition of New Mexico and California. I hold they are not worth a dollar.

Webster did not know it, but his words had already been proven wrong. In January of that same year, James Marshall (1810–1885) found some soft yellow flakes along the American River, near the sawmill in northern

California where he worked. He took the gold to his employer, John Sutter (1803–1880). Sutter received the news with excitement, but also with alarm. He had procured his land grants from the Mexican government some ten years before and did not think he could protect the find from greedy speculators.

Sure enough, despite his best attempts at secrecy, word leaked out. California prospectors, squatters, and thieves poured onto his land. "They left honesty and honor at home," Marshall said bitterly. Neither Marshall nor Sutter would profit much from their historic discovery. Sutter would later comment sadly on his new neighbors: "There is a saying that men will steal everything but a milestone and a millstone. They stole my millstones."

Gold Fever   The news traveled slowly across the United States. The *New York Herald* did not print the news until August. President Polk confirmed the news in his second inaugural address, and pandemonium seized the country.

Thousands of men made their travel plans. Some went alone; others formed companies to defray the cost.

The wealthy boarded ships that would take them around the southern tip of South America. Others sailed to Panama, crossed the isthmus by train, and then continued to San Francisco. Most took overland routes, often following paths that the U.S. Army had so recently tread.

All of the roads to California were long and difficult. The travelers risked storms around Cape Horn, Chile, and tropical disease across Panama. By land, they had to deal with harsh conditions, poorly charted trails, and hostile Native Americans. So many people suffered in one desert, on the doorstep of southern California, that the place was named Death Valley.

The Forty-Niners, as they were called, crowded into hastily constructed camps around San Francisco, Sacramento, and other small cities. New towns with colorful names like Poker Flat, Hell's Delight, and Whiskey Bar sprang up almost overnight. Within one year, the population of California jumped from less than 20,000 to over 100,000. San Francisco changed from a sleepy port village to a bustling metropolis.

In September 1849, a California constitutional convention met and applied for U.S. statehood. Its petition was accepted in 1850.

The New Culture   At first, "placer" gold—gold on the surface—could be found throughout California, especially in the streams and rivers. As these deposits were snatched up, individual panning gave way to larger mining operations. Everyone tried to tap the Mother Lode, a belt of quartz-encased gold almost two miles across and 120 miles long.

Mine temperatures could reach 150 degrees, and the mines were cramped, poorly ventilated, and dangerous. Nevertheless, a miner could make good money. At a time when the average American farm laborer made about ten dollars a month, a skilled or lucky miner could make sixteen dollars a day for an ounce of gold.

Many of the new arrivals set up businesses to exploit the new fortunes. By 1850, Sacramento housekeepers could make $150 a month. One woman made $100 a week by doing laundry. At the same time, the cost of living soared out of control. The average daily wage may have been ten dollars, but expenses could reach eighteen dollars a day. It is true that some vast fortunes were made in the gold rush, but most miners barely managed to survive.

Mining communities constituted a new, strangely egalitarian society. Almost exclusively male, this ragged band of adventurers lived on the edge of civilization. There was no way to distinguish between the newly wealthy and the newly destitute. The mayor of Monterey wrote of receiving a wild mountain man who looked like he had just crawled out of an animal lair and who held $15,000 of gold dust in his fist.

This equality did not extend to non-whites, however. The new settlers harassed Native Americans and

FEMINIST MOVEMENT

The hard life on the frontier stripped Americans of many artificial social niceties, not the least of which was the attitude that women were dependent. Women had to work hard to survive in the West, and they learned to value their abilities and their independence. Recognition of those abilities on a personal level led to demand for similar recognition on a public level.

In 1848, a group of women met at Seneca Falls, New York, for the first American convention on women's rights. Radical feminists, including Lucretia Mott (1793–1880) and Elizabeth Cady Stanton (1815–1902), demanded women's equal rights to education, property, and the vote. Stanton compared the feminist movement to the European revolutions of that year, saying, "Most cunningly [man] entraps [woman], and then takes from her all those rights which are dearer to him than life itself— rights which have been baptized in blood."

Some western states granted women the vote before the twentieth century, but American women did not win that right as a group until the Nineteenth Amendment to the U.S. Constitution was passed in 1920. Since then, movements for women's social, economic, professional, and personal freedoms have continued.

Mexican-Californians (Californios), chasing them from their land. Later, miners would riot against Chinese laborers who were brought to work on the transcontinental railroad.

The miners's camps were rough places, filled with rampant theft and vigilantism. One immigrant's wife, Louise Clapp (1819–1906), wrote letters (later published) to her sister in New England under the pseudonym Dame Shirley that described "murders, fearful accidents, bloody deaths, a mob, whippings, a hanging, an attempt at suicide, and a fatal duel." Yet California exerted its own kind of charm. As Clapp wrote to her sister, "I like this wild and barbarous life."

Metal Madness   The California Gold Rush slowly died down. Mines went deeper, and it became more and more expensive to extract the ore. But smaller migrations for precious metals cropped up periodically over the next decade. Between 1858 and 1859, almost 100,000 people rushed to Colorado, founding a shantytown called Denver. Another California rush happened in 1859, with the discovery of the Comstock Lode in the Sierra Nevada.

BIBLIOGRAPHY

Books

Chidsey, Donald Barr. *The War With Mexico*. New York: Crown Publishers: Harper Perennial, 1968.

Davis, William C. *Three Roads to the Alamo: The Lives and Fortunes of David Crockett, James Bowie, and William Barret Travis*. New York: Harper Perennial, 1999.

Eisenhower, S. D. *So Far From God: The U.S. War with Mexico 1846–1848*. New York: Random House, 1989.

Meed, Douglas V. *The Mexican War 1846–1848*. London: Routledge, 2003.

Quinn, John F. *Father Matthew's Crusade: Temperance in Nineteenth-century Ireland and Irish America*. Amherst, MA: University of Massachusetts Press, 2002, p. 10.

Truth, Sojourner. "Ain't I A Woman?", *Inquiry: Questioning, Reading, Writing*, 2d ed., edited by Lynn Z. Bloom and Edward M. White. Upper Saddle River, NJ: Pearson / Prentice Hall, 2004, p. 369.

Wheelan, Joseph. *America's Continental Dream and the Mexican War, 1846–1848*. New York: Carroll & Graf, 2007.

Periodicals

Anderson, Bonnie S. "The Lid Come Off: International Radical Feminism and the Revolutions of 1848." *NWSA Journal* (Summer 1998): vol. 10, p. 1.

Etcheson, Nicole. "Mistress of Manifest Destiny: A Biography of Jane McManus Storm Cazneau, 1807–1878." *Journal of Southern History* (November, 2002): vol. 68, p. 943.

Farrell, David R. "Slavery and the American West: The Eclipse of Manifest Destiny and the Coming of the Civil War." *Canadian Journal of History* (August, 2001) vol. 36, p. 383.

Gordon, Walter I. "The Capture and Trial of Nat Turner: An Excerpt from the Book: A Mystic Chord Resonates Today: The Nat Turner Insurrection Trials." *Black Renaissance/Renaissance Noire* (Spring–Summer 2006) vol. 6, p.132.

Hodgson, Godfrey. "Storm over Mexico" *History Today* (March 2005): vol. 55, p. 34.

Holden, William. "The Rise and Fall of 'Captain' John Sutter." *American History* (February 1998): Vol. 32, p. 30.

Jeffrey, Julie Roy. "The Transformation of American Abolitionism: Fighting Slavery in the Early Republic. (Book review)" *The Historian* (Fall 2005): vol. 67, p. 532.

Kinealy, Christine. "The Great Irish Potato Famine & Famine, Land and Culture in Ireland (Book Reviews)." *Victorian Studies* (Spring 2002): vol. 44, p. 527.

Mandelbaum, Michael. "In Europe, History Repeats Itself." *Time Magazine* (December 25, 1989).

Quinn, Peter. "The Tragedy of Bridget Such-a-one." *American Heritage* (December 1997): vol. 48, p. 36.

Rolston, Bill. "Frederick Douglass: A Black Abolitionist in Ireland: Bill Rolston Describes the Impact of an Erstwhile Slave, Who Toured the Emerald Isle Speaking Out Against Slavery in 1845." *History Today* (June 2003): vol. 53, p. 45.

Silvester-Carr, Denise. "Ireland's Famine Museum." *History Today* (December 1996): vol. 46, p. 30.

Web Sites

Jefferson, Thomas. "Second Inaugural Address." *The Avalon Project at Yale Law School*. <www.yale.edu/lawweb/avalon/presiden/inaug/jefinau2.htm > (accessed April 9, 2007).

Lincoln, Abraham. "Speech at Worcester, Massachusetts, September 12, 1848." *Collected Works of Abraham Lincoln*. <quod.lib.umich.edu/cgi/t/text/text-idx?c=lincoln;cc=lincoln;type=simple;rgn=div1;q1=fences;singlegenre=All;view=text;subview=detail;sort=occur;idno=lincoln2;node=lincoln2%3A2> (accessed April 9, 2007).

Lowell, James Russell. "War." *The Complete Poetical Works of James Russell Lowell*. <www.gutenberg.org/etext/13310> (accessed April 9, 2007).

"Mexican Colonization Laws." *The Handbook of Texas Online*. The University of Texas at Austin. <www.tsha.utexas.edu/handbook/online/articles/MM/ugm1.html> (Accessed April 4, 2007).

Polk, James K. "Polk's War Message Washington, May 11, 1846." *Berkeley Law School Foreign Relations Law*. <www.law.berkeley.edu/faculty/yooj/courses/forrel/reserve/Polk1.htm> (accessed April 30, 2007).

"Rufus King and the Missouri Controversy." *The Gilder Lehrman Institute of American History*. <www.gilderlehrman.org/collection/docs_archive/docs_archive_rufus.html> (accessed April 9, 2007).

Tallmadge, James, Jr. "Tallmadge's Speech to Congress, 1819." *Wadsworth Learning American Passages*. <www.wadsworth.com/history_d/templates/student_resources/0030724791_ayers/sources/ch09/9.3.tallmadge.html> (accessed April 9, 2007).

"Texas Declaration of Independence." *Texas A&M University*. <www.tamu.edu/ccbn/dewitt/decindepen36.htm> (accessed April 30, 2007).

Travis, William Barret. "Letter from the Alamo, February 24, 1836." *The History of the Alamo & the Texas Revolution*. Texas A&M University. <www.tamu.edu/ccbn/dewitt/adp/history/bios/travis/travtext.html> (accessed April 30, 2007).

Webster, Daniel. "Speech to the Senate, 1848." *The Great Speeches and Orations of Daniel Webster*. <www.gutenberg.org/etext/12606> (accessed April 14, 2007).

Introduction to the Civil War (1861–1865)

For decades, the issue of slavery threatened to push the fledgling United States into violent internal conflict. As the country's boundaries expanded, tensions increased. Each new territorial addition to the nation brought with it the question: Will slavery be allowed here, or forbidden? Legal compromises kept the controversy from boiling over for a time, but by the late 1850s, passions ran high on both sides of the Mason-Dixon Line. Still, a wary peace held. The country seemed to be holding its breath.

In 1859, militant abolitionist John Brown decided that the time had come for decisive action to end the institution of slavery. With a handful of followers, including his sons, Brown staged a raid on the federal armory at Harper's Ferry, West Virginia, hoping to begin an armed slave insurrection. He was captured in the attempt by forces led by future Confederate war hero Robert E. Lee, then serving in the U.S. Army. Reactions to John Brown's exploit split along geographic lines, further dividing the country. Those in the North, though concerned about Brown's violent tactics, were inclined to think of him as a hero with a noble cause. The slaves exalted him as a martyr and a liberator. White southerners, on the other hand, viewed the raid as an act of northern aggression.

Though Brown was tried and hanged, Southerners worried that the federal government would fail to protect them from further aggression by abolitionists—or, worse, might tacitly support the abolitionists' cause.

Within a year of John Brown's capture, Abraham Lincoln was elected president, and southern states began seceding from the Union. On January 9, 1861, the first shots of the Civil War were fired at Fort Sumter, South Carolina. By February 1861, the Confederate States of America was formed, with Jefferson Davis as its president.

The American Civil War went on to claim more than 600,000 lives, killing more Americans than all other American wars combined to that date. The South was doomed almost from the start: It was significantly outnumbered by the North, and the northern states were home to the industrial might of the nation. The South did have the benefit of excellent officers who managed a series of boldly executed victories in the first years of the war. Yet as the fighting wore on and control of the Union army was placed in the capable hands of General Ulysses S. Grant, the North's numerical advantage and industrial power prevailed. General Lee surrendered to General Grant on April 9, 1865. All fighting ended soon thereafter.

The turmoil, however, was far from over. The country was reunited, but the South was in ruins. The slaves were free, but their status was uncertain. An assassin's bullet claimed the life of President Lincoln just days after Lee's surrender, robbing the nation of his wise and generous leadership. Thus hobbled, the United States began to grope its way through a painful and tumultuous period known as Reconstruction.

The Civil War (1861–1865)

✪ Causes

The Compromise of 1850

By 1850, several slave states, led by South Carolina, were ready to secede from the United States. The United States annexed Texas in 1845. Annexation ignited a war between the United States and Mexico. That war yielded vast amounts of territory in what is now the American Southwest. Expansion of slavery had previously been limited to Missouri, Florida, and the Arkansas Territory. The Missouri Compromise of 1820 barred slavery in territories north of the parallel of 36 degrees, 30 minutes north. When the law was passed, slavery was viewed as a dying institution. In subsequent years, the economy of Southern states became more tightly bound to slavery. Free states held a majority in the House, while slave states held a majority of Senate seats. Prior to the Mexican-American War, it had become all but certain that free states would eventually outnumber slave states. The territory gained in the Mexican War was in the south. If slavery were expanded into these territories, the slave states could maintain a majority—in the Senate at least. When the issue of annexing Mexican territory first arose, David Wilmot, a Connecticut representative in the House, introduced a provision that any territory acquired from Mexico had to enter as free territory. Defeated in 1846 when it was first introduced, it was regularly introduced and defeated in subsequent sessions.

South Carolina was prepared to withdraw from the United States unless slavery was allowed to expand. Other states in the Deep South, notably Mississippi and Georgia, threatened to join South Carolina. Sensing a constitutional crisis, Representative Henry Clay of Kentucky proposed a compromise using paired bills that would give all parties some of what they wanted. The first pair admitted California as a free state and allowed slavery in territory gained in the Mexican-American War. The second settled the boundary dispute between New Mexico and Texas in favor of New Mexico. In exchange,

the federal government would assume debts that the state of Texas accumulated while a republic. The third pair of bills banned slave trading in the District of Columbia, but protected slavery in the district. Slaves could be owned but not bought or sold. The final pair of bills removed congressional authority over the interstate slave trade and strengthened the existing fugitive slave law by federalizing the recovery of slaves. These bills, introduced in January 1850, formed the basis of what was to be called "The Compromise of 1850." While all of the provisions underwent modification, the final version of the compromise was essentially unchanged from Clay's original proposals. It gave all parties some of what they wanted, enough to secure passage of the package.

At first it did not look as if the compromise would be passed. President Zachary Taylor (1784–1850) was ready to call the bluff of the slave states. When a delegation from New Mexico arrived with a petition for statehood, Taylor recommended the admission of both California and New Mexico as free states. He was ready to use force to keep unruly states in the Union if needed. Taylor fell ill and died shortly after Independence Day in 1850. He was succeeded by Millard Fillmore (1800–1874), a New Yorker who was willing to accommodate the South. He threw his support behind the compromise.

Advocates on both sides of the slavery issue condemned the package. Henry Calhoun of South Carolina gave a speech denouncing it the day before he died. He claimed it fostered Northern interests at the expense of the South. Too weak to read it, he had James Mason of Virginia read it to him. William Seward of New York, later Lincoln's secretary of state, gave a speech denouncing the compromise because it strengthened slavery. Many American statesmen, however, supported the package: Daniel Webster of Massachusetts, Sam Houston of Texas, and Stephen A. Douglas of Illinois worked with Clay to secure passage of the package. It was not passed as one big act, however. That effort fell apart on July 31, so the individual parts of the compromise were

Senator Henry Clay's Compromise of 1850 attempted to resolve the issue of slavery in lands taken from Mexico. *The Library of Congress*

shepherded through Congress by Stephen Douglas. The result was similar to Clay's omnibus proposal. The most controversial aspect of the act was the new Fugitive Slave Act, which brought the full weight of the federal government to assist slave owners seeking their "property"— their runaway slaves—in free states. That slaves could be taken into and out of free states without changing their status rubbed a raw nerve with many in the North.

Intended to prevent secession, the Compromise of 1850 forestalled it for only ten years. The pressures that threatened rupture in 1850 caused an explosion in 1860.

The Kansas-Nebraska Act

The Kansas-Nebraska Act, passed in 1854, nullified the Missouri Compromise and allowed new states entering the Union to decide the issue of slavery for themselves, but failed to satisfy Southern slave owners. It sparked civil conflict in Kansas that was a prelude to the American Civil War.

The architect of the Kansas-Nebraska Act was Sen. Stephen A. Douglas, an Illinois Democrat. He wanted a railroad connecting Chicago, Illinois, with San Francisco, California. The railroad needed a federal land grant. That could come as part of a bill to reorganize

the remaining territories of the Louisiana Purchase. Passage required the support of at least six slave state senators. They were willing to support Douglas—if the deal were sweetened by allowing slavery in the territories. The Missouri Compromise of 1820 forbade slavery in territories north of the 36 degrees, 30 minutes north parallel.

In January 1854, Douglas introduced a bill reorganizing the territories. It allowed states created from the Louisiana Purchase territories to be admitted to the Union with or without slavery. Popular sovereignty would settle the issue—letting the people living in the territory decide whether they wanted slavery or not. The compromise effectively nullified the Missouri Compromise because both Kansas and Nebraska extended north of the line beyond which slavery was forbidden by the earlier legislation. Unless slaves had been permitted prior to statehood, it was unlikely that a territory would attract enough supporters of slavery to vote for slavery. Southern senators refused to support the bill unless it explicitly repealed the Missouri Compromise's ban on slavery. Desperate to get the territorial reorganization passed, Douglas added language to do that.

The Kansas-Nebraska Act created two new territories: Kansas Territory opposite Missouri, and Nebraska Territory opposite Iowa. Slavery would be permitted while a territory. Whether slavery would be permitted after statehood was to be decided by popular sovereignty. The pairing implied that Kansas was to enter as a slave state and Nebraska as a free one.

The Act created a political firestorm that split the country. All of the Northern states, except Douglas's Illinois, either opposed or refused to endorse the bill. All Southern states supported it. Parties split along regional lines. Every Northern Whig voted against the bill. Twenty-four of the thirty-four Southern Whig party members in both houses of Congress voted for it. Southern Democrats overwhelmingly voted for the bill: seventy-two out of seventy-five. Only fifty-eight out of 108 Northern democrats supported it. The totals were enough, barely. It passed the Senate by forty-one to seventeen, but squeaked through the House. There it passed, on May 22, 1854, by a margin of 115 to 104.

The repercussions of the Kansas-Nebraska Act were felt in the 1854 elections. Only seven Northern Democrats supporting the Act were reelected. Many Northern Democrats that voted against the bill left the Democratic Party. The main opposition party, the Whigs, disintegrated. The Northern Whigs joined forces with the Free-Soil Party and disaffected anti-slavery Democrats to form the Republican Party. Most Southern Whigs were swept out of office by Southern Democrats. It was the biggest shift in the political landscape since the disappearance of the Federalists after the War of 1812.

Once the Act was passed, the issue of slavery would be settled upon the prairies of Kansas. Free-soil interests fostered Northern settlement of Kansas, primarily from the Midwest—Michigan, Ohio, Indiana, and Illinois. At the same time, pro-slavery settlers were pouring in from Missouri.

In November 1854, the first election was held in the Kansas Territory. Senator David Atchison, of Missouri, led an invasion of Kansas by thousands of Missouri pro-slavery activists—called "border ruffians" by abolitionists. Few of them owned slaves, but most were willing to resist the anti-slavery efforts by what they considered to be meddling Northerners. In an election later judged to be fraudulent by Congress, the Missourians elected a pro-slavery territorial delegate to the United States Congress. The pattern continued for much of the decade. In 1855, Missouri residents voted in pro-slavery candidates in territorial elections through the weight of illegal ballots. The territorial governor ordered new elections. Fair elections saw free-soil candidates chosen.

The territorial legislature seated the pro-slavery slate. It passed a slave code, criminalized criticizing slavery, and retroactively legalized the border ruffian vote. Free-soil Kansans formed their own territorial legislature and held a convention where they passed a free-soil territorial constitution. By 1856, Kansas had two competing legislatures. The two sides were soon shooting at each other. By 1856, the two sides were raiding the settlements of the other party. The newspapers began writing about "Bleeding Kansas," as the violence grew.

In 1856, two bills for the admission of Kansas as a state were introduced. The Republicans, controlling the House of Representatives, introduced a bill admitting Kansas as a free state. The Democrats, holding the Senate, offered one admitting Kansas as a slave state. Neither bill became law. The rhetoric in Congress turned to violence when Rep. Preston Brooks of South Carolina beat Massachusetts Sen. Charles Sumner unconscious on the Senate floor. In revenge for Sumner's beating, a group led by abolitionist John Brown (1800–1859) kidnapped five pro-slavery settlers from the village of Pottawatomie Creek. Brown's men murdered the settlers with broadswords.

For the next four years, Kansas bled. Pro-slavery forces won territorial elections through fraud. The territorial governor would hold new elections, which free-soil majorities won. An official, pro-slavery territorial legislature would be seated. An unofficial free-soil legislature supported by the majority of the territory's voters would challenge the official legislature. Congress would reject petitions for statehood as a slave state because they were based on patently fraudulent elections.

In 1858, Congress voted narrowly to admit Kansas as a slave state with a provision allowing Kansas voters to reject the pro-slavery constitution by voting on a land grant referendum. Kansans voted overwhelmingly against the referendum, and by extension, the pro-slavery constitution. This deferred statehood for at least two years. The scales were now heavily tipped in favor of free-

soil voters. Free-state Kansans organized a Republican party, electing two-thirds of the delegates to a new constitutional convention in 1859. They submitted a free-soil petition for statehood in 1860. Kansas entered the Union as a free state in January 1861. Popular sovereignty had triumphed.

The Dred Scott Decision

On April 6, 1846, Harriet and Dred Scott (1795–1858), slaves taken into free-soil territories, petitioned a Missouri court for their freedom. Dred Scott had also lived in a free state (Illinois) for two years. The case was ultimately decided over a decade later in 1857 by the U.S. Supreme Court. The court stripped blacks of American citizenship and declared the Compromise of 1850 unconstitutional, which resulted in permitting slavery in all U.S. territories. The decision made the Civil War all but inevitable.

In 1833, Dred Scott was purchased by St. Louis, Missouri, physician John Emerson. Missouri was a slave state, but Dr. Emerson was a surgeon in the U.S. Army. Assigned to Fort Armstrong, in Illinois, Emerson took Scott with him as a servant. After two years in Illinois, Emerson was reassigned to Fort Snelling in the Wisconsin Territory (later Minnesota). He again brought Scott with him. While at Fort Snelling, Scott married Harriet Robinson, another slave then living at the post. Emerson bought her. Emerson took the couple with him to Louisiana, and then back to Fort Snelling, before leaving the army and returning to St. Louis, Missouri. In 1843, Emerson died, and the Scotts became the property of Emerson's wife Irene.

Scott Petitions for Freedom Dred Scott lived for two years in Illinois, a free state, where slavery was illegal. He and his wife Harriet had also lived for several years in the Wisconsin Territory, where slavery was outlawed by the Northwest Ordinance—an act of Congress passed in 1787.

In 1846, the Scotts petitioned a Missouri state court to be declared free persons. They also filed assault and false imprisonment charges against Irene Emerson. Their case was not unusual. Before 1846, Missouri courts settled many similar cases involving slaves taken to free soil in favor of the plaintiffs. But the Scotts had filed suit at a bad time, because the Mexican-American War was beginning at the same time. That war made Texas a slave state and California a free state, and it hardened opinions about slavery on both sides of the issue.

By the time the Scotts' case was heard, in June 1847, Missouri courts were looking for excuses to refuse freedom to petitioning slaves. Title to the Scotts was clouded. The court dismissed the case on the grounds that the plaintiffs did not prove that they were suing their actual owner.

The two petitions were combined into a single case, which Dred Scott continued to pursue. The case wound its way up and down the state court system. Scott won

This 1854 map shows the division of the Kansas and Nebraska Territories from the controversial Kansas-Nebraska act of that year, which overturned the 1820 Missouri Compromise. *The Granger Collection, New York. Reproduced by Permission*

his freedom in the first case. Emerson appealed the decision. By the time the appeal was heard in 1851, the Compromise of 1850 had been passed. The pro-slavery Missouri Supreme Court viewed the Dred Scott case as a way to challenge the constitutionality of the Compromise of 1850. They returned Scott to slavery in March 1852. Scott then took the case to federal court. He had been sold to a man who lived in New York State but kept his property in Missouri. Since the case crossed state lines, Scott's attorneys claimed federal jurisdiction. In 1854, the federal court in St. Louis allowed Scott the legal standing to sue in federal court. In the subsequent federal case, the judge ruled that Scott was subject to the laws of Missouri, not Illinois, and remained a slave. In May 1854, the case was appealed, and on December 30, 1854, it went to the Supreme Court.

Supreme Court Ruling The Supreme Court heard the case two years later, in December 1856. Five justices were pro-slavery southerners, two were northern Dem-

ocrats sympathetic to the South, and two were anti-slavery Republicans. Three questions were involved: First, were African Americans citizens? Second, what was the status of slaves in free territories? Third, were congressional acts that banned slavery in territories constitutional? The verdict split along party lines.

The Supreme Court ruled on March 6, 1857, that blacks, free or slave, were not citizens of the United States and thus had no legal standing to sue in the courts. It also ruled that laws barring slavery in territories were unconstitutional, which eliminated the question of whether slaves taken to free territories became free themselves. Finally, the Supreme Court ruled that Scott's residence in a free state did not make him a free man because he was subject to Missouri laws and once again a slave when he returned to Missouri.

Implications and Consequences The ruling deprived free blacks of rights they had possessed since the

The 1857 Supreme Court case deciding the freedom or slavery of Dred Scott (lower left) was front-page news around the nation. *Getty Images*

establishment of the United States. It overruled state constitutions in five states that explicitly gave free blacks equal status with whites. In addition, it explicitly permitted slavery in all U.S. territories. According to the ruling, the Constitution's due process clause meant that a slave owner could not be deprived of property, even slaves, by simply moving it across state lines into a free state. Many in free states interpreted this as de facto legalization of slavery throughout the United States.

The Dred Scott decision meant that the Union would not long endure half-slave and half-free. It would have to become one or the other. The ruling forced the preferences of the slave-owning third of the population of the United States on the majority. With little room for compromise, a war to settle the issue became virtually inevitable.

After the decision, the Scott family was returned to Irene Emerson—who sold them to Taylor Blow, a friend of the Scotts (and their original owner) who had financed the initial lawsuits. Blow then set them free.

Dred Scott did not long enjoy freedom. He died in 1858, three years before the Civil War began.

The Harpers Ferry Raid

The Harpers Ferry Raid inflamed passions on both sides of the issue of slavery and hastened the start of the Civil War. On the evening of October 16, 1859, eighteen men entered Harpers Ferry, Virginia. Led by fanatic abolitionist John Brown, their goal was to capture the federal arsenal. With the weapons they obtained from the arsenal they planned to arm slaves in Virginia and ignite a slave rebellion. The raid failed. Within two days, the raiders were dead, prisoners, or fugitives.

The Plan The Harpers Ferry raid was conceived by John Brown, a militant abolitionist. Brown participated in violent antislavery activities in Kansas. By 1858, Brown left Kansas and was back East trying to get support for a slave revolt. His plan called for arming slaves in a mountainous section of the South and having them establish a mountain stronghold from which to spread rebellion.

To find sufficient arms for slaves willing to fight, Brown planned on capturing an arsenal. Brown's attention focused on the federal arsenal at Harpers Ferry, Virginia, (now West Virginia). In a slave state, near mountains, it was one of the largest and most modern munitions plants in the United States. It held a stockpile of 100,000 rifles.

Six prominent abolitionists—Franklin Sanborn, Thomas Wentworth Higginson, Theodore Parker, George Luther Stearns, Samuel Gridley Howe, and Gerrit Smith—helped support Brown's activities in Kansas. All were men of means. Several were quite wealthy. Known as the Secret Six or the Committee of Six, they financed Brown's raid. Stearns diverted money intended for Kansas to purchase arms for Brown's raid, including two hundred Sharp's carbines. Brown ordered one thousand pikes. The Sharp's carbines and pikes were to arm a "brigade" that would take and hold the federal arsenal.

In June 1859, Brown rented a farm in Maryland near Harpers Ferry for his "army." Brown found recruiting slow. By October, his force had but twenty-one men—sixteen whites and five blacks. Twelve had fought with Brown in Kansas. Three were his sons. Brown and his wealthy white supporters failed to rally blacks to Brown's cause. Brown attempted to recruit Frederick Douglass (1818–1895), a prominent ex-slave, abolitionist, and an old friend. Douglass, more pragmatic and realistic than the Secret Six, felt Brown's plan was doomed. Douglass discouraged other blacks from participating.

Douglass was right. Harpers Ferry was indefensible and difficult to escape from. Unfordable rivers ran on three sides of the town, trapping anyone in Harpers

John Brown led a group of white abolitionists and African Americans on an attack of the arsenal at Harpers Ferry, Virginia, on October 16, 1859. *Kean Collection/Getty Images*

Ferry. Even if Brown could raise a garrison large enough to hold the town, Harpers Ferry was surrounded by low mountains. Rifles and artillery on those heights would make defense of the town untenable.

The Raid   Leaving three followers to guard his base, Brown and seventeen others snuck into Harpers Ferry after dusk on October 16. Brown and his raiders quickly captured the arsenal. It was guarded by an unarmed night watchman. Brown sent a patrol out to round up hostages, including Lewis Washington, a great-great-grandnephew of President George Washington. By dawn he had over forty hostages.

The plan fell apart soon after the hostages arrived. An eastbound Baltimore and Ohio train approached the station at Harpers Ferry. The baggage master, a free black, tried to warn the train. He was shot dead by one of Brown's men. The train was allowed to proceed to Washington, D.C., after witnessing the shooting.By midmorning on October 17, the town and surrounding countryside were aware of the raid. Farmers, townsmen, and militia converged on the town. They occupied the heights around Harpers Ferry, sniping at the raiders.

Eight raiders and three townsmen were shot dead. Two of Brown's sons were killed.

By evening it was apparent the raid had failed. Seven raiders slipped out, including slaves impressed into Brown's army. Five made good their escape. Two were captured. Brown and the rest of the raiders retreated with their hostages into a brick fire-engine house and barricaded themselves in. That night, a company of U.S. Marines arrived from Washington, D.C., commanded by Army Colonel Robert E. Lee (1807–1870) and accompanied by Army Lieutenant J. E. B. Stuart (1833–1864). On the morning of October 18, the marines stormed the building. They used cold steel to avoid the risk of shooting the hostages. In a few minutes, two raiders were dead, Brown was badly wounded, and four men were taken prisoner.

Aftermath   Brown and the captured raiders were tried by the State of Virginia for murder, inciting slave rebellion, and treason against the State of Virginia. The trial lasted only a few days. All were convicted and sentenced to death. The sentences were carried out as quickly as the trial. John Brown was hanged December 2, 1859; four others were hanged on December 16, and the remaining two were hanged on March 16, 1860.

Attention turned to Brown's moneymen. One, Parker, was in Britain, dying of tuberculosis. Four others—Sanborn, Stearns, Howe, and Smith—fled to Canada. Higginson alone remained in Massachusetts, daring anyone to prosecute him. After Brown was hanged, the four in Canada returned. Sanborn again fled to Canada when a Senate committee began investigating the raid, searching for a conspiracy. Neither Sanborn nor Higginson testified before the committee. Sanborn got his subpoena voided. Higginson was not called. Howe and Stearns testified, but denied prior knowledge of Brown's plan. There the matter was allowed to lie. The senators realized that proving a conspiracy existed would cause serious problems.

Many Northerners viewed Brown as a martyr to the cause of freedom. Many Southerners viewed Brown's action as proof that the North would ignore the law to eliminate slavery. It set the stage for secession after the 1860 election.

✪ Major Figures

Abraham Lincoln

Abraham Lincoln (1809–1865) was the sixteenth president of the United States. He ascended to the presidency of the United States at a time of great crisis. He had the greatest plurality of the popular vote but got less than 40 percent of the vote in a four-way race. He did not receive a single popular vote in ten southern states. Nevertheless, he achieved an absolute majority of electoral votes, which gave him the presidency. It was the first time a candidate from the Republican party was elected president and only the second election in which that new party fielded a candidate for that office. Virtually as soon as the results became official, Southern states began seceding from the Union, beginning with South Carolina on December 20, 1860. The motivation was Lincoln's election.

A major plank in the Republican platform was abolition of slavery. The act of the nation's electing a president from an abolitionist political party was seen as sufficient justification for secession. Lincoln did not assume the presidency planning to enforce abolition—or even planning to contain slavery, except for preventing its spread into the territories. By the time Lincoln was inaugurated, in March 1861, however, seven states—the lower South and Texas—had seceded.

Initial Steps Lincoln initially sought non-confrontational means to preserve the Union. He was determined to keep under Union control all federal property, such as the national government, but virtually all mints, armories, custom houses, and military and naval installations in the seceding states had already been seized by the rebels. Only two offshore forts remained in federal con-

President Abraham Lincoln (1809–1865). *The Library of Congress*

trol: Fort Pickens, off Pensacola, and Fort Sumter, in Charleston Harbor.

When firebrands in South Carolina fired upon and then captured Fort Sumter, Lincoln called for 75,000 militia to put down the rebellion. This led four additional states from the upper south to secede. Lincoln was faced with the task of restoring a divided Union without having the means at hand to do so.

Restoration of the Union was the task that consumed the rest of his life. For Lincoln, the war was less about slavery than about the preservation of the Union. In an 1862 letter to New York City newspaper editor Horace Greeley (1811–1872), Lincoln wrote, "If I could save the Union without freeing any slave I would do it; and if I could save it by freeing all the slaves I would do it; and if I could save it by freeing some and leaving others alone I would also do that."

War Leader Lincoln's first job was to see that an army was built and to find a commander who was capable of doing that job. Initially impatient to achieve that goal, he made significant mistakes early in the war. He allowed political considerations to dictate the choice of leaders and also pressed the initial leader of the Union Army into precipitate action that led to the disaster at Bull Run.

He educated himself in military strategy as president using the same method by which he taught himself law as a young man—he pored over books of strategy and consulted with experts in military affairs. Lincoln realized that a Northern victory depended on destroying the Southern armies, not just occupying territory. He began searching for generals who shared this vision.

Lincoln kept trying out and discarding commanders for the Union armies until he found leaders who could fight—and fight effectively. Once convinced of a general's competence, he stuck with the man, despite any criticism. When others complained that General Ulysses S. Grant was a drunk, Lincoln stated: "I cannot spare this man—he fights."

Lincoln and Emancipation   As casualty lists mounted, especially after the Seven Days Battle campaign in 1862, Lincoln realized that reconciliation would not draw the seceding states back into the Union and that simple preservation of the Union did not justify the cost in blood. He then transformed the war into a crusade to abolish slavery.

Lincoln issued the Emancipation Proclamation, a document that was as much a military tool as a political one. It only freed slaves in territories under rebellion. It preserved slavery in portions of the nation then under federal control. It was issued as a military proclamation under his power as commander-in-chief. Doing this prevented a political fight in Congress. The Emancipation Proclamation was presented as a tool for depriving those states in rebellion of resources—their slaves. It also prevented European recognition of the Confederacy until the Confederate states eliminated slavery—the "state's right" over which the Southern states seceded.

When Lincoln's tenacity bore fruit after four years of bloody struggle with the military collapse of the Confederacy, Lincoln again opted for conciliation. In his second inaugural address, he called for an end to the conflict "with malice toward none; with charity for all." He endorsed the generous terms offered to Robert E. Lee's army at Appomattox Court House by General Ulysses S. Grant (1822–1885). Lincoln's vision of a charitable peace was forgotten after his death. Days after the Confederate surrender on April 9, 1865, Abraham Lincoln was assassinated. He was shot while attending a play on April 14 and died the next day. His death shifted government to the Radical Republicans who were more interested in retribution than reconciliation.

Early Years   The two men that led the United States and the Confederacy, respectively, during the Civil War, Abraham Lincoln and Jefferson Davis, had similar origins. They were born less than one hundred miles apart in central Kentucky and less than a year apart, both to farm families.

Lincoln was born seven months after Davis, on February 12, 1809, in a log cabin in Hardin County (now LaRue County), Kentucky. Lincoln came from humble origins. His mother, Nancy Hanks, was illegitimate, and his father, Thomas Lincoln, was illiterate. Lincoln's mother died when he was nine; his father

UNCLE TOM'S CABIN

Harriet Beecher Stowe was the daughter and wife of abolitionist Congregationalist clergymen. In reaction to the Compromise of 1850, especially the strengthened Fugitive Slave Act, she wrote a story dramatizing the plight of slaves. It was based, in part, on her experiences with slavery in Kentucky and with runaway slaves in Cincinnati, Ohio. The story was *Uncle Tom's Cabin*.

Stowe's story was originally serialized in an abolitionist newspaper. Stowe was encouraged to have it republished in book form. As a book, it quickly became very popular. In its first year in print, 300,000 copies were sold in the United States. By the start of the Civil War, two million copies—the equivalent of a book selling 20 million copies today—had been sold.

Uncle Tom's Cabin hardened opinions on slavery. While it is difficult to measure the number of Northerners it turned against slavery, it struck a raw nerve in the South. The book was denounced, and no fewer than fifteen novels defending slavery as an institution were subsequently written by Southern authors.

While its influence is hard to measure, it was real. When Lincoln met Stowe in 1862, he is reported to have joked, "So you're the little lady who started this great war."

remarried. The family had moved to Indiana when Lincoln was seven. A few years later, Thomas Lincoln moved the family to Illinois. After a few years in a one-room schoolhouse, Abraham Lincoln educated himself, eventually learning law and becoming a successful lawyer.

Lincoln was also fascinated with technology. He is the only president to have held a patent—for a never-manufactured device to help steamboats maneuver in shallow water. He carried this interest into the White House. Lincoln oversaw the enactment of legislation to authorize a transcontinental railroad and the land-grant college system.

Jefferson Davis

Jefferson Davis (1808–1889) was president of the Confederate States of America. He was no one's first choice to become president of the Confederate states—not even his own state's. Davis's ambition was to command the Army of the State of Mississippi and later, perhaps, become the supreme commander of the Confederate Army. Becoming a general was a goal of his youth.

Davis allowed himself to be appointed president—the compromise candidate who was acceptable to both radical and moderate politicians. He became the Confederacy's president on February 9, 1861, and served as interim president until he was elected to the position in October. Inaugurated in March 1862, he was the only president during the Confederacy's brief existence.

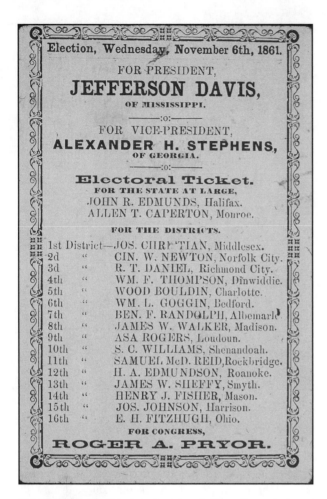

Election, Wednesday, November 6th, 1861.

FOR PRESIDENT,

JEFFERSON DAVIS,

OF MISSISSIPPI.

FOR VICE-PRESIDENT,

ALEXANDER H. STEPHENS,

OF GEORGIA.

Electoral Ticket.

FOR THE STATE AT LARGE,

JOHN R. EDMUNDS, Halifax.

ALLEN T. CAPERTON, Monroe.

FOR THE DISTRICTS.

1st District—JOS. CHRISTIAN, Middlesex.
2d   "   CIN. W. NEWTON, Norfolk City.
3d   "   R. T. DANIEL, Richmond City.
4th   "   WM. F. THOMPSON, Dinwiddie.
5th   "   WOOD BOULDIN, Charlotte.
6th   "   WM. L. GOGGIN, Bedford.
7th   "   BEN. F. RANDOLPH, Albemarle.
8th   "   JAMES W. WALKER, Madison.
9th   "   ASA ROGERS, Loudoun.
10th   "   S. C. WILLIAMS, Shenandoah.
11th   "   SAMUEL McD. REID, Rockbridge.
12th   "   H. A. EDMUNDSON, Roanoke.
13th   "   JAMES W. SHEFFY, Smyth.
14th   "   HENRY J. FISHER, Mason.
15th   "   JOS. JOHNSON, Harrison.
16th   "   E. H. FITZHUGH, Ohio.

FOR CONGRESS,

ROGER A. PRYOR.

This 1861 electoral ticket supports the candidacy of soon-to-be Confederate President, Jefferson Davis. *Kean Collection/Getty Images*

Strengths as President Davis oversaw the creation of both a national army and the civil branches of a national government. The South was handicapped in its fight with the North. The agrarian South had 40 percent of the population of the Union states and perhaps 10 percent of the industry. Davis began initiatives to overcome the manufacturing gap and prepared to fight a defensive war. The North had to invade in order to subdue the South.

Davis built a government, an army, and an economy. He appointed his initial cabinet from each of the other original Confederate states; no one else from his state, Mississippi, was appointed. His cabinet included several other politicians who had been considered for the presidency. He built a Confederate Army by nationalizing state forces into a national army. Davis also instituted a more rational system for the appointment of officers than was used in the North, one that valued military experience more than political connections.

Davis had opposed secession in 1860, but after Mississippi moved to secede, Davis became one of the foremost proponents of the Confederacy. As president,

Davis also put the Confederate economy on a war footing, using Southern exports as an economic weapon. He seized otherwise unavailable supplies from civilian owners when they were needed for military purposes. He encouraged the enactment of a conscription act in March 1862, a full year before the Union passed a similar national conscription act.

At the very end of the Confederacy, in 1865, too late to make a difference, Jefferson Davis pushed a bill through the Confederate legislature to permit black slaves to enlist in the Confederate Army. Blacks would receive freedom for enlisting. This voided the major reason for secession. But Davis had become so wedded to the cause of the Confederacy that he was willing to destroy the institution of slavery—the very cause of its existence—to see it continue.

Shortcomings Davis had significant weaknesses as president. He was autocratic and possessed a fiery temper. These traits served a military leader well, but the presidency was a civilian job. To work effectively with a legislature, a president needed to be a consensus builder and conciliator. Instead, Davis alienated many potential allies within the Confederacy's civil government. Davis also saw the president's role as commander-in-chief as a more active one than was appropriate. Davis wanted to be a battlefield general instead of a civilian president. He actively meddled in the tactical decisions of his generals, often to the detriment of events on the battlefield.

While Davis established commands spanning operational theaters, he failed to provide a grand strategic plan for the defense of the Confederacy. He also allowed personal pique to affect his choice of commanders. Several highly talented Confederate generals sat out critical parts of the war because Davis did not like them or was angry at them. Initially, these weaknesses were unimportant, because the Union lacked the army or military leaders to mount effective offensive operations. As time passed, Davis's strategic shortcomings combined with Lincoln's strength as a wartime president to undermine the Confederacy.

An example is the 1864 Atlanta campaign. The Union Army was led by William T. Sherman (1820–1891), a general plucked from professional obscurity—in part through Lincoln's efforts. He was opposed by an army led by Joseph Johnston (1807–1891), a man Davis disliked. Johnston delayed Sherman, refusing to fight pitched battles, except when he held an overwhelming advantage.

Frustrated by a summer of skirmishing as Sherman continued advancing toward Atlanta, Davis relieved Johnston, replacing him with the more aggressive John B. Hood (1831–1879). Hood sought battle with Sherman and was trounced. This allowed Sherman to take Atlanta. The victory shifted the victory in the 1864 presidential election in the North from peace candidate George McClellan (1826–1885) to Abraham Lincoln, who was reelected. Had Johnston remained in command, he might have lost Atlanta, but it would have fallen later, too late to affect the 1864 elections.

Early History   Jefferson Davis was born on June 3, 1808, in a farmhouse in Christian (now Todd) County, Kentucky, seven months before Abraham Lincoln's birth and less than one hundred miles away. Davis's family moved to Mississippi when he was an infant. Like Lincoln, Davis helped on the family farm, working in his father's cotton fields until he was sent to school at the age of eight.

After attending Transylvania University in his teens, Davis received an appointment to the U.S. Military Academy at West Point. After graduating in 1828, he served as a lieutenant in a post in the Northwest Frontier, where he met and married Sarah Knox Taylor, the daughter of post commandant Colonel (and later President) Zachary Taylor.

Sarah's father disapproved of Davis as a husband, so Davis left the army in order to marry her in 1835. Davis and his wife returned to Mississippi and established a plantation, Brierfield. His wife died of malaria only three months after returning. After living in seclusion at Brierfield for ten years after his wife's death, Davis remarried, entered politics, and was elected to the U.S. House of Representatives. He resigned in 1846, when the Mexican-American War began to command a volunteer regiment from Mississippi. He served under his first father-in-law, Zachary Taylor, at Monterey and Buena Vista during that war.

Returning to Mississippi a war hero in 1848, he spent the next twelve years in and out of politics. He served as a Mississippi's U.S. senator and as secretary of war during the Pierce Administration. As the secession issue heated up in the late 1850s, Davis cautioned against it. When Mississippi left the Union, however, he threw himself into the cause of the new nation that his adopted state joined.

Post-War Life   On May 10, Davis was captured in Georgia while attempting to flee the U.S. Army. He was held prisoner for two years and then released. The federal government decided not to try him for treason. He returned to Mississippi and wrote his memoirs. He died in New Orleans on December 6, 1889.

General Robert E. Lee

Robert Edward Lee (1807–1870) was the general in chief of the Confederate armies in the Civil War. Lee was born on January 19, 1807, in Stratford, Virginia. He was the son of American Revolutionary hero and former governor of Virginia Henry Lee (1756–1818)—known as "Light-Horse Harry"—and Ann Hill Carter, daughter of a respected Virginia landowner. By the time Robert, the couple's fifth son, was born, the Lee family had fallen on hard times. Lee's father had made a series of bad investments and lost the family fortune, and he was sent to debtor's prison when Robert was still a toddler.

Confederate General Robert E. Lee continued to be a heroic figure to many Americans long after the Confederacy was defeated.   *National Archives and Records Administration*

After his release, the family moved to Alexandria, Virginia, for a time, but Henry later moved to the West Indies for health reasons, leaving his family behind with young Robert as acting head of the household. Henry Lee died in 1818.

Without the benefit of financial support from his family, young Robert Lee decided on a career in the military. He entered the United States Military Academy at West Point in 1825, where he excelled as a student, both academically and militarily, graduating second in his class. Two years after graduating, he married Mary Custis, a descendant of Martha Washington. The couple had seven children together in their plantation home in Virginia.

U.S. Military Services Lee first distinguished himself as a man of unusual military talent during the Mexican War (1846–1848), where he served under General Winfield Scott (1786–1866), conducting scouting missions that led to the capture of Mexico City. Scott was impressed with the young captain and came to rely on his reconnaissance skills. It was during this war that Lee developed a reputation as a brave and capable leader.

In 1859, Lee took a central role in an event that pushed the nation down the path to civil war. Militant abolitionist John Brown and his followers raided the armory at Harpers Ferry, West Virginia, in an attempt to launch an armed slave insurrection. Lee and his troops were sent to Harpers Ferry to end the skirmish. Brown refused to surrender, and Lee's forces stormed the building. Within minutes, Brown and his small band were subdued. The event outraged southerners, who were concerned that Brown's violent attempt was the beginning of a northern effort to put an end to slavery. Southern states began to talk about secession.

Although Lee was a dedicated Virginian, he believed slavery was morally wrong. He had inherited slaves from his wife's father, but, following the dictates of his own conscience and the terms of his father-in-law's will, he freed them in 1862—before the Emancipation Proclamation, before the end of the war, and before many of his northern counterparts (including some top Union generals) freed their own slaves. He also found the idea of leaving the Union and rebelling against the federal government unthinkable, and he hoped Virginia would opt to remain part of the United States.

In 1861, the southern states began seceding from the Union. With civil war erupting, General Scott began gathering his most talented officers; Lee was at the top of his list. Scott recalled Lee to Washington with the intention of giving him command of the Union Army, a remarkable vote of confidence given that Lee was only a colonel at the time and had never commanded an army. The appointment could have been the crowning glory of Lee's thirty years of devoted service in the U.S. military.

Confederate Military Service When Virginia seceded on April 17, 1861, Lee was faced with a wrenching dilemma. He could either uphold his oath of loyalty to the U.S. government, accept Scott's commission, and lead forces against the South, or he could resign and fight for his home state against the army to which he had devoted his life. Lee decided he could not fight against the South, writing to his sister, "With all my devotion to the Union . . . I have not been able to make up my mind to raise my hand against my relatives, my children, my home. I have therefore resigned my commission in the [U.S.] Army." It was a decision of tremendous historical significance. Military historians count Lee as one of America's greatest generals; the top Union generals, however, ranged from mediocre to incompetent, a fact that quickly became apparent when hostilities broke out.

Had Lee accepted Scott's orders and commanded Union forces, it is likely the South would have been subdued quickly. As it was, the South moved speedily to recruit the talented Lee. By 1862, he was made military advisor to Confederate President Jefferson Davis.

In May 1862, General Joseph Johnston was seriously wounded at the Battle of Seven Pines in Virginia. General Lee immediately replaced him and enthusiastically took his new command, renaming Johnston's army the Army of Northern Virginia. By July, his forces stopped the Union Army from advancing on the Confederate capital of Richmond during the Seven Days Battles and forced Union General George B. McClellan to retreat.

Lee's army was always outnumbered and outgunned, but his attacks were strategically sound, aggressive, bold, and merciless. Before McClellan could reorganize, Lee swiftly attacked at the Second Battle of Bull Run (August 1862). An easy victory prompted Lee to march into Maryland—his first foray into northern territory. It was a bold move, but it proved disastrous. The Battle of Antietam (September 1862), fought near Sharpsburg, Maryland, was technically a wash, but since Lee had to retreat, it was viewed as a Union victory. It was also the bloodiest single-day battle in American history, costing Lee almost his entire army. France and Britain, which had been considering formal diplomatic recognition of the Confederacy, decided after the battle to wait a little longer to see how events played out. Sensing the momentum of the war had shifted in favor of the North, President Abraham Lincoln issued the Emancipation Proclamation on September 22.

Lee was down, but he was not yet defeated. In December 1862, he scored yet another victory, this time at Fredericksburg, Virginia, where Union forces hoped to crush his remaining army. Lee implemented a defensive plan that forced the Union to abandon its offensive, giving General Lee the rest of that winter to rebuild his army. By spring 1863, the Union was again on the attack. In April, General Joseph Hooker (1814–1879) was poised to take Chancellorsville, Virginia, but Lee made a surprise advance, putting Hooker on the defensive. After three days of furious fighting against a numerically superior force, Lee's troops forced a Union retreat. His improbable victory at Chancellorsville is considered his greatest triumph.

Emboldened, Lee again attempted to push the fighting onto northern soil. In June 1863, Lee marched his army into Pennsylvania. On July 1, 1863, he clashed with the forces of Union's new commander, General George Gordon Meade (1815–1872), in the small town of Gettysburg. The three-day battle was brutal. Lee was forced to retreat, leaving a third of his army (28,000 men) dead on the field.

In the spring of 1864, Lee met his match: General Ulysses S. Grant. The two engaged in small but deadly skirmishes and bloody battles as the two armies fought in Virginia, starting with the Battle of the Wilderness. President Lincoln sent Grant to take Richmond and squash Lee, but Lee was able to block Grant's maneuvers. Grant finally managed to force Lee to retreat to Petersburg, a town on the outskirts of Richmond.

Grant turned the battle into a nine-month siege. Although Lee's army did not starve, they were unable to participate in the war. In April 1865, Lee made an attempt to evacuate his men and head west, but Grant cut him off. On April 9, 1865, General Lee surrendered his tired and weak army to Grant at the courthouse in Appomattox, Virginia. Grant accepted Lee's surrender graciously, allowing his officers to retain their horses and sidearms. Lee returned home.

After the War Lee worked diligently to heal the wounds of the nation and to revitalize a shattered region. "Abandon your animosities," he famously urged southerners, "and make your sons Americans." Because of his concern for how the war would affect the younger generation, he accepted the position of president of Washington College, later named Washington and Lee University in his honor. He held the position until his death from heart failure on October 12, 1870.

Even before his death, Lee had become a legend. His renown only grew as years passed. To those in the former Confederate states, he was a potent symbol of the "Lost Cause." Stories of the valiant General Lee on his iron-gray horse, Traveller, thrilled generations in the post-war South, for whom Lee was like an idol. In the North and abroad, he came to be viewed as one of America's great leaders, admired by the likes of Theodore Roosevelt and Winston Churchill.

A few months after the Civil War, Lee submitted an application to have his U.S. citizenship restored. His wish was never granted during his lifetime. Somehow, the application was lost for more than one hundred years, only to be found by a clerk sorting through papers at the National Archives in Washington. The rediscovered application was approved by an act of Congress, and, with the support of President Gerald Ford, General Robert E. Lee once again became a U.S. citizen on July 22, 1975.

Ulysses S. Grant

Ulysses S. Grant (1822–1885) was the leading general of the Union armies during the Civil War and eventually the eighteenth president of the United States. Born Ulysses Hiram Grant, he had reversed his name to Hiram Ulysses when he received an appointment to the U.S. Military Academy at West Point. There, his name was listed as Ulysses S. Grant, and he remained Ulysses S. Grant for the rest of his life.

Two things where Grant did succeed were decisive—commanding an army in combat and defeating the Confederacy. These earned him a place in history and two

Civil War photographer Matthew Brady captured this image of Ulysses S. Grant at his headquarters in early 1864. *National Archives and Records Administration*

terms as the president of the United States—another thing at which he would fail.

Service in the Civil War When the Civil War began, Grant was working as a clerk in a leather goods store. He joined a company of volunteers in Galena, Illinois, and was elected captain on the basis of prior service in the U.S. Army. Primarily because of the shortage of trained officers, Grant was soon promoted to colonel, and he commanded a regiment of Illinois volunteers. He was given command of a brigade in Missouri a month later and then promoted to brigadier general. His promotion was more a sign of the desperation of the Union Army than an endorsement of him. He had left the Army abruptly amid rumors of drunkenness during the 1850s and had failed at various businesses after leaving.

Grant handled his brigade well at Belmont, Missouri, where they fought an indecisive action. Grant's commander, General Henry Halleck, then approved a plan drawn up by Grant to take two Confederate forts: Fort Henry on the Tennessee River and Fort Donelson on the Cumberland River. Working with naval river gunboats under the command of Flag Officer Andrew Foote, Grant and Foote forced the abandonment of Fort Henry and captured Fort Donelson in February 1862. Donelson's surrender yielded fifteen thousand

Confederate prisoners. It was the first significant military success by the North.

Grant pushed aggressively down the rivers to exploit his success. Surprised by a Confederate Army at Pittsburg Landing, Tennessee, and pushed back to the landing, Grant held his position at the end of the first day of the Battle of Shiloh. The next day, April 7, 1862, Grant counterattacked, scattering the Confederate Army facing him.

Late 1862 saw Grant marching against Vicksburg, on the Mississippi River. He was unsuccessful then, but he was tenacious. Working closely with the Navy, he besieged the river port, cutting it off from the Confederacy. Repelling Confederate attempts to relieve the siege, Grant starved the town into its surrender on July 4, 1863.

Lincoln was seeking aggressive, competent commanders for the U.S. Army. Grant was both. He had utterly destroyed two major Confederate armies at Fort Donelson and Vicksburg, in both cases accepting nothing less than unconditional surrender. He had demonstrated determination in the face of adversity at Shiloh. He had distinguished himself as a master of maneuver in the Vicksburg Campaign.

Lincoln promoted Grant to general-in-chief of the Army in March 1864. Grant attached himself to the Army of the Potomac, launching a series of new offensives intended to destroy the Confederacy. Grant led his army against Richmond, Virginia, the Confederate capital. Grant's goal was less the capture of the enemy's capital than the tying up of Confederate forces to defend this strategically unimportant but psychologically critical objective.

Grant realized that the war would be won west of the Appalachians, but he also knew that the Confederacy would focus its efforts on him. His grinding offensive on Richmond absorbed the attention of the South's most talented general, Robert E. Lee, and it forced the Confederates to commit reserves to defend Richmond rather than the rest of the Confederacy. Whether he won or lost each battle, Grant stuck to Lee after each engagement, preventing Lee's army from recovering.

By Grant's focusing the Confederacy's attention on him, he allowed the armies led by his lieutenants, the generals William T. Sherman, George H. Thomas, and Philip H. Sheridan to ravage the Confederacy. Sherman, commanding in the west, surrounded and captured Atlanta, Georgia, in September 1864. He then took one army and marched across the heart of Georgia to Savannah. Reaching Savannah, Sherman marched north, capturing and destroying Charleston, South Carolina, before going on to link up with Grant. Sheridan, in an independent campaign, marched through Virginia's Shenandoah Valley, using scorched-earth tactics to burn Lee's granary. Thomas repelled an offensive led by Confederate General John B. Hood. After destroying the

Confederate Army at Nashville in December 1864, Thomas marched into Alabama.

The combined effect of these offensives gutted the Confederacy. Before Sherman could reach Grant, Lee's army had collapsed, fleeing the Petersburg lines they held for over six months. With the war at an end, Grant offered Lee terms as magnanimous as his previous terms had been unconditional. He allowed Lee's men to return home on parole, Lee's officers to retain their personal arms, and everyone to keep their horses—so they could use them for the season's plowing.

Early Career Grant's career prior to the war had been undistinguished. Born in Ohio on April 27, 1822, Grant received an appointment to West Point in 1839. He graduated in 1843 in the bottom half of his class and was assigned to the Fourth Infantry. During the Mexican-American War, he served with General Zachary Taylor's army at Palo Alto, and then with Winfield Scott in the Veracruz-Mexico City campaign.

Post-War Life After that war, Grant served on various frontier posts in Michigan, the Oregon Territory, and California. Frustrated by lack of advancement and separation from his family, he quit the Army. He left under a cloud, dogged by accusations of drunkenness. He then started and failed at several businesses before finally being hired as a clerk in his father's store.

After the Civil War, Grant's reputation was quite good. Persuaded to run for president, he won that election and was reelected. He understood politics poorly and filled his cabinet with men more interested in serving themselves than the United States. While Grant was personally honest, his Administration was one of the nation's most corrupt.

After leaving office in 1876, a series of bad business decisions left him bankrupt. He restored his family's fortunes as a writer, first writing magazine articles about his Civil War experiences. Encouraged by Mark Twain, Grant finished his two-volume memoir on his deathbed. Grant died days after finishing the work on July 23, 1885.

John Brown

John Brown (1800-1859) was a staunch abolitionist. For some, the Civil War did not start with the first gun fired at Fort Sumter. They considered its starting point six months earlier, when Brown and eighteen others raided the federal arsenal at Harpers Ferry, Virginia, on October 17, 1859. Their objective was to arm slaves and start a slave revolt.

Early Life Brown was born on May 9, 1800, in Torrington, Connecticut, to a family with deep roots in Puritan New England. His father, Owen Brown, a tanner, moved the family to the Western Reserve region of Ohio in 1805. John Brown wanted to become a preacher, following the Calvinistic Protestantism of his

Abolitionist John Brown. *National Archives and Records Administration*

father. Eye problems forced him to withdraw from the seminary where he was studying. Instead, he followed in his father's footsteps, also becoming a tanner.

Brown inherited a dislike of slavery from his father, a dislike that grew into an obsession with the emergence of the abolitionist movement in the 1830s. His "Old Testament" Christianity led him into vigilantism. If a sin was committed, John Brown saw it as his responsibility to smite the wrongdoer.

Abolitionist Efforts

Brown allied with William Lloyd Garrison (1805–1879) in 1831, shortly after Garrison began publishing his abolitionist newspaper, *The Liberator*. By the middle of the 1830s, Brown was a stationmaster on an Ohio branch of the Underground Railroad, a conduit for spiriting runaway slaves to Canada. Throughout the 1840s, Brown's interest in the abolition movement grew, even as business failures bounced him from Ohio to Pennsylvania to Connecticut. He became increasingly radicalized, advocating violence in order to secure an end to slavery.

The passage of the Kansas-Nebraska Act in 1854 gave Brown a stage to test his theories. The law left the issue of slavery in Kansas and Nebraska to be decided by the inhabitants of the two future states. Kansas became the focus of both pro- and anti-slavery settlement in an effort to sway the state into one camp or the other. In 1855, John Brown, with his five sons, moved to Kansas to join the struggle. Missouri interests had established a pro-slavery territorial government through fraudulent means. Brown was determined to reverse that verdict through violence, if all else failed.

On May 23, 1856, Brown and seven men, including four of his sons, raided the pro-slavery community at Pottawatomie Creek. They hacked five pro-slavery men to death. In the months following the Pottawatomie Creek massacre, Brown and his band lived in the Kansas wilderness, conducting guerilla raids against pro-slavery settlements, helping "Bleeding Kansas" to bleed.

Harpers Ferry Raid

After a defeat at Osawatomie on August 30, 1856, Brown and his adherents left Kansas. Despite national notoriety and a federal bounty of $250 on his head, Brown lived unmolested by federal authorities for the next three years. Sheltered by influential abolitionists, Brown planned his next stroke—raising a slave rebellion in the South.

Six wealthy abolitionists funded Brown's plan and sheltered him. The "Secret Six" included Samuel Gridley Howe (husband of Julia Ward Howe) and Thomas Wentworth Higginson, a Transcendental minister who later commanded a black Union regiment in the Civil War. Brown was to raid a federal arsenal in the South, steal the arms in it, and distribute the arms to slaves willing to fight for their freedom. The plan called for the blacks to withdraw to the mountains, in imitation of successful slave revolts in both Haiti and Jamaica. Harpers Ferry, in the Appalachian foothills, was chosen.

The Secret Six, as well as Brown's commandos, were all white men. They failed to rally one black person to their cause. By 1858, Douglass was advocating armed resistance to slavery, but he viewed Brown's plan as foolish.

Ignoring the advice of their black allies, Brown's party pushed ahead. The raid was a dismal failure. The first man killed by Brown's party was a freed black. Harpers Ferry proved the "perfect steel-trap" Douglass had predicted. Brown was captured. The rest of his party was either killed or captured. The trial following the raid further inflamed passions on both sides of the slavery issue. Brown and his party were tried on charges of treason, murder, and fomenting rebellion. The trial was rushed in order to prevent a lynch mob's justice for Brown. The trial concluded on November 2 with Brown found guilty. Brown used the trial as a platform to play the Old Testament patriarch and martyr—a role given weight in the North due to the haste in which the trial was conducted. Brown was hanged on December 2, 1859. Nor did the trial satisfy the South. The Secret Six who financed the raid went untouched. This fact radicalized Southern secessionists and accelerated the pace towards war.

"THE BATTLE HYMN OF THE REPUBLIC"

After the Civil War started, John Brown was celebrated as a martyr in the North. Soldiers adapted the tune of a camp meeting hymn into a marching song, "John Brown's Body". The lyrics were uninspired. Each verse consisted of three repeated lines, such as "John Brown's body lies a-mold'ring in the grave." Every verse concluded with the line, "His soul goes marching on."

In November 1861, while working for the United States Sanitary Commission, Julia Ward Howe and some companions heard a group of soldiers singing the song and joined in. Afterwards, one companion urged Howe to write more fitting lyrics for the stirring tune.

The next morning, Howe rose at dawn and jotted down a new set of lyrics on a sheet of Sanitary Commission stationery. The result was the "Battle Hymn of the Republic", which was published in the February 1862 *Atlantic Monthly*. It captured the public's imagination and became the unofficial anthem of the Union Army.

Thomas "Stonewall" Jackson

Thomas J. Jackson (1824–1862) was a Confederate general. At the Civil War's outset, he was an obscure professor at the Virginia Military Institute (VMI). When Virginia joined the Confederacy in April 1861, the VMI Corps of Cadets was mobilized. Professor Jackson became Major Jackson and began his march into history.

Service in the Civil War   Jackson was soon promoted to colonel and sent to capture the U.S. Military Arsenal at Harpers Ferry. After that, he was promoted to brigadier general and given command of a brigade of Virginia volunteers. In July 1861, he commanded that brigade at the First Battle of Manassas (or Bull Run).

It was there that Jackson gained the nickname "Stonewall." His brigade stopped a Union assault that would have carried the day. Later, one of the regiments in his brigade, wearing blue uniforms that caused a Union battery to mistake it for Union troops, destroyed the battery, causing the disintegration of the Union line at that point. It was the assault that led to Confederate forces routing the Union Army. The victory led to Jackson's promotion to major general and an independent command in the Shenandoah Valley, the Confederacy's granary. Early in 1862, he launched an offensive against Union troops holding the Shenandoah. Outnumbered, he used a series of fast marches to outmaneuver his opponents and destroyed the Union forces.

In a brilliant campaign, he cleared the valley of Union forces by the middle of June 1862. He prevented reinforcement of McClellan's army in the Peninsula Campaign, threatened Washington, D.C., and crushed General Nathaniel Banks (1816–1894) at battles at Front Royal and Winchester. Jackson carried off so many Union supplies that thereafter, Banks was known as "Commissary" Banks, because he supplied Jackson's army.

Jackson's force was then moved by railroad to reinforce Robert E. Lee's troops facing McClellan in the peninsula. At the Seven Days Battle, Jackson and his force were uncharacteristically sluggish. Exhaustion was the best explanation. Despite this, Lee's army defeated McClellan. When Lee reorganized his army, Jackson was given command of one of the corps.

In August, Jackson was rested and back in form. He moved his infantry—which was being called "foot-cavalry" for the speed with which it moved—in a swift encircling march that allowed Jackson to destroy Union General John Pope's supply base at Manassas Junction on August 27. He held his position at Groveton over the next two days, after which Lee and the rest of the corps rejoined him. The Confederate victory at the Second Battle of Manassas (Bull Run) took place on August 29 and 30. This battle drove Union forces north of the Potomac

Jackson also participated in Lee's first invasion of the North, into western Maryland. Jackson occupied Frederick, Maryland, an event inaccurately memorized in John Greenleaf Whittier's (1807–1892) 1864 poem "Barbara Frietchie." (Frietchie actually waved her flag to Union troops a week after Jackson occupied the town, but it was romantically conflated with Jackson.)

Jackson fought stubbornly, but not brilliantly, at the Battle of Antietam (Sharpsburg) on September 17, 1862. Jackson's men bloodily repulsed numerous Union assaults, while the corps commanded by Longstreet was flanked. A Confederate route was prevented by reinforcements. Lee's army was in a precarious position at the end of the battle and quickly withdrew back to Virginia.

In May 1863, the Army of the Potomac again invaded Northern Virginia, commanded by a new leader, General Joseph Hooker. Lee's troops were outnumbered two to one. At Chancellorsville, Hooker attacked Lee. Lee sent Jackson on another flanking march. On May 2, Jackson fell upon the Union Eleventh Corps. One of the weakest corps in the Army of the Potomac, many of its regiments were made up of German immigrants who spoke English poorly. The Eleventh Corps had been placed on Hooker's right flank to keep it out of trouble. Surprised by Jackson's twilight attack, the corps panicked and fled the field. Hooker was forced to withdraw in order to save his army.

It was Jackson's last battle and his most brilliant. Jackson was shot and wounded by one of his own guards while conducting a reconnaissance. His left arm was amputated. While recovering from surgery, Jackson contracted

The sculptor of Mt. Rushmore, Gutzon Borglum, began carving this monument to Jefferson Davis, Robert E. Lee, and Stonewall Jackson in 1923 at Stone Mountain, Georgia. *PhotoDisc, Inc.*

pneumonia. Weakened from the wound and operation, he died on May 10, 1862. It was a loss that crippled Lee. Lee wrote of Jackson's injury "I have lost my right arm."

Early Life Jackson was born on January 21, 1824, in Clarksburg, Virginia, (now part of West Virginia). He was orphaned as a child and brought up by relatives. He received little formal education while growing up, but in 1842, at age eighteen, he received an appointment to the U.S. Military Academy at West Point. He graduated in the top third of his class in 1846, and was commissioned a lieutenant of artillery.

The Mexican-American War had started. Jackson was immediately sent to Winfield Scott's command. In Mexico, Jackson distinguished himself at the battles of Veracruz, Cerro Gordo, and Chapultepec. He was promoted to brevet major, a meteoric rise for someone right out of West Point. After the Mexican-American War, he remained in the Army until 1852, when he accepted a position as professor at VMI, in Lexington, Virginia.

Jackson was punctilious, eccentric, secretive, and a stern disciplinarian. His cadets considered him humorless, but he could be warm to his intimates. He was also

a devout Presbyterian who considered his victories to be bestowed by God and his enemies to be kin to the devil.

George B. McClellan

George B. McClellan (1826–1885) was a general in the Union Army. McClellan transformed the dispirited Union troops that lost the First Battle of Bull Run into a potent force. He created an army too strong for the Army of Northern Virginia to destroy. Ironically, McClellan could not defeat the Confederate Army, primarily due to his own timidity and indecisiveness.

In Western Virginia When the Civil War began, McClellan was president of the Ohio and Mississippi Railroad. He quit that position to accept a commission as a major general of Ohio volunteers.

With a small force of Ohio militia, he was given the task of securing the western portion of Virginia for the Union. It was mountainous territory, where plantation slavery was uneconomical, and its economy was tied to Pennsylvania and Ohio. McClellan was fortunate. The area had a large pro-Union population. Confederate forces there were commanded by two of the Confederate Army's lesser lights—Colonel John Pegram and General

President Lincoln and General McClellan meet at Antietam, after the famous battle, in 1862. *The Library of Congress*

John B. Floyd (President Buchanan's secretary of defense in 1860 and 1861).

McClellan's talented subordinate—William Rosencrans (1819–1898), then a colonel—defeated Pegram at Rich Mountain in July 1861 and Floyd, at Fairfax, in September. The campaign cleared the Confederates out of what later became West Virginia. McClellan got most of the credit.

Command of the Army The Union debacle at the First Battle of Bull Run was followed by continuing disorganization and demoralization in the Army of the Potomac. McClellan was then called east and was given command of the U.S. Army, relieving the retiring General Winfield Scott.

McClellan proved an excellent organizer and trainer. He reorganized the armies around Washington and regularized the Army's quartermaster corps to ensure his troops had adequate food and supplies. He also drilled and trained the Army of the Potomac, turning it into a powerful offensive weapon. He then proved unenthusiastic about using the weapon he had created. McClellan always had another reason to keep it in camp, training. At first, Lincoln encouraged McClellan. Then he prodded him. Finally, on January 27, 1862, Lincoln ordered McClellan to move.

It took McClellan another month to execute that order. He marched the Army of the Potomac out of Washington in early March. He stopped at Manassas after discovering that the Army of Northern Virginia, commanded by General Joseph E. Johnston, had withdrawn to Fredericksburg, Virginia.

The Peninsular Campaign On March 11, he moved the Army of the Potomac by sea to Fort Monroe, Virginia, at the tip of the Peninsula formed by the James and York Rivers. McClellan crawled up that peninsula at a snail's pace, intimidated by phantoms of superior Confederate forces. He spent one month, beginning on April 5, 1862, besieging lightly held Yorktown. Most of the rest of the next month was spent crawling to within ten miles of Richmond, Virginia, the Confederate capital.

The Army of Northern Virginia counterattacked at the Battle of Fair Oaks (or Seven Pines). McClellan's Army of the Potomac easily beat off the attack, and Joseph Johnston was injured during the battle. He was replaced by General Robert E. Lee, who held a staff position as an advisor to Confederate President Jefferson Davis.

McClellan slowly went about preparing the Army of the Potomac to besiege Richmond. Lee planned a counteroffensive intended to surround the Army of the Potomac and destroy it from behind. The result was the Seven Days Battle, fought between June 25 and July 1, 1862. A series of seven battles was fought during that time, most of which were won by the Army of the

Potomac. After each action, convinced that he had lost and was about to be surrounded, McClellan retreated. The Seven Days Battle climaxed with the Battle of Malvern Hill. McClellan's army crushed a Confederate attack against its fortified position. Against the desire of his Corps commanders, McClellan again retreated down the peninsula and finally withdrew the army back to Washington.

Lincoln did not formally relieve McClellan. Instead, Lincoln gave most of the Army of the Potomac to General John Pope. After Pope was defeated by Lee at the Second Battle of Bull Run (or Manassas), the Army of the Potomac was returned to McClellan.

Antietam and Its Aftermath In September 1862, Lee invaded western Virginia. McClellan went after Lee in a sluggish repetition of his behavior in the Peninsula. McClellan got a copy of Lee's orders to his subordinate commanders—it was captured from a Confederate courier. This allowed McClellan to trap Lee near Sharpsburg, Maryland, on September 17.

McClellan's army outnumbered Lee's by 90,000 men to 55,000, and Lee's total included reinforcements that arrived late during the resulting Battle of Antietam. Had McClellan attacked promptly, he would have outnumbered Lee three to one. Instead his hesitation caused a bloody and indecisive battle. Total casualties on both sides exceeded 3,600 dead and 17,000 wounded. McClellan's timidity reasserted itself. Instead of destroying the Army of Northern Virginia, McClellan was satisfied with holding the battlefield, and he allowed Lee's Army to escape. Having "defeated" Lee once, McClellan proved even more reluctant to risk another battle. Lincoln finally relieved McClellan in November 1862. McClellan never again served in an active role in the U.S. Army.

Although a strong supporter of the war, McClellan agreed to run as the Democratic candidate for president, on a peace platform. He lost the election, receiving 21 electoral votes to Lincoln's 212.

Early Life and Post-War Career Born on December 3, 1826, McClellan graduated from the U.S. Military Academy, second in the class of 1846. Receiving an engineering commission, he served with distinction in the Mexican-American War. Afterwards, he served as an engineering instructor at West Point.

Between 1850 and 1857, when he resigned from the Army, he participated in a number of significant engineering projects, served as an official observer from the U.S. Army during the Crimean War and designed the standard cavalry saddle used by the Army well into the 1880s—the "McClellan saddle." Between 1857 and the start of the Civil War, he was chief engineer and then vice president of the Illinois Central Railroad before becoming president of the Ohio and Mississippi Railroad.

After the Civil War, McClellan was chief engineer for the New York City Department of Docks and governor of New Jersey from 1878 to 1881. He died on October 29, 1885, in Orange, New Jersey.

Albert Sydney Johnston

Albert Sydney Johnston (1803–1862) was a general in the Confederate Army. Johnston refused an opportunity to serve as second in command of the U.S. Army in 1861. He then probably had more combat and campaign experience than any other officer in the U.S. Army except General Winfield Scott. Instead, after his adopted state of Texas left the Union, Johnston resigned his commission. He then accepted a commission as a general in the Confederate States of America. Johnston was sent west, with orders to raise a Confederate Army in Kentucky, a then-neutral border state. The expected pro-Confederate rising did not occur. Instead, the state was tipped into the Union camp.

Command in the West Johnston was placed in command of the Confederacy's western front (from the Appalachians to the Mississippi River valley). Despite a lack of troops, munitions, and supplies, Johnston patched together a defense. He relied on a series of riverfront fortifications to block a Union advance. These proved inadequate. The North built a series of river gunboats protected by iron armor or thick layers of wood. These ironclad and timberclad gunboats mounted guns heavy enough to defeat the earthwork fortifications the South could make. Because of superior mobility, the Union could mass forces to outnumber Johnston's individual garrisons.

Under Flag Officer Andrew H. Foote and Brigadier General Ulysses S. Grant, the Union mounted a series of combined operations on the Cumberland and Tennessee Rivers in February 1862. Johnston lost Forts Henry and Donelson, losing the Donelson garrison as well as the fort. He reorganized his remaining troops into the Army of the Mississippi and fell back on the railroad junction at Corinth, Mississippi. He was able to scrape together about fifty thousand men. Ten thousand were used for the garrison, leaving a field force of forty thousand men.

Shiloh Aware that he would be outnumbered by greater than two to one, after Union forces concentrated, Johnston resolved to attack first. He believed that Grant had 33,000 men at Pittsburg Landing, on the Tennessee River, about twenty-five miles from Corinth. Johnston marched quickly across the country, covering the distance in a day and a half.

His attack, which started hours before dawn on Sunday, April 6, 1862, was a total surprise. Grant actually had 39,000 troops at Pittsburg Landing, but 6,000 would reach the battlefield, later called Shiloh after a church there that was used as the Confederate headquarters, on the first day of the battle. Johnston's attack swept the Union Army virtually to the banks of the Tennessee. By nightfall, both armies were exhausted, and each side had suffered heavy casualties. Albert Johnston was among them. A wound years earlier had injured his sciatic nerve and left him insensitive to pain in his leg. A bullet had struck him in the leg during that first day of battle. Unaware of how serious the injury was, Johnston continued directing the battle until he passed out from loss of blood. He died soon after.

Johnston died at the apparent moment of triumph. Reinforced by fresh troops, Grant counterattacked the next day. Had Johnston been in command, Grant would likely still have won. Absent Johnston's leadership, the Confederate defeat was as total as it appeared the Union loss had been the previous day.

Early Life Johnston, born in Washington, Kentucky, on February 2, 1803, entered the U.S. Military Academy at West Point at age 19. Graduating in 1826, Johnston served in the Army for the next eight years, seeing action in the Black Hawk War. He resigned in April 1834 when his wife became ill. After she died, he became a farmer in Missouri, but soon moved to Texas. In Texas, he joined the army of the Republic of Texas. By January 1837, he was the senior brigadier general in that nation's army. He commanded the Texas Army and served as the Republic's secretary of war before returning to farming in Brazoria County.

Because of the American annexation of Texas, the Mexican-American War began. Johnston returned to the U.S. Army, commanding the First Texas Rifles. When that war ended, he alternated between farming and serving in the U.S. Army until the outbreak of the Civil War.

His most notable achievement in that period was commanding the expedition that reestablished federal authority in Utah in 1857–1858. Johnston's combination of firmness and tact brought the "Mormon War" to a blood-free conclusion. Johnston was then given command of the Department of the Pacific in 1860. He remained at that assignment until he resigned his commission in 1861 after Texas seceded from the Union.

David Farragut

David Glasgow Farragut (1801–1870), the adopted son of War of 1812 naval hero David Porter (1780–1843), served in the U.S. Navy for nearly sixty years. He contributed significantly to the Union victory in the American Civil War. Congress rewarded him by making him the U.S. Navy's first admiral.

In 1861, Farragut was living in Norfolk, Virginia, where he planned to retire. Although a Southerner by birth, and fifty-nine when Virginia seceded from the United States, Farragut's loyalty went to his country, not his state. To pro-secession neighbors pressuring him to "go South" he declared, "You fellows will catch the devil before you get through with this business." Then he moved to New York with his family and awaited a call from the Navy.

It took over six months. Farragut was suspected by some in the Navy Department of having Southern sympathies. Because of the recommendations of his foster brother, Commander David D. Porter (1813–1891) and Assistant Secretary for the Navy Gustavus Fox (1821–1883), the Navy finally offered Farragut command of the Western Gulf Blockading Squadron in December 1861. His foster brother commanded a flotilla of mortar boats in Farragut's squadron.

New Orleans and the Mississippi Farragut arrived in the Gulf in February 1862, assigned the task of capturing New Orleans. He first attempted to reduce the forts guarding the approaches to New Orleans, Fort Jackson and Fort St. Philip. A five-day bombardment by the mortar boats that consumed nearly seventeen thousand explosive mortar shells failed to reduce even Fort Jackson, down stream from Fort St. Philip.

Farragut had orders to reduce both forts before proceeding to New Orleans. Instead, he simply steamed past the the two forts, realizing they would fall if New Orleans was captured. He started his run at 2:00 A.M. on April 24, 1862, taking little damage. The Confederates in New Orleans sent a small force of steam rams and the ironclad *Louisiana* to oppose Farragut, but he brushed them aside. Farragut's fleet anchored at New Orleans at 1:00 P.M. on April 25. Aboard were six thousand Union soldiers led by Major General Benjamin Butler. New Orleans surrendered without resistance. Cut off, Forts Jackson and St. Philip followed suit. The capture had political as well as military significance. Farragut was promoted to rear admiral in July 1862.

Farragut then established control over the lower Mississippi River. He could reach Vicksburg, Mississippi, with his flotilla, and he did so. On several occasions he ran the Confederate batteries at Vicksburg, cooperating with General Ulysses S. Grant, whose campaign to capture Vicksburg ended with its surrender on July 4, 1863. This gave the Union control of the Mississippi River, splitting the Confederacy in two.

Mobile Bay In 1864, Farragut led a campaign to retake Mobile, Alabama. It was the last major Gulf Coast port east of the Mississippi that was still in Confederate hands. The approaches to Mobile Bay were blocked with pilings, were mined, or were under the guns of Fort Morgan, a pre-war coastal fortification that had been heavily reinforced.

As on the Mississippi River, Farragut chose to run the batteries. The safe channel was narrow. The monitor *Tecumseh* struck a mine (or torpedo as they were then called) when it came opposite Fort Morgan. Sinking instantly, it took most of its crew with it. The lead ship, steam sloop-of-war *Brooklyn* stopped, putting the line in confusion. Ignoring the mines, Farragut ordered his flagship, the *Hartford*, out of the safe channel and into the harbor. To a warning shouted from the *Brooklyn*, Farragut shouted, "Damn the torpedos, full speed

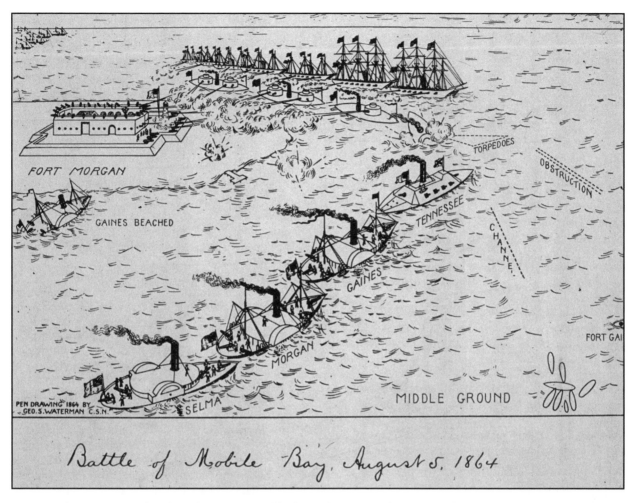

On August 5, 1864, Union Admiral David Farragut uttered his famous line, "Damn the torpedoes, full speed ahead!" during his victory in the Battle of Mobile Bay. *MPI/Getty Images*

ahead!" The rest of the column followed the *Hartford* into the harbor.

A few mines touched the *Hartford*. None exploded. In Mobile Bay, the squadron attacked a Confederate naval force that included the ironclad *Tennessee*. Farragut had three other monitors. The CSS *Tennessee*, commanded by Admiral Franklin Buchanan, and the rest of the Confederate ships, were battered into submission. As with New Orleans, once Mobile was captured, the forts defending Mobile Bay soon surrendered.

The Battle of Mobile Bay ended Farragut's active career. He was promoted to vice admiral in December 1864, and to admiral—a rank created for him—in July 1866. He made a goodwill tour of Europe in 1867–68, in failing health. He died visiting Portsmouth Naval Yard in New Hampshire on August 14, 1870.

Early Life James (later, David) Glasgow Farragut was born on July 5, 1801, near Knoxville, Tennessee. His father, Jorge Farragut, was an officer in the Revolutionary Navy, and a sailing master in the U.S. Navy. His father served at New Orleans, and the future David Farragut spent much of his youth there. Jorge Farragut's wife died in 1809, and thereafter James was raised by a close family friend, Captain David Porter. In 1814, to honor his foster father, James changed his first name to David.

In 1810, Farragut received an appointment as a midshipman in the U.S. Navy aboard Porter's ship, the frigate Essex. David Farragut served on the Essex during its Pacific voyage during the War of 1812. He was aboard the *Essex* in Valparaiso Harbor when it was captured by the British warships *Cherub* and *Phoebe*.

Farragut spent the rest of his life as a naval officer, mostly at sea. Promotion in peacetime was slow. He was promoted to lieutenant in 1825, commander in 1841, and captain in 1855. During that thirty-year period he served in the United States, the Mediterranean, the Caribbean, and the Brazil Station. Between 1854 and 1858 he was in California, where he established the Mare Island Navy Yard. In 1860 he was back at Norfolk, Virginia, where he established his home. During and after the Civil War, his residence was in Washington, D.C.

Jubal Early

Jubal Anderson Early (1816–1894) was an officer in the Confederate Army. Early began the Civil War strongly opposing secession. When Virginia joined the Confederacy, Early followed his home state. By war's end, he was a wholehearted believer in the Confederacy and remained so for the rest of his life. At his death nearly fifty years after the war's end, Early had emerged as the foremost proponent of the mythology of the "Lost Cause."

Early Confederate Service

Early was a lawyer in Virginia as the 1860s began. He had dabbled in politics as well, serving in the Virginia legislature in the 1840s. When Virginia held a convention in April 1861, to consider the issue of secession, Early attended as a delegate. Initially, he opposed secession—vociferously, as with everything about which he had an opinion. After South Carolina troops fired on Fort Sumter, in Charleston Harbor, Lincoln called for 75,000 militia to put down the rebellion. Early equally vociferously swung to supporting secession.

After Virginia seceded, Early offered his services as an officer to the Confederate government. Early had graduated from the U.S. Military Academy at West Point in 1837, and Virginia made him a colonel. Commanding the Twenty-fourth Virginia Infantry at the First Battle of Bull Run (or Manassas), he turned in a creditable performance and was quickly promoted to brigadier general.

He commanded a brigade in Ewell's Division of the Army of Northern Virginia for most of 1861 and 1862, fighting at Williamsburg, Malvern Hill, Second Bull Run (Manassas), and Antietam (Sharpsburg). After Brigadier General Alexander Lawton, commanding Ewell's Division (Ewell had been wounded at Groveton in August 1862), was wounded at Antietam, Early assumed command of the division during the battle.

Having done well as division commander at Antietam and Fredericksburg, in December 1862, Early was promoted to major general. He commanded Ewell's old division—now named Early's Division, at both Chancellorsville and Gettysburg in 1863.

Independent Command

During the Wilderness Campaign, Early received another battlefield promotion, taking command of A. P. Hill's Corps after Hill (1825–1865) was wounded. In May 1864 he was promoted to lieutenant general and then sent to an independent command in the Shenandoah Valley, Second Corps. His assignment was to relieve pressure from the Army of Northern Virginia, besieged at Petersburg. He carried out orders in spectacular fashion. Starting on June 12, 1864, Early swept down the Shenandoah Valley, chasing Union General David Hunter before him. Breaking out of the Valley at Harpers Ferry, Virginia, he crossed the Potomac River and struck for Washingtion, D.C., which was lightly defended.

A smaller Union force, commanded by Major General Lew Wallace, with six thousand men, met Early's Second Corps at Monocacy, Maryland. Wallace's troops were thrown together from two different corps, and many men were recruits. It took Early two days to defeat Wallace. At a terrible price to his own command, Wallace bought time for Grant to shift reinforcements to Washington.

Early reached the District of Columbia on July 11, but by then the capital's garrison had been reinforced and was too strong to defeat. After a few days of skirmishing around Fort Stevens, Early fell back to the Shenandoah Valley. Early had free reign in the Valley for the next few weeks. He ranged as far north as Chambersburg, Pennsylvania, which he burned on July 30, 1864. Finally, Grant tired of Early's raids. He sent Major General Philip Sheridan to take command of the Army of the Shenandoah, two corps totaling 43,000 men. After a few weeks of skirmishing, the two armies met at Winchester, Virginia, on September 19, and at Fisher's Hill on September 22. Early was defeated on both occasions.

Retreating south in the Shenandoah Valley, Early managed to surprise Sheridan's army at Cedar Creek on October 19, 1864. The Confederates routed the Union Army and took their camp. The starving Confederate soldiers then broke ranks to loot the Union camp. While they were doing that, Sheridan rallied his men and counterattacked. Early was defeated yet again.

Cedar Creek gave the Union the initiative in the Shenandoah for the rest of the war. Early fought on unsuccessfully. Finally on March 5, 1865, Early's Second Corps was destroyed at Waynesboro. Lee relieved Early, who headed for the west.

Early Life

Jubal Early was born on November 3, 1816, in Franklin County, Virginia. He attended West Point, graduated in 1837, and received an artillery commission. He participated in the Seminole War, in Florida. He remained in the Army until 1840, when he resigned his commission.

For the next twenty years, he was a lawyer in Virginia and a sometime politician. He served in the Virginia legislature in 1841 and 1842. During the Mexican-American War, he was a major in a Virginia militia regiment. Early saw little action. His regiment mainly served on garrison duty in northern Mexico. After the war ended in 1848, he returned to civilian life and his law practice.

Post-War Career

After the Confederate surrender, Early refused to surrender. He went to Texas and then to Mexico. After that, he sailed to Canada and lived there for two years. He wrote his war memoirs while in Canada, finally returning to the United States in 1867.

command of a brigade, which he led at the First Battle of Bull Run (Manassas) in July of that year. Burnside's brigade performed creditably, although it participated in the retreat at the battle's end.

After McClellan assumed command of the Army of the Potomac, Burnside proposed an amphibious operation to capture the Sea Islands off the Carolinas. Promoted to major general, he was given a division and captured Roanoke Island, New Berne, and Beaufort, North Carolina, between February and April 1862.

Ordered back to Washington in July after the Seven Days Battle, Burnside was given command of the Ninth Corps in September 1862, which participated in the Antietam Campaign. He commanded the Union right flank at South Mountain, on September 14. At Antietam on September 17, his Corps was on the Union left flank. He spent most of the battle trying to force a passage across a stone bridge on Antietam Creek. This was unnecessary. The creek could be forded without using the bridge. The time wasted allowed Confederate reinforcements to reach the field in time to prevent the Army of Northern Virginia from being defeated. This allowed Lee to slip away after dusk. The battle was the first indication that a command much larger than a division was beyond Burnside's capabilities.

Fredericksburg When McClellan was relieved of command of the Army of the Potomac in November 1862, Lincoln gave the Army to Burnside. Burnside accepted with great reluctance. He felt he was not up to the task. Burnside's instincts were right. He proved a failure. He reorganized the Army, creating three "Grand Divisions," each with two corps and a cavalry division or brigade. The organization proved unwieldy. He launched a December offensive, marching quickly to the Rappahannock River.

He launched an assault across the Rappahannock at Fredericksburg, Virginia, on December 13, 1862. Although Burnside successfully crossed the river, instead of reinforcing successes south of Fredericksburg, he concentrated his attack on a fortified Confederate position on Marye's Heights, behind the city of Fredericksburg. The assault on the bluffs was repelled. The Union Army took almost as many casualties as they did at Antietam; the Confederate forces had considerably fewer casualties.

Relieved of the Army of the Potomac after Fredericksburg, he was given command of the Army of the Ohio. He was more successful with a smaller command. Burnside stopped a Confederate cavalry raid into Ohio in July 1863, and then cleared Eastern Tennessee of Confederate forces. In November 1863, he stopped General James Longstreet outside Knoxville, preventing a junction between Longstreet and General Braxton Bragg at Chattanooga.

Later Career While in Ohio, he cracked down on people and newspapers critical of the war. This included

General Ambrose Burnside. *The Library of Congress*

He received a federal pardon in 1868 but remained an unreconstructed Confederate for the rest of his life.

Once back in the United States he began championing the "Lost Cause" movement. Early served as president of the Southern Historical Society. He never became reconciled to Confederate defeat. Early also led an effort to blame the defeat at Gettysburg on James Longstreet (1821–1904). Longstreet had accepted Reconstruction after the war, incurring the ire of unreconstructed Confederates.

Early spent much of his post-war life in New Orleans, participating with General P. G. T. Beauregard in running the Louisiana Lottery. Early died in Lynchburg, Virginia, on March 2, 1894.

Ambrose Burnside

Ambrose Burnside (1824–1881) was a general in the Union Army. Burnside served as a corps commander for much of the Civil War, briefly commanding the Army of the Potomac. While not the sole reason for a drawn result at Antietam, defeat at Fredericksburg, and disaster at the Battle of the Crater, his contribution to each of these outcomes was significant.

The Rising Star In 1861, Ambrose Burnside quit a position with the Illinois Central Railroad to raise a regiment of volunteers in Rhode Island, where he had run a factory in the 1850s. Burnside was then given

THE BURNSIDE CARBINE

Ambrose Burnside's most significant contribution to the Union victory in the Civil War came not from his battlefield performance but from the breech-loading carbine that he invented prior to the war.

Breechloaders could be used while mounted, giving cavalry units a reach they lacked with sidearms or sabers. Additionally, breech-loading carbines could be used from a covered position when dismounted. This allowed cavalry to ride to a defensive position, dismount, and then hold the weapon.

The first breech-loading carbines issued by the U.S. Army had one major problem. Cartridges would stick in the breech in combat, making the carbine useless. Burnside's design eliminated this problem. It used a tapered cartridge with an ejector. It fouled (became clogged with burnt powder) less than the earlier Hall's design.

The U.S. Army purchased over 43,000 Burnside carbines during the Civil war—enough to equip over fifty cavalry regiments. It was eventually superseded by the later Sharps and Spencer designs, which were the only two weapons more frequently used by Army cavalry units.

imprisoning Clement Vallandigham, a prominent war critic. Most of his actions were subsequently overruled by Lincoln.

In January 1864, he returned to the Army of the Potomac, again commanding the Ninth Corps. He initially did well. However, during the siege of Petersburg, he oversaw one last debacle—the Battle of the Crater, on July 30, 1864.

Burnside had a mine placed under the Confederate fortifications. While the Confederate line was successfully destroyed, the subsequent assault was repulsed and the Army suffered heavy casualties.

The attack failed for several reasons, not just Burnside's lack of skill. Burnside was forced to switch a brigade of black soldiers that had trained for the assault at the last minute because the government feared the political impact of high casualties in a black regiment. The new brigade, badly led and poorly prepared, was trapped in the crater formed by the mine. Burnside reinforced the failure by ordering reserves into the crater even after it became apparent success was impossible.

A court of inquiry blamed the failure on Burnside. He left the army in 1865.

Early Life   Burnside was born in Liberty, Indiana, on May 23, 1824. He graduated from the U.S. Military Academy at West Point in 1847, too late to serve in the Mexican-American War. He remained in the Army until 1853, when he resigned to open a firearms factory. He invented the breech-loading "Burnside" carbine and manufactured it in Bristol, Rhode Island. His factory

went bankrupt in 1857, and he got a position with the Illinois Central Railroad due to the influence of his friend, George B. McClellan.

He served as governor of Rhode Island from 1866 until 1869, and as senator from Rhode Island from 1871 until 1881. He died in Bristol, Rhode Island, on September 13, 1881.

Burnside wore long side-whiskers, which became known as "Burnside whiskers." The term later evolved into "sideburns," a term used today.

Joseph Hooker

Joseph Hooker (1814–1879) was the third commander—after George B. McClellan and Ambrose Burnside—of the Army of the Potomac. He is chiefly, and perhaps unfairly, remembered as the general who commanded the Army of the Potomac during its defeat at Chancellorsville.

He was serving as a colonel in the California militia when the Civil War began. A West Point graduate, he applied for and received a brigadier general's commission. He commanded a division defending Washington, D.C. Hooker distinguished himself as a division commander in the first half of 1862, fighting with distinction in the Peninsular Campaign and at the Second Battle of Bull Run (or Second Manassas). On May 5, 1862, after the Battle of Williamsburg in the Peninsula, he was promoted to major general. Following Second Manassas, he took command of the First Corps in the Army of the Potomac.

Corps Commander   His corps played an active role in the Maryland campaign of September 1862. Hooker aggressively led his corps at the battles of Stone Mountain (September 14) and Antietam (Sharpsburg, September 17), gaining the nickname "Fighting Joe." Though wounded at Antietam, he soon returned to active service.

At Fredericksburg, in December 1862, Hooker commanded the Center Grand Division. This consisted of two corps (Third and Fifth Corps) and a cavalry brigade. Hooker's force was given the most difficult task during the Battle of Fredericksburg—an uphill assault against entrenched Confederate positions at the top of Marye's Heights, which overlooked Fredericksburg, Virginia. Hooker opposed General Ambrose Burnside's battle plan prior to action, a position justified by the results at Fredericksburg. Most of the Union causalities were incurred during the failed assault on Marye's Heights.

Army Commander   Following Fredericksburg, Burnside was relieved of command and Hooker was given command of the Army of the Potomac. Hooker abolished Burnside's unwieldy "Grand Divisions." He concentrated the Union cavalry into a corps,

Columbia. "Where are my 15,000 Sons murdered at Fredericksburg?"   Lincoln. "This reminds me of a little Joke—   Columbia. "Go tell your Joke at Springfield!!"

In this Civil War-era newspaper cartoon, Columbia, the metaphorical embodiment of the United States, angrily scolds President Lincoln after the 1862 Union defeat at Fredericksburg.   *The Granger Collection, New York. Reproduced by permission*

establishing it as an independent command. Hooker instituted corps and division uniform patches. The distinctive insignia aided identification of units and built unit morale. Much of the Union Army soon imitated the practice.

In April 1863, Hooker marched the Army of the Potomac south. This new offensive to capture Richmond was stopped just after he crossed the Rapidan River on May 1, 1863. In a three-day battle centered on Chancellorsville, Virginia, General Robert E. Lee split the badly outnumbered Army of Northern Virginia into two parts. With the larger part, Lee held Hooker's army. The rest of Lee's forces, commanded by "Stonewall" Jackson, made a wide flanking march, hitting the Union Eleventh Corps from an unexpected flank. It routed, forcing the rest of the Army of the Potomac to retreat.

An enemy shell had landed near Hooker at the opening of the battle. Hooker probably suffered a concussion, leaving him incapable of running the battle at this critical stage. It also allowed Lee to hold Hooker while Jackson flanked them. Hooker's inactivity cost the North the battle and cost Hooker command of the Army of the Potomac. He resigned in June.

After Chancellorsville   In September 1863, Hooker was given the Eleventh and Twelfth Corps, sent to reinforce the Army of the Cumberland at Chattanooga, Tennessee. Hooker distinguished himself at Lookout Mountain on November 23, 1863.

General William T. Sherman took charge, after General Ulysses S. Grant moved east. Hooker's corps was part of Sherman's Atlanta campaign in 1864. Sherman had little faith in Hooker's abilities as an army commander. After capturing Atlanta, Sherman prepared for his march to the sea. Sherman named General William Howard commander of the Army of the Tennessee, passing over Hooker for this command. Hooker requested relief, and it was granted. From then until Hooker retired from the army in October 1868, he commanded various non-combat, administrative Army departments. He died in Garden City, New York, on October 31, 1879, eleven years after retiring.

Early Career   Joseph Hooker was born on November 13, 1814, in Hadley, Massachusetts. He attended the U.S. Military Academy at West Point, graduating in the upper part of his class in 1837. Appointed a lieutenant of artillery, he served in the Seminole War, as adjutant at West Point, and in the Mexican-American War. During that war, he served under both Generals Zachary Taylor and Winfield Scott, and was promoted to captain.

After the Mexican-American War, Hooker served the Army in various western posts until he resigned in 1853. Before the Civil War, he ran a farm near Sonoma, California, was superintendent of military roads in Oregon, and was a colonel in the California militia.

William Tecumseh Sherman

William Tecumseh Sherman (1820–1891) was the right-hand lieutenant of the Union's greatest general, Ulysses S. Grant, to whom Sherman was devoted. Sherman went on to lead a war-winning, major independent command.

At the start of the Civil War, Sherman was superintendent of the military academy in Alexandria, Louisiana, that later became Louisiana State University. When Louisiana seceded, Sherman quit his post and moved to St. Louis, Missouri.

In May 1861, Sherman received a commission as colonel and command of the Thirteenth Infantry. Given the Third Brigade, First Division, in the Army of the Potomac, he commanded the brigade at the First Battle of Bull Run (Manassas) in July 1861. In August, he was promoted to brigadier general, and in October, he was given an independent command in Kentucky.

Vastly overestimating Confederate capabilities, Sherman allowed uncertainty to paralyze him. He lost the confidence of the soldiers under his command, and in himself, suffering what some considered a mental breakdown. Relieved of command in November, Sherman was sent to the Western Department, where he commanded the District of Cairo (Illinois).

With Grant Sherman asked for and was given command of a division in Grant's Army of the Tennessee in March 1862. He allowed his division to be ambushed at Pittsburg Landing on April 6, 1862. At the resulting Battle of Shiloh, Sherman fought bravely and rallied his troops. At day's end, the Confederate Army failed to drive the Army of the Tennessee into the Tennessee River, in large part due to Sherman. Then, led by Grant, he participated in the next day's counterattack that swept the Confederates from the field.

For the next two years, Grant and Sherman fought as a team. He was Grant's leading lieutenant in the Vicksburg campaign. Sherman took part in the 1862 Corinth campaign and then moved to Memphis to transform that city into a Union stronghold. Sherman spearheaded Grant's first assault on Vicksburg, a direct attack from the north. There, Sherman was repulsed at Chickasaw Bluff on December 29, 1862.

The winter of 1863 saw Grant and Sherman attempt to move on Vicksburg several different ways. Finally, in late April, tired of unsuccessfully attacking Vicksburg from the north, Grant decided to run his army past the

William Tecumseh Sherman. *The Library of Congress*

Vicksburg batteries and attack the town from the south. Sherman, then commanding the Fifteenth Corps, diverted Confederate attention with a demonstration in front of Vicksburg as the rest of Grant's army slipped south. Sherman rejoined Grant at Port Gibson and participated in the subsequent Vicksburg campaign that led to the capture of the town on July 4, 1863. Following Vicksburg, Sherman was promoted to brigadier general of regulars. With Grant, he moved east, helping to relieve General William Rosecrans's army trapped in Chattanooga. Sherman became commander of the Army of the Tennessee in October, when Grant was promoted to command of all western forces.

After the Battle of Chattanooga on November 24–25, 1863, Sherman continued moving the Army of the Tennessee east. He relieved Ambrose Burnside, besieged in Knoxville by James Longstreet. In February 1864, Sherman led an inconclusive effort on Meridian, Mississippi.

In March 1864, Grant was promoted to commander of the Army. Sherman again replaced him, this time as commander of forces in the west. Sherman had command of 100,000 men in three armies: The Army of the Cumberland (General George Thomas), the Army of the Tennessee (General John McPherson), and the Army of the Ohio (General John Schofield).

Independent Command Grant moved the Army of the Potomac towards Richmond. To focus attention on this effort, Grant moved straight toward Richmond, without maneuvering. Grant's campaign was intended to suck up Confederate reinforcements. With the Confederates distracted by Grant and the siege at Petersburg, Virginia, Sherman went after Atlanta, Georgia.

The seventy-four-day campaign pitted two masters of maneuver—Sherman and Confederate General Joseph E. Johnston—against each other. Except for a disastrous frontal assault against a fortified Johnston at Kennesaw Mountain on June 27, Sherman attempted to maneuver around Johnston. Johnston skillfully parried in a series of running battles fought between Chattanooga and Atlanta. The duel might have continued until after the 1864 elections, but Jefferson Davis, frustrated by Johnston's refusal to strike at Sherman, replaced him with the pugnacious John Bell Hood, who did so. On July 28, Sherman defeated Hood's army at Ezra Creek, forcing Hood back into Atlanta. Atlanta fell to Sherman in September. The victory helped to power a Republican sweep of the November elections. On November 15, 1864, Sherman left Atlanta after burning buildings of military significance. The fires spread and consumed much of the town.

Sherman left a force under General Thomas to protect Tennessee from the Confederate Army. Sherman took 78,000 men, minimal food, and plenty of ammunition, and began a march to Savannah, Georgia. Abandoning supply lines, Sherman fed his men by raiding civilian food stocks. He also destroyed anything he encountered of military value. Sherman arrived in Savannah on December 10, reestablished supply lines, and then captured Savannah on December 21, 1864. He then turned his army north, capturing Columbia, South Carolina, on February 17. He continued north into North Carolina with the intention of joining Grant.

Sherman again faced Johnston, who had shifted to the Carolinas after Atlanta. Johnston surrendered to Sherman on April 26 at Durham Station, North Carolina. Sherman gave Johnston the same terms Grant offered Lee at Appomattox.

Postwar Career and Early Life After the war, Sherman continued in the army, rising to its commander in 1883. He retired from the army in 1884. When the Republican Party attempted to make him its presidential candidate, he refused. He wrote his memoirs in 1885, moved to St. Louis in 1886, and moved later to New York City. He died there on February 14, 1891. One of his pallbearers was his one-time enemy, Joseph Johnston.

Sherman was born in Lancaster, Ohio, on February 8, 1820. He was the son of a state supreme court judge. After his father's death in 1829, Sherman was raised in the home of a family friend, Senator Thomas Ewing. Sherman married Ewing's daughter Ellen in 1850.

Sherman graduated from West Point in 1840. He fought against the Seminoles in Florida. In 1846, at the outbreak of the Mexican-American War, Sherman was sent by sea to California. He remained in California until 1850, when he returned to Missouri. He quit the Army in 1853 to become president of a San Francisco bank. The parent bank in New York went bankrupt in 1857. In 1859, Sherman went to Alexandria, Lousiana, to become superintendent of a military academy there.

George Meade

George Gordon Meade (1815–1872) was a general in the Union Army and the last commander of the Army of the Potomac. Meade combined colorlessness with competence. He never gained his men's devotion the way Robert E. Lee or George McClellan did. He never gained a wide and favorable public reputation, as did Stonewall Jackson or Philip Sheridan. But no general was more respected by his peers than George Meade—even by his enemies. Confederate Lieutenant General Daniel Hill wrote, "Meade was one of our most dreaded foes; he was always in deadly earnest, and eschewed all trifling."

Brigade Commander At the beginning of the Civil War, George Meade was a captain in the topographical engineers. Initially, like many in the regular army, he was kept at his peacetime post in Michigan. In the expansion of the army after First Bull Run (or Manassas), Mead was promoted to brigadier general of volunteers and given command of a Pennsylvania volunteer brigade.

He took part in McClellan's Peninsular Campaign in 1862, demonstrating both competence and bravery. He fought at Mechanicsville, Gaines's Mill, and Glendale during the Seven Days Battle. At Glendale on June 30, he took command of his division after the loss of its commander and other officers more senior to Meade, leading it effectively before being badly wounded himself that day.

Despite the seriousness of the wounds he had suffered at Glendale, Meade was back in command of his brigade at Second Bull Run (Manassas) on August 29 and 30. During the Antietam campaign in September, Meade initially commanded the Third Division of General Joseph Hooker's First Corps. Meade took command of the First Corps at Antietam (Sharpsburg) after Hooker was wounded during the battle.

It was a temporary position. The Battle of Fredericksburg saw Meade back in command of the Third Division, First Corps. Hooker replaced Ambrose Burnside as commander of the Army of the Potomac after Fredericksburg. Hooker reorganized the Army of the

Potomac. Meade was given command of the Fifth Corps, which he led at Chancellorsville.

Gettysburg and Army Command Following the Battle of Chancellorsville, many leaders in the Army of the Potomac lost confidence in Hooker. On June 27, 1863, Hooker resigned as commander of the Army of the Potomac. Lincoln accepted the resignation and gave Meade command of the Army of the Potomac. It was an unpromising time to take command. General Robert E. Lee's Army of Northern Virginia was invading Pennsylvania. The Army of the Potomac was strung out along roads in both Maryland and Pennsylvania, reacting to the invasion. Meade had to fight the campaign using Hooker's disposition of the Army of the Potomac and choice of staff officers.

The two armies met at a Pennsylvania crossroads town, Gettysburg. In the three-day battle that took place from July 1 to July 3, Meade demonstrated great tactical skill. He chose excellent positions for the Union Army to fight and displayed shrewd judgment in committing reserves. The result was a significant tactical defeat for the Confederacy.

Meade was criticized for not conducting an aggressive pursuit after the battle. His decision not to pursue the enemy was due in equal part to his reluctance to endanger the victory won and his unfamiliarity with the Army he had just been given to command. He was fighting with someone else's army, one he had assumed command of a week earlier. It was not a job he had sought or really desired. After hearing the criticism, Meade offered to resign. Gettysburg proved a turning point. Meade's resignation was rejected, and he was voted the formal thanks of Congress in January 1864. Meade continued to command the Army of the Potomac until the end of the war in April 1865.

The Army of the Potomac remained an independent command for only a few months after Gettysburg. When General Ulysses S. Grant was given command of the Union Army in March 1864, he attached himself to the Army of the Potomac. From that point on, Meade was subordinate to Grant.

Meade filled that role ably and loyally. He managed the tactical dispositions of the army through the Battles of the Wilderness, Spotsylvania, Cold Harbor, and Petersburg, allowing Grant to focus on grand strategy. He was promoted to major general in the regular army in August 1864.

Post-War Career After the war, Meade had a variety of administrative roles, commanding the Division of the Atlantic (until August 1866), the Department of the East (August 1866 to January 1868, and from March 1869 until his retirement), and the Third Military District (January 1868 to March 1869). The Third Military District consisted of Georgia, Alabama, and Florida. Meade died on November 6, 1872, in Philadelphia from complications of the wound he had received at the Battle of Glendale in 1862.

Early Life Meade was born on December 31, 1815, in Cadiz, Spain, where his father was serving as a representative of the U.S. government. After returning to the United States, the family moved to Philadelphia, where he grew up.

George Meade did not intend to embark on a military career. He attended the U.S. Military Academy at West Point because it offered a free education. He graduated in 1835, receiving an artillery commission. He was immediately sent to Florida and served in the Seminole War. He resigned his commission in 1836 and spent the next six years doing surveying and engineering work for railroads. He also participated in surveying the borders of Texas and Maine.

In 1840, he married, and then, to better provide for his family, rejoined the Army in 1842 as a lieutenant in the topographical engineers. Except for military service during the Mexican-American War between 1846 and 1848, Meade remained in the topographical engineers until the start of the Civil War.

During the Mexican-American War, he served with General Zachary Taylor. Meade fought at Palo Alto, Resaca de la Palma, and Monterrey. He was brevetted first lieutenant at Monterrey for gallantry. After the Mexican-American War, he returned to engineering and surveying duties. He served in Philadelphia, in Florida, and in the years immediately before the Civil War, in the Great Lakes District.

John Wilkes Booth

John Wilkes Booth (1838–1865) assassinated President Abraham Lincoln at Ford's Theater in Washington, D.C., on April 14, 1865. Booth was tracked on April 26, 1865, to a tobacco shed in Port Royal, Virginia, by Army forces pursuing him. Rather than surrender, Booth chose to fight, and he was shot as the shed caught fire and burned down around him.

Booth was a well-known and well-regarded actor who performed in theaters in the central Atlantic states. He had appeared on stage between 1855 and 1864 in cities from Philadelphia to Richmond and had played leading roles for stock theater companies that circulated among the major cities in Pennsylvania, Maryland, and Virginia. Booth inherited the acting tradition. His father, Junius Brutus Booth was regarded as England's premier Shakespearian actor before emigrating to the United States. Booth's brothers, Edwin and Junius Brutus Jr. were also noted actors. His older brother Edwin assisted John Wilkes in starting his acting career.

The Kidnapping Conspiracy Born in Maryland, Booth strongly identified with the South. He sympathized with secession, as did many others in eastern Maryland. When the Civil War started, Maryland remained in the Union. Many pro-secession Marylanders

Painting showing President Abraham Lincoln's assassination by John Wilkes Booth.   *The Library of Congress*

went south and joined Confederate units. Booth did not. He apparently promised his mother that he would not become a soldier. He worked covertly for the Confederacy, though, providing aid and intelligence out of Washington and Baltimore.

In May 1864, Booth quit the stage. His stated reason was to run an oil business in Pennsylvania. It was more likely that he wanted extra time for the Confederate cause. He visited Montreal in October 1864, where Southern sympathizers in the North often met with Confederate agents. No record exists of what happened there.

Shortly after returning to Maryland, Booth moved to Washington and became part of a team of people planning to kidnap President Lincoln and exchange Lincoln for Confederate prisoners. The circle involved many who were later implicated in conspiring to carry out Lincoln's assassination: Samuel Arnold, George Atzerodt, David Herold, Dr. Samuel Mudd, Lewis Powell, Michael O'Laughlen, John Surratt, and John's mother, Mary Surratt. Mary Surratt ran a boarding-house where the conspirators would meet.

Louis Weichmann, a boarder in the Surratt house and wannabe conspirator, testified that they planned to kidnap Lincoln as he visited an Army hospital on March

17, 1865. Lincoln changed his plans that day, attending instead a luncheon at the National Hotel.

Assassination   The collapse of the Confederate lines at Petersburg, Virginia, the subsequent capture of Richmond, and the surrender of the Army of Northern Virginia overtook the kidnapping plan. By April 11 there was no Confederate government to negotiate an exchange of Lincoln for Confederate prisoners of war. The conspiracy changed to assassinating Lincoln and his cabinet.

Booth's bigotry partly motivated the assassination. Lincoln made a speech on April 11, stating his preference for enfranchising literate blacks and black veterans. Booth, in the audience, vehemently opposed this. He told a friend, "That is the last speech he will ever make." On Good Friday, April 14, 1865, President Lincoln attended a showing of the comedy *Our American Cousin* at Ford's Theater, near the White House. Booth, a friend of the owner, had a pass to the theater. Booth snuck into the Presidential box and shot Lincoln in the back of the head. Lincoln died the next day.

Booth leapt onto the stage from the box. He snagged his foot on a flag draping the box and landed heavily, breaking a bone in his foot. Before staggering offstage, he shouted, "Sic semper tyrannus" (Thus

THE FATE OF THE CONSPIRATORS

Mudd, Herold, Atzerodt, Powell, Mary Surratt, Arnold, Edmund Spangler (who aided Booth's escape in Maryland), and O'Laughlen were caught by the federal dragnet after Lincoln's assassination. John Surratt escaped to Canada and was eventually captured in 1866 in Alexandria, Egypt. The eight caught immediately after the assassination were tried by a military tribunal, an action to which even some of Lincoln's supporters objected. John Surratt was tried in 1869 in a civilian court in the District of Columbia.

All eight defendants in the military tribunal were convicted. The guilt of Herold, Atzerodt, and Powell was clear. They were condemned to death. Mary Surratt was convicted of aiding the assassination attempt by providing Booth with the weapons and supplies that he and Herold picked up at a tavern she owned. She, too, was condemned. All four were hanged on July 7, 1865.

The guilt of the others was more questionable. All had likely participated in the kidnapping conspiracy, although all denied it. Arnold and O'Laughlen almost certainly knew of the assassination plan, even if they did not participate in it. Mudd may not have known about it. Spangler probably did not. Arnold, O'Laughlen, and Mudd were sentenced to life imprisonment; Spangler was sentenced to six years in prison.

O'Laughlen died of yellow fever in 1867. The other three were pardoned by President Andew Johnson in 1869.

John Surratt, who participated in the kidnapping plot and probably knew about the assassination plot, was the luckiest conspirator. His trial on the assassination charge ended in a hung jury, and charges were dismissed. The statute of limitations had run out on other charges.

always to tyrants), the Virginia state motto. Booth left the theater, retrieved his horse, and then rode to the Washington Naval Yard. There he met David Herold and rode out of Washington.

Booth failed to recruit all of the kidnapping conspirators into the assassination plot. Besides Herold, Booth convinced Powell and Atzerodt to join him. Atzerodt was to kill Vice President Andrew Johnson (1808–1875), and Powell was to kill the Secretary of State William Seward (1801–1872). Atzerodt's nerve failed; he never attacked Johnson. Powell broke into Seward's house and badly injured Seward with a knife. Believing Seward mortally wounded, Powell left and fled Washington. Seward recovered, leaving Lincoln the only target killed.

Booth and Herold recovered supplies and weapons cached at a tavern in Surrattsville, Maryland (now Clinton, Maryland) and then fled into Virginia. En route,

they stopped at Dr. Mudd's house in Benedict, Maryland, and spent the night. Mudd splinted Booth's broken foot, unaware of Lincoln's assassination.

Booth and Herold left the next day, fleeing across the Potomac into Virginia. Mudd told authorities of Booth's visit to him on Easter Sunday, after Booth left his home the previous day. Union cavalry tracked Booth and Herold to a tobacco barn owned by Richard Garrett, in Port Royal, Virginia, on April 26, 1865. Herold surrendered. Booth refused to surrender. The barn was set on fire to drive Booth out. Spotted inside the barn, Booth was shot and wounded by one of the soldiers in the pursuit and dragged out of the barn. He later died in Garrett's house.

✪ Major Battles

Fort Sumter

When South Carolina artillery opened fire upon Fort Sumter in Charleston Harbor at 4:30 A.M. on April 12, 1861, the barrage was intended to start a war. Confederate forces had already been informed by Major Robert Anderson, Fort Sumter's commander, that he intended to surrender within the week if he was not resupplied. Although a supply ship was approaching Charleston, it was known to be unarmed and known to be carrying only food and other provisions for the garrison. It could have been turned away with a few warning shots, and Anderson would then have hauled down his flag.

Pro-secession firebrands were playing a larger game. By reducing the fort, they hoped to prompt a military counterreaction by the federal government. This would push the slave states that remained with the United States to join the Confederacy.

The Fort A masonry fort, Fort Sumter stood on an artificial island in Charleston Harbor. Started in 1829 and still incomplete in 1861, it dominated the approaches to Charleston. Even without its intended battery of guns, whoever owned Fort Sumter controlled the approaches to South Carolina's biggest seaport.

On December 20, 1860, South Carolina seceded from the United States and began seizing federal property. Major Anderson, a native of a slave state (Kentucky), commanded the Army's garrison in Charleston, sixty-five artillerymen. He was ardently pro-Union. The garrison was stationed at Fort Moultrie, a battery on Sullivan's Island, a sand spit attached to the mainland by swamp.

Moultrie protected Charleston from a seaward attack. It could not be defended against an assault from inland. Militia forces in both Charleston and Moultrieville on Sullivan's Island threatened Moultrie.

Evacuation and Siege Under cover of darkness, on December 26, 1860, Anderson evacuated Fort Moultrie, transferring his men to the unfinished Fort Sumter.

Union troops shot cannons in an effort to fight off a Confederate attack on a poorly equipped Fort Sumter. *MPI/Getty Images*

Local construction workers at Sumter were hustled into the boats used to transport the Union garrison to the island. Charleston exploded in rage. Three months of siege began.

One attempt was made to reinforce and resupply Fort Sumter by the outgoing Buchanan Administration. The unarmed *Star of the West* was sent, arriving on January 9, 1861. As it steamed down the main channel of Charleston Harbor to Sumter, a battery on Morris Island, south of the port, opened up. Warning shots splashed in front of the *Star of the West*. Anderson had mounted enough of Sumter's guns to have suppressed this battery. Unwilling to start a war on his own initiative, Anderson kept Sumter's guns silent. Unsupported, the *Star of the West* turned around and returned to Washington, D.C.

The North Considers Its Course of Action By Lincoln's inauguration, in March 1861, Fort Sumter was short on food and running low on necessities, items like candles and matches. Without relief, it would be forced to surrender. In his Inaugural Address, Lincoln pledged

to keep the remaining federal properties in the part of the United States that was revolting against the federal government.

Six states had joined South Carolina in forming the Confederate States of America. The federal government had lost control of all its possessions in those seven states, except for two remote naval anchorages in the Florida Keys, Fort Pickens in Pensacola Harbor, and Fort Sumter.

Lincoln's secretary of state, William Seward, on his own initiative, assured Southern authorities that the United States planned to evacuate Sumter. General Winfield Scott, the Army's commander, urged its abandonment. Sumter could not be held if subjected to a determined assault from the mainland. Yet it was federal property. Lincoln pledged to hold it. Evacuation would demoralize those in the North who wished to maintain the Union. It would embolden those in the Confederacy, fixing their determination to remain independent. Lincoln decided he could not give up Sumter without a fight.

Besides the southern states that were in rebellion, six of the seven remaining slave states were balanced on a knife's edge. If Lincoln ordered the Navy to shoot its way into Fort Sumter, they would probably succeed in relieving Sumter, but the North would carry the burden of being the aggressor. The remaining slave states would probably then join the rebellion.

On April 6, Lincoln announced that he was sending supplies to Sumter aboard an unarmed ship. It would only carry supplies—no ammunition or reinforcements—just food. It was a brilliant solution. The supplies, if delivered would sustain the garrison for months. Lincoln could use that time to work towards voluntary reconstruction of the Union. If the ship was fired upon, it would start a war, with the onus of starting it shifting to the South.

Southern Reaction   The rebelling states were in a precarious position. If the Upper South—with industrial centers in Missouri, Tennessee, Maryland, and Virginia, and the agriculture and population of Kentucky and North Carolina—remained in the United States, the seven states of the Confederacy would become weak and impoverished. Reconstruction would follow. To remain independent, the Confederacy needed war to force the Upper South out of its neutrality and into the Confederacy.

On April 9, the Confederate government ordered General Pierre Beauregard, the commander of Confederate forces at Charleston, to capture Sumter before the arrival of relief. Beauregard sent a summons to Anderson that demanded the fort's surrender. Anderson refused, stating he would not surrender before running out of food—which would happen in another week.

The Confederates could have starved the garrison out. They could also have driven away the *Star of the West* and kept it from reaching Fort Sumter, just as they had previously. The Confederate government did not want a peaceful resolution. Beauregard ordered his batteries to open fire at dawn on April 12. A thirty-six hour bombardment followed. Thousands of shells were fired at Sumter, crumbling the obsolescent masonry walls. The unarmed relief ship arrived during the bombardment, and it could not deliver its supplies to the fort.

On April 14, Anderson surrendered. It was more because Sumter was almost out of food and ammunition than due to the Confederate bombardment. It had failed to cause a single casualty. The garrison was allowed to fire a salute and was given passage back to the North.

Results and Aftermath   The battle had the desired result for the Confederacy—sort of. The Confederacy had the war it sought. Lincoln called for 75,000 volunteers to put down the insurrection, and Virginia, North Carolina, and Tennessee joined the Confederacy.

Missouri and Kentucky stayed with the Union, despite large pro-Confederate minorities. Maryland, the remaining land link to Washington, D.C., was not given a choice. Its pro-Confederate east was occupied. The result was a smaller Confederacy than the firebrands had sought—but one capable of fighting a long war.

The First Battle of Bull Run

The First Battle of Bull Run (or First Manassas), on July 21, 1861, was the first major battle of the Civil War. It was a contest of young armies in which the advantage swung wildly from one side to the other. At day's end, the Union Army—which had almost swept the Confederates from the field—was instead routed. A small battle by later standards, it was a warning to both sides of a long and bloody conflict.

As the spring of 1861 passed into summer, virtually everyone—North and South—expected a quick end to the Civil War. As July began, General Irvin McDowell had thirty thousand men in Washington. An additional Union Army, fifteen thousand men commanded by General Robert Patterson, threatened the Shenandoah Valley. Opposing McDowell were 21,900 men covering Manassas Junction in Virginia, commanded by Confederate General Pierre G.. T. Beauregard, a hero of Fort Sumter. General Joseph E. Johnston's 11,000 men guarded the Shenandoah Valley.

Lincoln's first militia call in April was for 75,000 men to serve for ninety days. Many of those answering that call would be back home at the end of July. They wanted the war settled. Northern newspapers urged "On to Richmond," the Confederate capital, in Virginia. Expectations were just as unrealistically high on the Confederate side. One Southerner was worth any ten Yankees, the belief ran. Beauregard urged a march on Washington. This became moot when he learned that McDowell was coming out to fight.

On To Richmond   McDowell was ordered to take Richmond. He marched twenty thousand men out of Washington on July 16, 1861. He left the rest to guard the capital. McDowell felt his army was unready. It took two days to reach Centerville, Virginia, twenty miles away, and an additional two days to prepare the army to attack across Bull Run—a creek seven miles to the west.

The delay proved fatal. On July 16, Beauregard had only ten thousand men covering Bull Run, near Manassas Junction, where roads from Washington to Richmond converged. The lull allowed time to shift eight thousand men from the Shenandoah to Manassas. Despite these reinforcements and the advantage of defending from prepared positions, Beauregard still almost managed to lose.

McDowell launched his attack before dawn on July 21. A flanking march took ten thousand Union soldiers across Bull Run north of the Confederate Army's positions. They surprised 4,500 Confederates on Beauregard's left flank. Both sides fought hard, with Union troops tenaciously attacking and Confederate troops doggedly yielding ground.

Civilians arrived with picnics at the Battle of First Bull Run, but the battle proved unexpectedly bloody.   *Battle of First Bull Run, 1861 (litho), American School, (19th century)/Private Collection, Peter Newark Military Pictures/The Bridgeman Art Library.*

By noon, Confederate forces had been pushed south of the Warrington Turnpike. The remainder of the Union Army, which had been marching up and down Bull Run against the Confederate right began crossing the creek and attacked. The Confederate line wavered. Men fled the field, carrying word of a Confederate defeat. The Confederate line was about to collapse.

The Tide Changes   Three things changed the course of the battle. In the center, holding high ground on Henry Hill, was a Virginia brigade commanded by Thomas Jackson, a Virginia Military Institute professor who had joined the Confederate Army. Using the natural advantage offered by the heights, Jackson's Brigade held. The rest of the Confederate line formed up around Jackson, whose stand earned him the nickname "Stonewall."

The Union troops were tiring. They had marched six miles in order to begin an attack at 2:00 A.M. By 1:00 P.M., most had been fighting for ten hours. Finally, fresh Confederate reinforcements were reaching the scene.

At 2:00 P.M., the Confederates counterattacked in an action started by brigade commanders on the scene. By this time, the battle was out of Beauregard's control. The first counterattacks ended in confusion. Units on

both sides shared uniforms of the same color or cut, and Confederate advances stalled twice due to a fear of firing on friends.

Fortune finally favored the Confederacy when a regiment in Jackson's brigade charged. Wearing blue uniforms, they were thought to be Union troops by an artillery unit providing support to the Union line. They realized their mistake when the Confederate regiment was on top of them. The Confederate regiment destroyed the battery and then rolled up the Union line. Panic ensued. Union troops had fought bravely all day, but they were tired. Union reserves were already committed, so McDowell lacked the force needed to plug the gap. The Union line collapsed and the troops fled. Some ran until they reached Washington. Part of then-Colonel William T. Sherman's brigade fell back slowly. Aided by several companies of regulars, they provided a rearguard. This allowed McDowell to establish a defensive line at Centerville the next day with his reserves.

Aftermath   There was little point to remaining in Centerville, so McDowell withdrew his force back to Washington. Richmond would not again be threatened with invasion for another eight months.

Both sides suffered significant losses. Each army committed around eighteen thousand men to the battle. McDowell's army experienced nearly three thousand casualties; among these casualties, thirteen hundred men were taken prisoner. Nearly two thousand of the Southern forces were killed or wounded. It was the first hint for either side that casualty rates would be much higher than in previous American wars of that century.

The Battle of Ball's Bluff

The Battle of Ball's Bluff, fought on October 21, 1861, was typical of minor actions fought in the Civil War's first year. A Union debacle, it was little different than many such debacles—for both sides—in the opening year of the war. It is memorable only because of its aftermath.

It led to the resignation of Winfield Scott as the U.S. Army's commander. Additionally, the general commanding the division to which the brigade that fought at Ball's Bluff belonged was arrested by order of the U.S. Congress. Imprisoned for over seven months, he was released without charges. This peculiar outcome was as much the result of the personalities involved as the events that occurred on October 21.

Guarding Washington, D.C. In October 1861, Brigadier General Charles P. Stone commanded a division in the Corps of Observation, defending Washington, D.C. Stone's division was guarding Potomac River crossings around Poolesville, twenty-five miles northwest of the capital. Responding to a reported Confederate movement near Dranesville, south of the Potomac, Stone pushed a small detachment across the Potomac. It occupied the heights above Ball's Bluff, threatening Leesburg. It was intended to draw Confederate forces away from Dranesville.

On October 21, Stone sent a brigade commanded by Colonel Edward D. Baker to support this detachment. Baker was a political supporter of Lincoln. He resigned as Oregon's senator to join the Union Army. With no formal military training, Baker served in the Black Hawk War and commanded a brigade in the Mexican-American War. Stone authorized Baker to either withdraw the detachment—which had succeeded in attracting the attention of a Confederate brigade—or reinforce the detachment with his brigade. He chose the latter course of action.It took a long time for Baker to move his brigade across the Potomac. He had one flatboat that could carry sixty men, two that could each hold twenty-five to forty men, and a skiff that could take four men. By noon, Baker had ferried fourteen hundred men across the Potomac to join the three hundred already there. He sent the rest of his brigade to Edward's Ferry with orders to distract the Confederates.

The diversion failed. A Confederate force commanded by Brigadier General Nathan Evans concentrated at Ball's Bluff. Both sides had roughly seventeen hundred troops, but Union forces were pinned to a thin crescent anchored on Ball's Bluff. They had no depth, no maneuvering room, and a broad river to their rear. The Confederate brigade was sheltered by woods around Ball's Bluff.

The Attack At 3:00 P.M., the Confederates attacked, pushing the Union forces back. The Union regiments began giving ground in good order, falling back slowly. Their problem was that they ran out of ground to give. Baker ordered his brigade back across the Potomac, but even overloaded, the boats could only take about one hundred men in one trip. A few hundred were able to escape to Harrison's Island in the middle of the river before Confederate pressure grew too strong.

Suddenly the Union line broke. The retreat became a rout, with every man for himself. Men fled to the river, swollen by recent rains. They threw themselves in, attempting to swim across. Forty-nine men were killed and over eight hundred captured or missing and presumed drowned. Of those that reached the other side of the Potomac, 158 were wounded. Among the dead was Colonel Baker.

The Aftermath The impact in Washington was out of all proportion to the casualties suffered or the military realities of the battle. Congress was shocked by the death of Edward Baker, a man well-liked by his former colleagues. Drowned soldiers from the battle washed up on the shores of the Potomac near Washington, further inflaming the emotions of Congress.

General George B. McClellan, General Stone's superior, considered the circumstances of the battle and concluded that Stone had done nothing wrong. Stone had given a subordinate a job—including the freedom to do the job as the subordinate best saw fit. That subordinate, Colonel Baker, made an error in judgment that led to defeat. That error illustrated the first rule of war—bad things happen.

McClellan refused to order an investigation into Stone's conduct at Ball's Bluff. because he believed that a formal inquiry was unnecessary. Congress was dissatisfied by this decision. Baker had been a good friend, and Congress felt that someone must be at fault. The Committee on the Conduct of the War—a joint commission of both representatives and senators—conducted its own investigation of Ball's Bluff. Sessions were held secretly. Witnesses were questioned, and cross-examination was not permitted. Stone was not permitted a defense, or even informed of who the witnesses were or what they said.

The Committee issued a warrant for General Stone's arrest on January 29, 1862. Over McClellan's protests, it was executed on February 9. Stone was imprisoned at Fort Lafayette, New York. He was later transferred to Fort Hamilton, New York. He was held in solitary confinement. No charges were filed against Stone. He was guilty of no crime—other than incurring congressional anger. After 189 days in legal limbo, Stone was released.

In the Battle of Hampton Roads, the CSS *Virginia* took on the USS *Monitor* in the first battle between ironclad ships. *Getty Images*

Other members of Congress passed a law in July 1862 that forbade any officer or soldier from being imprisoned for longer than thirty days without charges.

Monitor vs. Merrimac

On March 7, 1862, the CSS *Virginia* sailed from Norfolk, Virginia. The previous day it destroyed two Union warships blockading the Chesapeake River, the frigate *Congress* and the sloop *Cumberland*. Both were obsolescent wooden sailing warships. The Confederates had missed the real prize—the wooden steam frigate *Minnesota*, a sister to the USS *Merrimac*, from which the *Virginia* was built.

The *Minnesota* was hard aground. It could be sunk the next day, and the *Virginia* would then clear away the rest of the Union blockade. Lieutenant Catesby Roger Jones, who replaced the injured Captain Franklin Buchanan as *Virginia*'s commander, was startled when he neared the *Minnesota*. A craft was in front of it. It looked like a tin can box sitting on a raft. It was the Union ironclad *Monitor*. In the ensuing battle—the first between ironclad warships—naval warfare changed forever.

The Virginia When Virginia seceded from the United States in April 1861, it seized the Norfolk Naval Yard, the largest Navy installation in the Confederacy. The steam frigate *Merrimac*, one of seven screw-propelled wooden steam frigates in the U.S. Navy, had been undergoing refitting in Norfolk.

Before evacuating, Navy officials had burned the *Merrimac*. It sank at the dock, preserving the lower hull and engines. Confederate naval engineers raised the hull and found it was still useful. One wooden warship with unreliable engines—they had not been improved by three months underwater—was not going to be able to drive away the blockading Yankees.

The *Merrimac* was converted to an ironclad. The hull above the berth deck was removed and replaced with a long wooden citadel in which cannon could be mounted. This structure was rounded at the ends and sloped forty-five degrees. Four inches of iron armor—two layers of two-inch iron plate rolled at Richmond's Tredegar Iron Works—was bolted to the sides and the upper hull. The ship's deck was sheathed in a thinner layer of armor. The ship was armed with a battery of six nine-inch Dahlgren smoothbores and four seven-and-one-half-inch Brooke rifled cannon. Commissioned as the *Virginia*, the ship was ready for action at the end of February 1862.

The Monitor Secretary of the Navy Gideon Wells (1802–1878) heard rumors that the Confederates were building an ironclad. He responded by putting out a request for an armored warship. Three contracts were signed. Two were for ships like the *Virginia*. The third was revolutionary: an armored, rotating turret mounted on a low, flat iron hull.

The ship's designer, John Ericsson (1803–1889), was disliked by the Navy establishment. It took the intervention of both Lincoln and Wells to get Ericsson a contract. Even then, the terms were against Ericsson. He was given one hundred days to finish the ship and faced a penalty for every day it was late. He would not be paid in full until the Navy was satisfied with its performance. Ericsson signed the contract on October 4, 1861. Construction started in the Brooklyn Navy Yard on October 25, 1861. Coordinating the different subassemblies was at least as challenging an engineering feat as designing the ship. Eight inches of armor protected the turret. Two steam engines had a horsepower of 320.

The ship was launched on January 30, 1862, floating at exactly the draft Ericsson designed it for: eleven feet, four inches. It was named *Monitor*, because, in Ericsson's words, it "would prove a severe monitor" on the Confederacy. Outfitting took an additional month. The *Monitor* left New York Harbor on March 4.

The Battle The *Monitor* arrived at Hampton Roads at the entrance to the James River one day after *Virginia*'s first sortie. On March 6, the *Virginia*, commanded by Captain Buchanan, steamed out of Norfolk into Hampton Roads (the harbor). The *Virginia* first encountered two wooden sailing ships. It disabled the frigate *Congress* with a broadside of heated shot. Then *Virginia* turned and rammed the *Cumberland*, once a frigate but converted to a smaller sloop-of-war in the 1850s.

As the *Cumberland* sank, the *Virginia* turned its attention on the *Congress*. The frigate's captain had it run aground to keep the deep-draft *Virginia* from ramming it, but the *Virginia* fired red-hot shot at the wooden frigate until it caught fire and burned. Other Union warships, including the *Roanoke*, the *Minnesota*—sisters to the *Merrimac*—and the sail frigate *St. Lawrence* fled up Hampton Roads. The *Minnesota* ran hard aground, becoming easy prey for the *Virginia*. It was late in the day, and Buchanan was injured. The *Minnesota* would be there the next day. So was the *Monitor*. It had arrived during the evening of March 6 and positioned itself between the *Minnesota* and the enemy.

A long and indecisive duel between the two ironclads developed. Even at minimum range, the *Virginia*'s

Brooke rifles just dented the *Monitor*'s turret. The *Monitor*, ordered to use reduced charges with its untested eleven-inch Dahlgrens, could not penetrate *Virginia*'s armor. The *Virginia* was too unwieldy to ram the *Monitor*, and the *Monitor* lacked a ram. At noon, after nearly four hours of blazing away at each other, the *Virginia* turned towards Norfolk and sailed home.

Aftermath The two ships never met again. The *Virginia* was scuttled on May 11, 1862, when Norfolk was evacuated following McClellan's invasion of the James Peninsula. The *Monitor* sank in a storm on December 31, 1862, while being towed to South Carolina to aid in the blockade there. Yet the battle changed naval warfare forever. The wooden warship was obsolete. Armor and turrets would rule the seas for eighty years, until another technological revolution—aircraft—replaced the armored warship.

Shiloh

At dawn on Sunday, April 6, 1862, a Confederate Army was set to attack. A Union force camped near Pittsburg Landing on the Tennessee River was unaware of the enemy at its doorstep. Brigadier General William T. Sherman, who was commanding the camped force while General Ulysses S. Grant was away, ignored reports of a Confederate offensive. Union guards spotted the enemy. Shots rang out. The Confederate commander, Albert Sydney Johnston, ordered a general attack. He told his officers, "Tonight we will water our horses in the Tennessee." The battled remembered as "Bloody Shiloh" had begun.

The Situation Shiloh had its roots in Brigadier General Ulysses S. Grant's capture of Fort Donelson and Fort Henry, months earlier. The Union's first major offensive victory left the Cumberland and Tennessee River valleys open to the Union. Grant pushed down the Tennessee, establishing a camp at Pittsburg Landing near the Mississippi state border. Grant had 44,000 men and planned a summer offensive toward the Mississippi. He was waiting for reinforcements—25,000 men commanded by Don Carlos Buell—before proceeding.

General Albert Sydney Johnston, commanding the Confederacy's Army of the Mississippi, had forty thousand men. He knew that once Buell reinforced Grant, the Confederate Army would be badly outnumbered. Johnston decided to attack Grant before the reinforcements arrived. Marching overland from Corinth, Mississippi, his army camped in the woods around Shiloh church, on the evening of April 5, 1862. They set up to attack the Union position the next morning at dawn. The Union Army was unaware of its peril. Grant was absent, having gone to Savannah, Tennessee to confer with Buell. Sherman, in charge at Pittsburg Landing,

Johnny Clem became known as "Johnny Shiloh" after the battle, through a well-publicized story of his drum's destruction by artillery fire. *Hulton Archive/Getty Images*

had discounted rumors of a Confederate offensive. The six divisions were in camp formation.

The First Day—Confederate Attack

Johnston's army came screaming out of the woods just before sunrise. The attack was a complete surprise. Some Union regiments formed a line and fought. Others simply ran to the Tennessee River. Sherman, in the center, rallied the men in his division. Hotly pressed, they slowly fell back before the Confederate onslaught. On the left, anchored by the Tennessee River, the division commanded by General Stephen Hurlbut was pushed through a peach orchard and an oak thicket, where the firing was so thick that the place became known as "The Hornet's Nest." The division connecting the Union's center and left, commanded by Brigadier General Benjamin Prentiss, managed to hold the Confederates at a natural defensive line created by a sunken road. The Confederates massed sixty-two guns there and blew Prentiss's men out of the sunken road.

Once word of the attack reached Grant, he returned to Pittsburg Landing and took charge. By the afternoon, the Union Army had been pushed back two miles. It never came to a complete rout—mainly due to the tenacity shown by Sherman, Grant, and Hurlbut. They steadied their men, creating a new defensive line. The Union line was so close to the river that the timberclad gunboats *Lexington* and *Tyler* could provide artillery support.

The battle was not completely going the Confederate's way, however. Having cracked the Union center, Confederate troops swept over Prentiss's camp. Many Confederates had not eaten in over a day. They stopped to eat the food in the northern camp, giving Prentiss time to rebuild his line. Then General Johnston was wounded. Unaware of the wound's seriousness and eager to continue directing the battle, Johnston ignored the injury. As a result, he bled to death. Command fell to General Pierre G.. T. Beauregard.

The Second Day—Union Counterattack

As night fell and the fighting ceased, the Union line held. Sherman went to Grant. He wanted to urge a withdrawal and started by telling Grant, "Well, Grant. We've had the devil's own day of it, haven't we?" Grant simply replied, "Yes." After a moment's silence, Grant added, "Lick 'em tomorrow, though." And that is what they did. Reinforcements, supplies, and ammunition had poured into Pittsburg Landing. One of Grant's division's at Pittsburg Landing marched the wrong way and then countermarched back slowly. It had not fought at all the first day. That gave Grant 6,000 fresh troops. Additionally, Buell landed his troops—25,000 strong—during the night.

The Union soldiers had been fed and had full cartridge boxes. The Confederates were exhausted. They fought all day after marching twenty miles. They were low on ammunition and had no food. For many, all they had eaten that day was food taken from the enemy's campsites. Their sleep was disturbed by rain and by the Union gunboats, which fired into the Confederate camp throughout the night—one shell every ten minutes. Despite these disadvantages, the Confederates fought stubbornly on April 7, yielding slowly until the weight of the Union attack pushed them into retreat. Grant, uncharacteristically, did not order an aggressive pursuit. He viewed his men as being too tired for an effective pursuit. He had won a victory, but not annihilation of the enemy.

Results

Casualties were heavy. Both sides lost over seventeen hundred, and eight thousand were wounded. The South took nearly three thousand prisoners, the North almost one thousand. It was the largest, bloodiest battle of the war fought to that date. Strategically, Shiloh was a Union victory. The Confederacy was thrown on the defensive. Although some in Washington wished to relieve Grant after Shiloh, Grant was supported by

Lincoln and returned to the offensive. He was never again surprised on a battlefield.

The River Fleet A key to both the Union victory at Shiloh—and the Shiloh Campaign—was Union control of the navigable rivers in the Mississippi Basin. Early in the war, the U.S. Navy—and in some cases, the Army—commissioned construction of casemated gunboats, gunboats that were protected by either iron armor (ironclads) or thick layers of timber (timberclads). These ships carried batteries of heavy guns that were able to reduce earthwork forts and field artillery.

The Confederacy attempted to do the same, but the greater industrial capacity of the northern river ports won the production war for the Union. The Confederacy had to commit its naval forces piecemeal. They were quickly destroyed, captured, or neutralized. Except for places like Vicksburg, where high bluffs allowed Confederate batteries to be untouched by river gunboats, the Union ruled anywhere there was water to float a keel.

At Shiloh, this advantage gave Grant his victory. The timberclads *Lexington* and *Tyler*, immune to enemy fire from shore, gave Sherman's men cover under their heavy guns. This allowed the Union forces to re-form and regroup. Boats brought badly needed reinforcements, ammunition, and supplies for the next day's counterattack. The river fleet also allowed Grant to exploit his victory in the future by providing supply lines that the Confederates could not cut.

The Seven Days Battle

The Seven Days Battle was the climax of Major General George B. McClellan's Peninsular Campaign, his 1862 attempt to capture the Confederate capital at Richmond, Virginia. It also saw the emergence of Robert E. Lee as a battlefield force for the Confederacy. McClellan and the Union Army of the Potomac started the Seven Days Battle close enough to Richmond to hear its church bells. At its end, they were penned up at Harrison's Landing at the southern tip of the peninsula formed by the James and York Rivers.

The Union forces beat the Confederate armies commanded by Robert E. Lee in five of seven battles fought over the week of June 25 through July 1, 1862. Because of McClellan's timidity, each tactical success was transformed into a strategic defeat. It was one of military history's most powerful examples of the role psychology plays on the battlefield.

Lee took charge of Confederate forces in northern Virginia on May 31, 1862, when General Joseph E. Johnston, who had commanded the Army of Northern Virginia, was wounded at the Battle of Seven Pines. General McClellan pushed the Union Army of the Potomac to within ten miles of Richmond. While Richmond was not yet under siege, McClellan was preparing to attack the Confederate capital. Lee's forces

were outnumbered by McClellan, even after Lee withdrew forces from the Shenandoah Valley. Lee could not win a war of attrition with McClellan. He decided instead to destroy the Union Army through maneuver.

Mechanicsville Lee's attack started on June 26. Part of McClellan's army, Brigadier General Fitz John Porter's Fifth Corps, with thirty thousand men, was separated by the Chickahominy River. Lee decided to start by attacking it, to destroy the Army of the Potomac a piece at a time.

Part of Lee's army launched diversionary attacks against McClellan's main body. Lee sent four divisions to attack Porter. Stonewall Jackson's division was supposed to envelop Porter, but Jackson and his men were exhausted by previous fighting in the Shenandoah Valley earlier in June. They moved sluggishly. Instead, General A. P. Hill's division attacked Porter east of Mechanicsville. The Confederates threw ten thousand men against thirty thousand. Hill was repulsed with heavy casualties. McClellan, believing the Army of the Potomac was outnumbered, ordered a retreat. Porter fell back to Gaines's Mill.

Gaines's Mill Lee attacked Porter again on June 27. Jackson was again supposed to open the Battle of Gaines's Mill with a flank attack on the Union forces. Jackson again moved sluggishly. This time, Major General D. H. Hill's division launched a frontal assault on Porter. Hill's first assault was crushed, but Lee reinforced the attack Late in the day, Lee ordered a final assault. The Union line crumbled. Dusk ended the fight. Porter moved his corps south of the Chickahominy.

Savage Station McClellan, completely unnerved, abandoned his fortifications and ordered a general withdrawal early on June 28. McClellan pulled out so quickly that initially Lee did not realize what had happened. When Lee understood, he pursued the Union forces. As McClellan retreated to Glendale, part of Major General John B. (Jeb) Magruder's division encountered the Union rearguard: Brigadier General Edwin Sumner's Second Corps. Despite the disparity in force, Magruder's men attacked Sumner at Savage Station on January 29 and were repulsed.

Glendale McClellan continued his retreat anyway. On June 30, Lee attempted to cut off the Union Army from its supply line by attacking at Glendale. Jackson was again supposed to flank the Union right, while divisions led by A. P. Hill and Major General James Longstreet bulldozed the Union left flank.

Again, Jackson moved slowly. He parked his division at the edge of White Oak Swamp. His division remained a spectator to the day's events. Longstreet and A. P. Hill's divisions attacked, crushing the Union forces in front of them. Reinforcements that rushed from the Union positions in front of White Oak Swamp stabilized the Union line. By day's end, both sides took comparable casualties, and the Confederates were forced to regroup. Lee planned to resume the battle on the next day.

Malvern Hill On July 1, McClellan fell back to Malvern Hill, a superb defensive position. The Union artillery outnumbered the Confederate guns. They also had advantages of height and could see and hit anyone approaching with artillery fire from a long way off. Lee decided to attack anyway. He opted to precede any assault with an artillery barrage. An artillery duel developed in which Union counter-battery fire disabled many Confederate guns.

Lee initially canceled his assault on Malvern Hill. Late in the afternoon, he observed movement there. He decided that the Army of the Potomac was withdrawing. To keep the Union Army from escaping, Lee ordered an infantry assault on Malvern Hill. That decision was a mistake. Three Confederate divisions attacked the entire Army of the Potomac. The attacks were launched piecemeal and were uncoordinated. They were repulsed, and there were heavy Confederate casualties. Lee suffered 5,000 casualties to McClellan's 3,200. The Union won a decisive victory.

Despite this, McClellan—to the dismay of his Corps commanders—ordered yet another retreat. He was convinced that the Confederate Army, now three-quarters the size of the Army of the Potomac and exhausted by a week's worth of fighting, outnumbered him two to one. McClellan fell back to Harrison's Landing, where his supply base could be protected by naval power. The Peninsular Campaign was over.

Aftermath Lee's army suffered 20,000 casualties, including 3,300 dead. Union losses were lighter—only 16,000 casualties, with only 1,700 dead. However, nearly 6,000 men in the Army of the Potomac were missing; most were prisoners of war taken during the precipitous retreat. At the end of the Seven Days Battle, the Union was stronger, relative to the Confederate Army, than it had been when it started. They still had 90,000 effective soldiers. The Army of Northern Virginia had been reduced to 70,000. But the numbers did not matter. Neither did it matter that the Union won almost every battle fought during the Seven Days. Until the Army of the Potomac found leaders as resolute as Lee, they would continue losing battles that they should have won.

The Second Battle of Bull Run

Background The Second Battle of Bull Run (or Manassas), fought August 29–30, 1862, had significant results. It ended the first attempt to replace George McClellan as commander of the Army of the Potomac and set the stage for Robert E. Lee's 1862 invasion of Maryland.

The battle had its origins in McClellan's Peninsular Campaign. When McClellan took the Army of the Potomac to Virginia, the nation's capital and western Maryland were exposed. While in the field, McClellan could not discharge his responsibility as commander of the U.S. Army. Lincoln brought Major General John Pope from his Mississippi command and gave him command of the Army of Virginia. Initially, that army was made up of three corps—Nathaniel Banks's and John C. Fremont's corps covering the Shenandoah Valley, and Irwin McDowell's corps guarding Washington. Lincoln then transferred General Henry Halleck to Washington and made Halleck general in chief of the U.S. Army. Halleck had commanded forces in the West.

During the Seven Days Battle, Robert E. Lee's outnumbered Army of Northern Virginia hustled McClellan's Army of the Potomac from a position twenty miles from Richmond to Harrison's Landing at the tip of the Peninsula. The retreat had been mainly due to McClellan's timidity. McClellan was too popular to replace and too timid to produce decisive results. Halleck entrusted the more aggressive Pope with leading the next thrust on Richmond.

Pope had made enemies within his own ranks. When he arrived, Fremont, who was senior to Pope, quit in a huff. Franz Siegel replaced Fremont. Pope then alienated the common soldiers by giving a series of bombastic general orders and questioning their courage. Additionally, many officers loyal to McClellan were looking for ways to take this western interloper down a peg.

Pope's campaign got off to a good start. He began his advance in early August with his original three corps, around forty thousand men. Opposing him was General Thomas "Stonewall" Jackson with three divisions of around twenty thousand men. Banks' corps actually surprised Jackson at Cedar Mountain, Virginia, on August 6, 1862, even routing Jackson's original command, the Stonewall Brigade.

Jackson broke away, and both sides maneuvered for a week. In the interval, Lee brought up his army from the Peninsula, where it had been watching the Army of the Potomac. Now both armies numbered around 55,000, but Pope expected massive reinforcements from the Army of the Potomac. Rather than relieve McClellan, Halleck detached individual corps from the Army of the Potomac, transferring them to Pope's Army of Virginia. McClellan was left in Washington with an empty command.

Lee realized he had to strike before Pope received these reinforcements. He split his command, giving half to Jackson. On August 25, Jackson marched up the Rappahannock to Salem, Virginia, and then east through the Manassas Gap. Pope's cavalry failed to detect the movement, and Jackson moved his corps of 24,000 men a remarkable fifty miles in two days.

Jackson's "foot cavalry" fell upon the Union supply depot at Manassas Junction capturing it August 27. They gorged on the food there, carried off what supplies

Photographer Timothy O'Sullivan captured this grim image of Union and Confederate dead at Gettysburg.   *National Archives and Records Administration*

they could, and burned the rest. Jackson then disappeared again. While Pope's scattered cavalry sought in vain for Jackson, Pope dithered. He did not believe Jackson was at his rear until the telegraph line to Washington went dead. Pope marched and countermarched his men into exhaustion, chasing phantoms between Cedar Run and Bull Run. Finally, he fell back on Manassas.

McClellan suggested reforming the Army of the Potomac in Washington, under his command. Concentrating what forces were in the immediate vicinity would allow Lee to surround and destroy Pope. McClellan was willing for the Union to lose an army if it removed a rival general.

The Battle   By the evening of August 28, Pope made contact with Jackson, who had set up a defensive line west of the First Bull Run battlefield at Groveton. A fierce firefight developed at dusk. Pope force-marched his corps to Manassas in order to destroy Jackson before he slipped away. Jackson knew the corps commanded by Lieutenant General James Longstreet would join Lee on August 29, so Jackson baited Pope and enticed him to attack.

Pope launched his attack the next morning. He outnumbered Jackson by at least two to one. In his eagerness to beat Jackson before he could run, Pope launched a series of piecemeal attacks as each unit arrived. Jackson's 22,000 men had to fight only 32,000 Union troops on August 29. Jackson never felt the full force of the Union Army. The piecemeal attacks almost beat Jackson—a coordinated thrust would have succeeded.

The rest of Pope's army, an additional thirty thousand men, never engaged. Part of the problem was due to Fitz John Porter, commander of the Fifth Corps and a McClellan partisan. When first ordered to join Pope, Porter dawdled. On August 29, worried about Longstreet and contemptuous of Pope, Porter ignored the fighting to the north—waiting with ten thousand men for an attack from Longstreet that never came. McDowell's twenty thousand men on Porter's right were also tardy in reinforcing the battle. As night fell, a few of Jackson's brigades fell back a little into stronger defensive positions. Pope misinterpreted the withdrawal as a general retreat. The next morning he launched a general attack on Jackson.

Pope's attack almost succeeded, but Longstreet was now on the scene, flanking the Union left. When

Jackson was at the breaking point, Longstreet hit the Union left with everything he had—24,000 men in five divisions. The Union line reeled back. To prevent Longstreet from flanking them, the line bent like a fishhook around the Henry House—scene of some of the fiercest fighting of the First Bull Run battle. A twilight stand by Pope's men finally stopped the Confederate advance.

Pope pulled back across Bull Run that night. Lee attempted to trap his enemy as it returned to Washington, but his men were too tired, and the Union Army was too strong. Fresh troops were available from the Army of the Potomac. Lee finally pulled back on September 2.

Aftermath The Union suffered sixteen thousand casualties to the Confederacy's ten thousand. What was worse, the Union soldiers were sullen and demoralized. Lee's army, while tired, was still full of fight.

Despite McClellan's conduct, Lincoln believed McClellan wanted Pope to fail. Lincoln merged Pope's army back into McClellan's and sent Pope to the western frontier to fight Indians. McDowell was relieved of his command. Charges were filed against Porter. But McClellan was back, and the army loved it. Within days, the Army of the Potomac was ready to fight again. It was just as well, because Lee was invading Maryland.

Antietam

On September 17, 1862, two armies met at Antietam Creek, near Sharpsburg, Maryland, on what would prove to be the bloodiest day of battle in the Civil War. The Confederacy was never so close to winning the Civil War as it was when the sun rose that day. By the time the sun set, the Confederate offensive had been shattered. Lincoln used the result to issue the Emancipation Proclamation, transforming the war into a crusade against slavery and preventing European recognition of the Confederacy.

Lee decided to invade the North after Second Bull Run (Manassas). He planned to move into Maryland, which with luck would switch sides. Britain was ready to recognize the Confederacy as an independent nation. A successful invasion of the United States would convince Britain the Confederate States of America was a viable nation.

Lee marched north with 55,000 men on September 4, 1862. Desertion and straggling cost him 10,000 soldiers in the first week. By September 7, Lee was in Frederick, Maryland, upland country with few slave owners. The majority of the population supported the Union. Lee found few recruits. Lee learned that 10,500 Union soldiers still held the federal arsenal at Harpers Ferry, Virginia. He had expected the garrison to withdraw once he was in their rear, but it dug in. It was a poor defensive position. Harpers Ferry was surrounded by ridges and deep rivers. Whoever held the heights commanded Harpers Ferry. On September 9, Lee split

This statue commemorates the battlefield at Antietam, the first major battle to be fought in the North and one of the bloodiest of the war. *Scott Warren/Aurora/Getty Images*

his army into four parts. Three parts would surround Harpers Ferry. Lee, with the remainder of the army, would screen the mountain passes. By the time the Army of the Potomac figured out what was going on, Lee would be gone.

After Second Bull Run, morale in the Army of the Potomac collapsed. Lieutenant General George McClellan was restored to command of Union forces in the East. When McClellan learned that Lee was in Frederick, the Army of the Potomac began a lumbering pursuit. McClellan reached Frederick after a week's march, on September 13. The Marylanders in Frederick greeted the Union troops as liberators, restoring the Army's morale. McClellan got another gift in Frederick: Lee's plan of battle. Orders containing them were found in a nearby farm and sent to McClellan. McClellan knew where Lee was marching, when, and with what units.

McClellan moved swiftly (for him, that is) in pursuit. McClellan thought Lee outnumbered him two to one (in actuality, McClellan had 90,000 to Lee's 45,000). McClellan wanted to trap part of Lee's army

THE EMANCIPATION PROCLAMATION

Heavy casualties in 1862 left many fighting for the Union reluctant to return to the pre-war status quo. Some felt allowing slavery to continue in a reunited nation would court future ruptures. Many Northerners wanted the South punished for seceding. Depriving Southerners of their largest capital asset—the slaves they owned—would serve that goal.

Lincoln's overarching war goal was reestablishment of the Union. As the cost of the war increased, and more Northerners wanted more than just reunification, Lincoln sensed that emancipation would further that goal, not hinder it. Making abolition a war goal would make it difficult for European nations to recognize the Confederacy. England had been the leading proponent of abolition for over fifty years.

In July 1862, Lincoln proposed emancipation to his cabinet. William Seward, the secretary of state, objected—not to the concept, but to the timing. He stated that if Lincoln declared emancipation while the Union was losing battles, it would look like an attempt to stave off defeat. Wait for a victory, Seward urged. Lincoln agreed with the logic. He wrote the Emancipation Proclamation in July, but he put it in his desk to await the right opportunity. He waited until September 27, when Antietam finally provided the needed victory.

The Emancipation Proclamation was couched in military terms. Lincoln used his authority as commander-in-chief to deprive those in rebellion of property if they continued to defy federal authority. While unpopular in the loyal slave states, it did not deprive them of property—keeping them in the Union tent. Its chief effects were to keep Britain neutral (because the Confederacy would not abandon slavery) and to provide the Union Army with a new manpower pool—blacks who could now join as soldiers. By the war's end, over 175,000 blacks had joined the army—a total that was greater than both armies at Antietam.

chedsequentially by corps. First, Major General Joseph Hooker's First Corps launched an attack from the Union right. It fought unsupported for ninety minutes. About the time Hooker's attack petered out, Joseph Mansfield's Twelfth Corps, just to Hooker's left, renewed the attack. As they fell back, exhausted, it was the turn of the Second Corps.

The blows these attacks dealt shattered the Confederate line each time. Between attacks, Lee reformed his line and committed reserves to the most threatened areas. Many reinforcements came from the Confederate right. There, the Union Ninth Corps, commanded by Ambrose Burnside, spent the morning just listening to the gunfire to their right. When they finally attacked at 1:00 P.M., they stalled on a narrow bridge spanning Antietam Creek instead of fording the stream.

Despite Lee's best efforts, and the courage of his soldiers, by 1:00 P.M. the Confederate center collapsed. One final Union push would have crushed the Army of Northern Virginia, trapped as it was on the north bank of the Potomac. That final push never came. McClellan refused to commit his reserves. The battle continued on the Union left, where Burnside had finally pushed across the creek. As this attack was picking up steam, a fresh Confederate division arrived from Harpers Ferry. It proved to be just enough to stop Burnside.

Both sides had suffered enormous casualties by dusk, with approximately 23,000 dead and wounded. McClellan was content to let Lee withdraw back to Virginia across the Potomac the next day.

Fredericksburg

The Battle of Fredericksburg, December 13, 1862, was one of a series of bloody clashes fought between Richmond and Washington that ended virtually identically. Following a hard day's fighting, one of the two armies, generally the Army of the Potomac, was battered into defeat. The other army would be too exhausted to exploit the victory. Both armies would withdraw, regroup, and fight again in a few months.

In September 1862 at Antietam, it was the Army of Northern Virginia's turn to be defeated. Had General George McClellan, commanding the Army of the Potomac, followed up the victory on the next day, the war would have ended then and been a Union victory. McClellan allowed General Robert E. Lee's Confederates to slip back across the Potomac, where they were pinned. He then spent the next two months doing nothing. Lincoln, tired of trying to "bore with an auger too dull to take hold," relieved McClellan on November 7. Lincoln named Major General Ambrose Burnside as commander of the Army of the Potomac. Burnside accepted with reluctance. He had turned down the job twice before.

Burnside reorganized the Army of the Potomac into three "Grand Divisions" that contained two army corps, each with attached cavalry. It was an unwieldy structure

before it outnumbered the Union forces. McClellan pushed through at South Mountain and Crampton's Gap on September 14. Lee, realizing his danger, began gathering his scattered army near Sharpsburg, Maryland. Part of his army was stuck at Harpers Ferry and fighting the Union garrison.

Beaten at South Mountain, Lee wanted a battlefield victory before returning to Virginia. On September 15, Harpers Ferry surrendered. Lee decided these additional troops would enable him to fight it out with McClellan's larger force at Sharpsburg. McClellan arrived on September 16. He spent the day disposing his troops along Antietam Creek, east of Sharpsburg. The battle that was fought the next day was the war's only set-piece engagement voluntarily entered by both armies.

Despite a day to plan the battle, McClellan let control slip away from him. The Union attacks were laun-

that added another layer of command between combat units and Burnside's headquarters. Nevertheless, within a week of taking command, Burnside had the 110,000 men of the Army of the Potomac marching towards Richmond.

Lee took good advantage of the pause offered by McClellan. After Antietam, the Army of Northern Virginia had perhaps 35,000 effective soldiers. By adding troops left to cover Richmond, new reinforcements, and thousands of stragglers returning after the invasion of Maryland, Lee's army was up to 75,000 by early November. He had to scatter that army across Northern Virginia to cover all of the potential Union approaches.

The campaign began with Burnside outmaneuvering Lee. Burnside ignored the Orange and Alexandria Railroad route that was used in two previous invasion attempts. Instead, he moved the Army of the Potomac to Falmouth, Virginia, across from Fredericksburg. Burnside reached Falmouth on November 17. He caught Lee unprepared. The only thing between Burnside and Richmond was a thin screen of Confederate troops and the Rappahannock River. The pontoon bridges needed to cross the river got lost on the way and arrived a week later. Burnside's army camped on the Rappahannock's north bank while Lee moved his army to the heights behind Fredericksburg. By the time the pontoons arrived, Lee's 75,000 men were dug in.

Burnside considered his position for another week. Burnside had to attack. That is why he was given the army. Burnside could have shifted the Union Army above or below the Confederate Army and could have crossed unopposed. Burnside decided to again surprise Lee. Crossing the river at Fredericksburg was the last thing Lee expected. That is where Burnside crossed. He bridged the Rappahannock in the pre-dawn hours of December 11, using massed artillery to protect the engineers building the pontoon bridges.

The crossing was unexpected because it was foolish. Lee had General James Longstreet's corps dug into Marye's Heights behind Fredericksburg and Thomas "Stonewall" Jackson's corps on Prospect Hill to the south of Fredericksburg. Lee, never one to interrupt an enemy in folly, allowed Burnside's army to cross without real opposition.

Burnside had packed two Grand Divisions, "Right," commanded by Major General Edwin Sumner, and "Center," led by Major General Joseph Hooker, into Fredericksburg. He sent the "Left" Grand Division, commanded by Major General William Franklin, south of Fredericksburg, opposite Prospect Hill. The attack started early on December 13 but did not get moving until heavy fog lifted at about 10:00 A.M. The result was disaster. Franklin had an opportunity to push Jackson off Prospect Hill—or better yet, exploit the gap between the two Confederate corps and flank Longstreet. But Frank-

THE RIFLED MUSKET

The high casualty rates in the Civil War were due in part to new weapons. Artillery was still the battlefield's king, but development of the percussion cap and the minié ball increased the musket's deadliness.

The percussion cap replaced the flintlock, which struck a flint against steel to make sparks. Percussion caps contained a chemical that flared when struck, igniting the gunpowder in a rifle. Highly reliable, they worked even in a downpour. Flints were touchy, and often broke. They were less likely to work in damp weather.

The minié ball, invented by a French officer, Claude-Etienne Minié (1804–1879), was a conical lead bullet with a small steel ball in the base. The bullet, slightly smaller than the gun barrel, fell easily into the gun. When the gun was fired, the ball, forced against the lead, flattened the bullet, slightly widening it. If the barrel was rifled—that is, if it had spiral grooves that spun the bullet to stabilize it—the bullet spread into the rifling. This allowed a rifle to be loaded as quickly as a smoothbore musket. Everyone could be equipped with long-range rifles.

A rifled musket could fire almost as far as a field artillery piece. Long-range marksmanship by line soldiers was generally wretched, but the sheer volume of fire that was possible meant that inaccuracy did not matter. Infantry could hit the enemy effectively at ranges previously impossible. Tactics, especially at the start of the Civil War, were still based on the effective range of a smoothbore, and casualties multiplied as a result.

lin spent the day in half-hearted thrusts, ignoring orders from Burnside to attack.

Fredericksburg, where four Union corps charged up steep bluffs, became a slaughterhouse. All day long, brigades charged the approaches to Marye's Heights and were mowed down before they reached the enemy. Seventy percent of the nearly thirteen thousand casualties the Union Army suffered at Fredericksburg fell in front of Marye's Heights. As evening approached, Burnside, distraught at the losses, wanted to lead a final, desperate charge up the hill with his old command, the Ninth Corps. He was talked out of it by subordinates who realized it would only add more casualties.

Lee's army suffered less than 5,400 casualties, but they represented a large number of those committed to the battle. Because of the Union concentration at Marye's Heights and Franklin's reluctance to engage, only 20,000 of the 75,000 Confederate troops actively fought.

Burnside withdrew back to Washington the next day. He had not only lost a battle—he lost the confidence of his army. He attempted one more offensive in January 1863. It bogged down—literally. Roads disintegrated into mud. The "Mud March" created more bickering between Burnside and his generals. Burnside resigned thereafter and was replaced by Joseph Hooker.

The Battle of Chancellorsville

The Battle of Chancellorsville, fought May 1–4, 1863, was Robert E. Lee's finest victory. Badly outnumbered, Lee split his army. While Lee attacked the Union Army and prevented its advance, Lee's lieutenant, Thomas "Stonewall" Jackson, marched around the Union Army and struck from behind, routing it. The battle cost Joseph Hooker, the Union commander, his job. It cost Lee "Stonewall" Jackson, who was mortally wounded during the battle.

Union commanders started fighting among themselves after the disastrous Battle of Fredericksburg, in December 1862, and the demoralizing "Mud March" a month later. Army commander Ambrose Burnside felt, with some justification, that he had been badly served by his generals. General William Franklin ignored orders to attack at Fredericksburg. Franklin, loyal to the former commander of the Army of the Potomac, George McClellan, led a faction of officers seeking McClellan's reinstatement. A second faction grew around General Joseph Hooker, who wanted to replace Burnside. The acrimony exploded on January 24, 1863. Burnside demanded that Lincoln relieve the disloyal generals and threatened to resign if Lincoln did not do so. Lincoln removed Burnside and several officers more loyal to McClellan than to the army, including Franklin. Other officers resigned out of loyalty to Burnside, Franklin, or McClellan. Joseph Hooker replaced Burnside. Hooker reorganized the army, abolishing Burnside's unwieldy "Grand Divisions," and he also combined the cavalry into corps. Hooker overhauled the commissary structure, instituted leave policies, and restored the morale of the Army of the Potomac.

Lee spent the winter preparing his army. He reorganized his artillery. Lee wanted to attack, but two divisions of the Army of Northern Virginia, along with General James Longstreet, had been sent south. The Army of the Potomac was too strong for Lee to attack with the 55,000 men he still had. Lee's army waited in Fredericksburg, Virginia, opposite the Union Army camped on the north bank of the Rappahannock.

At the end of April, Hooker sent 10,000 cavalry on a wide sweep north across the Rappahannock. He sent General John Sedgwick's Sixth Corps to pretend to cross the Rappahannock south of Fredericksburg with 40,000 men. The rest of the army, Hooker and 75,000 men, went stealthily north, crossing the Rappahannock at United States Ford, north of Fredericksburg.

By April 30, Hooker's army was deep within thick woods, known locally as the Wilderness. The Army of the Potomac held the crossroads at Chancellorsville, controlling roads that were the only practical way of moving troops through the tangled thickets. Having flanked Lee's army, Hooker stopped and waited for the outnumbered Lee to retreat. Lee attacked. Leaving a thin screen of 10,000 men commanded by Major Gen-

This statue of Stonewall Jackson stands in Richmond, Virginia, the former capital of the Confederacy. *Hank Walker/Time Life Pictures/ Getty Images*

eral Jubal Early at Fredericksburg, Lee hustled west with 45,000 men. The armies made contact near the southern edge of the Wilderness late on May 1.

Hooker's generals wanted to push into the open fields south of the Wilderness in order to use the Union artillery superiority. Instead, Hooker pulled deeper into the Wilderness and waited for Lee to attack. Lee sensed that Hooker was going to remain inactive. He looked for a place to attack. Lee's cavalry commander, Major General J. E. B. Stuart, found it. The Union right flank—held by the Union Eleventh Corps—was hanging in the air. If they could reach it, they could hit Hooker from behind. Lee kept fifteen thousand men to focus Hooker's attention south. He then sent Stuart's cavalry, and thirty thousand infantry and artillery commanded by Stonewall Jackson, on a day-long march around the Union Army.

Hooker had no cavalry—it had been sent off on a useless raid. Union troops saw the Confederates moving to the west. Union troops attacked the tail of Jackson's column, which broke off to the north. Hooker convinced himself that Lee was finally retreating. Lee's hammer hit the Union Army at 5:30 P.M. on May 2. Jackson's men came screaming out of the woods, hitting the exposed flank of the Eleventh Corps. This corps was made up primarily of German immigrants. It had a poor reputation, and a commander, Major General Oliver Howard, with whom the men were at odds.

The corps routed, with Jackson's men in pursuit. Lee attacked from the south to pin down Union troops, adding pressure. The Confederates advanced two miles, stopped by darkness and a new defensive line. The line was cobbled together with elements from four corps. In the confusion, Stonewall Jackson was shot by one of his own men returning from a midnight reconnaissance. Jackson lost an arm and then contracted pneumonia while recovering. He died on May 11.

Hooker stayed on the defensive through May 3. Sedgwick, who had transferred ten thousand men to Hooker on May 1, pushed across the Rappahannock at Fredericksburg on May 3, launching three divisions against Marye's Heights. Sedgwick's men carried the Heights on their third assault. Sedgwick was in Lee's rear. An attack by Hooker would have won the battle. It never came. Hooker was knocked unconscious by a cannonball hitting his headquarters. Recovering consciousness, he refused to relinquish command. In a daze for the rest of the day, Hooker again withdrew.

Lee reacted to Sedgwick's threat, dispatching first one and then another division to Early. By afternoon, Lee had only 25,000 men opposing Hooker's 75,000. Hooker began withdrawing across the Rappahannock on May 4. Sedgwick, holding west of Marye's Heights, beat off an uncoordinated attack by 21,000 Confederates on May 4. Learning that Hooker was withdrawing, Sedgwick also withdrew north.

Lee's stunning victory was costly. Lee lost Jackson. Lee's army suffered 22 percent casualties—thirteen thousand men dead, wounded, or captured. The Union Army took seventeen thousand casualties in the fighting, but had started with more men. Additionally, the Army of the Potomac did not feel beaten. They felt cheated of a victory by Joseph Hooker's blunders.

Chancellorsville increased Lee's contempt for his enemy's abilities. He now believed one of his men could whip three Yankees. Lee knew he would lose a war of attrition—even at the exchange rates in Fredericksburg and Chancellorsville. Lee decided to take the offensive. He marched north, invading Pennsylvania.

The Battle of Jackson

The Battle of Jackson, fought on May 14, 1863, proved the key to Major General Ulysses S. Grant's attempt to isolate and capture Vicksburg, Mississippi. The capture of the vital Mississippi railroad junction at Jackson separated Confederate forces in the river port of Vicksburg from those in the field and cut off their supplies.

Grant spent the last half of 1862 and the first three months of 1863 trying to land an army on the Mississippi side of the Mississippi River in order to attack Vicksburg. He found no dry land north and east of Vicksburg suitable for safely landing his army and no way to reliably supply an army south of Vicksburg. He decided to move south of Vicksburg and travel light, bringing ammunition and a minimal amount of rations. He could move enough ammunition through the back bayous on the Louisiana side of the river and live off the land for food.

Grant ran the batteries of Vicksburg on April 16. He used the transports to ferry—from the Louisiana side of the Mississippi River across to the Mississippi side—an army that had marched overland, and he used river gunboats to protect the landing. By May 1, his army was sitting in Port Gibson, Mississippi, thirty miles south of Vicksburg. Grant soon had forty thousand men there. With those men, Grant had to besiege and capture the thirty thousand men in Vicksburg commanded by Lieutenant General John Pemberton (1814–1881). Pemberton's men were scattered among several garrisons, so until they concentrated—outside of Vicksburg—they were no threat. However, General Joe Johnston, commanding in the West, had an additional thirty thousand to forty thousand men that Pemberton could call upon. Johnston's field forces were scattered throughout Mississippi, but once he knew where Grant was going, he could concentrate them. The real threat was posed if Grant found himself trapped between Pemberton and Johnston.

Instead of moving directly against Vicksburg, which Pemberton expected, Grant decided to neutralize Johnston first. Key to this was Jackson, Mississippi, the state capital and a major railroad junction. If he destroyed the locomotives and rail yards there, it would be difficult for Pemberton to concentrate a field army against Grant and impossible to supply Vicksburg.

Grant marched from Port Gibson on May 7 and headed towards Jackson. He took a minimum of baggage—soldiers carried rations for three days, and the wagons that accompanied the army carried only ammunition. Food would be supplemented by foraging. Pemberton, expecting Grant to move against Vicksburg, held his forces behind the Big Black River. If the river protected Pemberton from Grant, it also shielded Grant from Pemberton. It was May 10 before Pemberton learned that Grant was headed towards Jackson. By the time Pemberton was moving, Grant was already at Raymond, Mississippi, twelve miles from Jackson. Grant's army brushed aside a Confederate brigade guarding that town.

On May 9, Richmond ordered Johnston to come to Pemberton's aid—but provided little other information. Johnston, in Tennessee, gathered up some forces and headed towards Jackson. On May 13, he was fifty miles east of Jackson when he received a telegraph from Pemberton. Sent May 1, it revealed that Grant was on the march. It was the first time Johnston learned about Grant's new offensive. He hustled to Jackson with what forces he had at hand—perhaps six thousand men. But it

THE RAILROAD WAR

The Civil War was the first war in which railroads played a major role. Only railroads and riverboats could carry the supplies needed for the tens of thousands of soldiers, and unlike riverboats, railroads could go anywhere.

Jackson, Mississippi, was important because it was a railroad junction—and because it was a Confederate railroad junction. The South had fewer miles of track and fewer locomotives than the North, and it had less capacity to replace losses. If a Union Army threatened a railroad junction, there would be a fight.

Consistently throughout the Civil War, the Union made better use of railroads than did the South. It forced northern railroads to cooperate by using a standard gauge. It also created the U.S. Military Railroad to operate trains in captured areas and a special branch of the Engineering Corps to keep railroads operating. If Confederate raiders destroyed a line, the Union could repair it in just days.

was too late. Grant had sent two corps to attack Jackson. Brigadier General John McClernand's corps was approaching from Corinth, Mississippi. Brigadier General William Sherman's corps was moving along the Raymond road. In all, the Union forces totaled 25,000 men.

The attack was launched in a driving rainstorm. McClernand hit first. General John Gregg, commanding the Confederate defenders, sent all his men against McClernand, unaware of Sherman. When Sherman's corps appeared on his flank, Gregg peeled off what troops he could muster to stop Sherman. The weight of Union numbers pushed the Confederates into prepared entrenchments. The battle raged all morning and into the early afternoon, and Gregg played for time as he evacuated supplies. Finally, at 2:00 P.M. he received word that the wagon train was gone, and he fell back, covering their retreat.

The Union Army spent the night in Jackson. The next day, Grant pulled most of his army out, marching west to face Pemberton, who was finally coming out to meet Grant. Grant left Sherman behind with orders to destroy the railroad yards. Sherman's men carried out those orders with enthusiasm. They wrecked railroad facilities and burned factories, machine shops, and foundries capable of producing military goods. A fair number of houses also caught fire. By the time they were done, Sherman's men were calling Jackson "Chimneytown." The damage was beyond the South's capability to repair with an enemy army nearby. Grant completed Vicksburg's isolation at the Battle of Champion's Hill two days later. Johnston and Pemberton were defeated. Johnston ordered Pemberton to abandon Vicksburg. Instead, Pemberton fell back to the Vicksburg fortifications.

Pemberton attempted to stop Grant's advance one more time at the Big Black River on May 17 and was equally unsuccessful. Grant successfully isolated Vicksburg and starved it into surrender six weeks later. Pemberton surrendered on July 4, 1863.

Gettysburg

After a surprising victory at Chancellorsville, General Robert E. Lee led his forces once more into northern territory. The Army of Northern Virginia (75,000 men)—organized into three corps under Generals James Longstreet, Richard Ewell (1817–1872), and A. P. Hill—marched into Pennsylvania. On June 30, 1863, Confederate and Union soldiers spotted each other just west of Gettysburg. Both sides returned to their camps without fighting.

The next day, the Battle at Gettysburg would begin, pitting Lee against General George G. Meade's Army of the Potomac, a force of 95,000.

Day 1: July 1, 1863 The first engagements of the battle were somewhat disorganized. Confederate troops, under Major General Henry Heth's command, struck General John Buford's cavalry early in the morning in an attempt to drive them out of Gettysburg. Buford was able to hold off the troops for a while, but he eventually retreated. At about the same time, Union General John F. Reynolds saw Confederate troops and committed his two corps (First and Eleventh Corps) to move into Gettysburg and engage in battle. By late morning, Heth was forced to retreat. The Union had gained the upper hand early, but Reynolds was killed early in the fighting.

After Heth's failed attack, Brigadier General Robert Rodes launched an immediate and uncoordinated attack on the First Corps. General Lee arrived on the battlefield after noon. He had hoped to delay or avoid battle, since he lacked information about the terrain and the size of the opposing force. Yet when he arrived, the fighting was in full swing, and he had no choice but to organize it as best he could. He allowed Heth to support Rodes in his fight with First Corps; both of their brigades took heavy losses in fierce fighting. At the same time, Lee sent Major General Jubal Early to attack the Eleventh Corps. Early quickly forced the federals to retreat to Cemetery Hill in considerable disorder. By late afternoon, both the First and Eleventh Corps were retreating. At the end of the first day of fighting, more than 9,000 Union soldiers and approximately 6,800 Confederate soldiers were dead or wounded, and Confederate forces had won the day—but not the battle.

General Meade received word of the day's events and readied reinforcements during the night. Fighting would resume the next morning, and six of the seven Union corps would be prepared for battle.

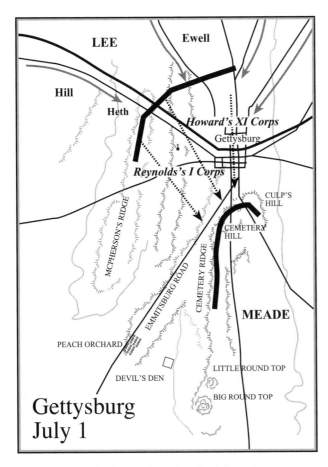

LEE

Ewell

Hill

Heth

Howard's XI Corps

Gettysburg

Reynolds's I Corps

MCPHERSON'S RIDGE

EMMITSBURG ROAD

CEMETERY RIDGE

CULP'S HILL

CEMETERY HILL

MEADE

PEACH ORCHARD

DEVIL'S DEN

LITTLE ROUND TOP

BIG ROUND TOP

Gettysburg
July 1

Despite advances in the two days prior, Confederate forces retreated from Gettysburg on July 3, 1863. This map shows the situation in Gettysburg on July 1. *Reproduced by permission of Gale, a part of Cengage Learning*

Day 2: July 2, 1863 General Lee was optimistic because of the previous day's success, but still troubled by his lack of information about the opposing army. Early morning reconnaissance had revealed that the Union Army was holding a horseshoe-shaped position along Cemetery Ridge. Lee planned his attack accordingly. He would send General James Longstreet with two divisions to attack the Union flank on the left. Lieutenant General A. P. Hill's men would follow and attack the center. Lieutenant General Richard Ewell was ordered to attack Cemetery Hill from the north and pin the Union in place. Lee gave Ewell instructions to engage in a full-scale attack for control of the hill "if practicable," but Ewell was overly cautious and did not press his attack. Historians consider Ewell's failure to gain control of Cemetery Hill one of the decisive tactical mistakes of the battle.

What Lee did not know was that Meade had regrouped overnight. Almost the entire Army of the Potomac was waiting for him. Meade had also positioned his troops to take advantage of the natural terrain, using small hills and the forests for cover. Longstreet

reached his position in the late afternoon. He charged and broke through the lines of Major General Daniel Sickles's troops at Peach Orchard and pressed the fighting on to Devil's Den and Little Round Top, where his advance was finally halted by the arrival of the Union's Sixth Corps. Just to the north, Ewell tried to take Culp's Hill, but was repelled. Early sent his brigades up Cemetery Hill, where he was attacked by Second and Eleventh Corps and driven back.

By then end of the second day of fighting, Lee's forces had gained little ground and more than 16,500 men, about equal numbers on both sides, were killed, wounded, or missing.

Day 3: July 3, 1863 Determined to continue striking, the still-confident Lee planned for an early attack on the Union center at Cemetery Ridge. Longstreet would lead the attack, while Ewell once again would try to take Culp's Hill. It was a well-designed plan, but General Meade was more than ready.

At 1:00 P.M., Longstreet began an artillery bombardment of the Union lines. The Union Army answered with its own cannons. For the next two hours, a deafening artillery duel ensued, with Confederate forces pitting their 140 cannons against the Union's 80. Thick clouds of smoke covered the field, hindering the view. The Confederate forces kept shooting blindly through the smoke and soon ran out of ammunition; the Union Army had stopped firing to conserve ammunition. When the smoke cleared, the Confederate infantry massed a desperate, doomed, legendary attack known as "Pickett's Charge" in which General George Pickett (1825–1875), with a farewell salute from Longstreet, led fifteen thousand men on a mile-long march across an open field and up toward Cemetery Ridge, where most of them met their death. The Union cannons tore the infantry to shreds, but the Confederates pressed on, engaging the Union troops in small-arms fire and hand-to-hand combat, all the way to the Union lines. By the time they got there, their forces had dwindled and they were unable to break the lines. The attack was a failure and the losses extreme: Nearly six thousand Confederate soldiers were killed or captured.

Attacks by Johnson, Ewell, and Stuart had also failed, and the battle was effectively over. The Union forces had handed General Lee a crushing defeat, crippling his army. Overall, Confederate casualties were close to 28,000. Meade's Army of the Potomac suffered horribly as well, with nearly 23,000 men—about one in four—lost.

Aftermath On July 4, Lee maintained his position, expecting that Meade would press his advantage. He did not. The battlefield was a disaster: dead bodies, blood-filled trenches, the wounded groaning in agony. That night, a heavy rain allowed Lee to make his retreat across the Potomac to Virginia. Meade slowly pursued him, but did not attack.

THE GETTYSBURG ADDRESS

President Abraham Lincoln's speech at the battlefield of Gettysburg, known as "The Gettysburg Address," is perhaps the single most famous presidential speech in American history. Lincoln made the speech just four months after the gruesome battle, and in just a few hundred words captured the nation's best hopes for a positive outcome to the devastating war:

> Four score and seven years ago our fathers brought forth on this continent a new nation, conceived in Liberty, and dedicated to the proposition that all men are created equal. Now we are engaged in a great civil war, testing whether that nation, or any nation, so conceived and so dedicated, can long endure. We are met on a great battle-field of that war. We have come to dedicate a portion of that field, as a final resting place for those who here gave their lives that that nation might live. It is altogether fitting and proper that we should do this. But, in a larger sense, we can not dedicate—we can not consecrate—we can not hallow—this ground. The brave men, living and dead, who struggled here, have consecrated it, far above our poor power to add or detract. The world will little note, nor long remember what we say here, but it can never forget what they did here. It is for us the living, rather, to be dedicated here to the unfinished work which they who fought here have thus far so nobly advanced. It is rather for us to be here dedicated to the great task remaining before us—that from these honored dead we take increased devotion to that cause for which they gave the last full measure of devotion—that we here highly resolve that these dead shall not have died in vain—that this nation, under God, shall have a new birth of freedom—and that this government of the people, by the people, for the people, shall not perish from the earth.

The Siege of Vicksburg

The capture of Vicksburg, on July 4, 1863, cut the Confederacy in two. It was the culmination of nearly nine months of campaigning and a six-week siege. It made Ulysses S. Grant's reputation and set him on the road to command of the Union Army. Combined with the Union victory at Gettysburg on July 3, Vicksburg was seen as the war's turning point.

Vicksburg, located on high bluffs above the Mississippi River, was called the Gibraltar of the West during the Civil War. Guarded by swamps impassable to an army on the north and its bluffs on the river side, it could only be approached from the south and east. Batteries mounted on the bluffs made passing Vicksburg hazardous, even for armored ships. The Confederacy held Vicksburg and Port Hudson, Lousiana, to the south, and it also controlled the two hundred miles of the Mississippi between the two. Food, supplies, and men from the Trans-Mississippi region could reach the rest of the Confederacy. Vicksburg was a prize the North wanted badly.

Grant tried to approach Vicksburg from the east in the fall of 1862. He found that his supply lines—which depended upon railroads rather than riverboats once south of the Tennessee River—were easily broken by Confederate raiders and guerrillas. For the rest of 1862, Grant sent a corps commanded by William T. Sherman up the Yazoo River, north of Vicksburg, and then across Chickasaw Bayou. On December 29, 1862, Sherman assaulted Confederate positions on the bluffs above Chickasaw Bayou and was repulsed. Grant tried moving south down the Yazoo, reaching it from Yazoo Pass. He was stopped at Greenwood, Mississippi. Grant established himself on the Louisiana side of the Yazoo, opposite Vicksburg, but could not run supplies past Vicksburg. He dug a bypass canal to allow his shipping to go around Vicksburg, but the canal would not fill.

Grant could get some supplies overland through Louisiana, but not enough to feed his army. He could bring only enough to supply it with ammunition. In April 1863, Grant made a bold move. On April 16, Grant had ships run the batteries at Vicksburg. Once south of Vicksburg, they ferried his army from Louisiana to Mississippi. The ships could probably not return north of Vicksburg, against the current. That would not matter—if Grant could take Vicksburg.

To confuse the Confederates, Grant made an infantry pretend to cross the Mississippi north of Vicksburg and sent a brigade of cavalry, commanded by Benjamin Grierson, to raid the Confederate supply lines to Vicksburg. Grierson's raid dispersed Confederate forces throughout central and southern Mississippi as they attempted to stop the Union cavalry from reuniting with Grant. Grierson took his brigade to New Orleans rather than return to Grant.

While the Confederates were vainly pursuing Grierson or reacting to the faked landing at Chickasaw Bayou, Grant landed 23,000 men near Grand Gulf, Mississippi. Grant soon had 40,000 men on the Mississippi side of the river and was on the march. He captured Port Gibson, ten miles inland, on April 30. Shielded by the Big Black River, Grant cut north, taking Raymond and then Jackson, Mississippi. Jackson, the state capital, was a railroad junction. Whoever held Jackson held the only supply line to Vicksburg. Grant's army fought and drove off a smaller force commanded by Joseph Johnston that was holding Jackson.

Grant had about forty thousand men. Johnston, who commanded Confederate forces in the west, could probably have concentrated seventy thousand men

Union troops, camped out in dugouts like those on this hillside, surrounded the city of Vicksburg for six long weeks in the summer of 1863. *MPI/Getty Images*

there. The Confederate forces were scattered all over Mississippi. General John Pemberton had thirty thousand defending Vicksburg. Johnston had twenty thousand scattered north and east of Grant. Johnston could have scraped together another twenty thousand elsewhere. Realizing he could not get enough men there fast enough, Johnston ordered Vicksburg abandoned. Pemberton could still get his army out of the city after Grant took Jackson, but once Grant crossed the Big Black River, Pemberton would be trapped. Pemberton disobeyed Johnston, choosing instead to hold Vicksburg. Leaving ten thousand men to garrison the Vicksburg fortifications, Pemberton moved east with twenty thousand men to rout Grant.

The two armies met at Champion's Hill on May 16. Grant had only two corps with him. (The third, Sherman's 11,000 men, was destroying the railroad yards at Jackson). Even then, Grant's 29,000 men outnumbered Pemberton nearly three to two. The battle cost Pemberton nearly four thousand casualties. At the end of the

battle, one of Pemberton's divisions had been separated from Pemberton. It joined Johnston's forces, but the rest of Pemberton's command was forced back to Vicksburg. By May 18, Grant had Pemberton trapped in Vicksburg.

Grant stormed the Confederate entrenchments on May 19 and May 22. Both attacks were repulsed, but Grant was not worried. He could starve his opponent in a short period of time. Once Vicksburg was surrounded, Grant controlled the approaches barred previously by Chickasaw Bluff. Grant reestablished a direct supply line using the Yazoo River. Grant sent part of his army to hold the Big Black River and prevent Johnston from lifting the siege. He then settled down to wait out Vicksburg. For the next six weeks, Grant waited while the Confederates tried to supply Vicksburg. They tried to capture the Union supply depots on the Louisiana side of the river. They were repulsed at both Milliken's Bend and at Miller's Point. Even if they had succeeded, it would not have mattered. Grant's supply line ran down the Mississippi side of the river. Johnston maneuvered along the Big Black River but was unwilling to attack across it without significant reinforcements. He never got them.

On July 2, Pemberton gave up. Surrender arrangements took an additional two days, so Vicksburg formally surrendered on July 4. Grant demanded—and received—unconditional surrender. He released the garrison of thirty thousand on parole—they pledged not to fight again until they were exchanged for Union prisoners of war. Doing that was easier than having to feed them as prisoners. Grant also hoped the released prisoners would discourage others from joining the Confederate Army.

The surrender of Vicksburg made Port Hudson untenable. The Confederate garrison there surrendered to Nathaniel Banks's besieging force on July 9. The capture of Vicksburg divided the Confederacy in two. While both sides of the Confederacy continued to fight, each half could no longer assist the other half. It marked the beginning of the end for the Confederacy.

Chickamauga

The Battle of Chickamauga, fought on September 19–20, 1863, reversed the tide of Confederate defeats in 1863. It revived Confederate spirits, which were flagging after Gettysburg and Vicksburg. The Confederate victory at Chickamauga allowed General Braxton Bragg's Army of Tennessee to besiege the Union Army of the Cumberland in Chattanooga.

Following Union victories at Gettysburg and Vicksburg, Lincoln felt that one more major Union victory would cause the Confederacy to quit. General William Rosecrans, commanding the Army of the Cumberland, was ordered to take Chattanooga, Tennessee. This would further divide the Confederacy, deprive them of a manufacturing center, and open pro-Union eastern Tennessee to the North. Rosecrans launched his offensive on August 16, 1863. He maneuvered the Confederate forces, commanded by Braxton Bragg, out of Chattanooga, by threatening Confederate supply lines through quick marches. Rather than allow himself to be trapped in Chattanooga, Bragg withdrew to northern Georgia.

The Chickamauga Campaign Rosecrans began an aggressive pursuit of what he assumed was a broken and retreating Confederate Army. Rosecrans broke the Army of the Cumberland into its corps, sending them independently in an attempt to encircle Bragg's army.

Bragg's army was neither broken nor demoralized. His 48,000 men were being reinforced by two divisions of men commanded by General James Longstreet, from the Army of Northern Virginia. With these, Bragg outnumbered the Army of the Cumberland, which had

56,000 men. Bragg began looking for ways to catch one of Rosecrans's corps, unsupported by the others.

Rosecrans occupied Chattanooga unopposed on September 9, 1863. Over the next four days, Bragg sprung two trapping attacks on Rosecrans's isolated corps. In both cases, the Union forces escaped destruction because Bragg's subordinate generals refused to press their attack. The attacks warned Rosecrans of his peril. Rosecrans concentrated his forces south of Chattanooga: the Fourteenth Corps, commanded by George Thomas; the Twentieth Corps led by Alexander McCook; and the Twenty-first Corps under Thomas Crittenden.

First Day's Battle Thomas force-marched his corps northeast along the Chickamauga Creek to join Crittenden's corps. Crittenden had been holding a position on the creek, exposing the road to Chattanooga. Thomas moved into the Union left, centered on the Lafayette-Roseville road during the evening of September 18, blocking the Confederate Army.

On September 19, the Army of Tennessee fell on Rosecrans's army. Bragg attempted to turn the Union left. Weakly held the day before, Thomas now anchored it. All day long, Thomas's men stood up against division-sized attacks. The terrain was woods that were so thick that regiments could not see or cooperate with each other.

Second Day's Battle The next day, September 20, Bragg gave General Leonidas Polk tactical command of the Confederate right, and Longstreet command of the left. Polk's assault started late. At 11:30 A.M., Bragg ordered Longstreet to attack. Longstreet charged. The woods had concealed a Union division from the eyes of Rosecrans's staff. Assuming there was a gap in the line, a second division had been ordered into the gap. Longstreet's charge hit the division as it was on the move and vulnerable. The Union soldiers broke and ran. Soon the entire Union right joined the panicked flight. Four divisions routed. Rosecrans's, Crittenden's, and McCook's headquarters were overrun, with the staff and commanders streaming north. Longstreet sensed an opportunity to destroy a Union Army. He sent in his reserves and asked Bragg for more men. Bragg had nothing to give Longstreet.

It should not have mattered. Longstreet was attacking George Thomas, though. Thomas was not panicked by the bad news to his right. Thomas sent what few reserves he had to form a new line to guard his open flank. Dug in, Thomas was determined to hold his position or die in place. Thomas was assisted by General Gordon Granger, commanding the Union reserve. As the rest of the Union Army streamed north in panic, Granger marched his men to the sound of the guns. His four thousand men gave Thomas the fresh troops he needed to stop Longstreet. Longstreet's men threw themselves against Thomas's line again and again that

The Battle of Chickamauga.   *MPl/Getty Images*

day. They were repulsed each time. Dusk ended the battle. Thomas took his command and fell back in good order to Chattanooga, joining the rest of Rosecrans's army.

Aftermath   Bragg did not immediately follow up. He had lost one-third of his army in the battle and was unnerved by the losses. Rosecrans was in no better shape and was soon relieved. Lincoln described Rosecrans as "stunned like a duck hit on the head." Rosecrans waited passively in Chattanooga. Union losses at Chickamauga totaled sixteen thousand dead, wounded, or captured.

Bragg besieged the Army of the Cumberland in Chattanooga, which was surrounded by mountains and rivers. Bragg cut off both river traffic and railroad communication with Chattanooga, to starve the Union Army into surrender.

Chattanooga

The Chattanooga campaign began with a Union Army besieged in a major city and ended with the Confederates beginning a long retreat to Atlanta, Georgia. In two decisive battles fought around Chattanooga, Tennessee— Lookout Mountain on November 24, 1863, and Missionary Ridge November 24–25—three Union armies,

with Ulysses S. Grant in overall command, routed the Confederate Army of Tennessee.

After Chickamauga, fought September 18–20, the Army of the Cumberland retreated to Chattanooga, Tennessee. Nestled in a bend in the Tennessee River, Chattanooga was at the bottom of a bowl formed by Raccoon Mountain to the northwest, Lookout Mountain to the southwest, and Missionary Ridge to the east and south. All roads and railroads to Chattanooga were south of the Tennessee River.

General Braxton Bragg's Army of Tennessee occupied Lookout Mountain and Missionary Ridge. This cut Union supply lines, both overland and on the river. He also sent fifteen thousand men under General James Longstreet to besiege the twelve thousand–man Army of the Ohio in Knoxville, Tennessee. The Army of the Cumberland had 30,000 to 40,000 men left after Chickamauga. Bragg had somewhere between 43,000 and 47,000 men. Bragg lacked the force to storm Chattanooga, but he had more than enough men to starve them out. He entrenched and waited for Union supplies to run out. The North did not wait inactively. Immediately after Chickamauga, the Union Eleventh and Twelfth Corps, commanded by Joseph Hooker, were detached from the Army of the Potomac and sent west. It took only eleven days to move them to central Tennessee.

Ulysses S. Grant was promoted to overall command in the west. He moved his headquarters to Tennessee, joining Hooker. Grant relieved Rosecrans, replacing Rosecrans with Major General George Thomas. From Mississippi, Grant ordered two corps of the Army of the Tennessee, commanded by Major General William Sherman to Tennessee. While waiting for Sherman to arrive, Grant sent Hooker and the Eleventh Corps, disgraced at Chancellorsville and Gettysburg, to capture Raccoon Mountain. In a hard-fought night action October 28–29, the Eleventh Corps took the mountain, opening a new supply line to Chattanooga. Grant then stockpiled supplies in Chattanooga until Sherman arrived in mid-November. By then Bragg's forces had been weakened by detaching Longstreet's two divisions. It was further demoralized by bickering among the Confederate commanders. Bragg suspended three generals due to sluggish performance and lost Nathan Bedford Forrest, who transferred out.

On November 23, Grant attacked. Thomas's Army of the Cumberland advanced onto Orchard Knob, clearing out the Confederate outpost line in front of Missionary Ridge. The next day, November 24, Grant had the wings of his army attack. To the right, Hooker, with the Eleventh and Twelfth Corps and two divisions of the Army of the Cumberland, attacked Lookout Mountain. Described later as "The Battle Above the Clouds," the battle was fought in a heavy mist that restricted visibility. Confederate forces on the mountain were outnumbered six to one, and Hooker rapidly took the crest. On the left, Sherman's army crossed the Tennessee and took Battery Heights on the Confederate far right. The Union Army was positioned to assault Missionary Ridge from both flanks on the next day.

The next day Sherman launched his assault on the Confederate right as scheduled in the morning. Hooker's attack on the Confederate left started off late and slowly. By mid-afternoon Sherman was slowly grinding up the northern slope of Missionary Ridge. Hooker was stalled. Grant decided that he needed a diversion to pin Confederate reserves. The Confederates had three lines of entrenchments in the center of Missionary Ridge. Grant felt a frontal assault would be suicide. He ordered Thomas to feign an attack on the Confederate entrenchments, and then withdraw.

Four Union divisions, 23,000 men, charged across an open field. Defying orders, they then pressed the attack, charging up the mountainside. Beaten at Chickamauga, they had something to prove. As the Union soldiers charged up the mountain, the Army of Tennessee panicked. They broke and ran. Thomas's soldiers charged after them screaming "Chickamauga! Chickamauga!" They soon cleared all three sets of entrench-

ments and held the ridge. The Confederate center routed, not regrouping until they retreated thirty miles. One Confederate division, Patrick Cleburne's, retreated in slowly, preventing the exhausted Northerners from immediately pursuing Bragg's army.

Longstreet was forced to lift his siege at Knoxville. He and his men rejoined the Army of the Northern Virginia. Bragg was relieved, replaced by General Joseph Johnston. Grant was promoted to General of the Armies, and then moved east. Sherman assumed supreme command in the west, controlling the Army of the Cumberland, the Army of the Tennessee, and the Army of the Ohio.

The Battle of Mobile Bay

By 1864, Mobile, Alabama, was the last remaining major Gulf Coast port west of the Mississippi still held by the Confederacy. The Battle of Mobile Bay led to the Union capture of the forts guarding the approaches to the port. It closed the last Gulf Coast destination for blockade runners wishing to offer succor to the eastern half of the Confederacy. It was Admiral Daniel Farragut's crowning victory.

Mobile was second only to Wilmington, North Carolina, as a destination for blockade runners. Blockade was ineffective at Mobile. There were too many ways to reach Mobile Bay. Once inside, Confederate batteries protected them. If these forts could be taken, Mobile could be blocked, but they could only be taken from inside Mobile Bay.

Admiral Daniel Farragut, commanding U.S. Navy forces in the Gulf, had his eyes on Mobile since capturing New Orleans two years earlier. He had only received permission to attack it in 1864. Farragut first moved against Mobile Bay in January 1864.

The approaches to Mobile were guarded by three forts. Fort Powell, an earthwork fortification with six guns, covered shallow Grant's Pass. Only light draft vessels could go that way. The main channel into Mobile Bay was protected by two prewar fortifications. Fort Morgan, on Mobile Point, was a powerful masonry star-shaped fort. It held forty guns in its casemates, and seven more on a water battery. On the opposite shore, on Dauphin Island, stood the smaller Fort Gaines. It held sixteen guns. Farragut planned to run the main channel between the forts, land soldiers in the rear, and take them from the Mobile Bay side. In January, the soldiers he needed were committed to General Nathaniel Banks's Red River expedition.

The Confederates had built a powerful ironclad, the *Tennessee* in Selma, Alabama. By March 1864, it guarded Mobile Bay. It had only seven guns and was slow, barely seaworthy, and difficult to maneuver. Despite that, it could destroy any fleet made up only of wooden vessels— all Farragut then had. The *Tennessee* was backed up by three paddle-wheel gunboats mounting four to six guns.

This fleet was commanded by Admiral Franklin Buchanan, the first captain of the CSS *Virginia*.

Farragut needed his own ironclads to force the channel. Promised four, it took until July before they began to arrive. A single-turret monitor, *Manhattan*, arrived on July 20, followed soon after by the twin-turret sister ships, the *Chickasaw* and the *Winnebago*. On August 2, the troops Farragut needed arrived, 2,000 men under Major General Gordon Granger. Farragut decided to launch his attack without waiting for the fourth monitor, the *Tecumseh*, a sister to the *Manhattan*.

On August 3, Granger's troops landed on Dauphin Island and surrounded Fort Gaines. Farragut spent the next three days sending parties into the main channel, removing the mines—or torpedoes, as they were then called—from the path he intended to take. While not all were removed, a clear path was found. Farragut learned that many of the torpedoes were inactive—incapable of exploding.

The *Tecumseh* arrived the night before Farragut intended to attack. Farragut added her to the attack plan, putting the *Tecumseh* ahead of the other monitors. Fog delayed Farragut's run until 5:30 A.M., after sunrise on August 5. The monitors approached in one column, and the rest of Farragut's fleet in a second column. These wooden ships were lashed together in pairs, with the larger ship in each pair on the starboard side, exposed to Fort Morgan. If one ship in a pair lost its engines in the channel, the other ship would pull it free.

For months, Farragut and his captains had been practicing his attack on a mapboard with wooden ships. The captain leading the line, Commander Tunis Craven of the *Tecumseh*, had missed those sessions, arriving the night before the battle. As he came to a buoy in the channel marking the edge of the minefield, he turned the wrong way—*into* it. Within a minute he struck a torpedo. A few seconds later, the *Tecumseh* sank, with most of its crew still aboard.

The Union line churned in confusion. The *Brooklyn*, leading the line of wooden ships, stopped with Fort Morgan at point blank range and blocked the channel to starboard. Farragut ordered his flagship, the *Hartford*, to steer left of the *Brooklyn*. Warned that this would take them into the minefield, Farragut shouted, "Damn the torpedoes! Full speed ahead!"

The *Hartford* cut a path through the field. The rest of the Union line followed exactly astern, letting Farragut sweep the course. The *Hartford* was more fortunate than the *Tecumseh* had been. The torpedoes that touched her hull were duds. The Union line was soon past the torpedoes and the guns of Fort Morgan. The *Tennessee* and its consorts then challenged the entire Union fleet. The three Confederate gunboats were quickly sunk, captured, or driven to Mobile. The *Tennessee* continued its fight alone. The *Tennessee* attempted

THE ATLANTA CAMPAIGN

Once Chattanooga was secure, the Union's next target was Atlanta. In May 1864, Sherman took the armies he commanded south. He had 110,000 men. His opponent, Johnston, had 65,000 men in two corps. Johnston, badly outnumbered, played for time. If he could keep the North from taking Atlanta before the 1864 election, a Peace Democrat might win and so would the Confederacy.

On May 4, Sherman started south. For seventy-four days Johnston fought a brilliant delaying campaign. Sherman fought an equally brilliant war of maneuver. Johnston fortified Dalton, Georgia. Sherman flanked Dalton. Johnston fell back to Resaca. Sherman marched around him. Johnston attempted a counterattack at Cassville, but General John B. Hood fell back when a column of lost Union soldiers appeared in Hood's flank.

Johnston found the defensive position he needed at Kennesaw Mountain. Sherman swung west to Dallas, Georgia. Johnston followed. The armies skirmished at New Hope Church on May 27. Sherman swung back to Kennesaw Mountain, made a frontal assault on June 27, and was bloodily repulsed. Sherman then flanked Johnston's army. It fell back to the Chattahoochee River, and then into strong fortifications north of Atlanta. It was mid-July. Sherman was at the end of a long supply line. With Johnston's army intact, Sherman could not storm Atlanta. The Confederates could hang on until winter.

On July 17, Jefferson Davis relieved Johnston, replacing him with Hood. Hood would attack instead of standing on the defensive. It was what Sherman wanted. Hood launched three sharp counterattacks against Sherman on July 20, 21, and 28. Each time he left his fortifications Hood got drubbed. Sherman began maneuvering around the weakened Hood. By late August, Sherman threatened the last rail line into Atlanta. Rather than allowing his army to be trapped, Hood evacuated Atlanta. Sherman occupied Atlanta on September 2, 1864, in time to lift Lincoln to victory in the November elections.

to ram the *Hartford*, but the wooden ship was faster and more maneuverable than the ironclad.

Buchanan broke off the attack, retiring under the guns of Fort Morgan. It was 8:30 A.M. Farragut anchored the *Hartford*, intending to send hands to breakfast before resuming his attempt to destroy the *Tennessee*. Buchanan returned at 8:50 A.M. He fought a long single-handed battle against three Union monitors and fourteen wooden warships. He had seven guns. Farragut's ships had 157, most of which were heavier than the guns of the *Tennessee*. The *Tennessee* fought the unequal contest for more than an hour. By the time it surrendered, it had lost steam, lost steering, and over half of its guns could no longer fire. It had been repeatedly rammed by Union warships. Buchanan was wounded. The captain, J.D. Johnson, surrendered the ship.

The Battle of Mobile Bay is shown in this line engraving. *AP Images*

The Union fleet turned its attention to the three forts. Fort Powell evacuated on the night of August 5 after being bombarded that day. Its magazines were exploded, to make it useless to the North. Fort Gaines, besieged by land and cut off by sea, surrendered on August 8. Fort Morgan took longer. Its commander initially refused to yield. He surrendered on August 23, after a two-week siege in which Granger's men pushed trenches up to the edge of the fort. With the forts held, there was no need to take Mobile itself. Mobile was closed to shipping. The islands and Mobile Point could easily be held with the small forces Granger had. Occupying Mobile would take a larger force.

The capture of Atlanta on September 2, 1864, and the Battle of Mobile Bay restored the flagging political fortunes of Lincoln and the Republican Party. The war looked winnable to Northern voters. The two victories powered a Republican sweep in 1864's November election.

Sherman's March

After Sherman took Atlanta, he had difficulty defending his supply lines. Rather than retreat to Chattanooga, Tennessee, he split his army in half. He sent half to Chattanooga. With the rest, abandoning his supply lines, he marched across country to Savannah, Georgia. In a five week campaign, he cut a swath across Georgia that

cut the heart out of the Confederate will to fight on. Then, having taken Savannah, Sherman took his army north to join Grant. It was the campaign that ended the war.

None of this was apparent in early November 1864. Sherman took Atlanta in September 1864, but he did not destroy General John B. Hood's Army of Tennessee. Sherman's narrow supply line ran over one hundred miles to Chattanooga. It was vulnerable to guerrillas as well as to Hood's army. Prudence dictated abandoning Atlanta. Sherman felt that withdrawing back to Chattanooga would send a message of weakness. Sherman wanted to abandon his supply lines and march through the Confederacy to the Atlantic coast with an army. On October 9, Sherman telegraphed his proposal to Grant:

> I propose that we break up the railroad from Chattanooga forward, and that we strike out with our wagons for Milledgeville, Millen, and Savannah. Until we can repopulate Georgia, it is useless for us to occupy it; but the utter destruction of its roads, houses, and people, will cripple their military resources. By attempting to hold the roads, we will lose a thousand men each month, and will gain no result. I can make this march, and make Georgia howl!

Sherman spent the month it took to get permission to make the attempt preparing. He had sent his sick and wounded north and divided his forces in half. He left sixty thousand men with Major General George Thomas, who was charged with shielding Tennessee and Kentucky from Hood. Sherman lightened the load of the army he was taking. Baggage was reduced to a bare minimum. Wagons carried mainly ammunition. Soldiers were issued rations for three days. The rest would come from the Confederates. It was harvest season in Georgia. On November 15, Sherman left Atlanta and headed toward Savannah. Before leaving, his Army burned every building of military value. The fires spread, and many private buildings and houses burned.

As Sherman moved south, Hood invaded Tennessee. The only forces opposing Sherman were 3,500 Confederate cavalry commanded by Joe Wheeler and several thousand members of the Georgia militia. Sherman broke his army into four infantry corps that marched independently along parallel courses. Sherman's army cut a lane of destruction across Georgia that was between twenty-five to sixty miles across. Along the way, farms were stripped of food. Railroads tracks were torn up—sometimes for tens of miles when the advance paralleled the railroad. Public buildings, warehouses, and any industrial buildings that could aid the Confederate military were torched. Livestock was "conscripted" into the Union Army. Slaves were freed. Young, able-bodied blacks were encouraged to join the march and serve as pioneers. In addition to the destruction wrought by Sherman's army, deserters from both the Confederate and Union armies, and runaway slaves, trailed behind Sherman. The deserters looted anything the army missed, and many of the slaves took their opportunity for revenge, burning whatever was still standing.

Sherman advanced five to fifteen miles each day. The Confederate Army could not stop Sherman. Their first-line troops were tied down on the frontiers of the Confederacy, fighting Union forces pressing on the Confederacy. What few local troops could be called upon were either teenagers or grandfathers. The one time the Georgia militia faced Sherman's army on the battlefield, on November 22 at Griswoldville, they experienced a bloody repulse. Sherman reached Savannah in mid-December. By then his army had exhausted the food they brought with them and were subsisting on anything they could capture, mainly rice. Sherman stormed Fort McAllister, which guarded Savannah, on December 13. He captured it, opening communications with the sea. Sherman resupplied his army in anticipation of storming Savannah. Instead, on December 20, the Confederates evacuated Savannah. Sherman sent a telegraph to Lincoln stating, "I beg to present you as a Christmas-gift the city of Savannah, with one hundred and fifty heavy guns and plenty of ammunition, also about twenty five thousand bales of cotton."

After resting a month in Savannah, Sherman left a garrison to hold the port. On February 1, 1865, Sherman took sixty thousand men north, heading to join Grant in Virginia. He left a path across South Carolina so destroyed that it made Georgia look untouched. His men blamed South Carolina for starting the war, and were determined to make the state pay for it. Sherman cut through South Carolina, avoiding the remnants of the Confederate Army, now commanded by Joseph Johnston. Bypassing Charleston for Columbia, he forced Charleston to surrender to blockading Union forces by destroying the railroads that supplied the city.

Sherman reached Virginia after the war ended, an end hastened by his march. By demonstrating the inability of the Confederacy to stop an army in its rear, he demoralized the Confederacy. Destruction of the Southern transportation and industrial infrastructure weakened the Confederate ability to react militarily.

The Siege of Petersburg

The siege of Petersburg, Virginia, lasted ten months, from June 1864 until the beginning of April 1865. Grant intended to pin down the Confederate Army at Petersburg. Petersburg was intended to deplete Confederate reserves throughout the South. The siege gave other Union armies, most notably that of Sherman in Tennessee and Georgia, freedom of movement. Grant got little glory from Petersburg, but Petersburg did what Grant intended.

With the spring of 1864, the Union launched a new grand strategy to destroy the Confederacy. Northern armies in Virginia, Tennessee, and Mississippi would launch simultaneous offensives. Grant stayed in the east, supervising a three-army drive to Richmond. Grant took the Army of the Potomac, commanded by George Meade, from Washington, D.C., to Richmond, Virginia. General Franz Siegel was to take the Army of the Shenandoah down the Shenandoah Valley, joining Grant at Richmond. General Benjamin Butler was to land the Army of the James at Bermuda Hundred, Virginia, south of Richmond and drive north.

Grant Moves South On May 1, 1864, Grant crossed the Rappahannock River with the Army of the Potomac and began his drive south. At The Wilderness, near Hooker's Chancellorsville battlefield, Robert E. Lee gave Grant a more severe trouncing than Lee had given Hooker the year before. Grant continued south. The two armies fought at Spotsylvania, Virginia, and Grant's men got the worst of it again. Grant continued south. So it went, through Virginia. The two armies would fight. Grant took heavier casualties than Lee. At the battle's end, Grant's army then sideslipped to its right, attempting to flank Lee. Lee marched past Grant to block the road to Richmond. The two armies fought again. The process was repeated. Grant could not crush Lee's army with a frontal assault. Grant had to flank it. The other

THE FORTY-EIGHTH PENNSYLVANIA, COLONEL PLEASANTS, MINING THE CONFEDERATE WORKS IN FRONT OF PETERSBURG, JULY 15-20, 1864.

The famous mine which was exploded before Petersburg July 30, 1864, was the work of a Pennsylvania regiment that included a large number of miners. Beginning in a little ravine where bushes hid them from the enemy, they dug a tunnel 500 feet long to a point under a salient of the Confederate works, and then a cross-gallery 70 feet long. In this gallery they placed 8000 pounds of powder with slow matches. The work occupied nearly a month. When the mine was exploded it sent the fort with its guns and men and great masses of earth 200 feet into the air, producing a crater 30 feet deep and 200 feet long. Every arrangement for taking advantage of the explosion seems to have been wholly mismanaged. The worst possible troops were chosen to lead the assault, and instead of going round the crater they simply precipitated themselves into it. where they became the easy target for musketry and hand grenades, as soon as the Confederates had recovered from their panic.

A soldier who had worked as a mining engineer in Pennsylvania suggested a way to end the trench stalemate at Petersburg: by tunneling under enemy lines with explosives.   © *Corbis*

two prongs of the attack went awry. Siegel got beaten in the Shenandoah, and Butler got unable to move at Bermuda Hundred.

Counterbalancing that, Union cavalry finally outclassed the Confederate horsemen. In one raid, Union cavalry under Sheridan destroyed most of Lee's stockpiled food, munitions, and half of the rolling stock in northern Virginia. They also killed Confederate cavalry genius J. E. B. Stuart. Grant was losing troops faster than Lee, but Grant could replace his losses. Lee could not.

Petersburg In mid-June, Grant reached Petersburg, a major railroad junction. Taking Petersburg would cut all but one of the railroads to Richmond. The remaining line could not carry enough. Richmond, the Confederate capital, would have to be evacuated.

On June 9, the Army of the James attacked Petersburg. Butler sent only 4,500 men against the Confederate defenders, one brigade with 2,500 men. Butler's attack should have succeeded, but he had not pressed hard. Then on June 15, the Army of the Potomac arrived. At first, Petersburg had only 5,500 defenders against two Union corps—one each from Butler's and Meade's armies. The Second Corps (Army of the Potomac) failed to arrive on the first day of the battle, June 15. Only the Eighteenth Corps (Army of the James) attacked. It captured part of the Confederate trenches but stopped after reports that Confederate reinforcements had arrived. Between June 15 and June 18, the entire Army of the Potomac reached Petersburg, ahead of Lee's men. Petersburg's defenders, led by General P. G. T. Beauregard, bluffed Grant with wooden cannon and by constantly moving the few troops he had. By the time Grant realized how weak the Confederate line was, Lee had arrived.

Both sides settled in for trench warfare. Grant began methodically extending his lines south of Petersburg, cutting off the railroads into the city one by one. He also kept testing the Confederate trenches, probing for a weak spot. The probing assaults included the Battle of the Crater, on July 30, 1864. A regiment made up of Pennsylvania miners dug a tunnel under the Confederate lines. Filled with explosives, the mine was set off in the pre-dawn hours of July 30, and the breach was stormed.

Originally, black troops were to have stormed the breach. They had trained for weeks. At the last minute, an untrained white regiment was substituted—for political reasons. The effect heavy black casualties would have in the North provoked the change. The white troops got stuck in the crater. The Confederates quickly recovered from their shock. Both the white troops and the blacks sent to rescue them were slaughtered.

Grant continued to probe the Confederate lines throughout the rest of 1864 and into 1865. He succeeded in bleeding Lee's army and forcing it to spread it thinly. Lee had to hold fifty-three miles of trenches with 44,000 men.

Five Forks

The Battle of Five Forks, fought April 1, 1865, ended the siege of Petersburg. It was a flanking attack, wide to the right of General Robert E. Lee's Petersburg, Virginia, entrenchments. In the battle, two corps commanded by Major General Philip Sheridan smashed Confederate forces anchoring Lee's right flank. The battle forced the Army of Northern Virginia out of its Petersburg fortifications and onto the road to Appomattox Court House and surrender.

Background By March 1865, General Ulysses S. Grant's armies outnumbered their Confederate enemies three to one. Grant could call on 128,000 men but Lee could get only 44,000. Despite that disparity, Grant could not force Lee out of Petersburg. The siege had begun the previous June, and the two armies had remained locked in those lines for ten months. At first this stalemate served Grant's strategic purpose of tying down Confederate reserves. By January 1865, the rest of the Confederacy was in disarray. Grant wanted to end the siege and capture or destroy Lee's army. Yet push as he might at the Petersburg lines, Grant could not crack them.

The last railroads linking Petersburg and Richmond, Virginia, with the rest of the Confederacy ran north of a crossroads town named Five Forks. Take Five Forks, and Richmond's supply line was cut. General Grant sent Sheridan with the Cavalry Corps and Gouverneur Warren's Fifth Corps to Five Forks. Sheridan's orders were not focused on capturing the railroad, however. Grant had a more ambitious goal. Sheridan was ordered to take Five Forks and move onto—not into—Lee's rear. Sher-

THE UNITED STATES, COLORED TROOPS

Petersburg saw the first large-scale use of black troops in the Union Army. When the war began, blacks were not allowed to join the army. It was a white man's war. Attitudes towards allowing blacks to fight shifted in 1862, due to the growing casualty lists. By the summer of 1862, increasing numbers of white Northern soldiers were willing to divide "the right to be killed" with blacks.

After the Emancipation Proclamation was issued, commanders began raising "colored" or "African-descent" regiments to fill out their lines. At first this was done unofficially, but after January 1, 1863, the U.S. Army began recruiting blacks in large numbers. They were organized into regiments of the U.S. Colored Troops. Men and non-commissioned officers were black. The officers were white, but all were combat veterans. All had to pass an examination demonstrating competence. The combination of enthusiastic men and experienced officers yielded outstanding units.

At first, few officers trusted the colored regiments. Their battlefield performance, however, converted many Army commanders, including George Thomas, Benjamin Butler, and Ulysses S. Grant into believers. By the time of the Petersburg Campaign, brigades and divisions of black soldiers were being used. By war's end, 178,975 blacks had enlisted in the U.S. Army. An additional 25,000 enlisted in the Navy (which had accepted blacks from the beginning). They provided the manpower needed to keep the Union Army going in the last year of the war.

idan was not just to block Lee's retreat. He was expected to attack Petersburg from the rear.

The Battle Sheridan began his march on March 31 across rain-sodden fields and roads. He crossed the Boydon Plank Road at Dinwiddie Courthouse, plodding northwest through muddy country. On the previous day, Grant cancelled the attack due to the rain, but Sheridan rode to Grant's headquarters and convinced Grant to allow Sheridan to continue. The delay caused by the weather and Grant's hesitancy allowed Lee time to react. He sent General George Pickett with twelve thousand men to guard Five Forks. To Sheridan, this was a plus—it gave him a bigger target to destroy.

Sheridan's cavalry hit Pickett's men at noon on March 31. Soon Warren's leading infantry on their right also made contact with Pickett. Two hard-fought actions ensued with the Confederates winning each. They inflicted four hundred casualties on the cavalry and fourteen hundred on the infantry, including eight hundred captured. The setbacks did not discourage Sheridan, who knew how limited Lee's manpower pool was. He planned to resume the attack the next day. When the sun rose on

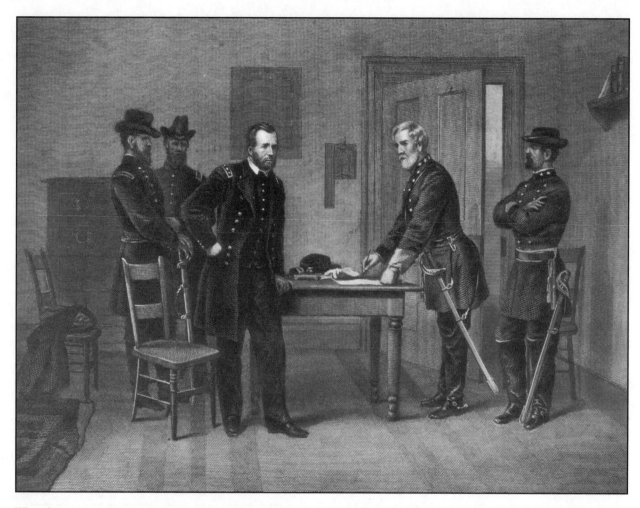

When the two generals met at Appomattox Court House in Virginia in 1865, Grant allowed Lee, in a gesture of respect, to keep his horse and saber. *Hulton Archive/Getty Images*

April 1, Warren's corps was not in position. The late arrival delayed the attack until afternoon. Warren reported that he would not be ready to attack until 4:00 P.M.

Pickett had fallen back to a position on the north side of White Oak Road, with orders to hold Five Forks at all cost. By 1:00 P.M., the Northerners had not arrived, and most were convinced they would not come that day. Pickett, with his staff, disappeared for a leisurely lunch without telling subordinate commanders where he was going. The Union line lurched into battle at 4:00 P.M. The Fifth Corps attack stalled in a confused tangle when one of its columns opened a gap in the Union line. At the point it was about to collapse in confused retreat, Sheridan rode to the front line and rallied the infantry. As the Union line steadied and resumed its advance, a late-arriving Fifth Corps infantry division arrived on the Confederate left, flanking the Confederate line. In the next half hour, the Fifth Corps cracked the Confederate line and took 3,400 prisoners, more than a quarter of Pickett's force. Union cavalry soon increased that num-

ber to 5,000 as the Confederate right gave way. Pickett returned from his meal only after half his command had been destroyed. Sheridan completed the rout by sending the Fifth Corps storming north to take the Southside Railroad. By now the Corps was commanded by General Charles Griffin. Sheridan was furious at what he perceived to be the dilatory behavior of the Corps under Warren. He summarily relieved Warren.

Lee counterattacked the next day—or tried to. Initially unaware of the magnitude of the disaster at Five Forks, Lee sent 2,000 men to reinforce Pickett and secure the Southside Railroad. It was too little, too late. Lee soon learned that his last rail line was about to be cut. He began to prepare his army to withdraw. As a result of Five Forks, both Petersburg and Richmond fell. With the last supply line cut, neither could be held. Lee's army, harassed by Sheridan's cavalry, fell back along the Appomattox River until it was trapped at Appomattox Court House, where Lee finally surrendered the remnants of the Army of Northern Virginia.

This photographs shows the camp site for the Chinese laborers who worked on the construction of the Pacific Railroad. *AP Images*

The War Ends Finally, on April 1, 1865, a flanking attack at Five Forks cut the last railroad to Petersburg. Lee prepared to retreat. Grant ordered a general assault on the Petersburg lines on April 2. The attack broke through the Confederate right. Petersburg fell that day. Richmond was evacuated the same day. Lee's army retreated up the Appomattox River valley, closely pursued by Grant. Finally it was trapped against the river at Appomattox Court House. On Palm Sunday, April 9, 1865, Lee surrendered his army to Grant. The surrender was one week after the assault that took Petersburg.

✪ The Home Front

The Pacific Railroad Acts

In 1862 and 1864, the U.S. Congress passed two Pacific Railroad Acts. Designed to foster the construction of a transcontinental railroad, the acts offered financial assistance and rewards to railroad companies building a railroad linking Omaha, Nebraska, with the California coast.

By the end of the Mexican-American War in 1848, the United States spanned the North American continent. States were established on the Pacific coast in the 1850s. Between the Pacific coast and the populated eastern half of the United States was a wide expanse of unpopulated prairie then called the Great American Desert. No navigable waterways crossed the mountains west of the plains. Reaching California or Oregon required an overland wagon ride, or months of travel by sea. A railroad spanning the continent would simplify communication and transportation. During the 1850s several plans were drawn up for such a railroad. The question was where to build it.

The Southern states favored a route across Texas, through the New Mexico and Arizona territories, and then to Los Angeles. In 1853, the United States even purchased the portion of what is now Arizona south of the Gila River to facilitate building a railroad along this route. The route went through some of the harshest deserts in the United States. It also failed to link the most heavily populated sections of California—around Sacramento and San Francisco—with the East. Northern interests favored a central route—preferably running from Kansas City, Missouri, to Sacramento. As with much involving sectional divides, nothing was settled in the 1850s.

Lincoln's election and the Civil War changed the situation. Lincoln was the most technologically oriented president of the nineteenth century. He owned a patent and had made most of his reputation and fortune as a lawyer in railroad cases. He knew as much about transportation systems as many engineers. He was also passionately committed to seeing a transcontinental railroad completed. The absence of Southern representatives and senators after the Civil War began had eliminated factional arguments in Congress about where to run the railroad. No one was much interested in the southern route.

The Act of 1862 In October 1861, a California railroad engineer, Theodore Judah (1826–1863), came to Washington with a plan for a transcontinental railroad—at least the California end. He surveyed a course through the rugged Sierra Nevada Mountains that looked achievable. All that was needed was a railroad from the east to link with.

Lincoln used Judah's concept as the basis for the Pacific Railroad Act. The Pacific Railroad Act of 1862 was passed on July 1, 1862. It authorized two railroads to build a line connecting California to the East. Judah's Central Pacific Railroad would start from Sacramento and follow the route charted by Judah. A second railroad would start from Omaha and build westward. The government would charter a new railroad, the Union Pacific, to build and run that railroad. Why Omaha and not Kansas City? Missouri was a battleground during the Civil War, so starting from Kansas City was not possible. The Hannibal and St. Joseph Railroad that ran to Kansas City later got land grants as a consolation prize.

The two railroads were to meet somewhere in the Utah Territory. To help each railroad, the Act provided loans, to be financed with government bonds, consisting of $16,000 for every mile of track laid on flatlands, $32,000 for every mile of track laid in the foothills, and $48,000 for each mile of track laid in mountainous terrain.

The bonds were financed with land grants. For each mile of track laid, a railroad would receive every other square mile for ten miles on each side of the track. Each mile of track laid gave the railroad ten square miles of public land.

The Act of 1864 By 1864, the Central Pacific had laid only eighteen miles of track. The Union Pacific had not

started building. A second Pacific Railroad Act was passed on July 2, 1864. It gave the railroads mineral rights on their land grants, allowed them to issue bonds equal in value to the government bonds, and increased the land grant from ten miles on either side of the track to twenty miles.

It authorized the Union Pacific to build track up to 300 miles west of Salt Lake City, and the Central Pacific to build up to 150 miles east of the California-Nevada border. The end of the railroad was ambiguous. These overlapped considerably. It was hoped the competition would speed construction. Finally, the act required the track to be completed by 1876—the nation's centennial.

Construction began almost immediately after the second act passed. Lincoln gave the railroad one more gift. He set the size of the track at four feet, eight and one-half inches, now "standard grade" for railroads. Construction took off after the Civil War ended. The Union Pacific and Central Pacific met at Promontory Point, in Utah Territory, on May 10, 1869.

Anti-Draft Riots

In 1863, the North was facing a manpower pinch. Most of those who were going to volunteer for service had done so. Congress passed a conscription act. It caused riots.

The Enrollment Act of 1863, passed on March 3, 1863, was not the first conscription act of the Civil War. The Confederacy passed a conscription act in 1862. Congress passed a militia conscription act on July 17, 1862. The militia conscription act of 1862 was an indirect draft. It levied a quota on each state, which could be filled by either volunteers or conscripts. The states were responsible for finding men, not the federal government. If they found enough volunteers—in 1862, most states found enough to fill their quotas—they need not use conscription. Four states—Pennsylvania, Ohio, Indiana, and Wisconsin—resorted to a militia draft to meet their quota. There were riots protesting the draft in all four. Resistance was centered in Irish Catholic areas of Pennsylvania, German Catholic townships in Wisconsin, and the "butternut" areas of Ohio and Indiana.

Butternuts, so-called from the butternut oil they used to dye their homespun clothing, were people who had moved to the counties along the Ohio River from Tennessee, Kentucky, Virginia and North Carolina. Poor, and insular, they resented the "Yankees" in the upstate areas who were from New England. They mistrusted abolitionism, disliked blacks, and opposed the war. Mobs in these areas killed two draft officers and wounded a commissioner. Lincoln instituted martial law and suspended habeas corpus in the rioting regions. Troops were sent in. The riots were put down, and the meeting of militia quotas proceeded. With the Enrollment Act, the reaction was more violent. The federal government was running it, not the states, and it was a

While the battle raged at Gettysburg, anti-draft rioters in New York City burned an orphanage for African Americans, expressing their unwillingness to fight to end slavery.   © *Bettmann/Corbis*

pure conscription law. All male citizens between age twenty-one and forty-five were subject to it. Volunteers did not count against the draft quota.

The law had clauses that inflamed class tensions. A man could buy exemption—called a commutation—from one draft call for $300.00. The bill authorized four draft calls. Someone paying for exemption in one call was still liable to be drafted in future ones. Alternatively, a drafted man could find a substitute. A substitute was someone not subject to the draft who agreed to serve in place of the drafted man. Generally, these were eighteen through twenty-year-olds or non-citizen immigrants. A substitute exempted a man from all future draft calls. The commutation fee—$300.00—equaled the working man's average annual wage in 1863. Substitutes charged at least as much. Many claimed the rich were exempt from fighting the war. "A rich man's war, but a poor man's fight" was a frequently used slogan. Southern conscription acts also included a substitution clause that excluded those in upperclass professions, including those who worked as government bureaucrats, doctors, and clergymen. Southern resistance to conscription was exercised by fleeing before being conscripted or deserting

afterwards rather than rioting. In the North, the Enrollment Act led to rioting.

The biggest riot took place in New York City and started on July 13, 1863. New York had a large concentration of unskilled workers. There was a labor shortage, but price increases had raced ahead of wage increases. Labor strikes left these workers in a sour mood. These laborers could afford neither substitutes nor the commutation fee. Many were Irish Catholics who viewed the war as being for the benefit of blacks who would displace them from their jobs. On July 11, a draft lottery was held in New York City. Most of the troops that normally garrisoned the city were in Pennsylvania, chasing the Confederate Army after Gettysburg. Laborers spent Sunday, July 12, in bars, drinking and nursing their resentments. They pledged to resist the draft.

Widespread rioting began Monday and continued for four days. Mobs attacked those they blamed for their problems: the government, the rich, blacks, and supporters of the war. Blacks were lynched or beaten. An orphanage for black children was looted and burned. Pro-war newspaper offices were attacked. People whose dress indicated they were well-to-do were attacked because they were "rich."

Opportunism and suspicion of industrialization accompanied the rioting. Stores were looted. Street-sweeping machines and self-loading grain elevators were burned, because they deprived unskilled laborers of jobs. Protestant churches were burned by Irish Catholic rioters. The city police lost control. By July 15, army regiments rushed in by the War Department arrived in New York City. Many had fought at Gettysburg two weeks earlier. Unamused by those unwilling to share the risks they faced on the battlefield, the soldiers in these units viewed the rioters as a different form of rebel. They settled the riots with massed rifle fire.

By July 17, an uneasy peace returned to New York City. Over one hundred people had died. The federal government packed the city with twenty thousand troops to enforce quiet and resumed the draft on August 19. The city council allocated money to pay commutation fees for drafted men—eliminating the need for further rioting.

✪ International Context

European Imperialism

The middle of the nineteenth century saw a rise in European imperialism. European technology had surpassed that of the rest of the world in the 1600s. Europe's military superiority over the rest of the world grew so large by 1800 that European nations could dominate the rest of the world—if they ever stopped fighting each other.

The end of the Napoleonic Wars in 1815 started such a period of domination. While wars were fought in Europe throughout rest of the nineteenth century, they were local and short. A nation might fight a neighbor, but other nations rarely joined in. Even when they did, such as during the Crimean War of the 1850s, where England, France, and some Italian states joined Turkey in a war against Russia, these European wars were limited in scope. The result was that European nations turned their efforts outward, attempting to control remote territories that held valuable resources. Some nations expanded overland. Russia moved east into Siberia and across the Bering Strait into Alaska. Most attempted to establish overseas empires. Britain expanded the overseas colonies that it had established previously in Australia, the Americas, and India. France began establishing colonies in Africa—most notably, Northern Africa, part of the former Barbary States—and in the Far East.

The Western Hemisphere was generally excluded from this expansion. Prior to the nineteenth century, much of North and South America had been colonized by Britain, France, Portugal, and Spain. Starting with the American Revolution in 1775, and ending with a set of revolutions against Spain in the 1820s, however, most of the countries in North and South America established

themselves as independent nations. By the 1840s, parts of North and South America that were still possessed by European powers—notably the British, French, and Spanish colonies in the Caribbean, along with Canada—wanted to remain attached to the colonizing nation. Cuba, for example, remained attached to Spain because it feared annexation by the United States. Canada had fought to remain British during the War of 1812.

The independence of nations in the Western Hemisphere was fostered by the Monroe Doctrine. It declared "that the American continents, by the free and independent condition which they have assumed and maintain, are henceforth not to be considered as subjects for future colonization by any European powers." The United States was willing to fight to enforce the Monroe Doctrine. Britain, the world's most powerful nation in the nineteenth century, supported the doctrine because it prevented European rivals from gaining a foothold in the New World.

When the United States became absorbed in the Civil War, it was too busy to worry about the Monroe Doctrine. Some nations took advantage of that in pursuit of their imperial ambitions in the Americas. One such nation was France. It was then ruled by Napoleon III (1808–1873), a nephew of Napoleon Bonaparte. It invaded Mexico in 1862, when the United States was fighting the Civil War. Trying to protect the nation's economy, the Mexican government of Benito Juárez (1806–1872) had suspended payment on foreign debts in 1861. To force payment, British and Spanish forces jointly blockaded the Gulf port of Veracruz in January 1862. France invaded and occupied the Yucatan port city of Campeche in March 1862. They then attempted to conquer Mexico.

Once it became clear that conquest, not payment, was France's goal, Britain and Spain withdrew from the endeavor. France persisted, despite initial defeats. The French attacked Veracruz in January 1863 and occupied Mexico City in June that year. By 1864, France controlled much of Mexico. In 1864, rather than set Mexico up as a French colony, France set up a puppet government. They installed Ferdinand Maximilian Joseph, Archduke of Austria as Emperor Maximilian I of Mexico (1832–1867). The United States objected to French intervention in Mexico but was unable to do much while the Civil War was raging. In 1864, Congress passed a resolution condemning France. Lincoln directed increased activity against Texas in an effort to return it to Union control, but he had limited success. By late 1864, the United States controlled the mouth of the Rio Grande River and not much more.

With the end of the Civil War in 1865, the United States began actively working to remove French influence from Mexico. General Philip Sheridan was sent to the Texas-Mexico border with an army of fifty thousand men. The army began patrolling the border and supplying

The impeachment voting for President Andrew Johnson. *The Library of Congress*

arms to Mexican nationalists opposing Maximilian and the French. Finally, in February 1866, the United States demanded that France leave Mexico. The U.S. Navy blockaded the Mexican coast, and the Army prepared to cross the border in support of Benito Juárez's government. Rather than fight the United States, Napoleon III yielded. He withdrew French troops from Mexico and urged Maximilian to leave. Maximilian chose to stay. Without French troops and support, his government was quickly defeated. The Mexican republic was restored in June 1867.

✪ Aftermath

The Impeachment of Andrew Johnson

The impeachment trial of Andrew Johnson marked the first time Congress attempted to remove a U.S. president from office. Johnson survived. His opponents fell one vote short of the necessary two-thirds majority required to convict and remove a president. The result led to the office of the president gaining strength, although Andrew Johnson was weakened by the trial.

Andrew Johnson After Abraham Lincoln's assassination, Vice President Andrew Johnson became president. Johnson was only the second man to assume the presidency in that manner.

Johnson, a Democrat from Tennessee, remained loyal to the United States during the Civil War. He was the only senator from a seceding state that remained in the United States Senate. He was subsequently appointed military governor of Tennessee, and Lincoln, a Republican, had picked Johnson as part of a wartime national-unity ticket in 1864. However, Johnson supported slavery. He cosponsored the 1861 Crittenden-Johnson resolution. Passed by Congress, it foreswore abolition, stating that the North had no interest in changing the domestic institutions of the seceding states.

By the end of the war, Johnson was still opposed to giving blacks rights equivalent to whites. Johnson favored a mild reconstruction. He wanted to return local control to the southern states quickly. Johnson wanted to restore full American citizenship even to those who had fought the United States if they swore an oath of loyalty. Lincoln also favored a mild reconstruction. Lincoln was the leader of the moderate wing of the

[From the Independent Monitor, Tuscaloosa, Alabama, September 1, 1868.]

A PROSPECTIVE SCENE IN THE CITY OF OAKS, 4TH OF MARCH, 1869.

"Hang, curs, hang! * * * * * *Their* complexion is perfect gallows. Stand fast, good
fate, to *their* hanging! If they be not born to be hanged, our case is miserable."

The above cut represents the fate in store for those great pests of Southern society—
the carpet-bagger and scalawag—if found in Dixie's land after the break of day on the
4th of March next.

A Facsimile put in Evidence before the Congressional Committee.

An Alabama newspaper published this cartoon in 1869, warning "carpetbaggers" (opportunists from the North) and "scalawags" (Southerners who collaborated with them) of the intentions of the Ku Klux Klan. © *Bettmann/Corbis*

Republican Party and had earned credibility and political capital as the president who led reunification. Johnson had no political base and was an outsider.

Conflict with Congress This put Johnson on a collision course with a more radical Congress. Congress was determined both to give blacks equality and use them to guard against future Southern separatism in the former slave states. When Johnson vetoed a civil rights act in 1866, Congress overrode the veto and then reintroduced the bill as the Fourteenth Amendment to the Constitution.

The elections of 1866 produced a Radical Republican landslide. Congress became more militant in its opposition to Johnson. It passed three acts intended to tie the president's hands. The one relevant to Johnson's impeachment was the Tenure of Office Act. It stated that any federal official who required Senate confirmation could not be removed from office without consent of the Senate. The act was ambiguous. It remained silent on whether it applied to those appointed by Lincoln and retained by Johnson. It also defined presidential defiance of the law as a "high misdemeanor." This gave grounds for impeachment and removal of a president who violated it. Johnson vetoed the law. His action was supported by his entire cabinet, including Edwin Stanton, the secretary of war. Stanton even helped Secretary of State William Seward write a veto message. The veto was overridden by Congress.

Stanton's later removal by Johnson in February 1868 triggered impeachment. Stanton and Johnson fought throughout Johnson's presidency. Johnson finally replaced

Stanton with General Alonzo Thomas in February 1868. Congress reacted by passing a bill of impeachment, citing Johnson's violation of the Tenure of Office Act. Eleven articles were included in the bill.

The Impeachment Trial A Senate trial started on March 5, 1868. The Senate then consisted of fifty-four members—forty-two Republicans and twelve Democrats. Thirty-six votes were required to convict the president of the impeachment charges. Johnson was given sixteen days to prepare a defense. The House impeachment managers argued that Johnson could be removed for violating the Tenure of Office Act.

Johnson's defense was based upon two major arguments. The first was that it was not clear that Stanton was covered by the Tenure of Office Act. Stanton had been confirmed by the Senate while Lincoln was president, and he was retained, without confirmation, by Johnson. Since Stanton had not been appointed by Johnson and subsequently confirmed, there was no need to have the Senate uphold the removal. Even if Stanton was covered by the Act, it was ambiguous. To remove a president for a violation that not even Congress could agree was violation was unfair. The second argument was that the Act violated the Constitution. Under the Constitution, a president had a duty to "take care that the laws be faithfully executed." Retaining a cabinet official in whom a president had lost faith conflicted with that responsibility.

Two extra-legal issues were involved in the impeachment. The first was whether impeachment could be used as a means of removing a president in whom confidence had been lost. Was impeachment the equivalent of a vote of no confidence? Was it predicated on presidential misbehavior? The second was the issue of who would replace the president. Johnson had been Lincoln's vice president, assuming the presidency when Lincoln was assassinated. He served almost all of Lincoln's second term and did so with no vice president. According to existing law, Johnson would be replaced by the president pro tempore of the Senate, Benjamin Wade. Wade was a Radical Republican and extreme abolitionist. Neither issue had the force of law. They were not raised at the trial. Both were considered by senators in voting to convict or not to convict.

On May 16, 1868, the Senate voted on one of the articles of impeachment. It was defeated by one vote (thirty-six votes for impeachment were needed). The vote was thirty-five to nineteen. All twelve Democrats voted against conviction. Seven Republicans joined them. The trial was then adjourned for ten days. On May 26, the trial reconvened. Two more articles of impeachment were defeated by an identical vote. A Senator then moved that the trial be ended. The motion carried thirty-five to nineteen vote. The Senate then voted to end the trial.

CARPETBAGGERS

The Carpetbaggers were Northerners who moved South during Reconstruction. The term was meant as an insult. It referred to a cheap piece of luggage used in the mid-nineteenth century, a soft-sided bag made of carpet fabric. The implication was that a carpetbagger was someone who could fit all of his possessions into one piece of luggage—the cheapest available.

Many carpetbaggers went south to invest in or develop new industries there. Others viewed reforming the South as a moral crusade. Some went to exploit the economic opportunities offered by the Northern occupation of the former Confederacy. As the Lost Cause myth—a romantic, nostalgic idea that tried to reconcile an idealized Southern past with the post-war reality of defeat—grew in the 1890s and 1900s, carpetbaggers were increasingly identified with the minority who cheated Southern whites during Reconstruction.

Most carpetbaggers were Republican. The majority made common cause with freedmen (former slaves) and scalawags (Southerners who joined the Republican Party and supported the Northern agenda). Carpetbaggers' influence vanished after Reconstruction ended.

What factors led to acquittal? The complexity of the law was one. Several senators agreed that no president should be removed for violating such a vague law. Others were reluctant to remove a president for political reasons. Overturning an election for non-judicial reasons was viewed as politically destabilizing. One or two may not have wanted Benjamin Wade as president. By the failure to get one more vote for conviction, Andrew Johnson remained president.

Reconstruction

Following the Civil War, the Union was left with the problem of governing the seceding states. There was general agreement that these states could not resume their previous status. The seceding states had to be reconstructed. Reconstruction became the process by which the states of the former Confederacy were readmitted to full statehood. It gave its name to the postwar era, from 1865 through about 1875.

Lincoln, leading the moderate Republicans, had originally planned a quick readmission to the Union of the rebelling states. He favored avoiding vengeance and quickly ending the bitterness—North and South—caused by the war. Lincoln's assassination prevented achieving this goal. It removed the leader of the moderate Republicans and created a reservoir of anger in the North.

Lincoln's successor, Andrew Johnson, attempted to follow the course set by Lincoln. His efforts were undercut both by his lack of standing in the Republican Party

(Johnson was a Democrat and had run with Lincoln on a "unity" ticket), and by the Southern states themselves. As the Reconstruction state governments—run by former Confederates—took over, they instituted "black codes." These laws limited the rights of freed slaves. In several states, blacks were slaves in every respect but name.

The black codes prompted a reaction in the North. In 1866, a Radical Republican flood swept the elections. It gave Congress the votes required to override Johnson's vetoes of civil rights legislation. Even before the election, Congress had passed a civil rights bill over Johnson's veto. It outlawed many of the provisions in the black codes. After the election, Congress took control of Reconstruction. It dissolved many of the southern state governments organized under Johnson and returned the South to military control.

Two new constitutional amendments were introduced. The Thirteenth Amendment had already been ratified in 1865 and had outlawed slavery. The Fourteenth Amendment guaranteed American citizenship to all people born in the United States or naturalized. It was ratified in 1868. The Fifteenth Amendment stated that the right to vote could not be denied because of race, color, or previous condition of servitude. It was ratified in 1870. These gave blacks unconditional rights of citizenship.

The Radical Republicans also reorganized the former Confederate states into five military districts run by the Army. Only Tennessee, in which a large minority had been Unionist during the Civil War, and a state that had been largely occupied by the Union Army during the war, escaped military rule. It was readmitted as a state in 1866.

The states in military districts were placed under martial law until they were readmitted to full statehood. The Army supervised local governments and elections. It also oversaw the process by which states were readmitted. It set the voter rolls and excluded from those rolls those who had sworn an oath to uphold the United States who subsequently rebelled against the United States. This effectively disenfranchised most prewar political office holders as well as former United States officers who resigned their commissions and served the Confederate Army. The Army also ensured that freedmen were allowed to vote.

At the time, this was a radical policy. Many whites did not then believe blacks to be fully human. Allowing blacks the vote—and the right to serve in state legislatures—created anger and even violent resistance by the white population of the former Confederacy. The Army protected both blacks and public office holders in military districts from this violence. The Army succeeded, but often at the price of further alienation of Southern whites.

Gradually, the rebelling states were restored to full statehood. This generally meant a state had to ratify the Thirteenth, Fourteenth, and Fifteenth Amendments to the U.S. Constitution, modify the state's constitution to recognize the rights granted in the U.S. Constitution, and hold free elections that were open to blacks. Between 1868 and 1870, all ten of the states under martial law were restored to full statehood. For blacks, it proved a hollow triumph. They enjoyed a brief decade of political relevance. Southern whites abandoned open resistance to the federal government and to black franchise for about as long as it took to remove martial law. Once civilian government was restored, it generally took only a few years for the Democratic Party—with its opposition to the black franchise—to reestablish its primacy. Between 1871 and 1877, the Democratic Party gained a majority in each of these ten states.

Reconstruction ended in 1877 when Democrats agreed to accept the disputed 1876 election of President Rutherford B. Hayes (1822–1893) on the condition that federal troops would be withdrawn from the South. Shortly afterward, barriers to black franchise would rise and laws that increasingly discriminated against blacks were passed. The Republican Party, with roots in emancipation and seen as the party that fostered the northern invasion, became marginalized in the South. It would not be until the 1960s that political balance appeared in these states again.

BIBLIOGRAPHY

Books

Ambrose, Stephen E. *Nothing Like It In The World: The Men Who Built the Transcontinental Railroad 1863–1869.* New York: Simon & Schuster, 2000.

Arnold, James R. *Grant Winds the War: Decision at Vicksburg.* New York: John Wiley & Sons, 1997.

Ballard, Michael B. *Vicksburg: The Campaign That Opened the Mississippi.* Chapel Hill, N.C.: The University of North Carolina Press, 2004.

Basler Roy P., ed. *Collected Works. The Abraham Lincoln Association, Springfield, Illinois.* New Brunswick, N.J.: Rutgers University Press, 1953–1955.

Brown, Dee. *Hear That Lonesome Whistle Blow: Railroads in the West.* New York: Holt, Rinehart and Winston, 1977.

Brown, William Wells. *The Negro in the American Rebellion: His Heroism and His Fidelity.* Boston: Lee & Shepard, 1867. New York: Johnson Reprint Corp., 1968.

Cadbury, Deborah. *Dreams of Iron and Steel.* New York: HarperCollins, 2003.

Canney, Donald L. *Lincoln's Navy: The Ships, Men and Organization, 1861–1865.* Annapolis, Md.: Naval Institute Press, 1998.

Catton, Bruce. *The Army of the Potomac: Glory Road.* Garden City, N.Y.: Doubleday, 1952.

Collins, Donald E. *The Death and Resurrection of Jefferson Davis.* Lanham, Md.: Rowman & Littlefield, 2005.

Daniel, Larry J. *Shiloh: The Battle That Changed the Civil War.* New York: Simon & Schuster, 1997.

Davis, Burke. *Sherman's March.* New York: Random House, 1980.

Davis, William C. *Battle At Bull Run: A History of the First Major Campaign of the Civil War.* Garden City, N.Y.: Doubleday, 1977.

———. *Duel Between the First Ironclads.* Garden City, N.Y.: Doubleday, 1975.

Dowdey, Clifford. *The Seven Days: The Emergence of Lee.* Boston: Little, Brown and Company, 1964.

Dyer, Frederick H. *A Compendium of the War of the Rebellion, Compiled and Arranged from Official Records of the Federal and Confederate Armies, Reports of the Adjutant Generals of the Several States, the Army Registers and Other Reliable Documents and Sources.* Des Moines, Iowa: Dyer Publishing, 1908.

Early, Jubal A. *Memoir of the Last Year of the War For Independence in the Confederate States of America Containing an Account of the Operations of His Commands in the Years 1864 and 1865.* New Orleans, 1867.

Fair, Charles. *From The Jaws of Victory.* New York: Simon & Schuster, 1971.

Farwell, Byron. *Stonewall: A Biography of General Thomas J. Jackson.* New York: W. W. Norton & Company, 1992.

Flood, Charles Bracelen. *Grant and Sherman: The Friendship That Won the Civil War.* New York: Farrar, Straus and Giroux, 2005.

Foote, Shelby. *The Civil War, A Narrative.* New York, Random House, 1958.

Gallager, Gary W. ed. *The Third Day at Gettysburg & Beyond.* Chapel Hill, N.C.: The University of North Carolina Press, 1994.

Grant, Ulysses S. *Personal Memoirs of U. S. Grant.* New York: C. L. Webster & Co., 1885–1886.

Hattaway, Herman, and Archer Jones. *How the North Won.* Urbana, Ill.: University of Illinois Press, 1981.

Johnson, Robert Underwood, and Clarence Clough Buel, eds. *Battles and Leaders of the Civil War, in four volumes.* New York: Thomas Yoseloff, 1956.

Johnson, Rossiter. *Campfires and Battlefields: The Pictorial History of the Civil War.* New York: The Civil War Press, 1967.

Kauffman, Michael W. *American Brutus: John Wilkes Booth and the Lincoln Conspiracies.* New York: Random House, 2004.

Lankford, Nelson D. *Cry Havoc! The Crooked Road to Civil War, 1861.* New York: Viking, 2007.

Lanning, Michael Lee. *The Civil War 100: The Stories Behind the Most Influential Battles, People and Events in the War Between the States.* Naperville, Ill.: Sourcebooks, 2006.

Leech, Margaret. *Reveille in Washington, 1860–1865.* New York: Harper & Brothers, 1941.

Leonard, Elizabeth D. *Lincoln's Avengers: Justice, Revenge, and Reunion after the Civil War.* New York: W. W. Norton & Company, 2004.

Long, E. B., and Barbara Long. *The Civil War Day by Day: An Almanac 1861–1865.* New York: Da Capo Press, 1971.

Lukes, Bonnie. *The Dred Scott Decision.* San Diego: Lucent Books, 1997.

Mahan, Alfred Thayer. *Admiral Farragut.* New York: D. Appleton and Company, 1892.

McHenry, Robert, ed. *Webster's American Military Biographies.* Springfield, Mass.: G. & C. Merriam, 1978.

McPherson, James M. *Battle Cry of Freedom: The Civil War Era.* Oxford: Oxford University Press, 1988.

———. *Crossroads of Freedom: Antietam.* Oxford: Oxford University Press, 2002.

Mitchell, Joseph B. *Decisive Battles of the Civil War.* New York: G. P. Putnam's Sons, 1955.

Navy Department Office of the Chief of Naval Operations Naval History Division. *Dictionary of American Naval Fighting Ships, vol. III.* Washington, D.C.: U.S. Government Printing Office, 1968.

Rehnquist, William H. *Grand Inquests: The Historic Impeachments of Justice Samuel Chase and President Andrew Johnson.* New York: William Morrow and Company, 1992.

Reynolds, David S. *John Brown, Abolitionist: The Man Who Killed Slavery, Sparked the Civil War, and Seeded Civil Rights.* New York: Alfred A. Knopf, 2005.

Rhea, Gorden C. *The Battle of the Wilderness: May 5–6, 1864.* Baton Rouge: Louisiana State University Press, 1994.

Rich, Joseph W. *The Battle of Shiloh.* Iowa City: The State Historical Society of Iowa, 1911.

Sandburg, Carl. *Abraham Lincoln.* New York: Charles Scribner's Sons, 1926.

Schneller, Robert J. *Farragut: America's First Admiral.* Dulles, Va.: Potomac Books, 2003.

Sears, Stephen W. *Chancellorsville.* New York: Houghton Mifflin, 1996.

———. *Gettysburg.* New York: Houghton Mifflin, 2003.

Sherman, General William T. *Memoirs of General William T. Sherman.* New York: D. Appleton and Company, 1889.

Swanberg, W. A. *First Blood: The Story of Fort Sumter.* New York: Charles Scribner's sons, 1957.

Sword, Wiley. *Shiloh: Bloody April.* New York: William Morrow, 1974.

Trudeau, Noah Andre. *Bloody Roads South: The Wilderness to Cold Harbor, May–June 1864.* Boston: Little, Brown and Company, 1989.

U. S. Congress, Joint Committee on the Conduct of the War. *Report of the Joint Committee on the War.*

1863–1866: The Battle Of Bull Run. Millwood, N.Y.: Kraus Reprint Co., 1977.

U.S. War Dept. *The War of the Rebellion: A Compilation of the Official Records of the Union and Confederate Armies.* Washington, D.C.: GPO, 1880–1901.

Introduction to the Conflicts with Western Tribes (1864–1890)

Native Americans traversed the vast American continent for thousands of years before Spanish explorers and missionaries arrived in the early 1500s. Three hundred years later, European Americans began what some historians call a "conquest" of those Indian lands. The westward expansion that took place between 1800 and 1900 was devastating to the Indians. The growing American capitalist economy, the Industrial Revolution, and the dramatic influx of European and Chinese immigrants effectively destroyed the Native American culture and way of life. During westward expansion, clashes over land rights caused the majority of battles that made up the Indian Wars. For fifty years, the U.S. military fought Native Americans, signed and broke treaties with them, and eventually subjugated them completed. By 1890, the last "free" Indians were rounded up and forced to live on reservations.

With the American Industrial revolution came dramatic urbanization in the eastern states, an influx of European and Chinese immigrants to both coasts, and rapid exploitation of the entire country's natural resources. Farmers and immigrants looking for a way to escape the surge in technology and wage labor in the east settled the uncharted western frontier with the help of the Homestead Act of 1862. Following the homesteaders were prospectors hungry for gold. Moving further west, these prospectors invaded Indian lands looking for routes to gold-laden hills, which were also located on or near Indian lands that were supposedly protected by treaties. The construction of the first transcontinental railroad brought further feuds between whites and Indians. The first waves of violence against immigrants came soon after. Chinese immigrants made up a majority of the laborers hired by the Central Pacific Railroad, and their willingness to work for paltry wages angered many white Americans anxious about the competition. Racist violence against the Chinese led to riots and the lynching of hundreds of these Asian immigrants in the 1880s.

The American cultural landscape changed almost overnight—immigrants from all over the world flooded the country's shores. The once-rural nation became an urban one, and mechanization created huge corporations and a new class of wage laborers that shifted the economy away from small farms and businesses. The get-rich-quick climate inspired political scandals, fraudulent business practices, and widespread layoffs. Goods were produced abundantly—and cheaply—so Americans became consumers for the first time. Despite the country's growth, city dwellers and farmers began to feel the pinch of unfair corporate business practices. The discrepancy inspired the formation of the most powerful third political party in the nation's history: the People's Party. The populists changed American politics forever.

On the international stage, the colonization of Asia and Africa, especially Africa, led to countless wars and land grabbing. British, Dutch, French, and Portuguese colonists, motivated by greed and a paternalistic belief in the superiority of white Europeans, displaced or ruled indigenous Asian and African populations simply by claiming sovereignty over them. This led to the destruction of native cultural traditions, the weakening of family ties, and the enforcement of alien systems of economy and law. Expansion, it seemed, was not limited to the American West.

Conflicts with Western Tribes (1864–1890)

✪ Causes

Settlement of the West

Westward expansion beyond the American frontier was one of the most significant historical events in North American history. The United States quickly became one of the twentieth century's most powerful nations after settling more than three million square miles of rich, diverse land. Despite the rewards, the expansion resulted in great destruction, suffering, and cultural loss to Native American peoples. Warfare between whites and Native Americans began as early as 1809 and ended in 1890, when the Indians were ultimately defeated and forced to live on reservations. Despite heavy military involvement in the Indian Wars, the final conquest of Native Americans rested squarely on the shoulders of the vast numbers of white settlers who wrested land from the native peoples.

Early Expansion The dream of westward expansion goes back to the American Revolution. Beginning with the Ordinances of 1785 and 1787, which encouraged the survey and sale of lands west of what had been the British colonies, the government promoted expansion while protecting Native Americans—an idea that would later prove quite contradictory. In the beginning, pioneers were motivated to buy and cultivate more and more land to grow crops to not only feed themselves, but to sell for a profit. This small but growing capitalist endeavor foreshadowed the direction westward expansion would take in later years.

Beyond the Mississippi The same things that drew pioneers west to the Mississippi—economic opportunity, the chance to buy and work their own land, and an escape from an earlier way of life—compelled them to continue heading ever westward. But the far West held vast resources of not just rich soil and immense grazing lands, but gold, silver, iron, copper, coal, and timber, too. The Louisiana Purchase heralded the first venture west of the Mississippi. President Thomas Jefferson's

(1743–1826) purchase of France's vast North American holdings in 1803 was characterized by a frontier ideology that included the following beliefs: Indians are to be treated as savages, American settlers are justified in dispossessing lands from previous inhabitants in the name of nation building, the government serves as the primary promoter of expansion and protector of the nation's economy, and conquered lands are to be incorporated into the United States.

Frontier expansion did not occur in a uniformly westward direction from the Mississippi. Advances in transportation, including the building of railroads, made it easier for pioneers to move both north and south so that by 1850, Arkansas, Michigan, Texas, Iowa, and Wisconsin had all been admitted as states. Parts of the Rocky Mountains and the Great Plains were settled less quickly due to the difficult, far-flung terrain. Movement was dictated by a number of factors, including resources that were taken and developed at different times and for different purposes. Frontier settlement, then, occurred in a series of explosive changes rather than a steady advance.

The Mining Frontier In January 1848, mill builders in a California settlement discovered traces of gold in the American River. Their find sparked the gold rush of 1849, an event that drew thousands of people from the eastern United States, Europe, Asia, and Australia. Over the next few years, hundreds of thousands of people flooded the gold fields. Although few found the fortune they sought and returned home, many stayed and established the state of California. Sadly, white settlers did so by wresting land claims from Hispanic inhabitants and killing many Native Americans. Before the end of the California gold rush, more than $1 billion in gold had been mined.

Believing that if gold could be found in California, it could be found in other parts of the West, prospectors began scouring neighboring states for the elusive and precious metal. In 1859, there was a gold rush in

This engraving shows a wagon train carrying settlers headed for a new life on the western frontier as it stops to make camp for the night.   *The Huntington Library. Reproduced by permission*

Colorado, followed by others in Idaho and Montana in the 1860s, and Arizona and Nevada in the 1870s. Even if gold was not to be found, sources of useful mineral deposits were discovered along the way. Silver was found in far-western Nevada, resulting in a silver strike that brought more than $300 million. Other silver strikes happened in Colorado, Idaho, Montana, and Arizona, which made the West one of the world's largest reservoirs of precious metals.

Railroad Expansion   On July 1, 1862, President Abraham Lincoln (1809–1965) signed the Pacific Railway Act into law. The law provided government support for the building of the first transcontinental railroad, an enormously complex and expensive undertaking deemed a necessity at the time. The explosive growth along the Pacific Coast demanded a means of transportation that would connect it with eastern states. Furthermore, the government saw the connecting of the Atlantic and Pacific coasts by railway as a natural and fitting product of the settlement of the West. The Central Pacific Company and the Union Pacific Railroad were chosen to construct the first transcontinental railroad, an endeavor

funded largely by the United States government. Congress loaned the two construction companies hundreds of millions of dollars to build it and also gave them millions of acres of western land they could then sell to settlers as a way of paying back their loans. The sale of the land also served to populate the West and established a market for freight services and railroad passengers. The Union Pacific Railroad was built westward from Omaha, Nebraska, while the Central Pacific was built eastward from Sacramento, California. The two met at Promontory Point, Utah, on May 10, 1869, to much fanfare. Over the next twenty years, other transcontinental railroads were built, connecting larger lines and reaching into remote areas. Of the many developments made manifest during westward expansion, the growth of the railroads ranks among the most significant.

Conflicts with Native Americans   Western settlement was, essentially, a conquest of lands once inhabited by Native Americans. Although efforts were made by white settlers to resolve conflicts with the Indians through treaties, these were regularly and promptly ignored by white settlers with the support of the United States government.

Hostilities between the two parties formed the basis of a series of battles that had their origins in the 1600s but escalated during westward expansion. These Indian Wars included the Sand Creek Massacre, the Sioux Wars, the Black Hills War, the Battle of Little Bighorn, and the Wounded Knee Massacre, among roughly thirty-five others. The final battle, the Wounded Knee Massacre, which occurred on December 29, 1890, was essentially the final Indian conquest. It resulted in the forced relocation of all Native Americans to reservations and marked the "closing" of the American frontier.

Transcontinental Railroad

The transcontinental railroad linked the Atlantic and Pacific coasts of the United States, making North America the first continent to boast such a rail line. It had been a national dream to connect the states of the vast country since the 1850s, so when the last tracks were laid on May 10, 1869, the war-weary nation had something to celebrate. Now the country had an efficient and reliable method of transporting goods, people, and raw materials great distances, something short-run rail lines built in the 1840s could not do.

Planning the Railroad   The scheme to build a transcontinental railroad was visionary in many respects. The distance it would have to cover was vast, the engineering obstacles it would have to overcome were huge, and the funds necessary to build it were phenomenally large. It was widely agreed that government funds would be required to complete the project. But first, the geographic location of the route had to be sorted out. Early planners felt the way to determine the best route would be to study the natural topography, climate, and terrain of a chosen few possibilities. In 1853, Congress authorized a survey of these possible routes to the Pacific Ocean to test the idea. The U.S. Army Topographical Corps was chosen to set out on expeditions across the country and returned with a multivolume report of its findings. The Corps discovered four particularly workable routes, with two standouts. One would link either Chicago or St. Louis with San Francisco; the other would run between New Orleans and Los Angeles. The railroad, it was decided, would travel, roughly, the forty-second parallel, from Omaha, Nebraska, to Sacramento, California.

On July 1, 1862, the Pacific Railway Act was signed into law by President Abraham Lincoln. The act provided government support for the building of the first transcontinental railroad. Congress decided to entrust the building of the railroad to two companies. The first, the Central Pacific Company, had previously constructed a railway crossing the Sierra Nevada mountain range east to Nevada in order to tap the Comstock mining trades. The second, the Union Pacific Railroad, was commissioned to build from the hundredth meridian westward to meet the Central Pacific on the California-Nevada border. The completion target for the transcontinental railroad was set for 1876.

Construction Begins   Union Pacific construction began in Omaha in December of 1863, but problems with financing forced delays for nearly two years. Congress agreed to double the land grants and agreed to a second mortgage on the original loan, which gave private lenders more confidence in helping fund the risky—and expensive—venture. The Central Pacific began construction the same year with monies funded by the Pacific Railroad Fund, which was collected through a special California property tax. Its progress was slowed not by financial need but by the difficult terrain presented by the Sierra Nevada. The railroad hired thousands of Chinese and other immigrants for the most dangerous labor, which they patiently and expertly performed from 1863 to 1867, the year they crested the Sierra Nevada. They were rewarded with easier downgrades after that and before too long, the endpoint was in their sights.

Successful Completion   The progress of building the railroad after 1867 picked up because of the end of the Civil War. Groups of men, especially Irish laborers, headed west after the war to seek work on construction crews. Grenville M. Dodge (1831–1916), an Army officer adept at command, took responsibility for organizing construction. His abilities occasionally included arming war veterans to fight Indians intent on interfering with railroad construction, though he focused his attention on coordinating an efficient line of surveyors, roadbed builders, spikers, and bolters. Before long, the line made its way into Wyoming. In the spring of 1869, Union Pacific and Central Pacific crews came within sight of one another. Congress decided that Promontory Point, Utah, would be the site of the junction of the two lines. To great fanfare and celebration, the connection of the rails took place on May 10, 1869. The completion of the transcontinental railroad was a truly nation-building event and the country, despite hardships and drawbacks, had been made better for it.

How the Transcontinental Railroad Changed America
To help fund the railroad, the government offered federal aid in the form of grants of public lands to railroad promoters. This benefited private investors who took on extensive construction costs with unprecedented profits from the sale of railroad land to settlers. The sale of the land raised capital for the railroad, served to populate the west, and established a lucrative market for freight services and railroad passengers. Many of the country's great fortunes were made by the men who helped build and control the transcontinental railroad. On the other hand, conflicts between Chinese and European railroad workers led to the pervasive and long-lasting anti-Chinese movement in California that began in the 1860s. The *Iron Horse*

Workers drove the last spike of the world's first transcontinental railroad in Promontory, Utah, on May 10, 1869. *Getty Images*

affected the Native American peoples, too, by displacing tribes along the transcontinental route. With the subsequent boom towns, construction, and the influx of settlers came the destruction of wild animals the native peoples depended on for their survival. This sparked friction between the Indians, U.S. troops, and settlers, which eventually exploded into full-scale warfare in the 1870s.

✪ Major Figures

Geronimo

Geronimo (1830–1909) was an Apache warrior and medicine man. Portrayals of him on film and in writing are numerous and wide-ranging, but Geronimo's fascinating life story is best told in his own words. First related to his second cousin, Asa Daklugie, Geronimo's life story was later told to S. M. Barrett, then superintendent of education at Lawton, Oklahoma. Barrett published *Geronimo, His Own Story* in 1906.

Early Life Geronimo was born just before 1830, the year President Andrew Jackson (1767–1845) introduced the Indian Removal Act. Although many historians claim the birth year as 1827, Geronimo claimed that he was born in June of 1829 in No-doyohn Canyon, Arizona.

His tribe, the Bedonkohe band of Apaches, inhabited the mountainous country that extended east and west of the state. The fourth in a family of four boys and four girls, Geronimo was called Goyathlay, or "One Who Yawns," for the first part of his life. Around 1846, Goyathlay joined the council of warriors and began fighting for his people. He soon exchanged a wealth of ponies for a wife, an Apache woman named Alope who bore Geronimo three children. He would go on to marry another three wives and father five more children.

Geronimo and the Mexican Raids In the summer of 1858, while Geronimo was away on a peaceful trading trip to Old Mexico, Mexican troops attacked the Bedonkohe campsite. The soldiers killed the warrior guards and most of the women and children, escaping with stolen ponies, supplies, and arms. Geronimo's mother, wife, and three children were among those massacred. Mangas Coloradas, a great Apache leader, instructed Geronimo to quietly return to Arizona. The warrior did so, while planning a way to avenge his people and his family.

In the summer of 1859, Geronimo approached Chiricahua Apache chief, Cochise, about joining forces. The chief agreed, later gaining additional support from

Nedni Apache chief, Whoa. The three tribes were on their way to Mexico when a battle broke out between the Apaches and a regiment of Mexican soldiers. Despite emerging victorious, Geronimo's taste for revenge was not appeased by the battle. Seeking to punish the Mexicans further, he persuaded two fellow Apaches to invade Mexico with him. As a result, Geronimo's friends were killed and Geronimo was blamed for their deaths. Undaunted, the warrior convinced twenty-five of his people to join him in another battle. This time Geronimo suffered a head injury that did not heal for months. Even though his people emerged victors from the battle, the loss of life was great enough to keep the Apaches from fighting for at least another year. After a string of unsuccessful invasions, Geronimo and his people finally enjoyed a string of successes in 1862 and 1863. During the summer of 1863, the Apaches conducted their most effective Mexican invasion, raiding enough food and provisions to last the Indians a year.

Geronimo conducted these yearly raids to great success year after year, until 1868, when the Apaches were attacked by Mexican troops. The Apaches retaliated by killing the cowboys responsible for watching the stock. Geronimo and his men then rounded up all the Mexican and cowboy stock and drove them back to the Apache camp. After 1868, Geronimo rarely ventured into Mexican territory, and the Mexican disturbances came to an end. In 1873, a Mexican attack occurred in the Sierra Madre Mountains, but it only lasted a few minutes and resulted in predominantly Mexican casualties.

Battling the White Man Geronimo and his warriors were forced by General George Crook (1828–1890) to surrender to government authorities in 1882. They were ordered to remain at the San Carlos Reservation, but Geronimo managed to escape. When, in 1883, most of his followers had returned to the reservation, Geronimo was persuaded to do the same. He explained the return of the Apache to San Carlos as being nothing more than an effort to persuade others to accompany him to Mexico. He wanted the white officers to know they had not come back simply because they had been ordered to.

When a rumor spread that white soldiers were planning to arrest Apache leaders, the Indians became tense. In a council meeting, Geronimo declared that it would be better to die on the warpath than be killed in prison, so he and 250 Apache warriors escaped the reservation. They met white opposition on the Apache Pass and once along the way to Old Mexico. Finally, the Apaches were left to peacefully roam the Sierra de Sahuaripa Mountains. For a year, Geronimo and his people kept horses and raised cattle rightfully obtained from Mexican farmers. When Geronimo returned to San Carlos, General Crook confiscated his livestock. The frustrated chief immediately set about making plans to travel to Fort Apache.

Geronimo, photographed here with rifle in hand, led Apache resistance to reservation confinement. *The Library of Congress*

Crook ordered his men to arrest the warrior if he tried to escape. If Geronimo resisted, Crook's men were told to kill him. Despite the general's threats, Geronimo escaped San Carlos with roughly four hundred Bedonkohe, Chokonen, and Nedni Apaches in tow. When government Indian scouts discovered the natives camping in the mountains west of Casa Grande, a battle erupted. During the fighting, a boy was killed, and most of the women and children were captured. When the Apaches were attacked again in the foothills of the Sierra Madre Mountains, they were forced to face the inevitable. Geronimo said that it was "senseless to fight when you cannot hope to win."

Geronimo and his followers initially joined General Crook on his way back to the United States and San Carlos, but fearing another attack, decided to remain in Mexico. After Geronimo and forty of his people escaped his grasp again, General Crook tendered his resignation. He was replaced by General Nelson A. Miles (1839–1925).

Although General Miles had promised Geronimo a new life on the reservation with his family in return for the warrior's promise to "quit the warpath," Geronimo and his followers were sent to Fort Pickens, Pensacola, Florida, instead. Many Apaches died of tuberculosis and other diseases, and Geronimo was held as a prisoner of war for the rest of his life. The Apache chief tried to adapt to reservation life by learning the white man's economic system. His livelihood later involved raising watermelon and selling his photograph and signature. Under the watchful eye of government officers, Geronimo traveled to fairs and exhibits in places like Omaha and St. Louis, earning twenty-five cents for every signed photograph he sold to the thousands of spectators who gathered to see him.

Geronimo joined the Dutch Reformed Church in 1903 and attended regular services until he was expelled for gambling. He died of pneumonia in 1909 and is remembered for his courage and for standing up for what belonged to him and his people.

Sitting Bull

Sitting Bull (around 1831–1890) was a tribal leader, warrior, holy man, and tenacious opponent of white settlement. Sitting Bull's legacy has been an inspiration to generations of Sioux.

The year of Sitting Bull's birth is widely disputed, though recent research holds that he was born in 1831. Unlike his birth year, his birthplace, the Grand River in present-day South Dakota, is not a subject of argument. He was called Jumping Badger until he was fourteen. That year, he proved himself a courageous and steady warrior during a battle with the Crow Indians. After the battle, his father named him Sitting Bull, taking the name Jumping Bull for himself. Sitting Bull and his people comprised the Hunkpapa band of Lakota Sioux and followed the old ways of the tribe, which included following buffalo herds, fighting enemy tribes, and performing spiritual rites handed down by their ancestors. The Hunkpapas were able to live according to these traditions until the 1850s, when the whites began to threaten the tribe's very existence.

New Enemies Before the 1850s, for as long as Sitting Bull could remember, the Hunkpapas traded with whites at posts along the Missouri River. This peaceful coexistence was shattered by several events, including the Minnesota Sioux uprising of 1862 and the discovery of gold in western Montana. The influx of white settlers into Sioux territory finally forced the Lakotas into an all-out war with the United States in the early 1860s.

Beginning with his first battle at the age of fourteen, Sitting Bull proved himself to be an especially talented warrior. By 1856, he had earned the distinction of being one of two honored sash-wearers of the Hunkpapa's Strong Heart warrior society. He soon rose through the ranks, becoming leader of the Strong Hearts and then cofounder of the elite Midnight Strong Hearts. As tribal leader, Sitting Bull was able to keep Hunkpapa tribal grounds free of competition from other tribes.

By 1862, Sitting Bull had earned a reputation for being both a respected tribal war chief and holy man. His leadership abilities were proven in 1863, when several bands of Sioux joined the Hunkpapas in a battle

with Generals Henry Hastings Sibley (1811–1891) and Alfred Sully (1821–1879) in Dakota. This initial skirmish set off a series of battles over the next few years, including clashes with General Patrick E. Connor (1820–1891) in the Powder River country in 1865. That year, Sitting Bull initiated a focused and deadly campaign against the forts along the Upper Missouri River. Two years later, the Lakota elected Sitting Bull leader of several Sioux bands. This type of political organization went against Lakota tradition, but illustrated the respect that many Sioux felt for Sitting Bull's leadership. With Oglala Chief Crazy Horse (1841–1877) as second in command, the Sioux continued their direct assaults on the Upper Missouri River forts, especially Forts Rice and Buford, until 1870.

Fighting Relocation The white plan to relocate all Lakota tribes onto reservation lands inspired the Treaty of 1868. Some tribes resisted the treaty and remained on the buffalo ranges of the Powder and Yellowstone valleys, while others acquiesced and settled the Great Sioux Reservation in western Dakota. Sitting Bull, now leader of all "nontreaty" Lakotas, opposed all U.S. government programs. He would have nothing to do with their treaties or rations or anything that stood in the way of living his life according to Sioux tradition. His steadfast renunciation of all things white helped him and Crazy Horse lead a united coalition of Lakota and Northern Cheyenne tribes for the next eight years.

On March 17, 1876, General George Crook and his troops attacked a Lakota encampment along the Powder River. Survivors joined Crazy Horse, who led them to Sitting Bull's village between the Little Missouri and Powder rivers. Among the many bands assembled at Sitting Bull's village were over ten thousand Lakota, including Hunkpapa, Oglala, Sans Arc, Minniconjou, Cheyenne, and Yanktonais. The massive group gradually made its way to the Rosebud and Little Big Horn rivers, where Sitting Bull anticipated a mighty clash. A series of visions had told him that a great Indian victory lay ahead, which reinforced his and his followers's sense of invincibility and outrage. Just as his visions had shown him, Sitting Bull and his thousands of followers easily overwhelmed General George Custer (1839–1876) and his troops on June 25. The historic defeat of U.S. troops at the Battle of Little Bighorn was a major Indian victory. Unfortunately, it shocked the American government into flooding the Sioux lands with soldiers hungry for revenge. Relentless military pressure forced many Sioux to surrender, while Sitting Bull and others retreated to Canada.

Sitting Bull's Final Years Sitting Bull and his people crossed the border into Canada in May of 1877. They were joined by Crazy Horse's followers after he was stabbed to death in September of that year. Life in Canada was hard for the Indians. Food was scarce, buffalo were few in number, and Sitting Bull's followers, threatened by Canadian officials, began defecting in large numbers. In 1881, Sitting Bull finally surrendered. After being held as a prisoner of war for two years, he joined his followers at Standing Rock Agency, Dakota Territory, where Agent James McLaughlin attempted to transform them into Christians, farmers, and American patriots. Sitting Bull resisted, so the agent, in retaliation, sent the warrior chief to tour with Buffalo Bill's Wild West show. Sitting Bull was a featured attraction in the exhibit for almost two years.

The 1880s saw a tremendous change in Native American life. With the vanishing buffalo went the tribal economy and culture. The U.S. military sought to shatter tribal relationships and strip all "nonprogressive" chiefs, such as Sitting Bull, of their power. Native children were sent to boarding schools and taught white traditions, while Christianity was forced upon native adults who were made to relinquish the ancient spiritual practices they called their own. The final straw came with the Sioux Act of 1889. It broke up the Great Sioux Reservation and allowed homesteaders to take over almost half of it. By 1890, the Sioux were a beaten people.

The Ghost Dance movement revived their hope for a short time, but when Sitting Bull became an apostle, McLaughlin and other military authorities decided he should be removed from the reservation and his people. This initiated a shootout that resulted in the death of the great chief and several of his followers. His body was originally buried without ceremony at Fort Yates, but the Hunkpapas requested it be moved to the Grand River. Some believe that Sitting Bull's nephew, Clarence Gray Eagle, buried the revered warrior's bones at a site near the river, but no one knows for sure. Sitting Bull is remembered as a man of great humanity and spirit, a powerful military and spiritual leader, and a tireless and uncompromising supporter of the Sioux people.

John Bozeman

John Bozeman (around 1835–1867) is credited with discovering a direct, efficient route from Montana to parts east, and for settling present-day Bozeman, Montana.

Not much is known of John M. Bozeman's early life, save for the fact that he was a native of the state of Georgia who abandoned his wife and three small children to try his luck at mining Cripple Creek, Colorado, in 1861. The twenty-six-year-old soon discovered that better gravel lands lay in Montana, so he and eleven companions set out for Virginia City where they arrived in June 1862. Thousands of gold seekers flooded places like Alder Gulch, Bannack, and Virginia City, Montana, despite the circuitous routes many had to take to get there—especially those traveling from the east. This led Bozeman and his partner, John M. Jacobs, to decide to set out to discover a more direct route east from Bannack in the winter of 1862. The two men initially took

the old trail leading into lands east of the Bighorn Mountains, ignoring the treaty that reserved use of the trail to the Sioux Indians. The dangerousness of their actions eluded them until the Sioux attacked Bozeman and Jacobs. The Sioux robbed them of their guns, ammunition, and horses, and left them to return to Montana on foot. Undeterred, Bozeman returned the following spring heading a group of emigrants and freighters. An Indian attack a hundred miles north of Fort Laramie persuaded the group to take a safer route west of the Bighorn Mountains into Virginia City via Bridger Pass.

The Bozeman Trail Bozeman remained persistent, altering his attempts to venture through Indian country by traveling primarily at night. In 1863, he and a party of men made their way through the Bighorn Basin to the Montana settlements. They entered the Gallatin River valley through a pass they named Bozeman Pass. A year later, Bozeman, Jim Bridger, and Allen Hurlbut established the Bozeman Trail. That year, four trains carrying fifteen hundred people traveled from the North Platte River at Richard's Bridge east of present-day Casper, Wyoming, to the Montana settlements via the trail. They encountered only one attack by a large Cheyenne and Sioux war party on the Powder River east of present-day Kaycee, Wyoming, but the Indians became increasingly frustrated at how their treaty lands were being invaded in the coming years. Attacks escalated, causing the American government to police the Bozeman Trail and erect Forts Reno, Phil Kearny, and C. F. Smith to protect civilian travelers. On December 21, 1866, combined forces of Sioux, Cheyenne, and Arapaho Indians massacred Captain William J. Fetterman's (around 1833–1866) entire command of eighty-one men near Fort Kearny. This led to the abandonment of the Bozeman Trail east and south of Fort C. F. Smith.

The Rise and Fall of John M. Bozeman In 1864, the year John Bozeman established the Bozeman Trail, he started an agricultural community in the Gallatin River valley. There, he raised wheat and potatoes to feed the Montana miners. That same year, the pioneer planned the town of Bozeman, Montana, around his farming colony. Elected the recorder of the district and appointed probate judge of Gallatin County in 1865, Bozeman used his influence to encourage the construction of the first flour-mill in the valley. This enterprise proved so successful, its capacity had to be doubled in 1866. After that time, he led no more wagon trains into Montana.

On April 16, 1867, a mere five months after the Fetterman Massacre, Bozeman and a companion departed Virginia City and headed into Indian territory. Two days later, at the crossing of the Yellowstone River, five Indians approached their camp. Bozeman, believing them to be friendly Crow, discovered too late that they were

Blackfeet. He was shot dead, while his wounded companion escaped.

Colonel John M. Chivington

John M. Chivington (1821–1892) is the infamous minister and military leader who, with the help of his regiment of Colorado Volunteers, slaughtered hundreds of Cheyenne Indians at their government-protected Sand Creek encampment in 1864.

Chivington was born into an Ohio farm family in 1821. His father died five years later, leaving the burden of the farm to Chivington's mother and older brothers. Because he was required to help out with the farming, Chivington received little in the way of a formal education. In his early twenties, he was drawn toward Methodism and was ordained in 1844. So began Chivington's long career as a minister. He took whatever assignment the church gave him, so he and his wife and children moved from Ohio to Illinois to Missouri within the span of four years. Being something of a frontier minister, he spent most of his time establishing congregations and supervising the construction of churches. In 1853, he participated in a Methodist missionary expedition to Kansas, preaching to the Wyandot Indians.

The Fighting Parson Chivington vehemently opposed slavery and the idea of secession, a position that brought him much trouble in Missouri in 1856. Pro-slavery congregation members sent him a threatening letter demanding that he stop preaching. That Sunday, Chivington approached the pulpit of his church armed with a Bible and two pistols. He declared, "By the grace of God and these two revolvers, I am going to preach here today." The statement earned him the nickname, the "Fighting Parson." Following the incident, the Methodist Church sent Chivington to Omaha, Nebraska, where he and his family stayed until 1860. He was then sent to Denver, where he was made presiding elder of the Rocky Mountain District of the Methodist Church.

Military Life In addition to serving his Denver congregation as minister, Chivington also volunteered with the Colorado Volunteer Regiment in his spare time. Because of his experience with the regiment, Colorado's territorial governor, William Gilpin (1813–1894), offered Chivington a position as chaplain when the Civil War broke out. Chivington declined, requesting a "fighting" instead of a "praying" position. In 1862, Chivington, who was now a Major in the regiment, played a leading role in defeating Confederate forces at Glorietta Pass in eastern New Mexico. He was widely regarded as a military hero after leading his troops in a surprise attack on the enemy's supply train.

After defeating the Confederacy's Western forces, Chivington returned to Denver and a promising future of great prominence. He was a likely Republican candi-

THE FETTERMAN MASSACRE

Despite the fact that the Bozeman Trail wended its way through traditional Sioux hunting grounds and that Sioux Chief Red Cloud (1822–1909) vowed to shut down the trail to defend the territory, the American government was determined to keep the road open at all costs. Fort Kearny—one of three forts erected to protect the passage—was run by Colonel Henry Carrington (1824–1912), a man inexperienced in dealing with both Indians and soldiers. In November 1866, shortly after Carrington had assumed his post at Fort Kearny, Captain William Fetterman joined the regiment. Unlike Carrington, Fetterman was an experienced fighter having served with the Eighteenth Regiment during the Civil War. He was well respected and believed that Indians, no matter how mighty or numerous, could not match the fighting skills of a regiment of well-trained United States soldiers. Soon, Fetterman was at the head of a rebellion against Carrington. He riled his fellow soldiers with talk of teaching the Indians a lesson and quickly convinced them that he could defeat the entire Sioux Nation with just eighty men.

While Fetterman boasted, Red Cloud was busy assembling a massive army of several thousand fighting men. On December 6, 1866, a sizeable party of warriors attacked an unescorted wood train departing the fort. Carrington attempted to retaliate, but was met by an imposing force that persuaded him to retreat back to the fort. Two died and five were wounded in the decoy strike. The Indians staged another decoy two weeks later, but Carrington did not fall for it. This forced Red Cloud to choose December 21, the last day of woodcutting for the winter, as the day he and his warriors would perform their major strike. At 11 A.M., the Indians attacked the wood train. Fetterman demanded the right to lead the rescue and Carrington allowed it. Fetterman rounded up seventy-nine men and set out to meet the warriors. Despite Fetterman's experience and ferocious hatred for the Indians, two thousand Indians soon surrounded the captain and his men. Within twenty minutes, all eighty men were dead. According to legend, as the Indians closed in for their final assault, Fetterman and his second in command, Captain Fred Brown, stood, placed their pistols at the side of each others' heads, and fired simultaneously. So ended Fetterman's boast about being able to defeat the entire Sioux Nation.

The Fetterman Massacre reestablished Indian claims to the area. Within two years of the battle, the forts along the Bozeman Trail were abandoned.

date for Colorado's first congressional seat and a leading advocate of statehood. While Chivington dreamed of a successful political future, tensions escalated between the burgeoning white population and the Cheyenne Indians. Chivington took advantage of the moment and publicly blasted anyone, including the territorial governor, who called for peace and treaty-making with the Cheyenne. In 1864, he announced, "I say that if any of them are caught in your vicinity, the only thing to do is

THE SAND CREEK MASSACRE

Black Kettle (around 1805–1868), the chief of the Cheyenne, had been attempting to keep peace with the whites of the southeastern Colorado Territory during a series of skirmishes between area gold miners and neighboring Indians. In a conference with the governor, the chief was instructed to take his people to a nearby encampment at Sand Creek where they were guaranteed safe conduct and placed under the protection of the fort. Black Kettle did so and the Cheyenne soon settled into peaceful village life. Then, at dawn on November 29, 1864, roughly 750 troops of the Colorado Volunteer Regiment attacked the Indians. Colonel John Chivington led the attack, ordering his men to kill, scalp, and mutilate every Indian they found. Because most of the young men of the camp were away hunting buffalo, the majority of Cheyenne murdered that day were women and children. In the middle of the massacre, Chief Black Kettle raised two flags of truce: a white flag and an American flag. President Abraham Lincoln had given the American flag to Black Kettle when the two met in Washington, D.C. The president promised the chief that the military would not harm his people as long as the stars and stripes flew above their village. Between two hundred and four hundred Indians were killed that day—estimates vary widely—while only nine militiamen died, mainly as a result of friendly fire. The wanton massacre inspired Sioux and Arapaho Indians to join Cheyenne warriors in new attacks against Plains settlers, which set off a winter war.

Although the Sand Creek Massacre was first heralded as a major victory, the attack soon became the subject of a military investigation and two congressional hearings. It attracted attention even in the midst of the Civil War, with thousands dying every day, and made American Indian policy and military brutality subjects of renewed scrutiny. Today, the tragedy remains a topic of bitter controversy among historians and a charged issue among American Indian activists.

kill them." He told a meeting of deacons a month later, "It simply is not possible for Indians to obey or even understand any treaty. I am fully satisfied, gentlemen, that to kill them is the only way we will ever have peace and quiet in Colorado." Several months later, Major Chivington made good on his genocidal promise when he led a regiment of Colorado Volunteers into the "battle" of Sand Creek, where they exterminated hundreds of peaceful Cheyenne.

After Sand Creek   Chivington was initially praised for the massacre at Sand Creek, but soon rumors of drunken soldiers butchering unarmed women and children began to circulate. Chivington arrested six of his men on charges of cowardice in battle, which seemed to confirm the rumors. The arrested men were in fact militia members who had refused to participate in the carnage and now spoke openly about the atrocities they witnessed. Soon, Congress prepared for a formal investigation into Sand Creek, and the U.S. secretary of war ordered the six men released.

No criminal charges were ever filed against Chivington, though he was forced to resign from the Colorado militia, withdraw from politics, and stay away from the statehood campaign. He moved back to Nebraska in 1865 and worked as a freight hauler. After that, he lived in California before moving back to Ohio, where he became the editor of a small newspaper. In 1883, he attempted to reenter politics but was forced to withdraw his campaign for a state legislature seat when word spread of his connection to Sand Creek. Before dying of cancer in 1892, he worked as a Denver deputy sheriff.

Red Cloud

Red Cloud (1822–1909) was chief of the Oglalas, the largest band of Teton Sioux. He worked tirelessly to promote peaceful relations between his people and the U.S. government, even though it meant losing the support of some of his people.

Facts about Red Cloud's early life are shrouded in mystery. The most colorful birth story holds that he was named after a meteor that slashed a red streak through the sky on September 20, 1822, the night he was born. Others maintain Red Cloud was a family name. His place of birth is also a source of conjecture. Red Cloud named the Platte River as his birthplace, but was accused of saying so only to justify his claim on the region. His father was called Lone Man and his mother was Walks as She Thinks.

A Born Warrior   Red Cloud revealed his talents as a skilled warrior early in life. He was just sixteen years old when he claimed his first scalp, a trophy taken from a defeated Pawnee. He received a near-fatal wound in the first war party he ever led, but went on to become a leading warrior by the time he was forty years old. Eventually, after claiming victory in bouts with the Crows, the Utes, and the Shoshonis, and after killing Bull Bear, chief of a rival band of Oglalas, he became head of the Oglalas.

Red Cloud's War   The Oglala were on friendly terms with whites traveling through their land up until the spring of 1865. That year, the white influx grew to unbearable numbers when gold was discovered in Montana. Gold diggers drove away precious buffalo herds as they crossed through Oglala hunting grounds; that changed the face of white/Oglala relations forever. On July 25 and 26 of 1865, the Oglala fought encroaching white trespassers at Platte Bridge. The next offensive came in mid-August and was fought against James A. Sawyer's Pumpkin Buttes surveying party. These initial skirmishes led the way for a series of battles from 1866 to 1868 that have become known as Red Cloud's War.

Red Cloud, who attempted to negotiate peace in Washington, is pictured here, center, with a Sioux delegation and their interpreter. *National Archives and Records Administration*

The Bozeman Trail, a passageway used by white settlers to reach Montana gold fields, was at issue due to the fact that it crossed supposedly "protected" Sioux hunting grounds. In the spring of 1866, Sioux and Northern Cheyenne were attempting to reach a peace agreement with U.S. government officials over the trail. Negotiations seemed to be going well until Colonel Henry Carrington and his troops arrived. Red Cloud grew suspicious. He believed the military sought to claim the trail for its own, despite what treaty agreements said. Red Cloud denounced the peace commissioners for taking lands and then trying to negotiate for them. He also persuaded fellow warriors to abandon diplomatic meetings with the whites and take up arms in defense of their homeland. Red Cloud then began a campaign of aggression against military troops posted at forts located on the Bozeman Trail. The most famous of these skirmishes happened on December 21, 1866. In a surprise attack, Red Cloud and a mighty army of two thousand Sioux warriors killed Captain William J. Fetterman and every one of his seventy-nine troops. The Fetterman Massacre was the beginning of the end for Bozeman Trail forts.

Prior to a treaty conference to be held at Fort Laramie in November of 1867, Red Cloud announced Fort Phil Kearney and Fort C. F. Smith, both situated along the Bozeman Trail, would have to be removed before he would sign anything. He had made his point after the Fetterman Massacre, so whites took his threat seriously. Because they would not feel comfortable until his name was on that treaty, and because a new road west of Fort Laramie, far from the disputed lands, was to be established in the near future, the forts were abandoned by August of 1868. Red Cloud finally signed the treaty, even though he did not agree with some of the terms. He made this known before signing, believing that his stated objections would become part of the treaty. In April 1870, Red Cloud went to Washington, D.C., to discuss the treaty and reservation plans with President Ulysses S. Grant (1822–1885). The trip was a success, and Red Cloud won many white supporters. The major point of dissension, the location of the Sioux supply distribution center, was negotiated to the approval of both Red Cloud and government officials. Although Red Cloud requested that the agency be located at Fort Randall on the Missouri River, it was finally decided that it would be moved to the Platte River near the present-day Nebraska-Wyoming border.

Red Cloud Negotiates A second trip to Washington in 1874 did not go as well. The government hoped to buy more Sioux land, specifically, Black Hills land, because gold had recently been discovered there. Red Cloud, on the other hand, came to Washington to protest the quality of agency goods being distributed to his people. Negotiations were chaotic because the Sioux were split over the decision to sell the Black Hills land. Red Cloud and Spotted Tail would sell the land, but only for the right price. Crazy Horse and Sitting Bull, though, preferred to go to war rather than lose more land. Red Cloud maintained his preference to make peace with the whites, even after they accused him of secretly supporting the warriors.

Many of Red Cloud's people lost faith in him after the Washington negotiations, but the Sioux leader continued to insist that the government honor the treaties and supply his people with higher-quality allotments. Although it looked to the Sioux like Red Cloud was giving in to white demands, he wrote many speeches decrying their treatment of his people. Alternately, the white government faulted Red Cloud for hindering the progress of the Sioux. By the end of the Indian Wars, the warrior had lost the support of the militant Sioux who forcibly removed him from the Pine Ridge Reservation. After his children secured his return and he was peacefully settled there, the government rewarded him with a two-story house. This did not keep the Sioux leader from biting the hand that fed him. He continued to decry the government for its treatment of Native Americans, speaking out against the whites whenever he could. He died on December 10, 1909, and is buried in the Holy Rosary Mission cemetery in Pine Ridge, South Dakota.

George Custer

George Armstrong Custer (1839–1876) is universally remembered for his role in the Battle of Little Bighorn, also known as Custer's Last Stand. The massacre in which Custer lost his life ranks as one of the greatest Native American victories of the Indian Wars.

Custer was born on December 5, 1839, to Emmanuel and Maria Custer in New Rumley, Harrison County, Ohio. Custer's primary ambition since childhood was to become a soldier. In 1857, after high school and a brief teaching career, Custer was admitted into West Point. Despite poor academic performance and a tendency toward wild behavior, he graduated at the bottom of his class. It was 1861 and the Civil War had just begun.

The Civil War Years From West Point, Custer was ordered to report for duty as a second lieutenant assigned to the Second Cavalry. He was immediately sent to fight in the Battle of Bull Run, one of the more

Besides his involvement in the Battle of Little Bighorn, George Armstrong Custer is remembered for his flamboyance and arrogance. *The Library of Congress*

significant battles of the Civil War. Custer proved a cool and steady leader in battle, which led him to jump four ranks, from captain to brigadier general, before the beginning of the Battle of Gettysburg. On the third day of the clash, twenty-three-year-old General Custer led a crucial charge that sent Jeb Stuart's Confederate Cavalry into retreat for the first time in the war. The battle wound up being one of the turning points of the Civil War, and Custer became known in the press as a "Boy General." By 1863, the swaggering, flashily dressed Custer celebrated another victory over Jeb Stuart, which helped secure his reputation as one of the finest cavalrymen of the Union armies.

In 1864, Custer married a judge's daughter from Monroe, Michigan. Elizabeth Bacon was beautiful and supportive and soon became Custer's greatest champion as well as a successful military hostess. In turn, Custer quit his hard-drinking ways and continued to rise in favor with his superiors. Commander Philip Sheridan (1831–1888) was most impressed with Custer's abilities. He became a lifelong admirer, awarding the young general with command of a division later that year. In early 1865, Custer brought the Shenandoah Valley war to its final, successful conclusion, and at the age of twenty-five emerged from the war an untarnished hero.

The Plains Wars Custer was not nearly as highly regarded after the war. When he was sent to the Southwest in 1866 to serve as captain in the Fifth Cavalry, Custer quickly earned a reputation for treating his animals better than he treated his men. He shot deserters without trial, shaved the heads of dissatisfied soldiers, and unfairly advanced favored friends and family. His conduct got him demoted to colonel, with little prospect of promotion. The "Boy General" was now widely regarded as a renegade. His bad behavior reached its pinnacle when he left his post in the thick of a campaign to meet his wife. For his absence without leave, Custer was court-martialed and found guilty. Despite the seriousness of the charges, which included "conduct to the prejudice of good order and military discipline," Custer received a light sentence. Thanks to friends in high places, the colonel faced a minor one-year suspension from command instead of the career-debilitating punishment his crime rightfully deserved.

Before the year was up, his greatest supporter, Philip Sheridan, called Custer to serve in a campaign in western Kansas. Army commanders Sheridan and William Tecumseh Sherman (1820–1891) were pressured to eliminate the Native American population from the Great Plains, so in the winter of 1868, Custer found himself tracking Indians trails through the snow. When he came upon a Cheyenne encampment along the Washita River, he ordered a surprise attack and got lucky. He and his men annihilated the entire village, capturing a significant number of women and children and destroying the winter food supply. The massacre became known as the Battle of the Washita.

For the next several years, Custer acted as commander of the Seventh Cavalry, leading them to victory in a number of Indian campaigns throughout North Dakota. In the summer of 1874, on orders from the War Department, he led a regiment of twelve hundred men on an exploration through the Black Hills. The massive expedition led to the discovery of Black Hills gold and the Sioux War some time later. In 1876, Custer was scheduled to lead a campaign against the Sioux and Cheyenne, but went to Washington, instead. He was called to testify before a congressional committee investigating Indian Bureau fraud. Custer's remarks shed an unfavorable light on Secretary of War

W. W. Belknap (1829–1890), which incensed President Ulysses S. Grant. The president ordered Custer's removal from command. This action inspired a vehement response from the public as well as from General Alfred Terry (1827–1890), who requested that Custer accompany him in the ongoing Sioux campaign. The outcry forced President Grant to restore Custer to commander of the Seventh Cavalry.

The Battle of Little Bighorn Custer arrived in Fort Lincoln, Dakota Territory, in the summer of 1876. He was to lead the Seventh in a campaign to corral all Indians found outside treaty area limits. Confident in his ability to defeat the Sioux and their allies if they were to fight, he and his regiment set out for the Little Bighorn River. On June 25, Custer's Indian scouts discovered an enormous Indian camp. Just as he had done at the Battle of Washita, Custer ordered a sudden surprise attack, splitting his force into three battalions in an effort to cut off any escape routes. His impetuosity caused him to underestimate the number and force of the well-armed warriors he soon met on the battlefield. Between 2,500 and 4,000 Sioux and Cheyenne overwhelmed the Seventh Cavalry, killing, stripping, scalping, and otherwise mutilating everyone. On June 26, Custer was driven onto the slope of what is now called Custer Hill and killed. His body was found stripped, not mutilated, and pierced by two bullets.

Custer's actions at the Battle of Little Bighorn inspired an instant firestorm of controversy that historians have debated and will continue to debate for many years. After his death, Custer was charged with disobeying orders and risking the lives of his men to allegedly regain President Grant's favor. Defenders reply that Custer was given the order of full discretion and little else. Republicans who long regarded Custer as a warmonger saw his death as a direct response to his own recklessness. Democrats, on the other hand, treated Custer as a martyr. Despite the debate over Custer's part in it, the Battle of Little Bighorn likely hastened the surrender of the Sioux in 1877, the event that marked the end of the Indian Wars.

Crazy Horse

Crazy Horse (1841–1877), the famous Oglala Sioux warrior, is best known for his role in the Battle of Little Bighorn, also known as Custer's Last Stand.

Born in the fall of 1841 in the Black Hills region of South Dakota, Tashunca-uitco, translated "Crazy Horse," was the son of an Oglala holy man, also called Crazy Horse. The child was originally given the name Curly because of his fair skin and light-colored, curly hair. He took his father's name after demonstrating great humility and bravery in a skirmish against the Arapaho in which he killed two enemy warriors. He was not quite sixteen years old at the time.

This pictograph, by Amos Bad Heart Bull, depicts Chief Crazy Horse in spotted war paint. *The Granger Collection, New York. Reproduced by permission*

Becoming a Warrior Crazy Horse became a young warrior during a critical moment in American and Native American history. The Oregon Trail, which opened in the early 1840s and served as a passage for white settlers heading west, crossed through the ancestral homelands of the Teton Sioux. After gold was discovered in California in 1848, whites flooded the Sioux territory, trampling the verdant grazing ranges of the Great Plains and driving away the buffalo in their quest for material wealth. The massive influx led to violent clashes between the Plains Indians and the soldiers sent to protect white settlers. It was during this dangerous time that Crazy Horse proved himself a legendary Oglala warrior. He was granted status as an *akicita*, or "shirt wearer," one who governs Sioux tribal councils and enforces tribal law. It was around this time that he also became known as a great military strategist and leader, showing skill and daring in battle. At thirteen, he stole horses from the Crow Indians. At nineteen, he led his first war party. Because he was quiet, kept to himself, and had few friends, Crazy Horse earned the nickname, Tasunke Witko, or the "strange one." Before riding into battle, Crazy Horse would attach a single hawk feather to his braided hair, paint his face with lightning streaks and hailstones, tie two small stones behind his ear, and brush dirt over himself and his horse. An early vision told him that if he did these things he would never be killed in battle.

Crazy Horse and Red Cloud It is widely known that Crazy Horse fought alongside Oglala Chief Red Cloud in the most successful war against the United States ever fought by an Indian nation, the Fetterman Massacre. Few know that it was Crazy Horse's strategic planning that led to the December 21, 1866, victory. The success of this alliance between Crazy Horse and Red Cloud led to the signing of the Fort Laramie Treaty, whose provisions mandated the abandonment of forts along the Bozeman Trail. More importantly, the treaty promised that the Sioux could reclaim possession of tribal lands, including the present-day western half of South Dakota and much of Montana and Wyoming.

Of course, the treaty did not hold. Custer's Black Hills expedition of 1874 brought war to the Plains and the eventual cessation of independent Indian nations. A year later, Red Cloud made a deal with the government and sold the rights to his people's sacred Black Hills. Red Cloud's apparent willingness to do so caused Crazy Horse to break ranks with him. They would never fight side by side again.

The Battle of Little Bighorn Crazy Horse played an important strategic role in the Battle of Little Bighorn, also known as Custer's Last Stand. The famous standoff began at the beginning of 1876 when federal authorities ordered Lakota chiefs, including Crazy Horse, Gall, and Sitting Bull, to report to their reservations by January 31. When the chiefs refused, General Philip Sheridan ordered General Alfred Terry, General George Crook, and Colonel John Gibbon (around 1827–1896) to form a combined assault and drive Sitting Bull and the other chiefs to the reservation. On June 17, Crazy Horse led five hundred warriors in a surprise attack on General Crook's troops on the Rosebud River, forcing the military to retreat. On June 25, a member of General Terry's force, George Armstrong Custer, discovered Sitting Bull's camp on the Little Bighorn River. Terry ordered Custer to force the enemy down the Little Bighorn to its mouth, where Gibbon's forces were waiting. When Custer charges the Indian encampment, his regiment of 225 troopers, the elite Seventh Cavalry, find themselves outnumbered four-to-one. The 2,500 to 3,000 Sioux and Cheyenne led by Crazy Horse, Sitting Bull, and Gall easily overwhelmed Custer's troops, killing every last man. After the battle, Sitting Bull and his Hunkpapas fled to Canada, leaving Crazy Horse and his small band of warriors to continue fighting through the harsh winter of 1876 and 1877.

Crazy Horse's Demise On May 6, 1877, Crazy Horse finally surrendered to General George Crook after receiving assurances that he and his people would be able to settle in Montana's Powder River country. Ever defiant, Crazy Horse and a band of eight hundred warriors arrived singing songs of war and brandishing weapons. Not surprisingly, he found it difficult to adjust to reservation life. Months later, rumors that Crazy Horse intended to take the younger men and return to battle compelled authorities to arrest him. Crazy Horse initially fled, but was finally convinced that he would be treated fairly if he complied. Upon his arrival at Fort Robinson, the warrior realized he had been betrayed when soldiers surrounded him. In an attempt to break free, Crazy Horse was bayoneted twice by a soldier and killed. His body was given to his mother and father, who buried Crazy Horse in a secret location in his precious Black Hills. The site of his grave remains a mystery.

Crazy Horse continues to live on in American popular culture. From the nineteenth-century dime novels that stereotyped him as a savage to increasingly sympathetic portrayals of him in films from 1926 to 1996, the story of Crazy Horse remains a subject of enduring fascination. The controversy that continues over whether or not the Sioux chief was ever photographed adds another distinct layer of interest to his legacy. The Lakota people maintain that Crazy Horse was never photographed because he would not allow anyone to photograph him. They maintain that his people protected him from people with cameras. Despite vehement claims, others still insist that a photo of Crazy Horse exists.

Bill Cody

Bill Cody (1846–1917), better known as Buffalo Bill Cody, created Buffalo Bill's Wild West, an outdoor frontier extravaganza that toured the United States and Europe from 1883 to the early 1900s. At the turn of the twentieth century, Bill Cody was one of the world's most famous Americans, having come to symbolize the American frontier.

William Frederick Cody was born to Isaac and Mary Cody in Scott County, Iowa, in 1846. After the Codys's eldest son, Samuel, died in 1853, the family headed west, settling in Kansas, where Isaac got a job supplying wood and hay to nearby Fort Leavenworth. After Isaac's death in 1857, young William and his sister Julia were left to care for their surviving siblings and ailing mother. To support the family, Cody worked as a mounted messenger and herder for Russell, Majors, and Waddell, a freighting firm that would go on to found the Pony Express. Cody honed his skills as a plainsman by spending two years trapping beaver and prospecting for gold in Colorado before being hired as a Pony Express rider—a dangerous job requiring skilled horsemanship and a love of adventure. The young man then served as a Union scout during the Civil War in campaigns against the Comanche and Kiowa tribes. In 1863, at the age of seventeen, Cody enlisted with the Seventh Kansas Cavalry, a post that took him as far as Missouri and Tennessee. After the war, Cody married Louisa Frederici and continued to work for the U.S. Army as a dispatch carrier and scout out of Fort Ellsworth, Kansas.

The Legend of Buffalo Bill Cody William F. Cody had already lived a full, exciting life before embarking on the career that earned him his nickname. In 1867, Cody began hunting buffalo to feed Kansas Pacific Railroad construction crews. Cody claimed to have killed 4,280 head of buffalo in seventeen short months on the job. Legend has it that Cody beat fellow hunter William Comstock for the name "Buffalo Bill" in an eight-hour shooting match. The name stuck, even when Cody went back to work for the Army as chief of scouts for the Fifth Cavalry. Between 1868 and 1872, Cody participated in sixteen battles, including a skirmish at Summit Springs, Colorado where he helped defeat the Cheyenne. For his dedicated service, he was awarded the Congressional Medal of Honor in 1872.

Becoming a National Folk Hero Buffalo Bill's real-life reputation for bravery and skill started to become the stuff of romantic fiction in 1869. Dime novelist Ned Buntline created a folk hero out of Cody's alter ego that year, one who ranked with Daniel Boone, Kit Carson, and Davy Crockett in the cultural imagination. Three years later, Buntline talked Cody into playing himself in

The world's enduring fascination with the romance of the Old West can be traced back to William F. Cody's outdoor extravaganza, "Buffalo Bill's Wild West." *The Library of Congress*

Buntline's play, *The Scouts of the Plains*. Even though Cody was no actor, audiences loved his natural showmanship and good humor. He continued acting for another ten seasons before becoming an author. In 1879, he produced the first edition of his autobiography and published the beginning of a series of Buffalo Bill dime novels. A total of seventeen hundred frontier tales were published, with as many as six hundred written by Prentiss Ingraham. These digressions could not compete with his love of hunting and scouting, though. Between theater seasons, Cody escorted elite Easterners and European royalty on hunting expeditions—excursions that helped spread his fame around the world. In 1876, Cody was called back to serve as an Army scout after Custer's defeat at Little Bighorn, the most famous battle of the Indian Wars. During this scouting mission, Cody killed a Cheyenne chief in hand-to-hand combat, an event he later wove into *Buffalo Bill's First Scalp for Custer*, a melodrama written and produced for the fall theater season.

Buffalo Bill's Wild West Beginning in 1843, popular entertainment took the form of frontier extravaganzas that glamorized life in the West. These vaudeville shows helped shape the romantic view of the Old West, but not as powerfully as Buffalo Bill's Wild West. Cody's celebration of the West combined his theatrical genius with his experience as hunter, scout, and horseman. Beginning in 1883, Buffalo Bill's Wild West took the form of spectacular outdoor theater that dramatized highlights of frontier life. Audiences were treated to buffalo hunts with real buffalos, Pony Express rides, Indian attacks featuring real Indians, and a reenactment of Custer's Last Stand, featuring participants of the actual battle. A stampede of buffalo, deer, elk, cattle, and wild horses herded by cowboys and Indians comprised the grand finale of most shows. In 1884, sharpshooter Annie Oakley, billed as "Little Sure Shot," became the star of the Wild West. A year later, it was Chief Sitting Bull, "the slayer of General Custer." The inclusion of authentic Western personalities was one of the hallmarks of Buffalo Bill's Wild West and a primary reason for its enthusiastic success. In 1887, Cody took the extravaganza to London to perform as part of Queen Victoria's Golden Jubilee celebration. Two years later, the Wild West toured the whole of Europe, beginning with a gala opening in Paris. It is widely held that this tour and Ned Buntline's Wild West dime novels are responsible for the enduring European fascination with the Old West. Buffalo Bill's Wild West returned to the United States in 1893 to great fanfare and economic success before beginning its slow decline. The show was managed by various entities and partners for another twenty-five years, finally ending a year after Cody's death on January 10, 1917.

Buffalo Bill and the Indian Wars Cody shared an interesting and somewhat controversial relationship with the Indians featured in Buffalo Bill's Wild West. Critics take issue—to this day—with the fact that they were depicted as dangerous savages, yet in reality, Cody was one of few whites willing to hire Native Americans at the time. This is due in large part to the fact that the Indian Wars were part of frontier life during Buffalo Bill's heyday. By 1890, Cody was living a celebrity's existence as Buffalo Bill, but the Army still considered him a vital resource in its dealings with the Indians. That year, Cody was called to serve during the last major Sioux uprising. He was accompanied by Indians from his troupe who proved effective peacemakers there and at Wounded Knee, where they helped restore order after the massacre. Cody freed a number of Indian prisoners after their defeat and included them in his show. Although it was considered dubious for Buffalo Bill to free Indian prisoners and include them in his show, the effort gave the Indians an opportunity to escape the terrible living conditions of the reservation and provided them with a view of the world beyond the American frontier.

George Crook

George Crook (1828–1890) was a West Point–educated career soldier who spent the majority of his professional life in the northwestern United States fighting in the Indian Wars. He is remembered as an unusually moral and friendly man whose beliefs on the subject of Native Americans were far in advance of other white men's of the times. He supported equal rights for Native Americans in legal matters and believed they deserved every privilege of citizenship.

George Crook was born on September 8, 1828, near Dayton, Ohio. On July 1, 1848, Crook entered West Point and upon graduation four years later was commissioned lieutenant of infantry. He engaged in explorations of the Northwest and protected settlers from occasional Indian raids there until the Civil War. In September 1861, he was named colonel of the Thirty-sixth Ohio Infantry, serving in West Virginia where, in May 1862, he was promoted to major in the regular army.

The Civil War Years Crook steadily rose through the ranks during his tenure as a soldier during the Civil War. As brigadier general of volunteers, he commanded

Despite his role as Indian fighter, General George Crook was a proponent of equal rights for Native Americans. © *Corbis*

a brigade that was attached to the Antietam campaign, an effort that led to the first major Civil War battle to be fought on Northern soil. For his conduct in the battles of South Mountain and Antietam, Crook was promoted to lieutenant colonel. In 1863, he took part in the Chickamauga campaign, leading a cavalry division of the Army. Soon after, he pursued General Wheeler's cavalry corps, for which he earned the title of colonel. In February 1864, he was back in West Virginia. Under the orders of General Grant, Crook interrupted railway communication between East Tennessee and Lynchburg. In so doing, he defeated the Confederates, captured the station at Dublin, and destroyed the railway and New River bridge. He was rewarded with a promotion to brigadier general. Several months later, Crook was placed in command of West Virginia, during which time he participated in three important battles, Winchester, Fisher's Hill, and Cedar Creek, and was again promoted. As major general of the regular army, he commanded one of General Grant's cavalry divisions, taking part in the final battles of the war.

The Indian Wars From West Virginia, Crook traveled to the district of Boise, Idaho, where he was assigned duties as lieutenant colonel of the Twenty-third Infantry. For three years he worked in that capacity to bring an end to the Indian War that had been raging in southern Oregon, Idaho, and northern California. He received the commendation of his superiors and the thanks of the Oregon legislature for his participation in the years-long campaign. It was during this time that Crook first confronted the moral dilemmas posed by Indian warfare. He understood that white aggression and expansion provoked Indian violence, but he also believed peace could only be achieved through force.

In 1871, President Grant sent Crook to end the war with the Apaches and various other violent northern Arizona tribes. He was so successful that he received thanks from the territory's legislature. In 1873, he was promoted to brigadier general in the regular army. Two years later, Crook was placed in command of the Department of the Platte. This assignment involved anticipating and quashing any trouble instigated by the Sioux and Cheyenne, who were becoming hostile over the gold diggers who were pouring into the Black Hills of Dakota. Crook played a prominent role in the great Sioux War of 1876, camping in the field for an entire year of daunting hardships. The most well-known conflict occurred in June of that year. Crook led a three-pronged attack on the Indians, only to be stopped at Rosebud Creek by Oglala Sioux warrior Crazy Horse. As Crook retreated, General George Armstrong Custer closed in on a Sioux encampment on the Little Bighorn River where he and his troops were soundly defeated. The Battle of Little Bighorn was a Sioux victory, but the tribe divided afterward, which left it vulnerable in future military conflicts.

Crook's Final Years Crook had little difficulty dealing with familiar tribes, but the same could not be said for those he had never before encountered. This was made plain when he was sent to Arizona in 1882 to suppress the Chiricahua tribe of Apaches who had taken refuge in the Sierra Madre Mountains of Mexico. Under Chief Geronimo, the Chiricahua had raided settlements on both sides of the boundary. No American or Mexican force had ever penetrated the mountains until Crook led an expedition there in 1883. He found and induced the tribe of some five hundred Chiricahua to return to their reservation. Two years later, Geronimo and a much smaller number of followers fled to the mountains and were pursued until only twenty-four were left. With the aid of his Indian scouts, Crook secured the Apache chief's surrender. General Sheridan, after deciding that Indian scouts were not to be trusted, persuaded President Grover Cleveland to refuse anything but Geronimo's unconditional surrender. When the chief slipped away, a frustrated Crook resigned his command. Sheridan replace him with rival officer Nelson Appleton Miles, who accepted Geronimo's final surrender. In response, all the Chiricahuas, even the devoted scouts, were sent to live on a reservation in faraway Florida. Crook was so incensed by this cruel and outrageous punishment that he spent his remaining years lobbying

unsuccessfully for the scouts's return to their native Arizona.

Crook returned to commanding the Department of the Platte. He stayed there until April 1888, when he was sent to Chicago as major general and assigned command of the Division of the Missouri. He died on March 21, 1890, and was survived by his wife, Mary Dailey Crook.

Despite the fact that Crook spent most of his life on the frontier, he did not participate in profane behavior or use rough language, he never drank alcohol, and he was sympathetic to the plight of the Native Americans. He leaned more toward pardoning than punishing Indians who struggled helplessly to protect their lands from white encroachment and became known during his lifetime for supporting and protecting the rights of Indian scouts. He was fearless both physically and morally and never ran from personal danger or responsibility. He was known for his modest and kind disposition and for making friends with people from every corner of society.

Chief Joseph

Chief Joseph (1840–1905) was a chief of the Nez Perce and is remembered as a gentle, intelligent, and articulate diplomat who spent much of his life petitioning the United States government for the right to return to his home in Wallowa Valley, Oregon. Although he was a skilled warrior, he preferred diplomacy to violence and was revered for his eloquence.

Chief Joseph was born in 1840 in Wallowa Valley, Oregon. He belonged to the Nez Perce, a band of the Shahaptian tribal family. His father, Old Chief Joseph, named him Hin-mah-too-yah-lat-kekht, or "Thunder Rolling in the Mountains," and taught him the traditional tribal lore of his family. He also allowed the Presbyterian minister Henry Spalding to name the baby Ephraim and to teach him the ways of the Christian faith. Before the first wagon train passed through their valley in 1843, the Nez Perce had befriended white explorers and surveyors such as Lewis and Clark and enjoyed friendly contact with white fur trappers and missionaries like Spalding. Soon, the few whites passing through on the Oregon Trail every year became thousands, and the Nez Perce braced themselves for the inevitable.

The Division of the Nez Perce In 1855, white politicians began trying to persuade the Nez Perce to hand over their lands to incoming white settlers. The Christian converts favored surrendering their lands in exchange for a reservation and money. The non-Christian Nez Perce, on the other hand, refused to negotiate. In the 1860s, when gold was discovered along the Clearwater River, white prospectors increased pressure on the native peoples. When a branch of the Nez Perce signed a treaty giving away a significant portion of their land, Old Chief Joseph called it the "Thief Treaty" and tore it up. He and

Chief Joseph. *Public Domain*

his son then renounced the Christian faith and the Nez Perce were forever divided into "treaty" and "non-treaty" factions. Unlike whites, the Native Americans did not abide by a defined institutional structure that allowed one leader to speak for the rest of the group. If members disapproved of a chief's decision, they simply disavowed themselves of that decision and dispersed.

War Begins

Old Chief Joseph died in 1871. The fate of the "non-treaty" Nez Perce now rested on Chief Joseph's shoulders. Despite the fact that he had his people's title to the Wallowa Valley confirmed by an 1873 treaty, the commissioner for Indian Affairs reversed the ruling two years later and allowed the building of a wagon road through it. Using diplomacy and intellectual persuasion, Chief Joseph convinced the U.S. Army commander, General Oliver Otis Howard (1830–1909), that the Native Americans were justified in claiming the valley for themselves. Even so, Howard felt compelled to follow orders and demanded that Joseph's band relocate to a reservation at Lapwai, Idaho, within thirty days. To ensure compliance, Howard took Nez Perce negotiator Toohoolhoolzote hostage.

Instead of fighting, Chief Joseph agreed to lead his people to the reservation and Toohoolhoolzote was released. The trek to Lapwai took the Nez Perce across the raging Snake River, a dangerous passage that cost

them many animals. As the band approached the reservation, Wahlitits, whose father was killed by settlers years prior, took revenge by killing four white settlers known to be Indian-haters. This ignited a war that Joseph had spent years trying to avoid. The Nez Perce easily overtook cavalry officer Captain Perry by killing over a third of his men in an ambush. Unfortunately, this prompted General Howard to call in a larger contingent, which caused the Nez Perce to flee.

For the next several months, Howard's troops tracked Chief Joseph's tribe, which increased in strength and number as they moved southeast. At the Big Hole River in Montana, Colonel John Gibbon, another Indian fighter, intercepted the tribe and killed one of Chief Joseph's wives. The Nez Perce retaliated by killing thirty cavalry members. From there, Chief Joseph led his people south and then east to Yellowstone, Wyoming, before heading north to Canada. At the end of September in 1877, just forty miles short of their destination, the Nez Perce were attacked by Colonel Nelson Miles and his cavalry. Chief Joseph instructed his twelve-year-old daughter to ride away as quickly as she could while he took up a gun and began fighting. The siege occurred during freezing conditions and lasted over a week. Toohoolhoolzote and Chief Joseph's brother, Ollokot, were among the many Indians to die. Colonel Miles promised the chief that his people would be allowed to return to Idaho if they ceased firing. In answer to Miles's deal, Joseph replied, "It is cold and we have no blankets. The little children are freezing to death. I want time to look for my children, and see how many of them I can find. Maybe I shall find them among the dead. Hear me my chiefs. I am tired; my heart is sick and sad. From where the sun now stands, I will fight no more for ever."

Becoming Famous, Respected, and Homeless

Colonel Miles was impressed by the Nez Perce and Chief Joseph. He publicly declared his admiration for the tribe's intelligence, self-reliance, and independence, and was therefore dismayed that the U.S. government would not allow him to honor his promise to escort the tribe back to Idaho. Instead, the Nez Perce were taken first to Bismarck, North Dakota, where Chief Joseph was honored by local townspeople, and then to swampy Fort Leavenworth, Kansas, where many contracted malaria. They finally ended up on a reservation in Oklahoma. Chief Joseph continued his steady stream of letters of complaint to the Bureau of Indian Affairs, to the several Army officers he had befriended along the way—including Howard and Miles—and to the president.

Chief Joseph's eloquent letters and speeches, whose echoes of familiar democratic themes struck a chord with educated Americans, won him a following of sympathizers. Despite the support of those who empathized with his plight and saw the justice in his point of view, Chief Joseph was never allowed to return to Wallowa Valley. In 1879, he met with President Rutherford

Hayes (1822–1893) in Washington, D.C., to plead for repatriation. He was rebuffed. Senior members of the government reassured the chief that he would be allowed to go home, but the bureaucracy of the system proved them wrong. In an article he wrote for the *North American Review*, Joseph wrote that he just wanted to live in the Wallowa Valley, the site of his father's grave, because "a man who would not love his father's grave is worse than a wild animal." The article ends, "We only ask an even chance to live as other men live. We ask to be recognized as men."

In 1885, the Nez Perce were finally granted the right to return to the Pacific Northwest, but reservation life at Colville—not Wallowa—was difficult and humiliating. In 1897, Joseph returned to Washington, D.C., to attend the dedication of General Grant's tomb with Howard and Miles, who continued to champion the chief's cause. He was treated like a social celebrity, even stayed with Buffalo Bill, but still made no progress. Chief Joseph died in 1905 after nearly thirty years on the reservation, his many decades of fruitless petitioning resulting in nothing more than broken promises.

Quanah Parker

Comanche leader Quanah Parker (around 1852–1911) is remembered for successfully straddling the divide between the traditional ways of his people and settled reservation life. His own mixed ancestry—his father was a Comanche war leader, his mother a white Texan—may have helped him adapt to the changing physical and cultural landscape brought on by white settlement.

Quanah, or Fragrant, was born to Peta Nocona, Comanche war leader, and Cynthia Ann Parker, a white woman raised as a Quahadi Comanche, in a Cedar Lake, Texas, encampment. Cynthia came from a prominent Texas family that settled Fort Parker before the territory was granted statehood. On May 19, 1836, a band of Comanches raided the fort, killing several family members and capturing nine-year-old Cynthia and her brother. The natives soon adopted the two white children, but Cynthia's brother died. She was renamed Preloch. She and Peta Nocona were married when Cynthia was in her mid-teens. Three years after Quanah was born, Preloch gave birth to Quanah's sister, Topsannah, or Prairie Flower. Preloch and Topsannah were recaptured by the Texas Rangers in 1861 and returned to the custody of the Parker family. Topsannah died a few years later, followed by Preloch, or Cynthia, in 1870. Having become a full Comanche, Cynthia spent her final years mourning the loss of her Indian family and friends.

Quanah's Early Years Quanah grew up during a particularly difficult moment in Quahadi Comanche history. White settlement had increased to such a degree that Indians of all tribes and nations, along with the buffalo herds they followed, had been almost completely crowded out. After losing his beloved mother and sister,

Quanah Parker, the mixed-race leader of the Quahadi Comanche, bridged the gap between devotion to traditional Indian ways and peaceable relations with whites. *Hulton Archive/Getty Images*

Quanah suffered the death of his father around 1866. The young Comanche with the gray eyes was raised by relatives and taunted by other Quahadi for his mixed ancestry. Despite physical characteristics that set him apart from his people, like his mother he felt fully Comanche and lived his life according to their cultural and spiritual traditions.

Relocation of the Quahadi The Treaty of Medicine Lodge, which outlined the resettlement of Arapaho, Kiowa Apache, Cheyenne, Riowa, and Comanche Indians onto reservations in present-day Oklahoma, was signed in 1867. Of these groups, the Quahadi Comanche resisted resettlement the longest, outlasting many other Comanche bands that accepted the terms of the treaty. The Quahadi punished whites that settled the frontier with seven years of sporadic raids, suffering occasional bouts of violent retaliation for their attacks. But the white settlers did less harm than the buffalo hunters, a growing population of professionals bent on making money at the expense of Plains

Indian culture. As the buffalo dwindled, Native Americans who relied on them faced starvation. In 1875, a united coalition of seven hundred warriors, including Quanah and fellow members of the Quahadi band, attacked buffalo hunters grouped at Adobe Walls, a trading post located in the present-day Texas panhandle. The fighting lasted three days, ending with the retreat of the Indian forces. The Quahadi leader of the Adobe Walls raid, medicine man Eschiti, was also thought to be responsible for the band's eventual agreement to reservation resettlement that same year.

Quanah's Rise to Power Reservation life was incredibly difficult for the Quahadi. Besides having to witness the death of their way of life, they had to face the death of their people as well. A shocking number of Quahadi became sick and died in the first several years of settlement, a fact that may have led to Quanah's eventual rise to power. With fewer competitors, he was able to rather quickly move from "ration chief," a fairly lowly position, to member of the Comanche Council. The council met to discuss decisions made by the reservation's Indian agent, with whom they consistently agreed throughout the late 1870s. The agent mistakenly believed Quanah's mixed race would make him an easy convert to white ways, and so he tried to get on Quanah's good side from the beginning. Quahadi members who were suspicious of Quanah's allegiance saw the agent attempting to groom Quanah for leadership, which caused further conflict. Luckily, Quanah sided with traditional Comanche leaders in the one council dispute they had with the agent. His detractors saw this as one of his last "loyal" acts.

In 1881, the Comanche Council protested the trespassing of Texas cattle barons and their stock on Comanche grasslands. Just as the Indian reservation agent had done, the cattlemen saw Quanah Parker as a man who might be persuaded to see their side of things. To convince him, they agreed to pay him and Eschiti to ride alongside white "cattle police" and make sure Comanche property lines were being respected. This promotion led to Quanah earning not only money but cattle and influence among the cattlemen. Before long, Quanah had enough money and pull to start his own ranch. He built Star House, a mansion decorated to suit decidedly wealthy, non-Indian tastes. Quanah's detractors saw Star House as an affront to other Comanche leaders. Others suggested he needed the space for his seven wives and seven children.

Influencing Two Worlds Despite his influence in the white world, his support of formal education for native people, and his advocacy of developing a money economy in the Indian Territory, Quanah was also a fervent supporter of polygamy and the Peyote Cult, a highly ritualized religious ceremony involving the ingestion of mescal buttons. Quanah was first introduced to the cactus and its medicinal attributes by a female Indian

healer. Soon, the peyote ceremony had swept through a number of Oklahoma tribes that quickly adopted its ritual songs and prayers. Oral historians indicate that Quanah may have been one of the first peyotists to integrate elements of Christian symbolism into the ceremony. His belief in the Peyote Cult was so powerful that he became a ritual leader, rejecting the Ghost Dance movement when it made its way to Comanche lands.

In 1884, Quanah traveled to Washington, D.C., to fight property changes that would divide tribal lands into individual plots. This was the first of twenty trips he would eventually make to secure a better land deal for the Comanches. Despite his attempts to bolster Comanche rights, many blamed Quanah for the eventual breakdown of ancient tribal traditions and the division of Comanche lands. His very public image as a "progressive" Indian made him a celebrity in the eyes of white America but caused many of his own people to grow increasingly bitter over his bicultural beliefs.

Quanah's Final Years Quanah Parker became seriously ill in early February of 1911. Suffering from a weak heart and rheumatism, the famous Comanche took to his bed at Star House. With Tonarcy, his principal wife, at his side, he died quietly on February 23. The procession to his final resting place is said to have stretched over a mile. Despite his many detractors and critics, Quanah Parker was highly revered during his lifetime. After a Christian funeral service, the controversial Comanche leader was buried beside his mother and sister in Cache County, Oklahoma. In 1957, all three were reinterred at Fort Sill Military Cemetery.

Wovoka

Wovoka (around 1856–1932) was the Paiute spiritual leader, known widely as the Paiute Messiah, who created the Ghost Dance religion of the late 1880s. Inspired by a vision that came to Wovoka during a serious illness, the Ghost Dance religion is blamed for events leading up to the Wounded Knee Massacre of 1890.

Wovoka, or "Wood Cutter," was born around 1856 to well-known Paiute medicine man Tavid, also called Numo-tibo, and his wife, Tiya. Wovoka and his three brothers were born in either Smith Valley or Mason Valley, Nevada. At around fourteen years of age, Wovoka began working for the Wilsons, a devout Presbyterian white family that may have previously employed Tiya. In addition to giving him work, the Wilsons allowed Wovoka to live on their land in Mason Valley. Wovoka also took meals with them and learned their religious ways. During this period of time, Wovoka took the name Jack Wilson. One day, while cutting trees for his adopted family, Wovoka fell ill and slipped into a coma. His recovery during a total eclipse of the sun on January 1, 1889, was not seen as a coincidence. He was instead credited for saving the universe by bringing back the sun.

Wovoka (l) a Northern Paiute religious leader founded the Ghost Dance Movement. *The Granger Collection, New York. Reproduced by permission*

The Birth of the Ghost Dance Religion

Wovoka, having already showed signs of sharing his father's shamanistic abilities, proclaimed that he had experienced a spiritual vision during his illness. In it, he said, God told him that a great transformation would come by the spring of 1891 if believers began dancing the Ghost Dance and following God's instructions. The transformation would bring the dead back to life, the buffalo back to fruition, and the elimination of the white man from the earth. God also said that Wovoka would be elevated to "President of the West," and that he would share political power with then-president Benjamin Harrison (1833–1901). In order for this to happen, Ghost Dance believers would have to live a morally pure life in harmony with the whites.

The vision was a much needed ray of hope for Native Americans of all tribes and nations. Most had already witnessed the death of their way of life and the near-extinction of the buffalo. They could no longer roam free, having been forced to live on U.S. government-run reservations. White settlement onto native lands had stripped them of their dignity, and years of fighting had left them tired and hopeless.

News of Wovoka's vision and its message of hope spread throughout the disheartened Indian Territory like wildfire. Soon, over thirty tribes had sent representatives to Wovoka to learn the Ghost Dance and its secrets. Sioux delegates, Short Bull and Kicking Bear, returned to South Dakota with the happy news that wearing a Ghost Shirt would keep battling warriors free from harm. Sitting Bull, the famous Sioux chief, quickly became a believer and proponent of the Ghost Dance and the wearing of the Ghost Shirt. His support, as well as the rampant acceptance of the new religion among almost all native peoples, struck fear in the hearts of white settlers and military personnel. Major Indian victories during the 1862 Minnesota uprising and the Battle of Little Bighorn were still fresh in their memories, and the anti-white message of the Ghost Dance "craze" reminded them that the future of the newly established states of North and South Dakota was still uncertain. In their minds, the Ghost Dance movement had to be stopped.

The Wounded Knee Massacre

In the winter of 1890, panicked Indian agents at the Dakota reservations demanded that Chief Sitting Bull be arrested for exciting his people with the Ghost Dance. The revitalized masses were witnessed dancing in the snow for days on end, which made the agents nervous. Soon, military personnel were ordered to arrest the chief at the Standing Rock Reservation. On December 15, 1890, Sitting Bull was shot and killed during the attempt. Hearing of Sitting Bull's death, Sioux Chief Big Foot decided to lead his people to safety at the Pine Ridge Reservation. On December 28, U.S. army troops intercepted them and brought them to an encampment along Wounded Knee Creek. The next morning, Colonel James Forsyth and his men arrived at the encampment. Forsyth demanded that all Indian firearms be relinquished. While disarming the Sioux, a scuffle broke out and a shot was fired. In less than an hour, close to five hundred military guards had massacred roughly two hundred unarmed Sioux women and children. Among the dead was Chief Big Foot (around 1825–1890). Colonel Forsyth was later charged for killing the innocents, but he was never punished. The Wounded Knee Massacre marked the end of the Indian Wars.

Wovoka's Life After Wounded Knee

By 1893, the Ghost Dance movement had ended. This did not diminish Wovoka's power or fame. His people continued to revere him as a great medicine man, while whites who knew him understood that his intelligence and peaceful nature kept him from inciting violence of any kind. Wovoka traveled from Nevada to reservations in the former Indian territory of Oklahoma and Wyoming, Kansas, and Montana. Admirers plied him with gifts and money wherever he went. In 1924, cowboy actor Tim McCoy invited him to visit the set of a movie he was making in northern California. While there, the

Arapahos hired to appear in the film showed the spiritual leader their utmost admiration.

Wovoka's fame and wealth did not keep him from living a simple life. He followed traditional Paiute customs and lived in a rough, two-bedroom house most of his life. Anthropologist Michael Hittman, a Wovoka scholar, has written that the medicine man believed in "the Great Revelation" until his death. He also provided shamanic services to a clamoring public for as long as he could. He lived long enough to see a Kaw from Kansas, Charles Curtis (1860–1936), elected vice president when Herbert Hoover (1874–1964) won the presidency in 1928.

Wovoka died on September 29, 1932, just a month after the death of his wife of over fifty years. After his death, some dismissed the spiritual leader as a fraud, but he was more widely remembered as an influential mystic who had a profound impact on American history.

Black Elk

Black Elk (1863–1950) was an Oglala Sioux, or Lakota, medicine man who devoted his life to the preservation of Native American peoples and culture. An account of his early life, as well as his philosophy, was written by John G. Neihardt in his book *Black Elk Speaks* in 1932.

Nicholas Black Elk, known more widely as "Black Elk," was born in December 1863 along the Little Powder River, which runs through Wyoming and eastern Montana. His father, also called Black Elk, was a Lakota Sioux shaman, or medicine man, in keeping with the rest of his paternal lineage. The elder Black Elk was wounded when the U.S. Cavalry fought the Oglala band, under the leadership of the great Oglala chief, Red Cloud, in 1866. After losing faith in his chief, Black Elk took his family to join another esteemed Oglala chief, Crazy Horse. The move allowed young Black Elk to participate in Custer's famous defeat at the Battle of Little Bighorn in June of 1876. A year later, after Crazy Horse was murdered, young Black Elk and the rest of his band fled to Canada to join Sitting Bull. There, for the next several years, he and his people witnessed the beginning of the reservation era and the extermination of the buffalo.

The most formative event of Black Elk's life occurred when he was nine years old. While suffering a serious illness, young Black Elk experienced a vision. In it, he was taken to the spiritual heart of the Lakota world and presented to the Six Grandfathers who symbolized The Great Mysteriousness, or *Wakan Tanka*. He was given instructions similar to those found in shamanic initiation rites, which he reenacted throughout his life as a way of preserving the survival and unity of his people. The vision was a spiritual calling, one that urged Black Elk to lead his people to keep the nation's "hoop"—thought of as a circle representing the traditional community identity

and the social and cultural coherence of the Sioux nation—intact by nurturing the sacred tree. The vision and its complex meaning were presented by Neihardt, Nebraska's poet laureate, in *Black Elk Speaks.*

Black Elk's Spiritual Faith After touring the United States and Europe with Buffalo Bill Cody's Wild West show from 1886 to 1889, Black Elk returned to his people, who were now forced to live in reservations. He found them suffering greatly, and they were placing their faith in a new religious movement called Ghost Dance. Black Elk was a respected spiritual leader of the Oglala who had led many dances and rituals, but the new messianic movement spurred by the Paiute Indian known as Wovoka was too powerful to ignore. Black Elk soon became a Ghost Dancer, believing in a dance that would bring about a day without white people and the reemergence of the buffalo. He even helped introduce the donning of Ghost Shirts, vestments that supposedly rendered bullets harmless to the wearer. The movement made U.S. soldiers in charge of keeping order on the reservations very nervous. Their panic led to the last and most horrible of Native American massacres: Wounded Knee.

The second most formative event of Black Elk's life occurred in 1904. After speaking with a priest from the Holy Rosary Mission, he decided he wanted to be baptized. This was after the death of his first wife, Katie War Bonnett, in 1903. She converted to Catholicism during their marriage and had all three of their children baptized. On December 6, 1904, the feast day of Saint Nicholas, Black Elk was accepted into the Catholic faith. From that day forward he was called Nicholas Black Elk. He soon became a catechist, responsible for instructing new converts, preaching, and if necessary, administering the sacraments. Black Elk's conversion did not lessen his devotion to his people or the vision that guided his native perspective, though. He saw no contradiction between his tribe's spiritual traditions and those espoused by Christianity. Instead, he sought answers to the mysteries of both belief systems with great zeal and energy and is, therefore, remembered as a holy man by both Native Americans and Christians alike.

His Literary Legacy In 1930, Black Elk met distinguished writer, poet, and critic John G. Neihardt on the Pine Ridge Reservation in South Dakota. Neihardt believed the story of Black Elk's life could serve humankind in a powerful and inspirational way, so the two began working together on the book that would become *Black Elk Speaks.* In it, Black Elk remembers pre-reservation Sioux life and spiritual practices at great length, but the core of the book centers on the vision that called the holy man to become a spiritual leader when he was just nine years old. Black Elk's vivid remembrance of the vision had the effect of resurrecting its power, despite his devotion to the Catholic faith for almost thirty years. Neihardt's description of its retelling remains a standard of visionary religious literature, attracting comparative mythology, symbology, and depth psychology scholars among its many readers. It has also prompted Native American revitalization movements and a renewed interest in traditional rituals.

It was Joseph Epes Brown's 1953 book *The Sacred Pipe* that made plain the traditional rituals referred to in *Black Elk Speaks*. Brown, one of the founders of Native American studies, renowned author, and professor of Religious Studies at the University of Montana, was keenly interested in the traditions and beliefs of the American Indian. His interest led him to Black Elk and the Oglala Sioux in 1947. Brown lived with Black Elk that year, interviewing the revered medicine man and recording the account of the seven rites of his people. Black Elk urged Brown to write a book so that the sacred beliefs of the Oglala Sioux could be preserved and understood by both native and non-native peoples. *The Sacred Pipe* details the purpose and function of the tribe's ancient ceremonies and explains the complexity, order, and beauty of the tribe's culture and past.

Black Elk's Final Years

Although Black Elk's life was riddled with ill health—he suffered from tuberculosis and poor eyesight—and economic difficulties brought on by a reservation existence, he continually maintained a spirituality infused with hopefulness. He devoted his life to improving, restoring, and preserving Native American culture, especially through his books with Neihardt and Brown, until his death on August 17, 1950. Before that day, Black Elk had told Brown that unusual phenomena would appear in the sky on the day he died. Those attending Black Elk's wake reported seeing the foretold "unusual phenomena" including a profusion of falling stars, particularly bright northern lights, and symbols, including a hoop and a figure-eight pattern that night. He continues to impact Native American culture, as evidenced by the resurrection of the Sun Dance within a decade of his death by his nephew Frank Fools Crow. By sharing such rituals of empowerment, he ensured they would not be dependent on oral tradition, thus giving them the opportunity to flourish.

✪ Major Battles

Sand Creek Massacre

The Sand Creek Massacre, a surprise attack on a peaceful Cheyenne camp, was a shocking and outrageous United States military action that led to congressional investigations of its perpetrators. The November 1864 event, part of the larger Colorado War, continues to serve as scathing evidence of the country's treatment of Native Americans during westward expansion.

Events Leading Up to the Massacre

Beginning in the late 1850s, white settlers began flooding the foothills and mountains of the Rocky Mountain range during the Colorado Gold Rush. The region, then part of the western Kansas territory, was home to both Cheyenne and Arapaho tribes, who soon found themselves in conflict with white gold diggers demanding the removal of Native American land claims. Despite the conflict, many Indians sought peace with the whites. Black Kettle, the chief of the Cheyenne, was especially interested in ending the fighting between the Indians and the whites. When he became aware of the fact that all citizens of Colorado had government-sanctioned permission to kill and destroy any Indians they discovered outside reservation boundaries, he held a council of Cheyenne and Arapaho chiefs. They agreed to comply with peace requirements defined by John Evans 1814–1897), the governor of the Colorado Territory.

The chiefs wrote a letter to Major Colley, the Indian agent at Fort Lyon, expressing their desire for peace and had the Indians One-Eye and Eagle Head deliver it on horseback. The Indians were intercepted by three soldiers who delivered them to Fort Lyon's commanding officer, Major Edward W. Wynkoop. A true Indian-hater, Wynkoop was suspicious of their motives, despite the contents of the letter, but decided to use One-Eye and Eagle Head as both guides and hostages on the expedition back to their Smoky Hill camp, where Black Kettle awaited. The chiefs's terms for peace included the release of white prisoners into Wynkoop's custody, so the major was forced to make the journey himself. It took One-Eye, Eagle Head, Wynkoop, and his troops five days on horseback to make the trek—enough time for the major to change his long-held beliefs about Indians. According to Dee Brown's book, *Bury My Heart at Wounded Knee*, Wynkoop is reported to have said, "I felt myself in the presence of superior beings; and these were the representatives of a race that I heretofore looked upon without exception as being cruel, treacherous, and bloodthirsty without feeling or affection for friend or kindred."

When Black Kettle and his chiefs met Wynkoop and his men for a council, both sides promised to do everything they could to keep the peace. As a result, Wynkoop and seven Indian leaders traveled the four hundred miles to Denver to meet with Governor Evans. Wynkoop had to beg the governor to meet with Black Kettle and his men. Finally, the governor agreed, and a council was held between him, Wynkoop, the Indian chiefs, and Colonel John M. Chivington, a Fort Leavenworth officer known for his ferocious hatred of Indians. The Indians, unsure of the final outcome of the meeting, were sure of one thing: The only real white ally they had was Wynkoop. They decided to stick with their friend, the one they now called Tall Chief Wynkoop, and move to a military encampment along Sand Creek, which was roughly forty miles northeast of Fort Lyon. They were treated so well that the seven Indian leaders made the decision to move their people to the encampment along Sand Creek. Their people consisted of Arapaho and Sioux Indians. The Arapaho, so comfortable with the United States military, decided to leave the encampment and move to the military fort where they were treated to regular rations. Soon, Wynkoop's friendly dealings with what Colorado and Kansas officials deemed "the enemy" led to his being replaced by Major Scott J. Anthony, one of Chivington's Colorado Volunteers. His first order was to cut the Arapaho's rations and demand the surrender of their weapons. Despite his brusque first remarks, he assured the Cheyenne camped at Sand Creek that they were under the protection of Fort Lyon and that they should continue to hunt buffalo until he received permission from the Army to begin issuing winter rations. This convinced Black Kettle to stay at Sand Creek through the winter.

The Massacre Itself Colonel Chivington never intended to keep the peace with the Indians. In fact, he had been preparing a force of Colorado regiments with the sole intent of bringing violence down upon their heads. Despite his calm words of reassurance, Major Anthony was also secretly hoping for a chance to attack the Indians assembled at Sand Creek. When Chivington and his officers arrived at Fort Lyon on November 27, the colonel talked excitedly about "wading in gore" and "collecting scalps," which Anthony supported. He assured his superior that the men at Fort Lyon were anxious to join Chivington's Indian attack. But not all the men shared their enthusiasm. Captain Silas Soule, Lieutenant Joseph Cramer, and Lieutenant James Connor protested the planned attack on the peaceful Sand Creek encampment. This infuriated Chivington, who threatened to court-martial the soldiers if they did not participate. Soule, Cramer, and Connor were forced to join the expedition, but secretly resolved not to order their men to attack unless it was in self-defense.

On the evening of November 28, Chivington led more than seven hundred men, including Anthony's Fort Lyon troops, toward Sand Creek. Because most of the young warriors were away hunting buffalo, the camp was comprised of six hundred Indians, two-thirds of which were women and children. The soldiers attacked at sunrise, the pounding of their horse's hooves the only warning of their sudden presence. Soon, women and children were heard screaming, terrified by the sight of hundreds of soldiers in their midst. Black Kettle raised an American flag above his lodge and called to his people to not be afraid, that the soldiers would not hurt them as long as the flag flew. Then the troops began firing from two sides of the camp. Hundreds of women and children huddled around Black Kettle's flag, still believing that the soldiers would stop firing once they saw the flag. Sadly, even after Black Kettle raised a white flag, the soldiers continued firing indiscriminately into the crowds of unarmed Indians.

In a few short hours, Chivington and his men had murdered 105 Indian women and children and 28 men. Many, including Black Kettle, escaped due to lack of discipline, drunkenness, and bad marksmanship on the part of the soldiers. As if the killings were not enough, the soldiers mutilated their victims in the most horrible ways. If the dead bodies were not scalped, they were sexually disfigured.

The Aftermath Black Kettle and every other Cheyenne and Arapaho chief who had attempted to negotiate with the white man for peace were stripped of their power after the Sand Creek Massacre. An alliance of revenge-seeking Cheyenne, Arapaho, and Sioux Indians launched a series of raids along the South Platte in January of 1865, signaling a new wave of violence between whites and Indians that would last for years. Despite its being initially heralded as a significant victory, the massacre quickly became the subject of a military investigation and two congressional hearings. It attracted nationwide attention, even in the midst of the Civil War, and led to renewed scrutiny of military brutality. Colonel Chivington, though forced to resign from the military, escaped criminal charges for his role in the massacre.

Red Cloud's War

Red Cloud's War is an umbrella term used to describe a series of battles that occurred between 1866 and 1868 between Oglala leader, Red Cloud, and the U.S. military. Red Cloud and the Indian Nation emerged as victors in what has since been described as the most successful campaign against the United States ever fought by Native Americans.

Oglala Sioux warrior, Red Cloud, gained prominence as a great leader in the territorial wars against the Pawnees, Utes, Crows, and Shoshonis before gold was discovered in present-day Montana. After the discovery in the late 1850s, Red Cloud was forced to fight a new enemy in a different kind of territorial war. The flood of Montana-bound white settlers trespassing through Sioux grazing lands was tolerated until their presence drove the buffalo away. Red Cloud knew that the buffalo were not the only creatures the whites would soon attempt to drive out.

Before the Wars The first sign of trouble came when the Bozeman Trail, which traversed the heart of Lakota territory, was "discovered" by John Bozeman. Bozeman had been looking for a direct passage to the Montana gold fields from the North Platte River in present-day Wyoming and found it, disregarding the fact that it cut straight through protected land. Cheyenne and Sioux war parties became increasingly frustrated over the invasion of their treaty lands and began attacking white Bozeman Trail travelers. In an effort to protect the whites from escalating Indian attacks, the U. S. military erected Forts Reno, Phil Kearny, and C. F. Smith along the trail. The forts, manned by armed military, served as policing stations. Now white settlers and miners, less fearful of vengeful Indians, came in caravans, all but wiping out the Sioux livelihood, the buffalo.

The Wars Begin   Red Cloud vowed to shut down the Bozeman Trail and defend his territory while the military stood firm, determined to keep the passage open at all costs. The Oglala leader was especially motivated to resist white settlement after witnessing the expulsion of the Eastern Lakota from Minnesota in 1862 and 1863. This travesty, he decided, would not be his people's destiny. Red Cloud and a united front of Sioux, Cheyenne, and Arapaho Indians began a focused and relentless assault on the forts beginning in 1865. On July 25 and 26 of that year, the Oglala attacked white trespassers at Platte Bridge. The next campaign, fought in mid-August, was fought against James A. Sawyer's Pumpkin Buttes surveying party. These initial skirmishes paved the way for Red Cloud's War. The climax of the strategic battles fought between 1866 and 1868 was the Fetterman Massacre of 1866.

The Fetterman Massacre   Fort Kearney was run by Colonel Henry Carrington, an inexperienced Indian fighter and military leader. In November of 1866, shortly after Carrington had assumed his post there, Captain William Fetterman joined the Fort Kearney regiment. Fetterman was a highly respected Civil War veteran who believed the Indians, no matter how fierce or numerous, were no match against a regiment of well-trained U.S. soldiers. Before long, Fetterman was the leader of an anti-Carrington rebellion. His followers believed him when he boasted of teaching the Indians a lesson. Fetterman convinced them that he could defeat the entire Sioux nation with just eighty men. Little he could not have known how quickly his boast would be put to the test.

On December 6, 1866, a mere fraction of the thousands of warriors assembled by Red Cloud attacked an unescorted wood train departing Fort Kearney. Carrington attempted to retaliate, but was met by a second imposing force that persuaded him to retreat back to the fort. Two weeks later, a contingent of Indians staged another decoy. This time Carrington did not fall for it. This forced Red Cloud to choose December 21, the last wood cutting day of the winter, as the day he and his warriors would launch their major strike. At 11 A.M., the Indians attacked the wood train, this time facing Fetterman, not Carrington, and seventy-nine of Fetterman's followers. The captain and his men were quickly overwhelmed by a massive army of two thousand Indians. It only took twenty minutes for all eighty men to be slaughtered.

The Fallout   Red Cloud and his allied forces continued their assaults on the three Bozeman Trail fort troops throughout the winter, which kept the regiments in a constant state of exhausting fear. The Fetterman Massacre made a profound impression on the military, as well as the white miners and settlers who had become accustomed to traversing the route. Red Cloud orchestrated a series of continued attacks over the next two years, which led to the government finally surrendering. The Fort Laramie Treaty of 1868 ordered the abandonment of the three forts along the Bozeman Trail and granted the Lakota possession of lands stretching from the Missouri River westward through the Black Hills of Dakota, or the western half of present-day South Dakota and much of Wyoming and Montana.

The signing of the Fort Laramie Treaty signaled the end of Red Cloud's War and marked Red Cloud as the only Indian leader to win an extended war against the United States. But his victory was bittersweet. Signing the treaty meant Red Cloud was essentially giving in to the white man's demands, despite the fact that he was signing on his own terms. Although he had forced the closure of the Bozeman Trail and the abandonment of its forts, he and his people were now under contract to remain on reservation lands, lands that were soon divided and taken away by the very government that assured their protection. General George Custer's 1874 Black Hills expedition brought an end to the peace the treaty promised and heralded the end of independent Indian nations. It was not long before Red Cloud, one of the most powerful and ferocious of Sioux leaders, began speaking out against the U.S. government in a tireless attempt to hold them to their promises. He kept up his nonviolent campaign for the rest of his life, losing the support of militant Sioux warriors who would have preferred war over years of treaty negotiations.

Red River War

During the Red River War of 1874, the U.S. Army and the Southern Plains Indians fought as many as twenty battles. The war's official end came in June 1875 when Quanah Parker, leader of the Quahadi Comanche Indians, surrendered at Fort Sill. The surrender marked the defeat of the Comanche Indians and the end of the Southern Plains' way of life.

The U.S. army was devoted to ridding the Texas panhandle region of Comanche, Kiowa, Southern Cheyenne, and Arapaho Indians during the summer of 1874. Like most anti-Indian campaigns, this one was inspired by westward-bound white settlers demanding protection against Indian raids. The army responded by establishing a series of frontier forts across the nomadic tribes's buffalo plains homeland.

The Medicine Lodge Treaty of 1867   The Medicine Lodge Treaty of 1867 created two reservations in Indian territory. The Comanche and Kiowa settled in one, while

The shooting of buffalo along railroads, as depicted in this 1871 wood engraving, contributed to the Red River War, also known as the Buffalo War. *The Granger Collection, New York. Reproduced by permission*

the Southern Cheyenne and Arapaho settled in the other. The whites promised that, in addition to receiving food, housing, and supplies—including guns and ammunition—the Indians would be allowed to hunt on any lands south of the Arkansas River "so long as the buffalo may range thereon in such numbers as to justify the chase." The plains between the Arkansas River and the Red River was thick with buffalo crowded out of the north, so the Indians consented and agreed to stop raiding and attacking white settlers. Ten chiefs signed the treaty and then voluntarily led their followers to the reservations.

But commercial buffalo hunters soon invaded the area promised to the Indians, ignoring the terms of the treaty. Between 1872 and 1874, 3.7 million buffalo were destroyed. Of that number, just 150,000 were killed by Indians. The buffalo, needed by white commercial hunters only for their hide, were slaughtered and stripped by the thousands. Their carcasses were left to rot on the plains. Without U.S. intervention, the buffalo herds grew thinner, forcing the Indians to rely on reservation rations.

Food was poor in quality and inadequate, but the Indians had nothing else. The restrictions of reservation

life were also confusing and almost impossible to follow. By the spring of 1874, the Indians were in poor shape. Discontented young warriors left for the Texas plains as conditions worsened. There was much talk of killing, driving the white man out, and war.

A War to Save the Buffalo Two Quahadi leaders spoke of supporting a war to save the buffalo. Isa-tai, a prophet and medicine man, was the first to suggest it. Quanah Parker, the young Quahadi chief, was the second. Parker suggested they strike at the hunters's base, the trading post called Adobe Walls, near the Canadian River. Everyone agreed that if the soldiers refused to drive the white hunters from Quahadi buffalo ranges, then the Indians must do it. In the early-morning hours of June 27, 1874, Isa-tai and Parker led some seven hundred warriors westward from Elk Creek. Isa-tai made medicine along the way, promising that it would keep the white men from being able to shoot the warriors. Before sunrise, they reached Adobe Walls, moved in, and attacked. After several hours of fighting, the Indians admitted that the whites were too well-armed and numerous to overwhelm. They retreated and then turned their frustration on Isa-tai and his broken promise.

The tribes separated after the attack on Adobe Walls. They spread out across the Texas panhandle region and attempted to live according to the old way of life, despite diminishing ancestral lands and buffalo. The heat made life on the plains difficult that summer. Streams dried up and grasshoppers consumed the dry grass. Most white hunters left the area, leaving the Comanche, Kiowa, Arapaho, and Cheyenne bands to wander the desolate landscape searching for buffalo. When forced to rely on rations, they were denied already inadequate portions as punishment for roaming beyond reservation borders. Their desperation forced them to fight, which gave the U.S. army reason to attempt to subdue them for good. The government responded to continued outbreaks with a new policy designed to drive the Indians from the area and make room for incoming white settlers.

The War Ends A military offensive was put together to enforce the new policy. In September of 1874, five officers led five columns of soldiers from different directions into the heart of the panhandle region. The troops were ordered to maintain a continuous offensive until the Indians were defeated. Colonel Nelson A. Miles traveled south from Fort Dodge; Lieutenant Colonel John W. Davidson moved westward from Fort Sill; Lieutenant Colonel George P. Buell went northwest from Fort Griffin; Colonel Ranald S. Mackenzie came northward from Fort Concho; and Major William R. Price traveled eastward from Fort Union.

Thousands of soldiers swarmed the Palo Duro Canyon, where hundreds of Comanche, Kiowa, and Cheyenne were camping. On September 26, Kiowa Chief Lone Wolf and his followers suffered a surprise military attack. The soldiers drove the Indians from the encampment by burning their teepees, slaughtering their animals, and destroying their winter supplies. Indians who escaped with their lives now had no food, clothing, or shelter. And still the military pushed. Thousands of troops in four separate columns continued to hunt for Indians, capturing as many as they could and returning them to Fort Sill. Lone Wolf and 252 Kiowa escaped capture but had no strength left. On February 25, 1875, they surrendered at Fort Sill. Quanah Parker and the Quahadis surrendered there three months later.

Indians who surrendered were disarmed and herded into a corral. Their horses were shot and all their other belongings were destroyed or burned. Indian chiefs and tribal leaders were confined behind high walls in an icehouse with no roof. They were thrown hunks of raw meat to eat, as if they were animals. Finally, twenty-six Kiowa were sent to faraway Fort Marion, Florida, as punishment for their crimes. Within ten years, all the

General George Armstrong Custer's Black Hills Expedition of 1874 violated the Fort Laramie Treaty with the Sioux Indians and brought about a gold rush. *© Corbis*

great leaders had either died or killed themselves. The Indians, unable to save the buffalo, also suffered the indignity of being stripped of their power. The Kiowas and Comanches would never again be able to live according to their traditions, and the buffalo had completely vanished.

The Black Hills War

The Black Hills War, a series of battles that took place between 1875 and 1877, began when General George Armstrong Custer and his Seventh Cavalry invaded protected Sioux land in search of rumored gold. The Treaty of 1868, which gave the sacred Black Hills, or "Paha Sapa," to the Sioux Indians, was blatantly ignored by a subsequent flood of gold-crazy white settlers and government officials who wanted the mineral-rich land for themselves. After two years of fighting, Chief Sitting Bull retreated to Canada, Chief Crazy Horse was killed, and the Black Hills, the material and spiritual center of the Sioux universe, was taken from the Indians and never returned.

In 1868, President Ulysses S. Grant deemed the Black Hills a worthless tract of land and so let the Indians have it. As a result, the Treaty of 1868 stated, "No white person or persons shall be permitted to settle upon or occupy any portion of the territory, or without consent of the Indians to pass through the same." But the Black Hills were considered holy by the Sioux. War-riors went there to speak with the Great Spirit and to experience visions. Ten nations of Sioux Indians had friends and family buried there. So when General Custer, the man who massacred Chief Black Kettle's Southern Cheyenne on the Washita River in 1868, had the audac-ity to intrude upon it without Sioux consent, Red Cloud, Spotted Tail, and other Cheyenne, Oglala, and Arapaho leaders became incensed.

Long Hair's Expedition The Black Hills, located along the border of present-day Wyoming and South Dakota, were a mystery to whites until General George Custer's famous 1874 expedition into their interior. Gold-hungry whites clamored to know what riches lay beneath the protected hills, so the U.S. army was ordered to make a reconnaissance to find out. Custer, known as "Pahuska," or Long Hair, by the Sioux, was chosen to lead the Seventh Cavalry, more than one thousand soldiers, across the plains to the Black Hills. Because they received no warning of his arrival, the Sioux could only watch as he and his blue-clad cavalry-men intruded upon their holy land. President Ulysses S. Grant, known to the Indians as "The Great Father," understood their rage and promised "to prevent all invasion of this country by intruders so long as by law and treaty it is secured to the Indians." Even Grant could not stop the frothing masses of white men after Custer announced that the Black Hills were filled with gold, "from the grass roots down." Before long, the trail that Custer had worn into the heart of Paha Sapa with the wheels of his supply wagons became known as Thiev-es's Road.

The War Begins By the spring of 1875, thousands of miners had stolen into the Black Hills by way of Thiev-es's Road. After the army failed to rid the hills of the lawbreakers, Red Cloud and Spotted Tail began sending strong protests to Washington. The Great Father responded with an order to set up a commission to meet with the Indians and negotiate a price for parts of their sacred land. The commission was composed, as usual, of politicians, missionaries, military officers, and traders. When they arrived at the White River meeting place on September 20, 1875, they found more than twenty thousand Sioux, Cheyenne, and Arapaho Indians wait-ing. Sitting Bull, Crazy Horse, and other non-agency chiefs refused to attend the council, claiming they would never sell Sioux land, especially the Black Hills.

It did not take long for the whites to realize the futility of trying to buy Black Hills land, so they switched tactics and began negotiating for mineral rights. This option seemed equally preposterous to the Indians. Red Cloud, who was not in attendance, sent a message to the proceedings requesting a recess. He felt the tribes needed time to hold councils of their own to discuss the whites's proposals. During the recess, some chiefs sug-gested that since the U.S. government had no apparent intention of enforcing the treaty, they should demand a great deal of money for the gold taken from their hills. Others argued that the hills were not for sale and that if the government would not keep the miners out, the warriors would. When the commission reconvened, Spotted Tail, chosen by Red Cloud to speak for all the Sioux, rejected offers to sell or lease the Black Hills.

The commissioners returned to Washington, reported their failure, and recommended that Congress offer the Sioux a final offer of a forced purchase. Frustrated by the Indian's noncompliance, the government demanded that all non-agency Indians and Indians roaming off the reser-vations hunting buffalo report to their agents by January 31. The independent Indians accepted the demand as a declaration of war against them. On March 17, 1876, General George Crook attacked a peaceful camp of North-ern Cheyenne and Oglala Sioux warriors along the Powder River. Although the soldiers destroyed their teepees, burned their food and saddles, and stole almost all their horses, many Indians escaped and recovered their horses later that night. Incensed by the attack, Crazy Horse led the Oglalas and Cheyennes to the Tongue River, where Sitting Bull and the Hunkpapas had spent the winter. The gath-ered tribes headed north when the weather warmed, join-ing bands of Brules, Sans Arcs, and Blackfoot Sioux who were camped along the Rosebud River. The group, num-bered in the several thousands and led by Crazy Horse, whipped Crooks's men on June 17, 1876. The skirmish became known as the Battle of the Rosebud. But the big-gest Indian victory was yet to come. The Indians decided to head west to Little Bighorn, where the antelope were plen-tiful and the grass lush and thick. The encampment at Little Bighorn spread for miles as the population of Indians had reached about ten thousand. On June 24, the Indians received word that General Custer and his Seventh Cavalry were marching toward Little Bighorn. Because he was unaware of the size of the Indian encampment, he was quickly overwhelmed. The Sioux killed every last white, including Long Hair, taking not a single soldier prisoner.

The War Ends After the Battle of Little Bighorn, the massive collection of Sioux tribes separated and went in different directions. In 1877, the U.S. government, maintaining that the Indians had violated the Treaty of 1868 by going to war with the United States, made a new law stating that they had to give up all rights to the Powder River country and the Black Hills. Further, the Sioux would have their reservations moved to the Mis-souri River, a region plundered by white miners. Presi-dent Grant then sent a commission to harass chiefs into signing away their rights to the Black Hills. Every chief responded by reminding the commissioners of the gov-ernment's many broken promises and the fact that it was

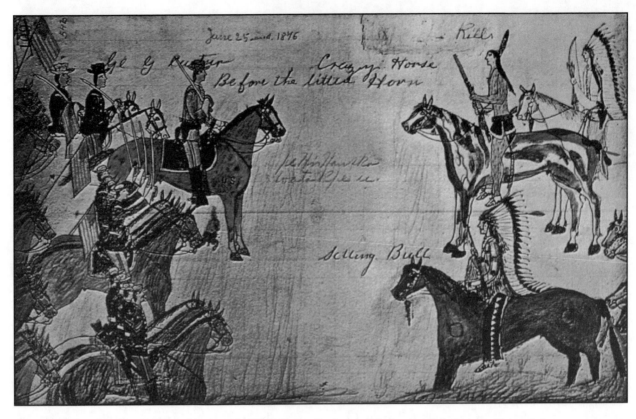

The Battle of Little Bighorn as depicted by Amos Bad Heart Bull. *The Granger Collection, New York. Reproduced by permission*

the U.S. that started the war with the Indians—not the other way around. Despite their protestations, they understood they had been defeated. The Black Hills had been stolen from them, the Powder River game had been driven out, and without rations or game they would starve. One after another chief reluctantly signed the commissioner's documents until the government secured the Black Hills treasures—the mysteries, vast forests, and billions of dollars of gold—for themselves.

Little Bighorn

The Battle of Little Bighorn, also known as "Custer's Last Stand," was the pinnacle of the Great Sioux War of 1876 and, ironically, the undoing of the Sioux people. Despite their victory over General George Armstrong Custer and his military forces on June 25 and 26, 1876, the Sioux were forced to surrender and settle into reservation life after the U.S. government took their sacred Black Hills from them just one year later.

The events leading up to the Battle of Little Bighorn mimic those of nearly every other battle fought during the Indian Wars. Like every significant engagement between Indians and the military, the fight was over land. This time, the Sioux were battling for the homeland of their ancestors, what was, to them, the sacred Black Hills of present-day South Dakota. In 1874, General Custer was ordered to lead an expedition

into the protected territory to see if rumors about gold being hidden there were true. Ignoring the Fort Laramie Treaty of 1868, which guaranteed the Sioux ownership of the Black Hills, U.S. Secretary of the Interior Columbus Delano sent Custer and his troops to invade the boundaries without Indian consent and find the gold they were looking for. Within the year, white gold prospectors were streaming into the area. According to the Fort Laramie Treaty, the military was responsible for keeping trespassers from invading protected lands, but they were unable to oust Black Hills intruders. The Sioux and Cheyenne Indians decided that if the U.S. government would not defend the Black Hills, they would.

Preparing for Battle The U.S. government had hoped to weaken the Sioux's ability to fight the imminent sale of the Black Hills by forcing them onto the Great Sioux Reservation, but the Indians maintained their resolve. Outraged by continued intrusions into their protected lands, Sioux and Cheyenne Indians left the reservation in late 1875. They met with the great warrior Sitting Bull in Montana to discuss a plan of attack. The following spring, the Indians had fought the U.S. cavalry twice, winning both times. These victories gave them the courage to continue fighting through the summer.

Meanwhile, the U.S. military was planning its own attack. To force the Indians back onto the reservations, the army ordered three separate columns of troops that would engage in coordinated fashion. Organized around Montana's Yellowstone River Basin, General George Crook was to advance to the south, Colonel John Oliver Gibbon was to advance from the west, and General Alfred Howe Terry was to advance from the east. Among Terry's regiment was the elite Seventh Cavalry, led by General Custer, an aggressive and flamboyant Civil War hero. On June 22, Terry sent Custer and his regiment to Rosebud Creek to look for Indians who may have gathered in the Little Bighorn Valley. Terry planned to accompany Gibbon along the Bighorn and Yellowstone Rivers. This way, they reasoned, they could head off any Indians that might try to escape northward if Custer struck from the south.

The Battle Begins Custer located the Sioux village along the Rosebud River about fifteen miles away on the morning of June 25. He also spotted a closer gathering of about forty Sioux warriors. Although he had been ordered to wait and attack the next day, Custer was afraid the warriors would alert the village of his location by then. He ignored his directive and divided his forces into three parties. Captain Frederick Benteen was sent to the upper valley of the Little Bighorn River to prevent any escape in that direction. Major Marcus Reno was supposed to cross the river and charge the Indian village directly. Custer planned to use the rest of the regiment to strike the encampment from the northern and southern ends simultaneously, but he made this decision without knowing what sort of terrain they would face. More importantly, he did not know the Indian army was three times the size of his meager force.

Reno and his troop of 175 soldiers attacked the northern end of the camp and were quickly overwhelmed. As soon as they became desperate, he ordered his men to cease charging, fought for ten minutes, and then withdrew into the brush along the river. They continued to be hunted by the Sioux and Cheyenne army, which chased the regiment uphill to the bluffs east of the river. After driving these forces out, the Indians saw 210 of Custer's men coming at the other end of the village. The Sioux and Cheyenne crossed the river and forced themselves into the advancing soldiers, driving them to a high ridge to the north. At the same time, Crazy Horse led his Oglala Sioux warriors downstream before doubling back in a sweeping arc, swallowing Custer and his men in one fell swoop. The Indians rained gunfire and arrows upon the soldiers, closing in on them with great force. Custer ordered his men to shoot their horses and use the carcasses as protection, but the bullets proved too powerful. Within an hour, Custer and his men were killed in one of the worst military disasters in American history.

After defeating Custer's regiment, the Indians continued to fight Reno and Benteen's now-united forces for another day. When they learned that two other columns of soldiers were headed their way, they decided to flee and let the soldiers escape. Once the battle was over, the Indians returned to strip and mutilate the bodies of the uniformed soldiers. They did this because they believed the soul of a mutilated body was not allowed to enter the kingdom of heaven, but forced instead to wander the earth for all eternity. For reasons that remain a mystery, the Sioux and Cheyenne warriors stripped and cleaned Custer's body, but they did not scalp or otherwise mutilate it. The general had been wearing buckskins instead of a uniform when he died, which may have led the Indians to believe that he was an innocent, not a soldier. If this were true, it would explain why his body was left intact. Others suppose that Custer's body was left alone because his usually long hair had been shorn before battle, which would make him hard to scalp.

The Battle of Little Bighorn was the Indian's greatest victory against the white man. Unfortunately for them, the slaying of a popular Civil War hero outraged American civilians and military troops alike. The country demanded retribution and took it by redrawing boundary lines and opening the Black Hills to white settlers. Within a year, the Sioux nation surrendered, accepted defeat, and settled into reservation life.

Nez Perce War

The Nez Perce War was fought in present-day Oregon, Idaho, Montana, and Wyoming in 1877 and was comprised of a series of battles between the Nez Perce and the U.S. government. It resulted in the surrender of the Nez Perce to military officers and the end of the tribe's way of life.

The Nez Perce were proud of the fact that they had not killed a white man in seventy years. After becoming friends with Lewis and Clark in 1805, the tribe had welcomed white visitors, offered them food, and looked after their horses. Sadly, beginning in 1855, the U.S. government began a campaign of harassment against the Nez Perce. Many chiefs were persuaded to sign treaties that gave away Nez Perce land and gold. Chief Joseph, leader of the Nez Perce, refused to sign any of the white man's treaties that included taking away his people's lands. After refusing to sign the 1863 treaty that would take away the Wallowa Valley and three-fourths of their remaining land, Chief Joseph planted poles along the boundary of those lands. In 1871, the whites simply came to the Wallowa Valley and ordered the Nez Perce to go to the Lapwai reservation. Again, Chief Joseph refused to pay attention to the military. He said, "we will defend this land as long as a drop of Indian blood warms the hearts of our men."

Before the War On June 16, 1873, President Ulysses S. Grant issued an executive order that withdrew Wallowa

This wood engraving depicts the surrender of Chief Joseph, Nez Perce leader, after his defeat and capture by U.S. Army General Nelson A. Miles.   *The Granger Collection, New York. Reproduced by permission.*

Valley from white settlement. Two years later he changed his mind. Now, the Wallowa Valley was open to white settlement and the Nez Perce were expected to move to the Lapwai reservation within a reasonable amount of time. In 1877, the government sent General Oliver O. Howard to remove all Nez Perce from the Wallowa Valley. Privately, General Howard believed it was wrong to take Chief Joseph's land from him. But he was eager to shed his reputation as an Indian-lover and so decided to carry out his orders in a swift and meticulous manner. In May 1877, he summoned Joseph to a council at the Lapwai reservation to discuss the date he and his people would surrender.

Chief Joseph chose Wallowa prophet, Toohoolhoolzote, as his council spokesman. The prophet began the meeting by informing Howard that they would never give up their land, even if other Nez Perce had. Howard responded by saying that the government had set aside a reservation for them and explained that the

Indians must go there to live. Toohoolhoolzote kept the officer engaged in an extended argument about land ownership until Howard became exasperated. He ordered the prophet be arrested and taken to the guardhouse. Then he told Chief Joseph that he and his people had thirty days to relocate to Lapwai.

Chief Joseph knew it was over. Military troops were stationed at their camp when he and his fellow leaders returned home. They held a council and decided to round up their stock and prepare to leave immediately. When Toohoolhoolzote was able to join them, he announced that only blood could cleanse him of his humiliation. He was not alone. Although Chief Joseph continued to press for peace, several young warriors were busy discussing war.

The War Begins   On the journey to Lapwai, several young warriors slipped away from camp and killed eleven white men in retaliation for their theft of land and stock. Chief Joseph wished the young warriors had not killed the white men, because he still preferred peace, but he understood his people's growing frustration. When they reached White Bird Creek, sixteen miles away, they were met by soldiers and the first real battle of the Nez Perce War.

After a series of victories, the Nez Perce grew to include 250 warriors, 450 noncombatants, and 2,000 horses. They had also assumed ownership of several rifles and a wealth of ammunition. On July 25, the massive band came upon Captain Charles Rawn and his regiment. Chief Joseph and two of his subchiefs approached the regiment while waving a white flag. Joseph calmly let Rawn know that he planned on passing through the barricade that the regiment was constructing without fighting—if Rawn's men allowed it. After days of deliberation and a half-hearted attempt to stop them, the Nez Perce were permitted to pass and head south. On August 9, U.S. military troops under the command of Colonel John Gibbon fired upon a Nez Perce encampment along the Big Hole River. Eighty Nez Perce were killed in the surprise attack. More than two-thirds of them were women and children. The Indians retaliated by attacking General Howard's troops and crossing into Yellowstone National Park on August 22. The Indians were forced to fight nearly every day for the next month. In a battle in the Bear Paw Mountains, where they believed they might be safe, the Nez Perce suffered a surprise attack that left Joseph's brother, Ollokot, and the prophet Toohoolhoolzote dead. The Indians were short of food, and their horses were terribly worn out, but they managed to secure the enemy's arms and ammunition. After dark, they attempted to slip away, only to find themselves surrounded. But instead of firing on the Indians, General Miles sent a messenger under a white flag to demand that Joseph surrender. Joseph replied that he would think about it. Later that day, a few of Miles's Sioux scouts rode out under another white flag. They assured Joseph that Miles was sincere in his desire for peace, which convinced Joseph to go to the commander's tent. The Indian chief was held prisoner while Miles resumed his attack. The military received reinforcements while the Nez Perce warriors dwindled in number. Joseph called his chiefs together for the last time. They wanted to continue fighting to the death. They had struggled for over thirteen hundred miles and they were not ready to give up. On the fifth day of the siege, Joseph went to Miles, gave up his gun, and delivered an eloquent speech that has since become the most quoted of all American Indian speeches. In it, he says, "Hear me, my chiefs! I am tired; my heart is sick and sad. From where the sun now stands I will fight no more forever."

The Wounded Knee Massacre

The Wounded Knee Massacre, which occurred on December 29, 1890, brought the Indian Wars to a violent close and ended the traditional Sioux way of life forever. Much like other Indian massacres that took place during westward expansion, the victims were mostly unarmed men, women, and children. Historians and Native American activists debate the events at Wounded Knee to this day while songs, books, poems, and visual art of all kinds keeps the slaughter in the public consciousness.

A People Retreats The Hunkpapa Sioux, demoralized by the assassination of their leader, Chief Sitting Bull, found solace in the Ghost Dance, the religious movement that promised the end of the white man and the resurrection of all buffalo and fallen Indians. The Hunkpapas were so devoted to the Ghost Dance and its prophecy that they decided not to retaliate against the whites who took Sitting Bull's life. They sought refuge with Red Cloud, one of the last remaining great chiefs instead. On December 17, 1890, about one hundred of the fleeing Hunkpapas reached Big Foot's Minneconjou encampment near Cherry Creek on their way to Red Cloud's Pine Ridge home. Unfortunately, Big Foot had just been placed on the U.S. War Department's list of "fomenters of disturbances," which led to an order being issued for his capture and arrest. Upon their arrival at Cherry Creek, the Hunkpapas shared the news of Sitting Bull's death, which prompted Big Foot and his people to head for Pine Ridge, too. On the way, Big Foot contracted pneumonia and began hemorrhaging.

The Military Intervenes On December 28, the Pine Ridge-bound Minneconjous spied four approaching cavalry troops. Big Foot promptly ordered a white flag be flown above the wagon he was traveling in. When the U.S. regiments reached the Indians, Big Foot left the comfort and warmth of his wagon sickbed to greet Major Samuel Whitside of the elite Seventh Cavalry. The major announced that he had orders to remove the chief to a cavalry camp on Wounded Knee Creek. Big Foot, blood dripping from his nose, replied that he was headed in that direction, because he was taking his people to Pine Ridge. The major arranged for Big Foot to travel in the Army ambulance, which was warmer and offered a smoother ride, and then told his half-breed scout to disarm the remaining Indians. John Shangreau, the scout, convinced the major to wait until they reached camp to take away the Indians's horses and arms. He explained that demanding these things from them now would only compel the Indians to fight. If that happened, the women and children would all be killed, and the men would get away. Whitside conceded, and once Big Foot was situated in the ambulance, formed a column for the trek to Wounded Knee Creek. Two

After the Wounded Knee Massacre of 1890, U.S. Army troops dumped the bodies of the fallen Sioux in a mass grave. © *Bettmann/Corbis*

cavalry troops led, followed by the wagons, the ambulance, and a compact group of Minneconjous. The other two cavalry troops and two Hotchkiss guns brought up the rear.

Arriving at Wounded Knee Creek The column reached Chankpe Opi Wakpala, or Wounded Knee, at twilight. The frozen, silent landscape served as a somber background to their arrival. The soldiers were ordered to take a careful count of the Indians and tallied 120 men and 230 women and children. Major Whitside was still anxious to disarm the Indians but decided to wait until the light of morning to do so. Tents were erected near the military camp, and rations were distributed among the hungry travelers. A stove was placed in Big Foot's tent, and a surgeon was summoned to examine the ailing chief. To discourage the Indian hostages from fleeing in the night, Whitside ordered his men to post the two Hotchkiss guns on the rises surrounding the encampment. The barrels of the rifled guns were pointed toward the Indian tents.

Later that night, Colonel James W. Forsyth, now commanding General George A. Custer's men, arrived with the rest of the Seventh Regiment. He took charge of operations at Wounded Knee, informing Whitside that he had received orders to take Big Foot's band to the Union Pacific Railroad. The Indians were to be shipped to a military prison in Omaha, Nebraska. Before settling in for a night of whiskey drinking—to celebrate Big Foot's capture—Forsyth and his officers placed two more Hotchkiss guns on the slope above the Indian encampment.

Despite their protective Ghost Shirts and their belief in the promises of the Ghost Dance, Big Foot's people were afraid of the soldiers that surrounded them. The Indians had killed many white military leaders fourteen years earlier at the Battle of Little Bighorn and feared that Whitside, Forsyth, and the Seventh Cavalry might still harbor vengeful feelings for them.

The Massacre Early the next morning, a bugle call woke the Indians, who were soon surrounded by mounted soldiers. The soldiers instructed the Indian men to meet in the center of the horses for a talk. After the talk, they said, they were to move on to the military headquarters at Pine Ridge. Big Foot was brought from his tent, and the older men gathered around him. After the Indians had received their breakfast rations, Colonel Forsyth, unconvinced that the Indians had handed over all their weapons, began searching the teepees and tents. Axes, knives, and tent stakes were added to the pile of guns, but the soldiers were still not satisfied. They ordered the warriors to submit to body searches. Although this angered every one of them greatly, only two Indians overtly protested. Yellow Bird, a medicine man, began chanting a holy song and dancing a few Ghost Dance steps, attempting to assure his fellow warriors that the soldiers' bullets would not hurt them. The second, a young Minneconjou named Black Coyote, rebelled when the soldiers attempted to take his Winchester rifle from him. He did not want to give up the rifle because it was expensive and it belonged to him, he said. As the soldiers grabbed him and spun him around, attempting to wrench the rifle from his hands, a shot rang out, followed closely by a large crash. No one knows who fired the first shot, but because the atmosphere was so tense, the lone, mysterious report led to a barrage of gunfire and indiscriminate killing.

Big Foot was among the first to fall dying into the snow. The first few seconds of fighting filled the air with powder smoke and the deafening sounds of firing carbines. Those Indians that had them fought with knives, clubs, and pistols at close range. The unarmed could do nothing but flee. The Hotchkiss guns tore the Indian camp to shreds, killing the men, women, and children who were attempting to escape. When the slaughter came to an end, Big Foot and more than half his people were dead or seriously wounded. Although 153 were counted dead, many of the uncounted wounded crawled away to die. The closest estimate reveals that of the original 350 men, women, and children, 300 lost their lives at Wounded Knee.

✪ The Home Front

American Industrial Revolution

The Industrial Revolution is widely regarded as one of the most crucial changes in human history. The Industrial Revolution (1790–1860) began in the early eighteenth century in England before spreading across Europe and Asia. Because it impacted nearly every facet of society, including economics, philosophy, politics, and culture, it quickly reached the Americas and the rest of the world. In America, the Industrial Revolution in the early decades of the nineteenth century exploited the country's rich store of natural resources, land, and immigrant labor. In a few short decades, the tremendous surge in technological and economic growth brought

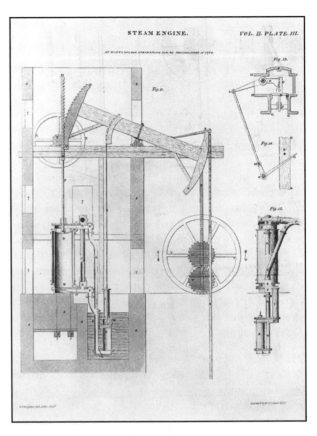

James Watt's invention of the steam engine, depicted here, paved the way for changes brought about by the Industrial Revolution. *The Library of Congress*

about by the Industrial Revolution changed American life forever.

In the Beginning The Industrial Revolution was the shift from home and hand production to machine and factory production of goods. Replacing skilled workers with machines allowed goods to be produced faster and cheaper. The shift from home to factory production changed predominantly agricultural societies into ones controlled by manufacturing and industry. As in England, textiles were the first manufactured product in the United States to be improved by a mechanical invention. Samuel Slater (1768–1835), considered by some to be the father of the American Industrial Revolution, secretly immigrated to this country from England in 1789. Believing that the textile industry had reached its apex in Britain, he took what he knew about textile machine production and opened the first American spinning mill in Pawtucket, Rhode Island, in 1790. Unlike others with textile manufacturing experience who had come to the United States before him, Slater knew how to build and operate the machines he would need in his water-powered mill. He also had a winning organizational system, a business component that would later prove to be as important to manufacturing as the machines that made production possible.

Once Slater established his mill, new inventions and production methods began to proliferate. In 1791, John Fitch received a patent for his steamboat design. In 1794, Eli Whitney (1765–1825) patented his cotton gin, which revolutionized the cotton industry and reinvigorated the slave trade in the American South. Five years later, Whitney invented the American system of manufacturing. His system used partially skilled labor, machine tools, and jigs to standardize interchangeable parts to be configured using an assembly line method. He later used the system to manufacture ten thousand muskets for the government. But it was not until the mid-1850s that the American Industrial Revolution began to permeate through all of society by means of the development of the railroad. Just as innovations in industry changed the country from an agrarian society into a mechanized one, the railroad system transformed more than just the actual American landscape. It transformed America.

How the Railroad Changed America

In 1815, John Stevens (1749–1838) received the first railroad charter in North America. Considered the father of American railroads, Stevens was instrumental in building the first operational railway systems on which steam locomotives would run. In 1830, the first American-built steam locomotive was operated on a common-carrier railroad. After that, railroads began transporting freight back and forth between the Great Lakes and the East Coast, paving the way for a growing network of rail lines that spanned relatively short distances. The preponderance of rail lines helped businessmen become rich, and they began dreaming of a railroad that would stretch from coast to coast. The opening of the country's western territories brought with it stories of the vast expanses of land, rich in minerals, to be found west of the Mississippi and these businessmen wanted a piece of it.

In 1863, construction began on the United States's first transcontinental railroad. Despite the Civil War, the challenges of the relatively unexplored western geography, and treacherous weather, the railroad was completed on May 10, 1869. Americans celebrated this profound achievement as a giant step forward in the country's westward expansion, but its impact on America's economic future turned out to be an added bonus. Many of country's greatest fortunes were made by the men who helped build and later control the transcontinental railroad. The ability to transport both goods and passengers to the West created and sustained tremendous growth and allowed new settlements and businesses to prosper. Capitalism and industrialization converged on the railroad system, which helped the American economy move to the forefront of world commerce.

City Life

As the Industrial Revolution developed, farmers found themselves in a precarious financial situation. New scientific cultivation methods and increased mechanization produced record crop yields, which caused prices to drop. As production costs increased and farmers's earnings plummeted, many found themselves in debt. When the Midwest and the East experienced the worst agricultural depression in the country's history in the 1870s and 1880s, farmers began looking to the citiess' urban centers for relief. Jobs with good wages, electricity, and wonders like the telephone persuaded agrarians to trade the countryside for city life. Joining the farmers were increasing numbers of immigrants from eastern and southern Europe. Upon arrival, both found hastily built cities rife with poverty, disease, and crime. Housing for most factory workers was usually in tenement buildings that quickly declined into slums. Living conditions were deplorable, and the slums were breeding grounds for typhoid, smallpox, cholera, tuberculosis, and other diseases that thrived in unsanitary environments. Layoffs were common, so much of the labor market was out of work at any given time, which contributed to an overall sense of uncertainty. Worst of all, child labor was rampant. In 1900, as many as three million American children worked full-time to help support their families.

The Legacy of the American Industrial Revolution

In the 1880s and 1890s, the social classes were divided by an extreme gap. The novel *The Gilded Age*, published in 1873 and written by Mark Twain and Charles Dudley Warner, criticizes the politics and rampant corruption that allowed some Americans to become incredibly rich while others were left in extreme poverty. The novel's title would later become synonymous with the age that saw the lower classes in cities such as Chicago and New York suffering in slums while the elite built lavish mansions beside them and enjoyed the fruits of industrialization. Farms and manufacturing plants produced an abundance of goods, especially products of convenience such as clothing and processed foods, which gave rise to a consumer culture that had not previously existed. Finally, revolutions in technology, urbanization, and transportation meant that Americans had the time and money to spend on leisure activities. Entertainment industries thrived as people from all classes became spectators and participants in organized sports, vaudeville shows, circuses, and theater of all kinds. The character of American life quickly changed in the last decades of the nineteenth century. Icons of popular culture, including the camera, the telephone, and the typewriter, proliferated and in some ways contributed to the America of the modern age.

Political Scandals

Despite a few notable successes, Ulysses S. Grant's two administrations, lasting from 1869 to 1877, were marked by massive corruption and indecisive leadership. The westward expansion that occurred during his presidency offered countless tempting opportunities for financial gain—both legal and illegal—and businessmen and government officials stood to gain the most. Vast resources like land, forests, oil, gas, iron, and gold were suddenly available to individuals and government entities whose discretionary powers had yet to be defined. Zoning changes, franchises, tax rulings, property assessments, operating permits, and the like became lucrative government favors awarded to the business firms most willing to resort to sordid methods. Once exposed, these methods became widely publicized political scandals. The "Gilded Age,"—so-called for its rampant corruption and profiteering—saw political scandals occurring mostly in urban centers where the Industrial Revolution had its greatest impact. Beginning in the 1860s with the Credit Mobilier scandal and the impeachment of Grant's secretary of war, William Belknap, corruption was a fact of life during the expansion of the United States.

Black Friday The earliest scandal in the first Grant administration involved the gold market. James "Diamond Jim" Fisk (1834–1872) and Jay Gould (1836–1892), two of the most notorious Wall Street speculators, came up with a scheme to buy up all the available gold and force the price to go up. Before the false rise in gold prices collapsed, Fisk and Gould planned to sell their gold to fellow speculators and walk away with a nice profit. Of course, they needed access to government information, which came in the form of Grant's sister Virginia. Virginia Grant's husband, Abel R. Corbin (1808–1881), was a New York financier with obvious ties to the White House and an acquaintance of Gould's. When Fisk and Gould learned through Corbin that Grant was planning on decreasing government sales of gold, the speculators began buying up all the gold they could. When Grant received a letter from Corbin asking him to disallow gold sales in the fall, the president began to suspect that his brother-in-law was speculating in the gold market. He had Virginia ask Corbin to cease speculating in a letter Corbin received on September 23, 1869. That was when Corbin, Fisk, and Gould realized their plan was about to come undone. Grant instructed his secretary of the treasury the next day to sell $5 million in gold, which ruined Fisk's and Gould's attempt to corner the market. On Friday, September 24, 1869, the value of gold fell drastically, wiping out speculators and causing many businesses and banks to fail. Since then, the date has been referred to as "Black Friday."

The Credit Mobilier Scandal The biggest political scandal of the mid-nineteenth century happened during the construction of the transcontinental railroad. The United States government was far more enthusiastic about a railroad running through the Rocky Mountains than investors were. The incredible risk inherent to the project forced Congress to make the deal as attractive as possible, so it gave the Union Pacific, one of two companies chartered to construct the railway, huge land grants, mineral rights to the land, and huge subsidies for construction. This assured investors that what had previously appeared quite risky was now a seemingly safe investment. But the controllers of Union Pacific were still wary about the profitability of actually running the railroad. In the beginning, Union Pacific Vice President Thomas Durant (1820–1885)believed the real money would be made in constructing the railroad, not operating it. So Durant and his fellow investors came up with what they believed was a foolproof plan. Instead of paying outside contractors to build the railroad, top Union Pacific stockholders would simply pay themselves. They did this by taking over the Credit Mobilier, a construction company that won a contract to build 667 miles of Union Pacific railroad. The company charged Union Pacific tens of millions of dollars more than the actual cost of construction, which went straight into the pockets of the men running Union Pacific and the politicians who had been either sold or given shares in the construction. By the time they were finished, the profiteers had made at least $23 million—probably much more than that in actuality—and bankrupted Union Pacific. Those who had invested in the railroad but not the construction company were left with almost worthless securities. *The New York Sun* broke the story of the scandal on the eve of the 1872 election. Speaker of the House James G. Blaine (1830–1893), a Republican from Maine, was implicated along with Grant's outgoing vice president, Schuyler Colfax, incoming vice president Henry Wilson (1812–1875), and congressmen Oakes Ames of Massachusetts and James Brooks (1810–1873) of New York. The 1872–1873 scandal was the biggest of the Gilded Age scandals. Despite the corruption behind the scenes, the railroad went on to transform the United States economy.

The Whiskey Ring Scandal The Whiskey Ring Scandal, exposed in 1875, was one of the longest running and most complicated of the nineteenth century political scandals. It involved a diversion of tax revenues in a conspiracy among politicians, government agents, distillers, and distributors. This system of fraud began in St. Louis and over time spread to Chicago, Milwaukee, and Cincinnati. Whiskey had been taxed since the late eighteenth century, but certain politicians saw an opportunity to profit by having revenue officers raise a sort of campaign fund among the distillers. These revenuers diverted the tax paid to the U.S. government to storekeepers, collectors, and political officials according to a fixed schedule of payouts. Newspapers and higher officials were bribed to keep quiet until the ring assumed national proportions. On May 10, 1875, the Treasury seized countless distilleries for failure to pay adequate taxes, arrested dozens of Treasury agents, and confiscated boxes of incriminating documentation. One of the highest ranking politicians involved in the fraud was Orville Babcock (1835–1884), personal secretary to President Grant. Grant was so sure of Babcock's innocence that he wrote a sworn deposition that was read at Babcock's trial. Despite overwhelming evidence against him, Babcock was saved from conviction. He did not return to the White House, though. Instead, Grant appointed him chief inspector of lighthouses.

The Collapse of Reconstruction

The Reconstruction of the South after the Civil War, though daunting, held the promise of real freedom for blacks across the country. Unfortunately, the passage of the Fourteenth Amendment in 1867, which defined American citizenship for the first time, did not guarantee that freedom. Though strides were made, Reconstruction inspired expressions of social and political backlash, including the rise of white supremacist organizations like the Ku Klux Klan and the Supreme Court decision to uphold the racist "separate-but-equal" philosophy behind *Plessy v. Ferguson.*

The War Ends The Civil War officially ended on April 9, 1865, when Union General Ulysses S. Grant accepted the surrender of Confederate General Robert E. Lee (1807–1870) at Appomattox Court House, Virginia. Lee's surrender marked the end of four years of the deadliest fighting in U.S. history—fighting that killed 620,000 men and brought economic devastation to the South. While Southern whites mourned their losses, blacks all over the country celebrated their victory. They believed that, finally, whites would recognize them as equal citizens. For the first time, former slaves were able to leave their masters, legalize their marriages, and shed their outwardly submissive behavior. But the process of Reconstruction was arduous and complicated, and former slaves found life after the war less rewarding than they had hoped. They soon discovered that whites cared more about their inalienable right to property than they did about black equality. President Lincoln's "10 percent plan" outlined the terms of readmitting the rebel states into the Union, but beyond announcing that former slaves could not be returned to bondage and calling for southerners to take an oath of loyalty and accept the abolition of slavery, he said little regarding former slaves. Had Lincoln the chance, he might have elaborated on a plan for integrating newly freed slaves into the Union. Unfortunately, John Wilkes Booth (1838–1865) extinguished that possibility when he fatally shot the president just five days after Lee's surrender.

Reconstruction Realities Radical Republicans unhappy with what they saw as moderate Reconstruction policies pushed for a complete Reconstruction of southern society, even before Lincoln's death. In early 1865, northerners such as Thaddeus Stevens and Charles Sumner led the congressional adoption of the Thirteenth Amend-

JIM CROW LAW.

UPHELD BY THE UNITED STATES SUPREME COURT.

Statute Within the Competency of the Louisiana Legislature and Railroads—Must Furnish Separate Cars for Whites and Blacks.

Washington, May 18.—The Supreme Court today in an opinion read by Justice Brown, sustained the constitutionality of the law in Louisiana requiring the railroads of that State to provide separate cars for white and colored passengers. There was no interstate, commerce feature in the case for the railroad upon which the incident occurred giving rise to case—Plessey vs. Ferguson—East Louisiana railroad, was and is operated wholly within the State, to the laws of Congress of many of the States. The opinion states that by the analogy of the laws of Congress, and of many of states requiring establishment of separate schools for children of two races and other similar laws, the statute in question was within competency of Louisiana Legislature, exercising the police power of the State. The judgment of the Supreme Court of State upholding law was therefore upheld.

Mr. Justice Harlan announced a very vigorous dissent saying that he saw nothing but mischief in all such laws. In his view of the case, no power in the land had right to regulate the enjoyment of civil rights upon the basis of race. It would be just as reasonable and proper, he said, for states to pass laws requiring separate cars to be furnished for Catholic and Protestants, or for descendants of those of Teutonic race and those of Latin race.

This newspaper article announces the verdict of the 1896 *Plessy v. Ferguson* case, in which Judge John Howard Ferguson ruled against Homer Plessy. *The Granger Collection, New York. Reproduced by Permission*

ment to the Constitution, which abolished slavery throughout the United States. In March of that year, Congress established the Freedmen's Bureau, an agency that helped establish schools, legalize marriages of former slaves, negotiate labor contracts for freed people, and distribute food to millions of white and black citizens. But by December of that year, southern states had already established laws that, while recognizing the abolition of slavery, prohibited blacks from voting, holding public office, assembling freely, or bearing arms. Most offensive were the vagrancy laws that held that blacks caught "strolling about in idleness" could be arrested and contracted out to planters. The First Reconstruction Act of 1867 countered the southerners's attempts to strip blacks of their right to equal citizenship. It initiated an unprecedented era of biracial democracy and allowed black men the right to vote, hold office, serve as jurors, and become police officers. Most importantly, many southern states, for the first time, provided state-funded public education to blacks. By 1877, more than six hundred thousand black children had enrolled in public schools.

While the federal government worked to protect black rights, white supremacist organizations rose up in an effort to reassert white dominance and racial superiority by terrorizing black southerners and their supporters. The Mississippi Plan emerged as a model to overthrow the Republican government, and through the use of violence and systematic repression, Democrats regained control of the state in 1875. Encouraged by President Grant's refusal to protect Republican voters, other southern states began instituting their own "Mississippi Plans." In less than twenty years, every southern state had followed suit and caused the near cessation of black voting.

By 1877, the period of Radical Reconstruction led by the Republicans had come to a close. "Jim Crow" laws legalizing racial segregation in every arena, including education, public facilities, and religion, became the norm. In 1896, the U.S. Supreme Court, in the case of *Plessy v. Ferguson*, decided that the concept behind "separate-but-equal" was valid and constitutional. By now, blacks were politically powerless and economically dependent. Those who achieved some measure of success were vulnerable to the wrath of racist whites who were determined to "keep blacks in their place." They did so with increasing physical violence, lynching thousands of blacks between 1889 and 1941. The dream of Reconstruction had become a nightmare.

Plessy v. Ferguson   In 1896, the U.S. Supreme Court established the constitutionality and validity of separate-but-equal accommodations for blacks and whites in its *Plessy v. Ferguson* decision. Essentially, the decision validated Jim Crow. Despite its significance, the decision was met with apathy at the time, was ignored by the press, and was relegated to a footnote by Supreme Court historians of the early and mid-twentieth century. The case was the second of two test cases planned to challenge the consti-

JIM CROW

The phrase "Jim Crow" has become shorthand for both the overt and subtle effects of racial segregation. Based on a slave character played by white minstrel performer Thomas "Daddy" Rice, the phrase "Jim Crow" was first popularized in 1828. To play Jim, a slave owned by a Mr. Crow, Rice blackened his face with burnt cork and wore a ragged costume. Mocking African Americans, he shuffled, danced, and sang a song called "Jump Jim Crow." His blackface minstrel show and the song became so popular that both quickly became part of American popular culture. Jim Crow later became synonymous with "separate-but-equal" racial designations given to such public places as schools, churches, residential areas, and cemeteries, as well as drinking fountains, restrooms, and restaurants. These designations signified whites's control over almost every aspect of public life and the belief that African Americans deserved the inferior and inadequate facilities they were forced to use.

Although the phrase alluded to the legal aspects of segregation, it also referred to symbolic patterns of behavior that framed black and white social relations. For example, blacks were naturally supposed to defer to whites, but never the other way around. Whether Jim Crow was manifested in signs or symbols, customs or laws, it affected the lives of every African American, regardless of class or gender. Jim Crow nurtured discriminatory practices, validated racism, and helped shape biased racial stereotypes. Rejection of these deeply entrenched racist beliefs and doctrines would soon inspire the Civil Rights Movement and the banning of racial segregation.

tutionality of an 1890 Louisiana state segregation statute. The events of the case began on June 7, 1892, when Homer Plessy (1863–1925) boarded the all-white car on a New Orleans train bound for Covington. After he was arrested and charged with violating Louisiana law, lead counsel Albion Tourgee, a white proponent of racial equality, appealed the state court conviction to the U.S. Supreme Court. *Plessy v. Ferguson* challenged the statute under the Fourteenth Amendment's equal protection, due process, and privileges and immunities clauses. It also argued that the segregation law constituted a badge of slavery, which violated the Thirteenth Amendment prohibition against slavery. The Court found a legitimate distinction between legal equality and socially acceptable segregation. This ruling continued to justify the doctrine of segregation in subsequent years. The one dissenting opinion was written by Justice John Marshall Harlan (1833–1911), who argued that the Louisiana statute violated the personal liberty of every citizen.

⭐ International Context

Decline of the Ottoman Empire

At its zenith in the seventeenth century, the vast political and geographic Ottoman Empire sprawled across southeastern Europe, southwestern Asia, and northern Africa. The empire came into being at the beginning of the fourteenth century and died out six hundred years later. Over the centuries, it was considered one of the world's most powerful and influential Muslim civilizations. While their military and cultural might allowed the Muslim Turks to rule several continents at one time, the Ottoman sultanate leadership and outdated economic structure were blamed for bringing about the empire's eventual downfall.

The Beginning of the End The sultanate began to weaken in the last decade of Sultan Suleyman's (1494–1566) reign. Known widely as "Suleyman the Magnificent," because of the many valuable improvements he made to the empire, the sultan accomplished much during his forty-six-year reign. He transformed the Ottoman judicial system and army, doubled his territory, and turned Istanbul, the heart of the empire, into a premier city featuring treasured buildings, aqueducts, and theological schools. Europe was unable to capitalize on the weakening sultanate because it was tied up in religious wars until the end of the seventeenth century. At that time, the Ottomans began negotiating treaties. The 1699 Treaty of Karlowitz, for example, handed over Austria and Poland to Christian Europe.

Despite such moves, Europe still respected Ottoman military might. For example, when Tsar Peter I sent troops into Ottoman Asia in 1696, he was able to successfully occupy the Sea of Azov and the Crimean rim. In 1711, though, the Ottomans restored the occupied lands to the empire and claimed the Black Sea for themselves. Russia continued to fight the empire for the Black Sea for another several decades until the Ottomans finally relinquished it with a treaty in 1792. Thus began an accelerated push for European expansion into the Ottoman Empire. When European countries formed what seemed to be a united front against the Turkish government, the Ottomans began to fear the worst.

European Powers Strengthen In 1818, the Concert of Europe, the self-styled coalition of Austria, Great Britain, Prussia, and Russia, admitted France to its ranks. The Bourbon monarchy was persuaded to join forces with Great Britain to form the Concert's primary maritime power. Between 1818 and 1914, the great powers resorted to war among themselves just once. In that instance, Great Britain, France, and Russia fought each other in the Crimean War between 1854 and 1856. Austria served as mediator, while Prussia remained neutral. Britain and France counted the Kingdom of Sardinia as an ally against Russia.

After the Crimean War, Russia revisited its obsession with the Black Sea and began taking over the property that surrounded it, both in Europe and in Asia. In 1856, Sultan Abdulmecit reinforced the Reform Edict, or Islabat Fermani, and briefly interrupted this Russian practice. At the same time, French investors, despite Britains's vehement opposition, created the Suez Canal Company. In 1869, the waterway was completed, and by 1914, Algeria and Tunisia had become part of France's empire. In a further step, France bankrolled Syrian, Lebanese, and Palestinian railways as well as harbors and became the dominant shareholder in the Ottoman Empire's official agent, the Ottoman Imperial Bank. The now Europeans effectively controlled the Ottoman Empire.

The Balkan Rebellion In the waning years of the Ottoman Empire, Russia reigned as its greatest enemy. Of all the key territories expansionist Russia desired, Istanbul, or Constantinople, was the jewel in the crown. If they could seize that city, they would control the Black Sea trade route between Europe and Asia. Because of the many defeats and stalemates in wars against Russia, the Ottomans had low morale. The once-confident military state that easily protected the Islamic world from European conquest was quickly crumbling.

In 1875, the Slavic peoples living in the Ottoman provinces of Bosnia and Herzegovina took advantage of the empire's weakness and led an uprising against it. Montenegro and Serbia, two neighboring Slavic states, joined the rebellion next, followed by Bulgaria a year later. The revolt was part of a larger political movement. The Pan-Slavic Movement sought to unify all Slavic peoples controlled by the Ottoman Empire, Austria, and Germany, and live as independent nations protected by Russia. Because Russia was eager to conquer the Ottomans and take Istanbul, it became an ally of the rebels and declared war on the empire. By 1878, the Ottomans had to admit defeat. They signed a peace treaty that released all the Balkan provinces—including Bosnia, Herzegovina, and Bulgaria—from Ottoman rule and were forced to hand over vast tracts of Ottoman territory to Russia.

The Balkan Wars The Ottoman Empire was dragged into further European land grabs in the latter half of the nineteenth century. By 1911, there was Italian and French competition for Ottoman-ruled Libya. The weakened empire was beaten and was forced to sign a peace treaty with Italy granting it Libya and the Dodecanese Islands. That Ottoman defeat inspired Greece, Serbia, Bulgaria, and Montenegro to fight the Ottomans for ownership of the provinces north of Greece, Thrace, and the southern European coast of the Black Sea. Their victory drove the Ottomans to the edge of Europe. Down, but not out, the Ottomans joined forces with

Students demanding German unification burn books at an October 18, 1817, Wartburg festival.   *The Granger Collection, New York. Reproduced by permission*

Greece, Serbia, and Montenegro in the Second Balkan War to roll back Bulgarian territorial gains. The battle resulted in the last military victory in Ottoman history.

By 1919, all that was left of the Ottoman Empire was Turkey, which extended from the southern European coast of the Black Sea west to Asia Minor, east to Iran, and south to Syria and Iraq. Three years later, the Ottoman Empire came to its official end when Turkey was declared a republic. Liberal nationalists, or "Young Turks," as they were called, staged an open revolt against the Ottomans in the early 1920s and brought the Ottoman Empire to its eventual conclusion. Their goal was to westernize and modernize Turkey, which they did.

Risorgimento

Risorgimento ("The Resurgence" in Italian), the name given the nineteenth century Italian unification movement, was a time of great cultural nationalism and political activism. Its roots go back to eighteenth century Italian cultural leaders such as Roman Catholic priest and Italian historian Ludovico Antonio Muratori (1672–1750), Italian tragic poet and dramatist Vittorio Alfieri (1749–1803), and economist and philosopher Antonio Genovesi (1712–

1769). Giuseppe Mazzini (1805–1872), inspired by the fervor of those cultural giants—Alfieri was a self-proclaimed prophet who used his gifts to revive the national spirit of Italy, while Genovesi was the first philospher to write in Italian instead of Latin—formed the secret society Giovine Italia, or Young Italy, and became a leading force behind unification. Mazzini's radical program was anticlerical and republican and only vaguely hinted at economic and social reforms. The more moderate and successful unification advocate was Victor Emmanuel II (1820–1878), the king of Sardinia. The king, due to his shrewd collaboration with Count Camillo di Cavour and Cavour's program of liberal reforms, became the central figure and symbol of Risorgimento and the first ruler of unified Italy. The fight for unification gathered momentum in 1831, the year Mazzini attempted to spark a war of liberation, and ended in 1870 when the Franco-Prussian war led to the withdrawal of French forces from Rome.

Early Nineteenth-Century Italy   The Italian peninsula was divided into eleven states by the late eighteenth century. France, after conquering the majority of the region in the 1790s, controlled most of these states until 1814. At that time, Viennese peacemakers, anxious to suppress revolutionary movements and future French domination, worked to ensure that Austria ruled the peninsula. The country directly controlled Lombardy and Venetia, while the ruling house of Europe, the Hapsburg monarchy, was chosen as the sovereign ruler of most of the other Italian states. By 1815, the idea of Italian unification was hardly considered. Local loyalties and hostile regional antagonisms so prominent in 1815 were momentarily forgotten during the revolutions of 1820 and 1821. Secret societies served to unite people who had grievances against the Austrian monarchies, but they were unsuccessful. Society members could not agree on either the means or the ends they hoped to achieve.

Mazzini and Young Italy

Giuseppe Mazzini started Young Italy, a secret society dedicated to making Italy a free, independent, republican nation, in 1831. He had little faith in the peasantry, so he focused his attention on urban artisans and the educated middle class, groups of people whom he believed were more interested in inciting a war against Austria. Had he been working for land reform, he might have sought to secure the support of the rural masses. His efforts to inspire a war of national liberation failed, and he was forced to disband Young Italy in 1836. Although his movement proved too idealistic, it did put the idea of unification on the political agenda. More importantly, the idea of an independent Italy captured the imagination of historians, writers, and composers who brought Italy's glorious past back to life in their operas, books, and poems.

The Revolutions of 1848 and 1849

Growing national awareness and poor harvests in 1846 and 1847 inspired a revolution in Paris in February 1848 and another revolution in Vienna in March of the same year. Despite rising nationalism, local grievances brought about these rebellions. Pope Pius IX (1792–1878), in fact, disassociated himself from the war against Austria and demanded that Italians remain loyal to their rulers. When Mazzini became the head of a Roman Republic, Pius fled to Naples and appealed to France, Austria, and Spain for assistance. Despite his valiant efforts, Italian patriot and military leader Giuseppe Garibaldi (1807–1882) could not defeat the decisive campaign of twenty thousand French troops that stormed the state. Rome fell on July 16, 1849. Afterward, the Pope returned and set up a reactionary government. From this point on, the Catholic Church served as a major obstacle on the road to Italian unification.

By now, the hopes of liberals and nationalists had been dashed. Revolutionary groups failed to cooperate effectively, Austrian military strength proved too overwhelming, and peasant masses that might have helped in the revolutions had been ignored. A new agenda was sorely needed.

The Fight for Unification

Popular in Sardinia for his respect for the constitution and liberal reforms, King Victor Emmanuel II devoted himself to the task of unifying Italy. In 1852, Emmanuel named Count Camillo di Cavour (1810–1861) as the prime minister of Piedmont. The two, despite Cavour's loyalty to the Piedmontese monarchy, would join forces to become the leaders of Risorgimento. In a July 1858 meeting, Cavour struck a deal with Napoleon III (1808–1873). Their combined efforts to oust the Austrians from Piedmont and share the spoils provoked the first war of unification. After several reorganizations of power and the installment of provisional governments in several regions, nationalists in central Italy picked up the fight.

Garibaldi, having abandoned his republican ideals, became a guerrilla leader in the fight for unification. Emmanuel supported Garibaldi, but Cavour made it clear that he did not. More importantly, the masses adored Garibaldi, and his troops were devoted to him. Unlike the wily Cavour, Garibaldi acted rather than thought. In May 1860, the military leader and 1,089 red-shirted volunteers sailed for Sicily. Upon arrival, Garibaldi won the support of Sicilian peasants by promising them land reform and tax reduction in exchange for their support. His plan led to success and he appointed himself dictator of Sicily. On September 7, after dodging a political attempt by Cavour to persuade Italians to credit Emmanuel for the takeover of Sicily instead, Garibaldi arrived in Naples and received a hero's welcome. By 1861, Garibaldi and his army of fifty thousand troops had secured every state in the peninsula. Instead of fighting Emmanuel's forces in Naples, Garibaldi handed over his conquests and saluted Emmanuel as the first king of Italy.

It would take another nine years to complete Italian unification. The rivalry between northern and southern states proved to be a major problem. Southerners found it difficult to distinguish unification from Piedmontese colonization. The Pope's hostility toward the new state was another obstacle. Garibaldi and his determination to bring Rome and Venice into the fold only added further difficulties. It took the Franco-Prussian war of 1870 to bring Risorgimento to its eventual conclusion. After French forces were forced from Rome, Italian troops occupied the city. Pope Pius IX refused to negotiate, but the Romans, in October 1870, voted overwhelmingly for unification and became the new country's capital.

Sino-Japanese War

The Sino-Japanese War of 1894–1895 was the culmination of two important nineteenth century East Asian events: the decline of China's Ch'ing Dynasty and

Japanese army passing the Triumphal Arch erected near Seoul, Korea after the victory at Asan, during the Sino-Japanese War.   *Vaughan/ Hulton Archive/Getty Images*

Japan's expanding military. The historic rivalry between China and Japan for control of Korea may have sparked the war, but larger, more complex developments in international politics provided the fuel.

The Origins of War   Japan had long sought to gain military control over the Korean peninsula due to its proximity to Japan. Finally, in 1875, Japanese designs on Korea exploded into a naval confrontation. Japan threatened to use force if Korea did not open relations with Japanese diplomats and merchants. This offended China because it saw Korea as a tributary state. Japan went one step further the following year and referred to Korea as an independent nation. Internal Korean conflicts resulted between conservatives who favored the Chinese and progressives who looked up to Japan as a model of modernization. Tensions between the two groups led to an anti-Japanese revolt in Seoul. When the Korean ruling family called for and received Chinese military assistance, Japan sent a force of fifteen hundred troops to occupy the Korean capital. Unprepared to fight China, Japan negotiated for the withdrawal of the forces of both countries. The 1858 Treaty of Tianjin, signed by Chinese and Japanese representatives, had declared that each power must notify the other if it intended to send military troops into Korea.

Korea continued to destabilize over the next nine years. During that time, Japan stepped up military preparations for war. Since the 1875 commercial invasion, Japanese merchants had glutted the Korean market with manufactured imports and rice. This led to an increase in anti-Japanese feeling as Koreans became more convinced that Japan was behind their growing economic problems. The Tong Hak Society, a decidedly anti-Japanese conservative religious group, promised peasants that if they opposed the government, the Japanese economic stronghold would end. This led to the Tong Hak peasant uprisings of 1894, the year the war started. When the southern Korean provinces exploded in riots, the government was again forced to call upon the Chinese military for assistance. China, according to the provisions of the Tianjin treaty, immediately notified Japan.

War Begins   Japan, confident in its military might this time, saw the anti-Japanese uprisings as an excuse for war. Although the riots had been suppressed by the time they got there, Japan sent five thousand troops to Seoul with orders to occupy the city. That provocation was further intensified when Japan ignored another provision of the Tianjin treaty. Instead of withdrawing immediately, as the treaty demanded, Japan stormed the Seoul palace and deposed the pro-Chinese Korean government. Effective immediately, all treaties were cancelled. The newly installed puppet government ordered all Chinese forces from the Korean peninsula. China responded by posting eight thousand troops along the Yalu River and called for another eight thousand from the Manchurian province. The war that had been avoided in 1858 had become a reality.

War was officially declared on August 1, 1894, but the first shots were fired almost a week earlier. On July 25, Japanese soldiers attacked a Chinese force at Asan, forty miles south of Seoul. The Chinese were defeated four days later at Songhwan, retreated to the north to Pyong-Yang, and waited for reinforcements. During this time, Japanese forces scored a major victory when they sunk a Chinese transport ship carrying the reinforcements bound for Asan. One thousand Chinese troops drowned in the attack. Within days, Japanese troops had gained control of the whole of southern Korea.

By September 15, more troops had swarmed the peninsula. Three Japanese columns bound for Pyong-Yang captured the city after fierce fighting. Meanwhile, Chinese forces along the Yalu were being reinforced by sea. A day after the Battle of Pyong-Yang, the Chinese fleet suffered a major defeat at Hai-Yang-Tao in what has become known as the Battle of the Yellow Sea. Survivors fled to Wei-hai-wei, where they were ultimately defeated in February 1895. This was not the decisive battle of the war, though. That occurred at Port Arthur, where the Second Japanese Army defeated a heavily fortified Chinese stronghold. This Chinese defeat occurred within a few days of the initial attack on November 21, 1894. The defeat convinced China to seek peace, but Japan rejected the initial offer. They hoped to better their position with future victories. A peace conference was forestalled until March 1895, resulting in the Treaty of Shimonoseki, which officially ended the war on April 17, 1895.

The Spoils of War Japanese Premier Ito Hirobumi (1841–1909) and Foreign Minister Mutsu Munemitsu (1844–1897) saw China's hopeless situation as an advantage and intended to make the most of it during peace talks. Japanese forces had reduced the Chinese forces by inflicting enormous losses and were prepared to march on Peking. They had achieved all of their objectives during the Korean occupation. China, on the other hand, had nothing—that is, until a Japanese would-be assassin shot Chinese statesman Li Hong-Zhang (1823–1901) in the face during the peace conference. The attack sent shock waves around the world and caused Japan great embarrassment. Li hoped Western leaders would intervene in the conflict and discourage Japan from making harsh demands, but the treaty that was drawn up during the peace talks, the Treaty of Shimonoseki, was a blow to China. The April 17 treaty

demanded that China recognize Korea as an independent Japanese protectorate. Further, it called for China's ceding of Taiwan, the Liaotung Peninsula in southern Manchuria, and the Pescadores to Japan. China also had to allow Japanese fishing vessels along the Yangtze River. Finally, the country had to open four additional ports to Japanese vessels, pay an indemnity of 360 million yen, and allow Japanese manufacturing within its borders.

The Fallout of the Sino-Japanese War The crippling blows dealt to China equaled the soaring benefits handed to Japan as a result of the war and the Treaty of Shimonoseki. The Chinese government was forced to incur foreign debt in exchange for further western economic exploitation, while Japan used the money to expand its military and industrial holdings. Clearly, the Sino-Japanese War resulted in the firm establishment of Japan as the leading political, economic, and military leader of all of Asia. China, on the other hand, became a lesser power and faced further internal political upheavals. Despite its obvious victory, Japan faced international pressure resulting from the imperialist overtones of the Treaty of Shimonoseki. Russia, which had its own obvious designs on Korea and Manchuria, persuaded France and Germany to join in its protest of the ceding to Japan of the Liaotung Peninsula. The "Triple Intervention," as it was commonly called, humiliated Japan. Over the next fifty years, the humiliation served to fuel Japan's imperialist resolve.

German Unification

On January 18, 1871, modern Germany was born. Prior to unification, the country was divided into independent states that comprised the sovereign regions of Prussia, the North German Confederation, the Confederation of German States, and the South German states. The rise of liberalism and German nationalism prompted the move toward unification, which was finally achieved—after several attempts—under the leadership of the first Prussian minister-president, Otto von Bismarck (1815–1898). Using unconstitutional and military methods, Bismarck, known as the "Iron Chancellor" after declaring that unification would come about by "blood and iron," used the Austro-Prussian, or Seven Weeks's War, which excluded Austria from the North German Confederation, to pave the way toward Germany's eventual unification. Appointed minister-president of Prussia in 1862, Bismarck devoted his energy to unifying Germany and successfully accomplished his goal in just eight years.

The Franco-Prussian War With Austria excluded from the North German Confederation, Bismarck was able to institute a new constitution that organized a strong federal union of twenty-two North German states. This new North German Confederation was designed to eventually include South German states, Baden, Wurtenburg, Bavaria, and Hesse-Darmstadt. Because the southern states were cautious about guarding their sovereignty, and because their liberal parties vehemently opposed the authoritarian and military Prussian system, Bismarck knew they would only be driven to unification out of necessity. This leads historians to argue over whether Bismarck planned a war with France to drum up the German support he eventually received. Some believe that it was a premeditated strategy, while others contend that the leader never planned the war. Regardless, on July 19, 1870, France declared war after a perceived insult from King William I of Prussia (1787–1888) via Bismarck about the question of the German influence over succession to the Spanish throne.

Within a few days, just as Bismarck had hoped, Bavaria, Wurtenburg, Baten, and Hesse-Darmstadt had joined Prussia in its war against France. After three months of victories, the German states met in the Palace of Louis XIV at Versailles to discuss the future of Germany. Bavaria and Wurtenburg were reluctant to join the North German Confederation, but Baden and Hesse showed no resistance. The foreign ministers of Bavaria and Wurtenburg met with Bismarck in conferences throughout the war. They expressed their fear of losing sovereignty and showed clear signs of resisting unification. But then, on September 1, the Germans captured Napoleon and one hundred thousand of his men at the battle of Sedan. The demonstrated intensity of German nationalism persuaded Bavaria and Wurtenburg that unity was inevitable.

Diplomacy Begins From September 22 to September 26, 1870, Bismarck conferred with representatives of the dissenting southern states. The representatives had by now accepted the idea of eventual inclusion in a vast German empire and used the constitution of the North German Confederation as a basis for talks. After proposing many special privileges and exceptions to the document, they realized unification would be a more diplomatic than constitutional effort. From that point on, Bismarck led a campaign of diplomacy that was met with a mix of strong support and bitter opposition. The National Liberal Party organized a campaign of support in the South German states, while the Crown Prince Frederick William of Prussia (1831–1888) waged his own military campaigns in France. When Bismarck met with the two reluctant states in Versailles, he found them divided. By pitting the split states against one another, a situation Bismarck both relished and exploited, the minister-president was able to persuade Wurtenburg to settle. After isolating Bavaria for ten days, Bismarck secured the state's signature on a treaty on November 25.

The treaty granted Bavaria "special rights" that seemed significant but meant nothing in reality. The "reserved rights" granted by the treaty were more substantial. They allowed Wurtenburg to control its own postal and telegraph systems and gave both Wurtenburg and Bavaria a degree of military independence. Bismarck recognized how costly these concessions were but decided they were worth the price. They did not fundamentally alter the Constitution, and every state agreed to accept the provision that made King William German Emperor, even though the South German states vehemently opposed the notion. Bismarck was able to secure the provision by bribing its most outspoken opponent, the king of Bavaria, Ludwig II (1845–1886). Until 1892, the Bavarian king received an annual thirty thousand marks from a special fund. Extending his diplomatic efforts even further, Bismarck used the king of Bavaria as an assistant in an endeavor to shield William I from embarrassment. Instead of making him emperor by act of parliament, Bismarck wrote a letter to the Prussian monarch asking him to accept the title instead. Then he sent the letter to Ludwig II for his signature. Having the request come from the king of Bavaria kept it from appearing unseemly.

Germany is Unified As king of Prussia, William I was disappointed by his new title. "German Emperor" did not appeal to him as much as "Emperor of Germany". The Constitution of the North German Confederation was amended so that "Emperor" replaced "President," and "Empire" replaced "Confederation," the new emperor insisted on waiting until January 18, 1871, the 170th anniversary of the Prussian Crown, to formally declare unification and his new title. He would thus begin his reign as a Prussian who ruled Germany. Bismarck enthusiastically supported the decision, because he was, above all else, a Prussian loyalist. In just eight years, Otto von Bismarck saved the Prussian monarchy and unified the German states. His anti-liberal, absolutist style symbolized a new type of nationalism that inspired even his most stalwart opponents.

European Colonization of Africa and Asia

Colonization, the ruling or displacing of indigenous populations by settler colonies claiming sovereignty beyond their national borders, usually refers to European imperialism, though colonization as a phenomenon is not limited to Europe. In the case of European colonization, though, most adventures into other continents were motivated by exploration and expanded by greed and a paternalistic belief in the superiority of white Europeans. This is especially true in the case of African colonization. European colonization of Africa began in the fifteenth century, when the Portuguese discovered a new trade route to India. Despite attempts to colonize the Indian and East Asian mainland, European interests only succeeded in controlling the ports—and that alone took two centuries. This was not the case in Africa. Missionaries came to the continent, in ever-increasing numbers beginning in the early 1800s, hoping to convert pagan, Muslim, and non-religious indigenous peoples to Christianity. Explorers came next, seeking raw materials and new industries. The largely unknown continent, with its

EUGENICS

Eugenics, the scientific and social movement that promotes racial "fitness" through selective breeding, gained widespread attention after Charles Darwin published *On the Origin of Species by Means of Natural Selection; or the Preservation of Favoured Races in the Struggle for Life* in 1859. The book and its findings inspired biologists to seek out the mechanisms of human heredity. Before long, the term "eugenics" was coined to describe the heritability of intelligence, and eugenicists, after years of research, determined that genes determined behavior. Further, they believed that mental and moral behavior was different among racial and ethnic groups. Eugenicists, then, took issue with Social Darwinism, the popular philosophy that applied Darwin's principles of evolutionary struggle and survival to human life. They argued that social policy initiatives inspired by Social Darwinism could not possibly benefit the poor or socially "unfit" if genes determined behavior.

In an attempt to gain scientific legitimacy, eugenicists in the late nineteenth and early twentieth centuries espoused a two-pronged program to preserve the most "fit" of the species. The first prong, "negative eugenics," would prevent reproduction among unfit stocks, while the second prong, "positive eugenics," would encourage breeding among morally and mentally superior stocks, which would, they believed, remove the threat of deleterious human traits from the race. "Racial hygiene," as the program was often called, was a response to increased waves of immigration into the United States during the early twentieth century. By 1912, the year of the first International Eugenics Congress, eugenic ideas had become socially accepted on a global scale. In 1907, Indiana became the first American state to enact a sterilization law. This opened the door to the formation of the Eugenics Records Office, which promoted aggressive negative eugenics campaigns championing sterilization measures and published extensive reports on the mental deficiencies of poor people, criminals, and various racial and ethnic groups. By 1911, the idea that disparities in health were genetically ordered, not influenced by environmental or socioeconomic factors, was widely accepted.

After World War I, studies relating IQ to race came into vogue, which shifted the focus of eugenics to define a genetic basis for intelligence. In 1927, the *Buck v. Bell* Supreme Court case gave further legitimacy to negative eugenics when it ordered compulsory sterilization of mentally handicapped citizens. This prompted the sterilization of thousands of people across the country. Popular and scientific skepticism of eugenic studies arose when news of experiments conducted by the Nazis during World War II became widespread. Anthropologists and biologists, armed with new data regarding genetic variation that challenged eugenics's rigid biological representations of race, bolstered the case against the movement.

and land grabs by Europeans. Beginning in the 1880s, a so-called "Scramble for Africa" was on. Germany, Italy, Great Britain, France, Portugal, Belgium, and Spain fought each other over African land and natural resources that they had stolen from the African people. Colonization led to the destruction of indigenous cultural traditions, the weakening of family ties, and the enforcement of alien systems of law and economy.

European Colonization of Asia In the fifteenth century, when Portugal discovered a new trade route to India, the Portuguese became zealous about seizing the most lucrative ports of East Africa, the Persian Gulf, and certain regions of India. The once-free ports were now controlled by the Europeans, who sought to eliminate any rivals. They attempted to enforce a monopoly in the spice trade by forcing local traders to pay customs duties in exchange for safe passage, but Asian maritime powers challenged the Europeans, ensuring the difficulty of a Western monopoly.

Centuries later, Dutch, French, and English traders began competing with the Portuguese for control over trade routes, textiles, and factory ownership. But India maintained political control over its interests by demanding gold and silver from the Europeans. As hard as they tried to expand their interests into the Indian mainland, the Europeans were overpowered by the might and organization of the Asians. When the Mughal Empire began to disintegrate, that might and organization was lost and the Europeans saw an opportunity to finally control Indian Ocean trade. By the 1870s, Britain had won the battle to become ruler of India, a position it held until August 15, 1947, when India won its independence.

European Colonization of Africa The first foreign colonies in Africa were formally established in Sierra Leone in 1787. After 1870, European intervention in Africa began its steady and rapid increase. King Leopold II of Belgium (1839–1909) began the accelerated race for African land and resource control in 1876. He organized the International Africa Association, which was supposedly created to serve humanitarian and scientific purposes. In reality, the association served as a cover for him to make bogus treaties with several African chiefs and snatch nine hundred thousand square miles of territory for himself. To squelch any further such land grabs, Germany called a conference in 1884, and twelve European nations and representatives from the Ottoman Empire and the United States attended. The African people were allowed no representation. Many rules were made during the conference, but few were followed. Instead, European colonizers continued to deceive African natives out of their land by forming treaties with chiefs who could not read or understand them. Europeans gave the Africans alcohol, fancy costumes, and trinkets in exchange for tribal lands. By 1914, Ethiopia

vast tracts of unspoiled land, proved a gold mine for foreign investors. Before long, advancements in technology and industrialization spurred further exploration

was the only African empire to remain independent from colonial rule.

✪ Aftermath

Immigration

The mass immigration of foreign citizens to the United States during the nineteenth century changed the country forever. The new arrivals brought ethnic and religious diversity with them, particularly to the crowded urban centers of New York and Chicago. Scandinavians were largely responsible for settling in the American Midwest. Despite their contribution to the geographic and cultural landscape, immigrants were treated with open hostility that bred anti-alien movements and exclusionary laws. The rapid rise in immigration after 1827 can be traced to U.S. economic expansion. In 1832, 60,000 foreigners arrived on Amerca's shores. In 1844, 75,000 more sought entry. The Irish and German potato famines and political upheavals, as well as failed revolutions in central Europe and Germany, drove those numbers up to 234,000 in 1847 and 380,000 by 1851. This unprecedented rate of immigration continued through 1854, by which time nearly 2.7 million people had entered the country. Immigration slowed during the Civil War years, 1861–1865, but it regained momentum afterward. Roughly 26.5 million foreigners became American immigrants between 1866 and 1914.

Anti-Catholic Sentiment   The majority of immigrants arriving at American ports throughout the nineteenth century were Catholic. British anti-Catholicism, fed by post-Reformation propaganda, had been rampant long before the first colonists came to America. The sentiment was carried to the New World. Bitter opposition greeted the notion of building Catholic churches and schools, and anti-Catholics disallowed the Mass from being celebrated publicly. This anti-alien feeling came from nativists who were largely American-born Protestants. They were convinced that opposing the desperately poor Irish and strange-tongued Germans somehow protected America.

In the first half of the century, nativists stepped up their anti-Catholic campaigns to include attacks on Catholic convents, schools, and churches; the publication of anti-Catholic newpapers and books; and massive demonstrations in which so-called "true" Americans assembled. By 1840, nativists channeled their hostility into political activism. The American Republican Party and the American Party, which later became known as the Know-Nothing Party, were two anti-Catholic, anti-immigrant groups to emerge during this time. By 1854, the Know-Nothings became the second most powerful political organization in the country. It enjoyed a very brief heyday—the party was in decline by 1856—that

revealed the intensity of anti-Catholic sentiment in the country at the time.

During the Civil War, all Union supporters—American-and foreign-born—called something of a truce. After the Confederacy surrendered, nativist activity went into sharp decline. But the economic expansion that followed the war brought a renewed and reinvigorated rise in anti-Catholic sentiment along with the staggering influx of immigrants seeking a better life. In response to the "new immigration" of the 1880s, a wave that brought southern and eastern European newcomers to the United States, many nativist fraternal groups were formed. The largest and most significant of these was the American Protective Association, or the APA. The APA, founded in Iowa in 1887, boasted 500,000 members bound by the belief that the "new immigrants" were the "refuse of Europe." The APA fizzled and disappeared by the end of the century.

Immigrants from Scandinavia   Scandinavian immigration began in the 1820s but reached its high point between 1861 and 1910. During this time, 1.9 million Danes, Swedes, and Norwegians settled in the United States. The causes for their emigration from their native countries included agricultural crises in those countries that had been caused partly by competition from imported goods and partly by surplus population. The Scandinavians also saw reverses in industrial and mining efforts during the late 1870s. The first Scandinavians to arrive in America made their homes in New York, but the majority that came later took advantage of the Homestead Act of 1862 and headed straight to the Midwest. Lured by the promise of cheap land, the Scandinavians were largely responsible for settling Michigan, Illinois, Wisconsin, Minnesota, Iowa, Nebraska, and the Dakotas.

Immigrants from China   Despite their intense impact on American finance and culture, the number of Chinese immigrants during the nineteenth century pales in comparison to other groups. Only about 41,000 Chinese came the United States before the Civil War, and just 284,567 arrived between 1861 and 1910. Many Chinese were forced to emigrate when their country's population doubled in the century before 1850. Political turmoil and openness to Western influence were other factors leading to an increase in Chinese emigration. In the 1850s, the majority of Chinese immigrants came to California—where they worked peripheral jobs in the gold mining industry—from the Pearl River Delta in southeastern China. In the 1860s, large numbers of Chinese found work with the Central Pacific Railroad as builders of the transcontinental railroad. Despite their heroic efforts, their stellar work ethic, and their willingness to labor for very low wages, the Chinese were widely despised by whites. The drive to end Chinese immigration began in 1873 with the California Workingmen's Party. Led by

Irish-born, anti-Chinese labor leader Denis Kearney, the party was supported by railroad employers who no longer needed an army of unskilled workers. Nine years later, the Chinese Exclusion Act, which banned further immigration of Chinese citizens, was passed.

Immigrants from Italy Three million Italians arrived on America's shores between 1881 and 1910. In the next decade, another one million came. Italians made up the largest number of immigrants and helped mark the shift between the "old" and the "new" immigration. The old immigrants came from northern and western European countries, while the new immigrants came from southern and eastern Europe, Asia, and Latin America. Unlike their precursors, Italian immigrants were able to temporarily migrate to America, earn money, and then return to their countries of origin— where the economic situation was quite dire but where they would not suffer from ethnic or religious persecution. They would then start businesses and buy land there. Atlantic crossings in modern ocean liners made remigration feasible—travel was relatively easy, and land in their native countries was modestly priced. But not all Italians remigrated. Those who tended to stay in America were driven from their homelands by high taxes, little access to rare fertile land, and the spread of disease throughout the country's vast vineyards.

Gilded Age

The era commonly referred to as the Gilded Age was a time of great anxiety and change for the United States. The quarter century from the end of the Civil War to the beginning of the twentieth century was marked by an accelerated pace that transformed the predominantly rural country into an industrialized urban nation. Almost overnight, the largely northern European and African populace came to include vast numbers of people from all over the world. The rise in mechanization created huge corporations and a new class of wage laborers, and shifted the economy away from small farms and businesses. The "get rich quick" climate of the era encouraged rampant political corruption and fraudulent business practices that led to White House scandals and widespread layoffs. These factors prompted a dramatic shift in social mores, politics, and economics. Historians alternately refer to this period as the Age of Energy, the Age of Excess, and the Age of Industry, but *The Gilded Age*, the 1837 book by Mark Twain and Charles Dudley Warren that satirizes the post-Civil War era and its wildly corrupt, excessive, and frenzied nature, is the name that best describes this truly unique period of American history.

Corporations The most significant development of the Gilded Age was the rise of large corporations. In just twenty-five years, Americans traded hand-made goods for those sold by bureaucratically managed companies. The implications of this shift were monumental. By 1900, every American bought products from companies, supplied them with raw materials, or worked for them in some capacity. Corporations created competition in the marketplace by increasing production and lowering prices, and gave rise to a vast labor class of wage earners that had not previously existed. For the first time, people who owned businesses did not run them. Instead, salaried managers and a hierarchy of personnel did the work of the company. The railroad industry revolutionized business management out of necessity. The successful coordination of crews, fuel, repairs, and schedules over large geographic areas necessitated the creation of systematic management. Business leaders like Andrew Carnegie (1835–1919) borrowed these management systems, which stressed cost accounting and undercutting competitor prices, and became quite successful. Unfortunately, this same system led to chronic overproduction in many industries, including the railroads. The combination of overproduction and rampant speculation led to a series of economic crises. The first so-called "panic" was precipitated by the 1873 collapse of the Jay Cooke and Company banking house. The collapse led to five and a half years of depression followed by a brief recovery, from 1879 to 1882. The national economy continued to move back and forth between boom times and depressions until 1898.

These economic downturns directly affected the new labor class of wage earners who worked for large industries and corporations. Chronic overproduction led to employee layoffs, wage cuts, and increased work for the same pay. Workers resisted these tactics by organizing unions and holding strikes. As a result, there were 9,668 strikes and lockouts between 1881 and 1890, with 1,400 of them happening in 1886 alone. Most of them were failures due to the violent suppression of workers's organizations, ethnic divisions in the labor force, and the avoidance of electoral politics by large unions.

Immigration In 1832, 60,000 foreigners arrived on America's shores. In 1844, 75,000 more of them sought entry. The Irish and German potato famines and political upheavals, as well as failed revolutions in central Europe and Germany, drove those numbers up to 234,000 in 1847 and 380,000 by 1851. This unprecedented rate of immigration continued through 1854, by which time nearly 2.7 million people had entered the country. Immigration slowed during the Civil War years but regained momentum immediately afterward. Roughly 26.5 million foreigners became American immigrants between 1866 and 1914. The dramatic spike in immigration during the Gilded Age led to a climate of hostility between American nativists and foreign newcomers. Sheer racism accounted for much of the hatred, but resentment toward common laborers, usually the Irish or the Chinese, was blamed on low wage competition. Anti-alien hostility sometimes turned violent.

In 1871, a white mob lynched eighteen Chinese immigrants in Los Angeles. In 1885, twenty-eight Chinese were murdered in Rock Springs, Wyoming, by another mob. Restrictive federal regulation followed in the form of the 1882 Chinese Exclusion Act, which banned further immigration of Chinese citizens. By 1890, nativistic fury was aimed at the "new immigrants" arriving from southern and eastern Europe, a group of people deemed "inferior" according to the quasi-scientific racism of the time. A rise in patriotism and Social Darwinism brought about a rise in exclusive hereditary societies such as the Sons and Daughters of the American Revolution, which was formed in 1889.

Victorian feelings about race, which tended to be harshly dualistic, caused European and Asian immigrants, and African American and Native Americans, to suffer equally. In the Victorian view, white, civilized, Protestant, American citizens were good, while non-white, savage, Catholic, and foreign citizens were bad. This belief system forced minority groups to the margins of society, where they stayed until the mid-twentieth century.

Urbanization

The combination of industrialization and immigration led to the dramatic rise of urbanization. In 1870, the nation boasted just fourteen cities with populations of 100,000 people. By 1900, it had thirty-eight, with Philadelphia, Chicago, and New York each claiming populations of over one million. The population of Chicago doubled between 1880 and 1890, and then doubled again by 1910. The concentration of new industries around transportation centers was the primary reason for the rise of the city. Mass transportation until 1890 was very slow because it relied on mules, horses, or mechanical cables for power. This meant that workers of all classes needed to live close to work. Urban wage-workers, despite working twelve- and fourteen-hour days, earned barely enough to live on. In 1890, the average non-farm worker labored over ten hours a day and made roughly $475 a year, far below nation's average poverty level. This left no money for entertainment, which usually consisted of a daily newspaper or a trip to the park. Domestic life was hard. Many workers walked to work to save streetcar fare or took in boarders to make ends meet. The latter practice became commonplace. The 1890 census found that twenty-three percent of all households contained seven or more people. This led to excessive overcrowding, illustrated by the fact that by 1900, the tenement district of Manhattan's Lower East Side claimed the dubious honor of being the most densely populated place in the world.

Populism

The term "populism" is rooted in the late nineteenth century political movement largely dominated by farmers, laborers, and radicals. Formed in the spirit of protest, the Populists sought to reform the political, economic, and monetary systems of the day. But populism has evolved over the years. Now the term refers to any political speech, style, or movement that appeals to the concerns of common people. This third party, born of anger, quickly became one of the most significant political movements in U.S. history, and its ideas continue to have power and appeal today.

The Origins of Populism The farmers saw the railroads, as well as the many corporations that handled distribution and processing of foods, as middlemen that fattened their own wallets while shortchanging the producers. As wage labor developed, they dreamed of being their own bosses and the long-term prosperity such a life would bring. Motivated by the promise of self-reliance and economic independence, they endured prairie fires, grasshopper infestations, droughts, frosts, and numerous other hardships without complaint. They could abide hard times brought by the hand of God, but when politicians, bankers, and railroad tycoons started to make life difficult, they became angry.

In 1873, more than 1.5 million farmers became members of the National Grange of the Patrons of Husbandry, or the Grange, as it was commonly called. The organization was founded by Oliver Hudson Kelley (1826–1913) in 1867 to serve as a secret society similar to the Masons that would educate farmers about the difficulties they faced and help ease their isolation. But farmers that signed on in 1873 sought more than education and social intercourse. They were concerned about the railroad's power to set the rates and control the costs of shipping their crops to market. The farmers saw the railroads, as well as the many corporations that handled distribution and processing of foods, as middlemen that fattened their own wallets while shortchanging producers and consumers alike. To fight back, Grange members first began forming their own cooperatives. Doing that allowed them to negotiate directly with manufacturers and buy necessities at lower prices. Then they tried buying their own grain elevators and packing plants to remove the middlemen from the process. That did not work as well as they had hoped, but it did prompt some Grangers to push for state-owned and/or state-regulated railroads and related corporations.

In the 1870s, some Grangers and Eastern laborers came together to form the Greenback Party, a political organization dedicated to creating economic expansion. Because the same amount of money had been in circulation since 1865, increased business activity since that time made the dollar worth more and debts harder to pay off. The Greenback Party proposed the continued use of the "greenbacks," or paper money, issued after the Civil War, or the creation of a gold and silver monetary system, or bimetalism. Despite its best efforts, the party failed to promote presidential candidates in the 1876, 1880, and 1884 elections and became largely defunct after 1884.

What the Grange and Greenback Party lacked was a truly broad-based, sustained political agenda. The political movement they needed, one founded on agrarian radicalism, was begun in Texas in the mid-1880s. Charles Macune and S. O. Daws formed the Farmers's Alliance and encouraged members to engage in cooperative purchasing, manufacturing, and lending. By doing so, they would forge a new "cooperative commonwealth" that would effectively take economic power from the corporations and put it into the hands of the individuals. The movement took on a resemblance to religious fervor. Instead of just talking about the alliance, farmers persuaded and convinced. They sat down in people's kitchens, hosted picnics, and sang songs. Soon, regular people, black and white, male and female, were speaking knowledgeably about the problems of monopolies, single currencies, and credit.

In 1889, the northern and southern halves of the Alliance met in St. Louis, Missouri, in a first attempt at becoming a unified, independent political party. An official organization was not formed at the meeting, but several common goals and political principles were decided. Alliance candidates in the 1890 election, even without the backing of a formal party, won four gubernatorial contests, the control of a handful of state legislatures, and more than fifty national House and Senate seats.

The People's Party is Formed

Thirteen hundred representatives of the northern and southern branches of the Farmers's Alliance inaugurated the People's Party, the largest third party in U.S. history in Omaha, Nebraska, in 1892. Populists, as People's Party members became known, believed in the principle that wealth belongs to the person that creates it, not corporations or middlemen who simply profit from the redistribution of the fruits of other men's labor. This powerfully simple guiding principle helped the Populists gain power fairly quickly. But as the party became more powerful, its detractors, especially elite land- and business-owning Kansans, Minnesotans, and Nebraskans, became more numerous. The vehemence of their opponents led Populist leaders to fuse with the mainstream Democratic Party after the 1896 Democratic convention. The decision, though controversial, was reached after Populists heard William Jennings Bryan (1860–1925) rail against Republican dependence on the gold standard. The bimetallist Jennings supported many other Populist ideals, which made him the perfect Democratic presidential candidate for Populists to support. But Bryan faced a formidable opponent in Republican William McKinley (1843–1901). He came to the campaign with more money and experience and was the first American politician to hire a professional fundraiser and campaign manager.

Populism Lives On

Because of McKinley's political strength and the fact that many Americans considered the Populist's ideas radical, threatening to the ideals of democracy and capitalism, and potentially dangerous, Bryan lost the 1896 presidential election. Although he was defeated, many Populist proposals were later taken over by progressive candidates in other parties. This shift brought about the rise of progressives who fought for a just and equitable society. Prompted by the desire to wipe out widespread corruption on the local, state, and national level, progressivism led to the formation of grassroots organizations that tackled the problems brought on by industrialization and rapid urbanization. Reformers continued to work on all levels to fight political, economic, and moral corruption. The People's Party's most enduring contribution to American politics might well be its use of populist rhetoric as an effective political tool. It has become a powerful political style that lives on to this day due to its belief in egalitarianism, honesty, democracy, and productivity.

BIBLIOGRAPHY

Books

Brown, Dee. *Bury My Heart at Wounded Knee: An Indian History of the American West.* New York: Viking, 1970.

Hoig, Stan. *Sand Creek Massacre.* New Norman, OK: University of Oklahoma Press, 1961.

Robinson, Charles M., III. *General Crook and the Western Frontier.* New Norman, OK: University of Oklahoma Press, 2001.

Periodical

Utley, Robert M. "The Bozeman Trail Before John Bozeman: A Busy Land." *Montana: The Magazine of Western History.* (Summer 2003).

Web Sites

"The Battle of Little Bighorn, 1876." *EyeWitness to History.com.* <www.earlyamerica.com/lives/franklin> (accessed April 8, 2007).

"Chivington, John M. (1821–1894)." *PBS.* <www.pbs.org/weta/thewest/people/a_c/chivington.htm> (accessed April 10, 2007).

"Durant's Big Scam." *PBS.* <www.pbs.org/wgbh/amex/tcrr/sfeature/sf_scandals.html> (accessed April 21, 2007).

Schultz, Stanley K. "The Gilded Age and the Politics of Corruption." *University of Wisconsin.* <us.history.wisc.edu/hist102/lectures/lecture04.html> (accessed April 21, 2007).

Introduction to the Spanish-American War (1898)

The American Revolution established the United States as an independent nation. A little over a century later, the Spanish-American War established it as a major world power. The conflict lasted four months in the summer of 1898, and ended in a resounding American victory. Led by President William McKinley, the U.S. government went to war for a variety of conflicting reasons, including humanitarian, economic, nationalistic, anti-imperialist, and imperialist feelings.

Cuban insurgents rebelled against Spanish rule in 1895, touching off a brutal guerrilla war. Because of slash-and-burn tactics on both sides, hundreds of thousands of Cubans died of hunger or disease over the next three years. The American press launched a strident propaganda campaign designed to rouse public outrage. Their newspapers stirred pro-Cuban sentiment by publishing sensational (and often exaggerated) accounts of Spanish atrocities. This inflammatory reporting, so-called "yellow journalism," was very effective. The American public began calling for the liberation of Cuba—by force, if need be.

Hostilities broke out after the sinking of the USS *Maine* in Havana Harbor. The battleship had ostensibly been sent to Cuba on a "friendship mission," but it was obviously there to safeguard American interests. On January 25, 1898, an explosion tore open the hull of the *Maine* and sank the vessel. Spain disavowed any involvement, but a U.S. naval review declared that the battleship had been breached from an external explosion.

Responding to public pressure, McKinley issued an ultimatum. He demanded, among other things, that Spain declare an immediate armistice with the Cuban rebels. The Spanish government accepted American arbitration in the conflict, but they insisted that the insur-gents should call for an armistice. The insurgents refused to do so.

Eager to avoid armed confrontation, Spain tried to be conciliatory. America, on the other hand, was spoiling for a fight. On April 19, Congress declared Cuban independence, and then approved military action to achieve it. Five days later, Spain declared war on the United States. Congress answered that a state of war had existed since April 21.

The war was fought on several fronts. The U.S. Navy blockaded Cuba, while the Army hastily assembled enough volunteers to storm the island. Joined by Cuban insurgents, American troops seized the San Juan Heights above the harbor of Santiago. The city surrendered after a crushing naval defeat.

After Cuba was taken, Major General Nelson Miles led a force to Puerto Rico, crossing the island from Ponce to San Juan. In the West Pacific, Commodore George Dewey captured the Philippines from the Spanish.

The fighting was short and, for America, relatively painless. Secretary of State John Hay called the venture "a splendid little war." His words reflected a rising sense of American nationalism and a growing confidence in the country's military strength.

McKinley and the Spanish ambassador signed a peace protocol on August 12. Four months later, the Treaty of Paris officially acknowledged the independent republic of Cuba. The United States assumed control of Guam, Puerto Rico, and the Philippines, and was already in the process of annexing Hawaii, moving the country's concerns beyond the North American continent. From that point on, America would take an increasingly prominent role in international affairs.

The Spanish-American War (1898)

✪ Causes

Imperialism

By the late nineteenth century, almost all of the world's powerful nations practiced imperialism, the economic and political control of foreign territories. Great Britain ruled an enormous number of countries around the world. France, Spain, Italy, Belgium, Germany, and Japan scrambled to compete with England, dividing the globe into their "spheres of influence." As the trauma of the Civil War faded, a strengthening United States also set out to create an empire.

Isolation and Expansion Since 1823, the United States had maintained a policy of isolationism, as defined by the Monroe Doctrine. This declared that the United States would remain neutral in any colonial quarrels outside the Western Hemisphere.

Following the Civil War, the United States generally stayed out of international affairs, devoting itself instead to Reconstruction at home. The country also turned to the West, following America's "manifest destiny." Expansionism provided opportunities for the unemployed and new markets for the enterprising. However, these benefits diminished as time went by. In 1890, the U.S. Bureau of the Census declared that the frontier no longer existed.

Imperialism Since the West was tamed, many Americans began agitating for new territories and protectorates. It was not without precedent. President Andrew Johnson (1808–1875) had bought Alaska from Russia in 1867. Between 1875 and 1887, the kingdom of Hawaii signed a series of treaties giving America substantial economic control of the island and use of the strategically important Pearl Harbor.

These new lands were not intended to become states. Imperialists simply wanted to acquire new markets, where merchants could dump excess American goods. Advocates of the growing navy wanted coaling ports around the world to fuel international ventures.

Nationalism also fueled the desire for empire. Americans disliked being overshadowed by the "Great Powers" of Europe. Imperialism was also motivated by a genuine, if misguided, altruism. Colonialists and missionaries believed that they could offer a better life to native peoples.

Not everyone shared these sentiments. President Grover Cleveland (1837–1908), in particular, opposed overseas involvements. He argued that colonialism was a betrayal of America's founding principles and would drag the country into unnecessary wars. One of his first acts as president was to reject the proposed annexation of Hawaii.

Anti-imperialists occasionally put forward arguments that were frankly prejudiced. They opposed closer ties with Cuba, for example, because they did not want any more "colored" races and Catholics in American society.

Cuba American empire builders were keenly aware of their late start. Most of the world had already been claimed. Nevertheless, the ambitious cast their eyes on the possessions of Spain. As Spain's power declined, its colonies began to break free of its control.

The Cubans had waged a ten-year war of independence from 1868 to 1878. That conflict erupted again in 1895. Spanish troops moved to crush the rebellion using methods that provoked widespread criticism in the U.S. press. In an attempt to starve out the insurgents, Spain moved thousands of villagers into urban centers. Then they destroyed the houses, fields, and livestock left behind. The result was a human and economic catastrophe.

The suffering of the Cuban people sincerely appalled many Americans. Remembering their own revolutionary heritage, they cheered on the Cuban patriots and condemned the tyranny of the Spanish imperialists. But other factors also swayed public opinion. America had invested $50 million in Cuba, and annual trade with Cuba was $100 million. The Cuban insurrectionists burned sugar cane plantations, factories, and mills in an

This 1898 print shows Uncle Sam looking over caricatures of the American peoples. © *Corbis*

attempt to make the island unprofitable for Spain. Investors begged the American government to protect their business interests.

On the other hand, many Americans did not believe that the Cubans could govern their own country, especially after centuries of Spanish misrule. Some industrialists wanted to help Spain regain control of the island in order to stabilize trade. Imperialists suggested that the United States should forcibly annex Cuba.

When legislators first asked for armed intervention in Cuba, President Cleveland stubbornly refused to get involved. Speaker of the House of Representatives Thomas Reed (1839–1902), a staunch anti-imperialist, effectively barred all discussion of the issue.

With the destruction of the USS *Maine* in 1898, the national will to fight became irresistible. When all attempts at diplomacy broke down in April, President William McKinley (1843–1901) reluctantly asked for a declaration of war. Congress happily obliged.

The American Empire Five months after the surrender of Santiago, Cuba, an official peace treaty was signed in Paris. The terms ceded Puerto Rico and Guam to the United States. Cuba was recognized as an independent

country. The United States bought the Philippines from Spain for $20 million and had annexed Hawaii in August. America was officially an imperial power.

War hero and future president Theodore Roosevelt (1858–1919) returned home with a reputation for boldness. He also brought back the conviction that American interests should be pursued abroad by vigorous means. Upon becoming president, Roosevelt would introduce "big-stick diplomacy," advancing American negotiations around the world with the threat of force.

Not everyone embraced American imperialism with Roosevelt's enthusiasm. Disgusted, Thomas Reed resigned from Congress. Ex-president Grover Cleveland helped found the Anti-Imperialist League, which would include Mark Twain and Andrew Carnegie.

Another malcontent was Emilio Aguinaldo (1869–1964), a Filipino insurrectionist who had helped the Americans. He had expected the Philippines to become independent after the war. Disappointed, he denounced the Treaty of Paris and declared a revolutionary government. The Filipinos launched a bloody war of resistance. In the next three years, over four thousand Americans died trying to keep control of the islands.

Yellow fever killed more Americans in the Cuba campaign than hostilities with the Spanish. This painting shows soldiers being inoculated under the supervision of Walter Reed. © *Bettmann/Corbis*

The Filipino insurrections employed savage guerrilla tactics such as torture and burying prisoners alive. The U.S. Army responded with atrocities of its own. During one attack, American soldiers were ordered to kill every male over ten years old. The rebellion was eventually crushed, but it haunted the American conscience.

Nevertheless, by 1915, the United States had extended its influence to Puerto Rico, Panama, the Dominican Republic, Nicaragua, Haiti, and the Virgin Islands. Cuba was made an American protectorate in 1903. The economic advantages of imperialism never really materialized, however, and eventually the drive for new territories slowed. The cataclysm of World War I ultimately destroyed the old world empires.

✪ Major Figures

Grover Cleveland

Grover Cleveland (1837–1908) was the 22nd and 24th President of the United States. He was an anti-imperialist who refused to let the United States become involved in Cuba, among other locations, in the years before the Spanish-American War. Born Stephen Grover Cleveland on March 18, 1837, in Caldwell, New Jersey, he was the son of Richard Falley Cleveland, a Presbyterian minister, and his wife, Anne Neal Cleveland. Raised in Fayetteville and Clinton, New York, Cleveland received his education at the Fayetteville Academy and the Clinton Liberal Institute.

Cleveland's father died in 1853, forcing Cleveland to give up hope of attending college. Instead, he worked to help support his family. He spent a year working at a school for the blind as an assistant teacher and then documenting the pedigrees of a herd of his uncle's dairy cows. By the end of 1855, he had settled on a legal career, working as a clerk for an attorney in Buffalo, New York, and studying law with him as well. Cleveland was admitted to the bar in 1859 and founded his own law practice.

Early Political Career Already active in the Democratic Party, Cleveland was named an assistant district attorney in Erie County, New York, in late 1862. Because he was still responsible supporting his mother and sisters, he avoided military service for the Union by borrowing funds to pay a substitute. Cleveland returned to his private legal practice after losing the election for district attorney in 1865.

Cleveland eventually won a series of elective offices on the local and state level, though he maintained his law practice through the 1870s. From 1871 to 1873, he served as Erie County sheriff. In 1881, Cleveland was elected Buffalo's mayor and promised to reform the corrupt government. He cleaned up the city successfully by vetoing questionable municipal contracts and also restrained public spending. A year later, he ran for and won the governorship of New York on the same platform of reform.

First Presidential Term Cleveland's political rise continued in 1884 when he ran for and won the American presidency, though he was a novice in national politics and his victory was by a narrow margin. The campaign was bitter, and his opponent, Republican James G. Blaine (1830–1893), was revealed to be corrupt. Cleveland faced challenges of his own relating to his financial support of his illegitimate child.

During his first term in office, Cleveland continued to be a civil-service reformer; he wanted lower tariffs, and he spent federal dollars conservatively. He also vetoed a bill that would have made many more Civil War veterans eligible for federal pensions. Passing his bills proved difficult, because the Senate was controlled by Republicans, and he also had to deal with Democrats who expected to be rewarded with offices by his administration.

The pension veto, along with Cleveland's support of a lower tariff, contributed to his loss of the White House in the 1888 election to Benjamin Harrison (1833–1901). Though Cleveland won the popular election in 1888, Harrison won the Electoral College and the presidency. After the loss, Cleveland returned to practicing law, in New York City. This time was but a respite, because he won the Democratic nomination in 1892 and defeated Harrison in the general election. One reason for Cleveland's victory was the high cost of the pensions and the drain they created on the federal budget.

Second Term in Office During Cleveland's second term in office, he again faced controversy because he would not allow the inflation of American currency by allowing notes, backed by silver, to be redeemed for silver. Cleveland also lost support by sending federal troops to bust the 1984 Pullman strike in Chicago and arresting the leaders of the strike. He intervened because the strike was harming the country's mail service. In addition, anti-Cleveland sentiments increased when the president seemingly worked with big business in creating deals with leading financiers like J. P. Morgan (1867–1943) to reinforce America's gold reserves.

Internationally, Cleveland went against the popular grain by holding anti-imperialist views and avoiding overseas involvement. He stopped American involvement in Cuba and Hawaii. In Cuba, the president did support the revolutionaries on the island fighting Spain, but he did not want to intercede. In Hawaii, Cleveland would not recognize the revolutionary government, which was encouraged by Americans who wanted the islands to be immediately annexed by the United States. He also forced a settlement with Great Britain over border issues between British Guiana and Venezuela in the Venezuela Boundary Dispute of 1895.

Cleveland left office in 1897 and moved with his wife, Frances Folsom, and their children to Princeton, New Jersey. He taught at Princeton University and later served on the school's board of trustees. Cleveland also remained nationally prominent. During the presidency of William McKinley, Cleveland was publicly critical of the new president's expansionist polices. Cleveland died on June 24, 1908, in his home in Princeton.

William McKinley

President William McKinley (1843–1901) was the 25th President of the United States and allowed America to become involved in the Spanish-American War, an early step in making the United States a player on the international stage. Born on January 29, 1843, in Niles, Ohio, he was one of nine children of William McKinley Sr., a Christian charcoal furnace operator, and his wife Nancy Allison. Raised in Niles and Poland, Ohio, McKinley was educated at public schools in Niles and at the Poland Academy, a Methodist seminary. He received some college education at Allegheny College and then worked as a schoolteacher and postal worker in his home state.

During the Civil War, McKinley fought in the Union army, which he joined in June 1861 as a private. He served with honor and distinction, showing bravery at the Battle of Antietam. By the time of his discharge in 1865, McKinley had reached the brevet rank of major. McKinley then continued his education by studying law for a short time at the Albany Law School and also clerked with a judge. In 1867, he began a legal practice in Canton, Ohio, and became active in the Republican Party.

Early Political Career McKinley's elective political career began shortly thereafter. He was elected prosecuting attorney of Stark County in 1869. Between 1876 and 1891, McKinley served several terms in the U.S. House of Representatives, ably representing Ohio. Because of his defense of the tariff policy, his administrative and organizational skills, and his ability to promote compromise among disharmonious elements among Republicans, he played a significant role in both the Ohio and national Republican Party. In 1890, McKinley devised the McKinley Tariff bill of 1890, which offered protection for U.S. interests, especially special interest groups.

After losing reelection to his congressional seat in 1890, McKinley ran for the governor's office in Ohio in 1891. He won and was reelected in 1893. McKinley's terms as governor were marked by public appearances at which he often spoke in support of tariffs and the passage of laws that favored labor interests.

Becoming President In 1896, McKinley secured the Republican nomination for president, in part because of his established public stature and his ability to transcend party politics. While McKinley's Democratic opponent, William Jennings Bryan (1860–1925), campaigned by traveling to spread his political message, McKinley remained in Canton and campaigned from his front porch. To the Americans who came to see him there, he emphasized his message of Republican victory equaling prosperity in the United States. He also believed in the United States expanding overseas, though preferably in a peaceful manner. Though the campaign was bitter, McKinley easily won the White House.

Support for the Spanish-American War While campaigning, McKinley emphasized domestic issues such as tariff reform and increasing tariffs. However, his presidency is better remembered for its international activities, especially in Cuba. Pressure had been building in the United States about the situation in Cuba since 1895, when Cubans rebelled against their Spanish overlords, sparking an ongoing internal conflict.

The Spanish army acted savagely to put down the Cuban rebels, and American business interests, primarily sugar companies, were hurt by the ongoing conflict. Some Americans also believed that the United States had to take a greater interest in leadership and politics on the world stage, and one way to do so would be by ending oppressive Spanish control in the Western Hemisphere. Yet McKinley did not immediately agree with congressional sentiments about declaring war. Instead, he negotiated with Spain to come up with a diplomatic solution. He was able to pressure Spain into some reforms, but they were not enough to satisfy Cubans or Americans.

More Americans called for war on Spain and U.S. intervention in Cuba after a stolen letter from the Span-

William McKinley campaigned for the presidency from the front porch of his Canton, Ohio, home. *The Library of Congress*

ish ambassador, Enrique Dupuy de Lôme, (1851–1904) was published. It implied that McKinley was only acting to satisfy public opinion and that Spain would not moderate its policies in Cuba. Then the USS *Maine*, an American battleship, exploded and sank while anchored in Havana Harbor, adding fuel to war-supporting Americans. Though McKinley still tried to avoid war by calling for a Spanish ceasefire and Cuban independence, he had no choice but to change his stance.

On April 11, 1898, McKinley asked Congress for the authority to go to war; on April 25, Congress declared that a state of war with Spain had existed since April 21. After winning the brief conflict, McKinley had to deal with the aftermath, primarily the question of what to do with the former Spanish colonies gained by the United States: Cuba, Guam, Puerto Rico, and the Philippines.

While some Americans wanted the nations to gain their freedom, those who supported annexation had their point of view generally supported by the president. With the Treaty of Paris, McKinley bought the Philippines from Spain for $20 million and also gained Puerto Rico and Guam. Cuba was freed, though the new country was forced to lease a naval base at Guantanamo Bay to the United States. McKinley believed that these choices would help further develop American trade, a keystone to his political agenda.

Second Presidential Term In 1900, McKinley again ran against Bryan for the presidency. American imperialism was still a significant political topic, though the country's course had already been decided. McKinley easily won reelection and began dealing with issues related to governing the new U.S. territories. Tariff reform was also on the agenda. Before he could fully address these issues, McKinley was shot by anarchist Leon F. Czolgosz (1873–1901) on September 6, 1901, in Buffalo, New York. He died from the wounds on September 14, 1901.

Henry Cabot Lodge

Henry Cabot Lodge (1850–1924) was an author, historian, and Republican Senator. Lodge was an enthusiastic supporter of American entry into the Spanish-American War in 1898. He was also an outspoken opponent of the Treaty of Versailles, which ended World War I, and the U.S. joining the League of Nations. Lodge was born in Boston, Massachusetts, on May 12, 1850, the son of John Ellerton Lodge, who worked in shipping and mercantile operations, and his wife, Anna Cabot Lodge. His family was socially prominent, and he received his education at Harvard. Lodge earned his undergraduate degree in 1871, his law degree in 1874, and his Ph.D. in political science in 1876. His doctorate in history was the first ever awarded in that discipline at Harvard.

While a graduate student from 1873 to 1876, Lodge was an editor of the *North American Review*, which later published his doctoral thesis, "The Anglo-Saxon Land Law." Though he was admitted to the bar in 1876, much of Lodge's time was spent on academic pursuits, including teaching American history at Harvard for three years. He also began writing books, including a biography of early American politician George Cabot (1752–1823), his great-grandfather, in 1877. In addition, Lodge served as an editor of the *International Review* from 1880 to 1881.

Early Political Career Lodge began his political career as an elected official in 1880 when he won a seat in the Massachusetts House of Representatives for two years. In 1883, Lodge successfully managed the Massachusetts Republican Party and continued to act as a loyal party member. Winning the Republican nomination for a seat in the U.S. House of Representatives in 1886, he won the close election and took office in 1887. While serving in these capacities, Lodge continued his writing career, penning biographies of Alexander Hamilton in 1882, Daniel Webster in 1883, and George Washington in 1889.

First elected in 1893, Henry Cabot Lodge served in the U.S. Senate for three decades, supporting the expansion of American interests through a powerful military and unilateral diplomacy. *The Library of Congress*

Serving in the House for three terms, Lodge was a persuasive voice for the Republican Party. He supported the African American right to vote, in part to help build up Republican Party backing in the South, and the 1890 Sherman Antitrust Act, which he helped write. In 1893, Lodge was elected to a seat in the U.S. Senate. He would keep this post for the next thirty years. After taking office, Lodge came to be regarded as an influential senator who counted Theodore Roosevelt among his close friends. Always defensive of the material interests of the United States, Lodge continued to believe that the American economy should be sheltered with a high protective tariff.

Support for the Spanish-American War Lodge supported American acquisition of others domains, primarily as means to ensure continued American economic progress. Thus, he was a leading backer of United States' entry into the Spanish-American War in 1898. Lodge was pleased with the American victory but understood that it came with responsibilities. At the end of the war, Lodge believed the Unites States should annex the Philippines, though this event did not come to pass. The war was also an illustration of some of Lodge's other beliefs, including the need for the United States to have a strong army and navy, and the need for the spending of federal dollars to build up these branches of the military. He believed a strong military would ensure peace. Lodge also continued to support Roosevelt's forceful Caribbean policies when he Roosevelt president in 1901.

Opposition to the Treaty of Versailles and League of Nations As World War I loomed in Europe, Lodge believed the United States should be prepared for action. He was against President Woodrow Wilson's (1856–1924) neutral stand on arming the country and opposing Germany. Lodge supported an early entry of the United States into World War I in support of the Allies because he believed a victorious Germany could hurt American economic interests in Latin America and other parts of the world. When World War I ended with a German defeat, Lodge was a powerful Republican voice in Congress, serving as both the chair of the Senate Committee on Foreign Relations and the Senate majority leader. He used his position to influence America's post-war stance.

While President Wilson played a significant role in crafting the Treaty of Versailles and the League of Nations, Lodge had a significant number of Republicans on his side in opposition to both plans. Lodge was a vocal opponent of both the Treaty of Versailles and the League of Nations because he believed the United States should control its own fate in international politics and stay away from alliances that would entangle the country into events it could not control. Lodge also believed the treaty would compromise American sovereignty and was especially opposed to the United States joining the League of Nations unless specific provisions were made to protect American interests.

After formally objecting to Wilson's treaty with thirty-six other Republicans in 1919, the tensions between Wilson and Lodge played out as the treaty was debated in the Senate. Lodge spoke out in favor of reparations against Germany and used his position as Foreign Relations Committee chairman to add amendments to the treaty. Both Wilson's and Lodge's versions were voted on in the Senate and neither passed, effectively spelling a victory for Lodge.

Neither the Treaty of Versailles nor the League of Nations were ratified by the Senate due to Lodge's workings, and a separate peace was made by the United States with Germany in 1921. For similar reasons, Lodge also opposed the United States joining the World Court in 1922, despite the support of Republican President Warren G. Harding (1865–1929). While still serving as a U.S. senator from Massachusetts, Lodge died on November 9, 1924, in Cambridge, Massachusetts, at the age of seventy-four.

William Randolph Hearst

William Randolph Hearst (1863–1951) was an editor, publisher, and newspaper magnate. Hearst was a propo-

Hogan's Alley first ran in black and white in Pulitzer's *New York World* and later in color in Hearst's *New York Journal.* The Granger Collection, New York. Reproduced by permission

nent of the Spanish-American War, advocating his position from the pages of his *New York Journal*. Hearst was born on April 29, 1863, in San Francisco, California, the only child of George and Phoebe (Apperson) Hearst. George Hearst (1820–1891) was a multimillionaire who gained his fortune in mining properties, while his wife worked as a schoolteacher before thier marriage. Hearst had an extensive education at private schools and with private tutors as befitting his family's wealth. He attended Harvard College until he was expelled in 1885 because of poor grades.

Early Newspaper Career Though George Hearst planned on leaving his fortune to his wife, not his son, Hearst asked his father for ownership of the *San Francisco Examiner* soon after his expulsion. George Hearst had bought the paper to further his own political ambitions and initially refused to hand the paper over to his son. Hearst then spent two years working as an apprentice for the *New York World*, then owned by Joseph Pulitzer, and learning about Pultizer's new journalism and its sensationalist techniques.

When George Hearst became a U.S. senator in 1887, he gave the *San Francisco Examiner* to his son. Experimenting with the journalistic ideas he learned in New York, Hearst used the paper as a means to shock readers by creating bogus news as well as embellishing real news. He attracted readers by recruiting well-known writers like Ambrose Bierce by offering them large salaries. Hearst's sensationalism and publicity stunts worked, and the paper became a success.

George Hearst died in 1891, and after his death, his wife sold $7.5 million of his mining interests and gave the money to Hearst. He used the funds to buy the *New York Journal*, a failing paper. In 1895, Hearst moved his headquarters to New York City. Using the same tactics in that paper as he had used in San Francisco, and by poaching the talent of rival Pultizer's *New York World* among other papers, Hearst was able to increase the circulation of the *Journal* from seventy-seven thousand to at least one million a year later.

Spanish-American War Coverage Hearst supported Cuban independence from the first edition of the *Journal*, and he spent significant sums of money to hire Richard Harding Davis (1864–1916) to report on the conflict and Frederick Remington (1861–1909) to create related illustrations for the *Journal*. When the pair arrived in Cuba in early 1897, they telegraphed New York that there was little conflict. Hearst assured them a conflict would be forthcoming. Hearst later claimed that he made the war, through the publication of the de Lôme letter.

Hearst continued to trumpet war after the USS *Maine* mysteriously exploded shortly after arriving in Havana Harbor. Though the president wanted to wait for the results of the investigation, Hearst used his newspapers to demand American intervention. When his wish was granted and the United States declared on April 25 that a state of war with Spain had existed since April 21, the newspaper magnate continued to support the war and used his newspaper to push his views.

Hearst also volunteered to fund an army regiment with which he would fight, but President McKinley declined the offer. Hearst later donated and armed one of his yachts for the U.S. Navy but was not allowed to serve on it. He was finally part of the action by acting as a *Journal* correspondent in Cuba during the conflict and was able to interview a number of top military leaders. The war also served as a means of increasing readership as part of his ongoing rivalry with Pulitzer and the *New*

THE DE LÔME LETTER

On February 9, 1898, William Randolph Hearst published the Lôme letter in his *New York Journal* and pushed forth the start of the Spanish-American War. The letter had its origins in President William McKinley's State of the Union address in December 1897. In the speech, he continued to push for Spanish reform of their corrupt government in Cuba and cessation of fighting the Cuban rebels. McKinley's actions did little to affect the situation, because the rebels did not want reform; they wanted independence.

Soon after McKinley's speech, Enrique Dupuy de Lôme, Spain's minister in the United States, sent a letter to an acquaintance in Cuba. In the letter, de Lôme stated that McKinley was ineffective and was leaving open the possibility of war only to increase American power worldwide. Furthermore, de Lôme revealed that Spanish reform efforts were insincere, because military victory in Cuba was Spain's only desired outcome.

De Lôme's letter was stolen by Cuban rebels and sent to the United States. In New York, it was given to the *New York Journal*. Without authenticating the letter or its contents, Hearst published the letter and added a sensational headline that emphasized that the Spanish insulted the United States. Hearst's publication of the de Lôme letter took the United States one step closer to entering the Cuban conflict.

York World. Hearst's coverage of the war brought many readers to the *Journal*.

Failed Political Career After the Spanish-American War ended and the twentieth century dawned, Hearst continued to expand his newspaper empire. He founded newspapers in Chicago, Boston, and Los Angeles between 1900 and 1904. Hearst bought these papers in part because he had decided to run for president and they provided a forum for his candidacy.

To that end, Hearst ran for and won a seat in the U.S. House of Representatives in 1902 and 1904. Hearst was a Democrat who represented New York. However, he failed his constituents and congressional colleagues by focusing his time and money on his failed 1904 presidential campaign. Hearst then ran as an independent candidate for mayor of New York City in 1905. A year later, Hearst was a Democratic candidate for governor of New York. He lost both elections and ran for office one more time a few years later. Hearst had another failed mayoral candidacy in 1909.

Hearst continued to expand his newspaper empire; by the 1920s, he was the owner of twenty daily papers and eleven Sunday papers. He also owned six national magazines, the King Features Syndicate, International News Service, and the syndicated Sunday supplement,

YELLOW JOURNALISM

At the end of the nineteenth century, Pulitzer's *New York World* and Hearst's *New York Journal* were in a fierce circulation battle. A comic strip called *Hogan's Alley*, better known as the "Yellow Kid," typified and named the war between the two publishing giants. Artist Richard F. Outcault (1863–1928) began publishing the strip in 1894 in *Truth* magazine. It moved to the *New York World* in 1895, and to the *New York Journal* (under the name *McFadden's Row of Flats* in 1897. Pulitzer hired another artist, George Luks (1866–1933), to continue drawing *Hogan's Alley*.

The cartoon's main character was Mickey Dugan, known as the "Yellow Kid," a bald child with big ears and buck teeth in a long, yellow shirt. He and his friends were lower-class New Yorkers who spoke in their own slang and satirized society from behind their facades of children's innocence—a tactic whose popularity has not since waned in comics and cartoons.

During the time leading up to and during the Spanish American War, both competing papers were running versions of "Yellow Kid" comics, and their tactics became known as "yellow journalism." Beyond dueling satire, both papers also competed for readers with sensational, emotional, exaggerated, and inflammatory news. Stories played on the public's emotions, focusing on suffering women and children in the brutality in Cuba. After the sinking of the *Maine* on February 15, 1898, that outrage was encouraged by a stream of sensationalistic front-page stories, editorials, and cartoons blaming Spain for the attack and demanding war.

the *American Weekly*. About 25 percent of Americans read a newspaper owned by Hearst during that decade.

Through his newspapers, Hearst lobbied against reform Democrats and American intervention in both World War I and World War II. His already shaky reputation took a further hit in 1927 when his newspapers printed fake documents that claimed that the government of Mexico paid more than $1 million to a handful of U.S. senators. The senators allegedly were going to throw their support behind a plot based in Central America that would start a war with the United States. Hearst's newspapers did not suffer as much of a fall in reputation as he did personally.

Empire in Decline   By 1937, the two corporations that Hearst owned to run his newspapers and other businesses were $126 million in debt. Hearst's company only avoided bankruptcy by his personal fortune and his stepping down as the overseer of his newspaper empire. However, Hearst was able to regain control by 1945.

After an illness, Hearst died on August 14, 1951, in Beverly Hills, California. He was survived by his long-time paramour, actress Marion Davies (1897–1961), and his sons from his marriage to showgirl Millicent Willson (1882–1974). At the time of his death, he was

still a media mogul, owning sixteen newspapers, King Features, magazines, the International News Service, and radio and television stations.

Joseph Pulitzer

Joseph Pulitzer (1847–1911) was an editor, publisher, and newspaper magnate. He is known for originating yellow journalism and posthumously establishing the Pulitzer Prizes. As the publisher of the *New York World*, Pulitzer pushed for the Spanish-American War and covered the conflict extensively as part of his rivalry with fellow newspaper magnate William Randolph Hearst. Born in Mako, Hungary, on April 10, 1847, he was the son of Philip Pulitzer, a wealthy grain dealer, and Louise Berger Pulitzer. As a child, Pulitzer was educated by tutors, but was physically weak, suffering from poor vision and frail lungs. Though he tried to enlist in three different militaries in Europe, his health issues prevented it every time.

Pulitzer immigrated to the United States in 1864, having been recruited to serve in the Union army during the Civil War. He was a member of the Lincoln Cavalry for less than a year. After his discharge, he settled in St. Louis, Missouri, where many Germans lived. Shortly after arriving, he held a number of jobs, including waiter, laborer, and hack driver.

Soon after being hired as a reporter for the *Westliche Post*, the German-language newspaper in St. Louis, Pulitzer was nominated by the Republicans for a seat in the state legislature. His candidacy was not taken seriously because his district was heavily Democratic, but by creating a focused campaign, he won the seat. While serving in office, Pulitzer attacked corruption.

Newspaper Fortune   In the 1870s, Pulitzer began building his newspaper empire. His first purchase came in 1872 when he bought the *St. Louis Post* for $3,000. After buying and selling a German newspaper for a profit, Pulitzer used the funds to establish a secondary career in law. He attended law school, passed the Missouri bar in 1876, and spent two years in his own legal practice.

Newspapers again became Pulitzer's primary focus after he bought the *St. Louis Evening Dispatch* in 1878 for $2,700 at auction. He then combined the *Post* and the *Dispatch*. The new *St. Louis Post-Dispatch* became a profitable success under the active leadership of Pulitzer and his editor-in-chief, John A. Cockerill. The paper promoted civic action against gambling and lotteries and pushed for cleaner streets. Pulitzer was also doing well because of the talent he recruited and paid well.

A success in St. Louis, Pulitzer used profits from the *St. Louis Post-Dispatch* to make the down payment on his purchase of the *New York World* for $346,000 in 1883. At the time, the paper was losing money, but Pulitzer was able to turn it around using the same formula that made him successful in St. Louis. One reason for his achievement was his paper's appeal to the common man by its battling fraud, public abuse, and generally supporting unions during strikes. Pulitzer also drew in readers with sensational stories and human interest pieces.

While Pulitzer's newspaper career was on the rise, he suffered some personal setbacks. After several years of increasingly poor eyesight, he was totally blind by 1889. Pulitzer also had an ever-worsening nervous condition, which was probably manic depression, as well as other health concerns such as diabetes, asthma, and insomnia. Pulitzer was unable to supervise the paper first-hand because of his illnesses. After 1890, he no longer went to the newsroom of *World*.

To run his empire, Pulitzer then depended on a number of secretaries and editors with whom he communicated continuously. They helped him battle William Randolph Hearst and the *New York Journal* for supremacy in the 1890s. Hearst imitated many of Pulitzer's innovations, but took the sensationalism to a new level as he tried to lure away Pulitzer's readers and employees. As the pair clashed, Pulitzer allowed the screaming headlines and sensational art that he had previously avoided to appear in his papers.

Support for the Spanish-American War Shortly before and during the Spanish-American War, the rivalry between Pulitzer and Hearst reached a new height. Both men supported the Cubans and American involvement in the conflict, but vied to produce the most sensational stories. The pair were competing to report on the acts of violence perpetuated on the Cuban rebels by the corrupt Spanish government ruling on the island.

After the explosion of the USS *Maine* in the harbor of Havana, Cuba, in February 1898, Pulitzer and Hearst published the belief that Spain was behind the explosion and that the United States must act. The pair continued their sensational coverage throughout the short conflict. By this time, the circulation of the *World* had reached fifteen million, a vast increase over the circulation of fifteen thousand that existed when Pulitzer purchased the publication in 1883.

Pulitzer soon lost his taste for the over-the-top journalism he and Hearst had been practicing. While still embracing sensationalism and the extensive reporting of crime, Pulitzer ended his more questionable journalistic practices. In 1902, he gave $2 million to establish a school of journalism at Columbia University to further legitimize his image.

By the end of his life, Pulitzer often traveled, primarily aboard his yacht, the *Liberty*. He died on October 29, 1911, while on his yacht, which was anchored in the harbor of Charleston, South Carolina. By the terms of his will, the well-known Pulitzer Prizes for writing excellence were established in 1915.

W. H. S.—"*Look, Uncle—there's a bully pear! let me pluck it for you.*"
UNCLE SAM—"*Wait a bit, Willy—when it's ripe t will fall into our grounds.*"

This 1868 cartoon depicts William H. Seward, the secretary of state in the Lincoln and Johnson administrations, urging Uncle Sam to pluck the "pear of Cuba." © *Corbis*

Admiral George Dewey

Admiral George Dewey (1837–1913) was a hero of the Spanish-American War who led the United States to victory in the battle of Manila. Born on December 26, 1837, in Montpelier, Vermont, Dewey was the son of Dr. Julius Y. Dewey and Mary Perrin Dewey. Dewey's physician father raised him after his mother's death when he was five years old, and the pair were close. After attending public schools, Dewey received the rest of his education at a Norwich, Vermont, military academy. Though Dewey hoped to attend West Point, the lack of vacancies forced his entry into the U.S. Naval Academy in Annapolis, Maryland. He graduated in 1858.

Civil War Service During the Civil War, Dewey served in the Union Navy as a lieutenant. His assignment was aboard the *Mississippi*, and he served on blockading fleets. His vessel was also involved with the Battle of New Orleans in 1862. His ship was then commanded by Captain David Farragut (1801–1870), whose tactics influenced Dewey's own tactical choices during his Spanish-American War victory in Manila. By the end of the Civil War, Dewey had been promoted to lieutenant commander.

After the Civil War, Dewey remained with the U.S. Navy, which saw significant expansion. Accordingly, Dewey's career progressed as well. He was promoted to commander in 1872, and then captain in 1884. By 1889, he was named the chief of the Bureau of Equipment. Four years later, he was serving as the president of the Lighthouse Board. By 1895, Dewey had been promoted to the president of the Board of Inspection and Survey. Dewey was named a commodore the following year, though he was unpopular with his fellow naval commanders.

In 1897, Dewey was given command of the U.S. Navy's Asiatic squadron, stationed in the Pacific Ocean. His appointment was probably influenced by the sway of Theodore Roosevelt, then the assistant secretary of the Navy, and President William McKinley. In early 1898, Roosevelt ordered Dewey to move his fleet to the Philippines and fight the Spanish navy, which controlled the area, if war was declared. Thus, Dewey was in a key position when the Spanish-American War broke out in the spring of 1898. Prepared for the events that followed, he was able to take charge of American interests in the Philippines.

Naval Leadership During the Spanish-American War Dewey guided the American fleet to the bay of Manila by May 1, 1898, about two weeks after war was declared on Spain. His forces attacked the Spanish fleet anchored in the harbor at dawn. The Americans had more modern ships and more arms than the Spanish, but were fewer in number—for every six Americans, there were seven Spanish. Spain also stationed its ships behind a minefield. In addition, heavy guns were positioned on the shore.

Using the Farragut-taught strategy, Dewey was able to destroy all of the Spanish vessels commanded by Spanish Admiral Patricio Montojo (1839–1917) within a few hours. He then controlled the Spanish naval base at Cavite, and the Spanish surrendered. Only eight American sailors suffered injury in the battle, and U.S. ships were essentially undamaged in the operation. This victory at Manila guaranteed that the United States would win the Spanish-American War. It also ended Spanish influence in Far East Asia and the Pacific.

Though Dewey controlled Manila because of his success at the Battle of Manila, he set up a blockade and stood ready for reinforcements. This situation proved difficult, as he had to deal with neutral ships. For example, five German ships did not want to consent to the rules of Dewey's blockade; though outnumbered, Dewey intimidated the Germans with the threat of force until they backed off.

Dewey also played a role in what happened on land as well. While waiting for backup forces, Dewey had the Filipino rebel Emilio Aguinaldo return to the Philippines from his exile in Hong Kong. Aguinaldo had worked against the Spanish while forced away from his home. The commodore wanted him to take charge of launching a revolution in his native country. Soon General Wesley Merritt (1834–1910) made it to the area with U.S. Army soldiers. Together, Merritt, and Dewey completed the capture of the city of Manila.

By winning Manila, the United States spent many years playing a significant role in the region. Dewey was also promoted to rear admiral for his dramatic victory at the Battle of Manila a short time later. After the conflict ended, Dewey received another promotion, to admiral of the Navy, a position created for him by an act of Congress.

An American Hero Dewey returned to the United States in the fall of 1899 to much acclaim and public admiration as a hero. Because of his high profile, some Democrats supported Dewey as a candidate for president in the 1900 election for a time, though this candidacy went nowhere because Dewey did not want—nor did he possesses the skill for—a political career. He withdrew his candidacy after a short time.

Instead, Dewey remained the highest ranking uniformed officer in the U.S. Navy. Dewey spent the next seventeen years as the president of the General Board of the Navy. In 1903, he was also named the Joint Army-Navy board's chairman. During these years, Dewey led the Navy on a massive expansion as the United States grew in world stature. The Navy built a number of modern warships and established a number of bases in the Pacific. Dewey remained General Board president until his death on January 16, 1917, in Washington, D.C., of the effects of a 1913 stroke, arteriosclerosis, and old age.

Emilio Aguinaldo

A leader in the Filipino insurrection during the Spanish-American War, Emilio Aguinaldo (1869–1964) worked in conjunction with American forces to win the Philippines from the Spanish. He was also technically and briefly the first president of the Philippines. Born Emilio Aguinaldo y Famy on March 23, 1869, he was part of large, Chinese mixed-race family of wealth. His father was a lawyer who once served as the mayor of Kawit. Raised primarily in the Cavite Province of the Philippines, Aguinaldo was educated in the Filipino city of Manila at the University of Santo Tomás. He also worked in the family businesses related to mining, cattle, and sugar. As an adult, Aguinaldo held an appointed municipal position in the Cavite Province. By 1895, he was serving as Kawit's mayor himself.

Revolt Against Spanish Rule In 1896, Aguinaldo took a leading role in the insurrection, the so-called Katipunan movement, against the Spanish government, which had controlled the Philippines for many years. The Katipunans did not want Spanish rule. Aguinaldo showed himself to be an outstanding military leader, expert in using guerrilla military tactics to attack the Spanish. After Spain essentially trapped Aguinaldo and his rebels in mountain terrain, both sides decided to settle, and a treaty was negotiated with rebel leaders. Spain remained in control of the territory but promised to put reforms into place as well as pay a significant

This wartime cartoon from *Puck* magazine shows the American image of erstwhile ally Emilio Aguinaldo once he began his rebellion against American occupation of the Philippines. © *Bettmann/Corbis*

amount of compensation for damages. Aguinaldo was forced to go into exile in Hong Kong in 1897 as part of the agreement.

Participation in the Spanish-American War   When the United States declared war on Spain in 1898 at the start of the Spanish-American War, Aguinaldo went back to the Philippines at the invitation of the United States. As American naval troops led by Commodore George Dewey attacked the Spanish troops, Aguinaldo reignited the Filipino revolt against the Spanish. On June 12, 1898, before the conflict ended, Aguinaldo declared the Philippines free from Spanish rule. He then founded a Philippine republic on January 23, 1899, complete with a national flag and a national anthem. Aguinaldo was proclaimed president and established his capital at Malolos.

The peace treaty negotiated between Spain and the United States undermined Aguinaldo's plans for an independent Philippines. The United States took over the Philippines as a possession from Spain. Aguinaldo started another rebellion, this time against the Americans already occupying his country. He eluded American forces for three years as he led other rebels in desperate guerrilla warfare. After being caught by the better-armed U.S. forces on March 23, 1901, Aguinaldo acquiesced to taking an

oath of allegiance to America. On April 19, 1901, Aguinaldo publicly proclaimed peace between his rebels and the Americans. Hostility towards the United States eased as the United States began working with Filipinos to make the Philippines an independent country.

Public Role in the Philippines   After spending some time in prison, Aguinaldo became a private citizen, primarily living in Kawit. He did return to public life several times over the years. In 1935, Aguinaldo ran for president in the Philippines. He lost the election to Manuel Quezon (1878–1944). During World War II, the Philippines were invaded and occupied by Japanese forces. Aguinaldo helped the Japanese publicly, and when American forces returned, he faced charges of helping the enemy. Though arrested, Aguinaldo was never tried, because he was freed as part of a general reprieve. Aguinaldo was able to witness the United States' granting independence to the Philippines a few years later, on July 4, 1946.

Aguinaldo continued to have public moments up to the 1950s. He was appointed to a presidential advisory body, the Council of State, in 1950. Seven years later, he became an author when he wrote *A Second Look at America* with V. A. Pacis. By the end of his life, Aguinaldo was a board chairman overseeing pensions for revolutionary veterans. He died on February 6, 1964, in Manila.

Theodore Roosevelt

Theodore Roosevelt (1858–1919) served as the assistant secretary of the Navy in the late 1890s and prepared the U.S. Navy for the Spanish-American War. He also was a member of the "Rough Riders," who fought in the conflict. Roosevelt also served as the Govenor of New York, Vice President of the United States, and later became the 26th President of the United States.

Born on October 27, 1858, in New York City, Roosevelt was the son of Theodore Roosevelt Sr. and Martha Bulloch Roosevelt. His family was wealthy, but the young Roosevelt suffered from health issues including severe asthma for much of his childhood. Despite his poor health, Roosevelt was able to pursue an interest in biology and geology, and he received an extensive education at home, overseen by his aunt, which was supplemented by his family's trips abroad. He was also able to conquer his poor health by taking up physical training and involvement in sports, such as boxing, as he grew older.

In 1876, Roosevelt entered Harvard and intended to become a scientist, but he became more interested in politics. Roosevelt graduated with honors from Harvard in 1880 and enrolled in Columbia Law School that fall. His law studies did not hold his interest, so Roosevelt finished a book he began writing while at Harvard, *The*

Naval War of 1812. He had dropped out of law school by the time the book was published in 1882.

Early Political Career

Though law school bored Roosevelt, politics remained an interest and his career choice. A Republican, he began his first political campaign when he was twenty-one years old. Roosevelt won a seat in the New York Assembly in 1882. When he took office, he was the youngest member of this legislative body. While serving in the assembly, Roosevelt was a reformer who wanted to root out corruption and improve conditions for workers.

After the deaths of his wife, Alice Lee (shortly after giving birth to their daughter, Alice), and his mother on the same day in 1884, Roosevelt left the baby with relatives and purchased a cattle ranch in the Dakota Territory. There, he educated himself about the cattle trade, hunted big game, and wrote three books about these subjects. After natural disasters a few years later that resulted in the loss of most of his cattle, he sold the ranch and moved back to New York. In 1886, after an unsuccessful bid for the office of mayor of New York, he traveled to London and married Edith Carow, his old childhood friend.

Throwing himself back into politics, Roosevelt supported the presidential campaign of Benjamin Harrison in 1888. After Harrison won, he appointed Roosevelt U.S. Civil Service commissioner by him. Roosevelt continued his reform activities from his federal office in Washington, D.C., where he ensured that federal employees were given their posts because of their abilities and not their social connections. He remained in the post when Grover Cleveland took office in 1893. No longer interested in the Civil Service Commission by 1895, Roosevelt took a position in the New York City Police Commission, and again targeted corruption.

Service in the Spanish-American War

When Republican William McKinley won the presidency in 1896, Roosevelt was named assistant secretary of the Navy. As soon as he took the post, Roosevelt wanted the U.S. naval fleet expanded and also wanted to build submarines on an experimental basis. He also became extremely interested in the Cuban rebellion against their Spanish colonial overlords. However, Secretary of the Navy John D. Long (1838–1915) did not have the same strong, war-promoting opinions as Roosevelt, which led to conflicts between them.

Because Roosevelt believed that the United States would have to become involved with the conflict, he was also sure that America would go to war with Spain. Roosevelt even drew up plans for a naval war with Spain. After Long's retirement, Roosevelt was left in charge of the Navy and began preparing naval ships for war. When McKinley finally declared war in the spring of 1898, the Navy was equipped and ready for action in Cuba as well as the Philippines, the other theater of battle in the Spanish-American War.

As assistant secretary of the Navy (1896–1898), Theodore Roosevelt believed war with Spain to be inevitable. *The Library of Congress*

The Rough Riders

Because Roosevelt wanted to see action in the conflict, he stepped down from his position in the Navy and took up an offer from the secretary of war for a commission in the army. Roosevelt was made a lieutenant colonel and helped organize the First United States Volunteer Cavalry Regiment, whose one thousand members soon became known as Roosevelt's Rough Riders for their intense bravery. The Rough Riders first saw frontline action in Cuba, fighting at Las Guasimas. After the skirmish at Las Guasimas, Roosevelt was promoted to colonel and named acting commander of the Rough Riders.

The unit continued to see action at the American assault on Santiago de Cuba, and, most famously, the Battle of San Juan Hill. With the help of a unit of African American soldiers, Roosevelt and the Rough Riders first took Kettle Hill and then San Juan Hill. Roosevelt considered the charge to capture San Juan Hill one of the best days of his life, despite the general lack of knowledge of events around them, the disorganization of the army, regular lack of supplies, and the fact that he and the Rough Riders sometimes had a hard time seeing the enemy. After the U.S. Navy completed the victory in the Spanish-American War, Roosevelt and the Rough Riders returned home to a hero's welcome. He later published a book about the experience, *The Rough Riders* (1899).

Elected Office Building on his fame as a war hero, Roosevelt ran for New York governor on the Republican ticket in 1898. He won the office, and, as with his earlier offices, pushed reform legislation as well as conservation. Because Roosevelt was unpopular with Republican leaders due to his new reform laws, they arranged for him to be selected as President McKinley's running mate when he ran for reelection in 1900. McKinley won, and Roosevelt became the vice president of the United States.

Though he was bored as vice president, Roosevelt's position soon changed when President McKinley was assassinated in September 1901. Roosevelt became the U.S. president, and he again championed reform and conservation issues as well as further expansion of the Navy. He also busted trusts (massive holding companies), which had created business monopolies, and he worked to increase federal regulation of businesses.

Roosevelt was reelected in 1904, and he selected his successor, William Howard Taft (1857–1930). In 1912, Roosevelt was dissatisfied with Taft's actions as president and challenged him for the Republican nomination. Because Taft essentially won the Republican nomination, Roosevelt formed the Progressive Party and ran for president again. He and Taft lost to Woodrow Wilson.

After the loss, Roosevelt traveled to Brazil and spoke out in support of the United States' participation in World War I. When America sent troops to Europe, Roosevelt's request to lead a volunteer division was denied. Because of declining health, he was unable to run for president again as he had hoped to in 1920. Well before the election, Roosevelt died in his sleep on January 6, 1919, at his home in Oyster Bay, New York.

John Hay

During the Spanish-American War, John Hay (1838–1905) served as the U.S. ambassador to Great Britain and then took the leading role in negotiating its peace treaty as secretary of state. John Milton Hay was born on October 8, 1838, in Salem, Indiana. Raised primarily in Warsaw, Illinois, Hay received his education at an academy in Pittsfield, Illinois, and then briefly attended a college in Springfield, Illinois. Though he was not sure of the vocation, Hay prepared for a law career at Brown University from 1855 to 1858.

Service to Abraham Lincoln Hay began his career as a lawyer in Springfield in 1859, working for his uncle, Milton Hay. During this time he met future president Abraham Lincoln, who was employed in the law office next to his. Hay worked on Lincoln's presidential campaign. When Lincoln won the presidency, Hay left Illinois for Washington, D.C., to serve as Lincoln's assistant private secretary. He remained in the position until Lincoln's assassination. Hay was also commissioned as a

KATIPUNAN

Founded in 1892, the full name for the Filipino rebel group known as Katipunan was the Kataastaasang Kagalanggalang Katipunan ng mga Anak ng Bayan, or the "Highest and Most Honorable Society of the Sons of the Country." This secret society was founded by Andrés Bonifacio (1863–1897) and had as its goal the overthrow of the Spanish colonial government controlling the Philippines. Inspired by the French Revolution, Katipunan represented the working peoples of the Philippines as they sought equality, independence, and freedom.

It was not until August 19, 1896, that Katipunan was exposed and its existence made public. A few days later, Bonifacio and many of the ten thousand members decided armed conflict would be their next step. They soon began guerrilla warfare assaults on the Spanish in the Philippines. Within a short time, there was conflict within Katipunan and the group split in two.

Because Bonifacio lacked skill as fighter and was unable to mediate a solution to the internal conflicts, Aguinaldo, by then a proven leader, had Bonifacio and others arrested. After being tried, Bonifacio was executed on May 10, 1897. The rebels continued to carry out their military plans under Aguinaldo until Spain forced a cease-fire later that year. When Aguinaldo returned from exile, he again headed Katipunan rebel forces who fought against the Spanish with American support during the Spanish-American War.

major in the U.S. Army—later promoted to colonel—and used his position to execute special missions as needed by Lincoln.

After Lincoln's assassination in 1865, Hay spent five years at American legations in Paris, France (as secretary), Vienna, Austria (as chargé d'affairs), and Madrid, Spain (as secretary of legation). In these minor posts, he displayed his social prowess more than foreign policy skills. Returning to the United States in 1870, he then spent the next four years as a New York City–based journalist and editor for the *New York Tribune*. A writer of some note, he published two volumes of poetry in 1871 that established his reputation as a writer, *Pike County Ballads and Other Pieces* and *Castilian Days*. Hay was also an author of other poems and novels that were well received.

In this time period, Hay married a wealthy, socially prominent woman, Clara Stone, who was the daughter of Amasa Stone, a Cleveland, Ohio, industrialist. This elevation in social status allowed Hay time to write and travel as well as take his political career to a new level. In 1878, Hay was appointed assistant secretary of state, a position he held until 1881. He also entertained the socially prominent at his home in Washington while

The U.S. 10th Cavalry, made up of African Americans, became known as "buffalo soldiers." They served with distinction in the capture of San Juan Hill. *The Granger Collection, New York. Reproduced by permission*

completing his then-important satirical novel *The Bread-Winners* in 1884.

Biography of Lincoln After five years of focused labor, *Abraham Lincoln: A History*, his influential biography, was published in 1890. This ten-volume work was written by Hay with John G. Nicolay, Lincoln's private secretary. The men had begun gathering materials for the project during Lincoln's presidency, with his blessing. Hay and Nicolay followed this book with a related two-volume work, *Abraham Lincoln, Complete Works: Comprising His Speeches, State Papers, and Miscellaneous Writings*, in 1894.

During William McKinley's campaign for president in 1896, Hay befriended the candidate and soon held positions of importance in his administration. Hay became the U.S. ambassador to Great Britain in March 1897. Hay was serving as the ambassador during the Spanish-American War and had to deal with related issues using his diplomatic skills. Though living abroad, he was an ardent support of the United States entering the war.

The Treaty of Paris When he returned to the United States in the fall of 1898, McKinley appointed him

secretary of state. Hay took office on September 20, 1898. He had an active role in making policy, including dealing with the events stemming from American victory in the Spanish-American War. Hay took charge of negotiating the peace treaty with Spain. The Treaty of Paris was signed in late 1898 and ratified by Congress in early 1899. The agreement saw Spain ceding Guam, Puerto Rico, and the Philippines to the United States. In return, the Americans gave Spain $20 million as compensation for the Philippines. While Hay had initially believed the Philippines should not be annexed by America, he later believed the islands should be annexed, because they would allow a U.S. presence in Asia and balance power between the West and the East (Japan and Russia).

Hay took a hard-line stance in the new American territory of the Philippines. When Filipino nationalists challenged American domination of their country during the Filipino Insurrection of 1899 to 1902, Hay supported their suppression. He also worked to better the position of the United States in Latin America. Secretary of State Hay was additionally responsible for the 1899 Open Door policy concerning China so that American merchants could continue to have needed trade rights while respecting China's sovereignty.

0014195 USS 'MAINE' HEADLINE, 1898.
Credit: The Granger Collection, New York

Joseph Pulitzer's sensational coverage of the sinking of the Maine helped push the nation towards war with Spain in 1898. *The Granger Collection, New York. Reproduced by permission.*

Service to Theodore Roosevelt After McKinley's assassination in 1901, Hay retained his post under President Theodore Roosevelt. While Hay had played an important role in foreign policy making under McKinley, he deferred to Roosevelt's lead after he took office. Hay actively worked to gain the land and the rights to build the Panama Canal during this time period. He negotiated the Hay-Pauncefote Treaties of 1900 and 1901 with Great Britain, which helped allow the Panama Canal to be built. He also negotiated the Hay-Bunau-Varilla Treaty with Panama, which created the Canal Zone and gave the United States the right to build the canal.

Hay became ill with uremia in 1902, and his health continued to decline in 1903. As Hay became more seriously ill, he held his political office in name only. While still serving as secretary of state, Hay died on July 1, 1905, in Newbury, New Hampshire, after suffering a pulmonary embolism.

✪ Major Battles and Events

Sinking of the *Maine*

The sinking of the U.S. battleship *Maine* drove the United States to declare war on Spain, launching causing the Spanish-American War. In January 1898, the *Maine* had been sent by the United States from Key West,

Florida, to Havana Harbor in Cuba. A so-called "act of friendly courtesy," the ship was stationed there as a means of safeguarding the lives and property of Americans in Cuba.

At the time, Cubans had been rebelling against the Spanish, who controlled Cuba as a colony. This revolutionary conflict had been going on and off for several years and was both bloody and costly to American business. The Spanish resented Americans on the island, but they had not taken action against them directly.

The Maine Explodes and Sinks The *Maine* was under the command of Captain Charles Sigsbee (1845–1923) and moored to a buoy about 500 yards away from the Havana arsenal when the incident occurred. The ship exploded on February 15, 1898, at 9:40 P.M., about three weeks after its arrival in Havana Harbor.

There were actually two separate blasts that happened in succession. The first was more muffled than the second, more powerful blast. The two explosions caused pieces of the ship to fly 200 feet in the air, and the steel of the forward half of the ship to be bent and twisted. Two hundred sixty sailors, including two officers, died in the blast. The ship's remains sank in Havana Harbor. Many of those killed were buried in a cemetery in Havana.

Blame Placed After the explosion occurred, Americans immediately believed that Spain was responsible for the sinking of the *Maine*. This idea was pushed by war-mongering newspapers in the United States. The newspapers, especially those owned by William Randolph Hearst and Joseph Pulitzer, believed the United States should declare war on Spain. They emphasized one of what would become the Spanish-American War's more popular rallying cries: "Remember the Maine!"

The U.S. Navy immediately began an inquiry into the matter, which was helmed by William T. Sampson (1840–1902). The report, released on March 21, 1898, concluded that the ship's sinking was caused by an external explosion, rather than an accident inside the ship. A floating submarine mine was blamed. However, the responsibility for the mine was not placed on Spain, Cuba, or anyone else, though the mine was probably of Spanish origin.

Spain's navy also conducted an investigation into the sinking. Its report concluded that there had been an internal explosion in the forward magazine of the ship that caused it to sink. This blast, they argued, was possibly caused by an unexpected fire in the coal bunkers. Regardless of the cause, the United States declared war on Spain in April 1898, and the American victory led to independence for Cuba.

Later Conclusions In 1912, what was left of the *Maine*—primarily the after hull—was raised from the floor of Havana Harbor by U.S. Army engineers. The ship was taken further out to sea and sunk again with appropriate ceremony. The remains of sixty-six sailors still on board were removed and buried at the Arlington National Cemetery. As the *Maine* was removed, another inquiry was made as to the cause of the explosion. This 1912 report found that an exterior explosive caused the first blast, which resulted in the ignition of the stored ammunition that caused the second explosion.

Throughout the twentieth century, other researchers have offered their own explanations about what caused the sinking of the *Maine*. Some believe a defective boiler caused an internal blast. It is more generally believed that the conclusions of the Spanish inquiry were correct. There was probably a fire in the coal bunkers that reached the ammunition and caused the ship to blow up and sink. The lack of conclusive evidence makes the actual cause forever uncertain.

Manila Bay

On May 1, 1898, U.S. Commodore George Dewey defeated the Spanish squadron defending Manila Bay. His quick and decisive victory thrilled the nation and paved the way for the capture of the Philippines.

Preparation   When the Spanish-American War was declared in April, Commodore Dewey was ready. Secretary of the Navy Theodore Roosevelt had given him instructions months earlier. If war were to break out with Spain, Dewey was to "see that the Spanish squadron does not leave the Asiatic coast" and undertake "offensive operations in Philippine Islands."

His squadron consisted of the flagship *Olympia*, the cruisers *Baltimore*, *Boston*, and *Raleigh*, and the two gunboats *Concord* and *Petrel*. They had all been carefully fitted out in the Hong Kong harbor when Dewey received his orders. He was to capture or destroy the Spanish squadron of Admiral Patricio Montojo.

As a state of war existed between Spain and the United States, Dewey could no longer legally use the neutral harbor of Hong Kong, or any port within seven thousand miles. He set out immediately to secure the harbor of Manila.

The attack was daring. Manila was a large city, with a defensive fleet and an arsenal. Thirty-nine heavy, land-based guns guarded the *Boca Grande*—the main entrance of the bay. The consul general of Singapore warned Dewey that the harbor waters had been mined. In the Hong Kong clubs, even the sympathetic British were betting heavily against American success.

Entrance   At midnight on April 30, Dewey's squadron reached Manila Bay. "Mines or no mines," the commodore said, "I'm leading the squadron in myself." The six ships steamed directly into the harbor. The land bat-

teries, poorly handled, only got in a few shots. All of them missed, and not a single mine exploded.

In fact, they could not have exploded. The Spanish were not as prepared as Dewey believed. They had no insulated wire and could not arm the mines.

If the Americans felt nervous about the upcoming battle, their enemies felt miserable. Admiral Montojo's squadron had seven cruisers to Dewey's four. But Montojo knew that his battleships were much smaller and older. The American ships carried fifty-three guns over four-inch caliber; the Spanish had only thirty-one. The Americans had larger and better-trained crews.

Montojo saw no hope for victory, but resolved to fight nonetheless. The Spanish squadron took a stand by the Cavite Navy Yard. They would have been better defended under the guns of Manila, but Montojo hoped to avoid civilian casualties in the city.

The Battle   At dawn, the Americans sighted the Spaniards and made straight for them. At 5:41 A.M., Dewey gave the order to the captain of the *Olympia*: "You may fire when you are ready, Gridley."

The American squadron formed a column moving south towards the Spanish, who were deployed in what the report of the engagement described as an "irregular crescent." When they drew close enough, the column turned sharply to the west, running roughly parallel to the enemy line. Firing their port broadsides, the Americans traversed the Spanish formation. At the other end, the battleships doubled back in an oval path. Looping back and forth, Dewey's squadron always presented a moving target. The range of the attack varied from 2,000 to 5,000 yards, which threw off inexperienced Spanish gunners.

At 7:00 A.M., Montojo's flagship *Reina Cristina* launched a spirited attack, but it was quickly repelled. Dewey's rapid-fire cannon did massive damage very quickly, while Spanish return fire was slower and less accurate. Their shore guns had almost no effect at all.

At 7:35, Dewey received an alarming (though incorrect) report that American ammunition had run out, so he ordered the squadron to withdraw. During the lull, it became clear that the Spanish fleet was crippled. The *Castilla* caught fire and sank. The *Reina Cristina* was also burning. Montojo ordered it to be scuttled before the magazines could explode. The *Don Antonio de Ulloa* alone kept its position while the smaller ships took refuge behind the arsenal.

Dewey renewed the attack at 11:16 A.M. The *Ulloa* was sunk, and the remaining ships were surrounded. In an hour, the entire Spanish fleet was "sunk, burned, or deserted." The shore batteries were quiet, and a white flag flew over Cavite.

The Spanish had fought fiercely, under orders to sink their ships before surrendering them. They suffered 161 dead and 210 wounded. In contrast, only nine

The naval battle off Manila Bay (Cavite) during the Spanish-American War. *The Library of Congress*

Americans were wounded, and their ships sustained only minor damage.

The Blockade   Dewey lacked the manpower to take the city, so he maintained a blockade of Manila until the U.S. Army arrived. Twenty thousand men arrived in late July, commanded by Major General Wesley Merritt.

While anchored off Manila, Dewey encouraged Emilio Aguinaldo, a Filipino resistance leader, to prepare his forces for a land battle against the Spanish. Aguinaldo later claimed that Dewey promised Filipino independence in exchange for their help. Dewey denied this. He insisted that he had offered only a military alliance.

Surrounded, the Spanish governor, Dom Fermín Jáudenes, struck a deal with Dewey. They staged a fake battle to preserve Spanish honor, and Manila formally surrendered on August 31.

In the meantime, Captain Henry Glass (1844–1908) of the USS *Charleston* captured Guam. Actually, the Spanish in Guam had not heard from Spain in months and did not know that they were at war. When the *Charleston* fired on their forts, Spanish officials rowed out to ask what was going on. Finding themselves prisoners of war, they reluctantly arranged for Guam's surrender.

When Dewey returned to the United States, a grateful public overwhelmed him with praise. They sold Dewey hats, Dewey cigarettes, and Dewey paperweights. Congress created a new Admiralty position just so that he could be promoted. There was even a serious, though short-lived, campaign to make him president.

Las Guasimas

The capture of Cuba was the first priority of the United States in the Spanish-American War. While the navy blockaded Santiago harbor, the Fifth Army Corps fought through the jungle hills to approach the city by land. Their first battle was a short but bloody skirmish at Las Guasimas.

The Amateur Army   The war found the U.S. Army relatively weak and outmoded, despite recent efforts to modernize it. It was also outnumbered. Cuba held around 150,000 regular Spanish troops, supported by 40,000 loyalist volunteers. The Cuban rebel army was about 50,000 strong. Only 26,000 men served in the U.S. Regular Army.

On April 22, Congress passed the Mobilization Act. This raised the regular army strength to 65,000 and called for a wartime volunteer force of 125,000. The new recruits were gathered into crude South Florida camps, awaiting deployment to Cuba. The camps were astonishingly undersupplied, unsanitary, and chaotic.

Theodore Roosevelt and his Rough Riders. *The Library of Congress*

Hundreds of the volunteers had never fired a gun in their lives.

This makeshift army included the First Volunteer Cavalry Regiment, called the "Rough Riders." When Spain declared war, Theodore Roosevelt had promptly resigned his naval commission in order to seek glory in combat. With his friend Colonel Leonard Wood (1860–1927), Roosevelt mustered about a hundred men—cowboys, American Indians, college football players, and policemen—into an unprofessional but wildly enthusiastic fighting force.

The Landing Spanish General Arsenio Linares (1848–1914) had spread his forces widely to intercept the expected American invasion. As a diversion, Cuban General Calixto Garcia (1839–1898) attacked a village outside of Santiago, drawing Linares's troops away. On June 22, the Fifth Army Corps landed near the village of Daiquiri, about fourteen miles east of Santiago. Only

three hundred Spaniards had remained to defend Daiquiri, and they abandoned their posts at the first round of American fire.

The Corps disembarked clumsily—two men and several horses drowned. Still, around 16,000 troopers made it to the shore. They could only bring enough horses for officers and for transportation. Most of the cavalry would have to fight on foot.

The Battle Commander William Shafter (1835–1906) made headquarters in a small town named Siboney. Before the army had completely settled there, however, Cuban intelligence reported a Spanish ambush at Las Guasimas. Spanish Brigadier General Antero Rubin (1851–1923) had a few thousand men in a strong position to the northwest of Siboney. They meant to delay the Americans; their orders were to retreat if attacked.

American Major General "Fighting Joe" Wheeler (1836–1906) was eager for action. He ordered the Las

Guasimas attack, knowing full well that Shafter was not ready to move. Three cavalry regiments fought under his command: the First Regular, the Tenth Regular and the Rough Riders.

On June 24, the three regiments advanced slowly but steadily through the thick jungle. Around 7:30 in the morning, an advanced patrol found Spaniards waiting at a crossroads, in deep pits or hidden in heavy undergrowth. Brigadier General Samuel Young (1840–1924) of the Tenth Cavalry discovered entrenchments and a small blockhouse along a high ridge.

Around 8:00, Young opened fire with Hotchkiss guns. These mounted cannons smoked a great deal, giving away their position. By contrast, the Spaniards carried Mauser "smokeless" rifles. The Americans took heavy fire, but they could not see where it came from. When his men began cursing in frustration, Colonel Wood snapped, "Don't swear—shoot!"

The First and Tenth Brigades approached the ridge from the north, the Rough Riders from the south. They lost a great number of men, but apparently proceeded calmly and in good order. When they had fought their way to an assault line, they charged the blockhouse. The Spanish withdrew around 11:00 in the morning.

After A few days later, Young succumbed to fever. Leonard Wood was given a field promotion, effectively leaving Roosevelt in command of the Rough Riders. Wheeler also fell ill, but he recovered in time to join the San Juan Heights battle a week later. It was said that the elderly ex-Confederate general became confused as he was watching the blue-coated Spanish retreat. "Come on boys!" he shouted. "We've got those damned Yankees on the run!"

The engagement at Las Guasimas raised American morale, but it was also sobering. The enemy was well seasoned, having fought in Cuba for three years. It knew the country and was accustomed to the climate. The Spanish were outnumbered, but better positioned. Their soldiers were brave and stubborn fighters.

The Americans, on the other hand, arrived with inexperienced troops, inferior weapons, and almost nonexistent supply lines. The next few weeks, however, gave them a chance to show their own courage and determination.

San Juan Hill

On July 1, 1898, U.S. Army troops captured the San Juan Heights after a confused and bloody battle. Possibly the most famous engagement of the Spanish-American War, this costly victory opened the path to Santiago de Cuba. It also made Theodore Roosevelt a national hero and propelled him to the presidency.

The Plan On June 22, the Fifth Army Corps, commanded by Major General William Shafter, arrived in Cuba. They landed about fourteen miles west of their

THE YELLOW FEVER

The Americans faced another enemy on the islands, one that would take far more lives than the Spanish. Through the entire Cuban campaign, the United States lost around 350 men in combat. However, more than 2,000 died of yellow fever and malaria.

The Cuban land campaign was not, on any level, well planned. Questionable decisions were made, not the least of which was the timing of the invasion. The Fifth Army Corps arrived in July—high season for tropical diseases.

The leadership perfectly understood the risk they were taking. Theodore Roosevelt wrote in a letter home: "The surgeons here estimate that over half the army, if kept here during the sickly season, will die."

Sure enough, sickness began to spread through the American camps in early July. Shafter divided the army. Hundreds of yellow fever victims remained in a hospital at Siboney.

The four African American Regular regiments had been nicknamed "Buffalo Soldiers," because of their bravery on the frontier. In Cuba they were also called "the Immunity Regiments." Americans mistakenly believed that blacks could not contract jungle diseases. Shafter ordered the Twenty-fourth Infantry, a black brigade, to care for the sick at Siboney. Over a third of that "immune" regiment fell ill and died.

Some good did come of the tragedy. The United States wanted to keep the army in Cuba long after the war ended. To do so, the devastating outbreaks of disease had to be stopped. Major Walter Reed (1851–1902) was commissioned to do a study of yellow fever. The Reed Commission discovered that mosquitoes transmit the disease, a revelation that would save innumerable of lives.

primary objective, Santiago. Two days later, American troops seized the Las Guasimas ridge.

The Fifth Army Corps consisted of the First and Second Infantry Divisions, commanded by Brigadier Generals Jacob Kent (1835–1918) and Henry Lawton (1843–1899), respectively, and the Calvary Division, commanded by Brigadier General Samuel Sumner (1842–1937). The cavalry included the First Volunteer Regiment, nicknamed "Roosevelt's Rough Riders."

While the troops waited, General Shafter took some time to assess their situation. Some 3,000 Cuban insurgents, under General Calixto Garcia, cut off Spanish reinforcements from the north. But Spanish General Arsenio Linares had placed a series of fortifications in the hills between Siboney and Santiago. In addition, 520 Spaniards waited in the sugar mill village of El Caney, threatening the army's right flank.

It was decided that Kent and Sumner would advance towards Santiago. After crossing the Aguadores River, Kent would bear left, while Sumner would bear right. Lawton would wipe out El Caney first (he thought it

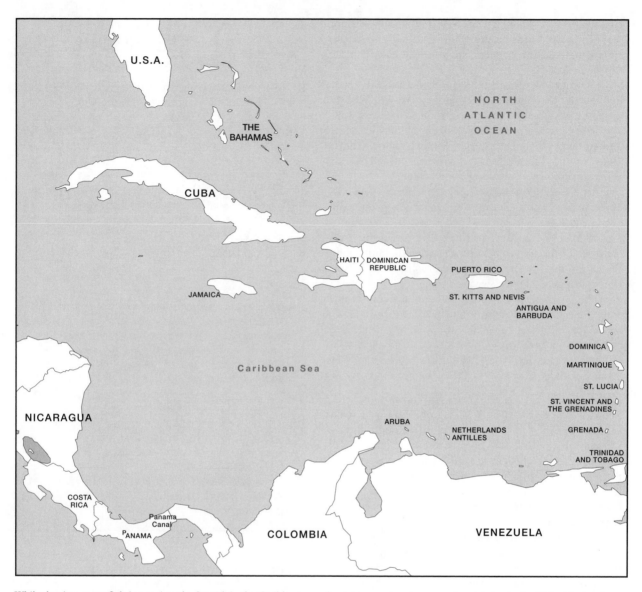

While the time spent fighting against the Spanish in the Caribbean was short, it opened up long-running debates in the United States about the definition and worthiness of empire. *Reproduced by permission of Gale, a part of Cengage Learning*

should take about two hours) and then come to reinforce the others. Captain George Grimes's howitzer battery would provide supporting fire.

On July 1, the troops began moving at dawn. Lawton began his assault on El Caney first at 7:00. An hour later Grimes's cannons opened fire. They battered the highlands for forty-five minutes, filling the valley with smoke. Then, around 9:00, the main attack moved forward.

San Juan Hill

Kent's First Brigade advanced through the jungle in stifling tropical heat. The objective was a cement blockhouse on top of San Juan Hill that was protected by trenches and eight barbed wire fences. From that position, the Spanish were able to pour continual rifle fire down on the attackers.

The American plan of attack almost immediately began to dissolve. Their brigades had been slowed on the narrow jungle paths and then separated. Chief Engineer Officer George Derby decided to go up in the Division's hydrogen balloon to get the lay of the land. The balloon immediately drew enemy fire and was shot down. The Seventy-first New York Volunteer Brigade froze under incoming fire, blocking the trail. Kent could not move them, so they were shoved aside.

By 1:00, the Sixth and Sixteenth Infantries had managed to take their assault positions. They found cover as they could along a little river valley, constantly losing soldiers under the Spanish guns. The men would later call the valley "Hell's Pocket."

Around the same time, Lieutenant John Parker arrived with four horse-drawn Gatling guns. "Where in the hell are the Spaniards?" he asked. "I've been fighting all day and haven't seen a damned one!" When someone pointed to the hilltop, Parker set the guns to work.

The officers waited for orders. Orders never came. The elderly, overweight General Shafter had collapsed from the heat. In the meantime, there was no sign of Lawton's reinforcements. He had encountered savage resistance from El Caney. Under their commander, Vara de Rey, the Spanish had fought almost to the last man. They would not give way until their ammunition ran out at 4:00 in the afternoon.

The senior commanders, mostly former Civil War officers, were trained to follow orders as part of a larger, disciplined force. Their junior officers, generally frontier soldiers, showed more independence and initiative. Lieutenant Jules Ord (1866–1898) begged his commanding officer, General Hamilton Hawkins (1834–1910), to let him lead an attack. "I will not ask for volunteers, I will not give permission and I will not refuse it," the general answered, after a long pause. "God bless you and good luck!"

What followed was a disordered, murderous, heroic scramble. Without orders, brigade after brigade followed Ord's screaming charge up the hill. Covered by Parker's Gatling guns, they cut through the barbed wire and ran forward. The defenders increased their fire.

The cavalry, having secured Kettle Hill, arrived at the top of San Juan Hill just before the infantry. When the Americans reached the trenches, the Spanish fled to the next line of hills. The infantry took the blockhouse, breaking in through the tile roof and fighting hand-to-hand. By 2:00 in the afternoon, San Juan Hill had fallen.

Kettle Hill A short distance to the north, Sumner's Calvary Division lined up to assault another hilltop entrenchment. (The Americans later named the place "Kettle Hill," for a large teakettle found at the top.) The volunteer Rough Riders took their positions behind the Ninth Regular Cavalry.

Taking fire, the calvary advanced but did not attack. Frustrated, losing men, and unable to find a ranking officer, Roosevelt took command and ordered a rush. The Ninth Regular captain balked, reluctant to follow a volunteer. "Then let my men through, sir." Roosevelt said, whereupon the Rough Riders took the lead.

Independently, other regiments also decided on a charge. Yelling, they ran full-tilt up the hill against bursts of artillery and small arms fire. The Americans overran the trenches and seized the small blockhouse.

Having taken Kettle Hill, they turned their attention to San Juan Hill across the road. They supported the American infantry charge by firing at the San Juan trenches and blockhouse.

The Ninth Cavalry Regiment then advanced across the valley to where the Spaniards had retreated from San Juan Hill. The black regular troops fought magnificently, driving the Spanish back. Roosevelt then rode out and took command of the regiment. By the end of the day, the U.S. Army controlled the highlands looking down on Santiago.

Exhausted, the U.S. Army did not continue to Santiago that day. Instead, they entrenched on the heights and waited for reinforcements.

The Fifth Army Corps suffered 205 dead and 1,180 injured in the battle. Many of the wounded would die in the next few days. Altogether, the Americans lost 10 percent of their force. The Spanish lost more than a third of their 17,000-man force.

Santiago Harbor

On July 3, 1898, the Spanish squadron at Santiago tried to break the American blockade and escape from the harbor. The battle ended with an overwhelming American victory, which destroyed Spain's naval presence in the Western Hemisphere.

The Blockade When war broke out between Spain and the United States, two U.S. naval squadrons were sent to the Caribbean. The first was the Flying Squadron, with the *Texas*, *Massachusetts*, and *Brooklyn*, commanded by Commodore Winfield Schley (1839–1911). The other was the Atlantic Squadron, commanded by Rear Admiral William Sampson. This included the armored cruiser *New York* and the battleships *Iowa* and *Indiana*. The *Oregon* arrived later, having come from San Francisco.

Rear Admiral William Thomas Sampson was officially in command of the naval forces at Santiago Harbor. *© Corbis*

THE NEW NAVY

In 1890, Captain Alfred Thayer Mahan (1840–1914) published *The Influence of Sea Power Upon History*, a book that was to change modern warfare. Using historical examples, Mahan argued that a nation's greatest military strength was its ability to control the sea with a strong navy.

At the time, the United States did not have a strong navy. Europe generally mocked the American fleet, which consisted almost entirely of wooden ships, leftovers from the Civil War. By 1889, the U.S. Navy was generally ranked twelfth in the world.

However, in the 1880s and 1890s, younger naval officers began to push for naval reform. In 1883, Congress approved funds for three all-steel plated cruisers. Three years later, Secretary of the Navy William Whitney (1841–1904) persuaded Congress into the construction of nine steel cruisers, including the *Maine* and the *Texas*. In 1885, the Naval War College was founded.

The 1890s saw the construction of huge, fully armored battleships and cruisers like the *Indiana*, the *Oregon*, and the *Massachusetts*. Equipped with the latest technology, these ships bristled with 13-inch rapid-fire guns, and could reach seventeen knots. Big-navy enthusiasts, such as Theodore Roosevelt, also pushed for more manpower and better training.

By 1898, most countries rated the U.S. Navy fifth or sixth in the world. Europeans generally placed America about on par with Spain. The Spanish-American War was to decisively end debate on the question of which navy was superior.

Sampson had overall command, even though he ranked lower than Schley.

At the same time, a Spanish fleet, led by Admiral Pascual Cervera (1839–1909), made its way to Cuba. Because of hesitancy on Schley's part, Cervera eluded the Americans and slipped into Santiago harbor. Annoyed at Schley, Sampson joined the blockade of Santiago on June 1.

A month later, William Shafter's Fifth Army Corps seized the San Juan Heights, only two miles outside Santiago. Shafter sent a message to the Spanish, threatening to bombard the city if they did not surrender.

Surrounded, Cuban governor-general Don Ramón Blanco (1833–1906) ordered Cervera to run the blockade. The admiral initially refused to leave. He knew very well that the Americans had larger, more modern ships with far greater firepower. "I have considered the squadron lost ever since it left Cape Verde," he wrote gloomily, "in view of the enormous disparity which exists between our own forces and those of the enemy." Even worse, the narrow mouth of Santiago Harbor forced the Spanish to leave in single file. They would have to run the American gauntlet one by one.

Nevertheless, Blanco overruled his objections. If the fleet were captured without a fight, he said, "Spain will be morally defeated." Cervera gave in, and he ordered a sortie on July 3.

The Sortie   At 9:00 A.M., Cervera led the squadron in his flagship, the *Infanta Maria Teresa*. In grim silence, the six ships steamed out, about ten minutes apart. Their goal was to escape to Cienfuegos or Havana.

On reaching the mouth of the bay, Cervera saw a weak point in the American blockade. Sampson had left that morning for a rendezvous with Shafter, taking his flagship, the *New York*. Four other ships had left to re-coal in Guantánamo. The Spanish fleet took advantage of their absence and made straight for a gap to the southwest.

The American ships, left under Schley's command, were taken by surprise. Most took a short time to swing around and pursue. Schley's flagship, the *Brooklyn*, found itself alone on an intercept course with the enemy column. Schley ordered a bizarre loop back, almost colliding with the oncoming *Texas*.

The Battle   For the Spanish, the battle went downhill from there. Within forty-five minutes, the *Infanta* had caught fire and was driven ashore. American fire concentrated on the flagship, allowing the two following vessels, the *Vizcaya* and the *Cristóbal Colón*, to pour on speed to the west.

The fourth ship in line, the *Almirante Oquendo*, took fifty-seven shells and was beached not far from the *Infanta*. The *Gloucester* ran the destroyer *Plutón* aground, and the *Furor* sank shortly afterwards.

The *New York* had been seven miles away when the engagement began. Sampson turned back immediately and returned in time to chase the *Vizcaya* and the *Colón*. A shell set off a huge explosion in the torpedo room of the *Vizcaya*, and she ran onto a reef. Watching the ship burn, the captain of the *Texas* said to his men, "Don't cheer, boys. Those poor devils are dying."

The *Colón* would probably have escaped if its supply of good coal had not run out. On inferior grade coal, she slowed and was overtaken, whereupon its captain deliberately beached the ship.

Surrender   The battle was a rout. The Spanish lost over 300 men in the engagement, with 157 wounded. Only one American died, and one other was hurt. The United States took 1,720 prisoners of war, including Admiral Cervera.

After a brief naval bombardment, Santiago de Cuba formally surrendered on July 17. Schley was popularly idolized at home, much to Sampson's disgust. Sampson claimed credit for the victory, since he had never officially turned over command. Schley, he claimed, had made serious errors before and during the engagement. The quarrel between the two commanders would become public, and embarrassing, after the war.

When he returned home, Cervera faced an inquiry regarding the loss of his squadron. He was honorably acquitted; it was evident that he had done all he could. American technological superiority—especially in gunnery—had carried the day.

✪ The Home Front

Immigration

From around 1890 to 1920, the United States experienced a huge inflow of immigrants, mostly from southern and eastern Europe. About a million newcomers arrived in 1889 alone. Their arrival threatened the Protestant Anglo-Saxon majority and changed the nature of America.

Causes The first great wave of immigration had washed over the country in the 1840s and 1850s. Irish and German farmers had flocked to the New World, escaping severe famine in their home countries. In the 1890s, a new influx began, this time caused not by shortage but by plenty. Thanks to the industrial revolution, Europe had made great strides in agriculture and medicine. As a result, the birth rate and the death rate dropped. At the same time, mechanized production made it more difficult to fully employ the burgeoning population.

In Italy and Eastern Europe, it was commonly believed that America was a land of plenty and opportunity. Young people would go to the United States to seek their fortunes. They wrote home, telling their parents and friends that there were, indeed, fortunes for the seeking. Most worked in sweatshops or as menial labor, but they often made far more money than they could have made in the old country.

While some people were drawn to America, others were pushed. Slavic Jews fled regimes that tolerated or even encouraged antisemitic violence. One Jewish intellectual wrote: "The only hope for Jews in Russia is to become Jews out of Russia." By 1898, half a million Jews had moved to New York City alone—about a third of Europe's Jewish population.

Backlash Many Americans were alarmed by the inflow of immigrants. They saw the United States as a British-born Protestant country. The new arrivals came from different ethnicities, spoke foreign languages, and embraced alien creeds.

People expressed frank contempt for the newcomers. The Irish were already despised as ignorant, lazy drunks. With the new wave of immigration, Americans adopted the European belief in Jewish greed and dishonesty. They mocked Slavs for stupidity, and they feared Italians as "Mafioso," criminals with no self-

The number of immigrants from Southern and Eastern Europe swelled dramatically between 1890 and 1920. Here, officers examine documents of immigrants at Ellis Island. *The Library of Congress*

control. The *Baltimore News* wrote, "The disposition to assassinate in revenge for a fancied wrong is a marked trait in the character of this impulsive and inexorable race."

Judaism, having just arrived, provided fresh fodder for American prejudices. But anti-Catholicism had blossomed in America from the beginning. Prior to the Revolutionary War, many colonies denied Catholics the vote and outlawed Catholic schools. Conflict with French Canada and Spanish Mexico only increased their antipathy. In 1875, President Ulysses S. Grant (1822–1885) openly declared: "If we are to have another contest . . . , I predict that the dividing line will not be Mason and Dixon's, but between (Protestant) patriotism and intelligence on one side, and (Catholic) superstition, ambition and ignorance on the other."

Protestant Americans tended to think of the Catholic Church as anti-democratic and tyrannical, the antithesis of American values. The Vatican, in their view, ruled over a cult that overlapped, and undermined, national loyalties. In New England, many communities celebrated an annual Pope-burning day as a kind of patriotic display.

Labor Relations   The willingness of immigrants to work for low wages also caused tension. Employers used the new labor to lower costs and to weaken the unions. Lower and middle-class Americans, fearing for their jobs, reacted angrily. The American Federation of Labor (AFL) vocally opposed immigration as a threat to the working class.

People also protested out of humanitarian concerns. Immigrants were often exploited by the practice of contract labor. Under this system, an immigrant was given free passage to the United States and then made to pay off the debt with free labor. In 1885, the Foran Act outlawed most forms of contract labor, but the practice continued illegally.

Finally, immigrants brought foreign economic and social doctrines. Socialist and communist movements thrived in Europe, and some sought to bring those revolutions to America. Anarchists assassinated several heads of states around the turn of the century, including U.S. President William McKinley.

Nativism   Various political groups attempted to resist the changes American society was facing as immigration boomed. In the 1840s, a group called the Order of the Star Spangled Banner had been active. Like many anti-Catholic societies, the Order feared being infiltrated by agents of the "romanish" conspiracy. To prevent this, they became secretive and conspiratorial themselves. If anyone asked about the group, its members were instructed to reply, "I don't know." As a result, they were known thereafter as the "Know-Nothing" party.

In 1887, a number of small nativist associations were absorbed into the American Protective Association (APA). This group, like the Know-Nothings, distributed anti-Catholic propaganda and promoted anti-Catholic politicians. They supported women's suffrage on the grounds that Protestant women would protect the country's youth.

The Ku Klux Klan, the largest of the nativist organizations, was founded in 1866. It faded during Reconstruction but was revived with vigor in 1915 as the Knights of the Ku Klux Klan. The first Klan had focused its animosity entirely on African Americans. The second incarnation opposed blacks, Catholics, Jews, and Communists.

Legislation   Though none of these groups were long-lived, they had an effect on the political scene. In 1882, Congress passed the Chinese Exclusion Act, which forbade Chinese immigration for ten years. In 1891, laws prohibited polygamists and people with contagious diseases to enter the country.

In 1892, the federal government established an immigration way station on Ellis Island in New York. Similar agencies for regulating immigrants were created in San Francisco, Boston, and Philadelphia.

In 1897, Congress passed a law requiring immigrants to be literate, but President Grover Cleveland vetoed the measure. William Taft and Woodrow Wilson also vetoed literacy bills, but the legislation was pushed through in 1915. In 1921, Congress drastically reduced immigration and imposed a quota system to limit entries from southern and eastern Europe.

✪ International Context

The Russo-Japanese War

At the dawn of the twentieth century, Japan was ready to take its place as a world power. Worried by Russian designs on Manchuria and Korea, the Japanese attacked Russia's forces in northeast Asia. After two years of fighting, Russia was soundly defeated. Japan's victory, costly to both sides, changed the balance of power in Asia.

Before the War   Since the establishment of the Meiji government in 1868, the Japanese had been building their industrial and military infrastructure. They were determined not to fall under a foreign empire and planned to forge one of their own. To these ends, Japan fiercely held to a doctrine of Korean interventionism. The Korean peninsula under foreign control, they contended, represented "a dagger pointing at Japan's heart."

This policy led to the Sino-Japanese war (1894–1895), which ended in a decisive Japanese victory over China. However, a "Triple Intervention" of Russia, Germany, and France forced Japan to return the Liaodong

This Russian postcard from the early 1900s depicts a dangerously expansionist Japan trampling over a helpless Korea. Russia, the card warns, appears to be next. *© Rykoff Collection/Corbis*

peninsula to China. The Japanese people felt deeply humiliated by this interference.

To add insult to injury, Russia took possession of Fort Arthur (Lushunkou), on the coast of Liaodong. Moreover, Russian troops began to move in Manchuria, just north of Korea. For ten years, Japan sought a diplomatic solution. It offered Russia a free hand in Manchuria if the czar would recognize Korea as a Japanese territory. Russia refused.

In 1902, Great Britain signed an alliance with Japan, promising to intervene if Russia allied itself to any third party. The treaty forced the Russians to fight alone, giving a strategic advantage to Japan. The Russians still did not back down. Civil unrest at home made the czar unwilling to show weakness abroad. He thought that the Japanese were bluffing. Even if it came to blows, his advisors believed that Russia would win quickly.

On February 8, 1904, Japan opened the war with a surprise torpedo attack on the Russian fleet at Port Arthur. Vice Admiral Togo Heihachiro (1846–1934), a former samurai, took the main Japanese fleet and blockaded the harbor. Japan declared war on Russia on February 10.

From the South In March, General Tamesada Kuroki's (c. 1844–1923) First Army landed at Chemulpo, Korea. From there they moved north to the Yalu River. Kuroki met a Russian advance guard under General Zasulich at the Yalu crossing. Vastly outnumbered, Zasulich was driven back.

From the North On May 5, the Japanese Second Army, under General Yasukata Oku (c. 1846–1930), landed northeast of Port Arthur. Moving towards the harbor, they encountered Russian resistance in the Nanshan Hills. After intense fighting, Oku drove back the Russians, opening the port of Dalny (Dairen) to the Japanese.

From the East Once Dalny was secured, General Maresuke Nogi (1849–1912) mustered the Third Army there. In July, with 80,000 men and 474 siege guns, Nogi moved to seize Port Arthur, an imposing complex of forts, walls, and trenches. It was manned by a large, well-armed garrison and commanded by the incompetent Anatoly Stoessel (1848–1915).

Nogi attacked the fortified hills east of the city. The fighting was long and brutal, but, one by one, the outer defenses fell. Surrounded and starving, Stoessel surrendered Port Arthur on January 2.

Manchuria In August, Marshal Iwao Oyama (1842–1916) took command of the Japanese forces north of Port Arthur. These were the combined armies of Generals Oku and Kuroki, along with fresh troops from the coast. They had 125,000 men in total.

This force bore down on Liaoyang, held by 158,000 Russians under General Alexei Kuropatkin (1848–1925). After ten days and 18,000 casualties, the Russians retreated. But the Japanese had lost even more men (23,600), and Oyama could not press his advantage.

When both sides had been reinforced, they clashed again at Sha He on October 5. The battle raged almost two weeks and claimed over 60,000 lives, without a decided outcome. Spent, both armies bedded down for the dreaded Manchurian winter.

In a late January snowstorm, Kuropatkin launched an assault on Oyama's position in Heikoutai (Sandepu). The battle turned into another stalemate, and the Russians were forced to withdraw to Mukden (Shenyang).

Joined by the Nobi province's Second Army and other troops, Oyama attacked Mukden in February. The battle was the largest in world history until that time—207,000 Japanese soldiers against 291,000 Russian soldiers. After losing 69,000 men, Kuropatkin fell back. The Japanese had lost 75,000 men. Both armies were too exhausted to continue.

On the Water On August 10, the Russian fleet tried to break out of the Port Arthur blockade. The excursion, known as the Battle of the Yellow Sea, ended in catastrophe for Russia. A few ships escaped, one sank, and most retreated back into the harbor.

In October, Russia's Baltic fleet set out from Europe with Admiral Zinovi Rozhdestvenski (1848–1909) in command. Refused passage through the Suez Canal, they did not reach Vladivostok until May. The force was large, but it was composed almost entirely of older, antiquated vessels.

On May 27, Togo's fleet pounced on Rozhdestvenski as he passed through the Tsushima Strait. Japan's ships were more modern, its sailors were better trained, and its commander was far more capable. By the next day, only six of thirty-tree Russian warships managed to escape; all of the others were sunk or captured. The Japanese lost three torpedo boats.

The Peace Japan was ready for peace. It had achieved superiority at sea, but the land campaign was deadlocked, and Russian reinforcements could eventually arrive. For their own part, Russians were sick of the war, and the czar had problems at home.

U.S. President Theodore Roosevelt brokered a deal that resulted in the Portsmouth Treaty. Russia pulled all troops out of Manchuria. They ceded Port Arthur and half of Sakhalin Island to Japan. However, the czar

refused to pay any indemnity money. Once again, the Japanese people felt cheated by an absurdly light peace settlement. Their resentment against Roosevelt and the United States would simmer for decades.

Japan emerged as a recognized world imperial power, challenging white people's assumptions about their own superiority. Western observers praised the Japanese commanders, but they were even more impressed by the fanatic courage of the Japanese soldiers. As the *New York Sun* observed: "The Russians were not so much outgeneraled as they were outfought."

The cost in human life was appalling. This was due to new methods of warfare—trenches, machine guns, barbed wire, mines, and distant artillery—which grimly foreshadowed the bloodbath of World War I.

✪ Aftermath

Annexation of Hawaii

For much of the nineteenth century, U.S. business interests sought to control the rich islands of Hawaii in the South Pacific. At the beginning of 1893, American citizens deposed the ruling Hawaiian monarch and took control of the country. Five years later, the U.S. formally annexed Hawaii.

Preachers The islands of Hawaii had been unified under the Hawaiian royal family since 1810, when King Kamehameha I (1758–1819) consolidated his reign over the other tribal chiefs. He was succeeded by his son, Liholiho, who ruled as Kamehameha II (1797–1824). Heavily influenced by American Protestant missionaries, Liholiho abolished the traditional Hawaiian religion.

On Liholiho's death, the crown passed to his brother, Kauikeaouli, known as Kamehameha III (c. 1813–1854). Also advised by missionaries, Kauikeaouli instituted a series of reforms, including a constitution and a legislature. He also ended feudalism, privatized land, and offered public education. The United States, Britain, and France officially recognized the kingdom of Hawaii under his rule, which lasted from 1824 to 1854.

Pirates Hawaii's relations with the U.S. Navy got off to a rocky start. In 1826, Captain James "Mad Jack" Percival (1779–1862) arrived in the schooner *Dolphin*, in search of some mutineers. His men had been looking forward to the famed hospitality of Hawaiian women. They were horrified to learn the missionaries had brought about a mass conversion of the island, and that Queen Kaahumanu (c. 1772–1832) had forbidden women to welcome sailors in the traditional way.

Enraged, Percival demanded that the queen release her girls, and threatened to shoot the missionaries if she did not. The queen loftily held her ground. The next day, 150 drunken sailors stormed Honolulu, rioting, breaking windows, and bullying clergymen. Reluctantly,

Queen Lilioukalani of Hawaii (1838–1917) clung mightily to Hawaiian independence against pressure for American annexation. *© Bettmann/Corbis*

to prevent further violence, Kaahumanu allowed Hawaiian women to visit the ship.

Planters Foreign influence was usually subtler. Over the years, more and more Americans moved to Hawaii, as missionaries and as planters. Sugar plantations thrived as owners imported cheap labor from China, Japan, and Portugal. Ships of every nationality, especially whalers, docked in Hawaii. The islands were strategically placed for any imperial nation with ambitions in the Pacific. With all of these considerations in mind, Americans began calling for the United States to annex Hawaii.

In 1876, King Kalakaua (1836–1891), the "Merry Monarch," signed a treaty that gave Hawaii a free sugar market in the United States. In exchange, Hawaii promised not to sell or lease any territory to any other nation. In 1887, Kalakaua leased Pearl Harbor to the U.S. Navy. In the same year, an American-backed revolution forced the king to accept a limited, constitutional monarchy.

Thereafter, American businessmen more or less ran Hawaii, because they controlled the local legislators. However, their comfortable rule was soon to be interrupted. The 1895 McKinley Tariff put duties on Hawaiian sugar. The law cost American companies almost $12 million. To make matters worse, Kalakaua died while visiting San Francisco in 1891, passing the crown to his independent-minded sister, Liliuokalani (1838–1917).

Politicians Liliuokalani tried to limit foreign interference in her country and to empower native Hawaiians. In 1893, foiled at every turn by American-controlled legislators, Liliuokalani announced a new constitution. She reversed the constitutional monarchy and returned power to the throne.

Alarmed, U.S. citizens in Hawaii took steps to overthrow her government. They formed the "Committee of Public Safety" and demanded that Liliuokalani step down. John L. Stevens (1820–1895), the U.S. envoy to Hawaii, sent for marines from the USS *Boston* to "protect American life and property." Threatened by a superior force, Queen Liliuokalani resigned under protest.

In her place, American sugar interests declared a provisional government under Sanford Dole (1844–1926), an American judge. Dole immediately sent a treaty to Washington, petitioning Congress for annexation. "The Hawaiian pear is now fully ripe," Stevens gloated, "and this is the golden hour for the United States to pluck it."

Unfortunately for Dole, Grover Cleveland, a staunch anti-imperialist, became president while Congress was debating the issue. Five days after taking office, he withdrew the treaty. He sent Commissioner James Henderson Blount (1837–1903) to investigate the matter.

Blount arrived in the islands to see the American flag raised over the government house. Already incensed by rumors of the coup, he ordered the flag lowered, and he sent the marines back to their ship. On receiving Blount's report, Cleveland wrote to Congress:

> By an act of war, committed with the participation of a diplomatic representative of the United States, and without the authority of Congress, the government of a feeble but friendly and confiding people has been overthrown. A substantial wrong has been done, which … we should endeavor to repair.

Following an appeal from Liliuokalani, Cleveland sent a letter to the Committee of Public Safety, calling for the restoration of the monarchy. Dole answered that the United States had no right to interfere with Hawaiian affairs. Although Cleveland condemned the "lawless occupation of Honolulu under false pretexts," he could not reinstate the queen without taking military action. He declined to do so.

The Committee of Public Safety drafted a new constitution, declaring the Republic of Hawaii on July 4, 1894. The next year, a group of Hawaiian loyalists attempted to overthrow the new government. The Republic captured them and threatened to kill them. To save their lives, Liliuokalani formally abdicated. She retired gracefully into private life, writing the following in her autobiography:

I would ask you to consider that your government is on trial before the whole civilized world, and that in accordance with your actions and decisions will you yourselves be judged. The happiness and prosperity of Hawaii are henceforth in your hands as its rulers.... May the divine Providence grant you the wisdom to lead the nation into the paths of forbearance, forgiveness, and peace, and to create and consolidate a united people ever anxious to advance in the way of civilization outlined by the American fathers of liberty and religion.

Annexation After the Spanish-American War, the United States was empowered. In a few brief months, its military had trounced that of Spain. People agreed that the newly prestigious U.S. Navy should have fueling stations around the world. Carried on a wave of national exultation, Congress approved the annexation of Hawaii on August 12, 1898. Hawaii was not made a state until 1959.

In 1993, the U.S. Congress passed a joint resolution apologizing for the illegal seizure of power from the Hawaiian royal family.

Gunboat Diplomacy

The Spanish-American War ushered in an era of unabashed American imperialism. During this time, the United States often used its impressive navy to intimidate and to control weaker nations, particularly in Latin America and the Caribbean. This kind of interventionism came to be known as "gunboat diplomacy."

America's Foreign Policy In the Monroe Doctrine, first formulated in 1823, the United States declared that she would fight any European colonial power that attempted to act in the Western Hemisphere. By 1904, however, several unstable Latin American governments had accumulated large foreign debts, which they were unable to pay. In response, European powers prepared to forcefully collect what was owed.

Determined to not give Britain or Germany an imperial foothold in the Americas, and never hesitant to assert American power, President Theodore Roosevelt expanded the Monroe doctrine. The "Roosevelt Corollary" declared America's right to directly interfere with

This 1904 cartoon illustrates President Theodore Roosevelt' foreign policy: "Speak softly, and carry a big stick."   © *Corbis*

Latin American nations. The United States was to act as a kind of police force, ensuring political and economic stability.

Much of America's subsequent domination was achieved not by force but by the threat of force. For a long time, U.S. foreign policy was guided by Roosevelt's famous dictum: "Speak softly, and carry a big stick."

Latin America

Most smaller countries did not have the faintest chance of challenging the United States militarily. Sometimes just the presence of a U.S. warship was enough to protect American interests. In 1903, the USS *Nashville* effectively removed Panama from Colombian control without firing a shot. This allowed America to buy, build, fortify, and control the Panama Canal.

Prior to this, Nicaraguans had hoped that the canal would run through their own territory—the project represented an enormous economic windfall for its host country. However, Nicaraguan President José Santos Zelaya (1853–1919) had refused to hand over land or sovereignty to the United States. Annoyed, the American government had shifted its attention to Panama.

Equally irritated, Zelaya declared his intention to build another canal, this time with the aid of Germany or Japan. The United States could not accept that scenario. In 1909, a revolt broke out against Zelaya, and the American government made sure that it succeeded.

Supposedly to protect American citizens, the United States sent gunboats and marines to Nicaragua. America also declared the Bluefields port on the Atlantic to be neutral territory, thus giving the rebels a safe haven and a source of supplies. Furthermore, the United States broke off diplomatic relations with Nicaragua after Zelaya executed two American citizens (they were caught laying mines in the San Juan River). Because America no longer recognized Zelaya's government, the Nicaraguan rebels were considered belligerents, not revolutionaries. This allowed them to legally import weapons.

Zelaya resigned, and his government collapsed. U.S. marines occupied Nicaragua almost continually until 1933. American banks virtually controlled the country's economy for decades. Though these measures did provide some civil order and financial stability, Nicaraguans increasingly resented these infringements of their national sovereignty.

The Caribbean

The United States had already exerted its power in much of the Caribbean. After the Spanish-American War, U.S. troops had remained in Cuba, and in 1903, the island was made an official protectorate of the United States. Puerto Rico had also been occupied in the war and was formally annexed in 1900.

The Roosevelt Corollary sanctioned American action in cases of "brutal wrongdoing or impotence." The fact was that political instability in neighboring countries threatened American interests. By 1915, Haiti had been ruled by twenty-two dictators in a span of thirty-two years. The last, General Vilbrun Sam, was assassinated in a public uprising. The very same day, President Woodrow Wilson sent 330 marines into the country. They established a U.S. military government that was to rule Haiti until 1933. In 1916, America also occupied the Dominican Republic. The next year, Denmark sold the Virgin Islands to the United States for $25 million.

The Good Neighbor Policy

Although American imperialism in the Western Hemisphere was seldom brutal, it was often exploitive and condescending. Latin American and Caribbean peoples disliked and distrusted American intrusion into their affairs. After a long series of protests, riots, and rebellions, President Herbert Hoover (1874–1964) officially renounced the Roosevelt Corollary. In 1933, President Franklin Roosevelt (1882–1945) announced a "Good Neighbor Policy." He vowed that America would no longer interfere in Latin American internal politics.

Nevertheless, during the twentieth century the United States continued to directly and indirectly intervene in countries such as Cuba, Nicaragua, Colombia, and Guatemala.

The Panama Canal

Since the European discovery of the Americas, ocean-going vessels had been the lifeblood of warfare and of trade. Yet to cross between the Atlantic and the Pacific in 1900, a ship had to sail six thousand miles around the tip of South America. In 1903, the United States undertook an ambitious engineering project: to build a water canal across the narrow isthmus of Panama.

Early Attempts The "Great Powers" had considered the idea of a Central American canal for centuries. The advantages were obvious. To journey around Cape Horn, Chile, was not only time-consuming, it was also expensive and dangerous. In Panama, less than fifty miles separated the two oceans.

In the 1850s, an American company constructed a railroad across that narrow strip of land. Passengers sailed to Panama, took the train across it, and then sailed to California.

In 1869, a French company, under the direction of Ferdinand de Lesseps (1805–1894), completed work on the Suez Canal in Egypt. Connecting the Mediterranean and the Red Sea, this man-made waterway allowed direct passage between Europe and Asia.

Emboldened by this success, de Lesseps turned his attention to the Americas. Visiting the Panama site, he declared that a canal could be built there without too

THE GREAT WHITE FLEET

After 1898, Americans felt justifiable pride in the U.S. Navy. In a little more than a decade, it had changed from a fossil into a fighting machine. Its superior gunnery, well-trained crews, and capable commanders earned significant international respect.

President Theodore Roosevelt could see no point in having a world-class navy if one never got to show it off. Between 1907 and 1909, he sent sixteen American battleships on a cruise around the globe. This "Great White Fleet" tour was meant as a good-will mission as well as a military training exercise.

In Asia, the fleet was also a demonstration of American strength in the Pacific. Nevertheless, the fleet was warmly welcomed in Yokohama, where thousands of schoolchildren waved American flags and sang "The Star-Spangled Banner." Chinese officials were embarrassed that only half of the fleet arrived in Peking harbor—the others had been sent for gunnery practice. To save face, the Peking government announced that the missing ships had been lost in a typhoon.

The fleet stopped in twenty-six countries altogether. In many ways, the trip proved a great success. The Navy demonstrated that it could effectively operate in both oceans, and its leadership gained a lot of operational insight. Diplomatically, tensions with Japan were eased for a time, and many foreign people formed favorable opinions of the U.S. Navy.

However, the expedition doubtlessly contributed to the ongoing European arms race. The competitive military buildup of the imperial powers would come to a head in World War I.

much trouble. He raised funds, assembled a team of top French engineers, and began construction in 1881.

He underestimated the difficulty of the project. Panama's muddy, rocky soil proved more intractable than Egyptian sand. Furthermore, the French were attempting to build a sea-level canal, which meant that they had to flatten seven miles of highland. They used dynamite to blast through 300-foot-high mountains. It was expensive, dangerous work, and landslides partially refilled the passage that they had cleared.

Accidents killed many men, but tropical diseases killed far more. In ten years, the company lost $287 million and almost 25,000 lives. They gave up, bankrupt, in 1889.

The "Phony" Revolution
At the beginning of the Spanish-American War, the USS *Oregon* took almost ten weeks to travel from San Francisco to the Caribbean. The war was almost over when she arrived in Cuba. Rattled by this strategic weakness, the U.S. government worked to create a Central American waterway.

Their first choice of location was Nicaragua, but they had found the Nicaraguan government too independent to cooperate. They had also attempted to buy the Panama site from Colombia, but Colombia had refused to sell. In 1903, a group of Panamanian separatists offered an alternative to these vexing negotiations.

Over the last few decades, rebels in Panama had repeatedly tried to gain independence from Colombia. They had no success, however, until they managed to contact U.S. Secretary of State John Hay and President Theodore Roosevelt. Both men were ardent expansionists and militarists. Roosevelt agreed to help the Panamanian revolution in exchange for a certain favor.

On November 4, Panama declared its independence. The announcement went virtually unopposed—the commander of Colombian forces in Panama had been bribed to not act. His men were further discouraged by the presence of the USS *Nashville*, docked in Colón. Moreover, the American railroad company kept all trains in Panama City so that Colombia could not mobilize its army.

Naturally, the Colombians were furious. They were to protest until 1921, when America agreed to pay Colombia $25 million for the loss of Panama.

In the meantime, having tidily secured the secession, the United States officially recognized the Republic of Panama in 1904. The new government immediately sold them a 10-mile-wide strip of land, called "the Canal Zone." Soon afterwards, American engineers poured into the country.

Construction
The Americans were more successful in Panama than the French had been, for several reasons. The Reed Commission had just discovered that mosquitoes carried yellow fever and malaria. Accordingly, Roosevelt appointed William Gorgas (1854–1920) to head a mosquito eradication program. Mosquitoes lay their eggs in standing water, so workers's residences were built with modern sewage systems. Exterminators fumigated buildings and sprayed larvicide on water surfaces. The sick were isolated behind mosquito nets. By 1906, these measures had wiped out yellow fever, and greatly reduced malaria, in the Canal Zone.

The American canal design was also superior to the French design. Chief Engineer John Stevens (1853–1943) decided, after study, that a sea-level waterway could not be done. Instead, he convinced Congress to build dams in the mountainous area. This would create a lake at a higher elevation, a "bridge of water." To adjust for the height, Stevens proposed a series of locks. These were to act like elevators, lifting ships from below at one end, and lowering them at the other.

Construction went well, not least because it was one of Roosevelt's pet projects. He visited in 1906—the first time a sitting U.S. president left American soil. When Stevens resigned in 1907, Roosevelt immediately found a replacement in Colonel George Goethals (1858–1928).

Goethals provided vigorous leadership and saw the work to completion. The project nevertheless experienced difficulties along the way. Mudslides, accidents, and

Construction of the Panama Canal cost over $300 million and 5,000 lives to complete.   *Archive Photos, Inc/Getty Images*

tropical disease still haunted the workforce. By the end of construction in August 1914, over five thousand men had died.

Nevertheless, the final price tag—$302 million—was $23 million less than had been estimated, and the canal opened six months ahead of schedule. It was widely acknowledged as a marvel of modern engineering. "A stupendous undertaking has been finally accomplished," U.S. Secretary of War Lindley Garrison (1864–1932) wrote, "[A] perpetual memorial to the genius and enterprise of our people."

Operation According to the Panama Canal Act of 1912, non-American vessels were to pay a toll. Despite this, commercial shipping of all kinds passed through the waterway—an average of ten thousand ships a year between 1914 and 1990.

After World War II, resentment grew in Panama over the continued presence of U.S. troops in the Canal Zone, which America claimed to own in perpetuity. In 1964, Panamanian nationalists rioted against American soldiers. Several people were killed, and diplomatic relations were temporarily cut.

In accordance with the U.S. "Good Neighbor" policy, President Jimmy Carter (1924–) signed a controversial treaty in 1978 with Panama. The canal was operated jointly until 2000, at which time Panamanians assumed full control.

BIBLIOGRAPHY

Books

Dalton, Kathleen. *Theodore Roosevelt: A Strenuous Life*. New York: Alfred A. Knopf, 2002.

Dolan, Edward. *The Spanish-American War*. Brookfield, CT: The Milbrook Press, 2001.

Jansen, Marius B. *The Making of Modern Japan*. Cambridge, Mass.: The Belknap Press of Harvard University Press, 2000.

Jones, Virgil Carrington. *Roosevelt's Rough Riders.*. Garden City, NY: Doubleday & Company, 1971.

Killblane, Richard E. "Assault On San Juan Hill". *Military History* (June 1998).

O'Toole, G. J. A. *The Spanish-American War: An American Epic 1898*. New York: W. W. Norton, 1984.

Traxel, David. *1898: The Birth of the American Century.* New York: Alfred A. Knopf, 1998.

Yans-McLaughlin, Virginia, and Lightman, Marjorie. *Ellis Island and the Peopling of America.* New York: The New Press, 1997.

Periodicals

Cavendish, Richard. "Japan's Attack on Port Arthur: February 8th and 9th, 1904" *History Today* (February, 2004)

Kennedy, Paul. "Birth Of A Superpower". *Time* (July 3, 2006).

Stoner, Lynn K. "The Santiago Campaign of 1898: A Soldier's View of the Spanish-American War". *Latin American Research Review* (Summer 1996).

Web Sites

"Anti-annexation Protest Documents: Liliuokalani to Albert Willis, U.S. Envoy, June 20, 1894." *University of Hawai'i at Manoa.* <libweb.hawaii.edu/digicoll/annexation/protest/liliu4-trans.html> (accessed April 4, 2007)

HistoryNet.com. "Spanish-American War: Battle of San Juan Hill" <www.historynet.com/wars_conflicts/19_century/3033026.html?page=1&c=y> (accessed March 26, 2007).

Liliuokalani, Queen of Hawaii. "My Cabinet—Princess Kaiulani." *Hawaii's Story by Hawaii's Queen.* Originally published in 1898. <digital.library.upenn.edu/women/liliuokalani/hawaii/hawaii-5.html> (accessed April 4, 2007)

The Navy and Marine Living History Association "The Battle of Honolulu" <www.navyandmarine.org/ondeck/1800battleofhonolulu.htm> (accessed May 2, 2007).

The Navy Department Library "The Cruise of the Great White Fleet" <www.history.navy.mil/library/online/gwf_cruise.htm> (accessed April 2, 2007).

Navy Historical Center. "Report of the Secretary of the navy, 1898" <www.history.navy.mil/wars/spanam/sn98-5.htm> (accessed April 2, 2007).

Roosevelt, Theodore. "General Young's Fight at Las Guasimas." *The Rough Riders.* Originally published in 1890. <www.bartleby.com/51/3.html> (accessed March 26, 2007).

The Spanish-American War Centennial Website. "The Official Report of Spanish Admiral Montojo on the Battle of Manila Bay" <www.spanamwar.com/mtreport.htm> (accessed March 26, 2007).

Introduction to World War I (1914–1919)

World War I, often referred to as "the Great War," was without precedent as nations around the world simultaneously took up arms against each other. The war's effects were vast and profound, with consequences that reverberated throughout the twentieth century. Human casualties were enormous. It is estimated that over ten million soldiers died and twenty million were wounded as a direct result of the war. The use of chemical weapons, bombardments from the air, and the century's first genocide account for the dramatic loss of military personnel. Civilians died in equally shocking numbers due to worldwide hunger and influenza epidemics. As a result of these vast casualties, Russia lost two million people and Serbia lost fully one-third of its population. The staggering loss of human life was just one aspect of the war that changed the world forever.

The assassination on June 28, 1914, of Austro-Hungarian Archduke Franz Ferdinand marks the beginning of World War I, but the underlying causes are debated. Historians provide a number of explanations, including the desire for greater wealth and territory, a massive arms race, a series of treaties that ensured that all of Europe would be dragged into a war begun by one nation, social turmoil brought on by the Industrial Revolution, and the simple miscalculation of ruling generals.

A complicated system of European alliances accounts for one of the leading causes of the war. A growing tide of nationalism, especially strong in the Balkan territories under Austro-Hungarian rule, also contributed to rising tensions. Nationalism had been a rising trend in Europe for several decades before the war, which causes some historians to wonder why the eruption of World War I did not happen sooner. Finally, the last leading cause of World War I was an unprecedented and aggressive pursuit of colonial holdings. Europe, Japan, and the United States were the primary competitors in this "empire for empire's sake" rivalry of the late nineteenth and early twentieth centuries.

World War I caused global change on three levels: political, cultural, and socioeconomic. After Germany surrendered and the war ended, reconstruction efforts were made. One of the results of those efforts was the Treaty of Versailles, the most significant and well-known of the postwar treaties. In it, Germany was forced to acknowledge responsibility for causing the war, among other things, and the League of Nations, decades in the making, was created. The map of the world was redrawn as a result of World War I and the many treaties that grew out of it. New nation-states emerged when boundary lines were redrawn, causing political and cultural struggles that linger to this day. The Russian Revolution and the appearance of waves of eastern and southern European immigrants on American shores immediately following the war led to a rise in Americans' fear of Communism. International anxiety, increased mechanization, and the spread of industrialization brought a fundamental shift in the way people perceived their places in the changing modern world.

World War I (1914–1919)

✪ Causes

European Nationalism

In the 1800s, Europe consisted of a patchwork of realms defined by historical kingdoms, ethnicities, and language groups. These were divided into small vulerable states and sprawling authoritarian empires. Many Europeans dreamed of uniting all their "people"—usually those who shared their culture—into one strong, independent nation. This impulse, called nationalism, dominated European politics throughout the nineteenth century and contributed directly to the outbreak of world war.

The Age of Metternich From 1796 to 1814, Napoleon Bonaparte (1769–1821) led the French army across Europe. He was, at first, remarkably successful—at its height, the first French Empire directly or indirectly controlled most of the continent.

As the war turned against France, the other major powers met in a series of meetings called the Congress of Vienna (1814–1815) in which they discussed the future of the war-ravaged continent. Largely due to the vision of the brilliant Austrian diplomat Prince Klemens Wenzel von Metternich (1773–1859), the map of Europe was re-drawn. Many small nations fell under the dominion of more powerful nations. Other countries ceased to exist. For example, Poland was divided and shared between Austria, Prussia, and Russia.

As a result, a great many Europeans found themselves ruled by large, multiethnic empires such as Hapsburg Austria or Czarist Russia. Their new governments often did not speak their language or share their culture.

In western and central Europe, native peoples had resented Napoleon's occupation, but they had also absorbed French soldiers' republican and egalitarian ideals. These notions made it more difficult for people to submit to the conservative foreign regimes under which they lived. Secret societies dedicated to self-rule, ethnic unification, and political liberalization sprang up in universities everywhere.

Metternich himself loathed radicals of all stripes, and he was convinced that nationalism would tear Europe apart. He declared that radical secret associations were "the gangrene of society." He instituted a system of censorship, spying, and repression to counter them.

Thus, the next twenty years of European history were marked by stubborn monarchist rule and rising populist discontent. In 1848, this tension led to revolutions throughout Europe. The uprisings were quelled, but nationalist and liberal movements persevered.

German Unification After the Congress of Vienna, several attempts were made to unify the thirty-eight independent states of the Germanic Confederation. None succeeded until the emergence of Otto Von Bismarck (1815–1898) as Chancellor of Prussia.

Bismarck represented a new strain of conservative nationalism. A religious monarchist, Bismarck had no interest in liberal politics. He was determined to unite Germany under King Wilhelm I (1797–1888) of Prussia.

A master political manipulator, Bismarck knew that the German states would unite against a common enemy. He engineered and won a conflict with Austria in 1866, which led to the formation of the North German Confederation. In 1870, Bismarck deliberately provoked a war with France. Even the southern Catholic German states, which had distrusted Protestant Prussia, joined in the effort.

The Germans easily overran the French, capturing their emperor, Napoleon III (1808–1873) at the Battle of Sedan. In January of 1871, Wilhelm was crowned kaiser (emperor) of a United Germany.

As spoils of the Franco-Prussian War, Germany absorbed the border states of Alsace and Lorraine. These "lost provinces" formed the focal point of the French nationalist movement. French patriots declared that there could be no peace with Germany while Frenchmen lived under foreign rule. *Revanchism* (revenge) became a major theme of French politics.

Nationalism surged in Germany and other nations in the years leading up to World War I, as testified to by the large crowd of Berliners watching a cavalry parade in the earliest days of the war. *The Granger Collection, New York. Reproduced by permission*

Italian Unification In the 1860s, the Italian peninsula was composed of several small nation-states, including the papal states around Rome. The northern Italian provinces fell under the Austrian empire.

Even after their defeat in 1848, northern Italian nationalists struggled to rid themselves of Austrian rule. One of the most important of these was Victor Emmanuel II (1820–1878), King of Sardinia, who devoted himself to the cause of Italian unity. His prime minister, Count Camillo di Cavour (1810–1861) proved a capable leader and diplomat. Through Cavour's efforts, Sardinia secured alliances with Britain and France. In 1859, with French military backing, Sardinia went to war with Austria. Though they were forced to abandon the campaign after France withdrew from the conflict, Sardinia eventually gained control of Lombardy, Parma, Modena, Tuscany, and Romagna.

In the meantime, General Giuseppe Garibaldi (1807–1882) drove out the Bourbon king of Naples,

King Francis II of the Two Sicilies (1836–1894). After securing most of southern Italy, Garibaldi's troops eventually decided to join the northern Sardinian movement. The Italian states pledged allegiance—one by one—to Victor Emmanuel II, and he was proclaimed King of all Italy in 1861. In 1870, the last holdout—Rome—joined the new nation.

The Eastern Empires While new empires sprung up in Europe, the sprawling Ottoman Empire of Turkey had begun to collapse. Greece and Serbia managed to break free in the 1820s. Britain and France tried to prop up Turkey because they did not want her territories falling under Russian control.

The Austrian empire faced nationalist groundswells in Hungary and the Balkans. In the end, Austrian Emperor Franz Joseph I (1830–1916) had to offer the Hungarian Magyars an equal place in his government in 1867. However, Serbian nationalists fiercely opposed Austro-Hungarian expansion into the Balkans.

SOCIAL DARWINISM

One of the most aggressive strains of nationalist thought sprang from the writings of English social philosopher Herbert Spencer (1820–1903). In his *A System of Synthetic Philosophy*, Spencer attempted to wed together modern understandings of biology and sociology. According to his theories, human civilizations follow evolutionary law, as do animal species. In an overcrowded population, he argued, the strongest, most intelligent, and most capable men would naturally triumph.

Although Spencer concentrated on individuals, many Europeans saw "survival of the fittest" as the root of all international conflict. Some ethnic groups used the theory to promote their own genetic superiority, and thus their right to conquer, or even eradicate, weaker peoples. The theory was widely used to justify the Nazi policies in World War II.

Russia itself controlled a large number of non-Russian territories, many of which writhed under the Czar's despotic government. In 1863, a Polish nationalist uprising was brutally supressed, but the forces of revolution throughout the empire grew more intense. The Russian government hoped that foreign wars would distract the country from their domestic difficulties. But the Russo-Japanese war ended in disaster for them, and the Czarist government was finally forcibly overthrown in the midst of World War I.

Competition for Colonial Holdings

Beginning in the late nineteenth century, imperialism—the acquisition and control of foreign territories—was pursued with great intensity by several European countries. Competition over key parts of Africa and Asia contributed to tensions in Europe, and war in Europe was subsequently exported to the whole world.

The New Imperialism In the 1880s, the world powers suddenly became aware of the existence of apparently unbounded wealth in Africa. Men like Cecil Rhodes (1853–1902) made enormous fortunes from the natural resources of the "Dark Continent." As a consequence, western countries flung themselves into "the scramble for Africa." By conquering, coercing, or buying tribal governments, European nations divided the continent among themselves.

In 1885, the imperialist nations signed the Berlin Act, which regulated free trade in the colonies. They also declared their roles as protectors of their new subjects. The signatories pledged to "watch over the preservation of the native tribes, and to care for the improvement of the conditions of their moral and material well-being."

Missionary David Livingstone (1813–1873) wrote that colonialism was driven by three C's: commerce, Christianity, and civilization. In addition, the colonial powers competed over the prestige conferred by a vast empire. They also struggled to achieve strategic military positioning around the globe.

Younger nations were eager not to be left out. Even the United States, with its anticolonial background, joined the rush for overseas colonies in the Spanish-American War of 1898. Only a few years out of feudalism, Japan also became an imperial power after it defeated Russia in 1905.

Britain Queen Victoria (1819–1901) celebrated her Diamond Jubilee in 1897 with an orgy of parade and spectacle. The British people were toasting her sixty years on the throne, but they were also congratulating themselves on their seemingly unassailable position of world power. The British Empire stretched across the globe and dominated Africa, Australia, Canada, India, and large parts of eastern Asia.

At the same time, a note of anxiety crept into these extravagant festivities. Rudyard Kipling (1865–1936), the unofficial poet laureate of imperialism, published the poem "Recessional," in which he warned against overweening confidence. Such boasting, he declared, smacked of the behavior of "lesser breeds without the law."

Two years later, Kipling published "The White Man's Burden." The poem was aimed at the United States, which was currently enmeshed in the Philippines War. Kipling exhorted Americans to do their duty, as Anglo-Saxons, and to help civilize the barbarous peoples of the world.

France Britain and France had clashed over their overseas dominions since the Nine Years War of 1688–1697, and their rivalry continued until the dawn of the twentieth century. By 1888, the French resented England for seizing control of the Suez Canal in Egypt, which a French company had built. In 1898, the two countries nearly came to blows over the Fashoda Incident, a skirmish of French and British forces in the Sudan.

However, politicians like Georges Clemenceau (1841–1929) began insisting that the French should not be preoccupied with colonial affairs. He argued that France should instead concentrate on reclaiming Alsace-Lorraine from the Germans. He and others accordingly promoted closer ties with Britain. In 1904, France and the United Kingdom—unified in their distrust of Germany—settled their territorial differences and signed the Entente Cordiale. England was given free reign in Egypt, and France was given control of Morocco.

Russia From 1813 to 1907, Britain fought a long cold war with Russia over the Middle East, specifically Afghanistan, Persia, and Tibet. England feared Russia's

This 1914 photographs shows locally recruited troops under German command in Dar Es Salaam, Tanzania (then part of German East Africa). *Hulton Archive/Getty Images*

expansion to the south—towards Britain's prize colonial possession, India. For decades, the two empires engaged in espionage and diplomatic intrigue, locked in a shadow conflict that Kipling called "the Great Game."

England had also sided against Russia in the Russo-Japanese War, essentially forcing Russia to fight alone. Also, Russian reinforcements arrived at the warfront months late because Britain had blocked the Suez Canal to Russian ships.

Nevertheless, Russia and Britain came to an accord in the face of the rising threat from Germany. The Anglo-Russian Convention of 1907 ended the Great Game and cemented the Triple Entente between Russia, Great Britain and Ireland, and France.

Germany In the beginning of the First German Reich, Chancellor Otto von Bismarck opposed the acquisition of overseas colonies, believing that they distracted attention from Germany's precarious situation at home. He once told an imperialist enthusiast, "Your map of Africa is very fine, but my map of Africa is here in Europe. Here is Russia and here is France and here we are in the middle. That is my map of Africa."

Nevertheless, as the race for colonies accelerated in the 1880s, Germany annexed parts of western, southwestern, and southern Africa, territories that now make up parts of Cameroon, Togo, Namibia, Tanzania, Rwanda, and Burundi.

When Kaiser Wilhelm II (1859–1941) forced the Iron Chancellor (as Bismarck was known) to resign in 1890, Germany adopted even more aggressive expansionist policies. Germany's watchword changed from *Realpolitik* (practical politics) to *Weltpolitik* (world politics).

The Entente Cordiale, between England and France, alarmed and offended Germany. In 1905, Wilhelm responded by delivering a speech in Tangiers in which he supported Moroccan independence. He was, in effect, staking a German claim for the territory. France reacted with predictable outrage, and both countries moved armies a little closer to the border.

Morocco had long been a bone of Anglo-French contention. Doubtless, the German government precipitated the crisis in order to test, and hopefully to break, the Entente. Instead, the Kaiser discovered the depth of his diplomatic isolation. At the international conference at Algeciras, only Austria-Hungary supported the Reich.

In 1911, Germany made another attempt to assert itself in Morocco, when the Kaiser sent the gunboat *Panther* to the port of Agadir. That action provoked resounding condemnation throughout the world. Nevertheless, Wilhelm did not relinquish his claim until France granted Germany economic rights in Morocco and ceded a large portion of the French Congo to German Kamerun.

The Moroccan crises greatly hastened the coming of World War I. For Britain and France, the crises had confirmed their suspicions about German aggression. The German public, in the meantime, felt put down and conspired against. The French and the English, they believed, were committed to stopping German advancement and were trying to deny them their place in the sun. All around Europe, politicians and generals began to seriously prepare for war.

Tangled European Alliances

In the late nineteenth century, the great powers of Europe involved themselves in a complex network of treaties and informal understandings. Most of these treaties were defensive alliances in which one party promised to come to the other's aid if either were attacked. In this way, diplomats strove to maintain the balance of power in Europe. In practice, the continent divided itself into two armed camps, a development that anticipated—and arguably caused—war.

The Central Powers Treaties among European nations were hardly new. In the wake of Napoleon's march across the continent, Austrian Prince Klemens Wenzel von Metternich constructed a diplomatic web of alliances among the aristocratic governments of Europe. The "Metternich system," as it was called, was meant to keep the peace in Europe not only by preventing wars between the nations, but by brutally suppressing liberal and nationalist movements.

Metternich was ousted, however, in the Revolutions of 1848—a wave of nationalistic and liberal insurrections. Although conservative forces put down the revolutionaries, their aspirations did not die. From 1815 to 1870, the various Italian states came together as one nation. In 1871, the unified German Empire was born when the northern German states pledged their allegiance to the Prussian King Wilhelm I.

The new nation of Germany emerged strong and victorious from the Franco-Prussian War. Nevertheless, Chancellor Otto von Bismarck, the architect of German unification, was very aware of its vulnerable position. Germany was surrounded by older world powers, and the defeated French made no secret of their thirst for revenge.

Because of a complex network of alliances, the 1914 assassination of Archduke Franz Ferdinand, pictured here with his wife Sophie, plunged Europe into war. *Getty Images*

In order to forestall a French attack, Bismarck in 1873 formed the Three Emperors's League, among Wilhelm I, Franz Joseph I of Austria-Hungary, and Czar Alexander II (1818–1881) of Russia. However, when the 1877 Balkan Crisis caused a diplomatic rift between Austria-Hungary and Russia, Germany had to choose one or the other. In 1879, Bismarck concluded the Dual Alliance between Germany and Austria-Hungary.

The new state of Italy also nurtured ambitions of world empire, particularly in northern Africa. Therefore, when the French occupied Tunis in 1881, the Italian government went so far as to approach their traditional enemy, Austria, for support. Thus, in 1882, the Dual Alliance became the Triple Alliance.

In 1887, the ever-cautious Bismarck engineered the Reinsurance Treaty with Russia, in which both countries promised to remain neutral if the other was attacked by a third party. But this treaty was not renewed after Kaiser Wilhelm II took power in 1888. Instead, Wilhelm gave his assurance that Germany would back Austria-Hungary no matter what, giving them a blank check for military support.

The Entente Forsaken by Germany, Russia found itself alone. Facing stubborn opposition from Austria-Hungary over the Balkan issue, the Czar entered into a military alliance with France in 1894. France found some measure of security in the arrangement—Bismarck had exerted considerable effort to keep the French diplomatically isolated since 1870.

If the French nursed bitter hatred towards Germany, the fact did not much bother the British—England and France had been persistent enemies for eight hundred years. However, Britain began to view Germany with alarm after the ascension of Wilhelm II. Even though the new emperor was the grandson of Queen Victoria, her government saw him as aggressive, anti-British, and unstable. Indeed, German statesman Friedrich von Holstein (1837–1909) commented that the young man was, "frankly, not quite right in the head."

Certainly, Wilhelm could behave erratically. In addition, he displayed a fierce Prussian nationalism, and he was unapologetically militaristic. He harbored a passion for martial uniforms; he once suggested that England make him a colonel in a kilt-wearing Scottish regiment.

Actually, while condemning Britain, Wilhelm seemed to long for English respect. He made several sincere—if gauche and impractical—overtures towards an Anglo-German alliance. His proposals were generally snubbed, and Wilhelm resented it. He felt that Britain looked down on him and on his people. This sentiment was shared by a great many of his subjects.

In 1896, Wilhelm sent a congratulatory telegram to one of the South African Boer Republics, who were in the midst of revolting against British rule. The British press exploded in anger, and anti-German feeling began to take root on the island.

The British government was far more alarmed by Germany's new expansionist foreign policy. When Wilhelm forced Bismarck to resign in 1890, he abandoned the Chancellor's restraint. Germany began actively seeking overseas colonies and protectorates. More ominously, Wilhelm built up the German navy, challenging England's supremacy at sea.

In 1904, Britain and France signed a series of agreements known as the *Entente Cordiale* (the cordial understanding). This was not a formal alliance, but it was extremely significant given the age-old enmity between the two nations.

After strenuous negotiation, Russia also entered into an informal agreement with Britain and France in 1907. The press quickly announced the "Triple Entente" as a counter to the Triple Alliance of Germany, Austria-Hungary, and Italy.

In 1902, Italy signed an agreement with France in which it promised to remain neutral should France be attacked. This directly contradicted Italy's commitments to Germany and Austria-Hungary. Nevertheless, the Triple Alliance was regularly renewed until 1914. As a result, when hostilities broke out, Italy was technically allied with both sides. Italy remained neutral at first and then joined the war in 1915 on the side of the Entente.

The Domino Effect When Austria-Hungary declared war on Serbia on July 28, 1914, Russia immediately mobilized its army to defend its Balkan commitments. Many top German officials were dismayed by their ally's actions, which were taken without consulting Berlin. Nevertheless, as they had promised, Germany declared war on Russia on August 1. In the meantime, Germany came to a secret alliance with the Ottoman Empire.

European generals had been preparing their war plans for years. The German army commanders had determined that their best hope for success lay in a lightning strike on Paris. The fastest path to Paris lay through Belgium.

When Germany attacked Luxembourg on August 3, Britain protested. The European nations, including Germany, had guaranteed Belgian neutrality by treaty in 1839. The German chancellor dismissed the neutrality agreement as "a scrap of paper." His words drummed up indignation in England and in America. The British were not obliged, under the terms of the Entente, to fight for France, but they were committed to defend Belgium.

That night, Sir Edward Grey (1862–1933) gloomily looked out the window of the London Foreign Office. "The lamps are going out all over Europe," he said sadly, "we shall not see them lit again in our lifetime." The next day, August 4, the United Kingdom declared war on Germany.

Assassination of Archduke Franz Ferdinand

In 1914, after years of nationalist posturing and unresolved disputes, Europe stood poised on the brink of war. Britain, Germany, and France had frantically built up their armies and navies while their military commanders had worked out detailed war plans. Diplomats had bound the great powers into a complex network of alliances, pledging their nations to fight. On June 28, 1914, a Serbian nationalist assassinated the presumptive heir to the Austrian throne, Archduke Franz Ferdinand (1863–1914). A month later, Austria-Hungary declared war on Serbia. One by one, the European powers were dragged into the conflict.

The Balkan Wars In 1908, the Dual Monarchy of Austria-Hungary annexed Bosnia, a former province of the rapidly dissolving Ottoman Empire. This move infuriated the neighboring Balkan states. Serbia protested particularly vigorously because of the large number of ethnic Serbs in Bosnia.

Although war was narrowly avoided in 1908, Serbians increasingly resented the continued Austrian, Turkish, and Italian incursions into Slavic territories. Backed by Russia, the Balkan League was formed, consisting of Bulgaria, Serbia, Greece and Montenegro. In

Police grab Gavrilo Princip after he assassinated Crown Prince Franz Ferdinand and his wife Sophie June 28, 1914, Sarajevo. © *Bettmann/Corbis*

1912–1913, the Balkan League fought and won a war against the Ottoman Empire.

Surprised and alarmed by Balkan strength, the Great Powers stepped in. Austria in particular could not permit Serbia to have a port on the Adriatic Coast. At the signing of the Treaty of London on May 30, 1913, the Balkan states were forced to accept—in their view—a thoroughly unsatisfactory set of peace terms.

In the summer of 1913, dissatisfaction with the new territorial assignments led to war between Bulgaria and the other members of the League. Bulgaria was soundly defeated. Serbia emerged from the Balkan Wars stronger and more antagonistic towards Austria-Hungary.

The Assassin Gavrilo Princip (1894–1918) was a young Bosnian Serb, the son of a postal worker. As a student, he had taken leadership of a national group called *Mlada Bosna* (Young Bosnia). From there he joined a secret society called *Ujedinjenje ili Smrt* (Union or Death), also known as the Black Hand. This organization dedicated itself to the creation of a Pan-Slavic state.

The Black Hand also fiercely opposed the Austrian Hapsburg monarchy. They suspected (quite rightly) that the Hapsburg monarchy wanted to absorb the Balkans. Princip was later to declare at his trial: "I am a Yugoslav nationalist, aiming for the unification of all Yugoslavs, and I do not care what form of state, but it must be free from Austria." When asked how he meant to achieve those ends, he replied, "By means of terror."

The Archduke Franz Ferdinand was the nephew of Hapsburg Emperor Franz Joseph. He did not expect to ascend to the throne himself, but Crown Prince Rudolf apparently committed suicide in 1889, making Ferdinand's father the next in line to be emperor. When his own father died in 1896, Ferdinand then became the heir apparent of the Austro-Hungarian Empire.

Ferdinand recognized the power of nationalism in modern Europe and considered it the defining issue of his day. He advocated several solutions to the problem, including a federal "United States of Austria," which would include Slavic Bosnia. He also suggested a "trialistic" Austria-Hungary-Yugoslav Empire.

As a political leader, Ferdinand was recognized as forceful and ambitious. By 1913, he had risen in the military and had been made inspector general of the armed forces.

The Murder Personally, Ferdinand despised Viennese high society, and he did not get along well with his uncle, the Emperor. The feeling was mutual, especially after Ferdinand fell in love below his station. He insisted upon marrying Countess Sophie Chotek (1868–1914), a lady-in-waiting, even though it meant that their children would not have the right to inherit the Hapsburg crown. Because of their difference in rank, Sophie could not appear with her husband on most public occasions.

However, Sophie did accompany her husband on June 28, 1914, when he visited Sarajevo. It is possible the Archduke did not recognize the significance of the date. By the Julian calendar, he arrived on the Feast of St. Vitus, the celebration of the 1389 Battle of Kosovo, a day with special significance for Serbian patriots. The day also had special meaning for Ferdinand and Sophie—it was their wedding anniversary.

Serbian nationalists received advanced word of the visit. They were outraged by what they considered to be a slap in the face to Slavic sovereignty. With members of the Black Hand, including Princip, they lined the street awaiting Ferdinand's motorcade. One of them managed to throw a hand grenade into his open cab. However, the archduke deflected the bomb. It exploded outside, wounding a few members of his entourage.

Shaken, the couple continued to City Hall, where they were greeted by the mayor. Later that day, Ferdinand left to visit the bombing victims in the hospital. Sophie insisted on coming with him. To be safe, they decided to take a different route through the city, but no one remembered to tell the driver. As a result, the car passed close to the site of the earlier attack, where members of the conspiracy were still loitering.

On realizing that they had gone the wrong way, the driver stopped the car to turn around. Princip, seizing the unexpected opportunity, stepped forward and shot both the Archduke and his wife. She was struck in the abdomen, he in the neck. Ferdinand cried: "Sophie dear, Sophie dear, don't die. Stay alive for our children." Bleeding heavily, he held on a little longer, but both of them died within the hour.

The crowd immediately seized Princip and then handed him over, beaten but alive, to the police. He was tried and found guilty. A discrepancy in his birth records made it questionable whether he had reached the age of majority at the time of the crime. The court gave him the benefit of the doubt and sentenced him to the maximum penalty—twenty years in prison. Princip died of tuberculosis in 1918.

The Fallout No proof has ever been found that the Serbian government conspired in the assassination (though the Serbian chief of intelligence was a member of the Black Hand). Nevertheless, on July 24, Austria issued an ultimatum to Serbia demanding certain measures to curb terrorist activities or face the end of diplomatic relations. It was sharply worded and almost impossible to accept. "It is clear," the letter read, "that the murder at Sarajevo was conceived at Belgrade."

As brutal as Austria-Hungary's demands—including suppression of press, education, organizations, and individuals deemed hostile to Austria-Hungary—were, Serbia agreed to most of them. The Austrian emissary to Belgrade, however, had been ordered to reject any response. On July 28 Austria declared war on Serbia. The fuse was lit; soon Europe would go up in flames.

✪ Major Figures

Kaiser Wilhelm II

Friedrich Wilhelm Hohenzollern ruled Germany as Kaiser Wilhelm II, from 1888 until his abdication in 1918.

A Child of Privilege Friedrich Wilhelm Hohenzollern (1859–1941) ruled Germany as Kaiser Wilhelm II, from 1888 until his abdication in 1918. Wilhelm was born to royalty, the son of Friedrich Wilhelm, crown prince of Prussia, and grandson of Wilhelm I, ruler of the German empire, and Queen Victoria of England. His mother, Victoria, daughter of the English queen, never shook off her obsession with what she considered the superiority of all things British, and her son grew to resent her controlling, critical, and domineering role in his life. His rebellion against her political teachings, all based on the comparatively liberal British system of government, drove him to pursue a pure authoritarianism during his own rule. The future kaiser's lack of personal insight, social skills, intellect, and foresight combined with a considerable narcissism to lead Germany into a war that eventually ensnared most of the Western world.

At his birth, attended by the British doctors beloved of his mother, the infant Wilhelm suffered an injury that resulted in a paralyzed, shortened left arm and hearing loss. Wilhelm forever blamed his mother and the British doctors for this disability, a resentment fed by Victoria's continual criticisms of the handicap. Wilhelm admirably overcame these physical obstacles and forced himself to become a good marksman, horseman, and swimmer.

Bitterness against the British His anger at British doctors was in no way diminished when they were brought in to attend to his father on his sickbed. Wilhelm's father had become king of Prussia on the death of Wilhelm's grandfather, Wilhelm I, but he survived only ninety-nine days as emperor. The disease that killed him

Kaiser Wilhelm II. *Getty Images*

was throat cancer, misdiagnosed by the English physicians as a lesser malady treatable with rest and proper diet. When Wilhelm's father succumbed after spending most of his time as ruler infirm in his bed, Wilhelm became kaiser and nursed in his heart a loathing for the British. This loathing extended to his own family, from his grandmother, Queen Victoria, to his many British cousins, with whom he had spent his childhood summers. His mother, the younger Victoria, fed this bitterness with frequent unfavorable comparisons between Wilhelm and his cousins.

Thus, the man who stepped up to the throne of the Hohenzollerns, a line of rulers that included Frederick the Great, was an unfortunate combination of internalized resentment, limited skills, and a powerful sense of entitlement. His strongest interest was the military, but even at these pursuits he was essentially mediocre, placing more emphasis on and deriving more delight from uniforms and parades than from military strategizing or drills.

Clashing with Bismarck   Ready at hand when Kaiser Wilhelm took the throne was Otto von Bismarck, the chancellor who had served for decades as Germany's chief policy maker. Part of Bismarck's policy was maintaining friendly relations with Russia, but for Wilhelm,

his Russian relatives were only second in line to the British as targets of his dislike. He disdained Czar Alexander and his successor, Czar Nicholas, both of whom considered Wilhelm mentally unstable. When it came time to renew Bismarck's secret nonaggression pact with Russia, Wilhelm, after consulting with his toadies, decided to let it lapse. A furious Bismarck, who considered this decision a fatal error, tendered his resignation as a mark of his disapproval, not actually intending for Wilhelm to accept it. But Wilhelm did accept it, and the intelligent, guiding mastermind of German international policy was chancellor no more.

One reason Wilhelm argued against renewing the pact was a concern that news of it would leak to Germany's ally in the "Dual Monarchy," the Austro-Hungarian empire. His loyalty to this other European empire would eventually set into motion the events that would build into World War I.

Attracting British Attention   Wilhelm, while not necessarily desiring military engagement with the other European powers, had an eye on England when he began building up the German navy. His goal was to make Germany a great naval power in European waters, and he succeeded in making it second only to England's legendary navy in size. The English warily watched this buildup, certainly with little trust in Wilhelm's motives, an attitude reinforced by the kaiser's unwanted interference in international matters. He often stumbled and bumbled his way into situations that did not involve or concern his empire, such as when he sent the infamous "Kruger Telegram," congratulating South African President Paul Kruger for his defeat of several hundred British raiders in 1895. To paraphrase Queen Victoria on another occasion, the British government was not amused.

Assassination of Franz Ferdinand   Wilhelm's lacking sense of propriety led him to errors such as the Kruger Telegram and to making dangerous public remarks, such as referring to Serbia as a nation with "her murderers and bandits" that deserved punishment. This latter comment was particularly incendiary because Serbia was an ally of the Russians, which had supported Serbia's agitation of the Slavs for freedom from Germany's partner in the Dual Monarchy, the Austro-Hungarians. When the heir to the Austro-Hungarian Empire, the Archduke Franz Ferdinand, was assassinated by a Bosnian Serb in Sarajevo on June 28, 1914, the first domino of war fell. Even though Serbia itself had nothing to do with the assassination, the Austro-Hungarians saw an opening that would allow them to subdue Serbia and possibly prevent their alliance with Russia to create a Slavic empire.

War   Acting on their hopes, the Austro-Hungarians delivered to the Serbs an ultimatum containing a list of demands. What Austria-Hungary really seemed to want was an excuse to go to war, and they grasped at the slimmest straw when Serbia accepted the ultimatum with the exception of a single condition: a provision allowing Austro-Hungarian officials to enter Serbia to find and punish the archduke's killer or killers. This lone equivocation was evidence enough for Austria-Hungary of Serbia's devious intentions, and not discouraged by Wilhelm himself, the Austro-Hungarians promptly declared war on Serbia. Wilhelm, the other part of the Dual Monarchy, in a fit of self-exoneration, said, "I can do no more." The second domino had fallen.

With the reality of war practically in his lap, Wilhelm recoiled from the idea of actual military conflict. It was one thing to encourage his ally in the Dual Monarchy from behind the scenes, or to withhold his advice and opinions, but something else entirely to join forces with that ally as it angered half of Europe. He immediately moved to keep the fighting limited only to Austria and Serbia, but he was too late. Russia, on the watch for just such an affront, had already mobilized on the eastern frontier. Wilhelm, unable to talk Russia into halting, was forced to declare war on the Czar as part of his agreement with his Austro-Hungarian allies.

The dominoes now fell apace. Russia had a pact with France that drew the French into the conflict, something the two countries had agreed on in an 1894 alliance. Flanked on the eastern and western fronts by hostile armies, Wilhelm sought to deal a swift blow to at least one of them. His strategy was to avoid a slog over the mountains and instead march directly through the flatter plains of Belgium to the western front and defeat the French. The only problem with this plan was that after the Belgian Revolution in 1830, European countries had recognized Belgium's long-standing neutrality and barring entry of any foreign army into the country. Wilhelm elected to ignore the treaty and sent his troops marching through Belgium.

With the Treaty of London in 1839, Britain and Prussia, together with other main European powers, made their recognition of Belgium's sovereignty official. Wilhelm's aggression was exactly what Britain had been waiting for. They now declared war on their German cousin for his blatant violation of international law. World War I had begun in earnest.

Failure, Armistice, and Exile As the fighting dragged on through bitter and agonizing trench warfare, Germany did not fare well. The much-vaunted navy could not leave the harbor, because it was trapped there by the British. The heavy losses wore on the German people, who grew disenchanted and fatigued from the hardships the war imposed. When the United States finally entered the war in April 1917 in response to German U-boat attacks, the war was near its end. Germany finally asked for an armistice, ending the fighting, and Wilhelm was forced to abdicate his throne. He was the last of the German emperors.

The deposed monarch fled to the Netherlands and was granted exile by Queen Wilhelmina (1880–1962). The Dutch refused to turn the exiled emperor over to international authorities for trial, and the former kaiser spent the remaining twenty years of his life in the Netherlands, a pathetic figure unable to acknowledge his personal role in any of the tragic events of his life. His wife, a German princess whom he married in 1881 and with whom he fathered seven children, died there in 1921. He wrote a memoir that focused only on the years preceding the war and blamed his defeat on Russian socialists, Jews, or his own relatives in Britain, but never on himself. When Hitler took France, the ex-emperor expressed his pleasure at the success, but Wilhelm did not live to see the outcome of World War II, dying at age eighty-two in the summer of 1941 in Holland.

Ferdinand Foch

Early Years Ferdinand Foch (1851–1929) was a French marshall and the commander in chief of the Allied armies in World War I. Foch was born on October 2, 1851, in the area of the Pyrenees where his family had lived for centuries. He was the sixth of seven children.

Obviously a bright young man, Foch attended college in Metz, a city in Lorraine. It was there, during a test on May 11, 1871, that he and his classmates learned that France had signed the Treaty of Frankfurt, which end the Franco-Prussian War and ceded the very ground on which the students sat to Germany. Northeastern Lorraine, including Metz, and Alsace now belonged to the Prussians. Undoubtedly, the sorrowful and angry students wanted to see the Germans someday be forced to return their territory, and Ferdinand Foch eventually became leader of the forces that would ensure that return and see France triumph, for a time, over the Germans.

Inspired by the cause of the Franco-Prussian War, Foch had enlisted in the army, but he never engaged in battle in that short conflict. Instead, he went on to the military École Polytechnique in Nancy, another German-occupied French town. After a year, he entered training school for artillery, graduating third in his class in 1872. He then received cavalry training and returned to a career as an artilleryman when he was promoted to captain in 1878. He was married in 1883 to Louise-Ursule-Julie Bienvenue.

An Officer and a Scholar In 1885, Foch attended the École Superieure de Guerre, a school intended especially for the most promising officers. He continued his streak of successes there, graduating fourth in his class and returning to the school as a professor. Even though he was physically unimposing at five feet, five inches tall, barrel-chested, and bow-legged, his square jaw and fiery way of speaking left a strong impression on anyone who met him. He was very much a student of war and all things military, approaching the execution of war with a scholarly, yet extremely practical, attitude. He argued that fighting was more important than strategy; that a leader must be more stubborn than his enemy; that offense, not defense, brings victory; and that shock is the tactic that wins battles.

His teachings were misinterpreted by some, leading to distortions that had disastrous consequences. In 1914, his followers twisted his ideas about offense before defense and used it as a guiding principle in their conduct of the early part of World War I. Ironically, defense won battles in that war far more frequently than offensive tactics did, and the offenses were often horrific bloodbaths rather than triumphant, shocking victories.

Religious Suspicion In 1901, Foch's familial connection to the Jesuits (his brother, Germain, was a Jesuit priest) proved to be a disadvantage. He suddenly stopped teaching at the École Superieure when the government became increasingly anticlerical. Adherence to Catholicism came to be viewed as disloyalty to the Republican government, and Foch was packed off under suspicion to various outposts in the provinces. To add insult to this unwarranted injury, he also saw his promotion to colonel delayed by two years. Through it all, he retained his glass-half-full view of things, telling other disgruntled officers that they would have to put up with a lot worse than that in a war.

Always busy, Foch managed to publish two books while he was banished, and waited for his country to realize how much they needed him. That realization came in 1907 when he was promoted to brigadier general and returned to the École Superieure as commandant, all by the order of a most unlikely comrade: Republican, Protestant, radical Georges Clemenceau, by then premier of France. By the time World War I began in August 1914, Foch had been promoted to division general and had taken leadership of the Twentieth Corps, the French Army's elite. He was close to retirement when Archduke Franz Ferdinand was assassinated in Sarajevo, which brought the long-simmering global conflict to a boil.

The Right Man at the Right Time Foch led his corps in Lorraine with relative success, fighting back the Germans, only to have them strike back. Foch was named to command the Ninth Army shortly after this engagement, and he and his regiment distinguished themselves at the first battle of the Marne, which lasted from September 6 through September 9, 1914. Foch never let up, pushing and pushing against the German onslaught. Four days after this triumph, however, he received the crushing news that his only son and his son-in-law had both been killed.

In October, the French commander in chief, General Joseph Joffre (1852–1951), appointed Foch leader of all of France's troops in the north. Joffre's intent was

for Foch and his men to keep the Germans away from the ports so that they could not cut the British off from their home base. Foch actually found himself organizing all of the Allied forces—the British, French, and Belgian armies—bolstering demoralized commanders with his own fire and will and, without the actual authority to do so, leading this multinational force to victory in horrendous battles that kept the Germans back and stalled out action on the western front.

Although he was appointed commander of the Northern Army Group in January 1915, Foch found himself relieved of that command in December 1916, just days after Joffre himself was fired. The firings were based on Foch's efforts to break the stalled action on the western front, where his forces had endured huge numbers of casualties during the battles of Artois and the Somme. After these catastrophic losses, Foch spent some time serving as an advisor until General Philippe Pétain (1856–1951) appointed him chief of the general staff on May 15, 1917, a post in which he served as the government's chief military advisor. He also proved his skills with multinational forces when he went to Italy with some British and French troops to slow down the Austro-German incursion at Caporetto. But the allies were officially on the defensive, and Foch, true to his philosophy, wanted to see them execute an offensive. His French superior and the British leader, Douglas Haig (1861–1928), were both doubtful about Foch's plans for an offensive, however, and refused to commit any men to it.

Commander of the Allied Forces The Germans launched their own offensive on March 21, 1918, ending any theoretical discussion about whether or not the Allies should plan one. Now, forced to maintain a defense to keep the Germans from splitting up the western front, the Allied leaders selected Foch to lead the multinational force, appointing him commander in chief of the Allied forces. After a narrowly won victory in a bloody battle at Chemin des Dames that involved the American forces as well, Foch saw the course of the war improve in France's favor with a subsequent defense against the Germans at Champagne and then his "shock," a counterattack that he and Pétain had carefully planned. This offensive led to a series of many more targeting Germany's supply routes, which pushed the German army further and further back toward the frontier. The beleaguered Germans finally asked for an armistice.

Foch was not enthusiastic about peace with the Germans, and at the Paris Peace Conference in 1919, he argued for a permanent military presence in the country and for drawing Germany's boundary at the Rhine. Clemenceau, however, was forced by the United States and Britain to accept an unsatisfactory compromise that many felt made too many concessions to Germany. Foch lamented the outcome, commenting that the agreement "is not peace. It is an armistice for twenty years." As subsequent events attest, his observation was remarkably prescient.

Foch himself did not live long enough to see World War II. He died of a heart attack in Paris at the age of seventy-seven on March 20, 1929. He lies entombed at Les Invalides, the final resting place of many of France's famous military leaders.

Czar Nicholas II

Nicholas II of Russia (1868–1918) was the last of the Russian czars and the last of the Romanov line, which had ruled the Russian empire for almost three hundred years. The dynasty collapsed under Nicholas in 1918, ending with his murder and those of his wife, their five children, two servants, and the family doctor.

Early Life Nicholas was born in Russia to Czar Alexander III (1845–1894), a powerful ruler who had suppressed rising discontent among his subjects during his reign. Twenty-six-year-old Nicholas came to the throne of a society with a rigid social structure and a chasm between the haves (the nobility) and the have-nots. He lit the differences in sharp relief by making several autocratic pronouncements, disdaining the idea that the people could at least to some extent rule themselves, and being intractable with the Duma, or Russian parliament, which he had reluctantly allowed to form. His autocratic approach to governing combined with some serious bad luck, a sick heir, and revolts from labor that shook governments across Europe and ultimately ended the rule of the Romanovs.

Troubled Monarch When his father died suddenly and unexpectedly in 1894, Nicholas came to rule the largest country in the world. Soon after, he fell in love with and married the German princess Alix Victoria Helene Luise Beatrix (1972–1918), granddaughter of Queen Victoria of Great Britain. Through her grandmother, she inherited the genetic mutation for hemophilia, which she would tragically pass to the only son she and Czar Nicholas would have. Alix converted to the Russian Orthodox Church, taking the name Alexandra. The two had been in the course of planning a huge, festive wedding when Czar Alexander died. The couple then had to marry quickly following the funeral. The coronation itself, intended to be a grand and gilded ceremony, ended in horror when thirteen thousand of the half million peasants in attendance were trampled to death in a rush for food stalls. Nicholas was blamed for not having the manpower for crowd control, and his reputation from that point forward with his commoner subjects was unfavorable.

Although Nicholas was a friendly fellow who loved his wife and family—which eventually consisted of four daughters (Anastasia, Tatiana, Olga, and Marie) and his son and heir, Alexis—he was not prepared for his new position. Most of his 130 million subjects were peasants laboring in rural villages, only recently freed from institutionalized serfdom. In spite of their newfound freedoms and small parcels of land to call their own, the peasant class remained constrained by the monarchy and forced to pay heavy taxes. In addition, the Russian population itself was booming.

A Nation in Transition Russia had fallen behind in the first half of the nineteenth century in terms of industrialization. Government-run efforts to catch up and industrialize led to the growth of large slums filled with underpaid factory workers who were supported by taxes paid by peasants—both the urban and rural working classes were angry about their predicament. The peasants themselves were receptive to the words of revolutionaries who were trying hard to foment rebellion and overthrow the aristocracy. When Czar Alexander died in 1894 at only forty-nine years of age, he left his son a nation made up of one hundred separate nationalities and increasingly open to the efforts of Marxist revolutionaries. Faced with this daunting prospect and the shock of his father's premature death, a worried Nicholas commented, "I know nothing of the business of ruling."

The Debacle with Japan On a visit to Japan two years before the death of his father, Nicholas had been attacked by a would-be assassin. The attempt to kill Nicholas was foiled by a cousin of the future czar, who happened to be with him, but the attacker left a scar across Nicholas's forehead, one that would always remind him of his hatred of the Japanese, against whom he harbored racist bitterness. His dislike of the Japanese led him to enter into war with Japan in 1904 over territories in the Korean peninsula and Manchuria. This ill-advised venture was a disaster. The Russians were overconfident and eventually lost the center of their power in the Pacific. They also suffered an embarrassing and devastating defeat at the hands of the Japanese fleet at the Straits of Tsushima. The Japanese had defeated the great Russian military.

This humiliating loss did nothing for Nicholas's reputation at home. Popular unrest intensified, leading to the "Bloody Sunday" in January 1905 when hundreds of the 200,000 Russians trying to peacefully petition for civil rights were shot down in front of the Czar's Winter Palace. Following this carnage, Nicholas and his family hunkered down in a palace outside St. Petersburg while unrest grew throughout the nation.

Tension over the Duma In an effort to appease the masses, Nicholas offered to set up a Duma, or parliament, but his terms were unacceptable. Rather than legislating as representatives of the people, this Duma would instead simply serve as advisors to the Czar. The half-hearted effort to appease his people failed miserably. Opposition arose on all sides and was followed by a general strike, in which workers from all levels, industries, and areas refused to work. Nicholas at first sought a military dictator to force the nation into submission. He then gave in and issued the "October Manifesto," granting the Duma legislative power and a constitution. Yet Nicholas himself insisted on keeping his traditional title of "autocrat," and was constantly at odds with the Duma, trying to restrict its powers and threatening to get rid of it completely. This attitude, of course, did nothing to improve relationships between the royal family and the people of Russia.

The Czarina Czarina Alexandra supported her husband's belief in the monarchy, reminding him of his ancestor, Peter the Great (1672–1725), a powerful monarch who ruled his people with an iron hand. Further undermining trust in the czar was the presence of one of her favorites at court, Grigori Rasputin (1869–1916), who arrived from Siberia in 1903. Rasputin had gained favor with Alexandra through his apparent success in treating Alexis's hemophilia. This blood-clotting disorder makes even the most minor wounds mortally dangerous, threatening not only the boy's life but the succession to the throne. As an autocrat, Nicholas could have overturned ancestral law disallowing a female ruler and ensured a Romanov sucession, given that he had four daughters and only one ailing son. But he never did, and Rasputin's powers over the couple only seemed to grow.

By 1913, the Russian public had had enough of Rasputin, who had gained considerable power as a result of his proximity to the throne. That year, celebrations of the three-hundredth anniversary of the Romanov dynasty were met with silence from the populace rather than with cheers.

When World War I broke out in 1914, in part due to bumbling diplomacy on the part of Kaiser Wilhelm of Germany, Nicholas was no better placed than he had been during his disastrous war with Japan. His army suffered defeat after defeat, and Nicholas himself deemed it right for him to go to the front lines and command his troops. This decision meant, of course, that the army's failures were now directly his, as well. Remaining behind in St. Petersburg, Alexandra ruled in her husband's place and was guided by the mysterious and strange Rasputin, disliked by many. Alexandra became the focus of rumors that, being German born, she was a traitor to the Russian people. Eventually, Rasputin was murdered by men tired of the influence he wielded over the royal family.

Downfall of the Romanovs Disruption and failure on the front lines translated into riots and strikes at home. Revolution was officially underway by March 1917. After even his military commanders refused to help him, Nicholas desperately cast around for a successor, someone who might appease the people. His own son, Alexis, was far too ill. His brother, Grand Duke Michael (1878–1918) refused. In the end, Nicholas was forced to abdicate on

March 15, 1917, ending the three-century rule of the Romanov line.

The former Czar had nowhere to go. He could not go to his wife's family in Britain without causing an international crisis and jeopardizing Britain's own need to maintain friendly relations with Russia, regardless of who was in charge. In the end, Nicholas and Alexandra and their children were placed under house arrest in Ekaterinburg. In the spring of 1918, the Russian Civil War broke out. The former czar and his family were kept in increasingly less comfortable surroundings. Finally, in the early hours of July 17, 1918, the family and their servants were awakened and marched into the cellar of the house. A firing squad awaited them. Nicholas was the first to be executed, requiring several bullets. His daughters had to be bayoneted after shots failed to kill them; the bullets were somewhat deflected by the jewelry they had hidden under their clothing. After the family, the servants, and the family's doctor had been executed, most of the bodies were burned with acid and thrown into a well. They later were moved to unmarked graves, where they remained until they were discovered in 1991.

David Lloyd George

David Lloyd George (1863–1945) was an English Liberal Party statesman and the prime minister from 1916 to 1922. He was instrumental in the formation of the Versailles Treaty. Welsh by ancestry, Lloyd George was born in Manchester, England, on January 17, 1863. His father, David George, was a school headmaster who became ill with tuberculosis and died in 1864, leaving Lloyd George's Welsh mother, Elizabeth, daughter of a Baptist minister, penniless. Her brother, Richard Lloyd, took in his sister and her three children in Wales. This uncle of Lloyd George's was a politically active Liberal and a Baptist preacher. Thus, early childhood influences molded Lloyd George into a political radical and fervent evangelical.

Early Years Lloyd George learned French and Latin from his preacher/shoemaker uncle, a passionate Welsh nationalist who spoke only Welsh at home, and he also attended the village school. Lloyd George most enjoyed geography, history, and Latin. Before he turned sixteen, he had passed the preliminary law examination. In July 1878, he began an apprenticeship in law; writing and speaking on temperance, land reform, and religion; and following in the footsteps of his grandfather and uncle by preaching in the church. He passed the Law Society exam in 1884, qualifying as a solicitor and at the young age of twenty-two, he set up his legal practice in Criccieth in North Wales, eventually opening branches in other villages. Much of his law business focused on defending accused poachers. He also worked to organize a farmers' union and campaigned against tithing, the practice of supporting the church by giving a portion

As prime minister, Lloyd George undertook efforts to build coalitions among Great Britain's liberals and conservatives, particularly for the sake of the war effort.   *Time Life Pictures/Mansell/ Getty Images*

of one's wages regularly. He became a growing force in the Liberal Party because of his legal skill and his public-speaking ability.

He married Margaret Owen, daughter of a Methodist farmer, in 1888, but they had an unhappy marriage because of Lloyd George's numerous affairs. In spite of this, they had five children, but lost a daughter to appendicitis in 1907.

Entering Politics As a Welshman brought up in Wales, Lloyd George felt strongly about the movement for Welsh home rule. He founded a newspaper he called the *Trumpet of Freedom* and hoped it would help him in his election to Parliament. He was selected to run for his borough in 1888, three years before the next general election. In spite of the time gap, he took the helm of the district party organization and kicked off his campaign. Within months he was rewarded with an appointment as alderman of his borough, Caernarfon.

The conservative incumbent of the borough died in 1890, leading to a by-election, which Lloyd George

won, squeaking by with an eighteen- or nineteen-vote lead. The moment was historic for him—he held the seat for the borough until he left the House of Commons in 1945.

His focus in the House was his homeland. He emphasized Welsh home rule, land reform, and disestablishmentarianism. He soon became leader of the radical faction of his own party, earning a reputation as an independent beholden to no platform. He gained a national profile by stumping as a pacifist against the Anglo-Boer War (1899–1902) in South Africa, asserting that Britain's involvement arose only from greed. This stance resulted in several serious threats on his life.

Growing Power The Liberals took power in the 1905 election, and Lloyd George's high profile earned him an appointment as president of the Board of Trade. He served his prime minister, Sir Henry Campbell-Bannerman (1836–1908), well in this appointment, creating the Port of London Authority, averting a major railway strike, and passing important reform legislation. Campbell-Bannerman died in 1908 and was succeeded by Lloyd George's future rival, Herbert H. Asquith (1852–1928), who promptly made Lloyd George chancellor of the exchequer, a powerful position.

As chancellor of the exchequer, Lloyd George found an ally in Winston Churchill (1874–1965). The two men drew up the "People's Budget," a plan for unemployment and health insurance modeled after a program Lloyd George had studied in Germany. After an initial defeat, this budget met with approval by the House of Lords in 1910, instituting duties on tobacco, gasoline, beer, and land. The passage of two acts initiated by Lloyd George—the National Health Insurance Act and the National Unemployment Insurance Act—formed the basis of the welfare state in Britain and cast Lloyd George to history as a social reformer.

Putting Pacifism Aside Because of his domestic focus, Lloyd George had very little time for foreign concerns, an exception being his passionate pacifism during the Anglo-Boer War. He broke with both his distance from foreign policy and his pacifism during the Agadir Crisis in 1911. Germany sent a warship into French-controlled territory in Morocco, triggering Lloyd George to warn the Germans that Britain had every intention of protecting its national interests. Nevertheless, he continued as an advocate of disarmament until as late as January 1914. By August 1914, World War I had broken out, and Lloyd George, driven by Germany's violation of Belgian neutrality, aligned himself against the kaiser.

Prime Minister In May 1915, the man who had thundered about pacifism was placed in charge of the new Ministry of Munitions, where he pushed for a massive output of munitions and an increase in conscription. A catastrophic loss at the Battle of the Somme, combined with other losses, undermined the people's faith in Asquith's government. After the death of Lord Kitchener (1850–1916), the secretary of state for war, Lloyd George was chosen to take his place. He immediately formed a coalition with conservative leaders. Asquith refused, however, to work with the coalition and resigned his office in protest in 1916. Some say that Lloyd George and his coalition pushed him out. Lloyd George reached the pinnacle of his rapid rise by taking Asquith's place, becoming prime minister on December 7, 1916, even though he was not even the leader of his own party. His accession relied instead on the support he received from the Conservative, and to a lesser extent, the Labor parties. His goal was to streamline the government, and he began by reducing the War Cabinet from twenty-three to five members. In addition, he applied his apparently inexhaustible energy, motivation, and courage to keep the nation inspired in the face of food shortages, military losses, and troubles among the Allies. His attitude differed significantly from that of his predecessor, who had come to be viewed as lacking drive and initiative in fighting the war.

Postwar Decline After the war, Lloyd George tried to maintain the Liberal-Conservative coalition he had forged, and he and his coalition members scored a significant victory in the 1918 election. Lloyd George was present at the Versailles Peace Conference, where he helped frame the treaty. But his overwhelming popularity of 1918 gave way to an erosion of support from 1919 to 1921, although he did fulfill some of his goals, including passage of the Housing Act of 1919 and establishing the Irish Free State. In spite of these successes, his administration also bore the repercussions of growing labor unrest, recession, and allegations of corruption. His coalition with Conservatives could not save him from Conservative ire at his spending, while radicals in his party rebelled against his austerity. The British populace and the coalition alike did not like his concessions to the rebellious Irish.

Lloyd George soldiered on through these trials, but he finally met defeat over yet another foreign policy problem: the Turkish crisis of 1922. He again found himself in disagreement with the coalition, and his pro-Greek stance almost resulted in another war for his country, this time with Turkey. Lloyd George, as a result, resigned his office on October 19, 1922, and was succeeded by Andrew Bonar Law (1858–1923). His Liberal party experienced a resounding defeat in the general election that same year.

An Elder Statesman The former prime minister remained a member of the House of Commons but failed to wield any particular influence for the remainder of his time there. For a short while, he also fell for Hitler's personal propaganda after meeting with the Nazi dictator in Germany in 1936. He obviously had changed his mind when, in 1938, he joined with Win-

Nicknamed the "Red Baron" in honor of his state-of-the-art red airplane, Richtofen inspired fear among Allied pilots until he was shot down in 1918. *AP/Wide World Photos. Reproduced by permission*

ston Churchill in decrying the appeasement policies of Neville Chamberlain (1869–1940), lambasting Chamberlain in May 1940. Chamberlain resigned as prime minister three days after Lloyd George's verbal attack, and Winston Churchill, Lloyd George's old ally, became prime minister. Irascible and unpredictable as ever, Lloyd George then proceeded to criticize many of Churchill's policies and refused two offers of a position in the War Cabinet.

In 1941, Lloyd George's wife died, and he was reportedly devastated at losing her, in spite of their tumultuous relationship. In 1943, the aging statesman married the woman who had been his personal secretary (and mistress) for thirty years, Frances Louise Stevenson. In 1944, he retired from the House of Commons and was elevated to the peerage, becoming the First Earl of Dwyfor, named for a mountain stream near his farm in Wales. The proud Welshman fittingly spent his final days in Wales, dying on March 26, 1945, at Ty Newydd.

Manfred von Richthofen

Manfred von Richthofen (1892–1918) was the top German aviator in WW I. Von Richthofen, more commonly known as the Red Baron, was credited with shooting down eighty enemy aircraft before being killed in action.

Von Richthofen was born on May 2, 1892 in Breslau, Germany an aristocratic family. His father was a major in the military, and he decided that his oldest son and second child would also be brought up to a military career. Von Richthofen was schooled at home, learning from tutors and enjoying hunting and horseback riding, before going to military school at age eleven.

Von Richthofen the Horseman Von Richthofen continued his athletic pursuits as a cadet but did not shine academically. He made few friends, disliked class work, and did only enough to scrape by. In 1909, when he entered the Royal Prussian Military Academy near Berlin, he settled in and began enjoying military life, still excelling in athletics and enjoying the companionship of his comrades. In 1911, he graduated and entered the cavalry, becoming a lieutenant in 1912.

Although his excellence as a horseman made him a natural for the cavalry, his first engagement in the Battle of Verdun showed him and the German commanders that horses were not going to be viable in modern warfare. The riders found themselves hunkered in trenches rather than on horseback, and soon von Richthofen had had enough. He requested transfer to the air service, or *Fliegertruppe*. He did not intend to become a pilot, because he thought the training would take too long.

Von Richthofen the Flying Ace Soon, von Richthofen could not resist the impulse to fly and moved from being an observer to flying his own missions, piloting the lightweight fighter planes. After only twenty-four hours of flight training, he took his first solo turn, crashing on landing but emerging unhurt and completely inspired. In 1916, he was assigned to a fighter squadron, making his first kill on September 17, 1916.

Within months, his kill tally had expanded to ten enemy planes shot down, qualifying him as an "ace" in the fighter-pilot lexicon. He loved the flying and the thrill of battle so much that for each plane shot down, he collected a souvenir and bought an engraved trophy to commemorate the event. After witnessing the deaths of many of the other pilots, his arrogance tempered only somewhat.

He earned greater fame in November 1916 for shooting down a famous British ace, Major Lanoe Hawker (1890–1916). In 1917, he took command of his own fighter squadron, which he immediately began to train in his own style. His squad's air victories escalated, and von Richthofen, still keeping score, had more kills than anyone. At about this time, he decided to paint his plane bright red. Although it seems like an invitation to trouble, his real reason was to let ground troops know not to fire on him. He also wanted any people watching from the ground to know who he was when he shot a plane down. Others in his squadron followed suit, painting their planes in signature designs. The colorful squadron became known as the "Flying Circus." Von Richthofen himself earned a nickname from the British, the "Red Baron," while the French called him "le petit rouge," or "the little red one." He achieved several kills almost every day.

Admiration in Life and Death Von Richthofen received a promotion to captain in April 1917. He was a valuable asset to his country both for his skill as a fighter pilot and for his image as a German hero. The German propaganda machine paraded him before crowds, threw parties for him, and urged him to write his life story. In spite of his thirst for fame and his obvious delight in his success, von Richthofen was not comfortable with all of the fawning and the other trappings of celebrity.

He returned to battle, and on July 6, 1917, just after he killed his fifty-seventh pilot, he himself was shot down. He was taken to the hospital with a gunshot wound to the head, which later was blamed for his uncharacteristic behavior when he returned to battle in August. His wound probably never truly healed, but he became known to history as an ace of aces by shooting down an overall total of eighty enemy planes. He did finally write his memoirs, calling them *The Red Fighter Pilot* (*Der Rote Kampflieger*).

On April 21, 1918, he was in pursuit of a British pilot, dipping and swooping his plane to keep the quarry locked on target. He broke his own rules in tailing the pilot, going too low and too fast, and his plane was shot down over the Somme River. Von Richthofen died in the crash—someone on the scene reported that his final utterance was the word, "kaput," German for "broken." British troops recovered his body and buried him like the warrior he was in a military funeral with honors.

Woodrow Wilson

A Rapid Rise Thomas Woodrow Wilson (1856–1924) was the twenty-eighth president of the United States, serving from 1913 to 1921. He was later awarded the Nobel Peace Prize for his work on the Versailles Treaty.

Wilson was born on December 28, 1856 in Staunton, Virginia. His father, the Rev. Dr. Joseph Ruggles Wilson, was a Presbyterian minister and founder of the Southern Presbyterian Church. Wilson's career trajectory was rapid and impressive. He graduated from Princeton University in 1879. A scholar before he became a politician, the future president then went on to earn a doctorate at Johns Hopkins in 1886, studying political science, history, and economics. Earlier in the 1880s, he studied law at the University of Virginia, a trade he practiced in Atlanta. His postdoctoral curriculum vita reads like an East Coast college guide; he taught history and political science at Bryn Mawr, Wesleyan, and Princeton. By 1902, Wilson took over leadership of Princeton at the age of forty-five. In 1910, Wilson became governor of New Jersey, running as a Democrat. He stunned some of his critics by actually fulfilling all of

Stop!

0002691   WILSON CARTOON, 1916.
Credit: The Granger Collection, New York

Despite his desire to stay out of war, President Wilson declared that "the world must be made safe for democracy." *The Granger Collection, New York. Reproduced by permission*

the pledges made as part of the Democratic platform for that election. By 1912, he was the U.S. president and was elected a second time to the office in 1916.

A Scholarly Approach to the Presidency   Wilson came into the presidency intent on establishing progressive domestic programs and reforms, but he found himself embroiled in a world war and gearing up the U.S. military for that and the other conflicts that marked his time in office. He considered himself a "liberal internationalist," one who believes that diplomacy, international law, and moral arguments should be brought to bear on a problem in order to achieve a peaceful solution. If that approach failed, then one could apply military force. He had come to his conclusions about the role of the president through his analysis of Theodore Roosevelt's (1858–1919) time in office. In 1908, Wilson wrote *Constitutional Government in the United States*, a book that presents what some scholars perceive as the classic view of the modern presidency. In it, he argues for the president as the nation's lone spokesman, representing the "people as a whole."

In the presidential election of 1912, Wilson beat Roosevelt, William Howard Taft (1857–1930), and Eugene Victor Debs (1855–1926). His first move as president was to demonstrate his role as spokesperson by holding the first in a series of regularly scheduled press conferences, setting a precedent that most presi-

dents have followed. He employed various outlets to shape public discourse, in addition to the press conferences, turning to newspapers and public statements, and he often claimed to speak not for himself, but for the people he led.

His parliamentary skills became as legendary as his use of words, the news media, and the "bully pulpit" supplied by his office. He used the principle of mutual respect between the executive office and the houses of Congress to reduce the barriers between the two branches of government while keeping himself the spokesperson for both, fulfilling his ideal of the president as representative of all.

Peace Without Victory   Wilson believed, on moral and religious grounds, that his nation existed to serve all of humankind. His initiatives and proposals, such as his "Peace Without Victory" plan, exemplified his belief that the strong and ruthless should never move to crush or exploit the helpless and weak, and he worked to avoid using violence abroad. In a speech to Congress, even as he asked for the authority to occupy Mexico to stop the attacks of Pancho Villa (1878–1923) on American interests, he thundered, "Do you think the glory of America would be enhanced by a war of conquest? Do you think that any act of violence by a powerful nation like this against a weak distracted neighbor would reflect distinction upon the annals of the United States?" He also, however, believed that sometimes force was required, and he turned to it often during his eight years in office.

Wilson's first use of U.S. armed forces occurred in 1914, when he sent troops to the Mexican port of Veracruz. They occupied the city for seven months in order to restore order and protect American economic interests while Mexican political factions fought one another. The president would most frequently use the armed forces in this way and for this purpose in Latin America, including another occupation in Mexico in which U.S. troops stopped Pancho Villa from continuing his attacks on towns on the New Mexico border. U.S. troops also occupied Haiti in July 1915 to restore order after the murder of its president, and they were deployed in the Dominican Republic in May 1916, again to restore order amid political upheaval.

Diplomacy with Germany   Despite his willingness to use force in the first years of his presidency, Wilson was reluctant to engage militarily when World War I broke out in 1914. For two years, he insisted on declaring U.S. neutrality, but economic factors and German aggression caused him to change his response in 1916. In May 1915, a German U-boat sank the British passenger liner *Lusitania*, which went down with 1,198 people, including 124 Americans. Wilson initially attempted personal intervention to stop the U-boat attacks, and his efforts had been effective by 1916. But 1916 was also an election year, and the pressures of politics led Wilson to expand the army and national guard, including establishing the Reserve Officer Training Corps (ROTC) program, which still exists today.

Wilson still held out hope for a compromise and for keeping his country out of the war. In May 1916, a year after the *Lusitania* sank, he came out in support of a postwar league that would ensure peace among nations. When he won reelection that November, he again looked for ways to end the war through diplomacy. His efforts failed, and in January 1917, he put forward his "Peace Without Victory" plan, his vision of achieving peace unaccompanied by national gain of land or claims of victory. The Germans were now intent on victory, however, convinced that with some well-applied force, they could overcome the British before any U.S. support could arrive from across the Atlantic. In their hubris, they rejected Wilson's overtures and accepted the probability that war with the United States would result.

Aggression against the Germans The Germans announced they would launch open submarine warfare on January 31, 1917. Wilson thus had to choose between continued, well-reasoned neutrality and all-out aggression. The people of the United States were similarly divided. Ultimately, Wilson chose the route of aggression, delivering a message of war in April lambasting the Germans for violating the rights of neutral nations and arguing for his vision of spreading democracy. His draft plan resulted in the rapid mobilization of the army. General John J. Pershing (1860–1948) led U.S. troops in Paris, engaging in the Second Battle of the Marne in 1918, and near the German frontier by September of that year, he led a force of 1.2 million men. Throughout U.S. participation in World War I, Wilson maintained that his nation was an associate power, not a member of the Allies, and that the United States could and would negotiate a separate peace if necessary.

Achievements and Failures Wilson's zeal in achieving his goals gave rise to outcomes both positive and negative. The institution of the draft became the model that the U.S. would use to constitute an army for many subsequent wars. Wilson used conscription to raise an army and war bonds to pay for it, tactics that would be used again during World War II. One of his greatest legislative achievements was the passage of the Federal Reserve Act, which he signed into law in 1913. This act, which combined private initiative with public oversight, established the Federal Reserve System, the most important economic institution in the United States. But Wilson never lost sight of his ultimate postwar goal: the creation of an international peace organization focused on cooperation and collective security.

What his administration did lose sight of was the necessity to maintain a nation's civil liberties, even in times of war. The wartime violations of civil liberties

WILSON'S WAR MESSAGE

The following is an excerpt of the president's address to Congress on April 2, 1917.

Neutrality is no longer feasible or desirable where the peace of the world is involved and the freedom of its peoples, and the menace to that peace and freedom lies in the existence of autocratic governments backed by organized force which is controlled wholly by their will, not by the will of their people. We have seen the last of neutrality in such circumstances. We are at the beginning of an age in which it will be insisted that the same standards of conduct and of responsibility for wrong done shall be observed among nations and their governments that are observed among the individual citizens of civilized states . . . .

A steadfast concert for peace can never be maintained except by a partnership of democratic nations. No autocratic government could be trusted to keep faith within it or observe its covenants. It must be a league of honor, a partnership of opinion. Intrigue would eat its vitals away; the plottings of inner circles who could plan what they would and render account to no one would be a corruption seated at its very heart. Only free peoples can hold their purpose and their honour steady to a common end and prefer the interests of mankind to any narrow interest of their own.

SOURCE: *Wilson, Woodrow. "War Message to Congress, April 2, 1917."* World War I Document Archive. *Brigham Young University Library. http:// net.lib.byu.edu/~rdh7/wwi/1917/wilswarm.html (accessed June 15, 2007).*

under the Espionage Act of 1917 and the Sedition Act of 1918, some of them extensive, triggered a reaction that ended in the postwar establishment of the American Civil Liberties Union.

Wilson and the Fourteen Points As a wartime president, Wilson was a forceful commander-in-chief, but he relied on the commander of the American Expeditionary Force, General John J. Pershing, to make decisions on the ground about America's army in France. Pershing was stopped by Wilson in 1918 when the Germans both begged for an armistice after the tide turned against them and cited Wilson's "Fourteen Points," which he had delivered as a presidential address in January 1918. The Fourteen Points included calls to end secret diplomacy, ensure freedom of the seas, reduce armaments, and create an independent Poland. In response to Germany's pleas, Wilson put a halt to Pershing's plans to invade Germany. He accepted Germany's request for an armistice and used his Fourteen Points as a starting point for the negotiations.

After the War President Wilson traveled to Europe in 1919, becoming the first sitting U.S. president to do so. At the peace talks in Paris, Wilson found himself giving up a number of his Fourteen Points in an effort to achieve his overarching goal of the creation of the League of Nations. The peace talk participants hammered out the Treaty of Versailles, but Wilson did not get a positive reception to it from home. The Republican-controlled Senate refused to ratify the treaty in July 1919 for reasons that included partisanship, fears that the United States would lose power, and concern over the concessions Wilson had made. Wilson's nemesis, Henry Cabot Lodge (1850–1924), happened to be chairman of the Senate Foreign Relations Committee, and he and his allies deplored the heavy international responsibilities the treaty would impose on the nation. In addition, Wilson, who had spent his terms in office emphasizing diplomacy, proved an intractable opponent.

Wilson suffered a massive stroke in October 1919. The stroke left Wilson paralyzed on his left side and was actually the largest of a series of small strokes and other vascular problems. He had suffered these problems so long that even as he was preparing to take office his first term, a prominent neurologist examined him and predicted that the new president would not survive to the end of the four years. He obviously did survive, even to complete a second term, but the large stroke left him unable to negotiate and use diplomacy in the old, familiar ways. In fact, through the remainder of his second term, the president did not function completely in mind, body, reason, or spirit. His second wife, Edith Bolting Wilson, whom Wilson had married after the death in 1914 of his first wife, Ellen Louise Axson Wilson, served as the conduit of all information in or out of the president's office. She blocked efforts to reveal the truth about the president's health and also refused to allow her husband to resign his office, even after he had agreed to do so at the behest of the doctors.

It was during this period of incapacity at the end of his term that the greatest social achievement of his administration occurred. The Nineteenth Amendment to the U.S. Constitution was ratified on August 26, 1920, conferring on women the right to vote. The outgoing president rode with his successor, Warren Harding (1865–1923), to Harding's inauguration on March 4, 1921. In spite of Wilson's physical frailty, however, he outlived the new president and attended Harding's funeral. Wilson died at home in Washington on February 3, 1924.

Erich Ludendorff

Early Life and Career Erich Ludendorff (1865–1937) was a German general and directed Germany's total war effort during the last two years of World War I.

Ludendorff was born on April 9, 1865, in Prussia, in an area that was primarily Polish. His mother was descended from aristocrats, and his father was a cavalry officer. In spite of his mother's connections, Ludendorff's family was not rich, although he is reported to have had a comfortable and pleasant childhood. He did well in school, earning a scholarship to a state military academy, and entered the army after he graduated in 1882. Ludendorff showed an aptitude for mathematics and was consistently first in his class, but he always knew that the military would be his career and intended to follow in the footsteps of both his father and grandfather.

Although his mother was of noble lineage, only men who were paternally noble could traditionally be promoted to general. He was taunted at school, where students made fun of him because he was a commoner. Ludendorff, known throughout his life for his dour severity, may have developed some of his personality traits because of this experience. At any rate, he excelled in the face of such obstacles and was appointed to the German general staff, a prestigious post, when he was only twenty-nine. One reason he climbed the career ladder so rapidly was that he disdained friendships, preferring to focus instead on forming himself into the best soldier he could be.

Military Leadership Ludendorff continued to exhibit this singular obsession with all things military. He read only books on military subjects and for two decades after his appointment to the general staff, where he spent most of his career, he closely studied all aspects of the German military. In spite of his almost religious military fervor, he was generally disliked even among the stereotypically arrogant and rude German officers for his unpleasantness. He is reported to have been filled with rage—he banged on tables, offended his superiors with his tactlessness, and was inflexible in thought. In spite of his obvious social deficiencies, he did marry, and his wife described him as "a man of iron principles."

Not surprisingly, Ludendorff actually looked forward to the onset of World War I, seeing it as his chance to finally earn the leadership position he had worked so hard to achieve—to the exclusion of almost everything else. At first, he was quartermaster general, ensuring food, clothing, transportation, and supplies got to the troops in Belgium. When a general died in battle at the Belgian line, Ludendorff quickly stepped in at the front to take his place. His first act was to drive a car up to a small tower that his army had been unable to capture. Reports state that he jumped from the vehicle, drew his sword, and banged on the door, yelling, "Surrender in the name of Kaiser Wilhelm!" It seemed like a foolish thing to do, but it had the effect of firing up the German troops, who surged against the outnumbered Belgians and defeated them. Ludendorff earned a medal from the kaiser himself for his audacity and became known as the

"Hero of Liege," after the town where he earned his honor. He also earned himself a place on the eastern front.

On the Eastern Front The only problem was that Ludendorff was not a noble and therefore could not command the troops on the front. To solve this problem, the general staff put the retired General Paul von Hindenburg (1847–1934) in charge with Ludendorff as second in command as chief of staff. In spite of what must have been a frustration to Ludendorff, the two men dovetailed their duties nicely, with Ludendorff planning and making decisions that von Hindenburg passed along as orders.

Ludendorff's decisions ended in a rout of the previously immovable Russian army at the Battle of Tannenberg. After this decisive victory, the two German leaders moved on, pushing the Russian forces all the way back across the front, in contrast to the stalemate that lingered on the western front. Ludendorff and von Hindenburg made such a great team that people started calling them simply, "The Duo."

Given their effectiveness at the eastern front, it was no surprise when they were moved to the western front in August 1916, where von Hindenburg became chief of the general staff, and Ludendorff his first quartermaster general. They planned together to remove from their path any military or political leader who disagreed with their plans, which included renewed, unrestricted submarine warfare. After they forced out Wilhelm's chancellor, who wanted to sue for peace, the two generals were essentially in charge of the country, which was now a military dictatorship with a figurehead kaiser.

On the Western Front Ludendorff and von Hindenburg now took up residence in comfortable headquarters while directing movements at the front. They got rid of any concerns about Russia by helping Vladimir Lenin (1870–1924) return from exile to lead the socialist revolution, a move that effectively removed Russia from the war equation for the moment. With the eastern front resolved for the time being, they began planning a huge German offensive on the western front. Their attacks starting in March 1918 leading to battles at Somme, Ypres, and Chemin des Dames were successes, sending the Allies into retreat, but those successes came with tremendous losses. The German Army lost more than 600,000 men in those three months of fighting.

In spite of the horrific losses, the two generals pushed forward with their offensive, launching two assaults that summer that were disastrous. Not only did they fail to push the Allies back any further, but they also saw many of their men desert, unwilling to again walk into a slaughter. The result was a massive midsummer German retreat, and Ludendorff and von Hindenburg knew the end was near—at least von Hindenburg did. Reportedly, when Ludendorff asked him what Germany

ought to do, the military nobleman replied, "Make peace, you idiot!"

Ludendorff agreed but knew that Germany had to position itself better on the battlefield before beginning negotiations. They did not want to enter armistice talks at a huge disadvantage and wanted Germany to appear as strong as it could. They attempted to achieve this by a slow retreat, but the Americans turned the slow retreat into a total defeat. Ludendorff was so distraught that those around him worried about his health. Some reported that when word came about Germany's complete loss, Ludendorff actually fell to the floor of his office, foaming at the mouth. It would have been a powerful emotional display from a man who had prided himself for his intractable strength.

Ludendorff's strategy of entering peace negotiations from a position of strength failed utterly, and Ludendorff himself was forced to resign in October 1918. The resignation of von Hindenburg followed in the next month, and the kaiser abdicated and fled to Holland. Germany had lost.

After the War The raging, unloved general ended up fleeing the country as well, ignominiously disguising himself with a wig and colored glasses and taking refuge in Sweden. While there, he engaged in the usual postwar pastime of writing his memoirs, which in his case laid the blame for Germany's loss on unpatriotic Germans. His argument attracted a certain nationalistic element in Germany, and he returned to his homeland in the 1920s, believing himself to be the living embodiment of Nordic virtues. There, he joined Hitler's National Socialist Party, was elected to Parliament as a Nazi, and even ran for president. Ironically, he lost the latter contest to the very man he had accused of being an unpatriotic German: Paul von Hindenburg. Ludendorff resigned from Parliament in 1928.

His tendency toward mental instability appeared to reemerge toward the end of his life. His second wife engaged in pseudo-religious, anti-Semitic, anti-Christian mystical teachings, and Ludendorff espoused beliefs that the Jews, socialists, Freemasons, Jesuits—anyone but him—were at fault for Germany's failure on the world stage. His essays and bizarre behavior eventually became so extreme that even Adolf Hitler (1889–1945) could no longer support him. Ludendorff died on December 20, 1937.

John Pershing

John Joseph Pershing (1860–1948) was a general in the Armies of the United States and went on to be commander in chief of the American Expeditionary Force in Europe during World War I.

Early Years Pershing was born on September 13, 1860 near Laclede, Missouri. Pershing was born almost on the eve of the Civil War, and his early memories of that conflict actually led him away from an interest in a

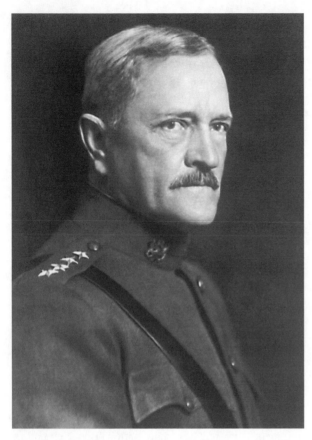

General John Pershing came to be regarded as the model modern general. *The Library of Congress*

military career. He planned instead to become a lawyer. His plans were put on hold, however, with the economic depression of the 1870s, and when his father's businesses (a store, lumberyard, and real estate) began to falter, he had to look for work. Pershing worked on his family's farm and attended public school. In 1878, he found a job teaching, and he studied for his degree during vacation, officially earning his teaching credentials in 1880. His first job was teaching at the school for the black children in his hometown. Racial tensions arose on both sides around his appointment, but Pershing handled them with calm, pointing out to one hostile former friend that Abraham Lincoln had given rights to black people, and it was his—Pershing's—job to teach these children.

Military Education In spite of his aspirations to the law, Pershing applied to the U.S. Military Academy at West Point in 1881. He was not suddenly interested in a military career, but he had realized that he could obtain a free college education via this route, one that might help him realize his dream of attending law school. Pershing flourished at West Point, achieving the highest student position possible at the academy and serving as class president, although public speaking made him

uncomfortable. His reputation at West Point set the tone for his future—that of a strong leader and strict disciplinarian. He had developed his interest in strict discipline as a child. He and his brothers had a near-fatal accident with a gun they were playing with, and since that incident, Pershing took guns and the details pertaining to them very seriously.

On the Western Frontier He left West Point in 1886 to go to New Mexico as a second lieutenant. In what would be a repeated scenario in Pershing's life, he just missed the main action in New Mexico; the Sixth Cavalry Regiment of the U.S. Army had just captured the elusive Geronimo, the Apache chief who had evaded army patrols for years. But after Pershing arrived, the Sixth simply engaged in routine patrols in New Mexico.

Pershing served with the Sixth in New Mexico for four years, until the regiment traveled to South Dakota to deal with another Native American leader, Sitting Bull, and with the Ghost Dance Rebellion of the Sioux tribe. Pershing arrived after the massacre at Wounded Knee and the shooting of Sitting Bull. His only involvement in the action was a short skirmish at Little Grass Creek on January 1, 1891.

Turning again to a teaching life, Pershing went to the University of Nebraska in the fall of 1891 to serve as a military instructor and to teach remedial math. While he was there, he finally achieved his lifetime dream of earning a law degree, an accomplishment that left him with the difficult choice of pursuing a legal career or continuing with the military. He decided to stick with the military.

While at the University of Nebraska, Pershing made a name for himself by whipping a group of undisciplined, uninterested students into a superior cadet corps. It was at this time that the future general first had his name associated with weaponry: his cadets became known as the Pershing Rifles, and they were good enough to win a national drill competition in Nebraska.

Military Command Pershing then moved on to Montana, where he commanded a unit of black soldiers with the Tenth Cavalry. Pershing spent only a year in Montana and then spent an unsuccessful year at West Point with the derisive cadets who resented Pershing for his strict attention to details about marching, saluting, standing at attention, and dress. This response to Pershing's close attention to military form would bring him criticism in later years, as well. It was at West Point that a group of white cadets he taught gave him the nickname "Black Jack," a reference to his command of the Tenth, meant to insult him.

The lieutenant finally got his chance to catch some of the action when he went to Cuba as the officer in charge of supplies (quartermaster) for the Tenth. Spain and the United States were at war over Cuba, and Pershing earned kudos for his bravery during the attack on San Juan Hill, the signature event of that war in Cuba.

The colonel of his regiment even said to Pershing that the lieutenant was "cool as a bowl of cracked ice" under fire.

Pershing continued his success in the Philippines, where he made captain and distinguished himself for suppressing uprisings. During an assignment in Washington, D.C., he met the daughter of a powerful Wyoming senator and told a friend that he had met the girl he was going to marry. After two years, he did marry Frances Warren, in 1905, and the two spent their honeymoon in Tokyo, where Pershing served at the American embassy.

His star was on a swift rise from then on, and in 1906, President Theodore Roosevelt chose Pershing over 862 officers with more seniority to become the youngest brigadier general in the U.S. Army. After his brief stint as an observer in the Russo-Japanese War, the new brigadier general returned to the Philippines, where he became, in addition to his military command, governor of the Moro province, which he and his forces had captured during his previous duty there. While the provincial governor, Pershing oversaw introduction of the minimum wage and initiated the building of new schools and medical facilities while still quelling the occasional rebellion.

After four years in the Philippines, the general found himself ordered to El Paso, Texas, to help battle the Mexicans, who were making border raids. Pancho Villa, the Mexican leader, led one raid in March 1916 that killed seventeen Americans. In response, Pershing led what President Woodrow Wilson referred to as a "punitive expedition" into Mexico on Villa's trail. Villa proved as elusive as Geronimo, and even after eleven months, Pershing still had not managed to capture or kill the Mexican rebel, although he did scatter the rebel army.

While he was in El Paso, Pershing's wife and three of his children died in a fire in their home in San Francisco; only his son, Warren, survived. The loss so devastated him that at his promotion to major general in 1916, he commented, "All the promotion in the world would make no difference now."

Command in Europe War in Europe pulled Pershing from the Mexican border to Paris, France. The United States finally declared war on Germany on April 6, 1917, after final attempts at diplomacy with the kaiser failed. Wilson, evidently still impressed with Pershing, selected the fifty-seven-year-old experienced general to command U.S. forces on the European continent. It was something the British and French had anticipated and had hoped for, but they soon became frustrated with Pershing's delay in engaging in battle. Pershing's reason for the delay was that he wanted his troops trained and fighting together as an American—not an Allied—army, and he forcefully refused to place them under Allied command. The United States insisted on remaining a separate party from the Allies, retaining its right to negotiate a separate peace, if necessary.

For almost a year after his appointment as commander, Pershing did not lead his troops into battle. He spent this time laying the groundwork carefully and completely for a full-scale invasion of Germany, including troop training and buildup, supply flow, intelligence gathering, and strategizing. He also spent much of his time inspecting his ever-improving soldiers, ruthlessly attending to the smallest details of their uniform and riding the division commanders without mercy.

In spite of the U.S. intention to maintain a separate presence, Pershing did allow some of his troops to fight alongside the British and French forces as the Germans began a major offensive in March 1918. Eventually, in August 1918, Pershing unleashed his forces, the First American Army, on the Germans, rooting them out of Saint-Mihiel in September and launching a major U.S. offensive later that month that drew German divisions away from other parts of the front where beleaguered Allied forces were faltering. In spite of American firepower, the U.S. force experienced a large number of casualties, but after an unsuccessful start, they finally began pressing down the German army as November began. Ten days after the tide turned in favor of the United States, on November 11, 1918, the Germans conceded and signed the armistice.

Pershing did not want the peace of the armistice; he wanted war, and hoped to continue the fighting and to force the Germans into unconditional surrender. His reason for wanting to avoid concessions to Germany was not a thirst for blood. With considerable farsightedness, Pershing worried that the Germans would rise again to threaten the world. In 1944, during World War II, the general commented, "If we had gone to Berlin then, we would not be going there now."

Later Years With his European aspirations thwarted, Pershing turned to politics. He did not, however, make a great politician and did not make it past the primaries in his two efforts to run for president. Eventually, he became the first possessor of a rank revived from the time of General Washington, General of the Armies, and became the Army's chief of staff, which he remained until 1924. Pershing published his memoirs in 1931, which although lacking in verbal flair, won the Pulitzer Prize in history. Ailing during his final years, he lived from 1941 until his death on July 15, 1948, at Walter Reed Hospital. General Pershing was buried at Arlington National Cemetery.

Georges Clemenceau

Georges Clemenceau (1841-1929) was a French journalist and statesman. He was twice premier of France, in 1906-1909 and 1917-1919, leading his country through the critical days of World War I and heading the French delegation to the Paris Peace Conference.

Prime Minister Georges Clemenceau's strong leadership style and many visits to the trenches proved to be inspirational to French troops as World War I dragged on.   *Time Life Pictures/Mansell/Getty Images*

A Study in Contrasts   Clemenceau (1841–1929) was was born on September 28, 1841, in Mouilleron-en-Pareds, a village on the French coast. Clemenceau was a man of contrasts and overwhelming energy who became the most famous political figure of his time in France. He was known for being strong-willed, tough, hard, and even cruel, and his rapier wit spared no one. As an able and wily politician, Clemenceau was renowned and feared as one of the greatest public speakers of his time, and as a newspaper columnist through much of his career, his wit gained him a wide audience.

On the outside, his roughness and cruelty earned him the nickname "The Tiger," but inside, as one friend once said, he had the "soul of an artist." A contradiction of a man, he was extremely well educated and highly cultured, a man who appreciated the liquid delicacy of the Impressionist artists, and exhibited enormous generosity, easily making and keeping friendships. But he also had a facility with making enemies, and he made many. In spite of his power and position, he never indulged in pretentiousness of person or lifestyle, living in a modest Parisian apartment even when he was France's premier.

Education and Early Career   Gifted with a brilliant mind, Clemenceau was educated at home, the oldest son and second of six children. His father Benjamin ceased his medical practice and retired to the family land. Clemenceau followed in his father's footsteps, earning a medical degree by studying at the school of medicine in Nantes, near the family home. He completed his studies at the University of Paris in 1865, a bright student but difficult to keep focused. Among his distractions were political activities, which at one point landed him in jail for two months for organizing a Republican demonstration.

Ultimately rejected by the leader of the Republican rebellion, however, and also by the lady of his heart, Hortense Kestner, Clemenceau made for the United States. He intended to settle there but remained only from 1865 until 1869, working as both a physician and as a political writer for French-language newspapers. Supplementing his income by teaching French at a girls' school, Clemenceau met the orphaned daughter of a dentist, Mary Elizabeth Plummer, who was one of his students. After overcoming reluctance on the part of her wealthy guardian, Mary finally married Clemenceau in 1869. The couple returned to France, where Clemenceau eventually found himself in Paris, participating in the overthrow of Napoleon III.

Winning Office   After establishment of the Third Republic in 1870, Clemenceau was elected to the National Assembly. He almost died at the hands of a lynch mob during a rebellion that broke out in his home district of Montmartre, in which radicals hanged two generals on behalf of the Paris Commune, which briefly governed Paris in 1871. According to Clemenceau, as he attempted to rescue the generals, he almost fell into the hands of the murderous crowd. He ended up resigning his office and failed to win reelection the following July.

Clemenceau then served on the Paris City Council after Paris returned to French governmental jurisdiction, where he became council president in 1875. In addition, he continued practicing medicine and fought a duel with a man who had insulted him over the revolt in Montmartre. It was not his first duel. His fame grew as a result of his tending to the poor and his more dramatic exploits, and he returned to national politics as a representative in the Chamber of Deputies for Montmartre in Paris. After a few more reelections, he established a newspaper, *La Justice*, and became a leader of the Radical Republicans, a party with a distinct socialist bent.

In keeping with his socialist nature, Clemenceau became politically quite like his future British counterpart, David Lloyd George. Like Lloyd George, Clemenceau argued for old age and unemployment insurance, nationalization of railroads, religious reform, and separation of church and state. His debating skills could reduce an opponent to his rhetorical knees, and he used his verbal fencing to knock out several successive moderate ministries. Yet he was consistently considered too radical to take the lead himself.

In the Private Sector Clemenceau had a bad few years as he weathered unsubstantiated charges of bribery over the failure of the Panama Canal Company, and he suffered an electoral defeat in 1893. A year earlier he had divorced his wife for adultery, although he was not faithful himself. To take refuge from his problems, he turned to writing for his and other papers, writing enough to combine his several thousand columns into sixteen books. Most of his writing was political, but some of it addressed art and literature. He also indulged in his love of the arts by writing a novel and a play.

He used his writing as a way to advocate for Captain Alfred Dreyfus, a Jewish officer accused on forged evidence of spying for Germany. Dreyfus was convicted but retried, due to Clemenceau's efforts. He was then reconvicted, and then finally declared innocent in 1906.

A Return to the Political Stage Clemenceau returned to politics in 1902 as a senator, and by 1906, he was a leading power in the Senate. At age sixty-five, he finally had begun to advance in politics, becoming a minister of the interior and then premier. In office from 1906 to 1909, he instituted a number of reforms and strengthened ties with Great Britain and Russia, a mark of foresight given future events. He suddenly lost a vote of confidence in 1909 and turned again to his writing, also doing a lecture tour.

War broke out in 1914, and Clemenceau hoped to be recalled to lead his country, but not being offered the top post, he declined any other appointment. He began politicking for a better conduct of the war through a new paper, *L'Homme Enchaine*, "The Chained Man," and as chairman of the Senate committees on foreign affairs and the army. Then came the darkest days of World War I in 1917, with the Allies failing on all fronts, and Clemenceau stepped to the forefront again. The French president, Raymond Poincaré (1860–1934), turned to him, and Clemenceau worked for his country with inspiring zeal. He toured the front dozens of times, negotiated improved cooperation among the Allies, named Ferdinand Foch commander of the allied forces, and generally proved himself, although a dictator of sorts, an effective wartime leader.

Forced to Compromise After the armistice, Clemenceau presided at the Paris Peace Conference that began in January 1919 and survived an assassination attempt the next month. In spite of his efforts with Great Britain and the United States at the conference, the legislative bodies of these two nations refused to ratify the treaty the Allies had hammered out. Some accused Clemenceau of being too easy on the Germans. In answer, he pointed out that regardless of personal feelings, Germany had sixty million men with whom the other European powers must try to get along.

His past and perceived compromising with the Germans caught up with him in his run for the presidency in 1920. He was defeated, and soon after, he retired from the premiership and the Senate. In his final years, he traveled and lectured, arguing powerfully against the increasing isolationism of the United States. As an octogenarian, he authored several more books, one of which he completed four days before he died, on November 24, 1929, of complications of diabetes. At his own request, he lies buried next to his father in a nameless grave in his home province of Vendée.

✪ Major Battles

Battle of the Marne

The Battle of the Marne was one of the first major confrontations in World War I on the Western Front. This horrific encounter between the allies of France and Britain against Germany took place in early September 1914 in France on the Marne River, east of Paris and west of the German border. The French Army and the British Expeditionary Forces proved strong enough to drive the Germans back, which signaled that the war would last longer than the German aggressors had planned.

The battle resulted from a long-standing German contingency plan for war known as the Schlieffen Plan. General Alfred von Schlieffen (1833–1913) had served as chief of staff to the German Army until 1906. Long before World War I began in August 1914, as alliances were developing between Britain, Russia, and France—Germany's adversaries at the turn of the century—the Germans saw a need for a war plan, and they began creating it. The Schlieffen Plan simply dictated that Germany would fiercely attack France, encircling Paris and the entire region with seven of the eight German armies. Then, once Paris was defeated, the German Army would quickly head across Germany on the country's advanced rails and roads to stop the Russian Army before it could get to Germany.

Soon after war was declared, Germany began to carry out this scheme with the Battle of the Marne near Paris. German General Helmuth von Moltke (1848–1916) succeeded Schlieffen and modified his plan somewhat. Moltke strengthened the left flank and sent thirty-two out of the seventy-eight German infantry divisions through Belgium. The French met the advancing Germans. From August 20 to 24, bloody battles between the two sides occurred along the border between Belgium and France. By August 25, French commander Joseph Jacques Cesaire Joffre ordered a retreat, and the Germans followed closely behind.

The French and their British allies soon regrouped. Within days, the British Expeditionary Force, under Field Marshall John French (1852–1925), landed in mainland Europe and began to assist the French forces.

The effort of Parisian taxicabs to rush French soldiers to the front during the Battle of the Marne would be celebrated.   © *Bettmann/Corbis*

Also, a new French Army was organized under Paris Military Governor General Joseph Simon Gallieni (1849–1916). Meanwhile, the Germans advanced toward Paris. General Alexander von Kluck (1846–1934) and General Karl von Bulow (1846–1921) were now both to the east of Paris but miles away from each other. When General Joffre got word of this separation, he ordered a counterattack and sought more support from the British. On the afternoon of September 5, the beginnings of this great battle began when the advancing French collided with Kluck's left flank north of the town of Meaux. By the next day, the Allies were waging an all-out assault. Kluck shifted his army to the west to begin a stern counterattack, which slowed the French advance for two days. But when Gallieni arrived with the newly formed Sixth Army, some of whom were in commandeered taxi cabs from Paris, the German advance was halted.

The gap between the two German forces had been enlarged, and it was now some thirty miles. The British forces and another French division marched right into this opening. General Molkte, disappointed and bewildered, had reached a point of mental collapse. By the afternoon of September 9, the Battle of the Marne was over and the Germans were headed back toward the Aisne River.

The battle resulted in heavy casualties on both sides. The German death toll is unknown, but fifteen thousand men were taken prisoner. The French losses over several days of fighting around this battle reached eighty thousand. It was also a reality check for the Germans. The Schlieffen Plan essentially failed for several reasons. Poor communication among the different German army divisions confused the attack. The French, with Paris close to their backs, were able to supply themselves during the onslaught. Moltke, who had become frantic during the conflict, was relieved of his command. Kaiser Wilhelm II fired him on September 14.

Though the Allies had successfully driven the Germans back, the impact of their victory is questionable. None of the generals on either side proved to be great leaders. The German army reorganized, and a stalemate of trench warfare followed on the Western Front.

The First Battle of Ypres

On October 20, 1914, General Erich von Falkenhayn (1861–1922), the relatively new chief of staff of the German Army, began executing his Flanders offensive. Falkenhayn's plan was to break through the enemy line and overtake the French ports of Dunkirk, Calais, and Boulogne on the English Channel. He thought he found a weak point—the Belgians defended a small position by the Yser River between Dixmude and Nieuport, where the river emptied into the sea. German heavy artillery bombarded the Belgians relentlessly, and they could not prevent the Germans from crossing the Yser River.

Belgium's King Albert I (1875–1934) personally commanded his country's army, which numbered only sixty thousand troops. King Albert knew he controlled the high ground and that the Germans were on land below sea level. He ordered the sluices opened on the dikes that held back seawater. Soon the ground the

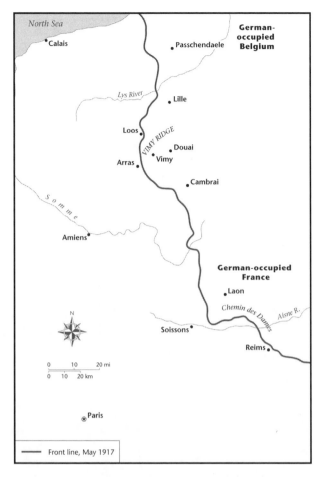

Calais

North Sea

Passchendaele

German-occupied Belgium

Lys River

Lille

Loos

VIMY RIDGE

Douai

Arras

Vimy

Cambrai

Somme

Amiens

German-occupied France

Laon

Chemin des Dames

Aisne R.

N

Soissons

Reims

0   10   20 mi
0   10   20 km

Paris

— Front line, May 1917

Ypres, Verdun, and the Somme witnessed bloody fighting in World War I because they stood along the path of a German invasion of France. *Reproduced by permission of Gale, a part of Cengage Learning*

Germans wanted to control was flooded—a twenty-mile stretch from Dixmude to Nieuport. This two-mile wide lake kept the Germans from attacking the Belgians for the rest of the war.

Falkenhayn was determined to reach the coast, and he focused his attention on the city of Ypres. The Allies chose to defend the high ground in a salient east of the city. The French held the line south of Dixmude—from the Yser River and the Ypres canal as far as Langemarck, in the suburbs of Ypres. The British had a thirty-five mile front around Ypres toward the low ridge of higher ground at Passchendaele. Sir John French led six British infantry divisions, one in reserve, and three cavalry divisions. For reinforcements, he had several divisions of Indian infantry and cavalry; however, they were not equipped or trained for winter weather. The Indians would later have to be thrown into the battle, and they were to fight bravely.

Field Marshal French and Field Marshal Ferdinand Foch had plans to attack and lead a breakout to Brussels,

but the Germans were better prepared for battle. The Allies were outnumbered, because Falkenhayn brought in the Duke of Württemberg's (1865–1939) Fourth Army and Prince Rupprecht's (1869–1955) Sixth Army from Lorraine. The British Expeditionary Force began by attacking toward the eastern part of Ypres. The Germans pushed back—sending the British Fourth Corps toward the city itself. Haig's First Corps arrived to relieve the Fourth Corps, and the British slowed to a crawl from exhaustion and high casualties. The Germans picked this time to attack. On October 20, 1914, twenty-four divisions of German troops lined up against nineteen Allied divisions. Haig showed his prowess at defensive warfare and held the Germans back, while the British sharpshooters slowed the German advance.

Falkenhayn began a new attack on October 31, with cavalry attacks at Messines Ridge in the southeast of Ypres. The British cavalry abandoned their positions there. Other German forces attacked General Sir Douglas Haig's First Corps in the north. They broke through at first, but were later pushed back by a British counterattack.

On November 11, the Germans tried again with an attack by only two elite divisions along the Menin Road. This surprised the British, and the Germans again made a short-lived breakthrough, but they were slow to exploit it. The British took every man available, including cooks and clerks, and sent them to the gap in the lines. The last-ditch effort worked to slow down the Germans. The fight see-sawed until November 22, with no side gaining an advantage. Winter came, and the fighting slowed down.

The British and French began to dig in. The French held territory they won in the north and south of the city. The Germans now held the high ground, but it was clearly a stalemate.

The first battle of Ypres symbolized more of the horror of World War I that was to come. Casualties were incredible on both sides, and the war was just beginning. At this battle, 134,315 German soldiers were killed or wounded, the British lost 58,155, and the French lost some 50,000. The British suffered the most because their army was the smallest.

Trenches now spanned 475 miles from the North Sea to Switzerland, and no attack could be successful without artillery. The winter of 1914 was mostly quiet. French Marshal Joseph Joffre tried two more unsuccessful and costly attacks in December, one in Artois and one in Champagne.

During Christmas of 1914, both sides declared a truce at many different locations in the trenches. Troops decorated Christmas trees and exchanged gifts. Both sides sang Christmas carols, and some even went out to No Man's Land and exchanged pleasantries and tobacco. In one place between the trenches troops from both sides even started a soccer game. They allowed each other to bury the dead in No Man's Land. The truce went on for a few days after Christmas until the generals ordered the men to cease these activities and begin fighting again. Many commanders from both sides believed the war could be won outright—that one decisive offensive in one battle could end the war. Others knew that the modern weapons—machine guns, magazine rifles, and quick-firing artillery—would only serve to lengthen the war of attrition.

Sinking of the *Lusitania*

On May 7, 1915, a German U-boat sank the *Lusitania*, a British passenger liner traveling from New York to Great Britain. Attacked off the coast of Ireland without warning, the ship sank in eighteen minutes, and 1,198 people were lost, including 124 Americans. Such tactics, essential to German submarine warfare, outraged the American public. While the incident did not cause the United States to declare war, it strained American-German relations and set the stage for America's eventual entry into the conflict.

Warning President Woodrow Wilson firmly believed that the United States should remain neutral in the European conflict. His attitude on this question perfectly reflected the prevailing mood of his country in 1915. It is true that a great many Americans, particularly on the East Coast, felt sympathy for the English. However, most Americans were disinclined to embroil their sons and brothers in a distant war.

Wilson also shared the average American's distaste for the rapidly developing field of underwater warfare. On the whole, Americans found ambush on the high seas (the submarine's entire raison-d'être) particularly dishonorable. On February 10, 1915, the American government declared unannounced U-boat attacks to be inhumane and illegal and vowed that the German government would face "a strict accountability" should it impede America's freedom on the water.

America's attitude left the Germans in a predicament. England's naval blockade had a stranglehold on their country. Germany had retaliated with a U-boat cordon around Great Britain. However, Germany's strategy was frustrated by neutral American merchant ships (and British passenger liners carrying American citizens), which brought foodstuffs and military supplies into Great Britain. The Germans dared not come down too hard on these leaks, for fear of bringing the United States into the war.

Nevertheless, on May 1, 1915, a German submarine attacked an American tanker, the *Gulflight*, on its way to the French coast. Three Americans were killed. The same day, New York newspapers ran an advertisement from the German Embassy in Washington that said: "Travelers intending to embark on the Atlantic voyage are reminded that a state of war exists between Germany and Great Britain and its allies." Americans were warned that any

This U.S. Navy recruitment poster's reference to the *Lusitania* illustrates the sinking's powerful influence on American public opinion. *© Swim Ink 2, LLC/Corbis*

ships flying Allied colors were "liable to destruction in those waters and that travelers sailing in the war zone on ships to Great Britain or its allies do so at their own risk."

Ambush The commander of the *Lusitania*, Captain William Turner (1856–1933), was more than aware of the risks he ran. The British would later deny it, but the *Lusitania* was carrying small arms ammunition into England. The British Admiralty had issued strict guidelines for all their national ships—they were to avoid headlands, around which submarines found their best hunting, they were to steam at full speed, and they were to follow a zig-zag course in the middle of the channel. For some unknown reason, Turner ignored all of these recommendations as he cruised past Old Head of Kinsale, Ireland, on May 7, 1915.

As it happened, the German U-boat *U-20* had been hunting in those very waters. Commanded by Captain Walther Schwieger (1885–1917), the *U-20* had sunk the British *Candidate* and the *Centurion* just the day before.

Around noon on May 7, Schwieger unsuccessfully chased the cruiser *Juno*. An hour and a half later, the *Lusitania* (traveling in a straight line at reduced speed) bore directly down on the submarine. The *U-20* fired a single torpedo into the hull of the *Lusitania*. The ship sank rapidly, and nearly twelve hundred passengers—including more than one hundred Americans—drowned.

Response The British and the American public reacted with predictable fury. Even if the *Lusitania* had been smuggling ammunition, they argued, that did not justify such wholesale slaughter of civilians. At the very least, tradition demanded that civilians should be given time to board the lifeboats.

Six days later, Wilson reprimanded the Germany embassy for their newspaper "warning" of May 1. He vigorously denied that the advertisement in any way absolved them of responsibility. Despite British hopes, however, Wilson declined to be pushed into a declaration of war. In a May 10 address to newly naturalized Americans at Convention Hall in Philadelphia, he reaffirmed American neutrality: "There is such a thing as being too proud to fight."

Nevertheless, Wilson continued to hound the Germans on the issue. The Reich reluctantly agreed to pay compensation for the lives lost on the *Lusitania*, and the kaiser ordered that passenger ships no longer be targeted.

Germany refused, however, to apologize for the sinking itself, pointing out that the *Lusitania* had been illegally carrying weapons into England. Schwieger's *U-20* was welcomed back into port with cheers, and the government even struck a celebratory medal to commemorate his attack. The *Kölnische Volkszeitung* newspaper proclaimed that "the sinking of the giant English steamship is a success of moral significance which is still greater than material success. With joyful pride we contemplate this latest deed of our Navy."

In the meantime, the Allies were disgusted by Wilson's reserve, as were some Americans. Former president Theodore Roosevelt launched his own propaganda campaign, calling stridently for immediate entry into the war.

Further Attacks On July 21, Wilson again condemned unannounced attacks, saying that they "must be regarded by the Government of the United States, when they affect American citizens, as deliberately unfriendly." Considering this last statement to be too strongly worded, Secretary of State William Jennings Bryan (1860–1925) resigned his post.

On August 19, the unarmed British *Arabic* sank with forty-four passengers, three of them American. In revenge, that same day the British *Baralong* approached the German *U-27*, flying American colors. When she came close enough, the *Baralong* lowered the Stars and Stripes, raised the Union Jack, and fired on the *U-27* and sank it.

While deploring this use of the American flag, Wilson pressured Germany into promising that "liners would not be sunk without warning and without safety of the lives of non-combatants, provided the liners do not try to escape or offer resistance."

Nevertheless, the issue continued to dog U.S.-German relations for the next two years. In 1917, Germany declared that its navy would resume unrestricted submarine warfare. Shortly afterwards, the United States officially entered World War I.

Gallipoli

The Battle of Gallipoli in 1915 resulted from a British plan to attack Turkey, an ally of Germany and the Central Powers. This strategic plan was developed and promoted largely by Winston Churchill, Britain's first lord of the admiralty at the time and prime minister during World War II. The Western Front had proven to be a stalemate, so Churchill and the British War Council decided to make use of Britain's strong navy to take the Dardanelles, the strategic straits connecting the Aegean Sea with the Sea of Marmara. The straits are also where Europe and Asia meet within Turkey. If successful, this strategy would have given the Allies a valuable link to Russian ports on the Black Sea. It was also planned to drive Turkey into submission and encourage the neighboring neutral nations of Romania, Bulgaria, and Greece to enter the war against the Central Powers.

The Allies began with a combined British and French naval attack on Turkey on February 19, 1915. The goal was to sail their fleets up the narrow straits, shelling Turkish forces and landing at the city of Gallipoli. The Allies, however, ran into some unexpected problems. Bad weather and a delay of the support from Australian and New Zealand forces arriving from Egypt postponed or canceled some of the plans. By March 18, another attack was planned. The Turks in many ways were ready for such attack. A series of underwater Turkish mines had been planted in the straits and were successful in damaging the Allied warships. One French ship, the *Bouvet*, was sunk, killing seven hundred men. Three others were partially destroyed and rendered useless.

Eventually, the combined forces decided to land on unoccupied beaches on Turkey's shore and then head uphill to take Turkish strongholds inland. The Allies never expected the fierce resistance they got from the Turks. Commander Mustafa Kemal (1881–1938), who would become Atatürk, the founder of modern Turkey, led the defense of his nation. Under his direction, the Turks dug machine-gun nests and bunkers atop the mountains and awaited the advancing British and French ground forces. The attackers landed on April 25, some on the open and unfortified beaches. But as many of these Allied soldiers charged uphill, carnage followed. Some waited quietly until their attackers charged the

As the war monument at Gallipoli suggests, the 1915 battle would loom large in the memory of World War I for Turkish and Australian and New Zealand Army Corps ("ANZAC") nation citizens. *© Roger Antrobus/Corbis*

hill. At other beachheads, Turkish machine guns and artillery fired into British boats as they hit land but before the soldiers ever departed. Soon these barges were filled with the dead and the water around the boats turned red from the spilled blood.

The British plan to take Turkey was far more difficult than they expected. They found themselves digging trenches not far inland and holding only what was open when they arrived. The stalemate near Gallipoli paralleled the one on the Western Front. Throughout May and June, the Allies tried to advance several times but were continually repulsed by the Turks. A war of attrition had developed. The final Allied assault on Gallipoli started on August 6, which resulted in small gains. Within three days, this attempt also failed. With no sign of change in sight, the allies withdrew from Gallipoli Peninsula in late 1915, and by January 9, 1916, the last Allied troops departed the area. The plan to divide and conquer had failed.

Verdun

In late 1915, the Allies and the Central Powers were both bewildered and frustrated at the progress of the war. Each front and each battle was inconclusive. Both

sides looked for the one decisive battle that would end the war quickly. The Allies thought 1916 would be the year for victory. French Marshal Joseph Joffre wanted a deliberate attack coordinated by all the Allied forces. He thought previous Allied operations lacked coordination. The Allies met on December 15 in Chantilly, twenty-six miles north of Paris, to plan their master stroke. The French hoped Britain and Russia would be better prepared in the summer. The British had to resort to a draft for the first time in their history. Their new soldiers needed to train and equip in the spring for operations on the continent in the summer. The Russians had to recover from dreadful losses of the previous year. They were also training with new equipment. Both the British and the Russians needed to close the gap in artillery pieces. The Germans had more heavy guns.

On February 14, 1916, Marshal Joffre and British General Sir Douglas Haig agreed that they would attack the Central Powers in June with a joint offensive near the Somme River, twenty miles east of the city of Amiens. They hoped that the Allies would have a surge in troops and equipment and that the combined personnel of France and Britain would overtake Germany.

Soldiers who were "going over the top" were climbing out of a trench to fight. Later, this World War I phrase took on a fitting connotation of heedlessness. © *Bettmann/Corbis*

The Germans had their own ideas for an offensive in 1916. Their strategy—"Starve Britain and Bleed France"—consisted of continued German submarine attacks against British shipping. These attacks would cut British supply lines and starve Britain. The Germans thought that destroying the French Army in 1916 would force the British to surrender, because the British Expeditionary Force would not be ready to fight in time. German General Erich von Falkenhayn figured that a war of attrition against France would bleed the French until they lost the will to fight. The Germans had inflicted great losses against the French in 1915 by staying on the defensive. It appeared Germany could continue to bleed the French that way.

However, Falkenhayn was under pressure to mount an offensive in 1916. The emperor and other German generals on the eastern front believed the time for a German offensive should come sooner rather than later. Falkenhayn wanted to break the will of the French with a decisive attack. He thought if the Germans attacked along a narrow front, the French would send their armies to reinforce the break-through point, and then the superior German artillery would destroy the French. Falkenhayn chose Verdun, near the Meuse River, as the target of his main effort. Verdun was a powerful symbol to the French and an important area in military history. Verdun played a pivotal role from the time of Atilla the Hun to the Franco-Prussian War. It was currently a fortress city made up of sixty forts and was part of a major line of defense between France and Germany. Falkenhayn believed France would overplay its hand to protect the city. The French would be lured into a killing ground for German artillery near Verdun.

Unfortunately, Falkenhayn did not communicate the subtleties of the German plan to his subordinate commanders, and the troops thought their objective was to take the city. The German Fifth Army was used to attack Verdun—six divisions with four more in reserve. The artillery collected for the attack was an awesome arsenal—1,100 pieces, including 542 heavy guns with two and a half million shells. There were thirteen "Big Bertha" siege howitzers, thirteen 420-mm guns, and seventeen 305-mm howitzers that had already been used to annihilate the Belgian forts. The German plan was simple. The French did not want to give up Verdun. They would have to keep sending reinforcements to the area of operations, and the Germans would use their artillery to cut the French to pieces.

On February 21, 1916, after delaying the attack because of the weather, the Germans began the artillery siege. However, the artillery attack did not kill as many of the French as planned. The German infantry did not attack in great strength, and the French fought back better than expected. But they eventually started retreating from many of the forts. Only Forts Vaux and Douaumont were left against the attacking Germans. These forts were on high points overlooking the Meuse and the city of Verdun; if the Germans took these objectives, they could fire at will into the city. When Fort Douaumont fell without firing a shot, the French situation looked bleak.

French General Noël de Castelnau (1851–1944) visited the front and decided that the Verdun salient could be held. This decision played right into the German strategy. Joffre agreed to raise a new French army to reinforce Verdun. He named Henri Pétain to lead this force. Pétain understood modern warfare better than many generals of his day. He had predicted that artillery and machine guns would destroy attacking infantry quickly. He also was a master of logistics. Pétain widened a main supply route and used trucks instead of the railways that the Germans already shelled. Soon the French were back in business as a steady stream of reinforcements and supplies reentered Verdun.

The German advance slowed on February 28 as French artillery were able to catch German infantry in the open on the west bank of the Meuse. Falkenhayn was again encouraged to attack by Kaiser Wilhelm and other generals. The Germans sought a hill called Le Mort Homme (Dead Man's Hill) that held most of the French artillery.

The German advance looked good at first, when three thousand French troops surrendered after the first German bombardment. But then French resistance stiffened, and the battle for Le Mort Homme lasted almost three months. Both sides engaged in ferocious hand-to-hand combat with bayonets, pistols, and grenades. An adjacent terrain feature called Hill 304 was actually reduced in height by twenty-five feet from the nonstop shelling. French casualties were 89,000; German casualties were 82,000.

The daily momentum swayed back and forth, but the overall stalemate lingered. Different French commanders attempted attacks. The Germans focused on Fort Vaux, to the southeast of Douaumont. The battle went down into the darkened underground tunnels of Fort Vaux. Only six hundred French soldiers held out there by fighting in the dark with pistols and grenades against German

troops armed with flamethrowers. The French finally surrendered. The Germans needed only one more French objective, Fort Souville, to be able to bombard the city of Verdun from the heights. The French were down to their last hope of resistance. But then the Germans shifted their attack. Falkenhayn had to redirect three of his divisions to the eastern front to help the Austro-Hungarian forces against the Russians. The German infantry made it to within twelve hundred yards before the last ridge in front of Verdun, but they could get no farther.

The failure of this attack helped the French gain momentum. Kaiser Wilhelm fired Falkenhayn and replaced him with General Paul von Hindenburg as the army chief of staff. Erich Ludendorff joined Hindenburg as chief of logistics, but they made the main operational decisions together. Once Hindenburg and Ludendorff visited the Verdun front, they were shocked at the carnage and stopped all German offensives in the area.

Meanwhile, Pétain began building up the French stock of artillery pieces. French Second Army Commander Robert Nivelle (1857–1924) used this artillery well. He perfected use of the "rolling" artillery barrage—firing on targets directly in front of the infantry as they charged the Germans. The artillery rounds served as a curtain of explosion that shielded the advancing French infantry. These soldiers could advance one hundred yards every four minutes. The Second Army began an attack using these tactics on October 19. The thick fog allowed the French to roll up on the enemy before the Germans knew what happened. The French won back Fort Douaumont on November 2 and Fort Vaux soon after the Germans retreated. The new lines formed with the Germans back two miles behind Fort Douaumont.

During the ten months of fighting, nearly one million men on both sides were killed or wounded. Verdun symbolized the horror and futility of World War I. There were heavy losses with hardly any decisive outcome. Many troops on both sides never saw the enemy. Heavy rains filled trenches and bomb craters with water, and soldiers drowned when they could not climb out of the muddy slopes. Some villages in the Verdun area were never rebuilt, and vegetation never grew again because the ground was so full of explosives.

Zimmerman Telegram

In February 1917, the German government announced its intention to recommence unrestricted submarine warfare. Knowing that this would almost certainly draw America into the war, German Secretary of Foreign Affairs Arthur Zimmermann (1864–1940) sent a coded message to Mexico proposing a military alliance against the United States. Germany promised to restore to Mexico the territories of Texas, New Mexico, and Arizona, which had been ceded to the United States in 1848.

The telegram was intercepted and decoded by the British, who immediately handed it over to Woodrow Wilson. The subsequent outrage helped to push the American public into World War I.

German Decision In August 1914, the kaiser had said that the war would be over before the autumn leaves fell. The British, French, and Russians had been equally sanguine, and equally wrong. By 1917, however, both sides were near exhaustion. The war had devolved into a bloody stalemate, expensive and apparently unwinnable.

The German high command reached a desperate decision. The British Isles, they reasoned, had not been self-sufficient for over a century. If the Reich's impressive U-boat fleet could effect a total blockade of the islands, the English would starve out of the conflict within a matter of months.

Germany knew that such a policy would cause the United States to join the war on the Allies' side. However, military leaders saw no other way to break out of the European impasse. They were encouraged by reports of Russia's imminent collapse, and they grossly underestimated America's possible impact on the war. German generals expected at most 100,000 American troops to join the war effort, and those would have to be transported through submarine infested waters. In any case, Germany hoped that the United States would not be able to fully mobilize in time to save Great Britain.

On February 1, 1917, Germany declared that any ship on approach to the British Isles, the coast of France, or the Mediterranean would be sunk. Two days later, the German *U-53* sank an American cargo ship, the *Housatonic*, off Great Britain's Scilly Islands. The crew was saved, but the grain cargo was lost. Apparently Zimmermann told the American ambassador in Berlin that, "everything will be alright. America will do nothing, for President Wilson is for peace and nothing else. Everything will go on as before."

The next day the United States broke diplomatic relations with Germany.

British Intelligence On February 23, British agents intercepted the encrypted "Zimmerman" telegram from Berlin to the German ambassador to Mexico. Because of the combined efforts of cryptanalysts and spies, they had been able to crack the code. It revealed Germany's plan to engage in all-out submarine warfare and suggested an alliance with Mexico. Germany offered to return Texas, New Mexico, and Arizona to Mexico in exchange for the country's help.

The intelligence break placed the British government in a quandary. On one hand, the Germans had just handed them a magnificent piece of propaganda. The Allies had campaigned to bring America into the war for two years; they could not pass up such a golden opportunity.

THE ZIMMERMAN NOTE

A transcript of the fateful telegram follows.

Berlin, January 19, 1917

On the first of February we intend to begin submarine warfare unrestricted. In spite of this, it is our intention to endeavor to keep neutral the United States of America.

If this attempt is not successful, we propose an alliance on the following basis with Mexico: That we shall make war together and together make peace. We shall give general financial support, and it is understood that Mexico is to reconquer the lost territory in New Mexico, Texas, and Arizona. The details are left to you for settlement . . . .

You are instructed to inform the President of Mexico of the above in the greatest confidence as soon as it is certain that there will be an outbreak of war with the United States and suggest that the President of Mexico, on his own initiative, should communicate with Japan suggesting adherence at once to this plan; at the same time, offer to mediate between Germany and Japan.

Please call to the attention of the President of Mexico that the employment of ruthless submarine warfare now promises to compel England to make peace in a few months.

Zimmerman (Secretary of State)

SOURCE: *"The Zimmerman Note to the German Minister in Mexico, January 19, 1917."* World War I Document Archive. *Brigham Young University Library. http://net.lib.byu.edu/~rdh7/wwi/1917/zimmerman. html (accessed June 15, 2007).*

On the other hand, if they published the note, Germany would know that Britain had cracked their latest codes. Furthermore, since the note had been sent to Mexico via Washington, the United States would know that Britain had tapped American communication channels.

To sidestep the problem, the British asked one of their Mexico City agents to intercept the message at the telegraph office. On February 24, the translated note was handed over to the U.S. ambassador in London.

American Reaction Woodrow Wilson had run his 1916 campaign with the slogan: "He kept us out of the war." However, he privately feared that American participation in the conflict was inevitable. The Reich's conduct of the war had convinced him that a victorious Germany would not be conducive to world peace.

Nevertheless, Wilson could not drag his country into war even if he had wanted to—he simply did not have popular or congressional support. The Zimmermann

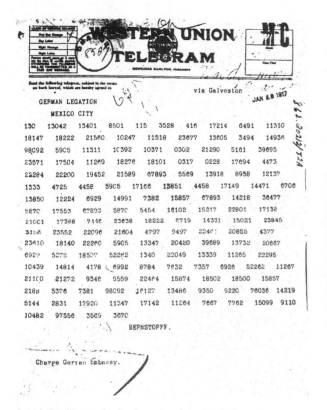

German machine guns proved costly to American lives at the Battle of Belleau Wood in 1918. Here is the American Military Cemetery in Belleau Wood. © *Corbis*

British Intelligence broke the code of the 1917 Zimmerman Telegram and publicized its inflammatory message in an effort to bring the United States into the war. *The Granger Collection, New York. Reproduced by permission*

telegram changed that. Midwestern Americans did not care much about the Somme or Verdun, but they minded about Mexico, which was just emerging from a long civil war. A southern attack on America did not seem too far-fetched. The United States had recently sent the Pershing Expedition into Mexico after a raid on New Mexico by Pancho Villa.

All the same, the popular outrage might have blown over if Germany had not vigorously resumed unrestricted submarine attacks. Five American ships were sunk in March alone. On April 2, Wilson went to Congress and asked for a declaration of war. "To such a task we can dedicate our lives and our fortunes, everything that we are and everything that we have, with the pride of those who know that the day has come when America is privileged to spend her blood and her might for the principles that gave her birth and happiness and the peace which she has treasured. God helping her, she can do no other."

On April 14, Mexican President Venustiano Carranza formally declined Germany's proposals.

Belleau Wood

The spring of 1918 saw the Germans mount what in some ways was one of their most successful offensives.

By April, the Germans had moved to within five miles of Amiens. Their front extended over twenty miles, but it was in danger of bogging down again. The original plan was a single, massive thrust north by northwest along the sea. But the German commanders changed this strategy and decided to divide the attacking forces into three prongs. They had hoped to take advantage of a break in the British lines near the old Somme battlefield.

Dividing the German troops in this way reduced the impact of the main attack. The three groups were not strong enough to create their own breakthrough in the Allied lines. To make matters worse, the Germans encountered obstacles from the Old Somme battle-field—craters, barbed wire, and unexploded ordnance. Some of the German units actually stopped to plunder Allied supplies of food and alcohol instead of resuming their attack. Others got lost and attacked the wrong sector.

The British and Australian troops seized upon the German disorganization and launched a counterattack on April 4. The Germans lost some of their most elite troops, and the pressure was on for German General Erich Ludendorff to act quickly. He proposed a new attack that was one of the contingency plans for the current operation. 'Operation George' would probe the British at the old Ypres battlefield. The British had improved their defenses at this location. They had worked on these positions since 1914, and it was probably their strongest defense on the whole western front. Field Marshal Sir Douglas Haig was concerned that this was the decisive point of the war. He sent a message to the troops in this sector known as the "Backs to the Wall" order, to fight to the end.

Luckily for the British, they had air support, and the Germans used unimaginative tactics with full frontal assaults. There were plenty of enemy targets for the British artillery and machine guns. There was even one of the first tank battles in history between the Germans and the British. The British tanks were superior in number and quality, and they were able to beat back the German attack. Ludendorff then decided to gamble, and he set his sights on Paris. He planned a hasty attack down the Oise Valley, because Paris was only seventy miles away. The German artillery now had six thousand guns with two million shells trained on the Allies. Fifteen divisions of the German Sixth Army began the attack. They were followed by twenty-five more divisions. The Germans had mass, speed, and momentum as they attacked from the heights of a ridgeline down to the reverse slope and the flatlands below.

Ludendorff's force got as far as Soissons and Château-Thierry; they were only fifty-six miles from Paris. The Allies began calling in their reserves, and this is how the Americans finally got in the fight. The U.S. Marine Corps had a brigade at Belleau Wood, along with the U.S. Army Second and Third divisions. The mission was to block the German advance at the road near Reims. The marines fought bravely and the German offensive ground to a halt. The U.S. Second Division counterattacked with the French at Belleau Wood. They stopped the Germans cold by June 6. However, the Germans were too close to Paris for comfort. Plans were made to evacuate the government and the people.

French Prime Minister Georges Clemenceau tried to rally his country with a rousing speech similar to Haig's "Back to the Wall" talk. One mass attack might have been too much for the Allies, because the Americans were not initially deployed correctly and were also inexperienced. But Ludendorff had decided to break his attacking force into three prongs and have one rush to Paris. Paris had looked like the lower-hanging fruit, but he was not able to grasp it. Now the Germans were again defending a narrow salient; they were overextended, and they invited more counterattacks. Unfortunately, they had broadcast what they thought was a successful attack to the citizens of Germany. Withdrawing now would look like defeat and hurt morale. Ludendorff felt he had no choice and decided on yet again another offensive.

During the preceding spring offensive, the Germans had lost another 100,000 troops. It seemed like the Allies could go on forever because reinforcements kept pouring in. The Americans now had twenty-five divisions in or near the area of operations. Fifty-five more were on their way. Despite a rocky start, General John J. Pershing had found a way to get along with Allied gen-

"BACKS TO THE WALL"

On April 11, 1918, British Field Marshal Sir Douglas Haig issued this special order to his troops in France and Flanders:

> Three weeks ago to-day the enemy began his terrific attacks against us on a fifty-mile front. His objects are to separate us from the French, to take the Channel Ports and destroy the British Army. moment.
>
> In spite of throwing already 106 Divisions into the battle and enduring the most reckless sacrifice of human life, he has as yet made little progress towards his goals. moment.
>
> We owe this to the determined fighting and self-sacrifice of our troops. Words fail me to express the admiration which I feel for the splendid resistance offered by all ranks of our Army under the most trying circumstances. moment.
>
> Many amongst us now are tired. To those I would say that Victory will belong to the side which holds out the longest. The French Army is moving rapidly and in great force to our support. moment.
>
> There is no other course open to us but to fight it out. Every position must be held to the last man: there must be no retirement. With our backs to the wall and believing in the justice of our cause each one of us must fight on to the end. The safety of our homes and the Freedom of mankind alike depend upon the conduct of each one of us at this critical moment.

SOURCE: *"Sir Douglas Haig's 'Backs to the Wall' Order, 11 April 1918."* FirstWorldWar.com. <www.firstworldwar.com/source/backstothe-wall.htm> (accessed June 15, 2007).

erals Foch and Haig. The American soldiers, known as "doughboys," were proving their mettle in combat. It finally appeared that the Allies were gaining momentum in the war. Belleau Wood appeared to be one of the decisive contests of the war. The American Expeditionary Force came to the aid of the French at the right time, and they were able to build momentum with further counterattacks against the Germans in their sector on the way.

The Battle of the Somme

The Battle of the Somme, fought from July 1 to November 18, 1916, was one of the costliest battles of the First World War. Long held up as a prime example of the futility of attritional warfare and the inability of the Allied leadership to capitalize on the rapidly shifting fortunes of battle, the battle did achieve some positive ends, but at an outrageous price in human life and misery.

Taken at the Battle of the Somme, this photograph of British soldiers testifies to the emergence of modern warfare, in the form of trenches, poison gas, and machine guns. © *Hulton-Deutsch Collection/Corbis*

1916 Battle Plans In December 1915, the Allies met in Chantilly, France, to decide on the general strategy for the coming year. They decided that simultaneous attacks would be launched on every front in order to overwhelm the German defenses—the British and French would attack in the west, the Italians in the south, and the Russians in the east.

For the British contribution to this plan, Douglas Haig, the newly appointed commander in chief of the British Expeditionary Force (BEF), favored an attack in northern Flanders along the Channel Coast, due to its proximity to British supply points and the chance it offered of driving the Germans from the Belgian ports from which they waged their devastating U-boat campaign.

At that time, however, the British were still unofficially considered the junior members of the Anglo-French alliance, and when General Joseph Joffre decided

to shift the planned British offensive south to the point where the BEF joined up with the French army, there was little Haig could do about it.

Verdun On February 21, as preparations were being made for three large Anglo-French offensives, the Germans launched their Verdun offensive. The French were suddenly committed to a major battle, one that would last the remainder of the year. They were in no position to participate in the planned Allied attack in any major capacity.

The promised French contribution to the British offensive (thirty-nine divisions attacking along a twenty-five-mile front) was reduced in April to thirty divisions along a fifteen-mile front. In the end, the actual French contribution at the opening of the battle was a mere twelve divisions attacking along ten miles of front. On the positive side, however, this reduced front allowed the French to more effectively concentrate their artillery.

Such small contributions were of little comfort to the British, who, after centuries of relying on their navy and an elite army to win wars, found themselves for the first time in history committing a huge army to war on the Continent.

Kitchener's Army   The Battle of the Somme would mark the debut of what was called the New Army, or Kitchener's Army, after Field Marshal Horatio Herbert Kitchener, the secretary of state for war who pushed through the policy to build the New Army. Thought laughable at the outset of the war, that policy was based on the idea that the Allies could only win by bringing overwhelming force to bear on the Germans. Thus, starting in August 1914, a massive army had been recruited and trained in England.

As more and more French units were pulled into the "meat-grinder" at Verdun, General Joffre began insisting that the British launch their planned offensive. The goal was no longer to put pressure on Germany and force a breakthrough but rather to pin down German reserves, preventing reinforcement elsewhere. Haig, however, was optimistic that a breakthrough could be achieved, especially in light of the German commitments at Verdun, and so he ordered the offensive planned accordingly.

The BEF committed 400,000 troops to the Somme sector, along with 1,400 guns, more than the Germans had deployed for their Verdun offensive. The attack, however, was to be carried out over a wider front, reducing the overall effectiveness of such a concentration.

Worse still, the terrain chosen for the offensive was not supportive of a major offensive. It was a quiet, rural sector that had seen little action so far and did not have the infrastructure that modern armies required. New railways, seventeen miles in all, had to be laid; unpaved gravel roads had to be shored up for the massive amounts of traffic they would soon be forced to bear; and British engineers even had to sink several dozen wells because the area was lacking in readily available sources of water. These preparations occupied the army's time and attention for three months, taking away from time that might have been spent in training and operational planning.

The First Day   On June 24, the preliminary bombardment of the Battle of the Somme began. It lasted a week and lobbed 1.5 million shells at the German lines. Simultaneously, four mines packed with TNT at the terminal points were dug from the British lines to positions directly under the German front line trenches.

The mines were detonated at 7:30 A.M. on July 1 as the artillery barrage lifted off the front lines and bombarded positions in the German rear. With those tre-

mendous blasts, the signal was given to go "over the top." Thirteen British and eleven French divisions left their trenches and moved forward.

Some British units actually had already done so. Tactics had been left up to individual regimental commanders, and some had ordered their troops to infiltrate "No Man's Land"—the area between the two forces's front lines—under the cover of darkness. Other commanders had their troops march forward from the trenches in waves, moving across hundreds of yards of shell-pocked earth at a walking pace.

The Germans, who had largely weathered the barrage in concrete-reinforced underground bunkers, quickly returned to their posts. At some points, where the British had been able to sneak up close enough during the night, the Germans were quickly overwhelmed. Elsewhere along the line, however, the advancing waves were mowed down by machine-gun fire. Those units that made it to the German positions were decimated and alone, and were quickly overwhelmed.

Communication with the rear areas was ineffective and confusing. German artillery, ignored by the preliminary bombardment, quickly sealed off No Man's Land with a curtain of fire, preventing reinforcements from moving up. Units were dispatched to reinforce nonexistent breakthroughs, and there were cases of some of these units, such as the First Newfoundland Regiment, being mowed down by German machine-gun fire before they even crossed their own front line.

The French, meanwhile, were meeting with considerably more success. Their concentrated artillery had battle-hardened crews and were much more effective. By the end of the day, they had met or even surpassed their objectives. But because they had outpaced their allies, they were forced to stop.

The setting sun marked the end of the bloodiest single day in British military history. Total BEF casualties were 57,740. Of that number, 19,240 were dead.

Haig ordered continued attacks over the next ten days. With many units still in disarray after the massive casualties of July 1, these attacks were launched sporadically and with little planning. A total of forty-six of these localized attacks took place over a ten-day period at a cost of 25,000 casualties and no gain.

Battle of Attrition   As the hoped-for breakthrough failed to materialize, the Allied commanders began to waffle, unsure of what their objectives were, moving between the extremes of seeking a breakthrough and waging a battle of attrition. Their tendency in one direction or the other would often be based upon the day-to-day events of the battle. A small success somewhere along the front would prompt hopes of a breakthrough, and reinforcements would be ordered in. But these uncoordinated, unsupported attacks were doomed to fail, and Haig and his generals then settled again on

THE TANK ROLLS OUT

Haig's decision to launch a final attack was no doubt influenced by the arrival of the new British "secret weapon": the tank. Impervious to rifle and machine-gun fire and able to cross wires and trenches with impunity, the new war machine carried with it high hopes.

On September 15, at the town of Flers, the first tanks to roll into battle seemed to achieve their promise. The German defenders, unsure of what to make of the metal monstrosities approaching them, fled in terror. An optimistic newspaper dispatch was filed from the front: "A tank is walking up the High Street of Flers with the British Army cheering behind."

Once again, however, the promised breakthrough failed to materialize. The new tanks were too slow and mechanically unreliable—only twenty-one of the initial forty-nine even made it past their starting positions—and there was no doctrine yet developed on how best to use tanks in battle. As rains set in, turning the ground to a morass of mud and slime, the Flers offensive ground to a halt.

the strategy of pinning the Germans in a bloody attritional battle.

From mid-July to mid-September, the British and the French, in exchange for an advance of three square miles, sustained a total of 82,000 casualties. Haig, finally resigned to a battle of attrition, began planning for another push, at Flers.

The offensive at Flers stalled in the mud, but Haig was still convinced he had the Germans on the brink of defeat. He would launch two more offensives along the Ancre River through October and into November, but with the failure of the second Ancre attack on November 18, the Battle of the Somme finally came to an end.

Casualties and Aftermath In all, fifty-one British and forty-eight French divisions participated in the battle's bloodbath. The BEF lost 420,000 men, and total Allied casualties were 614,000. German casualties are not known for certain, but estimates range between 465,000 and 650,000. Even at its most conservative estimates, total casualties in the Battle of the Somme were over one million men killed, wounded, missing, or captured, one of the gravest tallies of the war.

As the Battle of the Somme was winding down, the Germans were adopting a new strategy, constructing an elaborate trench system behind their current lines. In February 1917, the Germans withdrew to these new positions—the Hindenburg Line, as the British called it—abandoning the Somme battlefield, razing villages, and poisoning wells as they went.

Although some claimed that this retreat showed the Battle of the Somme's effectiveness, the Germans were simply shortening their lines, which had followed the irregular boundary of the 1914 advance, to free up units and resources. Nevertheless, the Germans had indeed suffered grave losses in the battle, losing more of its irreplaceable trained soldiers.

The Somme offensive also taught the British many important lessons that would bear upon the 1918 offensives, but the price in blood these lessons demanded was almost more than the BEF could endure. But with the French nearly knocked out of the war by Verdun, it fell to the British to continue the attacks. Once again meeting at Chantilly, plans were drawn up for the next year's offensives.

Argonne Forest

The Allies agreed on a major operation in September 1918. U.S. General John Joseph Pershing's First Army and French General Henri Gouraud (1867–1946) would mass their attack on September 26. Pershing would strike in the area surrounded by the Meuse River on the right and the Aisne River to the left. Gouraud would attack to the west of the Aisne. Both armies would seize Sedan and Mezieres. On September 27, British General Sir Henry Horne's (1861–1929) First Army and General Sir Julian Byng's (1862–1935) Third Army would move toward Cambrai. The next day, the Belgian Army and General Sir Herbert Plumer's (1857–1932) British Second Army would strike Flanders between the Lys River and the North Sea. General Sir Henry Rawlinson's (1864–1925) Fourth British Army and Marie-Eugene Debeney's (1864–1943) First French Army were ordered to attack St. Quentin.

The Allies now had the upper hand. German morale was dissipating. The Allies had 220 divisions to the 197 divisions for the Central Powers. Many of the German units were not full-strength, and only about fifty were ready for combat. The Allies had more artillery, tanks, and airplanes as well. However, the Germans were dug in and experienced in defense.

U.S. troops handled the portion of the offensive located near the Meuse River and the Argonne Forest. The Argonne was difficult terrain consisting of dense trees and thick underbrush. This area had been a quiet sector since 1914. Visibility and movement were difficult. The Germans took advantage of the natural obstacles and placed their defenses in the only avenues of approach—through the narrow Aire and Meuse valleys on two sides of the ridgeline.

Colonel George C. Marshall (1880–1959), a key officer on Pershing's staff, was assigned the job of moving the 500,000-man U.S. Army from the battle at Saint-Mihiel salient to the Argonne offensive. He completed these maneuvers in ten days, even though there were only three usable roads from Saint-Mihiel. The difficult terrain of the Argonne Forest made it a challenge to keep these troops resupplied. Four of the nine U.S. divisions had no combat experience and were

While the American troops in this photograph survived their trial in the Argonne Forest, others who were part of the "Lost Battalion" were not so fortunate. © *Bettmann/Corbis*

known as the "thin green line." Some of the experienced troops from Saint-Mihiel never made it to Argonne. The American troops had trouble with combat in the thick forest at first. But they made steady progress—four miles the first day and three miles the next. However, the Americans showed their inexperience by attacking in waves, shoulder-to-shoulder. They were easy targets for the German machine guns, and casualties were heavy.

On September 28, Pershing decided to bring in reinforcements. The U.S. First Division, or "Big Red One," joined the fight. The attack started again on October 4. Progress was still slow. Units had difficulty communicating and maneuvering in the Argonne Forest. Autumn brought nasty weather, fog and sleet. The First Battalion of Three-Hundred-Eighth Infantry Regiment of the American Seventy-seventh Division became lost and was cut off from friendly forces. It took two other American divisions to save it. Of the original 600 men in the battalion, only 194 troops survived.

But the battle also had the main American hero of the war—Sergeant Alvin York (1887–1964) from Tennessee. York's platoon was ambushed by German machine-gun

fire, and most of his fellow soldiers were killed. He then rushed alone to the German position, firing his rifle all the way. York killed twenty-five German soldiers and took an astounding 132 prisoners in actions he conducted by himself that day.

The battle of the Argonne continued to ebb and flow, but the Americans kept up their advance. The fresh troops with new equipment overwhelmed the exhausted Germans. By October 12, the Americans had moved through and cleared the Argonne and were now tracking toward the Meuse. Their front enlarged to ninety miles. Pershing now had enough replacements to create two separate armies. He remained the group commander over General Robert Lee Bullard (1861–1947), who commanded the Second Army, and General Hunter Liggett (1857–1935), who led the First Army. Although Foch complained that the Americans were moving too slow at first, German resistance began to weaken. The Americans had done what they set out to do, and by November 6, had come to a few miles of Sedan. Two days later, they shelled the city from the heights overlooking it.

The Germans had come to the end of their road. Since 1914, they had fought the Russians, the Italians, the Romanians, and of course the French and the British. After all that, the Americans were just too much for them at the end. The British and French were proficient at using their tanks with infantry attacks. This proved too much for the Germans at Amiens, who were now retreating to the Hindenburg Line. The Americans appeared, it seemed, out of nowhere.

The Hindenburg Line was one of the strongest German defensive systems of the war. The Allies had to bombard the barbed wire separately before they attacked. Natural obstacles remained, such as the Canal du Nord and the St. Quentin Canal. On September 27, the ground assault began. The Allied Fourth Army attacked, and the losses were heavy—5,400 Americans killed and 2,400 Australian lost. The Ninth Corps broke through at Bellenglise and Germany's allies were ready to call it quits. Bulgaria began negotiating for peace with the French and British on September 29. It was over for the Germans. They would soon begin the peace process as well, and their fate would be in the hands of Allied politicians and diplomats.

The Fourteen Points

On January 8, 1918, nine months after the United States entered World War I, President Woodrow Wilson went before Congress and presented his program for peace, which became known as the Fourteen Points. In it, Wilson outlined the basic principles he believed would bring about a just and lasting peace among the nations of the world. The Fourteen Points are significant because they translated many elements of American domestic reform, known as Progressivism, into foreign policy. Wilson argued that morality and ethics—not self-interest—serve as the basis for a democratic society's foreign policy. The program made clear that America's goals for the war differed from those that motivated France, Italy, and Great Britain. The United States, unlike its European allies, did not have imperial ambitions, designs on European territory, or desires for monetary reparations. The Fourteen Points profoundly affected the outcome of the war, the peace negotiations at the Paris Peace Conference of 1919, and the Treaty of Versailles.

Inspiration for the Fourteen Points The United States was a reluctant participant in World War I, and Wilson had tried to remain neutral for as long as he could. It was only after repeated entreaties from Allied forces and the resurgence of the German U-boat campaign, especially the sinking of the *Lusitania*, that Wilson finally gave in and declared war on the Central Powers in April 1917.

0015736   WOODROW WILSON HEADLINE.
Credit: The Granger Collection, New York

On January 8, 1918, the *New York Times* prints President Wilson's fourteen-point plan for peace in Europe after World War I. *The Granger Collection, New York. Reproduced by permission*

The European nations, on the other hand, had been preparing for war for many years. Motivated by aspirations of seizing enemy empires, both the Allied and Central Powers had, over time, managed to construct a complex web of secret treaties and agreements that served to bind various nations together. The United States had never been a party to any of these agreements, and Wilson desperately sought a basis for ending the war that would allow both sides to participate in building a lasting peace. He began by asking all combatants to state their war aims, but both sides refused, because many of their aims involved territorial ambitions. Frustration led Wilson to approach Congress with his Fourteen Points—basic principles, including freedom of the seas, geographic arrangements upholding the principle of self-determination, and the formation of a League of Nations, an organization designed to enforce global peace.

The Principles Behind the Fourteen Points More than just a shortsighted prescription for a peaceful resolution to World War I, Wilson's Fourteen Points captured the president's idealistic vision of future world diplomacy. As a progressive, Wilson promoted notions of free trade, open agreements, democracy, and self-determination in his domestic programs. Those notions were carried into the Fourteen Points and served to influence foreign policy beyond World War I. One of Wilson's more contentious motives behind the Fourteen Points, at least in the opinion of the many countries that let self-interest guide their foreign policy, was his belief that for democracy to endure, ethics and morality had to serve as the basis for foreign policy decisions. Many subsequent American presidents shared Wilson's view of morality and its role in foreign and domestic policy. Finally, the Fourteen Points constituted the only statement by any of the active World War I nations of its war aims. Therefore, they became the only standard with which to craft the peace treaty that would end the war.

The Fourteen Points, inspired by world events and Wilson's assessment of the path to a just and lasting peace, were these: 1) an end to secret treaties and the beginning of open agreements among nations; 2) freedom of the seas; 3) free international trade; 4) a reduction of armaments; 5) an impartial adjustment of colonial claims to respect the rights of both the colonizers and the colonized; 6) the evacuation (withdrawal of foreign forces) of Russian territory; 7) the evacuation of Belgium; 8) the evacuation of French territory and the return of Alsace-Lorraine to France; 9) the redefinition of Italian frontiers; 10) autonomy for Austria and Hungary; 11) the evacuation of Romania, Serbia, and Montenegro, and security for the Balkan states; 12) self-determination of the peoples of the Turkish empire; 13) independence for Poland; and 14) the formation of a general association of nations. Because Wilson knew his allies and Europe's neutral states would not be in favor of all of his points, he decided not to consult with those allies and states prior to his speech before Congress. Great Britain, for instance, would surely be wary of the second, "freedom of the seas" point. The island nation had long relied on the strength of its navy and its control of the seas for security reasons. According to the Fourteen Points, Britain would, for example, be unable to repeat the blockade of Germany that had successfully weakened that nation.

The Effect of the Fourteen Points

The Germans did not respond publicly to the Fourteen Points until late September 1918. At that time, it was becoming clear to the German forces that the Allied counterattacks in the summer and fall were having their desired effect. The German armies were being pushed back and their defeat seemed imminent. A new civilian government took office in Germany and appealed to Wilson directly for an armistice based on his Fourteen Points. Wilson and the new German administration under Prince Max von Baden (1867–1929) immediately began a complex and delicate series of negotiations while the Allies watched warily from the sidelines. In the end, Wilson

The original caption of this circa-1917 photograph read "Suffragists Besiege War Brides and Grooms at License Bureau, City Hall." © *Underwood & Underwood/Corbis*

negotiated a settlement that equaled a German surrender. In addition to evacuating all occupied territories, Germany agreed to the Allied occupation of portions of western Germany as a guarantee against the resumption of the war. The Fourteen Points, then, guided the end of World War I on November 11, 1918.

The Fourteen Points continued to play a vital role in negotiations for peace following the armistice. Wilson was one of the "Big Four" at the Paris Peace Conference of 1919, which was held in the Palace of Versailles. The other three leading negotiators for peace were David Lloyd George of Great Britain, Georges Clemenceau of France, and Vittorio Orlando (1860–1959) of Italy. Of the five treaties they wrote during the conference, the German treaty, more famously known as the Treaty of Versailles, was the only treaty to include any of Wilson's Fourteen Points. But it was one that meant a great deal to Wilson. Although it was a struggle, he had finally convinced his European counterparts that the formation of a general association of nations "for the purpose of affording mutual guarantees of political independence and territorial integrity to great and small states alike" was necessary. This association, the League of Nations, was the precursor to the United Nations, an institution that continues to work for international peace to this day.

✪ The Home Front

Women's Suffrage

During World War I, the decades-long effort by American women to capture the right to vote reached a new high. The war played a significant role in women's gaining enfranchisement a few years after its end with the ratification of the Nineteenth Amendment in August 1920.

Origins of the Movement After originally possessing the right to vote in several states in the late eighteenth century, women could not vote at all in the United States from 1807 onward. The modern call for American women's suffrage began in the mid-nineteenth century with the 1848 Seneca Falls Convention, also known as the first Women's Rights Convention. There, a group of women activists, primarily from the Northeast, resolved to pursue equality with men in a number of areas—political, social, economic, legal, and religious. The right to vote was a prominent issue. In Elizabeth Cady Stanton's (1815–1902) "The Declaration of Rights and Sentiments," a manifesto created for the convention, she stated that women had been denied their unassailable right to vote by men and that women were duty-bound to seek it.

For the next five decades, a number of American women promoted the idea of women's suffrage, often while campaigning for other causes like the temperance movement. They focused their efforts on the state level and sought changes to state constitutions. Suffragists also gave public speeches to other women explaining why the right to vote was important. After the Civil War, suffrage supporters equated freedom for slaves with the rights they desired for women.

Though Stanton and another prominent suffrage leader, Susan B. Anthony (1820–1906), hoped to gain the vote nationwide in the post–Civil War period, the courts denied their claims. Beginning in 1870, their National Woman Suffrage Association presented a resolution to Congress each year called the Susan B. Anthony Amendment to allow women's suffrage. It never received an affirmative vote. Only Idaho, Colorado, Utah, and Wyoming gave women the right to vote on a state level before the dawn of the twentieth century.

Twentieth-Century Division While the Susan B. Anthony Amendment continued to be presented to Congress annually through 1914, national women's suffrage was never really supported, though additional states gave women the right to vote. Soon, the women's suffrage movement became divided, with the National American Woman Suffrage Association (NAWSA), which had merged with the former rival American Woman Suffrage Association, retaining a more conservative approach to promoting their cause, focusing only on winning the right to vote state-by-state instead of any broader isues of women's rights. Other women's organ-

izations, such as the National Women's Party (NWP), formed in 1915 to promote a similar agenda, though often taking more controversial stances. The NWP, for instance, would be satisfied with nothing less than a constitutional amendment and often used tactics of civil disobedience to advance their cause.

The NWP consisted primarily of young women and took a more radical approach than NAWSA. Organized by Lucy Burns (1879–1966) and Alice Paul (1885–1977), the National Women's Party was inspired by the radical campaigns employed by the women's suffrage movement in Great Britain, which gained enfranchisement for British women over the age of thirty in 1918. The National Women's Party used such publicity techniques as parades, demonstrations, and rallies to garner attention for the movement. The group also organized in every state to ensure the suffrage issue remained at the forefront of the public's consciousness.

Importance of World War I As World War I began in the spring of 1917, NAWSA and the National Women's Party continued their contrasting approaches to gaining the vote. NAWSA focused on supporting the war cause and encouraging women to act patriotically. This included working for the war effort outside the home. The group's suffrage work was put aside for a time, believing that their show of patriotism in the short run would help further their cause in the long run.

The National Women's Party continued to push its suffrage agenda throughout the war in a very public way. Because President Woodrow Wilson declared that war was being waged for democracy in the world, the group used his words on banners to argue for the suffrage cause: "We shall fight for the things which we have always held nearest our hearts—for democracy, for the right of those who submit to authority to have a voice in their own government." Members also picketed the White House and were sometimes denounced as traitors. Some party members were arrested on charges like "obstructing traffic" during their demonstrations, and often convicted and sent to jail. During their incarcerations, privileges such as letter writing were denied. Alice Paul, one member who was imprisoned, claimed she and the other suffragettes in prison were political prisoners.

World War I helped the suffrage movement in another way as well. The war compelled many women to take jobs in businesses, industry, farming, and retail stores to support the war effort. Women also volunteered their skills where they might be needed. Such activities highlighted the changing role of women in American society and showed that the war's purpose of freedom and democracy also resonated at home. Opinions of many Americans on the subject began to change.

Passage of the Nineteenth Amendment The work of both NAWSA and the National Women's Party finally bore fruit in early 1918. President Wilson at that time modified his long-standing opinion that suffrage was a

After serving in Europe during World War I, African American soldiers returned to the United States with a new devotion to pursuing civil rights. © *Corbis*

state issue, not a federal one. He told Congress to make women's suffrage legal, and after failing to pass a measure in 1918, the constitutional amendment passed in June 1919. The Nineteenth Amendment was ratified by the thirty-sixth needed state (Tennessee) in August 1920.

National Association for the Advancement of Colored People (NAACP)

Founded early in the twentieth century, the National Association for the Advancement of Colored People (NAACP) worked to promote equality for African Americans. During World War I, the group dealt with discrimination faced by black soldiers and pursued litigation to improve the lives of all African Americans.

In the post–Civil War era, African Americans gained few real rights and freedoms, especially in the South. Jim Crow laws were particularly repressive, and blacks were often not allowed to vote. Some African American lead-

ers, like Booker T. Washington (1856–1915), believed that the best way to deal with the situation was to practice a policy of accommodation. Others, like W. E. B. DuBois (1868–1963), opposed this idea and formed a black civil rights group in 1905 called the Niagara Movement.

NAACP Begins Its Activities Because of funding and organizational issues, the Niagara Movement failed, but the recognized need for a national African American civil rights organization remained. This need intensified after a destructive race riot in Springfield, Illinois, in 1908. Labor leader William English Walling (1877–1936) wrote about the riot in the New York–based weekly the *Independent* and included a call for people to help African Americans fight for equality. Mary White Ovington, who was a white social worker, Walling, Du Bois, and other organizers both white and black met on February 12, 1909, and began a campaign to form such a group.

Additional leaders, including socialists, newspaper publishers, and religious leaders, joined the discussions about the focus of the new organization. Oswald Garrison Villard (1872–1949), the *New York Post*'s publisher, wrote a significant document that stated that the group should stress that African Americans had political and civil rights. Called the National Negro Committee when the group first met on May 31–June 1, 1909, the organization was renamed the National Association for the Advancement of Colored People when it was formally organized a short time later. In addition to the demand for rights, public education soon became important to the cause as well.

Based in New York City, Du Bois joined the NAACP in 1910 as the director of publications and research. He founded the group's primary publication, the magazine *The Crisis*. Its popularity contributed to the NAACP's becoming the primary African American group in the United States by 1915. The organization soon won significant victories in court.

Court Victories In 1915, Moorfield Storey (1845–1929), the first NAACP president, successfully argued a Supreme Court case, *Guinn v. United States*. The Court struck down an Oklahoma law that did not allow any man to register to vote who was illiterate or whose grandfather had not voted. At the same time, and in a related case, the Court *Beal v. United States*, struck down that state's "grandfather clause" in Maryland, stating that such voting restrictions were now illegal and violated the Fifteenth Amendment. These victories were the NAACP's first wins in court.

In 1916, the Supreme Court gave the NAACP another triumph in the case of *Charles Buchanan v. William Warley*. The court stated it was unconstitutional to pass ordinances that forced blacks to live in certain sections of cities—in this case, Louisville, Kentucky—because it violated the Fourteenth Amendment. While public restrictive covenants were illegal, the practice continued privately, with whites deciding only to sell or rent housing to members of their own race.

World War I and the NAACP World War I provided an opportunity for African Americans to make strides toward making the United States fully democratic, by drawing attention to racial inequality. The NAACP encouraged African American support for American military efforts in the belief that such support would lead to more backing for racial civil rights.

African American soldiers were specifically recruited by the American military during World War I, but they were forced to serve in units segregated by race and were generally limited to non-combat support roles. The NAACP kept "Soldier Trouble" files that recorded the organization's work to ensure that African American soldiers did not suffer further discrimination while acting in defense of their country.

Increased backing for African American civil rights, however, did not come with the end of World War I. Racial tensions had been growing during the war along with the migration of many African Americans from the South to jobs in northern urban areas. Blacks also became more assertive in their demands for full protection of their civil rights. The migration pattern continued after the war's end, and hostilities between blacks and whites led to race riots, especially during the summer of 1919.

The NAACP's numbers continued to increase. In 1917, there were over 9,200 members, but just two years later, more than 91,000 members belonged to 310 local branches. The organization was instrumental during the Civil Rights movement of the 1950s and 1960s, and remains active in promoting the rights of African Americans to this day.

Espionage Act

The Espionage Act (1917) and its modifying Sedition Act (1918) were both highly controversial measures passed by Congress that limited civil liberties in an attempt to protect the United States from German espionage during World War I. While the federal government greatly supported the laws, they were not backed unanimously by the American public. There were also significant numbers of radicals in opposition to the war. The laws were widely used to stifle criticism of the war.

Congress adopted the Espionage Act in response to demands that the security of the United States be guarded from its enemies, including Americans who might aid foreign enemies. The country's entry into World War I was not supported by all its citizens. There were pacifists who did not believe in military service and did not want to be part of the war. Others sympathized with Germany and its allies who fought against the American-supported side.

Rumors over the activities of foreign spies in the United States flourished. With the help of sympathizers, these spies were believed to be plotting to undermine and sabotage aspects of American life, including American industry. Though officially neutral when World War I began, American armaments and information were shared with Great Britain and France. Germany tried to damage America's support of these allies by sending spies to interfere with factories, warehouses, and ships in the United States that were involved in the production and distribution of munitions used against Germany. The Espionage Act was intended to offer a legal remedy for this situation.

Provisions of the Espionage Act As passed in 1917, the Espionage Act curbed freedom of speech and other civil liberties while affording the federal government the ability to ensure security matters were under control in the United States. Some of the provisions that were less controversial included making it a crime to impede

Under the terms of the Espionage Act, Eugene Debs, leader of the American Socialist Party, was sentenced to ten years in prison for criticizing the war. *The Library of Congress*

of spying or committing acts of sabotage under the Espionage Act, well-known anarchists Alexander Berkman (1870–1936) and Emma Goldman (1869–1940) were convicted and put in prison for putting together public assemblies at which participants spoke out against compulsory service in the military. At least 450 conscientious objectors were also successfully prosecuted for refusing military service.

Well-Known Cases Prosecuted Under the Law One of the most famous cases involving charges stemming from the Espionage Act involved Eugene V. Debs. He served as the leader of the American Socialist Party and was a significant person in the labor movement. Debs was charged with violating the Espionage Act after an appearance before a socialist meeting in Ohio at which he expressed the Socialist Party's doctrinal beliefs and offered his personal opinion on the war.

Debs was found guilty of violating the law under the military recruitment and mutiny-related provisions and sentenced to ten years in prison, although he received a presidential pardon and was released after less than three years. Debs attempted to get his conviction overturned, but the U.S. Supreme Court upheld it in 1919. A similar case involving the Socialist Party's general secretary, Charles T. Schenck, was also upheld unanimously by the Supreme Court in 1919. In the opinion, written by Associate Justice Oliver Wendell Holmes Jr. (1841–1935) freedom of speech was not absolute. If the speech would create a "clear and present danger," Holmes wrote, it was not protected speech.

The Sedition Act In 1918, before the Debs and Schenck cases were heard by the Supreme Court, Congress passed the Sedition Act, which further limited speech that criticized the government. This law stated that when the United States was at war, nothing "disloyal" or "abusive" could be stated or written about the government, the Constitution, the American flag, or any branch of the military. The passage of the Sedition Act created an even greater reaction among Americans than did the Espionage Act and resulted in a new wave of prosecutions. One conviction under the new law involved Robert Goldstein, a film director, who was given a ten-year prison sentence because his film *The Spirit of '76* showed Great Britain, the United States' ally in World War I, in somewhat of a negative light.

Other Americans were convicted under the Sedition Act for speaking out against American support for counterrevolutionary forces rising up against the Bolsheviks in Russia in 1918. Five men were convicted for passing out pamphlets that asked President Woodrow Wilson to change this policy and that criticized the militarism of Germany. Their leaflets were not written in English, nor were they clearly working against American interests in World War I, yet the jail terms of the men were upheld by the Supreme Court.

recruitment of soldiers by the military, to refuse to serve in the military if conscripted, or to start a revolution within the armed forces. The release of any information related to national defense as related to government or industry was also prohibited. In addition, the Espionage Act declared illegal any false newspaper reporting that could help the enemy.

The law's restrictions on what could be sent through the mail was even more controversial. People who sent any type of written item—from a newspaper to a book to a personal letter—through the mail that encouraged active resistance to any American law would be breaking the law. The Espionage Act stated that such lawbreakers could be punished not only with fines but with jail time as well. The law gave the federal government the ability to clamp down on nearly all dissent in the United States.

No longer could Americans speak out against the war or express their pacifism or beliefs that conscription was wrong. The Espionage Act was used to prosecute and imprison Americans, who faced a maximum $10,000 fine and/or twenty years in prison under certain provisions of this law. Though no one was convicted

Laws on the Books At the end of World War I, both the Espionage Act and the Sedition Act remained in force. By 1920, they were seen as necessary to preserve security in the United States during the Red Scare. In 1921, however, the Sedition Act was repealed. Americans convicted under it began to be pardoned around the same time.

The Espionage Act remained in effect for far longer. As written, the law continued to be enforced until March 1940. At that time, it was rewritten, and its provisions were similar to what had been the standard before World War I. The Espionage Act remained a law and was again modified at the end of World War II. It continues to be a viable law today.

✪ International Context

The Russian Revolution

By 1917, the Russian people were wearied by centuries of autocratic rule, confused by a rapidly changing society, and weakened by bloody external wars. In one year, two revolutions had completely changed the face of the country. First the February Revolution threw off the czarist regime, establishing a moderate provisional government. Then the October Revolution brought the Bolshevik Communist Party to power and established the Soviet Union.

The Czar Czar Nicholas II was by all accounts a loving and devoted husband and father. Unfortunately, as the heir of the three-hundred-year-old Romanov dynasty, he clung to political power despite his total lack of political ability. Nicholas had seen his progressive-minded grandfather, Alexander II, assassinated in 1881. The experience haunted the czar, and he swore not to repeat his grandfather's indulgence for reform.

Unfortunately, Russia was in desperate need of reform at the turn of the century. The country had only recently emerged from feudalism—serfdom had been abolished in 1861. This did not prevent landowners from exploiting their tenant farmers. Overcharged for land and constantly fighting against famine and crop failures, many peasants barely scraped by.

To escape the miseries of the country, many commoners fled to the miseries of the city. Urban centers like Moscow and Petrograd experienced population explosions. Thousands of unemployed Russians struggled to survive, while the employed had to endure long working hours, dangerous conditions, abusive bosses, and low wages.

Others were caught by military conscriptions. The army drafted millions of young men to fight, first in the Russo-Japanese War of 1904–1905, and then in World War I. The czar's government had entered these conflicts partially in order to distract the people from their grievances. The tactic backfired when the Russian military suffered costly defeat after costly defeat. The enormous army suffered from poor leadership and an appalling lack of supplies. Only one-third of its soldiers carried weapons—the others were sent onto the battlefield anyway and told to find a weapon among the dead bodies of those who had gone before.

Although the Russian people initially supported the war against Germany, their fervor quickly waned. Quite aside from the staggering casualty list, the war caused massive food shortages and deprivation. The cities grew even more overcrowded as refugees fled from the eastern war zone.

In 1915, Nicholas left Petrograd for the warfront, determined to personally lead his country to victory. He left his inept wife Alexandra in charge of the government. The czarina's most coherent political strategy was to consult "the Mad Monk," Grigori Rasputin, a drunken, sexually depraved mystic. Embarrassed, a band of Russian aristocrats murdered Rasputin in 1916, but only after he had severely damaged the monarchy's reputation.

February Revolution By February 1917, Petrograd had reached its breaking point. Starving women took to the streets, screaming, "End the war!," "Down with the autocracy!," and "Give us bread!" Demoralized troops deserted the army and joined the demonstrations. The president of the Duma, Mikhail Rodzianko (1859–1924) sent a telegram to the czar reporting, "anarchy rules in the capital. The government is paralyzed. The transportation of food and fuel is completely disorganized. Social unrest is mounting. The streets are the scene of disorderly shooting. Military units are firing on one another."

Apparently Nicholas waved aside the warning, saying, "once again, this fat-bellied Rodzianko has written me a lot of nonsense, which I won't even bother to answer."

Even the czar could not continue to ignore the problem for long. Realizing that his entire ministry and the military had turned against him, Nicholas abdicated on March 2. He offered the crown to his brother, Grand Duke Michael Alexandrovich. Wisely, Michael turned down the honor.

By default, the Provisional Government took control of Russia, initially headed by Prince Georgy Lvov (1861–1925). Before long, a young lawyer in the Social Revolutionary Party named Alexander Kerensky (1881–1970) took power. He faced a difficult task. Czarist loyalists threatened the new government, as did the communist Social Democratic Labor Party (SDLP). In addition, a workers's association, the Petrograd *Soviet* (labor council), gained power in the capital. Soon the association was functioning as a kind of rival government.

An even more lethal threat entered the country in the person off Vladimir Ilyich Ulyanov (1870–1924), better known as Lenin. The February Revolution had found the famed communist agitator exiled in Switzerland. The Germans, knowing that a communist government would not pursue the war, allowed Lenin rail passage back to Russia. They insisted that he travel in a sealed train, worried that he would infect Germany with his subversive ideas.

The October Revolution Kerensky made the fatal mistake of continuing the war effort. England and France exerted heavy pressure for Russia to remain in the fight. Victory—which alone would justify the deaths of nearly 1.7 million Russians—seemed possible once America declared war on Germany in April. Kerensky spurred the military on to one more offensive in June. This proved a miserable failure. Deserting troops streamed back into Russia, sowing chaos wherever they went.

As public sentiment turned against the Provisional Government, increasing numbers of Russians turned to the communists. Lenin headed up the Bolsheviks, an extremist branch of the SDLP. Their slogan, cheered across Russia, was "Peace, land, and bread."

In October, the Bolsheviks pulled off a well-organized coup, seizing the Winter Palace and other major government buildings. The Bolsheviks, who owed much of their success to the disgruntled military, unconditionally withdrew from the war. They also executed Czar Nicholas and his family, which had been kept safe until then by the Provisional Government.

Lenin proclaimed a new policy for Russia: "All Power to the Soviets!" Thus the Soviet Union was born. The nation almost immediately plunged into a civil war between the counterrevolutionary "White Army" and the communist "Red Army" that lasted until 1921. The Bolsheviks emerged victorious. Soon they established a regime that would surpass the czar's in oppression and bloodshed.

The Mexican Revolution

From around 1910 to 1920, Mexico underwent a series of revolutions and coups d'état. These struggles involved a large number of separate factions: conservatives, moderates, radicals, nationalists, opportunists, and bandits. Throughout the prolonged (though sporadic) fighting, the United States interfered on a regular basis, trying to protect American investments in Mexico. In more subtle ways, Germany also meddled in the affair, trying to distract American attention away from Europe.

Porfiro Diaz Porfiro Diaz (1830–1915) served as president of the Republic of Mexico from 1877 to 1880. He then stepped down from office, true to his belief that no president should serve more than one term. Because of the incompetence of his successor, however, Diaz returned to office in 1884 and occupied it continually for the next twenty-six years. The president-turned-dictator abandoned the liberalism of his early career on the grounds that Mexico was not yet ready for true democracy.

Mexican revolutionary Pancho Villa's raids across the U.S. Southwestern border contributed to the wartime fears about Mexico unleashed by the Zimmerman Telegram. *© Corbis*

While in power, Diaz opened the country both to laissez-faire capitalism and foreign investments. By 1910, foreigners (particularly Americans) owned the vast majority of mines, rubber plantations, and petroleum reserves in Mexico. Diaz's legislation allowed a small band of wealthy landowners (*haciendados*) to put small farmers out of business, turning the peasants into poor tenants or ranchero employees.

An economic downturn in 1908 prompted a wave of discontent, particularly among the rural poor. In the north, reformer Francisco Indalécio Madero (1873–1913) founded the National Anti-Reelectionist Party and announced his candidacy for the presidency. His speeches began attracting large, enthusiastic crowds.

Diaz, despite having promised open elections in 1910, became intimidated by Madero's popularity. The president had his rival arrested before the election. Shortly afterward, however, Madero escaped and fled into exile. From San Antonio, Texas, he urged his countrymen to "throw the usurpers from power, recover your rights as free men and remember that our ancestors left us a heritage of glory which we are not able to stain. Be as they were: invincible in war, magnanimous in victory."

Across the country, a multitude of small, disunited rebel forces organized to support Madero as a means of opposing Diaz. Radical Emiliano Zapata (1879–1919) led a group of *zapatistos* in the south. Zapata, who had been born in a poor farming village, vowed to return Mexican farmland to the peasants. Meanwhile, former bandit Francisco "Pancho" Villa (1878–1923), sometimes called the "Robin Hood of Mexico," commanded guerrilla fighters in the north. Under this mounting pressure, Diaz resigned on May 25, 1911.

Francisco Indalécio Madero

Francisco Indalécio Madero led the provisional government, but his policies did not make him popular. A cautious reformer rather than a radical revolutionary, Madero did not hold Diaz's hard line. He also did not implement land reform or industry nationalization, as socialists like Zapata had demanded. This moderation cost him a great amount of support on both sides.

Madero's clearest and most enduring reform was to limit the presidency to one term of service. His own presidency was cut short in 1913, during the *Decena Tragica* (Ten Tragic Days), when reactionary General Victoriano Huerta (1850–1916) pulled off a coup d'état. Huerta had Madero and his vice president executed. Eight months later, he arrested 110 members of the Mexican Congress, establishing himself as military dictator.

Victoriano Huerta

The newly elected American president, Woodrow Wilson, could not countenance the summary murder of the Mexican head of state. Brushing aside the advice of American businessmen, who wanted stability in Mexico at any price, Wilson refused to "recognize a government of butchers."

In the meantime, Mexicans throughout the country rose up against Huerta's regime. To the north, Venustiano Carranza (1859–1920) gathered a group of "Constitutionalists" and formed an alternate provisional government at Hermosillo. (His was not the only one—at one time, more than two hundred revolutionary groups had declared Mexican governments.)

Eventually, the southern Zapatistas also allied themselves with the Constitutionalists. President Wilson sent a representative to meet with Carranza and offered to declare war on Huerta, to blockade Mexican ports, and to supply the Constitutionalists with American troops. Carranza flatly refused. He felt that to accept Wilson's offer would be to bargain away Mexican sovereignty. Wilson bristled at the snub but nevertheless lifted the arms embargo against Carranza's forces.

The United States' navy seized the port of Veracruz in 1914. Its justification for this action was patently ridiculous: the local representative of the Huerista government had accidentally arrested two American sailors. The commander had released the prisoners and apologized, but he had refused to salute the American flag with a twenty-one gun salute. By May, more than six thousand American troops occupied the city.

The Veracruz episode demoralized Huerta and cut off his supply of arms. Carranza's forces, working with both Villa and Zapata, toppled his government in August.

Venustiano Carranza

The revolution had bound together the ultranationalist Carranza, the radical Zapata, and the bandit-populist Villa. With victory, their shaky coalition soon crumbled. Both Villa and Zapata broke with Carranza and orchestrated sporadic violence against his government.

After Wilson recognized Carranza's regime in 1915, Villa led an attack on Columbus, New Mexico, killing seventeen Americans. No one knows precisely what motivated the Columbus raid, but the incident almost brought about another Mexican-American war. In March 1916, Wilson sent a punitive expedition after Villa, led by Brigadier General John Pershing. The Americans quickly scattered the ragged little army of the *Villistas*, but Villa himself escaped. Undaunted, Pershing and his men pushed deep into the heart of Mexico, searching for the rebel leader. Despite furious complaints from Carranza and armed resistance from Mexican villagers, Pershing did not withdraw his troops until February 1917.

Despite these difficulties, Carranza drafted an important new constitution that included significant political and economic reforms. With the help of his very capable general, Álvaro Obregón, (1880–1928), he managed to fend off continued attacks by Villa and Zapata.

Unfortunately, Carranza's career followed those of his predecessors. In 1920, he tried to impose Ignacio Bonillas as his hand-picked successor. Obregón, who had already announced his own candidacy, found himself threatened by federal troops.

Obregón and his political allies, known as the "Sonora Clique" launched a new revolution, announcing that Carranza was unfit for office. The country rallied behind him. Carranza was driven out of the capital and killed in May 1920.

The newly elected Obregón served the country faithfully, tackling many of its intractable problems. He managed to bring some stability and order back into Mexican life. Villa was assassinated in 1923; Zapata had already been killed by one of his followers in 1919.

The Irish Revolution

Long-standing tensions between the Irish and the English turned violent toward the end of World War I and eventually burst into open warfare. The Irish War of Independence, characterized by guerrilla warfare, police action, and military reprisals, ended with a truce in 1921. The Irish Free State was founded, but the violence flowed over into the Civil War, which lasted until 1923. Fighting also broke out over Unionist Northern

Ireland. The bitterness of the conflict haunts Irish politics even today.

The Easter Uprising

In 1914, the British Parliament voted for Home Rule to Ireland, granting a measure of self-governance to the island. However, the outbreak of World War I delayed its implementation.

In Northern Ireland, Protestants did not want to become a minority under Catholic rule and preferred union with Great Britain. So-called Unionists organized the Ulster Volunteer Force to fight Home Rule. They were backed by a Protestant society known as the Orange Order. In response, the ultranationalist Catholic Irish Volunteers were formed. Another radical group, Sinn Féin (Ourselves Alone), established by Arthur Griffith (1871–1922) in 1905, vowed "to make England take one hand from Ireland's throat and the other out of Ireland's pocket."

World War I deeply divided the Irish. Many initially supported Britain's war aims. Others believed that the European conflict provided the perfect opportunity for a definitive break with England. In 1916, one of these extremist groups declared the Irish Republic and launched the Dublin Easter Uprising.

The English responded quickly and with a heavy hand. Within a week, the insurrection had been quelled. Under the umbrella of martial law, the British troop executed nationalist leaders, made sweeping arrests, and even murdered some civilians. These deaths deeply shocked the Irish, who began to lean more towards independence.

Before long, the people of Ireland had tired of the seemingly pointless war in France. Furthermore, they bitterly resented the United Kingdom's conscription of young Irish men. In the general elections of 1918, voters sent a majority of Sinn Féin members to Parliament.

Armed with this mandate, the newly elected representatives refused to travel to London. Instead they reaffirmed Irish independence and created their own Parliament (the Dáil Éireann or First Dáil) and ministry (the Aireacht). The Irish Volunteers became the Irish Republican Army (IRA). In early 1919, members of the IRA killed two members of the Royal Irish Constabulary (RIC), the loyalist Irish police force.

The next two years witnessed an escalating pattern of guerrilla attacks and reprisals. The IRA, led by Michael Collins (1890–1922), attacked police barracks and tax offices across the island, seizing weapons and driving out Crown officials. The Dáil established an alternate police force and tax collection agency. In this way, the nationalist Irish government slowly but surely took practical control of the country.

Bloody Sunday

The British reinforced the besieged RIC with two paramilitary units: the "Black and Tans" and the Auxiliaries. These groups were largely composed of soldiers newly returned from World War I. Shell-shocked, cynical, and contemptuous of the Irish, the new policemen were often drunk and disorderly. Their reprisals against the civilian population went largely unpunished by the British government.

On November 21, 1920, Collins organized the assassination of fourteen Dubliners who had been identified as British spies. Later that day, Auxiliaries drove trucks onto a local Gaelic football field and fired into the crowd. Fourteen civilians were killed, and over sixty were wounded.

The incident, known as "Bloody Sunday," precipitated a sharp increase in violence. Only a week later, the IRA ambushed and slaughtered an Auxiliary patrol in County Cork. The English responded by burning seven houses in Midleton, and then setting central Cork on fire.

Casualties on both sides mounted as skirmishes broke out across the country. The IRA mounted a bloody series of ambushes on British targets that culminated in the burning of the Dublin Customs House. Frustrated by their losses, the British executed Republican leaders, and the IRA executed suspected English informers.

In the meantime, the largely Protestant northern Irish felt threatened by the rebellion, and they lashed out against their Catholic neighbors. What followed was a kind of civil war between the IRA and the Ulster Volunteer Force (UVF). Riots seized Belfast and Derry. Revenge killings and mob violence quickly spiraled out of control.

The Truce

England faced an embarrassing dilemma. By 1921, it was clear that the Crown security forces could not suppress the Irish nationalists, and the British people viewed royalist tactics with increasing dismay. A full-scale British military invasion would have only deepened the public disapproval.

On June 22, 1921, King George V (1865–1936) delivered a speech in Belfast in which he urged that a truce be agreed to. He asked "all Irishmen to pause, to stretch out the hand of forbearance and conciliation, to forgive and to forget, and to join in making for the land they love a new era of peace, contentment, and good will."

In July, British Prime Minister David Lloyd George and First Dáil President Éamon de Valera worked out a ceasefire. Some members of the IRA refused to honor the truce, and sporadic attacks against RIC barracks and Protestant loyalists continued.

The Treaty

The Anglo-Irish Treaty of 1921 established the Irish Free State, which was to be a Dominion of the British Empire. Members of the new Irish government were asked to swear allegiance both to the Free State and to the Crown. In practice, however, the Dáil and the Aireacht ruled southern Ireland.

The northern counties, given the choice, opted to remain with England. Violence continued almost unabated between the Catholics and Protestants in the north.

The compromise agreement did not suit all of the revolutionaries. While Collins viewed the treaty as a stepping-stone towards true independence, de Valera saw it as a betrayal of the Irish Republic. He angrily resigned as president, taking an anti-treaty faction of the IRA with him. Even when elections made it clear that the majority of Irishmen supported the treaty, de Valera and others continued to fight it.

In June 1922, the Irish Civil War broke out and continued for eleven months. Michael Collins, after a lifetime of service, was murdered by Irishmen in 1922. Ireland approved a new constitution in 1937, and it left the Commonwealth and became the Irish Republic in 1949.

✪ Aftermath

Treaty of Versailles and Its Implications

The Treaty of Versailles, which sealed the defeat of Germany and officially ended World War I, was the result of the arduous and often bitter negotiations of the Paris Peace Conference of 1919. Signed in the Hall of Mirrors of the Palace of Versailles on June 28 of that year, the treaty also represented the attempt of the winning powers to regulate the radical and far-reaching social, political, and cultural changes that emerged during the last two years of the war. The most significant of these changes was the actual or impending political and territorial collapse of the Russian, German, Austrian, and Ottoman Empires—and their ruling dynasties.

The primary negotiators of the treaty—the "Big Four," as they were known—were Georges Clemenceau, premier of France and president of the peace conference; David Lloyd George, prime minister and chief representative of Great Britain; Woodrow Wilson, president and chief representative of the United States; and Vittorio Emanuele Orlando, prime minister of Italy and head of the Italian delegation to the peace conference. But the Treaty of Versailles was not the only treaty drawn up at the Paris Peace Conference. Five treaties, one for each of the Central Powers, were created. The Treaty of Versailles just happens to be the most well-known and significant of the five. Besides calling for Germany to admit guilt for starting the war and payment of reparations that were unspecified in the terms of the treaty, the treaty realigned geographic boundaries of certain European countries and set the specifications for the establishment of the League of Nations, an organization created to foster international cooperation by offering a forum for peaceful settlement of international disputes.

The negotiators of the Treaty of Versailles have been criticized for focusing on "vendetta" rather than peace, while the League of Nations has been blamed for behaving as an international body that officially sanctioned imperialism. Frustrations related to these points and others eventually led to events resulting in World War II.

The Fourteen Points President Woodrow Wilson delivered an address to the U.S. Congress in January 1918, long before the surrender of the Central Powers, that outlined a proposal he called the Fourteen Points. The proposal detailed goals the Allies should aim for when they approached international conflict resolution after the war. In essence, the Fourteen Points captured Wilson's idealistic vision of future world diplomacy. His plan to make the world "safe for democracy" included the key principles of national self-determination, disarmament as a means of preventing future armed aggression, the fair treatment of people in colonial-ruled countries, just terms for peace (including justified punishment and free trade), and the creation of the League of Nations. Wilson's idealistic vision was largely rejected both by the victorious Allied nations, which were stunned by the devastating effects of war on their countries and by the U.S. Congress, which was entering an era of isolationism. The Allies' refusal to accept Wilson's Fourteen Points would be a major obstacle to progress in the Paris Peace Conference.

The Peace Conference of Paris On January 18, 1919—the anniversary of the 1701 proclamation of the Kingdom of Prussia and of the 1871 proclamation of the German Empire—the Peace Conference of Paris officially convened in the Hall of Mirrors at the Chateau of Versailles. After the armistice on November 11, 1918 (the surrender of the Central Powers), the Allies had agreed, in opposition to President Wilson's desire for both Central Powers and Allied nations to be present, that the Allied nations of Italy, Japan, the United States, Great Britain, and France would alone dictate the terms of peace to the Central Powers. The European Allies, embittered by the war, felt that the aggressors should be punished. Five treaties, one for each of the Central Powers (Germany, Austria, Bulgaria, Hungary, and the Ottoman Empire) were to be drawn up.

At the beginning of the conference, major decisions were made by the Council of Ten—two representatives from each of the five Allies. After March 24, the Council of Ten became the Council of Five when the foreign ministers of the great powers withdrew and left negotiations to their respective heads of state. The Big Four, intent on expediting the completion of the German treaty (the Treaty of Versailles), constituted themselves the Council of Four (all the Allies except Japan). The delegates labored over the provisions of the treaty for three months.

The League of Nations President Wilson came to the Paris Peace Conference determined to make creating the League of Nations a top priority. On January 25, 1919, creation of the organization was approved by the Allies. Its purpose was to provide safeguards against future wars

Though Woodrow Wilson celebrated the Treaty of Versailles alongside David Lloyd George and Georges Clemenceau, the negotiations ultimately proved satisfactory neither to his ideals nor the U.S. Congress's reservations.   *The Library of Congress*

and to serve as an integral part of treaty negotiations. Wilson was appointed chair of the commission chosen to draft the new organization's covenant. The draft was finished in record time. The covenant's text was adopted by a unanimous decision on April 28, 1919, and was incorporated into the Treaty of Versailles on January 10, 1920.

Germany's Treaty and Its Implications The dual goal of the Big Four during the drafting of the Treaty of Versailles was to provide safeguards to ensure the perpetuation of peace and German contrition. Beyond these generalities, Wilson, Clemenceau, Lloyd George, and Orlando found it difficult to agree on the provisions of the treaty. Clemenceau vigorously opposed German annexation of the new state of Austria. Lloyd George rejected the French effort to perpetuate a fragile Germany and called for restoration of the traditional European balance of power along with guarantees that Germany would not again attack France. Wilson was

prepared to sacrifice most of his Fourteen Points, except the fourteenth—the creation of the League of Nations. Orlando played a relatively minor role in negotiations, asking only to secure the territories in the Adriatic region that had been lost during the secret Treaty of London in 1915. His bid was unsuccessful. Despite their disagreements, the Big Four completed the German treaty by the end of April.

The major provisions of the treaty included the covenant of the League of Nations, territorial arrangements affecting Germany's frontiers and former colonies, German disarmament, and the payment of reparations. Germany had suffered tremendous territorial losses along its western and eastern frontiers. To the west, the Saar Valley was surrendered to international control for fifteen years; at the end of that time period, its citizens could decide whether they wanted to join France or Germany. To the east, Germany was obliged to recognize a new Polish state that included substantial portions of Prussian territory. With regard to disarmament, German military and naval forces were reduced considerably. The army was not to exceed 100,000 men, and the navy was reduced to a token force that could not use submarines. More dramatically, the treaty forbade a German air force. In addition to the reparations Germany was forced to pay, the country had to acknowledge its responsibility for starting the war and for all the destruction caused by it.

On May 7, the Allies presented the Treaty of Versailles to the newly arrived German delegation, which was led by the country's foreign minister, Count Ulrich von Brockdorff-Rantzau (1869–1928). He was given three weeks to provide a written response to the harsh treaty. After denouncing, among other things, the provision forbidding the German-speaking peoples of Czechoslovakia and Austria from uniting with Germany, the Germans finally accepted the terms. The treaty was signed on June 28, 1919, the fifth anniversary of the assassination of the Archduke Franz Ferdinand. The United States was the only great power that refused to ratify the Treaty of Versailles.

The Treaty of Versailles remains a subject of great debate. Great Britain and France, the major guarantors of the peace settlement, found their task difficult to accomplish due to conflicting foreign policies. Bolshevik Russia, besides never fully recognizing the treaty, promoted worldwide revolution—the opposite of the peace the Treaty of Versailles was meant to ensure. The United States, which contributed so much to the final draft, wound up turning its back in isolation against Europe. Against great odds, the Treaty of Versailles held until 1935.

Map of the World Redrawn

The most significant consequence of World War I was the demise of the German, Austro-Hungarian, Russian, and Ottoman empires. New states, ostensibly nation-states bound by common ethnicity, arose in their place. These territorial changes resulted in the map of Europe being redrawn significantly. Boundaries were changed in Africa, the Middle East, and eastern and western Europe. These redrawn borders resulted in political and geographic consequences that in some instances continue to reverberate throughout the world to this day. Peace settlements lasting from 1918 to 1923 physically and politically shaped the modern Middle East, for example. Treaties decided during the Paris Peace Conference of 1919 contributed greatly to the redrawn world map, but secret agreements during World War I also affected the political and geographic outcome. Historians still debate the wisdom of using some of these secret commitments as the basis for certain postwar settlements. These same historians point to the conference's controversial preference for soothing the victorious Allies' differences, appeasing their territorial desires, and punishing Germany instead of reaching a just and lasting resolution to the war.

The Paris Peace Conference of 1919 Following the official surrender of the Central Powers (Germany, Austria-Hungary, the Ottoman Empire, and Bulgaria) on November 11, 1918, President Woodrow Wilson expressed a desire for both the Central Powers and the Allied nations to meet at the Paris Peace Conference in January 1919 to discuss reconstruction efforts. European allies, embittered by the ravages of the war, opposed the idea and insisted that they should dictate the terms of peace. They relished the opportunity to punish the Central Powers for being aggressors during the war. In advance of the official negotiations, the "Big Four,"—British Prime Minister David Lloyd George, French Premier Georges Clemenceau, Italian Premier Vittorio Orlando, and United States President Woodrow Wilson—discussed settlement terms. It was decided that five treaties, one for each of the Central Powers, would be drawn up. France demanded the return of its former provinces of Lorraine and Alsace and required possession of territories west of the Rhine River and the Saar Valley. Great Britain insisted on the German-held African territories of German East Africa, German West Africa, the Belgian Congo, Angola, Algeria, and Morocco. Italy fully expected to gain possession of the Tirol region and the cities of Fiume and Trieste, but Wilson disputed the country's claim to Fiume. Orlando, frustrated by the refusal, left the conference in anger. Japan, despite not having representation at the conference, was given the formerly German-held territories of the Caroline, Mariana, and Marshall Islands, Quindau, and the Chinese peninsula of Shandong. Russia, also not represented, lost territories that became the states of Finland, Estonia, Latvia, and Lithuania. The Treaty of Versailles, which officially ended the war and is the most well-known and significant of the five treaties, took the Saar Valley from Germany. This territory was occupied by the League of Nations for fifteen years, during which time the coal mine from the region was given to France. The formerly German territory of Poland was restored and given access to the Baltic Sea. This move created a geographic split between East Prussia and Germany. Finally, it was decided that the League of Nations would occupy the German city of Danzig.

Eastern Europe Eastern Europe experienced the most drastic post–World War I territorial changes. The Austro-Hungarian Empire which had existed since 1526, was reduced to two truncated states, Austria and Hungary. Poland, for the first time since 1795, reappeared as an independent entity. The peoples of Ruthenia and Slovakia, who had not enjoyed self-government since the remote past, joined with Bohemia and Moravia—Habsburg-ruled since 1620—and became the new state of Czechoslovakia. Serbia, the fate of which had started the war, rose to become part of the Kingdom

Yugoslavia, today recognized as the Republic of Serbia. Romania greatly increased its territorial base after seizing Transylvania from Hungary and Bessarabia and Northern Bukovina from the Russian Empire.

The new states required governments that would satisfy all the constituents within their borders. Because the populations of states such as Romania, Yugoslavia, and Poland had such diverse social, territorial, and political traditions, majority interest and coalitions were difficult to create. Many new states could not agree on even a basic system of government. Beyond their political problems, the new states were fraught with socioeconomic crises. Despite declarations to the contrary, the United States and Western Europe failed to assist and support the development of these states during this difficult time.

The Middle East The 1918 defeat of the Ottoman Empire marked the end of an era. Postwar peace settlements, with origins in secret wartime agreements made by France, Russia, Italy, and Great Britain, shaped the modern Middle East—politically as well as geographically. Historians note that the geographic partitioning of the Ottoman territories by victorious Allied forces was less important in the long term, though, than the introduction of a new system of political organization based on the European nation-state.

One of the first secret agreements between France, Great Britain, and Russia was the 1915 Constantinople Agreement. In it, Russia was offered one of the most highly prized regions involved in the whole war—Istanbul and the Turkish Straits. In another secret treaty, the 1915 Treaty of London, Italy was urged to join the war after claiming the Dodecanese Islands and Libya. The country was also given political and economic influence over Adalia in western Asia Minor. The 1916 Sykes-Picot Agreement, which later became the key to the future settlement of Ottoman Arab lands, gave France Cilicia, coastal Syria, and Lebanon. Great Britain received Basra, Baghdad, and the Palestinian lands of Haifa and Acre. Four years later, at the Conference of San Remo, Great Britain and France agreed to modify the lines of the Sykes-Picot Agreement slightly. France was given command of Syria and Lebanon and waived claims to Mosul in exchange for shares in the Turkish Petroleum Company. Great Britain received command of Iraq, Transjordan, and the whole of Palestine. During the 1920 Treaty of Sévres, the victorious Allies attempted to enforce a similar settlement on the defeated Ottoman government. The Allies tried to partition Turkey into very small units, taking Anatolia and Thrace. But Turkish nationalists challenged the settlement and regained the whole of Anatolia in the Treaty of Lausanne in 1923. Turkey's resistance against the humiliating terms of Sévres offered a glimpse of future challenges to the newly formed nation-states.

League of Nations

The League of Nations, an organization intended to preserve international peace and serve as a forum for open diplomacy, came about as a result of World War I. U.S. President Woodrow Wilson, its most vocal supporter, played a leading role in its creation. Although the League of Nations was a product of the 1919 Treaty of Versailles, it was planned years before World War I even started. In the waning years of the nineteenth century, many governments predicted the coming of a major war and began taking steps to avoid it.

Prewar Planning In 1899, twenty-nine nations came together at the First Hague Peace Conference to explore ways to preserve international peace and reduce armaments. The scale of the conference was unprecedented, and its goal of maintaining a stable and peaceful international order was unique. That governments were acting proactively, not reactively, was a sign of real progress. But because the real threat of war was not present, and no major international tensions existed at the time, the participants were not compelled to devise any radically innovative plans. The only attempts they made to reduce the risk of war came in the form of improved international arbitration. The issue of armaments was not even addressed. Finally, and rather ironically, the representatives codified various laws and customs of war in an effort to reduce its devastation but did not adjust or modify the right of states to resort to war. The most tangible and progressive effect of the conference was the unanimous agreement that conferences of its kind should be repeated. Again, because they were not driven by circumstance, the Second Hague Peace Conference did not take place for another eight years. Even then, when the international political climate was tense, delegates failed to devise new ways of protecting world peace and reducing armaments. They agreed to meet again in another eight years, but World War I changed their plans.

Post–World War I The magnitude of World War I forced Hague Peace Conference representatives to rethink their objectives and perceptions. Toward the end of the war, it was clear that some kind of international organization was needed to prevent another world war. U.S. President Woodrow Wilson supported the idea enough to include it in his January 1918 speech to Congress that outlined his strategy—the Fourteen Points—for postwar international conflict resolution. In that speech, Wilson laid out a plan to make the world "safe for democracy" and listed national self-determination, fair terms for peace, and the creation of a forum for open diplomacy—the League of Nations—as its key principles. As one of the "Big Four" at the Paris Peace Conference of 1919, he insisted the issue of the League of Nations be one of the first considered. On January 25, 1919, the Big Four decided that the League of Nations

The Palais des Nations in Geneva housed the League of Nations from 1919 to 1936.   *The Granger Collection, New York. Reproduced by permission*

should be created and that it should be an integral part of the Treaty of Versailles.

Creating the League of Nations

Wilson was appointed chairman of the commission charged with drafting the covenant of the new organization. The covenant was created quickly, and the text was unanimously approved on April 28, 1919, but went into effect as a part of the Treaty of Versailles on January 10, 1920. In the meantime, a preparatory committee was appointed and Englishman Sir Eric Drummond (1876–1951) was named the organization's first secretary general so that implementation work could begin immediately.

During the Paris Peace Conference, they decided that League headquarters would be in Geneva; that the main branches would be the Assembly, the Council, and the Secretariat; and that the Assembly would be composed of the entire membership. The Assembly was to meet once a year, when members could discuss any issue deemed worthy. Nonbinding resolutions required a unanimous vote, which meant that any member could veto any recommendation, though this rarely happened. The Council initially contained four permanent members—France, Great Britain, Italy, and Japan—and four nonpermanent members. The number of nonpermanent members was subsequently increased to six, then nine, and finally, eleven. The Council met four times a year and gathered for special meetings as needed. Each League branch adhered to the rule of una-

nimity, and there was no clear differentiation of duties between the Assembly and the Council specified in the covenant.

The covenant also provided for the establishment of the Permanent Court of International Justice. The League of Nations was responsible for creating the Court, and its structure was approved by the Assembly in 1920. The Court was kept independent from the rest of the League and was highly respected for the quality of its decisions. Another body kept separate from the League was the International Labor Organization (ILO), which promoted the rights of working people around the globe. Like the Permanent Court of International Justice, the ILO later became an agency of the United Nations, the organization that replaced the League of Nations after World War II.

Despite its international intent, the League did not achieve global membership. Ironically, the U.S. Congress refused to ratify the Treaty of Versailles, and therefore never joined the League of Nations. When Japan, Germany, and Italy put into place expansionist policies, they decided to leave the organization. The Soviet Union was expelled from the League when it invaded Finland in 1939.

The League Grows

The League of Nations became an increasingly complex structure as subsidiary groups were created to meet the Assembly's various needs. Bodies dealing with economic and social matters grew the fastest and often included subsidiary groups of their own. As the League grew, members came to realize that peace could not be achieved by dealing with power relationships, armaments, and political resolutions alone.

Its Legacy The League of Nations became defunct during World War II. Despite its inability to prevent that war from occurring, the League acted as a stepping-stone toward a more elaborate international peace organization. As imperfect as it was, the League provided a forum where weak nations as well as strong, could have a voice. More importantly, it allowed organized society the right to assess the legitimacy of aggression. For the first time in the history of international affairs, public agencies served the economic and social needs of a global society. For these reasons and more, the League of Nations is remembered as a success.

Communism in America

Fears about the threat of Communism in post–World War I America led to the Red Scare of 1919–1920. Two events, the rise of organized labor during World War I and the Communist Revolution that took place in Russia in 1917, created an atmosphere of anxiety that led to the Red Scare. The great waves of southern and eastern European immigrants arriving on American shores at the time only intensified the rampant fear and suspicion. Thousands of foreign-born residents accused of being sympathetic to leftist causes were detained and eventually deported. Left-wing organizations became more secretive, and many groups and individuals were accused of supporting communism—including such famous Americans as actor Charlie Chaplin and educator John Dewey. The Red Scare made even the most innocent citizens afraid to express their ideas for fear of being labeled a communist. Fortunately, the Red Scare ended almost as quickly as it began. The U.S. government, especially the attorney general's office, had overstepped its authority in many cases, and the citizenry had tired of their unlawful conduct. When leading Americans stood up and demanded that the Justice Department obey the law, they effectively turned the tide of communist fear that had gripped the country. The Red Scare was over.

Communism Communism is the social and political system that calls for all property to be communally owned and the distribution of wealth among citizens to be determined by need. Outlined by Karl Marx (1818–1883) and Friedrich Engels (1820–1895) in their 1848 publication, *The Communist Manifesto*, communism is most often associated with the 1917 Russian revolution and the establishment of the federalist Soviet Union (USSR) in 1922. Vladimir Ilyich Lenin, the first Soviet head of state, espoused his own version of Marxism, known as Marxism-Leninism. His particular brand of communism became the dominant economic and political theory adopted by communist groups around the world. A product of nineteenth-century industriali-

zation, communism profoundly influenced global politics and economics. Communists and communist parties first appeared in the United States in 1919.

The Labor Movement In 1905, the International Workers of the World (IWW) organized thousands of immigrants working as unskilled labor in the country's growing industries. During World War I, the IWW led a number of strikes in an attempt to get employers to improve working conditions. Although President Woodrow Wilson was a longtime supporter of organized labor, he objected to strikes that shut down factories that produced goods necessary for the war effort. Further, striking foreigners provoked the ire of nativists who deemed the international working class unpatriotic and disloyal for putting their needs above the country's. The workers heeded the president's request to wait until after the war to demand better pay and working conditions, but the damage to the reputation of the largely southern and eastern European populations had already been done.

As soon as the war ended in 1918, laborers of all kinds began striking in huge numbers. In 1919, almost two million workers went on strike. Meat cutters, house builders, steelworkers, and train operators went on strike. Walkouts occurred in shipyards, shoe factories, telephone companies, and even police departments. Coal miners demanded government control of their industry. Even conservative farmers, numbering in the hundreds of thousands, organized and demanded major economic changes. Traditionalists saw little need for labor unions and were frightened by the rising tide of revolt. Recalling Lenin's warning that the Bolshevik Revolution would spread to workers around the world, they feared a communist revolution in their own country.

The police strike in Boston in 1919 brought their fear to a fever pitch. When the Boston police chief refused to negotiate with policemen demanding higher wages, the policemen walked out. As a result, thieves began breaking into unprotected homes and businesses. Massachusetts Gov. Calvin Coolidge was forced to call on state troops to protect the city, an action that ended the strike. It seemed to most Americans that labor unions and union sympathizers were planning a revolution. A campaign to protect the country from these radicals and extremists was launched. Leaders of the campaign blamed the communists, or "Reds," and so the "Red Scare" was on.

The Red Scare Individuals and groups suspected of being communist extremists were violently attacked across the country. In Centralia, Washington, four people were killed in a fight between union members and their opponents. In New York City, a group of men attacked the office of a socialist newspaper, destroying the equipment and beating the people working there. The growing violence exacerbated public feeling against political leftists and labor unions. People with leftist views were thought to be revolutionaries bent on overthrowing the government. Soon, local and state governments began passing laws making it illegal to belong to revolutionary groups.

Americans demanded the national government step in. President Wilson was ill and distracted by the League of Nations, but Attorney General A. Mitchell Palmer (1872–1936) saw an opportunity to gain public support for his upcoming presidential bid. He believed that taking strong action against communism would gain the attention of voters, so he ordered a series of raids on leftist leaders. Many of these people, guilty or not, were arrested and jailed for weeks without being charged. Foreigners accused of participating in revolutionary activities were expelled from the country. Eight thousand foreign-born residents supposedly sympathetic to leftist causes were deported. Among them was famed anarchist Emma Goldman. Palmer and many others believed that communists were criminals intent on overthrowing the U.S. government.

The Red Scare effectively tied immigrants to radicalism, but white Americans of northern European descent were not immune to suspicion. Many innocent people began keeping their views to themselves for fear of being labeled a communist. The entire country was suffering from violence wrought by the Red Scare. Palmer's extreme actions left a bad taste in the mouths of Americans tired of social change. They were eager to enjoy postwar peace, the return of free speech, and the rule of law. Palmer could no longer be trusted, so political leaders, including Republican Charles Evans Hughes (1862–1948), demanded that the Justice Department stop illegal actions against suspected communists. By the summer of 1920, the Red Scare had effectively ended, for the time being.

Modernism in the Arts

Modernism refers to the post–World War I international cultural movement that deliberately shunned tradition in favor of innovations in literary and artistic expression. Influenced by the political and cultural fragmentation of Europe, the resulting rise of nationalism, and revolutionary changes in scientific thought, modernism reflected the dramatic changes of the late nineteenth and early twentieth centuries. Impressionism was the first visual art form to break with tradition. The emergence of this style led to the birth of the other major modern art forms of the early twentieth century, including post-impressionism, expressionism, cubism, abstractionism, surrealism, and socialist realism. Music also underwent a revolutionary change after World War I. Modern music, like the visual arts, abandoned tradition and traded harmony and tonality for abstract mathematical patterns, atonality, and dissonance. Literature and drama followed suit. Writers of the time rejected romantic themes of liberty and progress; they instead began to explore realistic depictions of life, including social problems and family tensions. Realism, as this literary and dra-

Ernest Hemingway, who became known for his distinctive, clipped, modern style of fiction, served during World War I in an ambulance brigade. © *Corbis*

matic form came to be known, paved the way for the philosophy of existentialism, another modern innovation.

Modernism and Visual Art Impressionism was the first art form to challenge the strict representation of external forms of objects, people, and nature in paintings. As its name implies, impressionism was more interested in capturing the overall feeling or impression of what the artist saw in a particular moment than in representing the realistic appearance of the subject. One of the first impressionist painters was Claude Monet. His *Impression: Sunrise*, painted in 1873, lent the movement its name. The use of color and a heightened sensitivity to composition and light helped impressionist painters like Edoard Manet, Claude Monet, Edgar Degas, and Pierre-Auguste Renoir convey impressions rather than depictions of what they painted. But realism was not totally abandoned.

The post-impressionists broke with the tenets of realism altogether. Instead of representing or interpreting the world, these artists believed the function of art was to create a new world with its own meaning. From about 1870 onward, this way of thinking influenced many artists. They experimented with styles that allowed them to create new worlds on canvas. Paul Cezanne, one of the leaders of the post-impressionist movement, for instance, chose to depict objects as patterns of flat surfaces and forms, pushing painting to near abstraction. Paul Gauguin fled his native France, immigrated to Tahiti, and painted a series featuring vivid colors, distorted figures, and nearly nude indigenous people. Vincent Van Gogh's painting of a common starry night, for example, reveals a vivid mental state with its movement, vibrancy, and swirling colors.

The next modern artistic leap came in the form of expressionism, a trend that found artists expressing emotion in more nonrepresentational and abstract ways. Borrowing from Van Gogh's emotional intensity and Gauguin's bold lines and colors, expressionist artists, writers, and musicians attempted to express hidden human drives rather that surface realities. Vasily Kandinsky, the founder of expressionism, experimented with disassociating shape, color, and line from his subject. The resulting paintings were wildly colorful and complex abstractions that reflected Kandinsky's background as a musician. Pablo Picasso, another expressionist, pushed the movement further by inventing cubism, a visual style that breaks up, analyzes, and reassembles objects into abstracted, largely geometric forms. Art historians link Cezanne's reliance on the cone, the sphere, and the cylinder to cubism and credit the artist for giving the movement its roots. American artists, like Georgia O'Keeffe, pushed expressionism into abstractionism, a style that interpreted rather than represented everyday objects and scenes. Her flowers and southwestern landscapes, for instance, are richly depicted examples of abstract symbolism. Salvador Dalí, on the other hand, used expressionism as a jumping off point for surrealism, a literary and artistic movement that drew heavily from Sigmund Freud's theories concerning the unconscious mind. Surrealism, therefore, sought to unite conscious and unconscious realms of experience and inspired painters like Dalí and Renee Magritte to depict fantastic dreamscapes loaded with complex symbols.

In Socialist countries, modern art took a different path—and served as political propaganda. The Socialist principle that art must glorify political and social ideals of communism led state-controlled artists to paint idealized scenes of Soviet building projects and political leaders. Socialist realism, as it was known, influenced Mexican painter Diego Rivera, who painted murals aimed at inspiring the illiterate masses to revolt.

Modernism in Music

As with modernism's new visual and literary art forms, modern music relied on experimentation and a heightened awareness of the unpredictable nature of the universe to create new sounds. Expressionist composer Arnold Schoenberg, for example, led the musical movement to abandon traditional harmony in favor of abstract mathematical patterns. Claude Debussy and Igor Stravinsky were more impressionistic, composing music that inspired listeners to imagine the sounds of springtime or other natural

sounds, such as running water. One of the most significant modern musical innovations was jazz, a style of music influenced by the Harlem Renaissance, the flourishing of African American art and culture centered in New York's Harlem between the first and second World Wars. Defined by its improvisational methods, the artistic, cultural, and social movement that became jazz grew out of African American participation in World War I.

Modernism in Literature

The literature of the post–WW I to pre–WW II era clearly reflects the worldwide shock and postwar disillusionment brought on by World War I. From this period of lost innocence emerged the Harlem Renaissance, the all–encompassing artistic movement that exalted the unique culture of African–Americans; the radical literary innovations of Gertrude Stein, Virginia Woolf, James Joyce, William Faulkner, and Marcel Proust; and modernist poetry by Ezra Pound and T. S. Eliot.

In the 1920s, a period widely known as the "Jazz Age" and/or the "Roaring Twenties," the United States experienced a radical cultural shift. Americans enjoyed the world's highest national average income in the world at the time and celebrated the fact by frequenting nightclubs, listening to jazz music, drinking cocktails, touring in automobiles, and dancing like never before. The exuberance—and the lost sense of identity—inherent to the age are reflected in the work of F. Scott Fitzgerald and Harlem Renaissance writers like Langston Hughes and Zora Neale Hurston. Fitzgerald, widely regarded as one of the greatest writers of the twentieth century, wrote four novels and dozens of short stories that deal with the extravagance and disillusionment of the age known as the "lost generation," including *The Great Gatsby* (1925), the epitome of the age. Hughes, one of the many talented poets of the Harlem Renaissance, incorporated blues, spirituals, and colloquial speech into his poetry. "The Negro Speaks of Rivers," which was published in 1921 and became one of his most beloved poems, explores the journey of African–Americans through history. Hurston, a strikingly gifted storyteller, wrote from the perspective of a folklorist. Her most important work, the novel *Their Eyes Were Watching God* (1937), vividly portrays the lives of African Americans working the land in the rural South. Hurston was a harbinger of the women's movement and an inspiration to contemporary writers Alice Walker and Toni Morrison.

Writers like Ernest Hemingway and Erich Maria Remarque pushed the boundaries of Realism to include works about the war itself. Hemingway, arguably the most popular American novelist of his generation, brought the horrors of war to life in his trademark understated, clean style in *A Farewell to Arms* (1929). Remarque, badly wounded in World War I, presented a grimly realistic portrayal of a soldier's experience during wartime in his staunchly anti–war *All Quiet on the*

Western Front (1929). Virginia Woolf, remembered as both a feminist and a modernist, ignored traditional plot structure and focused on the inner lives and musings of her characters. An innovative novelist and perceptive critic and essayist, Woolf made a major contribution to the development of the novel with *Mrs. Dalloway* (1925), *To The Lighthouse* (1927), and *Orlando* (1928). Each writer of the period was, in his or her own way, experimenting, forging a new path during a critical time in world history.

Two of the most influential poets of the era were Ezra Pound and T. S. Eliot. Pound founded a new school of poetry known as Imagism, which championed a clear, highly visual style that drew on classical Chinese and Japanese poetic techniques. His most famous work is the encyclopedic epic poem entitled "The Cantos". Besides advocating a thoroughly modern aesthetic in poetry, Pound was responsible for nurturing an exchange of work and ideas between British and American writers. Famous for advancing the work of contemporaries such as William Carlos Williams, Robert Frost, James Joyce, and Marianne Moore, Pound was especially moved by the poetry of T. S. Eliot, whom he regarded as a genius. Eliot, an American who became a British citizen in 1927, received the Nobel Prize for Literature in 1948. His first book of poems, *Prufrock and Other Observations* (1917), immediately established him as a leading poet of the avant-garde. By the time *The Waste Land* was published in 1922, Eliot had secured his standing as the most influential writer of poetry and literary criticism in the English–speaking world.

BIBLIOGRAPHY

Books

Cowley, Robert, ed. *The Great War: Perspectives on the First World War.* New York: Random House, 2003.

Evans, Martin Marix. *Passchendale and the Battles of Ypres 1914–18.* London: Osprey Publishing, 1997.

Keegan, John. *An Illustrated History of the First World War.* New York: Alfred A. Knopf, 2001.

Kirchberger, Joe H. *The First World War: An Eyewitness History.* New York: Facts on File Ltd., 1992.

Lyons, Michael. *World War I: A Short History.* Upper Saddle River, N.J.: Prentice Hall, 2000.

Seligmann, Matthew S., and Roderick R. McLean. *Germany from Reich to Republic, 1871–1918.* New York: St. Martin's Press, 2000.

Strachan, Hew. *The First World War.* Viking Penguin: New York, 2003.

Periodicals

"Courageous Leadership Will Be Able to Eradicate Partition." *Irish Examiner* (October 02, 2006).

Hergesell, Alexandra. "Echoes of World War I." *Europe* (October 2001).

Hull, William. "The Scramble for Africa: White Man's Conquest of the Dark Continent from 1876–1912." *The Historian* (Summer 1993): vol. 55, p. 80.

"In Harm's Way; The Sinking of the Lusitania." *The Economist* (April 20, 2002).

Low, D.A. "The Scramble for Africa: 1876–1912." *The English Historical Review* (November 1994): vol. 109, p. 1319.

Otte, T.G. "'The Winston of Germany': The British Foreign Policy Elite and the Last German Emperor." *Canadian Journal of History* (December 2001): vol. 36, p. 471.

"The Foundation of Sinn Fein: November 28th, 1905." *History Today* (November 2005): vol. 55, p. 61.

Web Sites

"The Austro-Hungarian Ultimatum to Serbia, English Translation (23 July 1914)." *World War I Document Library.* Brigham Young University Library. <http://net.lib.byu.edu/~rdh7/wwi/1914/austro-hungarian-ultimatum.html> (accessed April 22, 2007).

Jarmul, David "America's Fear of Communism in 1920 Becomes a Threat to Rights." *VOANews.com* (May 17, 2006) <www.voanews.com/specialenglish/archive/2006-05/2006-05-17-voa2.cfm> (accessed May 2, 2007).

Jevtic, Borijove. "The Assassination of Archduke Franz Ferdinand (28 June 1914)." *World War I Document Library.* Brigham Young University Library. <http://net.lib.byu.edu/~rdh7/wwi/1914/ferddead.html> (accessed April 22, 2007).

Kipling, Rudyard. "Recessional (1897)." *The Oxford Book of English Verse.* Originally published in 1919. <www.bartleby.com/101/867.html> (accessed June 4, 2007).

"The Narodna Odbrana (1911)." *World War I Document Library.* Brigham Young University Library. <http://net.lib.byu.edu/~rdh7/wwi/1914m/odbrana.html> (accessed April 22, 2007).

"Modernism and Experimentation: 1914–1945." *Outline of American Literature.* <http://usinfo.state.gov/products/pubs/oal/lit6.htm> (accessed June 6, 2007).

"The Story of Africa: Between World Wars (1914–1945)" *BBC.* <www.bbc.co.uk/worldservice/africa/features/storyofafrica/13chapter11.shtml> (accessed May 4, 2007).

"WWI—The Great War Remembered" *United States Department of Defense.* <www.defenselink.mil/home/features/2005/WWI/index.html> (accessed April 22, 2007).

Further Reading

BOOKS

Adams, Henry. *History of the United States of America During the Administrations of James Madison.* New York: Library of America, 1986.

Ambrose, Stephen E. *Nothing Like It In The World: The Men Who Built the Transcontinental Railroad 1863–1869.* New York: Simon & Schuster, 2000.

Arnold, James R. *Grant Wins the War: Decision at Vicksburg.* New York: John Wiley & Sons, 1997.

Ballard, Michael B. *Vicksburg: The Campaign That Opened the Mississippi.* Chapel Hill, N.C.: The University of North Carolina Press, 2004.

Barson, Michael and Steven Heller. *Red Scared! The Commie Menace in Propaganda and Popular Culture.* San Francisco: Chronicle Books, 2001.

Basler, Roy P., ed. *Collected Works. The Abraham Lincoln Association, Springfield, Illinois.* New Brunswick, N.J.: Rutgers University Press, 1953–1955.

Boettcher, Thomas D. *Vietnam: The Valor and the Sorrow.* Boston: Little, Brown and Company, 1985.

Borneman, Walter R. *1812: The War That Forged A Nation.* New York: Harper Collins, 2004.

Brown, Dee. *Bury My Heart at Wounded Knee: An Indian History of the American West.* New York: Viking, 1970.

———. *Hear That Lonesome Whistle Blow: Railroads in the West.* New York: Holt, Rinehart and Winston, 1977.

Brown, William Wells. *The Negro in the American Rebellion: His Heroism and His Fidelity.* Boston: Lee & Shepard, 1867. New York: Johnson Reprint Corp., 1968.

Buell, Hal, ed. *World War II: A Complete Photographic History.* New York: Black Dog & Leventhal, 2002.

Cadbury, Deborah. *Dreams of Iron and Steel.* New York: HarperCollins, 2003.

Caffrey, Kate. *The Twilight's Last Gleaming: Britain vs. America 1812–1815.* Briarcliff Manor, N.Y.: Stein and Day, 1977.

Calloway, Colin G. *New Worlds for All: Indians, Europeans, and the Remaking of Early America.* Baltimore: Johns Hopkins University Press, 1997.

Canney, Donald L. *Lincoln's Navy: The Ships, Men and Organization, 1861–1865.* Annapolis, Md.: Naval Institute Press, 1998.

———. *Sailing Warships of the U.S. Navy.* Annapolis, Md.: Naval Institute Press, 2001.

Carlisle, Rodney, ed. "Israel." *Encyclopedia of Politics,* vol. 1: The Left. Thousand Oaks, Calif.: Sage Reference, 2005.

Catton, Bruce. *The Army of the Potomac: Glory Road.* Garden City, N.Y.: Doubleday, 1952.

Chandler, David G. *The Campaigns of Napoleon.* New York: Macmillan, 1966.

Chapelle, Howard I. *The History of the American Sailing Navy.* New York: W. W. Norton, 1949.

Chidsey, Donald Barr. *The War With Mexico.* New York: Crown Publishers: Harper Perennial, 1968.

Clowes, Wm. Laird. *The Royal Navy: A History From the Earliest Times to the Present,* Vol. 6. London: Sampson Low, Marston and Company, 1901.

Collins, Donald E. *The Death and Resurrection of Jefferson Davis.* Lanham, Md.: Rowman & Littlefield, 2005.

Cowley, Robert, ed. *The Great War: Perspectives on the First World War.* New York: Random House, 2003.

Dalton, Kathleen. *Theodore Roosevelt: A Strenuous Life.* New York: Alfred A. Knopf, 2002.

Daniel, Larry J. *Shiloh: The Battle That Changed the Civil War*. New York: Simon & Schuster, 1997.

Davis, Burke. *Sherman's March*. New York: Random House, 1980.

Davis, William C. *Battle At Bull Run: A History of the First Major Campaign of the Civil War*. Garden City, N.Y.: Doubleday, 1977.

———. *Duel Between the First Ironclads*. Garden City, N.Y.: Doubleday, 1975.

———. *The Pirates Laffite: The Treacherous World of the Corsairs of the Gulf*. Orlando, Fla.: Harcourt, 2005.

———. *Three Roads to the Alamo: The Lives and Fortunes of David Crockett, James Bowie, and William Barret Travis*. New York: Harper Perennial, 1999.

Dillon, Richard H. *North American Indian Wars*. New York: Facts on File, 1983.

Dolan, Edward. *The Spanish-American War*. Brookfield, Conn.: The Milbrook Press, 2001.

Dorland, Gil. *Legacy of Discord: Voices of the Vietnam War Era*. Washington: Brassey's, 2001.

Dowdey, Clifford. *The Seven Days: The Emergence of Lee*. Boston: Little, Brown and Company, 1964.

Dudley, William S., ed. *The Naval War of 1812, A Documentary History, Vols. 1–3*. Washington, D.C.: Naval Historical Center, Department of the Navy, 1985.

Dupuy, Ernest. *World War II: A Compact History*. New York: Hawthorn Books, 1969.

Durand, James R. *The Life and Adventures of James R. Durand*. Sandwich, Mass.: Chapman Billies, 1995.

Dwight, Theodore. *History of the Hartford Convention: with a review of the policy of the United States Government, which led to the War of 1812.*. Freeport, N.Y.: Books for Libraries Press, 1970.

Dyer, Frederick H. *A Compendium of the War of the Rebellion, Compiled and Arranged from Official Records of the Federal and Confederate Armies, Reports of the Adjutant Generals of the Several States, the Army Registers and Other Reliable Documents and Sources*. Des Moines, Iowa: Dyer Publishing, 1908.

Early, Jubal A. *Memoir of the Last Year of the War For Independence in the Confederate States of America Containing an Account of the Operations of His Commands in the Years 1864 and 1865*. New Orleans: Blelock, 1867.

Eisenhower, S. D. *So Far From God: The U.S. War with Mexico 1846–1848*. New York: Random House, 1989.

Evans, Martin Marix. *Passchendale and the Battles of Ypres 1914–18*. London: Osprey Publishing, 1997.

Fair, Charles. *From The Jaws of Victory*. New York: Simon & Schuster, 1971.

Farwell, Byron. *Stonewall: A Biography of General Thomas J. Jackson*. New York: W. W. Norton & Company, 1992.

Fleming, Thomas. *Liberty! The American Revolution*. New York: Viking, 1997.

Flood, Charles Bracelen. *Grant and Sherman: The Friendship That Won the Civil War*. New York: Farrar, Straus and Giroux, 2005.

Foote, Shelby. *The Civil War, A Narrative*. New York: Random House, 1958.

Gallager, Gary W. ed. *The Third Day at Gettysburg & Beyond*. Chapel Hill, N.C.: The University of North Carolina Press, 1994.

Gardiner, Robert. *The Naval War of 1812*. London: Chatham Publishers, 1998.

Gilbert, Martin. *The Second World War: A Complete History*. New York: Henry Holt, 1989.

Grant, Ulysses S. *Personal Memoirs of U. S. Grant*. New York: C. L. Webster & Co., 1885–1886.

Green, Michael D. "Alexander McGillivray." *American Indian Leaders: Studies in Diversity*. Lincoln, Neb.: University of Nebraska Press, 1980.

Griffith, Benjamin W., Jr. *McIntosh and Weatherford, Creek Indian Leaders*. Tuscaloosa: University of Alabama Press, 1988.

Halbert, H. S., and T. H. Ball. *The Creek War of 1813 and 1814*. Tuscaloosa: University of Alabama Press, 1969.

Harvey, Robert. *Cochrane: The Life and Exploits of a Fighting Captain*. New York: Carroll & Graf, 2000.

Hattaway, Herman, and Archer Jones. *How the North Won*. Urbana, Ill.: University of Illinois Press, 1981.

Hickey, Donald R. *Don't Give Up The Ship!: Myths of the War of 1812*. Champaign, Ill.: University of Illinois Press, 2006.

Hiro, Dilip. *Iraq: In the Eye of the Storm*. New York: Thunder's Mouth Press/Nation Books, 2002.

Hoig, Stan. *Sand Creek Massacre*. Norman, Okla.: University of Oklahoma Press, 1961.

Hoxie, Frederick E. *Encyclopedia of North American Indians*. Boston: Houghton Mifflin, 1996.

Isaacs, Jeremy, and Taylor Downing. *Cold War: An Illustrated History, 1945–1991*. Boston: Little, Brown, 1998.

Isserman, Maurice. *The Vietnam War: America At War*. New York: Facts on File, 1992.

James, William. *The Naval History of Great Britain: From the Declaration of War by France in 1793 to the Accession of George IV*, Vol. 6. London: Richard Bentley, 1859.

Jansen, Marius B. *The Making of Modern Japan*. Cambridge, Mass.: The Belknap Press of Harvard University Press, 2000.

Johnson, Curt. *Battles of the American Revolution*. New York: Bonanza Books, 1984.

Johnson, Robert Underwood, and Clarence Clough Buel, eds. *Battles and Leaders of the Civil War, in four volumes*. New York: Thomas Yoseloff, 1956.

Johnson, Rossiter. *Campfires and Battlefields: The Pictorial History of the Civil War*. New York: The Civil War Press, 1967.

Jones, Virgil Carrington. *Roosevelt's Rough Riders*. Garden City, N.Y.: Doubleday & Company, 1971.

Kaplan, Robert D. *Imperial Grunts: The American Military on the Ground*. New York: Random House, 2005.

Karnow, Stanley. *Vietnam: A History*. New York: Viking Press, 1983.

Karsten, Peter, ed. *Encyclopedia of War and American Society*, Thousand Oaks, Calif.: Sage Reference, 2005.

Katz, Solomon H., ed. "Rationing." *Encyclopedia of Food and Culture*. New York: Charles Scribner's Sons, 2003.

Kauffman, Michael W. *American Brutus: John Wilkes Booth and the Lincoln Conspiracies*. New York: Random House, 2004.

Keegan, John. *An Illustrated History of the First World War*. New York: Alfred A. Knopf, 2001.

———. *The Second World War*. New York: Penguin Books, 1989.

Keenan, Jerry. *Encyclopedia of American Indian Wars*. Santa Barbara: ABC-CLIO, 1997.

Kimball, Warren. *The Juggler: Franklin Roosevelt as Wartime Statesman*. Princeton, N.J.: Princeton University Press, 1991.

Kirchberger, Joe H. *The First World War: An Eyewitness History*. New York: Facts on File Ltd., 1992.

Kutler, Stanley I., ed. *Dictionary of American History*. New York: Charles Scribner's Sons, 2003.

Lankford, Nelson D. *Cry Havoc! The Crooked Road to Civil War, 1861*. New York: Viking, 2007.

Lanning, Michael Lee. *The Civil War 100: The Stories Behind the Most Influential Battles, People and Events in the War Between the States*. Naperville, Ill.: Sourcebooks, 2006.

Leech, Margaret. *Reveille in Washington, 1860–1865*. New York: Harper & Brothers, 1941.

Leonard, Elizabeth D. *Lincoln's Avengers: Justice, Revenge, and Reunion after the Civil War*. New York: W. W. Norton, 2004.

Levinson, David, and Karen Christensen, eds. *Encyclopedia of Modern Asia*. New York: Charles Scribner's Sons, 2002.

Lewis, James. *The Louisiana Purchase: Jefferson's Noble Bargain?* Chapel Hill, N.C.:The University of North Carolina Press, 2003.

Long, E. B., and Barbara Long. *The Civil War Day by Day: An Almanac 1861–1865*. New York: Da Capo Press, 1971.

Lukes, Bonnie. *The Dred Scott Decision*. San Diego: Lucent Books, 1997.

Lyons, Michael. *World War I: A Short History*. Upper Saddle River, N.J.: Prentice Hall, 2000.

Mahan, Alfred Thayer. *Admiral Farragut*. New York: D. Appleton, 1892.

Mahon, John K. *The War of 1812*. Gainesville, Fla.: University of Florida Press, 1972.

Markham, Felix M. *Napoleon*. New York: New American Library, 1964.

Marrin, Albert. *The War for Independence: The Story of the American Revolution*. New York: Atheneum, 1988.

McHenry, Robert, ed. *Webster's American Military Biographies*. Springfield, Mass.: G. & C. Merriam, 1978.

McNeill, William, Jerry Bentley, and David Christian, eds. *Berkshire Encyclopedia of World History*, vol. 4. Great Barrington, Mass.: Berkshire, 2005.

McPherson, James M. *Battle Cry of Freedom: The Civil War Era*. Oxford: Oxford University Press, 1988.

———. *Crossroads of Freedom: Antietam*. Oxford: Oxford University Press, 2002.

Meed, Douglas V. *The Mexican War 1846–1848*. London: Routledge, 2003.

Merriman, John, and Jay Winter, eds. "Eastern Bloc." *Encyclopedia of Modern Europe: Europe Since 1914: Encyclopedia of the Age of War and Reconstruction*. Detroit: Charles Scribner's Sons, 2006.

Miller, Donald. *The Story of World War II*. New York: Simon and Schuster, 1945.

Minks, Louise, and Benton Minks. *The Revolutionary War*. New York: Facts on File, 1992.

Mitchell, Joseph B. *Decisive Battles of the Civil War*. New York: G. P. Putnam's Sons, 1955.

Moore, Robin. *The Hunt For Bin Laden: Task Force Dagger*. New York: Random House, 2003.

Morgan, Edmund S. *The Birth of the Republic, 1763–1789*. Chicago: University of Chicago Press, 1956.

Muir, Rory. *Britain and the Defeat of Napoleon, 1807–1815*. New Haven, Conn.: Yale University Press, 1996.

Navy Department Office of the Chief of Naval Operations Naval History Division. *Dictionary of American Naval Fighting Ships, vol. III*. Washington, D.C.: U.S. Government Printing Office, 1968.

Nies, Judith. *Native American History*. New York: Ballantine Books, 1996.

O'Toole, G. J. A. *The Spanish-American War: An American Epic 1898*. New York: W. W. Norton, 1984.

Overy, Richard. *Why the Allies Won*. New York: W. W. Norton, 1995.

Painter, Sue Ann. *William Henry Harrison: Father of the West*. Cincinnati: Jarndyce and Jarndyce, 2004.

Philbrick, Nathaniel. *Mayflower: A Story of Courage, Community, and War*. New York: Viking, 2006.

Pickett, Albert J. *History of Alabama, and Incidentally of Georgia and Mississippi, from the Earliest Period*. Charleston, S.C.: Walker and James, 1851.

Pickles, Tim. *New Orleans 1815*. Oxford: Osprey Publishing, 1993.

Pope, Dudley. *Life in Nelson's Navy*. London: Chatham Publishing, 1997.

Porter, Roy. *The Enlightenment (Studies in European History)*. Hampshire, UK: Palgrave, 2001.

Powaski, Ronald E. *The Cold War. The United States and Soviet Union 1917–1991*. New York: Oxford University Press, 1998.

Purdue, A.W. *The Second World War*. New York: St. Martin's Press, 1999.

Quinn, John F. *Father Matthew's Crusade: Temperance in Nineteenth-century Ireland and Irish America*. Amherst, Mass.: University of Massachusetts Press, 2002.

Ralfe, James. *The Naval Biography of Great Britain: Consisting of Historical Memoirs of Those Officers of the British Navy Who Distinguished Themselves During the Reign of His Majesty George III*, Vol. 2. Boston: Gregg Press, 1972.

Ramsay, Jack C., Jr. *Jean Laffite: Prince of Pirates*. Austin, Tex.: Eakin Press, 1996.

Rehnquist, William H. *Grand Inquests: The Historic Impeachments of Justice Samuel Chase and President Andrew Johnson*. New York: William Morrow and Company, 1992.

Reilly, Robin. *The British at the Gates: The New Orleans campaign in the War of 1812*. New York: Putnam, 1974.

Remini, Robert V. *Andrew Jackson and His Indian Wars*. New York: Viking, 2001.

———. *The Life of Andrew Jackson*. New York: Harper and Row, 1988.

Reynolds, David S. *John Brown, Abolitionist: The Man Who Killed Slavery, Sparked the Civil War, and Seeded Civil Rights*. New York: Alfred A. Knopf, 2005.

Rhea, Gorden C. *The Battle of the Wilderness: May 5–6, 1864*. Baton Rouge: Louisiana State University Press, 1994.

Rich, Joseph W. *The Battle of Shiloh*. Iowa City: The State Historical Society of Iowa, 1911.

Ricks, Thomas E. *Fiasco: The American Military Adventure in Iraq*. New York: Penguin Press, 2006.

Robinson, Charles M., III. *General Crook and the Western Frontier*. Norman, Okla.: University of Oklahoma Press, 2001.

Rodger, N. A. M. *The Wooden World: An Anatomy of the Georgian Navy*. Annapolis, Md.: Naval Institute Press, 1986.

Rommel, Erwin. *Attacks*. Provo, Utah: Athena Press, 1979. Originally published in 1935.

Sandburg, Carl. *Abraham Lincoln*. New York: Charles Scribner's Sons, 1926.

Schneller, Robert J. *Farragut: America's First Admiral*. Dulles, Va.: Potomac Books, 2003.

Sears, Stephen W. *Chancellorsville*. New York: Houghton Mifflin, 1996.

———. *Gettysburg*. New York: Houghton Mifflin, 2003.

Seligmann, Matthew S., and Roderick R. McLean. *Germany from Reich to Republic, 1871–1918*. New York: St. Martin's Press, 2000.

Sherman, General William T. *Memoirs of General William T. Sherman*. New York: D. Appleton, 1889.

Smith, Page. *A New Age Now Begins: A People's History of the American Revolution*. New York: McGraw Hill, 1976.

Stephen, Sir Leslie, and Sir Sidney Lee, eds. *The Dictionary of National Biography*. Oxford: Oxford University Press, 1917.

Strachan, Hew. *The First World War*. Viking Penguin: New York, 2003.

Summers, Harry G., Jr. *Historical Atlas of the Vietnam War*. Boston: Houghton Mifflin, 1995.

Suskind, Ron. *The One Percent Doctrine: Deep Inside America's Pursuit of its Enemies Since 9/11.* New York: Simon & Schuster, 2006.

Swanberg, W. A. *First Blood: The Story of Fort Sumter.* New York: Charles Scribner's sons, 1957.

Sword, Wiley. *Shiloh: Bloody April.* New York: William Morrow, 1974.

Traxel, David *1898: The Birth of the American Century.* New York: Alfred A. Knopf, 1998.

Trudeau, Noah Andre. *Bloody Roads South: The Wilderness to Cold Harbor, May–June 1864.* Boston: Little, Brown and Company, 1989.

Truth, Sojourner. "Ain't I A Woman?," *Inquiry: Questioning, Reading, Writing,* second edition, edited by Lynn Z. Bloom and Edward M. White. Upper Saddle River, N.J.: Pearson/Prentice Hall, 2004.

U.S. Congress, Joint Committee on the Conduct of the War. *Report of the Joint Committee on the War. 1863–1866: The Battle Of Bull Run.* Millwood, N.Y.: Kraus Reprint Co., 1977.

U.S. Department of the Navy. *Official Records of the Union and Confederate Navies in the War of the Rebellion.* Washington, D.C.: GPO, 1922.

U.S. War Dept. *The War of the Rebellion: A Compilation of the Official Records of the Union and Confederate Armies.* Washington, D.C.: GPO, 1880–1901.

Vietnam: A Television History. Boston: WGBH Video, 1983.

Ware, Chris. *The Bomb Vessel: Shore Bombardment Ships of the Age of Sail.* Annapolis, Md.: Naval Institute Press, 1994.

Wheelan, Joseph. *America's Continental Dream and the Mexican War, 1846–1848.* New York: Carroll & Graf, 2007.

Woodward, Bob. *Plan of Attack.* New York: Simon & Schuster, 2004.

———. *State of Denial: Bush at War, Part III.* New York: Simon & Schuster, 2006.

Yans-McLaughlin, Virginia, and Marjorie Lightman. *Ellis Island and the Peopling of America.* New York: The New Press, 1997.

Zobel, Hillard B. *The Boston Massacre.* New York: W. W. Norton, 1970.

PERIODICALS

Anderson, Bonnie S. "The Lid Comes Off: International Radical Feminism and the Revolutions of 1848." *NWSA Journal* (Summer 1998): vol. 10, p. 1.

Cavendish, Richard. "Japan's Attack on Port Arthur: February 8th and 9th, 1904" *History Today* (February 2004).

"Courageous Leadership Will Be Able to Eradicate Partition." *Irish Examiner* (October 2, 2006).

Etcheson, Nicole. "Mistress of Manifest Destiny: A Biography of Jane McManus Storm Cazneau, 1807–1878." *Journal of Southern History* (November 2002): vol. 68, p. 943.

Farrell, David R. "Slavery and the American West: The Eclipse of Manifest Destiny and the Coming of the Civil War." *Canadian Journal of History* (August 2001) vol. 36, p. 383.

"The Foundation of Sinn Fein: November 28th, 1905." *History Today* (November 2005): vol. 55, p. 61.

Gordon, Walter I. "The Capture and Trial of Nat Turner: An Excerpt from the Book *A Mystic Chord Resonates Today: The Nat Turner Insurrection Trials.*" *Black Renaissance/Renaissance Noire* (Spring–Summer 2006) vol. 6, p.132.

Hergesell, Alexandra. "Echoes of World War I." *Europe* (October 2001).

Hodgson, Godfrey. "Storm over Mexico." *History Today* (March 2005): vol. 55, p. 34.

Holden, William. "The Rise and Fall of 'Captain' John Sutter." *American History* (February 1998): vol. 32, p. 30.

Hull, William. "The Scramble for Africa: White Man's Conquest of the Dark Continent from 1876–1912." *The Historian* (Summer 1993): vol. 55, p. 80.

"In Harm's Way; The Sinking of the Lusitania." *The Economist* (April 20, 2002).

Jeffrey, Julie Roy. "The Transformation of American Abolitionism: Fighting Slavery in the Early Republic. (Book review)" *The Historian* (Fall 2005): vol. 67, p. 532.

Kennedy, Paul. "Birth Of A Superpower." *Time* (July 3, 2006).

Kinealy, Christine. "The Great Irish Potato Famine & Famine, Land and Culture in Ireland (Book Reviews)." *Victorian Studies* (Spring 2002): vol. 44, p. 527.

Low, D.A. "The Scramble for Africa: 1876–1912." *The English Historical Review* (November 1994): vol. 109, p. 1319.

Mandelbaum, Michael. "In Europe, History Repeats Itself." *Time Magazine* (December 25, 1989).

Martin, Susan Taylor. "Writers Reassess Franks's Days as Iraq Commander; Authors Claim Errors During and After the Invasion." *Houston Chronicle,* (October 15, 2006).

Mazzetti, Mark. "General Starwars." *U.S. News & World Report* (September 3, 2001): 20.

McCarthy, Rory. "Taliban Under Siege." *The Guardian* (November 30, 2001).

McCarthy, Terry "A Volatile State Of Siege After a Taliban Ambush." *Time Magazine* (November 18, 2001).

Moniz, Dave. "Stakes in Iraq Rival Those in WWII, Gen. Myers Says." *USA Today* (September 27, 2005): 6A.

Norton, Graham Gendall. "Toussaint Louverture." *History Today* (April 2003).

Otte, T. G. "'The Winston of Germany': The British Foreign Policy Elite and the Last German Emperor." *Canadian Journal of History* (December 2001): vol. 36, p. 471.

Quinn, Peter. "The Tragedy of Bridget Such-A-One." *American Heritage* (December 1997): vol. 48, p. 36.

Rolston, Bill. "Frederick Douglass: A Black Abolitionist in Ireland: Bill Rolston Describes the Impact of an Erstwhile Slave, Who Toured the Emerald Isle Speaking Out Against Slavery in 1845." *History Today* (June 2003): vol. 53, p. 45.

Schultz, Eric B. "Time Line of Major Dates and Events." *Cobblestone* 21.7 (2000).

Silvester-Carr, Denise. "Ireland's Famine Museum." *History Today* (December 1996): vol. 46, p. 30.

Stievermann, Jan. "Writing to 'Conquer All Things': Cotton Mather's *Magnalia Christi Americana* and the Quandary of Copia." *Early American Literature* 39.2 (2004): 263–98.

Stoner, Lynn K. "The Santiago Campaign of 1898: A Soldier's View of the Spanish-American War." *Latin American Research Review* (Summer 1996).

Utley, Robert M. "The Bozeman Trail Before John Bozeman: A Busy Land." *Montana: The Magazine of Western History* (Summer 2003).

WEB SITES

The Afghanistan War Evolves" *New York Times* (December 9, 2001). <http://www.pulitzer.org/year/2002/public-service/works/story3b.html> (Accessed September 1, 2007.)

"The Air Campaign." *Conduct of the Persian Gulf War*. Intelligence Resource Program. <www.fas.org/irp/imint/docs/cpgw6/>(accessed June 6, 2007).

"The American Experience, MacArthur, Korean Maps." *PBS*. <www.pbs.org/wgbh/amex/macar thur/maps/koreatxt.html> (accessed May 16, 2007).

"American War and Military Operations Casualties: Lists and Statistics." *Navy Department Library*. <www.history.navy.mil/library/online/american%20war%20casualty.htm>(accessed June 20, 2007).

"Anti-annexation Protest Documents: Liliuokalani to Albert Willis, U.S. Envoy, June 20, 1894." *University of Hawai'i at Manoa*. <libweb.hawaii.edu/digicoll/annexation/protest/liliu4-trans.html> (accessed April 4, 2007)

"The Austro-Hungarian Ultimatum to Serbia, English Translation (23 July 1914)." *World War I Document Library*. Brigham Young University Library. <http://net.lib.byu.edu/~rdh7/wwi/1914/austro-hungarian-ultimatum.html> (accessed April 22, 2007).

"The Battle of Little Bighorn, 1876." *EyeWitness to History.com*. <www.earlyamerica.com/lives/franklin> (accessed April 8, 2007).

BBC News. "7 October: US launches air strikes against Taleban". <http://news.bbc.co.uk/onthisday/hi/dates/stories/october/7/newsid_25 19000/2519353.stm> (Accessed June 5, 2007).

"Bill Clinton: A Life in Brief." *AmericanPresident.org*. Miller Center of Public Affairs, University of Virginia. <www.millercenter.virginia.edu/index.php/Ampres/essays/clinton/biography/1> (accessed June 8, 2007).

Boot, Max. "Special Forces and Horses." *Armed Forces Journal*. <http://www.armedforcesjournal.com/2006/11/2146103> (Accessed June 9, 2007).

Calvert, J. B. "William Henry Harrison and the West." University of Denver, 2001. <www.du.edu/~jcalvert/hist/harrison.htm> (accessed March 9, 2007).

"Chivington, John M. (1821–1894)." *PBS*. <www.pbs.org/weta/thewest/people/a_c/chivington.htm> (accessed April 10, 2007).

Churchill, Winston S. "Iron Curtain Speech, March 5, 1946." *Internet Modern History Sourcebook*. <www.fordham.edu/halsall/mod/churchill-iron.html> (accessed May 11, 2007).

Doser, Mark. "Black Monday—The Stock Market Crash of 1987." *4A Economics*. Holy Trinity School. <www.newlearner.com/courses/hts/bec4a/ecoho16.htm> (accessed June 8, 2007).

"Durant's Big Scam." *PBS*. <www.pbs.org/wgbh/amex/tcrr/sfeature/sf_scandals.html> (accessed April 21, 2007).

Estes, Kenneth W. "Iraq Between Two Occupations: The Second Gulf War (1990–1991)." *International Relations and Security Networks*. <http://se1.isn.ch/serviceengine/FileContent?serviceID=PublishingHouse&fileid=FB678761- 6586-38 F1-EFA6-21799C0D073E&lng=en> (accessed June 6, 2007).

Feltus, Pamela. "The Gulf War." *U.S. Centennial of Flight Commission*. <www.centennialofflight.

gov/essay/Air_Power/gulf_war/AP44.htm>
(accessed June 6, 2007).

Fowler, Mariam R. "Menawa: A Chief of the Upper Creeks." Shelby County Museum, Columbiana, AL. <www.rootsweb.com/~alshelby/Menawa. html>(accessed March 22, 2007)

Frahm, Jill. "SIGINT and the Pusan Perimeter." *National Security Agency.* <www.nsa.gov/publications/publi 00024.cfm#5> (accessed May 19, 2007).

Franklin, Benjamin. *The Autobiography of Benjamin Franklin.* Reprinted at Archiving Early America. <www.earlyamerica.com/lives/franklin> (accessed March 10, 2007). Originally published in 1793.

Guardian Unlimited. "Fears grow over true intentions of Northern Alliance." <http://www.guardian. co.uk/afghanistan/story/0,,566005,00.html> (Accessed September 1, 2007.)

Hamilton, Alexander. *The Works of Alexander Hamilton, (Federal Edition),* Henry Cabot Lodge, ed. Vol. 7. (18thc). Reprinted at The Online Library of Liberty. <oll.libertyfund.org/Home3/HTML.php?record ID=0249.07> (accessed March 27, 2007).

"Henry R. Luce and the Rise of the American News Media." *PBS.* <www.pbs.org/wnet/american masters/database/luce_h.html> (accessed May 9, 2007).

Hermansen, Max. "Inchon—Operation Chromite" *United States Military Logisticsin the First Part of the Korean War.* University of Oslo. <http:// vlib.iue.it/carrie/texts/carrie_books/hermansen/ 6.html> (accessed May 17, 2007).

HistoryNet.com. "Spanish-American War: Battle of San Juan Hill" <www.historynet.com/wars_conflicts/ 19_century/3033026.html?page=1&c=y> (accessed March 26, 2007).

"History of Korea, Part II." *Life In Korea.* <www. lifeinkorea.com/information/history2.cfm> (accessed May 15, 2007).

"INDEPENDENCE: The Birth of a New America." *Time* (July 4, 1976). Reprinted at <www.time. com/time/magazine/article/0,9171,712235- 1,00.html> (accessed March 10, 2007).

Internet Movie Database <http://www.imdb.com> (accessed May 29, 2007).

"Interview with Lt. Col. Charles Bussy, U.S. Army." *CNN.* <www.cnn.com/interactive/specials/ 0005/korea.interviews/bussey.html> (accessed May 19, 2007).

Jarmul, David "America's Fear of Communism in 1920 Becomes a Threat to Rights." *VOANews. com* (May 17, 2006) <www.voanews.com/ specialenglish/archive/2006-05/2006-05-17- voa2.cfm> (accessed May 2, 2007).

Jefferson, Thomas. "Second Inaugural Address." *The Avalon Project at Yale Law School.* <www.yale. edu/lawweb/avalon/presiden/inaug/jefinau2. htm> (accessed April 9, 2007).

Jevtic, Borijove. "The Assassination of Archduke Franz Ferdinand (28 June 1914)." *World War I Document Library.* Brigham Young University Library. <http://net.lib.byu.edu/~rdh7/wwi/ 1914/ferddead.html> (accessed April 22, 2007).

Kipling, Rudyard. "Recessional (1897)." *The Oxford Book of English Verse.* Originally published in 1919. <www.bartleby.com/101/867.html> (accessed June 4, 2007).

"The Korean War Armistice." *BBC News.* <http://news. bbc.co.uk/1/hi/world/asia-pacific/2774931. stm> (accessed May 18, 2007).

"The Korean War—The Inchon Invasion." *Naval Historical Center.* <www.history.navy.mil/photos /events/kowar/50-unof/inchon.htm> (accessed May 16, 2007).

Liliuokalani, Queen of Hawaii. "My Cabinet—Princess Kaiulani." *Hawaii's Story by Hawaii's Queen.* Originally published in 1898. <digital.library.upenn. edu/women/liliuokalani/hawaii/hawaii-5.html> (accessed April 4, 2007)

Lincoln, Abraham. "Speech at Worcester, Massachusetts, September 12, 1848." *Collected Works of Abraham Lincoln.* <quod.lib.umich.edu/cgi/t/text/text- idx?c=lincoln;cc=lincoln;type=simple;rgn=div1;q1= fences;singlegenre= All;view=text;subview=detail; sort=occur;idno= lincoln2;node=lincoln2%3A2> (accessed April 9, 2007).

Lowell, James Russell. "War." *The Complete Poetical Works of James Russell Lowell.* <www.gutenberg. org/etext/13310> (accessed April 9, 2007).

"Mexican Colonization Laws." *The Handbook of Texas Online.* The University of Texas at Austin, <www. tsha.utexas.edu/handbook/online/articles/ MM/ ugm1.html> (Accessed April 4, 2007).

"Modernism and Experimentation: 1914–1945." *Outline of American Literature.* <http://usinfo. state.gov/products/pubs/oal/lit6.htm> (accessed June 6, 2007).

"The Narodna Odbrana (1911)." *World War I Document Library.* Brigham Young University Library. <http:// net.lib.byu.edu/~rdh7/wwi/1914m/odbrana.html> (accessed April 22, 2007).

The Navy and Marine Living History Association. "The Battle of Honolulu." <www.navyandmarine.org/ ondeck/1800battleofhonolulu.htm> (accessed May 2, 2007).

The Navy Department Library. "The Cruise of the Great White Fleet." <www.history.navy.mil/library/on line/gwf_cruise.htm> (accessed April 2, 2007).

Navy Historical Center. "Report of the Secretary of the navy, 1898." <www.history.navy.mil/wars/spanam/sn98-5.htm> (accessed April 2, 2007).

Paine, Thomas. "Common Sense." Reprinted at the Constitution Society <www.constitution.org/tp/comsense.htm> (accessed March 10, 2007). Originally published in 1776.

———. "The American Crisis: 1, December 23, 1776." Reprinted at the Constitution Society <www.constitution.org/tp/amercrisis01.htm> (accessed March 10, 2007). Originally published in 1776.

PBS.org. "Frontline: Campaign Against Terror: Interviews: Lt. Colonel David Fox." <http://www. pbs .org/wgbh/pages/frontline/shows/campaign/inter views/fox.html> (Accessed September 1, 2007.)

Peace Corps. <www.peacecorps.gov> (accessed June 1, 2007).

Polk, James K. "Polk's War Message Washington, May 11, 1846." *Berkeley Law School Foreign Relations Law.* <www.law.berkeley.edu/faculty/yooj/courses/forrel/reserve/Polk1.htm> (accessed April 30, 2007).

Roosevelt, Theodore. "General Young's Fight at Las Guasimas." *The Rough Riders.* Originally published in 1890. <www.bartleby.com/51/3.html> (accessed March 26, 2007).

"Rufus King and the Missouri Controversy." *The Gilder Lehrman Institute of American History.* <www.gilder lehrman.org/collection/docs_archive/docs_archive_rufus.html> (accessed April 9, 2007).

"The S&L Crisis: A Chrono-Bibliography." *FDIC.* <www.fdic.gov/bank/historical/s&l/> (accessed June 8, 2007).

Schultz, Stanley K. "The Gilded Age and the Politics of Corruption." *University of Wisconsin.* <us. history.wisc.edu/hist102/lectures/lecture04.html> (accessed April 21, 2007).

Smith, Adam. "An Inquiry into the Nature and Causes of the Wealth of Nations by Adam Smith." Project Gutenberg <www.gutenberg.org/etext/3300> (accessed March 27, 2007). Originally published in 1776.

The Spanish-American War Centennial Website. "The Official Report of Spanish Admiral Montojo on the Battle of Manila Bay" <www.spanamwar.com/mtreport.htm> (accessed March 26, 2007).

State of the Union Addresses of James Monroe. <www.gutenberg.org/dirs/etext04/sumon11.txt> (accessed April 8, 2007).

"The Story of Africa: Between World Wars (1914–1945)." *BBC.* <www.bbc.co.uk/world service/africa/features/storyofafrica/13chapter 11.shtml> (accessed May 4, 2007).

Tallmadge, James, Jr. "Tallmadge's Speech to Congress, 1819." *Wadsworth Learning American Passages.* <www.wadsworth.com/history_d/templates/student_resources/0030724791_ayers/sources/ch09/9.3.tallmadge.html> (accessed April 9, 2007).

"Texas Declaration of Independence." *Texas A&M University.* <www.tamu.edu/ccbn/dewitt/decindepen36.htm> (accessed April 30, 2007).

"Thomas Jefferson's Account of the Declaration." Reprinted at USHistory.org. <www.ushistory.org/declaration/account/index.htm> (accessed March 10, 2007).

Travis, William Barret. "Letter from the Alamo, February 24, 1836." *The History of the Alamo & the Texas Revolution.* Texas A&M University <www.tamu.edu/ccbn/dewitt/adp/history/bios/travis/travtext.html> (accessed April 30, 2007).

Treaty of Ghent. <www.loc.gov/rr/program/bib/our docs/Ghent.html> (accessed April 5, 2007).

Truman, Harry S. "The Truman Doctrine, President Harry S. Truman's Address Before a Joint Session of Congress, March 12, 1947." *The Avalon Project at Yale Law School.* <www.yale.edu/lawweb/avalon/trudoc.html> (accessed May 18, 2007).

Utz, Curtis A. "MacArthur Sells Inchon." *Assault from the Sea, Amphibious Landing at Inchon.* Naval Historical Center. <www.history.navy.mil/download/i-16-19.pdf> (accessed May 17, 2007).

Voltaire. "The Philosophical Dictionary." H.I. Woolf, ed. New York: Knopf, 1924. Reprinted at Hanover Historical Texts Project <history.hanover.edu/texts/voltaire/volindex.html> (accessed March 27, 2007).

"Walton Harris Walker, General, United States Army." *ArlingtonCemetery.net.* <www.arlingtoncemetery.net/whwalker.htm> (accessed May 19, 2007).

"War Chronology: February 1991." *U.S. Navy in Desert Storm/Desert Sheild.* <www.history.navy. mil/wars/dstorm/dsfeb.htm> (accessed June 6, 2007).

Webster, Daniel. "Speech to the Senate, 1848." *The Great Speeches and Orations of Daniel Webster.* <www.gutenberg.org/etext/12606> (accessed April 14, 2007).

Wormser, Richard. "Harry S. Truman Supports Civil Rights (1947–1948)." *PBS.* <www.pbs.org/wnet/jimcrow/stories_events_truman.html> (accessed May 24, 2007).

"WWI—The Great War Remembered." *United States Department of Defense.* <www.defenselink.mil/home/features/2005/WWI/index.html> (accessed April 22, 2007).

Index

Matsui, Iwane, 2:459

Mayflower (ship), 1:6–7

Mazari Sharif, Battle of, 2:**639–640**

Mazzini, Giuseppe, 1:275–276

McAuliffe, Tony, 2:436

McCarthy, Eugene, 2:*560*, **560–561**

McCarthy, Joseph R., 2:**512–514**, *513*

McClellan, George
  Antietam, Battle of, 1:*207*, **207–208**
  Ball's Bluff, Battle of, 1:200
  Bull Run, Second Battle of, 1:205–207
  Civil War, 1:**183–185**, *184*
  Fredericksburg, Battle of, 1:189–190, **208–209**
  Seven Days, Battle of, 1:**204–205**

McClellan, John, 2:558

McClernand, John, 1:212

McCook, Alexander, 1:216

McCord, James, 2:588

McDowell, Irvin, 1:198–200

McGillivray, Alexander, 1:80

McGovern, George, 2:588

McIntosh, William, 1:80, 88, *93*

McKenzie, Ranald S., 1:262

McKinley, William
  and Cuba, 1:287
  and populism, 1:284
  Spanish-American War, 1:**289–291**, *290*

McKinley Tariff Bill (of 1893), 1:290

McNamara, Robert, 2:552, **555–557**, *556*, 571, 580

McQueen, Peter, 1:91

Meade, George G., 1:**193–194**, **212–213**

Mechanicsville, 1:**204**

Medicine Lodge Treaty (of 1867), 1:254, **260–261**

Medina, Ernest "Mad Dog," 2:577

Meiji Constitution, 1:386

Meiji (Emperor), 2:386

Mein Kampf (Hitler), 2:383, 461

Melville, Herman, 1:160

Menawa (Chief), 1:*87*, **87–88**

Mengele, Josef, 2:462

Merritt, Wesley, 1:296, 303

Metacom, 1:**9–11**, 11–13

Metternich, Age of, 1:320

Metternich, Klemens Wenzel von, 1:162, 320, 324

Mexican-American War
  Adams, John Quincy, 1:125, 130, 163
  Austin, Stephen F., 1:**131–133**, *133*, 135

Bowie, James, 1:**138**

Cherokee Tribe, 1:133–134

Clay, Henry, 1:141, 157–159, *158*

Crockett, David, 1:**136–138**, *137*

Goliad, 1:147–148

Grant, Ulysses S., 1:131

Houston, Sam, 1:*133*, **133–134**, 147–148

Jackson, Thomas "Stonewall," 1:183

Jefferson, Thomas, 1:158

Lee, Robert E., 1:178

Lincoln, Abraham, 1:131

Manifest Destiny, 1:**130–131**

Missouri Compromise, 1:**156–159**, *157*

Native Americans, 1:142

Polk, James, 1:126, 130, *140*, **140–141**, 159

"Remember the Alamo!," 1:148

Republic of Texas, 1:*133*, 134, 142–143, 146, *155*

Santa Anna, Antonio López de, 1:**138–140**

Scott, Winfield, 1:**143–145**, *144*

Taylor, Zachary, 1:**141–143**, *142*, *149*, 149–151

and Tecumseh, 1:142

Texas annexation, 1:155–156

Texas Declaration of Independence, 1:134

Texas Rangers, 1:138

Texas Revolution, 1:132–133

Travis, William Barret, 1:**134–136**, 146

U.S. campaigns in, 1:*151*

U.S. territorial conquests, 1:*153*

Mexican-American War, Battles
  Alamo, 1:*145*, **145–146**
  Buena Vista, 1:*140*, *142*, 143, **150–152**
  Cerro Gordo, 1:153–154
  Chapultepec, 1:154
  Palo Alto, 1:*149*, **149–150**
  Resaca de la Palma, 1:143
  San Jacinto, 1:**146–149**, *147*
  Veracruz, 1:**152**

Mexican-American War, Treaties
  Gadsden, 1:140
  Guadalupe Hidalgo, 1:141
  Velasco, 1:139

Mexican raids, 1:239–240

Mexico
  Mexican Revolution, 1:365–367
  Mexico City, 1:153–155
  Mexico Movement, 1:131
  raids, 1:239–240

Miantonomoh, 1:**3–4**

Michael of Russia (Grand Duke), 1:332

Middle East, 1:371, **681–682**

Midway, Battle of, 2:**422–424**

Midway Island, 2:392–393

Mikoyan, Anastas, 2:537

Miles, Nelson A., 1:252, 262, 267

Military Assistance Advisory Group Vietnam (MAAGV), 2:568

Military Assistance Command, Vietnam (MACV), 2:567–568, 573

Millard, Henry, 1:148

Mineta, Norman Y., 2:454

Mining frontier, 1:236–237

Minutemen of Massachusetts, 1:49

Mississippi
  Mississippi Plan, 1:273
  Mississippi Territory, 1:87, 91
  riverboat travel, 1:122
  settlement in, 1:236

Missouri Compromise, 1:**156–159**, *157*

Mitchell, John N., 2:581

Mitscher, Marc, 2:402

Mobile Bay, Battle of, 1:186–187, *187*, **218–220**, *220*

Modernism, U.S., 1:**374–376**

Mogadishu, Battle of, 2:672

Mohammed, Khalid Shaikh, 2:620

Molotov-Ribbentrop Pact, 2:388, 411, 427, 441

Moltke, Helmuth von, 1:343

Mondale, Walter, 2:527

Monet, Claude, 1:374

Monitor vs. The Merrimac, 1:**201–202**, *210*

Monroe, James, 1:74, 115, 125–126

Monroe Doctrine, 1:**125–126**, *126*, 673

Monte Cassino, 2:**430–432**

Montgomery, Bernard, 1:387, 2:**393–394**

Montojo, Patricio, 1:296, 302

Moore, Harold, 2:572

Morales, Juan, 1:74, 152

Morgan, J. P., 1:289

Morgenthau Plan, 2:441–442

Moroccan crisis, 1:324

Morse, Samuel, 1:160

Mosley, Samuel, 1:13–15

Mott, Lucretia, 1:165

Mountbatten, Louis, 2:471

Mrs. Dalloway (Woolf), 1:376

Munemitsu, Mutsu, 1:278

Munich Pact, 2:**409–411**

Muratori, Ludovico Antonio, 1:275

Murrow, Edward R., 2:417, 457

Musharraf, Pervez, 2:*628*, **628–630**, 646

Mussolini, Benito, 2:384, **385**

My American Journey (Powell), 2:605